THE LETTERS OF ERNEST HEMINGWAY, VOLUME 1: 1907–1922

"A fascinating new volume that peels away at a young Hemingway different, richer, more tender than the machismo-encrusted persona we've come to know through his published works."
The Atlantic

"The delight of these letters and the sheer quantity of useful editorial material . . . should entice even the most ardent Papa-reviler to delve into the spontaneous words of a creative genius."
Publishers Weekly, starred review

"The existence of some of these documents (pre-dating Hemingway's fame) is close to a miracle, and the Letters is without question a spectacular scholarly achievement."
Arthur Phillips, *New York Times*

"A work of monumental authority, shrewd and sympathetic, which will be indispensable for anyone delving into Hemingway's childhood affections, adolescent bravura, and the hope, enthusiasm and disgust of his early manhood."
The Spectator

"[A] superbly edited volume."
Times Literary Supplement

"His letters burst off the page with all his swaggering vigour, brio, brilliance, wit and rage, uncensored and unrestrained."
Sarah Churchwell, *The Guardian*

"[Hemingway's] letters were never intended for publication, and they are surprising . . . Behind the hard-living, hard-loving, tough-guy literary persona we find a loyal son pouring his heart out to his family, an infatuated lover, an adoring husband, and a highly committed friend."
Robert McCrum, *The Guardian*

"Hemingway admirers, scholars, and students will find the book essential. The letters fill in abundant biographical and intellectual details, and readers will revel in the young man's exuberant wordplay, private language, and slang."
Booklist

"Magnificently edited . . . [this volume] is a work of true literary scholarship . . . what makes this first volume more than a mere collection of juvenilia is that here is all the evidence of the writer – and the man – that he was to become."
Literary Review

"The collected Hemingway letters will be enthusiastically welcomed by the scholarly world as well as the legion of Hemingway enthusiasts around the world. He is not only one of the most important twentieth-century writers in the world, but a fascinating and frank letter writer. This collection will be an invaluable addition to the world of letters."
Noel Riley Fitch

"By any measure it's a Very Big Deal."
Roger Cox, *The Scotsman*

"And so begins the ambitious – and highly anticipated – publication of The Letters of Ernest Hemingway, a vast collection that proves to be both a revealing autobiography and the passkey to his literary works. This first volume is a vibrant portrait of the artist as a young man, striking all the notes that will resonate as themes in the epic life and epochal literature that lie ahead."
A. Scott Berg, *Vanity Fair*

"To know what Ernest Hemingway was really like, don't read biographies of him. Read his letters."
Chronicle of Higher Education

". . . a major project in literary scholarship . . . left me eager to read more."
National Post

"An intriguing insight into the evolving personality before it entered the public arena."
Dublin Review of Books

"This book combines the most serious scholarship with great readability – the perfect Christmas present."
Standpoint

THE LETTERS OF ERNEST HEMINGWAY, VOLUME 2: 1923–1925

"This essential volume, beautifully presented and annotated with tremendous care and extraordinary attention to detail, offers readers a Hemingway who is both familiar and new."
Times Literary Supplement

"Hemingway did not want his letters published, but this carefully researched scholarly edition does them justice . . . devotees will find this and future volumes indispensable."
Library Journal

"With more than 6,000 letters accounted for so far, the project to publish Ernest Hemingway's correspondence may yet reveal the fullest picture of the twentieth-century icon that we've ever had. The second volume includes merely 242 letters, a majority published for the first time . . . readers can watch Hemingway invent the foundation of his legacy in bullrings, bars, and his writing solitude."
Booklist

"It would be hard to find a more crucial three year period in a writer's life."
Independent on Sunday

"This second volume of The Letters of Ernest Hemingway documents the years in which he became himself . . . His style is at once close to and yet unutterably distant from that of his fiction."
Michael Gorra, *New York Times*, Editor's Choice

"Roughly written as they are it is fascinating to watch the private rehearsal of what would become public performances."
Daily Telegraph

"The volume itself is beautifully designed and skillfully edited . . . As a book, it is perfect."
Los Angeles Review of Books

"Never is Hemingway more fascinating or in flux than in these letters from his Paris years, that dark and dazzling confluence of literary ascendancy and personal maelstrom. Bravo to Sandra Spanier for giving us this dazzling gem of literary scholarship, and the young Hemingway in his own words—unvarnished, wickedly funny, mercilessly human."
Paula McLain, author of *The Paris Wife*

"Warmly unpretentious and frequently playful."
The Spectator

"[T]he newly published letters are bracingly energetic and readable, and they add depth and detail to the already vast biographical record of Hemingway's early years."
Edward Mendelsohn, *New York Review of Books*

"Two thirds of these have never seen the light of day before. A great continuing literary project."
Jeff Simon, *Buffalo News*, Editor's Choice

"Bawdy, humorous, linguistically playful."
Literary Review

"The volume's 242 letters, about two-thirds previously unpublished, provide as complete an account of Hemingway's life during the Paris years as one could ask for."
John Reimringer, *Star Tribune*

"For those with a passion for American literary history and an interest in the machinery of fame, these letters, ably and helpfully annotated by a team of scholars led by Sandra Spanier of Penn State University, provide an abundance of raw material and a few hours' worth of scintillating reading."
Kansas City Star

"This expertly edited and annotated volume will be devoured by fans eager to learn how the literary titan came into his own."
Publishers Weekly

"The editors of this project have much to celebrate. Volume 2 is an exceptional collection, magnificently collated and, in Papa's words, 'exciting as hell'."
James McNamara, *The Australian*

THE LETTERS OF
ERNEST HEMINGWAY
VOLUME 3
1926–1929

The Letters of Ernest Hemingway, Volume 3: 1926–1929, featuring many previously unpublished letters, follows a rising star as he emerges from the literary Left Bank of Paris and moves into the American mainstream. Maxwell Perkins, legendary editor at Scribner's, recognized and nurtured the young Hemingway's talent, accepting his satirical novel *The Torrents of Spring* (1926) in order to publish what would become a signature work of the twentieth century: *The Sun Also Rises* (1926). By early 1929 Hemingway had completed *A Farewell to Arms*. Hemingway's letters of this period also reflect landmark events in his personal life, including the dissolution of his first marriage, his remarriage, the birth of his second son, and the suicide of his father. As the volume ends in April 1929, Hemingway is setting off from Key West to return to Paris and standing on the cusp of celebrity as one of the major writers of his time.

THE

CAMBRIDGE EDITION OF

THE LETTERS OF
ERNEST HEMINGWAY

General Editor
Sandra Spanier
The Pennsylvania State University

Editorial Advisory Board
Linda Patterson Miller, Chair
The Pennsylvania State University–Abington

Jackson R. Bryer
University of Maryland

Scott Donaldson
College of William and Mary

Debra Moddelmog
The Ohio State University

James L. W. West III
The Pennsylvania State University

May 5, 1926

Dear Mr. Perkins:—

The title will be The Sun Also *Rises* — I see nothing to be gained by using the archaic Ariseth of the King James version. as the title is ~~supported by the quotation from Ecclesiastes~~ ~~neither it is taken~~ ~~exactly~~.

I am enclosing a story which I hope you and the magazine will like. I'm glad Professor Copeland liked the In Our Time and I'm pleased about Galsworthy. La Nouvelle Revue Française are going to publish ~~it~~. Has there ever been any news of it from ~~the~~ Perkins? I wrote you that It has rained here for 21 days and I'm feeling very low with no exercise and consequent insomnia etc. Have started another story. We go to Spain a week from today.

I hope you like this story Corriere della Sera of Milano — which is the best and the biggest paper in Italy — has published a 2 column review of In Our Time. I would send it to you — and will if you like — but have been keeping it to impress the wop bartender at the Bar Torino in ~~Madrid~~ which is located just under the place we live in at Madrid.

Thanks very much for the check for 600 dollars. With best regards
Ernest Hemingway

Ernest Hemingway to Maxwell Perkins, 5 May 1926 from Paris. Archives of Charles Scribner's Sons, Box 768, Folder 3; Manuscripts Division, Department of Rare Books and Special Collections, Princeton University Library.

THE LETTERS OF
ERNEST HEMINGWAY

VOLUME 3
1926–1929

EDITED BY

Rena Sanderson

Sandra Spanier

Robert W. Trogdon

VOLUME ADVISORY EDITORS

J. Gerald Kennedy

Rodger L. Tarr

CAMBRIDGE
UNIVERSITY PRESS

CAMBRIDGE
UNIVERSITY PRESS

University Printing House, Cambridge CB2 8BS, United Kingdom

Published in the United States of America by Cambridge University Press, New York

Cambridge University Press is part of the University of Cambridge.

It furthers the University's mission by disseminating knowledge in the pursuit of education, learning and research at the highest international levels of excellence.

www.cambridge.org
Information on this title: www.cambridge.org/9780521897358

First published 2015

Printed in the United States of America

A catalogue record for this publication is available from the British Library

ISBN 978-0-521-89735-8 Hardback

Cambridge University Press has no responsibility for the persistence or accuracy of
URLs for external or third-party internet websites referred to in this publication,
and does not guarantee that any content on such websites is, or will remain,
accurate or appropriate.

CONTENTS

PLATES

The plates are located between pages 268 and 269.

1 Hadley Hemingway and Pauline Pfeiffer in Schruns, Austria (c. December 1925–January 1926).
2 Pauline Pfeiffer and Ernest Hemingway in Schruns (c. December 1925–January 1926).
3 Hadley, Bumby, and Ernest in Schruns (March 1926).
4 Maxwell Perkins, Hemingway's editor at Scribner's.
5 Hemingway with Frau Lent, John Dos Passos, and Gerald Murphy in Austria (March 1926).
6 Gerald and Sara Murphy at Cap d'Antibes (summer 1926).
7 Zelda, Scottie, and F. Scott Fitzgerald in Juan-les-Pins (summer 1926).
8 and 9 Bumby with Ernest and with Hadley on the beach at Juan-les-Pins, where the Hemingways stayed from late May to early July 1926. Ernest enclosed both photos in a letter to his father of 24 July 1926.
10 Gerald and Sara Murphy, Pauline, Ernest, and Hadley in Pamplona (July 1926).
11 Separation agreement written by Hadley (c. November 1926).
12 Ernest with Virginia Pfeiffer at Gstaad, Switzerland (February 1927).
13 Hemingway skiing at Gstaad, inscribed to Maxwell Perkins (February 1927).
14 Ernest and Pauline at the time of their wedding in Paris (May 1927).
15 Bumby at the Hemingway family home in Oak Park, Illinois (May 1927).
16 Hemingway posing with a steer near Pamplona (July 1927).
17 Myrsine and Hélène Moschos, Sylvia Beach, and Hemingway outside Shakespeare and Company in Paris, inscribed to Beach (March 1928).
18 Portrait of Hemingway by Helen Breaker, Paris (March 1928).
19 Pauline at the Hotel Ambos Mundos in Havana, Cuba (April 1928).
20 Clarence Hemingway and Ernest in Key West (April 1928).
21 Willoughby Hemingway, Ernest, Grace Hall Hemingway, and Pauline in Key West (April 1928).
22 Hemingway with a barracuda, inscribed, Key West (spring 1928).

These illustrations appear courtesy of the following:

Hemingway Collection, John F. Kennedy Presidential Library, 1–3, 5, 10–16, 18–22, 26, 29; Special Collections Library, The Pennsylvania State University Libraries and Ernest H. Mainland, 8–9; Manuscripts Division, Department of Rare Books and Special Collections, Princeton University Library, 4, 7, 17, 23–24, 27–28; Beinecke Special Collections, Yale University Library and The Estate of Honoria Murphy Donnelly/Licensed by VAGA, New York, NY, 6; Special Collections, Colby College, 25; National Portrait Gallery, courtesy of Karin Peirce, 30.

MAPS

GENERAL EDITOR'S INTRODUCTION

Sandra Spanier

By early 1926, Ernest Hemingway was already a figure of note on the literary Left Bank. His return from a winter vacation in Schruns, Austria, where he had just finished revising a novel about a group of dissipated expatriates in Spain, attracted attention in the "Latin Quarter Notes" column of the 30 March 1926 Paris *Tribune*. "Home-comers are beginning to wander to the Quarter in increasing numbers, and, what with the tourists and 'regulars,' will soon give Montparnasse the proper atmosphere once more for the sight-seeing squad," the columnist observed. "Ernest Hemingway reported yesterday with an extra pound or two under his belt."

At the time, Hemingway had to his credit two slim books published in Paris by small avant-garde presses, and a short-story collection, *In Our Time*, released in October 1925 by New York publisher Boni & Liveright. In the spring of 1925 he had assisted in launching the modernist magazine *This Quarter*, shepherding the first number through production with a Paris printer on behalf of co-editors Ernest Walsh and Ethel Moorhead, who were living in the South of France. The first number included Hemingway's now classic story "Big Two-Hearted River" alongside works by Gertrude Stein, William Carlos Williams, James Joyce, and Ezra Pound.

The second number of *This Quarter* (Autumn–Winter 1925–1926) featured a poem by Walsh titled "Ernest Hemingway." It begins:

> Papa soldier pugilist bullfighter
> Writer gourmet lionhead aesthete
> He's a big guy from near Chicago
> Where they make the shoes bigger and
> It's a good thing that because he aint
> Got french feet Napoleon and him
> Wouldn't have said much together
> He'd have pulled Buonaparte's nose
> And absolutely ruined french history

Archibald MacLeish's poem "Fragment of a Biography," published in the 1927 *American Caravan*, was dedicated to Ernest Hemingway. By the following year, Hemingway (and his passion for the bullfight) was famous enough to be the subject of a caricature by popular cartoonist Ralph Barton, published in the January 1928 issue of *Vanity Fair*. The cartoon depicts Hemingway in a puffy-sleeved matador's costume smoking a cigarette and sharing a bottle of wine at a café table with a bull.

Volume 3 of *The Letters of Ernest Hemingway* (1926–April 1929) traces the trajectory of a rising star as he emerges from the coterie of postwar expatriate literati and moves into the American mainstream. Having been introduced to his work by F. Scott Fitzgerald, Maxwell Perkins, the legendary editor at Scribner's, recognized the young Hemingway's talent and nurtured it, accepting his satirical novel *The Torrents of Spring* (1926) in order to publish what would become one of the signature works of the twentieth century, *The Sun Also Rises* (1926). The short-story collection *Men Without Women* (1927) followed. By early 1929, Hemingway had completed the manuscript of *A Farewell to Arms* and accepted a lucrative serialization offer from Scribner's, which would be his lifelong publisher.

Hemingway's letters of this period reveal the progression of his relationships with other major literary figures of the day, including Pound, Fitzgerald, MacLeish, John Dos Passos, Sherwood Anderson, James Joyce, and T. S. Eliot. The letters reflect the landmark events in his personal life as well: the dissolution of his first marriage to Hadley Richardson, his affair with their friend Pauline Pfeiffer, his marriage to Pauline, the birth of his second son, Patrick, and the suicide of his father.

Returning from Europe in the spring of 1928 to spend a year in the United States, Hemingway took up residence in Key West, developed a passion for big game fishing, and discovered the American West, a landscape that reminded him of his beloved Spain. As the volume ends in early April 1929, Hemingway is setting off with his family on the return to Paris and standing on the cusp of celebrity as one of the major writers of his time.

Volume 3 includes 345 letters, more than 70 percent of them previously unpublished. Whereas each of the previous two volumes represents some sixty correspondents, the letters in this volume are directed to ninety-nine recipients. Maxwell Perkins is far and away Hemingway's most frequent correspondent of this period, the recipient of seventy-four letters in this volume. Others represented most frequently include Hemingway's parents, Clarence and Grace Hall Hemingway (twenty-two letters, addressed to them individually and together), the painter Waldo Peirce (nineteen letters), Ezra Pound (eighteen letters), F. Scott Fitzgerald (thirteen letters), Archibald

MacLeish, journalist Guy Hickok of the *Brooklyn Eagle*, and artist Henry Strater (nine letters each), and Pauline Pfeiffer (eight letters).

Among those who received at least four letters from Hemingway included in this volume are his sister Madelaine (nicknamed "Sunny"); his new in-laws, Mary and Paul Pfeiffer; the young poet Evan Shipman; Sylvia Beach, owner of the Left Bank bookshop Shakespeare and Company and publisher of Joyce's *Ulysses*; Owen Wister, author of the bestselling 1902 novel *The Virginian*; Bill Smith, Hemingway's close friend from summers of his youth up in Michigan; Isabelle Simmons Godolphin, his next-door neighbor in Oak Park, Illinois; and Pierre Chautard, his disgruntled Paris landlord.

As Hemingway's circle of renown expanded, so did the number of correspondents with whom he had only brief exchanges. Nearly two-thirds of those represented in this volume received only one or two surviving letters from Hemingway, as he responded to fans, collectors, teachers, and aspiring writers who wrote to seek his autograph, buy a manuscript, or solicit his advice on writing.

Hemingway's letters chart the course of his relationships, personal and professional, and map the ever-widening web of his associations. Comparing the roster of his correspondents from one volume of letters to the next, we can track the ebb and flow of friendships. Those new to the roster in volume 3 include Peirce, Shipman, Wister, publisher Charles Scribner, and expatriates Sara and Gerald Murphy.

Notably absent is Gertrude Stein, his influential early mentor. "Gertrude Stein and me are just like brothers," Hemingway wrote to Sherwood Anderson on 9 March 1922, shortly after meeting her in Paris.[1] She soon became one of Hemingway's most frequent correspondents, the recipient of five letters in the final year of volume 1 (1907–1922) and twenty-six letters in volume 2 (1923–1925). They detail the progress of his writing, his efforts to get her 900-page novel serialized in the *Transatlantic Review*, and his son Bumby's teething, until Hemingway broke with Stein in the fall of 1925 after she declined to review *In Our Time*.

Of course, the number of surviving letters to any given recipient is not always a reliable indication of that person's importance in Hemingway's life—or of the numbers of letters they actually exchanged. The thousands of incoming letters that Hemingway saved, including some 9,500 in the Hemingway Collection of the John F. Kennedy Library in Boston, help us gauge the intensity and volume of a correspondence, even when Hemingway's outgoing letters do not survive or remain unlocated.

Among the most lamentable lacunae are his letters to two of the most important women in his life, his wives Hadley and Pauline. Hadley burned most of Hemingway's letters to her after their marriage collapsed, "one of the few outward signs of her rage and sorrow," in the words of her biographer Gioia Diliberto. Pauline left instructions that all of her correspondence be destroyed after her death, and after she died suddenly in 1951, her wishes were observed. Nevertheless, a few of Hemingway's letters to them survived, and included in this volume are two to Hadley and nine to Pauline. As a measure of the original magnitude of these correspondences, among Hemingway's papers at the Kennedy Library are 69 letters he received from Hadley during this period, totaling 198 pages, and 80 letters, totaling 289 pages, from Pauline.

Hemingway thrived on the contact of correspondence. He eagerly solicited letters, even as he sometimes apologized for the quality or frequency of his own. "This is a rotten letter but if you write I'll write a good one. I cant write letters but have better luck answering them," he told Ernest Walsh in a letter of 7 April 1926.[3] About to sail for Europe after a ten-day trip to New York City to change publishers, he wrote to Bill Smith and Harold Loeb on 18 February 1926, "A screed to the boat would materially shorten the passage." To his sister Sunny, then working in a dentist's office in Oak Park, he wrote on 1 October 1928 from Pauline's family home in Piggott, Arkansas, "Tear a little time from your tooth extracting and write me again. A letter in Arkansas is worth nine any place else."

Hemingway was always hungry for the news, the inside scoop. "Send on all the dirt. Hotel Rossli until the end of the month," he wrote to Pound from Gstaad, Switzerland, on 13 February 1927. "Slip me the dope," he told Bill Smith in a letter of 28 July 1927. In a letter to Fitzgerald of c. 15 September 1927, Hemingway entreated his friend for gossip and preemptively returned the favor:

> Love to Zelda and Scotty—write me all the dirt. The Murphies have been in Antibes all summer I think. Have heard nothing from Don Stewart since he left last fall. Nothing from Benchley. Letters from Dos pretty often. MacLeishes are in America. Pat Guthrie after Duff got her divorce wouldn't marry her because she had lost her looks and now lives with Lorna Lindsley who saved him from jail on a bad check and who can let him go to jail at any time. Duff is on the town.

He signed off, "What the hell. Please write. I would like to hear all about Liteary Affairs—wish I could see you and talk."

Patrick Hemingway, the author's surviving son, has remarked that his father "probably could have earned his living as a gossip columnist," noting that for most of Hemingway's lifetime, newspaper and radio personalities like Walter Winchell "gave you the latest word on who was sleeping with who and all that stuff." Patrick added, "I mean, it's in the letters. What's the gossip? What's going on? And he was very good at it."[4]

Responding to a newsy letter from Isabelle Simmons Goldophin listing fifteen numbered nuggets of Oak Park gossip, Hemingway declared (c. 12 August 1928), "Well that was a <u>grand</u> letter." He was on page 574 of his novel-in-progress (*A Farewell to Arms*) and hoped to finish soon. "All I do is work and work—Never write letters—but love to get them— You certainly presented the town in a masterly way—," he wrote. "Got to stop— All the juice has to go in the book—" Yet he added, "Please write again—"

As much as he enjoyed receiving them, writing letters was a distraction from his serious writing, and Hemingway's priorities were clear. A flurry of correspondence with publishers vying for the British rights to his work was "All damned annoying when you are writing a novel and don't want any business of any sort," he complained to Perkins on 19 October 1927. "It's gotten now so I won't open any letter or cable until the end of the day and the day's work finished. Always excepting your own letters none of which have come."

To Bill Smith, he wrote in a letter of 1 November 1927 in their characteristic personal slang, "The writer has been playing the role of son of a bitch with you again Smith due to nonwritage—but it has been due to working on a novel which has emptied the writer like a sink or watercloset every day and made screeding near an impossibility."

Working steadily on *A Farewell to Arms*, he apologized to his father on 1 June 1928, "I am sorry not to have written more and oftener but it is almost impossible to write a letter when you are writing as hard as I am on this book. I am apalled at the urgent letters I should write." To Archibald MacLeish, he wrote on 15 July 1928, "Once I get this fooking book done (it rides me and poops me all day and all night) I will write you out of house and home wit letters."

In contrast to the painstaking craftsmanship of Hemingway's published work, the letters are unpolished, unselfconscious, candid, and casual. He dashed off letters on whatever paper was handy. A letter of 11 January 1929 to Henry Strater is written on the back of a discarded draft page from the typescript of *A Farewell to Arms*.

His running remarks on the circumstances of composition imbue the letters with a sense of immediacy. A letter of 4 January 1929 to "Mother Pfeiffer and Patrick's Grandfather" evokes an intimate domestic scene in a household with two small children. "Pat has gotten his second tooth through today," he told his in-laws. "He is very happy and reasonable and good and inherits from his mother the ability to let it be known if he is mistreated." Thanking them for their Christmas gifts and reporting Bumby's delight in his new accordion, Hemingway wrote, "This letter had better stop because everyone is going to bed and the typewriter is noisy."

Typewriter malfunctions were also cause for comment and curses. "My own typewriter is broken and this borrowed one has so many wretched individual traits that my mind is half occupied all the time I'm writing with the malignancy of the machine," he told Maxwell Perkins in a letter of 6 December 1926. To Guy Hickok he wrote (c. 27 July 1928), "this typer is not mine and I don't know where the margin release is—am not trying to pull an ezra on you with fancy spellings," joking about the erratic phonetic spellings characteristic of the letters of Ezra Pound.

A series of letters he wrote in February 1927 from the Hotel Rössli in Gstaad are typewritten in red ink, with portions of some characters appearing in black—the result of a jammed ribbon holder causing the keys to misstrike the standard red and black ribbon. In a 14 February letter to Perkins outlining the stories to be included in *Men Without Women*, Hemingway parenthetically interjected, "(Please pardon this ribbon)." Writing to Pound the day before, he had been less polite. Referring to the new dust cover design for Scribner's latest printing of *The Sun Also Rises*, he wrote, "They have sent me a wrapper—admirably conceived—beautifully executed (fuck this typewriter) for the 5th printing."

Hemingway's some 6,000 surviving letters located to date are directed to more than 1,900 recipients. When asked what it was like to write a letter to his father, Patrick Hemingway responded, "Easy. Easy because he directed his letters to whoever he was writing with the perception of the correspondence that had taken place over the years and the things that you had in common."[5]

Hemingway was a natural rhetorician, always aware of his audience and tailoring each letter to its reader. Sometimes he would write letters in clusters, even writing individual letters to each of his parents and mailing them in separate envelopes to the same address on the same day. In a letter of 1 June 1928 to his father, a physician who taught him to fish and hunt and love the outdoors, Hemingway reported the size, numbers, and species of fish he caught in the teeming waters off the Marquesas Islands. He also sought obstetrical advice as to where Pauline should go for the birth of their child. That same day, in a separate letter to his mother, who had taken up painting, he inquired, "How is ART?" adding, "Literature is very hot and sweaty today."

In later years, Hadley said of Ernest, "He was so complicated; so many sides to him you could hardly make a sketch of him in a geometry book."[6] Taken together, his collected letters reveal the many facets of Hemingway that too often have been obscured by the one-dimensional public persona—the mythical macho figure that sometimes threatens to overwhelm our view of Hemingway the human being and the writer.

Certainly the letters show Hemingway the bon vivant, organizing outings with comrades, whether on the ski slopes of Austria and Switzerland, in the bullring of Pamplona, in the mountains of Wyoming, or in the waters off the Florida Keys— making preparations, anticipating the provisions they will need, taking inventory of his alcohol supply, boasting of the bounty of the catch or the hunt. He also had a wicked wit, particularly on display in letters to Pound, as in the letter of 5 January 1928 in which he expressed his contempt for Wyndham Lewis by referring to Lewis's magazine, *The Enemy*, as "The Enema."

Yet in his letter to Hadley of 18 November 1926, we hear his expression of contrition and tenderness for the woman he knows he has deeply wronged and is leaving for another. "I think perhaps the luckiest thing Bumby will ever have is to have you for a mother," he wrote, "and I pray God always that he will make up to you the very great hurt that I have done you—who are the best and truest and loveliest person that I have ever known." Writing to Pauline, an ocean away during the three-month separation that was Hadley's requirement for granting a divorce so they could marry, Hemingway expressed his agonized loneliness and thoughts of suicide. "I've felt absolutely done for and gone to pieces," he confessed to Pauline in a letter of 12 November 1926. In a letter of 9–14 September 1927, written five months after his wedding to Pauline, we hear the voice of the wayward son attempting to explain to his respectable Midwestern parents why he had not told them of his divorce before they read about it in the newspaper.

The letters also show Hemingway's practical side. In a letter to his sister Sunny of 13 November 1928, he gave detailed instructions for preparing his Model A Ford for their drive together from Oak Park to Florida, stipulating that she take it to the Snow Brothers garage and get "5 quarts of Mobiloil A."

Among Hemingway's underappreciated qualities are his lively sense of humor and gift for parody. Bragging about his infant son Patrick in a 1 October 1928 letter to his sister, he mimics the rhetoric of contemporary advertising while lightly mocking their mother: "I am thinking of advertising as a male parent— Exceptional children for All Mothers—are your children deformed, underweight, rickety? E. Hemingway son of Grace Hall Hemingway the Paintress— Perhaps He can help You."

Hemingway liked his joke so much that he also used it in a letter to F. Scott Fitzgerald (c. 28 September 1928): "I am thinking of advertising in the Nation or some such suitable medium. Are your children Rickety, deformed, in any way unsatisfactory. See E. Hemingway (then pictures of the product—all by different Mothers) Perhaps He can help You . . . Tear off the enclosed coupon and mail it in a plain stamped envelope and you will receive his booklet Perfect Children for You All."

And although Hemingway could gripe in a letter of 23 July 1928 to Waldo Peirce about "muchachos yelling all the time" as he was trying to write, his letters also express a father's tender love and pride in his offspring. Shortly before returning with his family to Europe, Hemingway wrote affectionately to his devout mother-in-law on 4 March 1929, "[Patrick] and Bumby are both too good to be true and I'm glad you go to the retreat and pray a great deal so that you will have enough credit stored up so that we may deserve, through you, to have them. I feel about them as when I'm fishing and have some gigantic and unbelievable fish—knowing that if anything happens no one will ever believe it— but think of you as a lying fisherman or only a fond father."

The range of Hemingway's voices is demonstrated most dramatically when he writes of his father's suicide. On 13 December 1928, a week to the day after Clarence Hemingway fatally shot himself in the family home, Ernest wrote openly and without pose to his mother-in-law, whom he trusted with his emotions. "I was awfully fond of my father—and still feel very badly about it all and not able to get it out of my mind and my book into my mind," he wrote. "I fixed the practical side of things up in Chicago as well as I could—got it organized . . . Also got them pretty well cheered up but couldn't cheer my self up after I went away. My father had been having much pain and hadN't been able to sleep and the poison of all that knocked him out of his head . . . He was going through that time of a man's life when things are liable to seem the very blackest and most out of proportion too."

A week later, writing to his own mother and youngest siblings on 19 December 1928 in his new role as head of the family, he put on a brave face: "Best love and again wish you as merry a Christmas as I know Dad would have wanted you and us all to have."

Hemingway's correspondence with Archibald MacLeish about his father's suicide illuminates the closeness of their friendship. "You must not let your mind work over and over the way it happened," MacLeish advised Hemingway in a letter of 14 December 1928. "I know how your mind works round and round your pain like a dog in cover going over and over the same track and what a torment it is to you. But now you must not" (JFK). Hemingway responded with appreciation (c. 23 December 1928), "You wrote a swell letter—you were right about what I shouldnt do— Am keeping my mind on my work but what socks on the jaw this book has taken!"

"My old man shot himself as you may have read in the paper," Hemingway wrote to Waldo Peirce on 4 January 1929. "Hell of a lonely way to die. Combination of losing all his money, not being able to sleep, finding he had diabetes and the good old pain of Angina pectoris. Poor old boy." Yet on the very same day, writing to John Dos Passos, he adopted a startlingly callous tone, focusing on the financial strains imposed by his father's death: "Every other day we shoot snipe for the day after. My old man shot himself on the other hand (not in the other hand. In the head) as you may have read in the paper."

In what is perhaps their greatest value, the letters are revealing of Hemingway's creative process, his aims, his assessments of his own writing and that of others, his keen competitiveness, and his high ambitions. After rereading his own story "The Undefeated" in the second number of *This Quarter*, Hemingway told Ernest Walsh (c. 15 January 1926):

> Disliked it when I read the proof. I thought it was a great story when I wrote it. Don't think I am getting vacillating or doubtful about my stuff and do not, for instance, think it is a hell of a lot better story than my well known contemporaries can write. But the hell of it is that I am not in competition with my contemporaries but with the clock—which keeps on ticking—and if we figure out some way to stop our own particular clock all the other clocks keep on ticking . . . Oh Christ I want to write so well and it makes me sore to think that at one time I thought I <u>was</u> writing so well and was evidently in a slump.

Hemingway never shied from the hard work of writing or disguised its difficulty. "My god it is hard for anybody to write," he told Waldo Peirce in a letter of c. 1 October 1928, as he encouraged his friend to do some writing:

> I never start a damn thing without knowing 200 times I can't write— never will be able to write a line—can't go on—can't get started—stuff is rotten—can't say what I mean—know there is a whole fine complete thing and all I get of it is the bacon rinds— You would write better than anybody but the minute it becomes impossible you stop. That is the time you have to go on through and then it gets easier. It always gets utterly and completely impossible. Thank God it does—otherwise everybody would write and I would starve to death.

Soon after completing the draft of *A Farewell to Arms*, Hemingway wrote to Maxwell Perkins in early September 1928, "Writing whether you want it or not is competitive— Most of the time you compete against time and dead men— sometimes you get something from a living (contemporary | competitor) that is so good it jars you." He cited as an example a chapter of Thornton Wilder's 1927 novel *The Bridge of San Luis Rey*. "But as you read them dead or living you unconsciously compete—" he wrote. "You know the ones you have no chance against and the others that, with luck, you can beat. Living and dead. Only never tell this to anyone because they might call it the megalomania or simply swollen head."

And in a letter of 11 March 1929, the novel finished, pronounced by Max Perkins "a most beautiful book," and about to be serialized in *Scribner's Magazine*,

Hemingway wrote to the older writer Owen Wister, who had taken an interest in his work, "I hope so that you'll like the book—" Hemingway described the course of its composition over the past year and the gamut of his own emotions along the way. "I worked like a horse from the end of January until nearly the end of August— then the devils own re-writing from Thanksgiving day until the end of January—," he wrote:

> It seems that much better book—but I'm still so close to it that can't tell if I've made it or only think I've made it— So now we fish and when an installment comes it seems all new and grand—it can't be as good as it seems—and I know the time is coming when it all goes to ashes—that is probably reserved for when it's between covers—but in the meantime there are no worries—finances, nothing can touch me—and my only worry is that I'll die or drown or someone shoot me or some such silly thing before I can write another book. Then, of course, the awakening is when you sit down and are utterly unable to write a story or a line of anything.

The letters testify to Hemingway's dogged discipline as a writer. They log his progress almost daily, as he tallies and reports the running page counts of his novel. In the letters Hemingway expresses his frustrations, anxieties, and satisfactions with his writing. But rarely, if ever, does he discuss the work itself. "It's a terrible mistake to talk about a book," he told Max Perkins (c. 12 August 1928).

Through the letters we live in the landscapes, meet the people, and witness events unfold that provided fodder for his fiction. Hemingway's letters narrate in real time the life experiences that inform his work. In the case of *A Farewell to Arms*, the letters provide immediate accounts of his being wounded in Italy in 1918 while serving as a volunteer with the American Red Cross Ambulance Service, his falling in love with nurse Agnes von Kurowsky at the hospital in Milan, and, ten years later, Pauline's difficult labor and the Caesarean delivery of their son.

But in the very language of the letters, too, we can sometimes see the genesis of his art. Lines he dropped into a letter with apparent spontaneity echo later in his published work, as though letters served him unconsciously as a sounding board for his craft. A single letter of c. 15 January 1926 to editor Ernest Walsh, dashed off in response to the issue of *This Quarter* that had just arrived in the mail that morning, almost uncannily presages two later works. Taking issue with Walsh's claim in the magazine that expatriate writer and publisher Robert McAlmon was a better writer than Mark Twain, Hemingway declared:

> Mark Twain wrote great, vast quantities of Hog Wash. He also wrote one, and one only very wonderful thing—Huck Finn. And if you will,

now, read Huckleberry Finn, honest to God read it as I re-read it only about three months ago, not anything else by Mark Twain, but Huckleberry Finn, and the last few Chapters of it were just tacked on to finish it off by Howells or somebody. The story stops when Jim, the nigger, is captured and Huck finds himself alone and his nigger gone. That's the end. Well you read Huckleberry Finn and if you really, honest to ourselves believe MacAlmon has ever written anything or everything together that deserves to be mentioned in the same room, house, city, continent or magazine with Huckleberry Finn I will stop writing because there will be no damn use to write if such a state of things can be.

Nearly a decade later, in the opening chapter of *Green Hills of Africa* (1935), Hemingway would famously proclaim, "All modern American literature comes from one book by Mark Twain called *Huckleberry Finn*. If you read it you must stop where the Nigger Jim is stolen from the boys. That is the real end. The rest is just cheating. But it's the best book we've had. All American writing comes from that. There was nothing before. There has been nothing as good since."

In the same mid-January 1926 letter to Walsh, Hemingway also objected to Walsh's dismissal of all but modern poetry. "This is my idea of Poetry—" he said, quoting the sixteenth-century lyric that begins "O western wind, when wilt thou blow" and naming "Andy Marvell To His Coy Mistress somewhere in 17th century." Lines from both poems would reverberate in *A Farewell to Arms*, which he would not begin to write for two more years.

While Hemingway was writing the first draft of that novel, Pauline gave birth to their son Patrick on 28 June 1928 by Caesarean section after a dangerous protracted labor. In a letter of 4 July 1928, Hemingway reported to his parents, "He is very big strong and healthy. He is too big in fact as he nearly killed his mother." In the final chapter of *A Farewell to Arms*, shortly after Catherine Barkley's Caesarean delivery and shortly before her death, a nurse asks the protagonist Frederic Henry if he is proud of his newborn son (neither yet realizing the baby was dead): "'No,' I said. 'He nearly killed his mother.'"

Hemingway claimed he never wanted his letters to be published and typed out a 1958 directive to his executors to that effect. During his lifetime he had, in fact, consented to the publication of a handful of his letters.[7] He wrote others expressly for publication, including letters to the editor, book jacket blurbs, and occasional commercial endorsements, including ones for Parker Pens, Ballantine's Ale, and Pan American Airlines.[8] After Hemingway's death in 1961, a trickle of additional letters appeared in print, and the following years saw increasing calls for publication of his letters—not to bend to "a demand for literary gossip or prurience," in the words of scholar E. R. Hagemann, but to satisfy the "demand of literary history."[9]

Finally the author's widow, Mary Hemingway, in consultation with her attorney, Alfred Rice, and Hemingway's publisher, Charles Scribner, Jr., authorized publication of a volume of letters. To edit the book they chose Carlos Baker, the Princeton professor who had written the 1969 authorized biography, *Hemingway: A Life Story*. Baker's edition of *Selected Letters 1917–1961*, encompassing 581 letters, was published by Scribner's in 1981. Since then a few other clusters of Hemingway correspondence have been published, including letters he exchanged with Maxwell Perkins, his sister Marcelline, Sara and Gerald Murphy, and A. E. Hotchner.[10]

Of his father's directive that his letters not be published, Patrick Hemingway said in a 2015 interview, "I find that puzzling. He surely was pretty savvy about these things. He must have known there wasn't a chance that his letters wouldn't be published. I mean the sign that you're destroying your letters is that you're destroying them." "We had specific conversations on letters, my Dad and, I," he recalled. He recounted with a hearty laugh his father's admonition comparing their correspondence to the letters from the English statesman Philip Dormer Stanhope, fourth earl of Chesterfield (1694–1773), to his son—posthumously published in 1774 and widely read as a guide to the manners and morals of the era. "'You know, Mouse,' he said, 'We're really in the position of Lord Chesterfield's letters to his son.' And he said, 'It doesn't really matter what you write to me, but it's *very important* what I write to you.'"[11]

When the Cambridge Edition of *The Letters of Ernest Hemingway* was launched in 2011 with the publication of the first volume, only about 15 percent of Hemingway's some 6,000 known surviving letters had previously seen print. The project was authorized by the Ernest Hemingway Foundation and the Hemingway Foreign Rights Trust, holders, respectively, of the U.S. and international copyrights to the letters.

It is the express wish of Patrick Hemingway that this edition be as complete a collection of his father's letters as possible. "I felt that if they were going to publish his letters at all, there shouldn't be any picking and choosing, that you either got the whole picture of him as a correspondent, as a letter writer, or nothing at all," he said.[12]

The Cambridge Edition aims to be as comprehensive as possible, affording readers ready access to the entire body of Hemingway's located surviving letters, those previously published as well as those appearing here in print for the first time. The letters are presented complete and unabridged, arranged in chronological order of their composition. Although we do not publish the letters that Hemingway received, they inform our editorial comments on his outgoing letters.

Fortunately for posterity, Hemingway was a packrat. Like many writers, he saved drafts, manuscripts, and galley proofs of his published work, manuscripts of work-in-progress, and occasional carbon copies of business letters. But over the years he also preserved drafts and false starts of letters, completed letters that he decided not to mail (sometimes scrawling "Unsent" across a dated envelope), and outtakes from letters that he scissored off or tore away before sending.

We define "letters" broadly to include postcards, cables, identifiable drafts and fragments, letters Hemingway wrote for publication, and those he thought better of sending but nevertheless saved.

As a rule we do not include book inscriptions, except those the editors consider substantive or of particular interest. For the most part only one authorial copy of each letter exists; thus we have faced few problematic issues of textual history and textual variants. When such issues do arise, they are addressed in the notes that follow each letter.

Letters are transcribed whole and uncut whenever possible. However, when letters are known only through facsimiles or extracts appearing in auction catalogs or dealer listings, or through published quotations, we present whatever portions are available, citing their source. While they are no substitute for the original documents, such extracts can serve as place markers in the sequence of letters until such time as complete originals may become available.

Because Hemingway did not routinely keep copies of his letters and because they are so widely dispersed, simply locating the letters has been a massive undertaking. It helps that Hemingway was famous enough at an early enough age that many of his correspondents beyond his family saved his letters. Furthermore, many recipients of his letters were sufficiently well known themselves that their own correspondence has been preserved in archival collections, with Hemingway's letters among their papers. His letters to Maxwell Perkins, F. Scott and Zelda Fitzgerald, Sylvia Beach, and Henry Strater survive at the Princeton University Library; his letters to Ezra Pound primarily at the Beinecke Library at Yale; those to Archibald MacLeish at the Library of Congress; and letters to Waldo Peirce, along with photographs and scrapbooks, at Colby College. The Pennsylvania State University Special Collections Library holds a collection of more than one hundred previously inaccessible family letters acquired in 2008 from Hemingway's nephew Ernest Hemingway Mainland, son of Hemingway's sister Sunny, along with a trove of other family materials he donated, including several volumes of scrapbooks that Grace Hemingway compiled for Sunny (as she did for each of her six children).

To date we have gathered copies of letters from some 250 sources in the United States and abroad. These include more than seventy libraries and institutional archives. The world's largest repository of Hemingway papers, the John

F. Kennedy Presidential Library in Boston, has donated copies of all outgoing letters in its collection (some 2,500 letters) for the benefit of this project. The edition has benefited from the generosity and interest of scores of scholars, archivists, aficionados, book and autograph specialists, collectors, and surviving correspondents and their descendants, including members of Hemingway's extended family, who have provided valuable information or shared copies of letters. As an important part of our editorial process, our transcriptions, initially made from photocopies or scans provided by institutional repositories and private owners, have been meticulously compared against the original documents on site visits whenever possible.

Since the Hemingway Letters Project was initiated in 2002 to produce this edition, I have learned that it is almost impossible to overestimate public interest in Hemingway and the broad appeal of his work. Dozens of people from around the world have contacted us to share information or copies of letters, and new letters continue to surface. Recently we heard from a woman in Idaho whose father ran the Hertz Rent-a-Car franchise in Boise. While cleaning out her garage, she discovered her father's battered old briefcase containing a letter from Hemingway dated 7 November 1959. It concerned a mixup in payment for the automobile he drove from Sun Valley to Key West the previous spring. ("I always pay my bills and pay them promptly and I feel very badly about this matter," Hemingway wrote, offering to reimburse any expenses incurred by the delayed payment).[13]

Based on the estimated number of letters we expected to find, we initially planned a twelve-volume edition. We now project the complete edition to run to at least seventeen volumes to hold the nearly three million words Hemingway wrote in letters, along with our own introductory materials, annotations to the letters, chronologies, maps, and other editorial apparatus. The final volume will feature a section of "Additional Letters," for those that come to light after publication of the volumes in which they would have appeared chronologically.

Hemingway's letters present more challenges to the reader and editors than one might expect from a writer so renowned for simplicity. Obscure personal references, ever-evolving nicknames, in-jokes, and offbeat private lingos that he shared with particular correspondents are at times perplexing, if not virtually impenetrable. As a rule we leave it to readers to experience Hemingway's language on their own as he wrote it, without editorial intervention or attempts at explication. In transcribing the letters, we have preserved exactly Hemingway's idiosyncrasies of spelling, punctuation, syntax, and style, including his well-known habit of retaining the silent *e* in such word forms as "liveing" or "desireable."

The letters display Hemingway's love of wordplay and linguistic inventions. "God Nose I havent been writing letters," he commented in a letter of 7 April 1926 to Ernest Walsh. In a 31 May 1928 letter to Maxwell Perkins, he wrote from Piggott, Arkansas, "Am now at the above address—a christ offal place." In a letter of 15 July 1928 to Archibald MacLeish, whose third child would be born the next month, Hemingway wrote, "If you aren't writing litrachur (Influence of Pound on Hem's style) or doing obstetrics write me another letter." Having completed the draft of *A Farewell to Arms*, he told Sylvia Beach in a letter of 24 September 1928, "My book, (first draft) is finally done (or dung)."

As Hemingway lived in Paris and traveled in Austria, Switzerland, Spain, and Italy, he seasoned his letters with words and phrases of French, German, Spanish, and Italian, with various degrees of grammatical precision. He had an ear for idiomatic expressions and slang, including the off-color. He would mix languages in a single sentence, anglicize foreign words, and give English words a foreign flair. He took great amusement in the sayings of his French-speaking three-year-old son, Bumby, quoting them in letters to friends. In a 5 March 1927 letter to Isabelle Simmons Godolphin, Hemingway reported that upon arriving in Switzerland by overnight train, Bumby had pronounced, "'La Suisse est vraiment magnifique papa!' So now I'm teaching him English and he goes around to everyone saying 'I spik Englich.'"

In letters to the burly painter Waldo Peirce, a fellow hispanophile and bullfighting aficionado who had just come into an inheritance, Hemingway employed a whimsical array of Spanish-sounding salutations. He variously addressed Peirce as "Capitalista enorme," "Muy Waldo Mio," or "Muy borracho y bangoristo mio—" ("muy borracho" meaning "very drunk," and the invented "bangoristo" a reference to Peirce's hometown of Bangor, Maine). Hemingway sometimes addressed Ezra Pound, who lived in Italy, as "Il Duce," in joking reference to Benito Mussolini, whom Pound admired and Hemingway scorned. In a letter of c. 14 November 1926, he addressed the multilingual Pound as "Dear Herr Gott"—literally, "Dear Mr. God," a pun on *der Herrgott*, a German expression for God or the Lord.

When not taking deliberate liberties with the English language or experimenting in another, Hemingway generally was a sound speller. His handwritten letters exhibit few errors, apart from occasional slips of the pen. But his typewritten letters are often riddled with mechanical errors that he did not bother to correct. When he mistyped a word or phrase, rather than stop to erase and retype it accurately, he typically would type a string of x's through the mistake and continue on, or sometimes simply retype his correction or revision over the original attempt with more forceful keystrokes.

To silently correct Hemingway's spelling and punctuation or to regularize capitalization in the letters would strip them of their personality and present a falsely tidy view of the letters his correspondents received. Such cleaning-up also would render meaningless his own spontaneous metacommentary on the imperfections of his letters or his likely misspellings.

Of F. Scott Fitzgerald, Hemingway wrote to Maxwell Perkins in a letter of 21 April 1928, "He is prolific as a Guinea pig (mis-spelled)." Concerning Thornton Wilder's changing publishers, Hemingway speculated in a 7 June 1928 letter to Perkins that "he must have some reason or have fallen among peculiarly plausable thieves. I have heard several of them talk and they are all plausible (I'll try it with an i)—" In a letter to Perkins of 23 July 1928, he reported on Patrick's birth, saying, "Pauline had a very bad time— Cesaerian (can't spell it) and a rocky time afterwards—"

Hemingway also made wry remarks about his own grammar. Concerning *transition*, the new literary review being edited by Eliot Paul and Eugene Jolas, he commented in a letter to Pound (after 20 January 1927), "No matter who or whom, for all I know of grammar whom is the feminine of who, the literary journalists Messers Paul and Peter Jolas get for their first number a review can't be run without intelligence."

Yet even as we attempt to preserve the idiosyncratic flavors of Hemingway's letters, we strive to make them as accessible and readable as possible. We have regularized the placement of such elements as dateline, inside address, salutation, closing, signature, and postscripts. We also normalize Hemingway's often erratic spacing and paragraph indentation. For example, sometimes he would type a space both before and after punctuation marks or hit the space bar two or three times between words, creating a visual quirkiness that we do not attempt to reproduce in print. No published transcription of a typed or handwritten letter can ever fully capture its actual appearance on the page. This is not a facsimile edition, and for those wishing to study in depth the physical characteristics of a letter, no printed rendition can substitute for an examination of the original.

We rely primarily on notes, rather than on intrusive symbols within the text, to supply necessary contextual information, translations of foreign words and passages, and first-mention identifications of people in each volume. Annotations appear as explanatory notes immediately following each letter. A more detailed description of our editorial practices and procedures appears in the Note on the Text in this volume. Our aim is to produce an edition that is at once satisfying to the scholar and inviting to the general reader.

Hemingway always drew a clear distinction between writing letters and writing for keeps. He liked to write letters, he told Fitzgerald in a letter of 1 July 1925, "because it's such a swell way to keep from working and yet feel you've done something."[14] Hemingway did not recognize the letter as one of his strongest and richest genres.

When asked what role he thought the publication of the collected letters would play in his father's legacy, Patrick Hemingway replied:

> I think it will make him much more accessible. When we read a really fine work of fiction, I think we're always interested in the author. We think, how did this man gain the insights and the knowledge to write so well? There must be something about him that's interesting for himself or herself alone. And the letters of Hemingway will supply them with all the information they want as to why he wrote the way he did, for the insights he had and his abilities.[15]

Yet the insights afforded by Hemingway's letters extend beyond the biographical. Patrick likened his father's letters to the seventeenth-century diary of Samuel Pepys, whose personal observations of such events as the Plague of London and the Great Fire of London constitute a primary record of the history of his times. As for why he wanted his father's letters to be published, "My feeling was that really for the first half of the twentieth century, they are a unique record because he was a writer and also a newspaper person, as well," Patrick said. "And he was involved in so much of it, so that his letters are a portrait of the first half of the twentieth century."[16]

Pulitzer-prize winning biographer A. Scott Berg wrote of the collected letters:

> Their value cannot be overstated. Where Hemingway's published works had all been so deliberate and painstakingly chiseled, his letters were free-form and expansive—unsanded and unvarnished. "I would write one true sentence, and then go on from there," he famously said of the process he had applied to a lifetime of literary efforts. In the final analysis, however, his letters may prove to be the most honest log of Hemingway's fascinating life voyage, the truest sentences he ever wrote.[17]

"Writing a novel if you write hard instead of easy is a hell of a job," Hemingway told Waldo Peirce in a letter of 17 June 1928 as he was deep in drafting *A Farewell to Arms*. He considered letter writing as writing "easy." It is their very lack of polish that gives Hemingway's letters their unique value as background and counterpoint to his published works and as a running record of his age.

NOTES

1 Sandra Spanier and Robert W. Trogdon, eds., *The Letters of Ernest Hemingway*, Volume 1 (1907–1922) (New York: Cambridge University Press, 2011), 330.
2 Gioia Dilberto, *Hadley* (New York: Ticknor & Fields, 1992), xii.
3 Unless otherwise cited, all letters quoted in this introduction are included in this volume.
4 Patrick Hemingway, interview with Sandra Spanier, Bozeman, Montana, 8 June 2011.
5 Ibid.
6 Quoted in Denis Brian, *The True Gen: An Intimate Portrait of Ernest Hemingway by Those Who Knew Him* (New York: Grove Press, 1988), 52.

7 In part or in full, these include letters to Stein, to critic Edmund Wilson, to his Italian and German publishers, and to the Oak Park Public Library on the occasion of its fiftieth anniversary. They appear, respectively, in Donald Gallup, ed., *The Flowers of Friendship: Letters Written to Gertrude Stein* (New York: Knopf, 1953); Edmund Wilson, *The Shores of Light: A Literary Chronicle of the Twenties and Thirties* (New York: Vintage Books, 1952); *Il Cinquantennio Editoriale di Arnoldo Mondadori*, 1907–1957 (Verona: Mondadori, 1957); *Rowohlts Rotblonder Roman* (Hamburg: Rohwohlt, 1947); and *Library Journal* 79 (December 1954): 292. The history of publication of Hemingway's letters and the genesis of the Cambridge Edition are discussed in more detail in the "General Editor's Introduction to the Edition" in *The Letters of Ernest Hemingway*, Volume 1 (2011) and Volume 2 (2013), and also in my "Letters" chapter of *Ernest Hemingway in Context*, ed. Debra A. Moddelmog and Suzanne del Gizzo (Cambridge: Cambridge University Press, 2013), 33–42.

8 Collected in Matthew J. Bruccoli and Judith S. Baughman, eds., *Hemingway and the Mechanism of Fame: Statements, Public Letters, Introductions, Forewords, Prefaces, Blurbs, Reviews, and Endorsements* (Columbia: University of South Carolina Press, 2006).

9 E. R. Hagemann, "Preliminary Report on the State of Ernest Hemingway's Correspondence," *Literary Research Newsletter* 3, no. 4 (1978): 163–72; 165.

10 Matthew J. Bruccoli, ed., with Robert W. Trogdon, *The Only Thing That Counts: The Ernest Hemingway–Maxwell Perkins Correspondence* (New York: Scribner's, 1996); Marcelline Hemingway Sanford, *At the Hemingways: With Fifty Years of Correspondence Between Ernest and Marcelline Hemingway* (Moscow: University of Idaho Press); Linda Patterson Miller, ed., *Letters from the Lost Generation: Gerald and Sara Murphy and Friends*, Expanded edn. (Gainesville: University Press of Florida, 2002); and Albert J. DeFazio III, ed., *Dear Papa, Dear Hotch: The Correspondence of Ernest Hemingway and A. E. Hotchner* (Columbia: University of Missouri Press, 2005).

11 Patrick Hemingway, interview with Sandra Spanier, Boston, Massachusetts, 20 April 2015.

12 Patrick Hemingway, interview with Sandra Spanier, Bozeman, Montana, 8 June 2011.

13 EH to Gordon C. Smith, Jr., 7 November 1959. Courtesy of Paige McKee.

14 Sandra Spanier, Albert J. DeFazio, and Robert W. Trogdon, eds., *The Letters of Ernest Hemingway*, Volume 2 (1923–1925) (New York: Cambridge University Press, 2013), 359.

15 Patrick Hemingway, interview with Sandra Spanier, Bozeman, Montana, 8 June 2011.

16 Patrick Hemingway, interview with Sandra Spanier, Boston, Massachusetts, 20 April 2015.

17 A. Scott Berg, "The Hunt for Hemingway," *Vanity Fair* (October 2011): 290.

ACKNOWLEDGMENTS

The Cambridge Edition of *The Letters of Ernest Hemingway* owes its existence to the authorization and kind cooperation of the Ernest Hemingway Foundation and the Hemingway Foreign Rights Trust, which hold, respectively, the U.S. and international copyrights to the letters. It was Patrick Hemingway who originally conceived of a complete scholarly edition of his father's letters, and he has been most generous and supportive of this effort, meeting with the general editor on several occasions and graciously answering questions, identifying references, and sharing stories illuminating the letters that no one else can tell. For their roles in securing permissions, we extend special thanks to Michael Katakis, representative of the Trust, and to Kirk Curnutt, permissions officer for the Foundation.

From the start the Hemingway Letters Project has benefited immensely from the sound guidance and strong support of our Editorial Advisory Board, whose members have given generously and tirelessly of their time and expertise. Headed by Linda Patterson Miller, the advisors include Jackson R. Bryer, Scott Donaldson, Debra Moddelmog, and James L. W. West III. They deserve special recognition for their exceptional commitment and active involvement, including advising in the establishment of editorial policies and reading the manuscript of this volume at several stages. The edition is much the stronger for their contributions. We are most grateful, too, to J. Gerald Kennedy and Rodger L. Tarr, who have brought to bear their deep knowledge and meticulous attention to detail and have made vital contributions in their capacity as volume advisory editors.

The Hemingway Letters Project has been supported in part by Scholarly Editions grants from the National Endowment for the Humanities. We are honored to have been designated a *We, the People* project, "a special recognition by the NEH for model projects that advance the study, teaching, and understanding of American history and culture." (Any views, findings, or conclusions expressed in this publication do not necessarily represent those of the National Endowment for the Humanities.)

We deeply appreciate the generosity of those organizations and endowments that have supported the Project through grants and gifts: AT&T Mobility, the Heinz Endowments, the Michigan Hemingway Society, the Dr. Bernard S. and Ann Re Oldsey Endowment for the Study of American Literature in the College of the Liberal Arts at The Pennsylvania State University, and the Xerox Corporation, which has contributed copying, printing, faxing, and scanning equipment as well as a DocuShare database management system that has been customized for our needs. We are grateful, too, to individual donors, including Ralph and Alex Barrocas, Linda Messer Ganz, Eric V. Gearhart, Walter Goldstein, Gary Gray and Kathleen O'Toole, Harold Hein, Bill and Honey Jaffe, Lewis Katz, Ira B. Kristel, Mary Ann O'Brian Malkin, Randall Miller, Barbara Palmer, Graham B. Spanier, David A. Westover III, and Mark Weyermuller.

For fellowships and grants to support travel to archives and other research activities by Project scholars, we also wish to thank the Bibliographical Society (U.K.), the Bibliographical Society of America, and the John F. Kennedy Presidential Library. We are grateful to the Idaho Humanities Council for its support of Rena Sanderson in her work on Volume 3 in particular.

The Pennsylvania State University has provided indispensable institutional support and an ideal home for the Project from its inception in 2002. We particularly wish to thank the following, in addition to those named in earlier volumes: Dean Susan Welch, College of the Liberal Arts; Dean Barbara Dewey and Dean Emeritus Nancy Eaton, University Libraries; Nicholas P. Jones, Neil Sharkey, and Henry Foley, Offices of the Provost and of the Vice President for Research; Mark Morrisson, head of the Department of English; and Michael Bérubé, director of the Institute for Arts and Humanities. Rodney Erickson strongly supported the project from the beginning, and for that we are most appreciative. We also wish to thank Rodney Kirsch, senior vice president for Development and Alumni Relations, and Joanne Cahill, Beth Colledge, and John Dietz; Ron Huss and the Intellectual Property Office; Associate Deans Raymond E. Lombra, Denise Solomon, and Eric Silver, and Trish Alexander, Sandra Balboni, Shane Freehauf, Mary Kay Hort, Mark Luellen, Michael Renne, John Taylor, Morgan Wellman, and Chris Woods in the College of the Liberal Arts; English Graduate Studies program director Garrett Sullivan, internship coordinator Elizabeth Jenkins, and the staff of the Department of English; Roger Downs and Deryck Holdsworth of the Department of Geography; and cartographer Erin Greb and the Peter R. Gould Center for Geography Education and Outreach.

We thank Boise State University for its generous support of the work of Rena Sanderson on Volume 3, with special thanks to the English Department and department chair Michelle Payne; and to Albertson Library, especially Alan Virta, former head of Special Collections. We also wish to acknowledge support provided to Robert

W. Trogdon by Kent State University, with particular thanks to Dean James Blank, College of Arts and Sciences; Wesley Raabe, director of the Institute for Bibliography and Editing; and Cathy Tisch, secretary for the Institute for Bibliography and Editing.

In addition to those named on the title page of this volume, we owe special thanks to Hemingway Letters Project editorial team members Mark Cirino, Albert J. DeFazio III, and Miriam B. Mandel for their contributions to its preparation. Hilary K. Justice and LaVerne Maginnis merit recognition for their earlier contributions to this volume. Stacey Guill, Verna Kale, and Ellen Andrews Knodt provided valuable assistance by traveling to archives to perfect transcriptions of Volume 3 letters against original documents. Other consulting scholars to the Project who deserve thanks include Edward Burns, Rose Marie Burwell, Mark Ott, Gladys Rodríguez Ferrero, Chtiliana Stoilova Rousseva, and Lisa Tyler.

We are deeply indebted to the dozens of libraries, museums, and institutional archives that have supplied copies of letters in their collections and assisted in research for the edition.

The John F. Kennedy Presidential Library, the world's largest repository of Hemingway papers, has been particularly generous in its support of the Project, donating copies of its entire holdings of some 2,500 outgoing letters, providing a number of images for illustrations free of charge, and responding tirelessly to our requests and queries. Special thanks are due to Director Thomas J. Putnam; Hemingway Collection Curator Susan Wrynn; Chief Archivist Karen Adler Abramson; Amy Macdonald; in Reference, Stacey Chandler, Christina Fitzpatrick, Kelly Francis, Stephen Plotkin, and interns Suzanna Calev, Elyse Edwards, Tara Mayes Munro, Samuel Smallidge, and Marti Verso-Smallidge; in Audio-Visual Archives, Laurie Austin, Maryrose Grossman, Kora Welsh, Mel Taing, Steve Brannelly, and John Buzanga.

We also gratefully acknowledge the outstanding support of the Pennsylvania State University Libraries, with warmest thanks to Timothy Pyatt, head of Special Collections; William L. Joyce, former head of Special Collections; Sandra Stelts, curator of Rare Books and Manuscripts; and William S. Brockman, Paterno Family Librarian for Literature. Mark Saussure, Steven Baylis, Shane Markley, and Peggy Myers of Digital Libraries Technologies have provided indispensable technical and database management support. We also wish to thank Timothy R. Babcock, Sandra Ball, Shirley Davis, Catherine Grigor, Susan Hamburger, Nicole Hendrix, Sally Kalin, Curtis Krebs, and Albert Rozo.

For supplying copies of letters in their collections and granting permission for their publication in Volume 3 of *The Letters of Ernest Hemingway*, we acknowledge the following libraries and archives, with special thanks to the individuals named here for their assistance: Colby College Special Collections— Patricia Burdick and Erin Rhodes; Columbia University, Rare Book and

Manuscript Library—Michael Ryan, director, Susan G. Hamson, Jennifer B. Lee and Karla Nielsen; Cornell University Library, Division of Rare and Manuscript Collections; Historical Society of Oak Park and River Forest—Frank Lipo; Indiana University, The Lilly Library—Rebecca Cape, Zachary Downey, David K. Frasier, Breon Mitchell, Saundra Taylor, and Cherry Williams; Ernest Hemingway Collection at the John F. Kennedy Presidential Library and Museum; Knox College Library, Special Collections and Archives—Carley Robison, Mary McAndrew, and Kay Vander Meulen; Library of Congress— Frederick W. Bauman; Newberry Library, Chicago—John H. Brady, Martha Briggs, Jo Ellen McKillop Dickie, Alison Hinderliter, John Powell, and Liesl Olson, director of the Scholl Center for American History and Culture; New York Public Library, Berg Collection—Isaac Gewirtz, curator; New York Public Library, Manuscripts and Archives Division, Astor, Lenox, and Tilden Foundations—Tal Nadan; Ohio State University Libraries; Pennsylvania State University Libraries; Princeton University Library Manuscripts Division, Department of Rare Books and Special Collections—Don C. Skemer, curator of Manuscripts, Anna Chen, Sandra Calabrese, Charles E. Greene, AnnaLee Pauls, Chloe Pfendler, Ben Primer, David Dressel, Megan Malta Scauri, and Gabriel Swift; Southern Illinois University, Carbondale, Special Collections Research Center—Pam Hackbart-Dean, director, and James Bantin; Stanford University Libraries, Special Collections and University Archives—Larry Scott and Mattie Taormina, head of Public Services; University of Delaware Libraries, Special Collections—Laurie Rizzo; University of Maryland Libraries, Hemingway Collection, Special Collections—Beth Alvarez; State University of New York, University at Buffalo, The Poetry Collection at the University Libraries, James Maynard; University of North Carolina at Chapel Hill, Wilson Library; University of Texas at Austin, Harry Ransom Humanities Research Center—Jean Cannon, Richard W. Oram, and Rick Watson; University of Virginia Library, Albert and Shirley Small Special Collections— Bradley J. Daigle, Margaret D. Hrabe, Edward F. Gaynor, George Riser, and Heather Riser; University of Wisconsin-Milwaukee, Golda Meir Library, Archives/Special Collections; Yale University, Beinecke Rare Book and Manuscript Library—Nancy Kuhl, curator of the Collection of American Literature, and Anne Marie Menta.

The following also provided special assistance in the preparation of Volume 3: University of South Carolina Library—Elizabeth Sudduth, director of the Irvin Department of Rare Books and Special Collections, Kate Boyd, Ashley Knox, Jeffrey Makala, and Bill Sudduth; and University of Tulsa, McFarlin Library, Department of Special Collections—Marc Carlson.

The many additional libraries and archives whose contributions of materials and assistance pertain primarily to later volumes of the edition will be acknowledged there.

The following manuscript specialists and dealers have been most helpful in a variety of ways: Bart Auerbach; David and Natalie Bauman, Ernest Hilbert, Bauman Rare Books; Patrick McGrath, Christie's New York; Steve Verkman, Clean Sweep Auctions; Edward Ripley-Duggan, Director, Book Department, Doyle, New York; Alexander Buchlis, Ernestoic Books; David Bloom, Freeman's Auctions; Thomas A. Goldwasser; Glenn Horowitz Bookseller, Inc.; George R. Minkoff; Stuart Lutz, Stuart Lutz Historic Documents Inc.; David Meeker, Nick Adams Rare Books; James Pepper; Kenneth W. Rendell Gallery; Selby Kiffer, Sotheby's New York; David Rivera, Swann Galleries; and Gary McAvoy, Vintage Memorabilia.

We are extremely grateful to those individuals who have generously shared copies or transcriptions of letters with the Project. Those who provided letters appearing in or pertaining to Volume 3 include Herbert S. Channick, Andrew Cohen (with thanks also to Sarah Mugnier and Bruno Rivière), Robert K. Elder, Mark Hime, Ernest H. Mainland, Jeffrey Marks, David Meeker, Maurice F. and Marcia Neville, James Sanford, and John E. Sanford.

We also thank the following for sharing copies of letters, photographs, and other materials pertaining to other volumes in the edition: Nick Angell; James Arsenault; Nat Benchley; Brent Benoit; Carl Butrum; Tsuri Bernstein; Nancy Brannan; Benjamin C. Bruce; Kelly and Xan Pugh Carnes; Clackamas Community College, Clackamas, Oregon—Greg Fitzgerald, Robert L. Glass, Martha Ramsdell Johnson, Larry Peterson, Joanne Truesdell; Bernard Dew; Caroline R. Donhauser, Peter L. Donhauser, and the late Rosine Lambiotte Donhauser; Elizabeth Fajans; Virginia Fritch, trustee of the Jean Breeden Estate Collection; Tom Fuller; David Gonsior; C. Edgar Grissom; Paul Heidelberg; Angela Hemingway; Mina Hemingway; Patrick and Carol Hemingway; Wayne Horne; Walter Houk; Finn-Olaf Jones; Declan Kiely, Morgan Library and Museum; Mary Kiffer, John Simon Guggenheim Memorial Foundation; Sean D. Kirkland; Larry E. Kirkland; Jobst Knigge; Evelyn Marques; Paige Smith McKee; Jonathan and Elisabetta Mennell; Liborio Ruíz Molina; Charles Oliver; David Petruzelli; Michael Schnack and family; Steve Soboroff; the Helen Guffey Weaver Estate; and Billy Woodward. We remain grateful to those named in previous volumes and to the donors of letters who wish to remain anonymous.

In order to inform our annotations and ensure accuracy in the transcriptions of letters that Hemingway wrote from a range of locales, addressing an array of specialized topics, and employing various languages, we have called upon the particular expertise of a number of willing volunteers. The following deserve special thanks for the information and insights they have provided relative to Volume 3.

Brewster Chamberlin, Key West Arts and Historical Society, generously shared successive drafts of his detailed Hemingway Chronology, recently published as *The Hemingway Log: A Chronology of his Life and Times* (University Press of Kansas, 2015). We are also grateful to Tom Hambright for his assistance with Key West details. Michael Culver kindly provided important information drawn from his unpublished manuscript, "Sparring in the Dark: The Art and Life of Henry Strater."

Ruth Hawkins and Adam Long of the Hemingway-Pfeiffer Museum and Educational Center were most helpful in addressing our questions and providing materials concerning Pauline Pfeiffer, her family, and Hemingway's time in Piggott, Arkansas. Channy Lyons provided valuable information about Grace Hall Hemingway as an artist. Shari Baeth assisted with volume illustrations.

Steve Paul of the *Kansas City Star* was, as always, a fount of information about Hemingway's Kansas City connections. Bill Schiller of the *Toronto Star* generously shared information on Hemingway's associations with Toronto. Members of the Ernest Hemingway Foundation of Oak Park also deserve thanks: Barbara Ballinger, John W. Berry, Virginia Cassin, Kurt and Mary Jane Neumann, and Alison Sansone. Bart H. Ryckbosch, Glasser and Rosenthal Family Archivist at the Art Institute of Chicago, provided information about paintings that Hemingway particularly admired during his 1928 visit.

We are most grateful, too, to those who shared their language skills and local knowledge.

For French language and Parisian references, Thomas Austenfeld, Stéphan Garnier, Solange Garnier-Fox, Kathryn Grossman, Monique Jutrin, J. Gerald Kennedy, and Anne Reynes.

For German language and references to Germany, Switzerland, and Austria, Thomas Austenfeld and Rena Sanderson.

For Hemingway's Italian, Mark Cirino, Sherry Roush, and Marica Tacconi.

For Spanish language questions and references to Spain and bullfighting, Hjalmar Flax, Miriam B. Mandel, Pablo Pésaj Adi, and Enric Sullà.

For assisting the Project in various other ways, we also wish to thank the following: Kerry Ahearn, Jonathan Bank, A. Scott Berg, Christian M. Brady, Silvio Calabi, Nancy Chiswick, Suzanne Clark, George C. Colburn, Kirk Curnutt, Donald Daiker, John Delaney, Joseph Distler, Stephen Ferguson, Cheryl Glenn, Lavinia Graecen, James Vol Hartwell, John Harwood, Hilary Hemingway, John Hemingway, Sean and Colette Hemingway, Valerie Hemingway, Paul Hendrickson, Steve Hersch, Jonathan Hutchinson, Rosalind Jacobs, Allen Josephs, Donald Junkins, Alessandro Kechler, John King, Brent Kinser, Jeremiah Kitunda, Sara Kosiba, Douglas LaPrade, David Lorigliola, Jeffrey Malala, Alice Anne Martineau, James McClay, Ronald McFarland, David Morrell, John Mulholland, David Murad, Robert M. Myers and sons Bruce and

David Myers, Michael Oriard, Sean O'Rourke, Sally Pemberton, Tony Penrose, Catherine Carino Pescatore and son Joe Pescatore, Thomas H. Reed, Jack Repcheck, John Robben, David Robinson, David and Nanette (Strater) Ruppert, Gary Scharnhorst, Virginia Schmidt, Robert Schwartz, Charles Scribner III, Gail Sinclair, Jean Marilyn (Sewall) Strater, Katherine Strater, Nick Strater, Neil Tristram, Matt Turi, Alex Vernon, Samuel Untermyer III, William B. Watson, Steve Weinberg, and Gene Youtz, as well as those named in previous volumes.

For their parts in preserving Hemingway's letters and other documents at Finca Vigía, his longtime home outside Havana, the 2009 and 2013 opening of these materials to researchers by both the Museo Hemingway in Cuba and the Kennedy Library in Boston, and the continuation of the preservation efforts, the following deserve recognition: in Cuba, Gladys Collazo, President, Consejo Nacional de Patrimonio Cultural (National Council of Cultural Patrimony); Gladys Rodríguez Ferrero, Ana Cristina Parera, Ada Rosa Alfonso Rosales, Isbel Ferreiro Garit, Néstor Álvarez, and the staff of the Museo Hemingway; in the United States, Congressman Jim McGovern, Jenny and Frank Phillips, Bob Vila, Mary-Jo Adams, Thomas D. Herman, Consuelo Isaacson, and the Finca Vigía Foundation. For their ongoing help in enhancing our understanding of Hemingway's life in Cuba we also are grateful to Ana Elena de Arazoza, Enrique Cirules, Esperanza García Fernández, Oscar Blas Fernández, Victor Pina, Raul and Rita Villarreal, and René Villarreal, who for many years served as Hemingway's dedicated mayordomo and as first director of the museum after the author's death.

The Hemingway Letters Project is most fortunate to have the benefit of the skills, professionalism, and dedication of project assistant editors Jeanne Alexander and Bryan Grove. For their excellent service as project assistants, David Eggert and Linnet Brooks deserve many thanks.

Those who have served as graduate and post-graduate research assistants at Penn State deserve much appreciation for their many valuable contributions to the edition. They include Jace Gatzemeyer, Mike Hart, Michelle Huang, Bethany Ober Mannon, Justin Mellette, Katie Owens-Murphy, Krista Quesenberry, and Robert Volpicelli, in addition to those named in previous volumes. We particularly wish to honor the memory of Michael DuBose, who was passionate about the project and contributed so much, always with enthusiasm and good humor. We appreciate, too, the fine work of these undergraduate and post-baccalaureate assistants at the Project center involved in the preparation of this volume: Coral Flanagan, Samantha Gilmore, Julia Kelsey, Adam Virzi, and Victoria Woods.

We thank the following Boise State University graduate students for their enthusiastic assistance: Lauren Allan, Tyler A. Bevis, Nicole Christianson, Daniel Clausen, Victoria L. Grabowski, Ryan Holman, Nathan Green, Marek Markowski, Kathryn Railsback, Linda Gail Smith, Christy C. Vance, and Kristin

W. Whitting. We also thank Kent State University graduate assistants Jennifer Beno, Jennifer Butto, Ben Gundy, Adam McKee, and Rachel Nordhoff.

We are most grateful to our publisher, Cambridge University Press, for its commitment to producing this comprehensive scholarly edition. We wish to express our particular thanks for the vision and support of publisher Linda Bree and the expert assistance of Anna Bond. It has been a great pleasure, too, working with Rachel Ewen and earlier with Frances Bajet and Melissanne Scheld in the New York office. We also wish to thank the following for their roles in the preparation and publication of this volume: in the United Kingdom, Elizabeth Davey, Jessica Ann Murphy, and Hilary Hammond; and in New York, Michael Duncan, Christine Kanownik, and Thomas D. Willshire. For his cover design, we warmly thank Chip Kidd.

Finally, we are deeply grateful for the interest and support of other colleagues, family members, and friends too numerous to name, but who, we trust, know of our appreciation. The editors wish to express special appreciation to the following: Rena Sanderson to Ken Sanderson and Jane Woychick; Sandra Spanier to Graham, Brian, and Hadley Spanier, and to her parents, Richard and Maxine Whipple; and Robert Trogdon to Sara Kosiba. The list of those to whom we owe thanks inevitably will grow much longer as publication of the edition proceeds, and we will continue to acknowledge our accumulating debts of gratitude in subsequent volumes.

SANDRA SPANIER

NOTE ON THE TEXT

RULES OF TRANSCRIPTION

As a rule, the text is transcribed exactly as it appears in Hemingway's hand or typewriting, in order to preserve the flavor of the letter—whether casual, hurried, harried, inventive, or playful (as when he writes "goils" instead of "girls," refers to his cats as "kotsies," remarks "we cant stahnd it," or exclaims "Goturletter thanks!"). When his handwriting is ambiguous, we have given him the benefit of the doubt and transcribed words and punctuation in their correct form.

Special challenges of transcription are treated as follows:

Spelling
- When a typed character is incomplete, distorted, or visible only as an impression on the paper (whether due to a weak keystroke, type in need of cleaning, or a worn-out ink ribbon) but nevertheless is discernible (as ultimately determined in the field checking of the original document), the intended character is supplied without editorial comment.
- When a blank space suggests that an intended letter in a word is missing but no physical trace of a keystroke exists on the manuscript page, or when Hemingway types a word off the edge of the paper, the conjectured missing letter or portion of the word is supplied in square brackets: e.g., "the[y] are trying," or "meningiti[s] epidemic."
- Similarly, when a word is incomplete due to an obvious oversight or a slip of the pen, and the editors deem it advisable for clarity's sake, we supply missing letters in square brackets: e.g., "I[t] makes no difference."
- Because typewriter keyboards varied over time and from one country to another and did not always include a key for every character Hemingway wished to write, he necessarily improvised: e.g., for the numeral one he often

typed a capital letter "I," and for an exclamation point, he would backspace to type a single quotation mark above a period. We have not attempted to reproduce those improvisations or conventions of the day but have silently supplied characters that Hemingway would have typed himself had his keyboard allowed.

- We have not attempted to reproduce in print the appearance of mechanical malfunctions. For example, when jammed typewriter keys cause two letters to appear superimposed in a single letter space, such errors are silently corrected, the letters transcribed without comment in the sequence that makes sense.

Capitalization

As a rule, Hemingway's usage is preserved exactly. However, while his handwriting is generally open and legible, his uppercase and lowercase letters are sometimes indistinguishable (the letters "a" and "g," for example, almost always take the form of the lowercase, with capital letters often differentiated only by their size relative to other letters). In ambiguous cases, we have silently followed correct usage in the context of the sentence.

Punctuation

Whether Hemingway is writing by hand or on a typewriter, there is no apparent pattern to his use or omission of apostrophes, and in handwritten letters he frequently marks the end of a sentence with a dash rather than a period. Hemingway's often erratic punctuation—or lack thereof—has been strictly preserved, except in the following instances:

- In handwritten letters Hemingway sometimes marked the end of a declarative sentence with a small "x" (likely a carryover from his early habits as a newspaper reporter), a wavy flourish, or another mark difficult to render in print. Rather than attempting to reproduce these markings, we have normalized them without comment as periods.
- Hemingway sometimes wrote parentheses as vertical or slanted lines; these have been normalized as curved parentheses.
- Hemingway often neglected to put a period at the end of a paragraph's last sentence (as indicated by indentation of the following line) or at the end of a sentence enclosed in parentheses. Other sentences simply run together. To routinely insert ending punctuation for the sake of grammatical correctness would alter the letters' pace and tone: masking Hemingway's carelessness or breathlessness, erasing both the inadvertent charm of some childhood letters and his intentional wordplay, and imposing an arbitrary logic or false clarity on

some ambiguously worded passages. Generally we do not supply missing full stops, except when the editors deem it necessary for clarity or when Hemingway's intention seems obvious: e.g., as indicated by extra spacing after a word and capitalization of the following word to mark the beginning of a new sentence. In such cases, we supply a period within square brackets.

- Whenever the editors have supplied punctuation for clarity's sake, those punctuation marks are enclosed within square brackets: e.g., as when Hemingway neglected to use commas to separate proper names in a list.

Cancellations and corrections

Hemingway rarely bothered to erase errors or false starts in his letters, typically canceling or correcting written material either by drawing a line through it or typing over it. Usually his intent is clear, and we have not reproduced every cancellation and correction. However, when deleted or altered material is legible and the editors deem it of significance or interest, a cancellation or correction may be retained in place, with a line drawn through the text that Hemingway canceled, as the reader would have encountered it in the letter.

When he typed over his misstrikes with more forceful keystrokes so that his intended phrasing appears in darker type, we present only his corrected version. When he canceled words and phrases by backspacing and typing over them (usually with strings of the letter "x"), he occasionally missed a letter at the beginning or end of the canceled material; we do not reproduce stray characters that he obviously intended to cancel. Nor do we transcribe stray characters, inadvertently repeated words, and false starts that he simply neglected to cancel: e.g., a portion of a word typed off the right margin of the page, followed by the complete word on the following line.

Interlineations, marginalia, and other markings

Hemingway's insertions, whether they appear as interlineations or marginalia, have been transferred into the text at a point that, in the editors' judgment, most accurately reflects his intended placement. However, when the insertion would render a sentence or passage confusing if simply transcribed at the indicated point without comment, we enclose the inserted material within square brackets and provide a brief editorial explanation in italics: e.g., [*EH insertion:*]. When the intended position of any material is questionable or an insertion merits editorial comment, the situation is addressed in a bracketed in-text notation or in an endnote.

When Hemingway's markings indicate that the order of letters, words, or phrases should be transposed, we have done so without comment. When he uses ditto marks to indicate repetition of a word or phrase appearing on a previous line of the original text, we have supplied the word or phrase within square brackets at the indicated place: e.g., "Did you write the Steins? [*Ditto marks*: Did you write the] Ford Maddox Fords."

Whenever possible, Hemingway's occasional sketches or drawings are reproduced as they appear in the text of the letter. Otherwise, brief descriptions are provided in square brackets where such graphic elements appear in the text: e.g., [*Drawing of a sleeping cat*], and any commentary that the editors deem necessary is supplied in a note.

Other markings in the text that are difficult to render in print, such as stray doodles, demarcation lines underneath the letter date or return address, or flourishes following his signature, are not noted unless the editors deem them to be of particular interest. We do not transcribe Hemingway's page numbering.

Indentation and spacing

In both handwritten and typewritten letters, Hemingway's indications of paragraph breaks are irregular. Sometimes, instead of indenting, he signaled a paragraph break by starting a new page, leaving a gap between lines, or ending the previous sentence in midline. The editors have indicated new paragraphs by regular indentation of the first line.

In typewritten letters, Hemingway's spacing is erratic. Frequently he hit the space bar both before and after punctuation marks or several times between words, and extraneous blank spaces occasionally appear in the middle of a word. The spacing around punctuation marks and between words has been normalized, and extraneous blank spaces appearing within words have been silently eliminated.

However, when Hemingway ran words together with no space between, they are transcribed exactly as they appear, as it is often impossible to determine whether he did this accidentally or intentionally for effect. Run-together words also may indicate a mood of haste or excitement that would be lost to readers if conventional spacing were editorially inserted.

Compound words

Transcriptions follow Hemingway's treatment of compound words exactly, with no attempt made to impose consistency or to correct or standardize hyphenation or spacing: e.g., there is no apparent pattern to his usage of such compounds as "good-bye," "goodbye," and "good bye," or "someone" vs. "some one."

In handwritten letters, Hemingway's "y" is often followed by a space that might or might not mark a gap between words: e.g., it is sometimes difficult to tell if he intended to write "anyway" or "any way." When Hemingway's handwriting is ambiguous, we transcribe the word as it would be used correctly in that sentence.

Underlined words
Words underlined by Hemingway are underlined in the transcriptions; the double, triple, and quadruple underlining he occasionally employed also is indicated in order to capture his emphasis or exuberance.

Missing portions of text
Square brackets are used to indicate illegible, damaged, or missing text at the point of occurrence, with a description of the manuscript's condition in italics: e.g., [*illegible*], [*MS torn*], [*MS razor-cut by censor*]. Any conjectured reconstruction of missing text is supplied in roman type within square brackets.

Date and place of writing
The date and place of origin (often a specific return address) as supplied by Hemingway in the text of his letters are transcribed exactly as he wrote them; however, we have standardized the line placement of these elements so they appear flush to the right margin. The use of letterhead is indicated in the source note following the complete text of a letter, and letterhead address information also is recorded there rather than transcribed as part of the text of the letter.

Valediction and signature
Hemingway's valediction and signature are transcribed as he wrote them, whether on one line or two, but their position on the page is standardized so that they appear flush to the right margin.

Postscripts
Regardless of where a postscript appears in the manuscript (in a margin, at the top or bottom of a letter, or on the back of a letter's final page), it is generally transcribed as a new paragraph following the signature, reflecting the probable order of composition.

Joint letters
Letters that Hemingway wrote with another person or to which he adds a postscript are presented in their entirety so as to preserve the context of his portion, with the point at which one writer takes over from another indicated in

brackets: e.g., [*EH writes*:] or [*Hadley writes*:]. Where one writer inserts a brief remark into the text of another, the point of interjection as well as the remark itself are indicated in brackets: e.g., [*EH interjects*: I doubt this.].

Foreign languages

Any portion of a letter written in a language other than English is transcribed exactly as Hemingway wrote it, with no attempt to correct errors or to supply any missing diacritical marks.

When a word, phrase, sentence, or passage within a letter is in a foreign language, a translation is supplied in a note preceded, when deemed necessary for clarity, by the correct spelling or diacritical form of a word. Translations are not supplied for words or phrases presumably familiar to most readers: e.g., *adios, au revoir*. When Hemingway wrote an entire letter in another language, the transcription of the original text is followed by an English translation in square brackets.

We do not attempt in our translations to replicate Hemingway's foreign-language grammatical errors: e.g., in conjugation of verbs and in gender agreement of nouns and adjectives. Rather, we provide a translation that conveys the sense of the message, while briefly noting the presence and nature of such errors. Similarly, we do not attempt to replicate the exact syntax and mechanics (e.g., capitalization and punctuation) of Hemingway's use of a foreign language, but rather aim in our English translation to convey the style and tone of his usage, whether formal or colloquial.

EDITORIAL APPARATUS

Heading

Each letter is preceded by a heading indicating the recipient and date of the letter, with any portion supplied by the editors enclosed in square brackets.

Source note

A bibliographical note immediately following each letter provides information about the source text upon which the transcription is based, including the location and form of the original letter. Abbreviations used are described in the list of Abbreviations and Short Titles in the front matter of each volume. Information appears in this order:

(1) Symbols indicate the location and form of the original letter. For example, "JFK, TLS" indicates a typed letter signed that is located in the collections of

the John F. Kennedy Library. When the original letter cannot be located and the transcription derives from another source (e.g., a photocopy, a recipient's transcription, a secretary's transcription of dictation, an auction catalog, or another publication), that source is indicated. When Hemingway closed a letter with a "mark" instead of writing his name (as when he drew a beer stein to signify his nickname "Stein," short for "Hemingstein"), we have considered the letter to be signed, describing it, for example, as "TLS" rather than "TL."

(2) The use of letterhead stationery is noted and the address information supplied. Additional letterhead elements tangential to the study of Hemingway (e.g., an advertising slogan, description of a hotel's facilities, proprietor's name, phone number) are not generally recorded. However, in the rare cases when Hemingway provides commentary on these elements, the situation is described in a note. If the text is from a picture postcard, a brief description is provided: e.g., A Postcard S, verso: Sun Valley Lodge, Idaho.

(3) Surviving postmark information is supplied. When a postmark stamp is incomplete or illegible, portions of place names or dates supplied by the editors are enclosed in square brackets: e.g., SCH[RUN]S. When the original letter cannot be consulted and postmark information derives from another source (e.g., a description in an auction catalog), we enclose that information in square brackets.

Endnotes

Annotations appear as endnotes following each letter. In notes Ernest Hemingway is referred to as EH. Initials are not used for any other persons, but editors frequently use the short names that Hemingway would have used: e.g., Hadley for his first wife, Elizabeth Hadley Richardson Hemingway; or Buck Lanham for his friend General Charles T. Lanham. Recipients of letters included in a given volume are identified in the Roster of Correspondents in the back matter of that volume. Other people are identified in endnotes at first mention. There necessarily may be some duplication and cross-referencing as we aim to make the volumes useful to readers, not all of whom will read the letters strictly chronologically within a given volume or across the edition.

In determining which references merit annotation, we have been mindful of the international audience for the edition and, in consultation with the publisher, have provided notes for some references likely to be familiar to U.S. readers: e.g., Karo syrup, Old Faithful geyser. We do not generally attempt to explicate EH's inventive expressions, private slang, and other wordplay, leaving it to readers to experience and interpret his language as he wrote it.

The editors have made every effort to identify EH's references to people, places, events, publications, and artistic works. However, the identities of some are inevitably lost to history. When a note is not provided at the first mention of a reference, the reader can assume that it remains unidentified.

SANDRA SPANIER

ABBREVIATIONS AND SHORT TITLES

MANUSCRIPT SOURCES AND LOCATIONS

Biblioctopus	Biblioctopus Books, Mark Hime
Channick	Herbert S. Channick Collection
Cohen	Andrew Cohen Collection
Colby	Special Collections, Colby College; Waterville, Maine
Columbia	Rare Book and Manuscript Library, Columbia University; New York, New York
Cornell	Rare and Manuscript Collections, Carl A. Kroch Library, Cornell University; Ithaca, New York
HSOPRF	Historical Society of Oak Park and River Forest; Oak Park, Illinois
IndU	Lilly Library, Indiana University; Bloomington, Indiana
JFK	Ernest Hemingway Collection at the John F. Kennedy Presidential Library and Museum; Boston, Massachusetts
Knox	Special Collections and Archives, Knox College Library; Galesburg, Illinois
LOC	Library of Congress; Washington, D.C.
Marks	Jeffrey H. Marks Rare Books
Meeker	David F. Meeker Collection
Neville	Maurice Neville Collection
Newberry	Newberry Library; Chicago, Illinois
NYPL	Genevieve Taggard Papers, Manuscripts and Archives Division, New York Public Library, Astor, Lenox, and Tilden Foundations; New York, New York
NYPL-Berg	The Berg Collection of English and American Literature, New York Public Library, Astor, Lenox, and Tilden Foundations; New York, New York
OSU	Rare Books and Manuscripts, Ohio State University Library; Columbus, Ohio

PSU	Rare Books and Manuscripts, Special Collections Library, Pennsylvania State University Libraries; University Park, Pennsylvania
PUL	Department of Rare Books and Special Collections, Princeton University Library; Princeton, New Jersey
James Sanford	James Sanford Collection
SIU	Special Collections Research Center, Morris Library, Southern Illinois University; Carbondale, Illinois
Stanford	Department of Special Collections and University Archives, Stanford University Libraries; Stanford, California
SUNYB	The Poetry Collection of the University Libraries, University at Buffalo, The State University of New York; Buffalo, New York
UDel	Special Collections, University of Delaware Library; Newark, Delaware
UMD	Special Collections, University of Maryland Libraries; College Park, Maryland
UNC	Manuscripts Department, Wilson Library, University of North Carolina at Chapel Hill; Chapel Hill, North Carolina
UT	Harry Ransom Humanities Research Center, University of Texas at Austin; Austin, Texas
UTulsa	Department of Special Collections, McFarlin Library, University of Tulsa; Tulsa, Oklahoma
UVA	Special Collections, University of Virginia Library; Charlottesville, Virginia
UWMil	Division of Archives/Special Collections, Golda Meir Library, University of Wisconsin-Milwaukee; Milwaukee, Wisconsin
Yale	Yale Collection of American Literature, Beinecke Rare Book and Manuscript Library, Yale University; New Haven, Connecticut

FORMS OF CORRESPONDENCE

The following abbreviations are used in combination to describe the form of the original source text (e.g., ALS for autograph letter signed, TLS for typed letter signed, ACD for autograph cable draft, TLcc for typed letter carbon copy, phJFK for a photocopy at the John F. Kennedy Library):

A	Autograph
C	Cable
cc	Carbon copy

D   Draft
Frag   Fragment
L   Letter
N   Note
ph   Photocopy
S   Signed
T   Typed

Other abbreviations

b.   born
c.   circa
d.   died
n.p.   no pagination

PUBLISHED WORKS

Works by Ernest Hemingway

The following abbreviations and short titles for Hemingway's works are employed throughout the edition; not all of them appear in the present volume. First U.S. editions are cited, unless otherwise noted.

ARIT   *Across the River and into the Trees.* New York: Scribner's, 1950.
BL   *By-line Ernest Hemingway: Selected Articles and Dispatches of Four Decades.* Edited by William White. New York: Scribner's, 1967.
CSS   *The Complete Short Stories of Ernest Hemingway: The Finca Vigía Edition.* New York: Scribner's, 1987.
DIA   *Death in the Afternoon.* New York: Scribner's, 1932.
DLT   *Dateline: Toronto: The Complete "Toronto Star" Dispatches, 1920–1924.* Edited by William White. New York: Scribner's, 1985.
DS   *The Dangerous Summer.* New York: Scribner's, 1985.
FC   *The Fifth Column and the First Forty-nine Stories.* New York: Scribner's, 1938.
FTA   *A Farewell to Arms.* New York: Scribner's, 1929.
FWBT   *For Whom the Bell Tolls.* New York: Scribner's, 1940.
GOE   *The Garden of Eden.* New York: Scribner's, 1986.
GHOA   *Green Hills of Africa.* New York: Scribner's, 1935.
iot   *in our time.* Paris: Three Mountains Press, 1924.

IOT	*In Our Time.* New York: Boni and Liveright, 1925. Rev. edn. New York: Scribner's, 1930.
IIS	*Islands in the Stream.* New York: Scribner's, 1970.
Letters vol. 1	*The Letters of Ernest Hemingway: Volume 1 (1907–1922).* Edited by Sandra Spanier and Robert W. Trogdon. New York: Cambridge University Press, 2011.
Letters vol. 2	*The Letters of Ernest Hemingway: Volume 2 (1923–1925).* Edited by Sandra Spanier, Albert J. DeFazio III, and Robert W. Trogdon. New York: Cambridge University Press, 2013.
MAW	*Men at War.* New York: Crown Publishers, 1942.
MF	*A Moveable Feast.* New York: Scribner's, 1964.
MF–RE	*A Moveable Feast: The Restored Edition.* Edited by Seán Hemingway. New York: Scribner's, 2009.
MWW	*Men Without Women.* New York: Scribner's, 1927.
NAS	*The Nick Adams Stories.* New York: Scribner's, 1972.
OMS	*The Old Man and the Sea.* New York: Scribner's, 1952.
Poems	*Complete Poems.* Edited, with an Introduction and Notes by Nicholas Gerogiannis. Rev. edn. Lincoln: University of Nebraska Press, 1992.
SAR	*The Sun Also Rises.* New York: Scribner's, 1926.
SL	*Ernest Hemingway: Selected Letters, 1917–1961.* Edited by Carlos Baker. New York: Scribner's, 1981.
SS	*The Short Stories of Ernest Hemingway.* New York: Scribner's, 1954.
TAFL	*True at First Light.* Edited by Patrick Hemingway. New York: Scribner's, 1999.
THHN	*To Have and Have Not.* New York: Scribner's, 1937.
TOS	*The Torrents of Spring.* New York: Scribner's, 1926.
TOTTC	*The Only Thing That Counts: The Ernest Hemingway–Maxwell Perkins Correspondence, 1925–1947.* Edited by Matthew J. Bruccoli with Robert W. Trogdon. New York: Scribner's, 1996.
TSTP	*Three Stories and Ten Poems.* Paris: Contact Editions, 1923.
UK	*Under Kilimanjaro.* Edited by Robert W. Lewis and Robert E. Fleming. Kent State University Press, 2005.
WTN	*Winner Take Nothing.* New York: Scribner's, 1933.

Selected reference works cited in this volume

Baedeker's *Paris*	Baedeker, Karl. *Paris and its Environs with Routes from London to Paris: Handbook for Travellers.* Leipzig: Karl Baedeker, 1924.

Baker *Life* Baker, Carlos. *Ernest Hemingway: A Life Story*. New York: Scribner's, 1969.

Brasch and Sigman Brasch, James D., and Joseph Sigman. *Hemingway's Library: A Composite Record*. New York: Garland, 1981.

Bruccoli and Baughman Bruccoli, Matthew J., and Judith S. Baughman, eds. *Hemingway and the Mechanism of Fame: Statements, Public Letters, Introductions, Forewords, Prefaces, Blurbs, Reviews, and Endorsements*. Columbia: University of South Carolina Press, 2006.

Bruccoli *Fitz–Hem* Bruccoli, Matthew J. *Fitzgerald and Hemingway: A Dangerous Friendship*. New York: Carroll & Graf, 1995. (Paperback edition with appendices.)

Bruccoli *Sons* Bruccoli, Matthew J., ed. *The Sons of Maxwell Perkins: Letters of F. Scott Fitzgerald, Ernest Hemingway, Thomas Wolfe, and Their Editor*. Columbia: University of South Carolina Press, 2004.

Grissom Grissom, C. Edgar. *Ernest Hemingway: A Descriptive Bibliography*. New Castle, Delaware: Oak Knoll Press, 2011.

Hanneman Hanneman, Audre. *Ernest Hemingway: A Comprehensive Bibliography*. Princeton, New Jersey: Princeton University Press, 1967.

Hanneman *Supplement* Hanneman, Audre. *Supplement to Ernest Hemingway: A Comprehensive Bibliography*. Princeton, New Jersey: Princeton University Press, 1975.

L. Hemingway Hemingway, Leicester. *My Brother, Ernest Hemingway*. Sarasota, Florida: Pineapple Press, 1996.

P. Hemingway Hemingway, Patricia S. *The Hemingways: Past and Present and Allied Families*. Rev. edn. Baltimore: Gateway Press, Inc., 1988.

Mandel *HDIA* Mandel, Miriam B. *Hemingway's "Death in the Afternoon": The Complete Annotations*. Lanham, Maryland: Scarecrow Press, 2002.

Mellow Mellow, James R. *Hemingway: A Life Without Consequences*. Boston: Houghton Mifflin, 1992.

L. Miller Miller, Linda Patterson. *Letters from the Lost Generation: Gerald and Sara Murphy and Friends.*

	Exp. edn. Gainsville: University Press of Florida, 2002.
M. Miller	Miller, Madelaine Hemingway. *Ernie: Hemingway's Sister "Sunny" Remembers*. New York: Crown Publishers, 1975.
O'Rourke	O'Rourke, Sean. *Grace Under Pressure: The Life of Evan Shipman*. Santa Monica, California: Harvardwood Publishing, and Nashville, Indiana: Unlimited Publishing LLC, 2010.
Reynolds *AH*	Reynolds, Michael S. *Hemingway: The American Homecoming*. Cambridge, Massachusetts: Basil Blackwell, 1992.
Reynolds *PY*	Reynolds, Michael S. *Hemingway: The Paris Years*. Oxford: Basil Blackwell, 1989.
Reynolds *Reading*	Reynolds, Michael S. *Hemingway's Reading, 1901–1940: An Inventory*. Princeton, New Jersey: Princeton University Press, 1981.
Sanford	Sanford, Marcelline Hemingway. *At the Hemingways: With Fifty Years of Correspondence Between Ernest and Marcelline Hemingway*. Moscow: University of Idaho Press, 1999.
Smith	Smith, Paul. *A Reader's Guide to the Short Stories of Ernest Hemingway*. Boston: G. K. Hall, 1989.
Trogdon *Racket*	Trogdon, Robert W. *The Lousy Racket: Hemingway, Scribners, and the Business of Literature*. Kent, Ohio: Kent State University Press, 2007.
Trogdon *Reference*	Trogdon, Robert W., ed. *Ernest Hemingway: A Literary Reference*. New York: Carroll & Graf, 1999.
Winnick	Winnick, R. H., ed. *Letters of Archibald MacLeish: 1907–1982*. Boston: Houghton Mifflin Company, 1983.

INTRODUCTION TO
THE VOLUME

Rena Sanderson

Ernest Hemingway's letters in Volume 1 and Volume 2 trace his life through 1925, covering his youth through World War I, his work as a journalist for the *Toronto Star*, his marriage to Hadley Richardson, the birth of his son John Nicanor Hemingway (nicknamed Bumby), and his apprenticeship as a writer in the expatriate community of Paris. During those years he formed a network of acquaintances and friendships with writers and artists such as Sherwood Anderson, Ezra Pound, Gertrude Stein, Sylvia Beach, F. Scott Fitzgerald, Archibald MacLeish, John Dos Passos, Gerald Murphy, and Joan Miró. A quick learner who knew how to make the most of his opportunities, Hemingway emerged by the end of 1925 as a promising young writer. His poems and stories had appeared in European magazines, and he had two small books published in Paris—*Three Stories and Ten Poems* (1923) and *in our time* (1924). A larger book of stories, *In Our Time*, was published in the United States in 1925.

This third volume presents the letters Ernest Hemingway wrote during an immensely productive period, from January 1926 to the beginning of April 1929, when he fulfilled his early promise and became a major author. Bracketing the period are two of his most widely recognized and enduring novels, *The Sun Also Rises* (published in 1926) and *A Farewell to Arms* (completed in early 1929 and published later that year). His satirical novel, *The Torrents of Spring*, came out in 1926, and his short stories appeared in American and foreign magazines as well as in his collection *Men Without Women* (1927). British editions of *In Our Time* (1926), *The Sun Also Rises* (titled *Fiesta*, 1927), and *Men Without Women* (1928); a book of six of his stories in French, *Cinquante mille dollars* (1928); and a German translation of *The Sun Also Rises* (titled *Fiesta*, 1928) further advanced his reputation.

In spite of this impressive publication record, success did not come easily. There were triumphs but also setbacks, including events in his personal life that made writing difficult. These included a divorce, a second marriage, the birth of a second son, personal illnesses and accidents, family tensions and tragedy, and new responsibilities. The letters in this volume show Hemingway managing these complications while never losing sight of his high ambitions and emerging, at almost thirty years of age, as a more mature person and author.

Hemingway was no ordinary correspondent but a gifted writer with exceptional skills of observation and unusual sensitivity to his times. One of the distinguishing characteristics of his early fiction is its contemporary quality—its depiction of modern life during the early twentieth century. The letters, like his fiction, reflect his sharp eye and capture an era. They constitute a rich social and historical record covering a wide range of topics: the weather (snow in Madrid in May 1926); geography and landscapes (descriptions of towns, rivers, cathedrals, vegetation, and wildlife); travel and transportation conditions; patterns of tourism; historical and political events and figures; economic details (prices, exchange rates); social customs; sports; and entertainment. We are given insights into a time when cars were a luxury, travel and mail between the United States and Europe took at least one week and often longer, and transatlantic phone service, nonexistent until 1927, was very expensive. Literary production depended largely on manual typewriters (without correction ribbons) and on the frustratingly slow delivery and turnaround of proofs.

During the 1920s silent and talking movies had arrived, but literature was still a major form of entertainment, instruction, and social criticism. Writers were seen as people of significance, and successful ones came under close public scrutiny. Hemingway was immersed in this culture not only as a writer but also as an avid reader. His letters to Isidor Schneider (his contact at Boni & Liveright) include requests for books to be sent to him, and his literary commentary and assessments recur throughout this volume.

As the Roster of Correspondents at the end of the book shows, Volume 3 includes letters written to ninety-nine people representing a broad range of backgrounds, including publishers, writers, editors, and artists as well as family members, old and new friends, and his readers. Hemingway tailored his letters, adopting dramatically different voices depending on the recipient and the purpose of the letter. As a result, the letters vary widely in topic, language, and tone. These distinctly contrasting styles reflect the various sides of Hemingway's persona and the nuances of his various relationships.

It takes two to create a correspondence, and Hemingway's letters ought to be understood, whenever possible, in light of the letters he is answering. During this period he received hundreds of letters, many of which were tracked down and examined during the production of this volume. Often these letters have supplied details not found in biographies; they have helped to confirm the chronology of Hemingway's life and have assisted with dating his undated letters. The explanatory notes that accompany the letters provide readers with further information about this incoming mail.

Of the 345 letters that appear in this volume, 76 were previously published in *Ernest Hemingway: Selected Letters, 1917–1961*, edited by Carlos Baker, while 243 letters appear here for the first time.[1] The letters in Baker's collection primarily address Hemingway's professional life, while those first printed here not only advance our understanding of that professional life but also provide fresh revelations about Hemingway's personality and private life. As a result, this volume offers a fuller picture of Hemingway, the writer and the man.

The figure we come to know through these letters is a man of many passions who lived with gusto. If his bluntness offends at times, his charisma is hard to resist. We see a dynamic, energetic Hemingway in his twenties, a man of extraordinary stamina. He liked to balance his work as a writer with a full slate of physical and social activities as well as intellectual and creative interests. He traveled by ship, train, and automobile at a time when such travel was time-consuming and exhausting. He craved physical challenges—demanding ski trips in Schruns and Gstaad, long bike rides in Paris or on the French Riviera, deep-sea fishing in Key West, horseback riding, hunting, and fishing in Wyoming and Montana—and he regularly attended spectator sports, from six-day bicycle races to boxing matches to bullfights. Most often he enjoyed these activities in the company of family and friends.

Certain letters reveal Hemingway's most private emotions, including the intensity of his feelings during the transition from his first to his second marriage. Others show how sociable he was, how much he valued friendship and good company. In numerous letters, including ones from the fall of 1928 and early 1929 (absent from Baker's *Selected Letters*), he reached out to friends, inviting their visits and arranging get-togethers. He enjoyed making new friends, but he also remembered old friends and responded with sensitivity to those who felt that their lives were not as exciting as his. Evidence of his kindness and support of friends and of family appear throughout the correspondence.

In general, his letters to women show Hemingway in a good light. As her older brother, he warmly invited his sister Madelaine ("Sunny") to visit him in Paris and to join him for the 1927 Fiesta of San Fermín at Pamplona, "at my expense naturally" (6 May [1927]).[2] He stayed in touch with childhood neighbor Isabelle Simmons Godolphin, asking her for the latest gossip in Oak Park. In communications with his mother, Grace Hall Hemingway, he vigorously defended *The Sun Also Rises* against her sharp criticism. Later, he addressed her artist-to-artist about her painting. "That catalogue of your show looks very exciting," he wrote to her disarmingly on 1 October (1927). "I would rather see the whole show than anything that there will be in Paris this fall."

Of special scholarly interest are the letters related to his writing career. The early ones vividly portray a young Hemingway—cocky one moment, giddy as a schoolboy the next, then again reflective and mature—eager to make a name for himself in the literary world. The letters document his career moves: strategically submitting magazine stories, switching to a new publisher, promoting his books (by sending his publisher lengthy lists with the names and addresses of potential reviewers), and negotiating over censorship, revisions, and publicity. They also express his values and habits as a writer, his disappointment over rejections, and his frustration at misleading publicity and unfavorable reviews. In spite of setbacks and occasional fallow periods, he was determined to continue writing, as is illustrated by his work on an unfinished novel and by his persistent endeavors, in different locations, to complete *A Farewell to Arms*. The letters also demonstrate that he was being courted by competing publishers, even after he switched to Scribner's in early 1926. Several previously unpublished cables and letters show that Hemingway first accepted and then rejected an offer from a reputable British publisher in the fall of 1927, a development missing from the major biographies.

Some letters offer insight into Hemingway's personal relationships with other writers. In several, he expressed support and encouragement. And competitive though he certainly was, in letters published here for the first time, he recommended the work of Archibald MacLeish, Morley Callaghan, and Evan Shipman to editors and publishers. In a letter of 13 May 1926 to Robert McAlmon, he offered "to go 50–50" on the publication costs for Callaghan's book and explained: "I think once he gets published . . . he can go on and not worry about this stuff. I know thats the way it made me feel."

Hemingway adopted widely varying voices, depending on the fellow author he was addressing. His eighteen letters to Ezra Pound, which appear here for the first time, are thick with intellectual sparring, linguistic playfulness, and blasé weariness. The more intimate letters to Fitzgerald swing from warm expressions of friendship to amusing braggadocio and hurtful barbs. In letters to veteran author Owen Wister, he adopts a tone of mutual respect and collegiality. And he strikes an apologetic note in his letter to T. S. Eliot expressing remorse for having insulted him in two separate articles about two years earlier. We learn a great deal, reading these letters, about Hemingway's writing community and about the literary views, practices, and market conditions of the time.

****

Of the years covered in Volume 3, 1926 was the most volatile. The year started with change in the air. On 31 December 1925, Hemingway, his wife Hadley, and son Bumby celebrated New Year's Eve at the Hotel Taube in Schruns, a small village in the Montafon Valley of Austria where they had spent a skiing vacation the previous year. They had arrived in Schruns on 12 December and on Christmas Eve were joined for the holidays by Pauline Pfeiffer. The daughter of a wealthy family from Piggott, Arkansas, Pauline, at thirty, was four years older than Hemingway but four years younger than Hadley. The Hemingways had met her the previous spring in Paris, where she was working as a writer for *Vogue* and, having become close friends in the ensuing months, they wanted to share with her a special place they had discovered. This particular guest would soon turn their lives upside down.

Hemingway's mind was on his career. On that final day of 1925, he wrote F. Scott Fitzgerald that Horace B. Liveright, his New York publisher, had just rejected *The Torrents of Spring*, Hemingway's parody of Sherwood Anderson's *Dark Laughter*. Anderson was also a Boni & Liveright author, and a prominent one the publishers were loath to offend. Hemingway understood the situation, knew that a rejection would void his contract with Boni & Liveright, and had other options in mind. In April 1925 he had promised Maxwell Perkins, an editor at Charles Scribner's Sons, that he would give Scribner's the first chance to make him an offer were he to leave Boni & Liveright. More recently, two other New York firms (Knopf and Harcourt, Brace) had expressed interest in publishing his fiction, especially *The Sun Also Rises*, his novel-in-progress. In his New Year's Eve letter Hemingway told Fitzgerald, himself a Scribner's author who had initially recommended Hemingway's work to his publisher, that he was determined to keep his promise to Perkins. The next morning, he added a P.S.: "Got to worrying last night and couldnt sleep. Do you think I ought to go to N.Y?" Answering his own question, he listed good reasons for going.[3]

Once he received his new passport (dated 6 January 1926), Hemingway left in early February for an exhilarating eleven-day stay in New York. He successfully switched from Boni & Liveright to Scribner's without offending either Liveright or Harcourt. After meeting Perkins, Hemingway was delighted at his arrangement with Scribner's. His contract for both *The Torrents of Spring* and *The Sun Also Rises* provided for royalties of 15 percent and an advance of $1,500— excellent terms for the time. In addition, as he wrote Bill Smith and Harold Loeb (18 February 1926), it looked as if *Scribner's Magazine* was ready to buy "all the stories I can give them."

On his way back to Hadley and Bumby in Schruns, Hemingway stopped in Paris to see Pauline Pfeiffer. In *A Moveable Feast* he would write, "I should have caught the first train from the Gare de l'Est . . . to Austria. But the girl I was in love with was in Paris then, and I did not take the first train, or the second or the third. When I saw my wife again . . . I wished I had died before I ever loved anyone but her."[4]

In mid-March, John Dos Passos and the wealthy American expatriates Gerald and Sara Murphy joined the Hemingways for skiing. But Schruns also proved to be "a good place to work," Hemingway found.[5] His stay there inspired the story "An Alpine Idyll." And it was in Schruns that spring that he undertook the task of revising *The Sun Also Rises*, which he had drafted in ten weeks the past summer and fall.

His contract with Scribner's kept Hemingway professionally on track. In March he and Perkins began a regular correspondence that would last for twenty-one years, until Perkins's death in 1947. Everything was progressing smoothly with the books' publications. In March and early April 1926 author and editor corresponded about relatively minor changes in *The Torrents of Spring* and about publicity matters prior to its publication on 28 May. On 24 April, Hemingway put the typescript of *The Sun Also Rises* in the mail.

In March the French magazine *Le Navire d'Argent* featured a translation of "The Undefeated," a story that had appeared in German in *Der Querschnitt* the preceding summer. But Hemingway had a hard time placing his stories in American magazines. In his letter of 2 January 1926 to Ernest Walsh (co-editor with Ethel Moorhead of *This Quarter*), Hemingway explained that he was "trying the Fight Story ["Fifty Grand"] . . . on the big money market." *Cosmopolitan* magazine had already rejected it, but he decided "to try it on the other 3 magazines who pay lots of money because I cannot pass up the chance of what $1,000 in the hand would mean if any of them would take a chance and buy it." Large-circulation magazines such as *Cosmopolitan* appealed to a rapidly growing middle-class readership during the 1920s and were paying high prices for stories by popular fiction writers. This was the "big money market" Hemingway hoped to enter, one that provided a major source of income for writers of fiction throughout the first half of the twentieth century. Magazine publications paid better than books, whose yields were spread out over extended periods of time. However, magazines were not yet ready to publish Hemingway's work.

By April 1926, "Fifty Grand" had been rejected by the three magazines Hemingway had targeted: *Collier's Weekly*, *Liberty*, and the *Saturday Evening Post*. *Scribner's Magazine* also turned it down and in June rejected "An Alpine Idyll" as well. The rejections by *Scribner's Magazine* of the first two stories he submitted came as a considerable disappointment. During his February meeting with Perkins in New York, Hemingway had learned that *Scribner's Magazine* would pay him roughly $200 to $250 per story, much less than the rates offered by the *Saturday Evening Post*, but he had assumed that it represented a ready market for his stories.[6]

Meanwhile, there were unsettling developments in Hemingway's private life as his marriage to Hadley started to unravel. In late April or early May, while on a trip through the Loire Valley with Pauline Pfeiffer and Pauline's sister, Virginia Pfeiffer (known as Jinny), Hadley discovered that Ernest and Pauline were having an affair.

The situation was complicated by illness. By mid-April Bumby had developed whooping cough, and Hadley herself had been coughing for weeks. Hadley had planned to go to Spain with her husband, but instead she accepted Gerald and Sara Murphy's invitation to stay with Bumby at the Villa America, their home in Antibes, so that she and her son could recuperate in the mild Mediterranean climate. On 13 May, Hemingway boarded the night train for Madrid alone. He still expected Hadley to join him in Madrid and sent her their joint passport so she could do so. However, this plan was abandoned after a doctor officially diagnosed Bumby's whooping cough and insisted on quarantine. Hadley moved with Bumby and his nanny into the Villa Paquita, a house in Juan-les-Pins leased by the Fitzgeralds and turned over to Hadley.

On 21 May 1926, Hadley wrote to her husband, addressing him as "Dearest + still-beloved Waxin," and told him that she had invited Pauline to "stop off here if she wants—it would be a swell joke on tout le monde if you and Fife and I spent the summer at Juan les Pins or hereabouts instead of Spain—"[7] On 28 May, the day after he received the passport that Hadley returned to him, Hemingway set out on the long train ride to the French Riviera. By the time he arrived in Juan-les-Pins, Pauline was already there, and he, Pauline, and Hadley occupied the same lodgings throughout June. The three of them rode bicycles, swam, and shared meals together, a situation Hemingway later fictionalized in the posthumously published novel *The Garden of Eden* (1986). After attending the fiesta at Pamplona in early July with the Murphys, the Hemingways followed the bullfight circuit in Spain and Pauline left for Paris. About 12 August, Ernest and Hadley returned to Paris to set up separate residences.

After his stay in Madrid in May, where he worked on three stories ("The Killers," "Today Is Friday," and "Ten Indians"), Hemingway did not write anything new before August, but he worked hard on further revisions of *The Sun Also Rises*. Following advice from Fitzgerald, expressed in person at Juan-les-Pins and in a letter of June 1926, Hemingway cut the opening section of the novel entirely.[8] In addition, he dealt with revision requests from Perkins. In a letter of 27 May 1926 to Charles Scribner, Perkins had explained that Hemingway's work would help to counteract Scribner's reputation as "ultra-conservative."[9] However, the publishing house was not ready to challenge censorship. Writing to Hemingway on 18 May, Perkins called the novel "a most extraordinary performance," but he insisted that the passage referring to Henry James's sexual impotence could not be printed and that "one or two other things" would need to be addressed later.[10] In a letter of 20 July he specifically asked for revisions to prevent libel charges and suppression of the book.[11] Somewhat grudgingly, Hemingway agreed to make the changes as he corrected the proofs. Early in his relationship with Scribner's, he was demonstrating his flexibility while trying to hold the line for artistic autonomy. Discussions between Hemingway and Perkins regarding objectionable scenes and obscene language would continue for years.

As he reported to Fitzgerald in a letter of c. 1 December 1926, Hemingway enjoyed "a grand spell of working" in the fall of 1926. From mid-August through December he sent out and placed two of the stories he had worked on in Madrid, returned the corrected proofs of *The Sun Also Rises* (on 27 August), and composed five new stories and one parodic article. Encouraged by his placement of "Today is Friday" with The As Stable Publications in August and by the first acceptance of one of his stories ("The Killers") by *Scribner's Magazine* in September, he wrote "A Canary for One," a story often discussed as a fictional treatment of the Hemingways' August train trip from the Riviera to Paris to set up separate residences. He also wrote three war stories—"In Another Country," "Now I Lay Me," and "A Simple Enquiry"—depicting soldiers, their physical and psychological wounds, and their conflicts. The fifth story, "A Pursuit Race," details one man's personal failure. The stories center on loss, betrayal, deception, loneliness, fear, and crises of conscience, themes obviously related to Hemingway's own situation.

That autumn the domestic drama involving Hemingway, Hadley, and Pauline played itself out, as the letters of that period attest. On 24 September, Pauline left for the United States in order to comply with Hadley's stipulation that she would agree to a divorce if Pauline and Ernest still wanted to be together after a separation of three months. The letters record Hemingway's response to the separation, including his longings for Pauline, feelings of guilt toward Hadley, and bouts of depression. On 16 November, Hadley asked him to initiate divorce proceedings. Responding on 18 November, he promised her all royalties, British and American, from *The Sun Also Rises*, except for Scribner's advance.

With that crisis resolved, a sense of relief seems to pervade the correspondence. Hemingway immediately turned back to work, on 19 November sending Perkins "How I Broke With John Wilkes Booth," a light-hearted piece on breakups that would be published in the *New Yorker* the following spring as "My Own Life." He also engaged in a spirited exchange of letters with Ezra Pound, who had written him on 28 October inviting a contribution for a new literary journal to be called *The Exile*, then in the planning stages. Subsequently Pound asked for Hemingway's advice regarding the scope, funding, distribution, and likely success of the periodical. In a noteworthy reversal of roles, Hemingway confidently advised his former mentor, served as mediator between Pound and MacLeish, and teased Pound about his politics.

Scribner's Magazine accepted two more stories that fall—"A Canary for One" and "In Another Country." In addition, both Jonathan Cape and William Heinemann offered to publish a British edition of *The Sun Also Rises.* (Hemingway stuck with Cape, which had brought out the British edition of *In Our Time.*) Most important, of course, was Scribner's publication of *The Sun Also Rises* on 22 October 1926. In mid-November, Hemingway thanked Perkins for sending him clippings of positive reviews. Very soon, however, he bemoaned the fact that he had written a novel depicting actual living people and started to resent the comparison of *The Sun Also Rises* to Michael Arlen's *The Green Hat.* Hemingway's reactions to the reviews are scattered throughout his letters. Without a doubt, the novel made a splash, and the spotlight fell on Hemingway as never before.

The year of 1927 was generally a quiet, stabilizing period for Hemingway. He recovered from the turmoil of 1926, regained his equilibrium, settled into his new life with Pauline, and continued writing.

Once again Hemingway spent Christmas and New Year's Eve at a ski resort, this time in the more upscale Gstaad, Switzerland, where he joined Archibald and Ada MacLeish and Pauline's sister Jinny. He stayed in Switzerland for skiing until early March, retrieving Pauline when she returned to France on 8 January and bringing Bumby from Paris in late February. In a letter of c. 18–20 January to Isidor Schneider, Hemingway wrote that he was MacLeish's guest and that he was living on "$1.50 a day with wonderful food and fine ski-ing. I have a good sunny room with a reading light and a comfortable place to work." Alternating work with skiing, he was writing well.

Meanwhile, *The Sun Also Rises* enjoyed good sales, with 11,000 copies sold by the end of January. That month Perkins reminded Hemingway to start thinking about the story collection Scribner's had agreed to publish in the fall. This commitment allowed Hemingway to concentrate on writing well without undue worrying about the marketability of the stories. In mid-February he sent Perkins a title for this volume—*Men Without Women*—and a list of ten stories for possible inclusion. Subsequent letters to Perkins provide a behind-the-scenes look at the preparation of the book, which was published in October.

In the spring, Hemingway's work began to appear for the first time in American magazines, including the *New Yorker, Scribner's Magazine,* and the *New Republic.* In addition, early in the year two stories with a long history of rejection were accepted for later publication—the *Atlantic Monthly* took "Fifty Grand," and the *American Caravan* accepted "An Alpine Idyll."

Magazine editors were also asking Hemingway for contributions. In a letter of 19 February to Perkins, Hemingway wrote that he had received "requests for articles stories or serials from New Yorker, Vanity Fair, Harper's Bazaar, Hearst's etc.," but to him the offers looked "like the fast smooth flowing shutes that I've watched so many of my ancestors and contemporaries disappear over." By this time, he had grown wary of "the money making trap which handles American writers like the cornhusking machine," as he explained to his parents in a letter of 5 February.

He thought that popular magazines would limit his freedom to write as he pleased. In January, *Vanity Fair* had assured Hemingway that he could write stories "about pretty nearly anything . . . except abortion and allied subjects."[12] In May, as if to demonstrate his artistic independence, he wrote "Hills Like White Elephants," a story about abortion, although the word is never mentioned. In August, "Hills Like White Elephants" appeared in *transition*, an expatriate literary journal, but it stood little chance of appearing in a commercial American magazine. As he had told Fitzgerald in a letter of c. 1 December 1926, Hemingway also had "two other stories that I know can't sell so am not sending them out—but that will go well in a book." One was "A Simple Enquiry," a story about homosexuality, no doubt one of the "allied subjects" *Vanity Fair* would not have accepted; the other was "A Pursuit Race," a story featuring drugs and alcoholism as well as language (the word "shit") that even Perkins questioned. All three of these stories appeared in *Men Without Women*, illustrating that material too controversial for American magazines could usually be included in books.

During his first year with Scribner's, Hemingway had learned important lessons from responses to his work and had grown familiar with the American literary marketplace. He developed as a writer and established himself with Scribner's, where he enjoyed an excellent rapport with Perkins, who always seemed to understand his concerns and requests. Of course, Hemingway was being courted by various publishers by this time, and he made sure to tell Perkins. Liveright attempted to gain him back with an appealing proposal in May, and other publishers also made generous offers that year, but Hemingway declined. He was smart to stay with Scribner's, a financially conservative publishing house where Perkins was always his loyal advocate. Horace B. Liveright's extravagant spending and poor investments would lead to Boni & Liveright's bankruptcy in 1933.

Early in 1927, Hemingway was preparing for his new life with Pauline. Writing to his parents on 5 February, he informed them of his separation and forthcoming divorce from Hadley, making sure to mention that he had turned over to her all the royalties from *The Sun Also Rises*. He also told them to expect a visit from

Hadley and Bumby, but he did not mention his forthcoming marriage to Pauline. During this time, he and Hadley remained good friends. In his letters, Hemingway sounds relieved that everything was working out, including Bumby's visits and interaction with Pauline. The divorce became official on 21 April, and he and Pauline were married three weeks later, on 10 May. After their honeymoon in Le Grau-du-Roi in southern France, they returned to Paris in early June and settled into their new apartment at 6, rue Férou, on the Left Bank.

Since 1923, Hemingway had gone to Spain in the summertime for the bullfighting in Pamplona, bringing his wife and friends along. In 1927, however, he broke that pattern, attending the fiesta at Pamplona in early July not with his new wife but with his new friend Waldo Peirce, a painter from Maine. In a letter of 6 May, Hemingway encouraged his sister Sunny to accompany him there. "You will be a god send to me," he wrote, adding that he could not bring Pauline because he had been there with Hadley the preceding year. As Peirce explained in a letter to his own mother, Hemingway wanted to keep his second marriage secret in Pamplona because the Spanish did not approve of divorce. Pauline, therefore, stayed in San Sebastian where Hemingway joined her for a ten-day stay after the fiesta at Pamplona.[13] From there the couple followed the bullfights from town to town. However, on 28 July, Hemingway wrote his friend Bill Smith from Valencia that the whole bullfight season was "gone to hell," with several matadors wounded or ill, a disappointment he mentioned in several letters. Still, there were good times ahead that summer. In August Hemingway especially enjoyed his stay with Pauline in Santiago de Compostela, a place that enchanted him.

In September, Hemingway wrote his father a long letter from the French resort town of Hendaye, finally telling him all about the divorce, his marriage to Pauline, and his situation as a writer: "We are going to Paris next week and I am starting a novel and will work very hard until Christmas vacation." Writing to Perkins in a letter of 15 September, Hemingway promised to go on a "six hour a day regime in Paris" to complete the novel, noting "99/9/10 remains to be written." Once he started, Hemingway made good progress and by October was writing steadily, following the adventures of a boy called Jimmy Crane and his father. In his letters he recorded the increasing number of pages and chapters.[14]

Following the publication of *Men Without Women* on 14 October 1927, Hemingway was irritated by some negative reviews. Sales were strong, however, especially for a book of stories, with 10,000 copies sold within the first month. His reputation was growing. That fall, he began to receive and answer letters from fans and collectors wanting to buy first editions and manuscripts or autographs, from students and teachers asking for comments on his craft, and from others requesting permission to publish his advice and reprint his work. Later that winter recognition also came in the form of parodies, caricatures, and extravagant book reviews in such prominent American magazines as *The Bookman, Vanity Fair,* the *New Republic,* and the *New Yorker.*

The year 1928 was generally productive in spite of its rough start and tragic end. That winter Hemingway suffered from a series of illnesses and accidents, including sore throats and colds, to which he was prone. In addition, Bumby accidentally scratched the pupil of his father's right eye. After recuperating during a skiing vacation with family and friends in Gstaad, Hemingway returned to Paris in February to find burst pipes and no heat at the apartment, and he caught another cold. Then, on 4 March, in a well-publicized accident, the skylight in the apartment's bathroom crashed down on him, and the resulting gash in his forehead required stitches. Scribner's touched up its publicity photos, taken in Paris by Helen Breaker, to remove the scar that remained.

On 17 March, Pauline and Ernest left France and sailed for Key West via Havana, Cuba. That same day, before their departure, Hemingway wrote Perkins that he had completed twenty-two chapters and 45,000 words of the novel begun the preceding fall, which he now called "a sort of modern Tom Jones." He was thinking of setting it aside, however, so that after his arrival in Key West, he could continue work on a story that he had started only two weeks earlier but that was going "wonderfully." This was the start of *A Farewell to Arms*, the novel of love and war inspired by Hemingway's experiences in Italy during World War I. The novel he set aside was never completed.[15]

The letters of April and May capture Hemingway's excitement at his discovery of Key West, a town not yet spoiled. Writing to Waldo Peirce in April, he described it as "a grand place. Population dropped from 26,000 to 10,000 in last ten years. Nothing can stimulate it . . . No mosquitos Fine breeze—hot as Spain and cool at night." As Pamplona was made special by bullfighting, a sport and art form requiring bravery and a code of conduct appreciated only by aficionados, and as Schruns and Gstaad were made special by exhausting ski excursions and the risk of avalanches, so Key West appealed to Hemingway because it offered another demanding sport—deep-sea fishing—requiring a new set of skills and extraordinary physical strength and stamina. In Key West, as earlier in Pamplona, Schruns, and Gstaad, Hemingway happily slipped into the role of lead explorer and urged friends to join him. John Dos Passos, Bill Smith, and Waldo Peirce all paid visits to Key West that spring for fishing expeditions. Best of all, Hemingway could write as well as fish and socialize. As he wrote artist friend Henry Strater on 13 May, he was "working like a bastard at 7 till 1 a m and then going fishing every day."[16] By the time he left Key West at the end of the month, Hemingway had completed about two hundred pages of his novel-in-progress—with "200 words or so to a page," as he wrote Perkins on 31 May.

As much as Hemingway enjoyed Key West, he stayed there for only a few months in 1928—April, May, and December. The rest of the year he spent on the road, crossing the United States either in the new Model A Ford (a gift from Pauline's Uncle Gus Pfeiffer) or by train, staying in temporary quarters and living out of his suitcase. The letters of 1928 thus provide an interesting record of travel conditions at that time and more specifically of Hemingway's journeys and of his work on the novel along the way. To document his progress, in his letters he often reported the mileage on the odometer as well as the number of pages he had completed.

Pauline was pregnant that spring, and in preparation for the impending birth, she departed by train for her parents' home in Piggott, Arkansas, on 19 May. Hemingway followed with father-in-law Paul Pfeiffer, driving the Ford from Key West to Piggott in six days. The Hemingways stayed in Piggott through early June and then went to Kansas City, where Pauline was scheduled to give birth. On 28 June, after a long and difficult labor, she gave birth to Patrick, Hemingway's second son, by Caesarean section. While she and the infant remained in the hospital for several weeks that sweltering Midwestern summer, Hemingway stayed in Kansas City and continued writing.

After returning with Pauline and the baby to Piggott, Hemingway reported to Waldo Peirce on 23 July that he was "on page 478 or something like that" and expected "six weeks more work" to finish his love-and-war novel. With the royalties from *The Sun Also Rises* going to Hadley and no story written or sold in 1928, he was "about broke" and needed an advance for the novel he was having trouble finishing. The "bloody heat"—temperatures "over 90 all the time"—and the newborn's crying made work difficult. He decided to leave Pauline and Patrick behind and drive to Wyoming with Bill Horne of Chicago, his World War I buddy, to "fish ½ day and work the other half. Will finish book." Pauline was scheduled to join him there later.

After a three-day road trip in the Ford, Hemingway and Horne arrived at Folly Ranch in the Bighorn Mountains (near Big Horn, south of Sheridan) at the end of July. Needing more solitude to complete the novel, Hemingway quickly relocated to quieter lodgings. By mid-August he was feeling lonely and looking forward to Pauline's arrival. On 18 August, the day she arrived by train, Hemingway wrote his journalist friend Guy Hickok that he was "on page 600 and only about 2 days from the end—The bloody end."

With the first draft of *A Farewell to Arms* completed, he and Pauline traversed Wyoming, fishing and hunting, and along the way visited Owen Wister, the author of *The Virginian*, at a guest lodge in Shell. Before finishing the trip with a hunting excursion to the Crow Indian Reservation in Montana, Hemingway wrote from Sheridan to Perkins and to Sylvia Beach (in Paris) regarding business matters. Clearly eager for social interaction, he also sent off letters to several friends that September, including MacLeish, Peirce, and Strater, to arrange for get-togethers.

During his days in the remote American West, Hemingway's literary prominence was steadily growing. His American book sales were strong, and his works appeared in French and German translations that summer and fall. In several letters that summer, Perkins had written of Scribner's keen interest in serializing the novel-in-progress, and in a letter of 8 August he explained that he expected Scribner's to pay $10,000 for the serial rights: "A top price, for us," Perkins said.[17] Soon after Ernest and Pauline arrived back in Piggott on 25 September (with 9,200 miles on the odometer), Perkins sent Hemingway a check for $5,000 as a nonbinding advance to be applied either toward serialization or publication of the novel still in draft stage.[18] Having promised Ray Long, editor of *Cosmopolitan*, the serial rights to his next novel, Hemingway was initially reluctant to accept the advance, but Perkins assured him that Long would understand.

In mid-October, Hemingway drove on his own from Piggott to Oak Park to visit his parents for a few days, then left to stay with Bill Horne in Chicago. Pauline joined him there at the end of the month, and by train they traveled east to make a series of social calls, starting with the MacLeishes in Conway, Massachusetts, followed by a stay in New York City, and concluding with a get-together with Scott and Zelda Fitzgerald for a Princeton football game and an overnight stay at the Fitzgeralds' rented mansion near Wilmington, Delaware. By late November, after a three-day journey from Piggott that included Hemingway's sister Sunny, the Hemingways were back in Key West.

Just days after their arrival, Hemingway left for New York to pick up Bumby, who had been ill and was coming from France for an extended stay. On the morning of 6 December 1928, the day Hemingway boarded a train with Bumby to head back to Key West, his father committed suicide in Oak Park. The letters and cables provide intimate glimpses of what happened on that day and subsequently. Within twenty-four hours after the funeral, Hemingway began the return journey to Key West. There he fought off his usual winter cold and settled into a routine of revising the novel, with Pauline and Sunny typing the pages. By 23 January 1929 he had finished the semi-final draft of *A Farewell to Arms*, with a revision of the ending to come later that spring.

In 1929 there were again visitors, and even more than in the previous year. Perkins came for the first week of February. He joined Hemingway in fishing the Gulf Stream, and he read and liked the novel. Aboard the Havana Special, heading back to New York, Perkins reread the typescript and on the train's stationery penned a glowing letter to Hemingway, calling it a "most beautiful book."[19] On 13 February he cabled an offer of $16,000 for the rights to serialize the novel in

Scribner's Magazine, an unprecedented amount in the firm's history.[20] Hemingway cabled his acceptance the next day.

The letters of 1929 included in this volume show a busy Hemingway stretched in new directions and responding to changes in his professional and personal life. While entertaining friends and hosting fishing expeditions, he was also making travel plans for a family trip to Europe and correcting galleys of the serial installments of *A Farewell to Arms.* Corresponding with Owen Wister, he asked for professional advice regarding various matters, including how to respond to an invitation from the Authors' League of America and to Scribner's handling of omissions in the serialization. Among his personal letters that spring, those to his mother reveal a dramatic change in their relationship. With Grace Hall Hemingway struggling financially because of her late husband's bad investments, her son stepped in as the new head of the family, directing from afar how other family members could help and providing her with emotional support as well as substantial financial assistance of his own.

****

The letters of Volume 3 trace Hemingway's "American Homecoming," the apt subtitle of Michael Reynolds's biography of this period.[21] Early in 1926, young Hemingway found the publisher and the editor with whom he would stay for the rest of his career. Signing on with Scribner's secured his entry into the American literary market, something he very much desired. At the same time, after a long period of expatriation, he was eager to return to his homeland. Unexpected developments of 1926 and 1927 kept him in Europe, responding to ups and downs, illnesses and accidents. When he did return to the United States, later than expected, in March 1928, it signified a major turning point in his life.

The return to America was in some ways an errand into the wilderness and a rebirth. He left behind an expatriate life and society that had facilitated his break with Oak Park and served him well during his apprenticeship as a writer. Upon coming back to the United States, he reclaimed what he had missed—the purity and excitement of the outdoor life he experienced as a boy while camping, fishing, and hunting with his father and friends. Both in Key West and out West, he found again the rush of new discoveries, the joy of learning new skills, and the pleasure of fishing and hunting in unspoiled territory. No longer a boy in flight from the game warden or a son being chased out of the house by his mother for bad behavior, he reclaimed as an adult what he valued and what he had missed during his stay in Europe.

Hemingway returned to his homeland in 1928 an experienced man of the world, with a network of accomplished friends and, through his second marriage, a prominent and welcoming second family. However, with the expectant eyes of the Pfeiffers (especially Pauline and Uncle Gus) upon him, he still had to establish his worth as a person and his significance as a writer. By the time he left for Europe a year later, on 5 April 1929, he had lost his father but had reconnected with his mother and siblings. He had learned to live with the emotional, legal, and financial challenges of a growing family—with old responsibilities for his first wife, Hadley, and their son Bumby; new responsibilities for his second wife, Pauline, and their son Patrick; and, after the suicide of his father, additional responsibilities for his mother and younger siblings. During his year back home, Hemingway worked hard at his craft, with handsome results. Although at times he bemoaned the number of dependents and the weight of his responsibilities, he had risen to the occasion, providing the necessary financial and emotional support. He had even made his mother proud of him.

The rest of 1929 would include new challenges, but photographs of Hemingway aboard the SS *Yorck* that April show a confident, happy man. The promising young writer giddy over his first contract with Scribner's in early 1926 returned to Europe in 1929 an accomplished author, wise in the ways of contracts, censorship, magazine serialization, and publishing politics. Not yet thirty, he had already written several of the books and stories that would become classics and had established a substantial record of American and international publication. Still ahead was the serialization of *A Farewell to Arms* in *Scribner's Magazine*, which would gain much attention, especially after the second installment was banned in Boston in June. Published as a book by Scribner's on 27 September 1929, the novel would draw rave reviews, sealing Hemingway's position as a major American writer.

NOTES

1 Carlos Baker, ed., *Ernest Hemingway: Selected Letters, 1917–1961* (New York: Scribner's, 1981).
2 Unless otherwise cited, all letters quoted are included in this volume.
3 Sandra Spanier, Albert J. DeFazio III, and Robert W. Trogdon, eds., *The Letters of Ernest Hemingway, Volume 2 (1923–1925)* (New York: Cambridge University Press, 2011), 462.
4 Ernest Hemingway, *A Moveable Feast* (New York: Scribner's, 1964), 210.
5 *Ibid.*, 202.
6 In 1926 the average net income for a United States taxpayer was $5,306.43, roughly $442 per month. (*Statistics of Income for 1926* [Washington, D.C.: United States Government Printing Office, 1929], 3).
7 Hadley Richardson Hemingway to Ernest Hemingway, 21 May 1926 (JFK).
8 F. Scott Fitzgerald to Ernest Hemingway, [June 1926] (JFK), in Matthew J. Bruccoli and Margaret M. Duggan, eds., *Correspondence of F. Scott Fitzgerald* (New York: Random House, 1980), 193–96.
9 Maxwell Perkins to Charles Scribner, 27 May 1926 (PUL; *TOTTC*, 38–39).
10 Maxwell Perkins to Ernest Hemingway, 18 May 1926 (PUL; *TOTTC*, 38).

11 Maxwell Perkins to Ernest Hemingway, 20 July 1926 (PUL; *TOTTC*, 41–43).

12 *Vanity Fair*, Lewis Galantière to Ernest Hemingway, 6 January 1927 (JFK).

13 William Gallagher, "Waldo Peirce and Ernest Hemingway: Mirror Images," *Hemingway Review* 23, no. 1 (Fall 2003): 31.

14 For a more detailed description of the story, see Michael S. Reynolds, *Hemingway: The American Homecoming* (Cambridge, Massachusetts: Basil Blackwell, 1992), 145–52.

15 A manuscript of twenty chapters survives at the JFK Library as Item 529b, listed under the title "Jimmy Breen."

16 Waldo Peirce captured the adventure of one fishing expedition in a manuscript with watercolor illustrations titled "Hemingway among the Sharks," set in the "Marquesas Keys—Gulf of Mexico" and dated "May 10, 1928," which depicts Bill Smith, Peirce, and Hemingway in action aboard a small boat (Sotheby's catalog, New York, 5 December 2013, Lot 114).

17 Maxwell Perkins to Ernest Hemingway, 8 August 1928 (PUL; *TOTTC*, 75). In 1928 the average net income for a United States taxpayer was $6,196,81. (*Statistics of Income for 1928* [Washington, D.C.: United States Government Printing Office, 1930], 3).

18 Maxwell Perkins to Ernest Hemingway, 2 October 1928 (PUL; *TOTTC*, 80–81).

19 Maxwell Perkins to Ernest Hemingway, [9 February 1929] (JFK; *TOTTC*, 86).

20 Maxwell Perkins to Ernest Hemingway, 13 February 1929 (PUL; *TOTTC*, 86). In 1929 the average net income for a United States taxpayer was $6,132.22 (*Statistics of Income for 1929* [Washington, D.C.: United States Government Printing Office, 1931], 4).

21 Reynolds, *Hemingway: The American Homecoming*.

VOLUME 3 (1926–1929) CHRONOLOGY

12 December 1925–25 January 1926	EH, Hadley, and son John (nicknamed "Bumby") are on a skiing vacation at the Hotel Taube in Schruns, Austria, where EH also works on revising *The Sun Also Rises*. Pauline Pfeiffer joins them for Christmas, returning to Paris in mid-January.
	Boni & Liveright rejects *The Torrents of Spring* on 30 December, freeing EH from his contract and allowing his move to Scribner's.
	"The Undefeated" appears in the Autumn–Winter 1925–1926 number of *This Quarter*.
25 January 1926	EH leaves for Paris en route to New York City to meet with publishers; Hadley and Bumby remain in Schruns.
3 February 1926	EH sails from Cherbourg for New York aboard the *Mauretania*.
9–20 February 1926	In New York, EH visits the publishing houses of Boni & Liveright, Harcourt, and Scribner's. He meets editor Maxwell Perkins and signs contract with Scribner's for *The Torrents of Spring* and *The Sun Also Rises*.
20 February–1 March 1926	EH sails to France aboard the *President Roosevelt* in the company of Robert Benchley and Dorothy Parker.
2–3 March 1926	In Paris, EH and Pauline pursue their love affair; EH sees F. Scott and Zelda Fitzgerald.
5 March 1926	EH rejoins Hadley and Bumby in Schruns.

12–17 March 1926	After John Dos Passos and Gerald and Sara Murphy join the Hemingways in Schruns, the group stays at the Hotel Rössle in Gaschurn.
23 March 1926	EH finishes rewriting *The Sun Also Rises*.
29 March 1926	The Hemingways are back in Paris, staying at the Hôtel Vénétia until subtenants vacate their apartment at 113, rue Notre-Dame-des-Champs.
1 April 1926	Perkins recommends literary agent Paul Reynolds to EH after "Fifty Grand" has been repeatedly rejected.
5–11 April 1926	EH and Hadley attend the Paris six-day bicycle races. Jonathan Cape offers to publish a British edition of *In Our Time*.
14 April 1926	Chink Dorman-Smith arrives in Paris; the next day he and EH attend a rugby match between the military academies Sandhurst and Saint-Cyr.
24 April 1926	EH sends Perkins the typescript of *The Sun Also Rises*.
c. late April–early May 1926	Hadley learns of EH and Pauline's affair while traveling in the Loire Valley with Pauline and her sister, Virginia (Jinny) Pfeiffer.
14–28 May 1926	EH is alone in Madrid, where he attends bullfights and, according to his Madrid log, works on "The Killers," "Today is Friday," and "Ten Indians."
c. 15 May 1926	Hadley travels to Antibes with Bumby, who has been ill, to visit the Murphys at their Villa America.
20 May 1926	Bumby is diagnosed with whooping cough and quarantined. Hadley, Bumby, and the Hemingways' longtime housekeeper Marie Rohrbach move into the Hôtel Beau-Site, Cap d'Antibes.

28 May 1926	*The Torrents of Spring* is published in New York by Scribner's. EH leaves Madrid for the French Riviera.
30 May–5 July 1926	EH, Hadley, Pauline, and Bumby share lodgings at the Fitzgeralds' leased Villa Paquita in Juan-les-Pins.
5 June 1926	Following F. Scott Fitzgerald's advice, EH cuts the original opening of *The Sun Also Rises*.
c. 10 June 1926	EH, Hadley, and Pauline move from Villa Paquita to the Hôtel de la Pinède, Juan-les-Pins; Marie Rohrbach and Bumby move into a nearby bungalow.
Spring–Summer 1926	"A Banal Story" appears in the *Little Review*.
6–12 July 1926	EH, Hadley, Pauline, and the Murphys attend the Fiesta of San Fermín in Pamplona, staying at the Hotel Quintana. Bumby is in France in the care of Marie Rohrbach and her husband.
13 July 1926	EH and Hadley stay at the Hotel Suizo in San Sebastian.
15–21 July 1926	EH and Hadley stay at the Hotel Aguilar in Madrid.
20 July 1926	Perkins sends galley proofs of *The Sun Also Rises* to EH in Paris, asking for changes.
24 July–c. 1 August 1926	EH and Hadley are in Valencia for the eight-day fiesta, staying at the Hotel Valencia.
c. 2 August 1926	EH and Hadley are back in Antibes as guests of the Murphys at Villa America.
c. 12 August 1926	Upon returning to Paris, EH and Hadley separate. She moves into the Hôtel Beauvoir and EH into Gerald Murphy's studio at 69, rue Froidevaux. Bumby is in Brittany with Marie Rohrbach.
31 August 1926	Cape has rejected *The Torrents of Spring*.
23 September 1926	British edition of *In Our Time* is published in London by Cape. EH and Pauline travel to Boulogne and stay at the Hôtel Meurice; the next day, Pauline boards the *Pennland* to New York, on her way to Piggott, Arkansas, beginning the

	three-month separation from EH that Hadley has stipulated as a condition for granting him a divorce.
7 October 1926	Anson Hemingway, EH's paternal grandfather (born 1844), dies in Oak Park, Illinois.
12–c. 18 October 1926	EH and Archibald MacLeish are in Zaragoza, Spain, for the Fiesta of El Pilar.
16 October 1926	*This Quarter* editor Ernest Walsh dies at the age of thirty-one.
22 October 1926	*The Sun Also Rises* is published in New York by Scribner's.
November 1926	*Today is Friday* is published in the pamphlet series of The As Stable Publications of Englewood, New Jersey.
3 November 1926	The effective date of Hadley's handwritten and signed statement extending the period of EH and Pauline's separation, specifying "a leave of absence without communication" between them until 3 February 1927. EH and Pauline agree to comply.
c. 6 November 1926	Hadley embarks on ten-day trip to Chartres with Winifred Mowrer, staying at the Hôtel de France, where Paul Mowrer visits them; Bumby stays with EH in Paris.
c. 16 November 1926	Hadley releases EH from separation agreement and says she is ready for divorce.
December 1926	Both Cape and William Heinemann have made offers for British rights to publish *The Sun Also Rises*; New York producer Dwight Deere Wiman expresses interest in theatrical and film rights.
4 December 1926	"The Undefeated" appears in *The Best Short Stories of 1926*.
8 December 1926	Hadley files for divorce in Paris.
25 December 1926	EH leaves for Gstaad, Switzerland, where he joins Jinny Pfeiffer and Archibald and Ada MacLeish at the Grand Hotel Alpina.

30 December 1926	Pauline sails from New York to France aboard the *New Amsterdam.*
8 January 1927	EH meets Pauline at Cherbourg.
19 January 1927	EH, Pauline, and Jinny are in Gstaad, staying at the Hotel Rössli.
27 January 1927	Hadley receives judgment of divorce granting her custody of Bumby.
12 February 1927	"My Own Life," a humorous article, appears in the *New Yorker.*
27 February 1927	EH returns to Paris to bring Bumby back to Gstaad.
Spring 1927	EH's "Neo-Thomist Poem" appears in *The Exile* under the misprinted title "Nothoemist Poem."
March 1927	"The Killers" appears in *Scribner's Magazine.*
5 March 1927	EH, Pauline, Jinny, and Bumby have moved to the Hotel Eiger in Wengen, Switzerland.
6 March 1927	"A Protest against Pirating 'Ulysses'" appears in *New York Herald Tribune Books*; EH is among the 162 signers.
10 March 1927	EH, Pauline, and Bumby return to Paris.
c. 15–26 March 1927	EH and Guy Hickok take a road trip around Italy in Hickok's Ford, visiting Ezra and Dorothy Pound at Rapallo and priest Don Giuseppe Bianchi near San Marino.
April 1927	"In Another Country" and "A Canary for One" appear in *Scribner's Magazine* under the heading "Two Stories."
1 April 1927	EH pays three months' advance rent and subleases an apartment at 6, rue Férou, after Gerald Murphy asks him to vacate his studio by 1 May.
4–10 April 1927	EH attends six-day bicycle races in Paris.
14 April 1927	Divorce decree is final for Hadley; on 21 April the decree releases EH, and he is free to remarry.
16 April 1927	Hadley and Bumby sail from France aboard the *Berengaria* for a six-month stay in the United States to visit family and friends. In New York

	Hadley meets Perkins and receives a $1,000 royalty check for *The Sun Also Rises* as part of the divorce settlement.
10 May 1927	EH and Pauline are married in Paris in a civil ceremony, followed by a Roman Catholic ceremony at the Église Saint-Honoré-d'Eylau, Place Victor Hugo.
11 May 1927	EH and Pauline leave Paris for their honeymoon at Le Grau-du-Roi in the South of France.
18 May 1927	"Italy, 1927" (later retitled "Che Ti Dice La Patria?" in *Men Without Women*) appears in the *New Republic*.
25–26 May 1927	Grace and Clarence Hemingway meet their grandson Bumby when Hadley and Bumby visit Oak Park.
7 June 1927	EH and Pauline are back in Paris in their new apartment at 6, rue Férou.
9 June 1927	*Fiesta*, the British edition of *The Sun Also Rises*, is published in London by Cape.
24 June 1927	EH rejects an offer from Hearst's International Magazine Company for British and American rights for his next ten stories, novel, and the novel's film rights.
July 1927	"Fifty Grand" appears in *Atlantic Monthly*.
5–12 July 1927	EH and Pauline travel to Spain, where EH and Waldo Peirce attend the Fiesta of San Fermín in Pamplona while Pauline stays in San Sebastian.
c. 12 July 1927	EH joins Pauline in San Sebastian, where they stay at the Hotel Biarritz.
21–30 July 1927	EH and Pauline stay at the Hotel Inglés in Valencia.
31 July–4 August 1927	EH and Pauline stay at the Gran Hotel Biarritz in Madrid, then travel to La Coruña.
August 1927	"Hills Like White Elephants" appears in *transition*.

16–31 August 1927	EH and Pauline are in Santiago de Compostela, staying at the Hotel Suizo.
September 1927	"An Alpine Idyll" appears in the first volume of *The American Caravan: A Yearbook of American Literature.*
2 September 1927	EH and Pauline arrive in Hendaye, France, and stay at the Ondarraitz Hotel (owned by R. Barron) for about two weeks.
23 September 1927	EH and Pauline are back in Paris. Through literary agent Eric Pinker, EH accepts Heinemann's offer for British rights for his next novel and book of stories.
October 1927	"The Real Spaniard," a parody by EH of Louis Bromfield, appears in the *Boulevardier*, with unauthorized revisions by editor Arthur Moss.
7 October 1927	EH cancels the deal with Heinemann and decides to keep British publication rights with Cape.
8 October 1927	Hadley and Bumby sail from New York for France aboard the *Tuscania.* EH has completed nine chapters of a new novel with a father–son theme, which he would later call a "sort of Tom Jones" book. Working titles included "A New Slain Knight" and "Jimmy Breen."
14 October 1927	*Men Without Women* is published in New York by Scribner's.
16 October 1927	EH meets Hadley and Bumby in Le Havre; Bumby stays with EH and Pauline in Paris while Hadley moves into an apartment at 98, boulevard Auguste-Blanqui.
3–c. 12 November 1927	In Berlin, EH and Pauline attend the six-day bicycle races.
16 November 1927	EH is back in Paris.
27 November 1927	"The Killers" appears in *The Best Short Stories of 1927.*
5 December 1927	EH has written 20 chapters of the new novel.

13 December 1927	EH (ill with the grippe), Pauline, Bumby, and Mr. House and his son (of Horton Bay, Michigan) leave Paris to meet Jinny Pfeiffer and the MacLeishes at Gstaad. During the journey, Bumby accidentally scratches the pupil of EH's right eye.
6 January 1928	EH is awarded a second place prize of $250 by the O. Henry Memorial Committee for "The Killers."
31 January 1928	Pauline, Jinny, and Bumby return to Paris; EH remains in Switzerland for a skiing excursion to Lenk and Adelboden.
early February 1928	Returning to Paris, EH finds burst pipes and no heat in the apartment and again falls sick with the grippe.
4 March 1928	EH is injured by a falling skylight that gashes his forehead; he receives stitches at the American Hospital at Neuilly. Around this time, he begins writing what will become *A Farewell to Arms*.
17 March 1928	EH and Pauline sail from La Rochelle bound for Havana aboard the *Orita*. With 22 chapters and 45,000 words written, EH is ready to set aside his novel in progress and plans to continue work on the new novel in the United States.
1 April 1928	EH and Pauline arrive in Havana when the *Orita* docks at 10:50 p.m. They stay at the Hotel Ambos Mundos.
4 April 1928	EH and Pauline depart from Havana and arrive in Key West, Florida, aboard the *Governor Cobb*. They move into an apartment above the Trevor and Morris Ford automobile agency at 314 Simonton Street.
10 April 1928	EH's parents and uncle Willoughby Hemingway stop in Key West while on a vacation in Florida and Cuba that started 19 March.

20 April 1928	British edition of *Men Without Women* is published in London by Cape.
c. late April–May 1928	John Dos Passos, Bill Smith, Waldo Peirce, and Kate Smith visit EH and Pauline in Key West. EH writes in the mornings and goes deep-sea fishing with his friends in the afternoons.
19 May 1928	Pauline leaves Key West by train for Piggott; a few days later, EH and Paul Pfeiffer, Pauline's father, follow in the Hemingways' Model A Ford coupe, reaching Piggott in six days.
1 June 1928	EH is in Piggott; he has written 238 pages of *A Farewell to Arms*, almost 200 of them in Key West.
12 June 1928	EH and Pauline are in Kansas City, staying with EH's cousin Ruth Lowry and her husband Malcolm.
28 June 1928	Pauline delivers Patrick by Caesarean section after eighteen hours of labor. For the next three weeks EH stays in Kansas City, working on his novel while Pauline recuperates in the hospital.
28 June 1928	*Cinquante mille dollars*, a collection of six stories in translation, is published in Paris by Éditions de la Nouvelle Revue Française.
21 July 1928	EH, Pauline, and Patrick are back in Piggott.
25 July 1928	EH travels back to Kansas City.
28 July 1928	EH and Bill Horne leave Kansas City in EH's Ford, arriving three days later at Folly Ranch, outside Sheridan, Wyoming.
3–7 August 1928	EH stays at the Sheridan Inn and works on *A Farewell to Arms*.
8 August 1928	EH moves to Eleanor Donnelley's more isolated Lower Ranch and continues writing.
18 August 1928	Pauline arrives in Sheridan, having left Patrick in her parents' care in Piggott.
c. 23 August 1928	First draft of *A Farewell to Arms* is finished.

30 August 1928	*Men Without Women* has sold 20,000 copies, and *The Sun Also Rises* 26,749 copies.
late August–18 September 1928	EH and Pauline travel in Wyoming and Montana, fishing and hunting; they also visit Owen Wister in Shell, Wyoming.
23–25 September 1928	EH and Pauline return to Kansas City, then drive on to Piggott, arriving with 9,200 miles on the odometer.
11 October 1928	EH receives a $5,000 advance from Scribner's for his drafted novel.
16 October 1928	EH drives the Ford from Piggott to Oak Park and stays for a week in his parents' home. This is his second visit home since he and Hadley moved to Paris in 1921. EH made a brief visit by himself at Christmas in 1923 when he and Hadley were living in Toronto.
23–c. 31 October 1928	EH stays at Bill Horne's home in Chicago, where Pauline joins him, leaving Patrick in Piggott.
25 October 1928	*Fiesta*, the German edition of *The Sun Also Rises*, is published in Berlin by Rowohlt Verlag.
1 November 1928	EH and Pauline leave Chicago by train to visit the MacLeishes in Conway, Massachusetts, for about a week.
mid-November 1928	In New York City, EH and Pauline stay at the Hotel Brevoort. They see Perkins, Waldo Peirce, and Mike Strater, and attend boxing matches at Madison Square Garden.
17 November 1928	EH and Pauline attend the Princeton–Yale football game in Princeton, New Jersey, with the Fitzgeralds and Mike Strater. After the game, the Hemingways stay overnight at Ellerslie Mansion, where the Fitzgeralds lived, near Wilmington, Delaware.
18 November 1928	EH and Pauline leave Philadelphia by train; EH proceeds to Oak Park to pick up the Ford and drive with his sister Madelaine ("Sunny") to Piggott.

c. 24–c. 27 November 1928	The Hemingways move to Key West: EH and Sunny travel to Florida by car and Pauline and Patrick by train, meeting in Jacksonville, where Sunny joins Pauline and the baby, and EH continues the drive alone. In Key West, the Hemingways rent a house at 1100 South Street.
3 December 1928	EH rides the Havana Special train for almost forty hours from Key West to New York to meet Hadley and Bumby, who arrive on 4 December on the *Île de France*.
6 December 1928	Clarence Hemingway (born 1871) commits suicide at home in Oak Park. That afternoon, EH and Bumby depart from New York by train, bound for Key West. Near Trenton, New Jersey, EH receives a telegram with the news of his father's death. Leaving Bumby in the care of a porter to complete the trip to Key West, EH takes an overnight train to Chicago.
8 December 1928	EH attends his father's funeral in Oak Park. The next day he boards a train to return to Key West.
13 December 1928	EH is back in Key West sick with the grippe and sore throat, but he works steadily revising the novel.
22 January 1929	Typewritten draft of *A Farewell to Arms* is finished.
31 January–7 February 1929	Perkins visits EH in Key West, joining in fishing expeditions and reading the typescript of the novel, which he takes with him to New York.
c. 4–22 February 1929	Mike and Maggie Strater and Denny and Edith Holden visit Key West.
13 February 1929	Perkins wires offer to serialize *A Farewell to Arms* in *Scribner's Magazine* for $16,000; EH accepts the next day.
27 February 1929	Waldo Peirce and Kate Smith arrive in Key West.

6 March 1929	EH sends his mother money for overdue taxes and the first of the monthly $100 checks he will send her until 1930.
14 March 1929	Perkins sends EH a contract for *A Farewell to Arms*, although EH does not sign it before leaving for France.
c. 19 March 1929	Dos Passos arrives in Key West.
c. 19–25 March 1929	EH and companions on fishing trip to Dry Tortugas.
3 April 1929	EH mails the corrected fourth magazine installment of the novel to Perkins; he will complete the remaining segments in Europe.
5 April 1929	EH, Pauline, Bumby, Patrick, and Sunny sail from Havana aboard the *Yorck*, bound for Boulogne.

MAPS

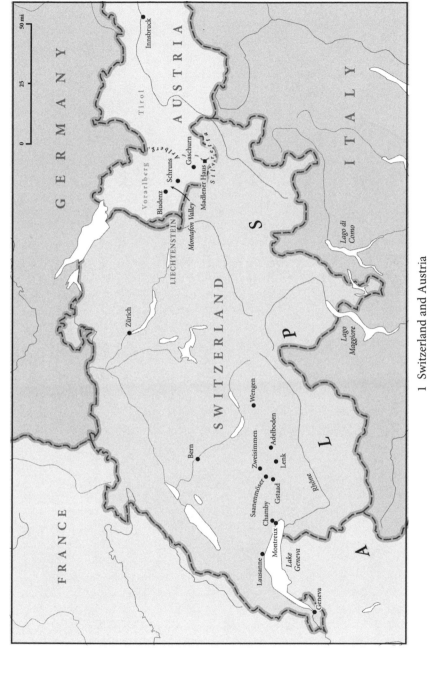

1 Switzerland and Austria

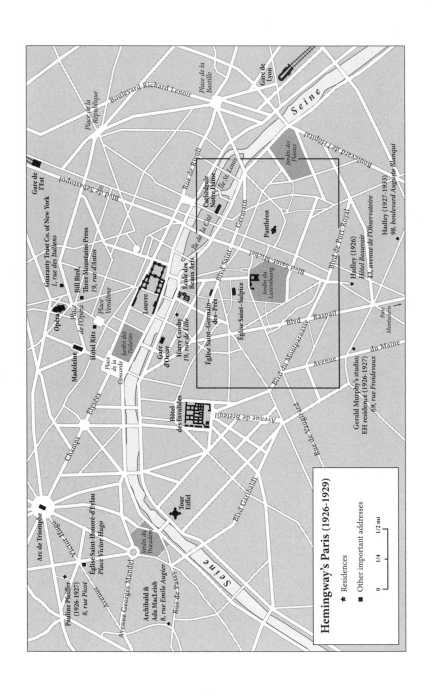

Hemingway's Paris (1926–1929)

★ Residences
■ Other important addresses

0   1/4   1/2 mi

Residences and important addresses:

Guaranty Trust Co. of New York
1, rue des Italiens

Bill Bird
Three Mountains Press
19, rue d'Antin

Harry Crosby
19, rue de Lille

Hadley (1926)
Hôtel Beauvoir
43, avenue de l'Observatoire

Hadley (1927–1933)
98, boulevard Auguste Blanqui

Gerald Murphy's studio;
EH residence (1926–1927)
69, rue Froidevaux

Pauline Pfeiffer
(1926–1927)
8, rue Picot

Archibald &
Ada MacLeish
8, rue Emile Augier

Map labels:

Place de la Bastille · Gare de Lyon · Seine · Boulevard Richard Lenoir · Place de la République · Gare de l'Est · Blvd de Sébastopol · Boulevard de l'Hôpital · Jardin des Plantes · Rue de Rivoli · Cathédrale Notre-Dame · Île St. Louis · Île de la Cité · Germain · Panthéon · Blvd de Port-Royal · Opéra · Place de l'Opéra · Place Vendôme · École des Beaux Arts · Blvd Saint-Germain · Blvd Saint-Michel · Madeleine · Hôtel Ritz · Louvre · Jardin des Tuileries · Gare d'Orsay · Église Saint-Germain-des-Prés · Église Saint-Sulpice · Jardin du Luxembourg · Place de la Concorde · Blvd Raspail · Blvd du Montparnasse · Avenue du Maine · Parc Montsouris · Hôtel des Invalides · Avenue de Breteuil · Champs Élysées · Rue de Vaugirard · Arc de Triomphe · Victor Hugo · Église Saint-Honoré-d'Eylau · Place Victor Hugo · Avenue Georges Mandel · Rue de Passy · Jardin du Trocadéro · Tour Eiffel · Blvd Garibaldi · Seine

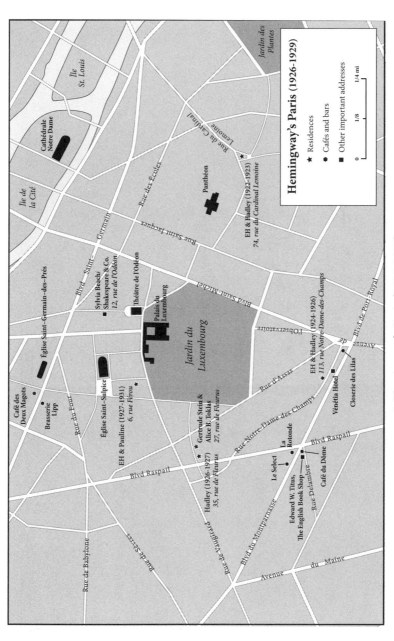

2 Hemingway's Paris (1926–1929)

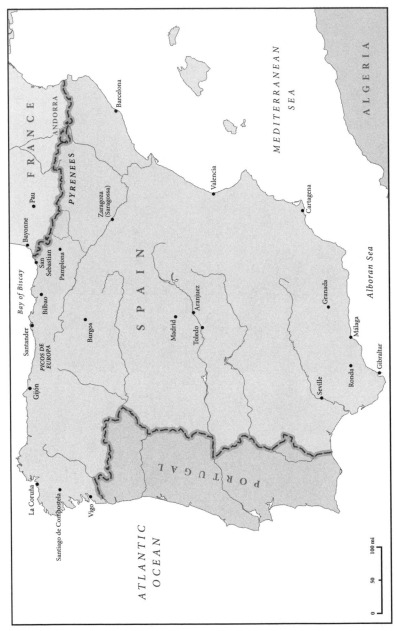

3 Spain

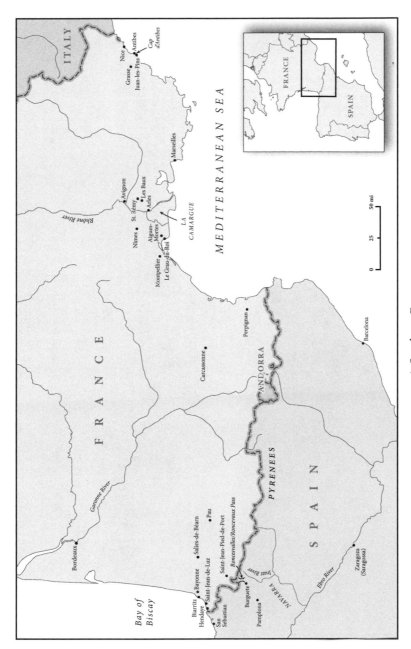

4 Southern France

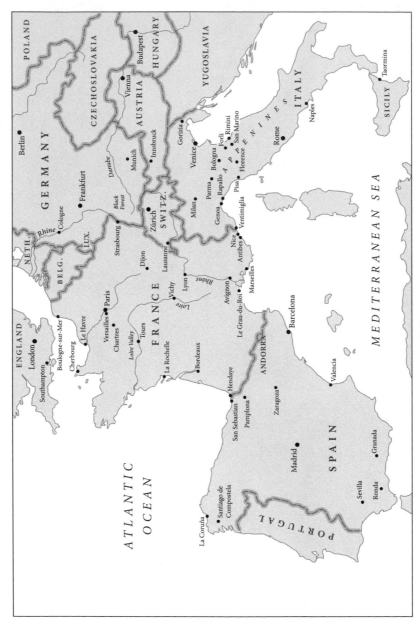

5 Europe

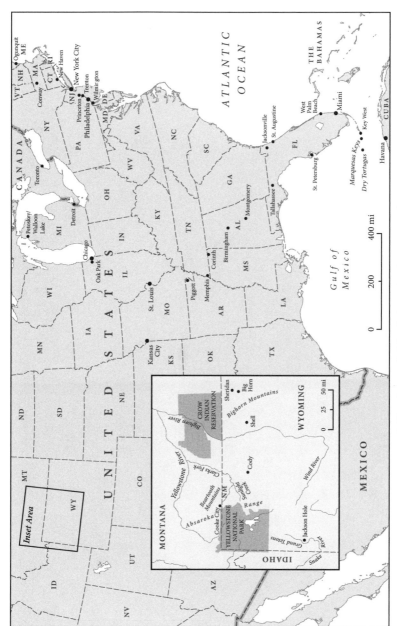

6 Hemingway's North America (1926–1929)

THE LETTERS
1926–April 1929

To William B. Smith, Jr., 2 January 1926

Jan 2, 1926

Dear Boid—

That's rotten hard luck about the leg but hope by now it's in swell shape. It will be a swell relief to have that knee finally O.K. anyway. Wish I would have known of it so I could have flooded the hospital with screeds.[1] We had an Xmas cable from Don but as it came through the bank there was no address.[2]

Pauline's been here since Xmas and we've had foul weather steadily.[3] Gawd if there was someway of getting the weather not to bear down. It's the only thing left that hasn't been fixed.

Schaekels has won championship of Mexico. Ko-ed 9 boys in 9 fights in Mex City. All of which makes it appear that Alf Ross were tough. He's winning right along.[4]

Jeest Pauline is a swell girl. Anybody who goes big through seven consecutive rainy days when they expected skiing has got something in addition to the usual christian virtures.

When we got here on the 12th of Dec. was 14° and 2 1/2 feet of powder snow. Europe was swept by spring wave about Dec 22.

Yest was New Year. They got a Kirch down here that you cant taste the alc in at all. No burn to it. But grand wallop. We punished 18 of them yest while shooting cards over at the Adler.[5]

Hope you've vended. You have them rising like a warm spring evening on the Black anyway. It's just a ? of time till you land. If you got any carbonics I would like to see any of them you favour.[6]

The Gerald Murphys are coming here in Feb. and we are all going to Munich and fly from there to <u>Madlener Haus</u> 2,000 meters, in Silvretta[.] Plane loaded with blankets, rich foods, wines, and condiments. Ski from there in all directions. Dos is coming too. We are going to visit Murphy's at Antibes in April.[7]

Jeest if you want to read a swell book get Peter Simple by Capt Marryat in Dutton's Everyman Library.[8] Greet any hapgoods you see for me.[9] Greet Kate from group of young people in heart of old world Austria.[10] If it keeps on Spring we are going on walking trip over the passes and down into

Innsbruck. It cleared off yest and started to get cold then is warming up again today. We walk 14–15 kilometers a day and finish at some inn with beer and kirsch. I am getting like a horse in the legs. Christ I hope the knee is all right.

Will screed again shortly. Did you get bovine reproductions?[11]

Yrs. always, Miller

Hash sends her love.[12]

Evan has gotten rid of Marcelle—gave her a $1000 bucks I believe— That must have made Marcelle believe in God. And is staging a Rake's Progress. He gets his dough every Monday and is broke every Tuesday. Well he'll get it as long as he lives.[13]

Scott's been staking Harold Stearns. Harold's been sick.[14]

Jo Bennett is back in Paris from States and sent you her best.[15]

Private Collection, ALS

1 EH is responding to a letter of 15 December 1925 that Smith wrote from the hospital in Boston where he was recovering from knee surgery (JFK).

2 In his letter, Smith asked if EH had heard from their mutual friend Donald Ogden Stewart (1894–1980). Stewart wrote a series of humorous books in the 1920s, including *Mr. and Mrs. Haddock Abroad* (1924) and *The Crazy Fool* (1925). After meeting EH in Paris in spring 1923, Stewart joined him for the Fiesta of San Fermín in Pamplona in 1924 and 1925. EH's comic story "My Life in the Bull Ring with Donald Ogden Stewart" (first published in *Letters* vol. 2, 191–95) is based on the madcap adventures at Pamplona in 1924. Stewart also served as a model for the character Bill Gorton in *SAR*. Because EH was often away from Paris, he used his bank, the Guaranty Trust Company of New York at 1, rue des Italiens, Paris, as his permanent address for mail delivery.

3 EH is writing from Schruns in the Austrian state of Vorarlberg. EH, his wife Hadley (née Elizabeth Hadley Richardson, 1891–1979), and their son "Bumby" (John Hadley Nicanor Hemingway, 1923–2000) were staying at the Hotel Taube, where they had also spent three months the preceding winter. They were joined for the holidays by Pauline Pfeiffer (1895–1951), who worked for *Vogue* in Paris, had befriended EH and Hadley in 1925, and would marry EH in 1927.

4 Belgian boxer Arthur Schaekels (also known as Arturo Schackels or Shackels, b. 1904) won the Mexican welterweight championship on 12 December 1925 by decision over Mexican-born U.S. boxer Tommy White (b. c. 1898), who had held the title for three years and had twenty-five victories in 1925, including several in Mexico City. Algerian-born welterweight Alfred (Alf) Ros (b. 1903) had defeated Schaekels in Paris on 2 September 1925.

5 *Kirsch* or *Kirschwasser* (German), a dry, colorless brandy distilled from cherries. In a joint letter to Sylvia Beach that EH and Hadley had written from Schruns [14 December 1925], Hadley noted they had been warmly welcomed by old friends, including "one old Austrian gentleman who runs the rival of the Taube, the Adler in the next village" (*Letters*

vol. 2, 438–39). A 1925–1926 travel brochure that survives among EH's papers at JFK lists lodgings called Adler in both Schruns and the nearby village of Tschagguns.

6 In his 15 December letter, Smith reported on his efforts to "vend" his stories to popular magazines. EH and Smith had often fished the Black River in the Pine Barrens region of northern Lower Michigan east of Horton Bay. "Carbonics" refers to carbon copies.

7 American artist and expatriate Gerald Murphy (1888–1964), his wife Sara (1883–1975), and American writer John Dos Passos (1896–1970) joined EH and Hadley for skiing in Schruns and nearby Gaschurn in March 1926. The Madlener Haus, an Alpine lodge (elevation about 6,500 feet) in the Silvretta mountain range, which lies south of Schruns and extends along the border of Austria and Switzerland. In February 1925, EH and Hadley had spent a week at the Madlener Haus, using it as a base for their skiing excursions. The Murphys owned a villa at Cap d'Antibes, on the French Riviera.

8 *Peter Simple*, a novel by English sea captain and author Frederick Marryat (1792–1848), originally published by E. L. Carey & A. Hart in Philadelphia (1833–1834) and by Saunders & Otley in London (1834). Everyman's Library, a series of reprinted literary classics published in England by J. M. Dent and distributed in the United States by New York publisher E. P. Dutton since 1906. The Everyman's Library edition of Marryat's novel was published in 1907.

9 Smith was then living in Provincetown, Massachusetts, as were members of the Hapgood family. Writers Hutchins Hapgood (1869–1944) and Neith Boyce (1872–1951) were married in 1899 and had four children, Harry Boyce (1901–1918), Charles Hutchins (1904–1982), Miriam (1906–1990), and Beatrix (1910–1994). The family lived in New York and summered in Provincetown, where in 1915 Hutchins Hapgood had helped to found the Provincetown Players theater troupe. EH met Miriam in late 1922 while she was a student in Lausanne.

10 Katharine Foster (Kate) Smith (1891–1947), Bill Smith's sister and one of EH's closest friends before his marriage to Hadley, was also living in Provincetown. Natives of St. Louis, Kate and her brothers had spent summers at Horton Bay, where EH first met them. Kate was also a school friend of both Hadley and Pauline, having met first Hadley at Mary Institute in St. Louis and later Pauline at the University of Missouri. After graduating with an A.B. degree in English and Journalism, Kate pursued a writing career.

11 Probably the bullfight pictures taken in Pamplona that EH enclosed in his letter to Smith of 3 December 1925 (*Letters* vol. 2, 431).

12 "Miller," EH's middle name, was a nickname used in his correspondence with Smith. Hash, a nickname for Hadley.

13 Evan Biddle Shipman (1904–1957), American poet and horse-racing expert, had arrived in Paris in October 1924 accompanied by a Belgian bar waitress named Marcelle, with whom he lived in an apartment on the Île Saint Louis (O'Rourke, 52). EH also reported in his 3 December 1925 letter to Smith that Shipman had broken with Marcelle (*Letters* vol. 2, 430). *A Rake's Progress* is a series of eight paintings completed in 1735 by English painter William Hogarth (1697–1764). It depicts the decline and eventual madness of Tom Rakewell, who loses his fortune through extravagant living. Shipman had received an inheritance of $5,000 on his twenty-first birthday, 23 October 1925 (O'Rourke, 9).

14 F. Scott Fitzgerald (1896–1940) lent money to Harold E. Stearns (1891–1943), expatriate American journalist, writer, and editor. Stearns was the author of *America and the Young Intellectual* (New York: Doran, 1921) and editor of *Civilization in the United States: An Inquiry by Thirty Americans* (New York: Harcourt, Brace, 1922). A contributor to the *New York Herald* European edition (commonly known as the Paris *Herald*) and Paris correspondent for *Town & Country*, Stearns also wrote a racing column for the European

edition of the *Chicago Tribune* (commonly known as the Paris *Tribune*) under the name "Peter Pickem."

15 Josephine (Jo) Beach Day Bennett (1880–1961), American activist who worked for women's suffrage, racial justice, and labor rights and ran for U.S. Senate on the Farmer-Labor ticket in 1920. In 1926 she divorced her husband, a Connecticut attorney with whom she had three children, and lived off and on in France, where she became romantically involved with Harold Stearns. In spring 1925 she and Dorothy (Dossie) Moffat Johnston (1896–1987) had joined EH and Hadley at Schruns for a skiing vacation.

To Ernest Walsh, 2 January 1926

January 2, 1926

Dear Ernest—

Glad to hear This Quarter is on the stocks. Sure I'll be as brutal and candid as you like. I look forward like hell to seeing the Wolumne.[1]

About McAlmon: As you know I have always backed him up, touted his stuff to people and defended him.[2] I dont mind him hating me or being jealous a damned bit. It's quite natural as you say. When you say McAlmon will outlive Dickens you are simply talking horse shit as I believe you'll admit yourself.[3] Not that I give a damn who outlives who. It's more important to me to live than to outlive. When I get sore is when anybody, nothing to do with their being brother artists, brother officers, brother bricklayers or what have you, tells little knifing lies behind your back.[4] The instant reaction is to push such a ones face in. This reaction having passed, none of it makes any god damned difference. Let's not talk about McAlmon. The last day I was in Paris I went around looking for him intending, when I found him, to beat him up, not regarding the transaction as in anyway creditable to myself, but because I figured that was the best way to show my contempt—that I wouldnt be ashamed of beating him up, even though he's half my size, anymore than I would feel any remorse at squawshing a bed bug which is even less than half my size. And I suppose that, had I found him, I wouldnt have had the guts to do it—being lousy with christian precepts and inhibitions. And I dont think old Benvenuto Cellini, or Ben Jonson or anybody else that could drink would have been a comrade with McAlmon.[5] And I dont think Mac would have had any more friends, nor as many friends in any other age than our own. Being always lousy when drunk and always vomiting after your 4th or 5th whiskey never made for comradeship.

There is comradeship today and I have it with Don Stewart and Dos Passos and a guy named Chink and a guy named Howy Jenkins and several other guys and would have it with you if we could bum around together.[6] And whether they can write or not makes no bludy difference. Most writers and artists—most, not the exceptions, are just social climbers and swell to be near.

I've always given you my best stuff and always will. At present I'm trying the Fight Story—about 15,000 words, on the big money market. It's come back from Hearst. Ray Long said he would buy it if there was woman interest in it. They would pay me $1200. I'm not putting in any woman interest and not changing one word to suit anybody. But have to try it on the other 3 magazines who pay lots of money because I cannot pass up the chance of what $1,000 in the hand would mean if any of them would take a chance and buy it.[7] Needless to say I would prefer 1,000 times over to be published in This Quarter than in The Dial.[8]

I had an offer of several hundred dollars for the Bull Fight story from Scribners 2 months ago. They had heard about it and Scott Fitzgerald offered me $250 down and thought he could get more. Scribners dont spend much on stories. I wrote Scott that you were publishing the bull fight story in This Quarter and that settled that.[9]

Without doubt I will get the fight story back—and then I will send it to you—but first I must expose it to the chance of making me immediate cash. Am still re-writing on the novel which is called The Sun Also Rises.[10]

If I am anything I am a catholic. Had extreme unction administered to me as such in July 1918 and recovered. So guess I'm a super-catholic. Why do you ask. It is most certainly the most comfortable religion for anyone soldiering. Am not what is called a "good" catholic. Think there is a lot of nonsense about the church, Holy Years etc. What rot. But cannot imagine taking any other religion at all seriously[11]

It certainly will be swell to see the Review. Shoot me one right away—will you? I may have to go to America in January. Hope to hell not. Steerage in the winter. Still the sea is always worth it.

We had a fine drunken New Year. I also won 1,230,000 kronen at cards. That's over 400 francs in French money.[12]

Hadley and I send our love to Miss Moorhead and a great New Year to you both

Yours always,

Ernest

JFK, ALS

In a letter to EH of 9 January 1926, Walsh would acknowledge receipt of this letter and promised to answer "when I get a few worries off my mind" (JFK), but any additional response from Walsh remains unlocated.

1 *This Quarter* (1925–1932) published a wide range of work by many prominent new writers, including Ezra Pound, James Joyce, Gertrude Stein, H.D. (Hilda Doolittle), and EH. After meeting Ernest Walsh in Paris in 1922, Scottish feminist and painter Ethel Moorhead (1869–1955) provided financial backing for the magazine. The first issue, published in Paris in spring [May] 1925 with considerable help from EH, included his story "Big Two-Hearted River." The second number (Autumn–Winter 1925–1926), published in Milan, included EH's "The Undefeated." EH had returned the corrected proofs of the story with his letter to Walsh and Moorhead of 30 November [1925] (*Letters* vol. 2, 420).

2 American expatriate writer and publisher Robert Menzies McAlmon (1895–1956), who published EH's first book, *TSTP* (1923). A year earlier, EH had written to McAlmon enthusiastically praising his novel *Village: As it Happened Through a Fifteen Year Period* (1924) and had recommended McAlmon's work to others, including anthologist Edward J. O'Brien, Sylvia Beach, and Ezra Pound (*Letters* vol. 2, 228–29; 154, 223, 395).

3 Reviewing McAlmon's story collection *Distinguished Air* (Paris: Three Mountains Press, 1925) in *This Quarter* no. 2, Walsh called McAlmon "one of the most astonishing writers since the fathers of English literature," declaring, "If you care for Shakespeare, if you care for Dickens, if you care for Conrad, you will care more for McAlmon" (331).

4 By the end of 1925, EH's relationship with McAlmon had soured. In a letter to Fitzgerald [c. 24 December 1925], EH called McAlmon "a son of a bitch with a mind like an ingrowing toe nail" and reported that McAlmon was claiming responsibility for starting EH's writing career and accusing EH of exploiting people emotionally (*Letters* vol. 2, 455–56).

5 Benvenuto Cellini (1500–1571), Italian sculptor, goldsmith, and writer; Benjamin (Ben) Jonson (c. 1572–1637), English dramatist, poet, and critic.

6 Eric Edward "Chink" Dorman-Smith (later Dorman-O'Gowan, 1895–1969), British Army career soldier in His Majesty's Fifth Fusiliers, had befriended EH in Milan in November 1918 while EH was recovering from his war injuries. The two men renewed their friendship after EH returned to Europe with Hadley in December 1921, and Chink was godfather to their son, Bumby. Howell G. Jenkins (1894–1971), a native of Evanston, Illinois, served with EH in the American Red Cross (ARC) Ambulance Service Section 4 in Italy, and the two maintained a friendship for several years following the war. He was one of EH's fishing and camping companions in Michigan in the summer of 1919 and a member of EH and Hadley's wedding party in 1921.

7 EH is referring to his long boxing story "Fifty Grand." On 3 December 1925, EH had written to Bill Smith that a representative of media tycoon William Randolph Hearst (1863–1951) "took Fifty Grand story back with him. Said he was sure Ray Long would like it as much as he does" (*Letters* vol. 2, 428). Ray Long (1878–1935) was vice president and editor in chief of Hearst's International Magazine Company and editor of *Cosmopolitan* magazine from 1919 to 1931. The story would be rejected by *Cosmopolitan*, *Collier's Weekly*, *Liberty*, the *Saturday Evening Post*, and *Scribner's Magazine* before it finally appeared in the *Atlantic Monthly* in July 1927 and in *MWW* that October.

8 *The Dial*, first established as a Transcendentalist magazine in 1840 by Margaret Fuller (1810–1850) and Ralph Waldo Emerson (1803–1882), went through two more iterations before it was purchased in 1919 by American poet Scofield Thayer (1889–1982) and James Sibley Watson, Jr. (1894–1982). It had rejected EH's poetry in 1922 as well as his bullfighting story "The Undefeated" in 1925.

9 New York publishing house Charles Scribner's Sons was named in 1878 by brothers John Blair Scribner (1850–1879), Charles Scribner II (1854–1930), and Arthur Hawley Scribner (1859–1932), whose father, Charles Scribner (1821–1871), had founded the firm with Isaac D. Baker (1819–1850) in 1846. After meeting EH in the spring of 1925, F. Scott Fitzgerald recommended EH's work to his own editor at Scribner's, Maxwell Perkins (1884–1947). Any written record of Scribner's offer to buy "The Undefeated" or letter from EH to Fitzgerald concerning *This Quarter*'s publication of the story remains unlocated.

10 EH had drafted the novel between 13 July and 21 September 1925; it would be published by Scribner's on 22 October 1926. For detailed discussion of the novel's composition, see Frederic Svoboda, *Hemingway and "The Sun Also Rises": The Crafting of a Style* (Lawrence: University Press of Kansas, 1983); and Matthew J. Bruccoli, ed., *"The Sun Also Rises": A Facsimile Edition* (Detroit: Omnigraphics, 1990).

11 EH was raised as a Protestant, attending the Third Congregationalist Church in Oak Park, Illinois. While serving with the American Red Cross (ARC) Ambulance Service in Italy, he was wounded near Fossalta di Piave on 8 July 1918 and transported to a field hospital, where the Florentine priest Giuseppe Bianchi (d. 1965) administered extreme unction, the Roman Catholic sacrament of anointing those who are seriously ill or dying.

12 The currency of the Austro-Hungarian Empire, the Krone, remained the national currency following the empire's demise in 1919 but became so devalued by postwar inflation that a larger monetary unit, the Schilling, was introduced in 1922 to stabilize it. In 1926, 1,230,000 Kronen were worth 123 Schilling—equivalent to about 533.80 French francs or 17.31 U.S. dollars.

To Ernest Walsh, [c. 15 January 1926]

[*Ethel Moorhead autograph notation above first line*: Criticism etc of our 2nd No. T. Quarter printed in Milan][1]

Dear Ernest—

I don't write Dear Ernest and Dear Miss Moorhead because you wanted me to write you nothing but the truth and as soon as I start to write the truth in large chunks I always get very profane, not to mention obscene and I have a low middle class upbringing that makes me uncomofortable if addressing such remarks as horse shit to a lady.

This Quarter came this morning. [*Moorhead marginal notation*: (No. 2 T.Q.)] IT IS SPLENDID. Looks fine, comfortable to handle, the right kind of paper, bound right, grand cover, supplement printed separately—as it should be—and mechanically a hell of a fine performance. As for what is in it: it is the first exciting magazine I have read since I was 13 and used to wait for the baseball magazine to come out. That's god's truth. And you know I'm not lying when I tell you I don't get excited about something simply because it is printing stuff of mine or stuff about me.

The poetry is the best bunch of poetry I've ever seen in a review. I wish you had something of Isador Schneider, your last time's Irish poet, and the late Mr. Eliot and you could call it an Anthology and let it go at that.[2] With maybe one by Bill Williams, one by H.D., if she can still write them, and about two lines by Marianne Moore which is about what Marianne rates. And ask her to make the lines her own.[3]

Have not yet read Boyle, Knister prose, Ethel Moorhead prose. Will report on that later.[4]

Joyce is swell. I would always rather know what it is all about but I like Joyce straight, with orange juice, with Liffey water or what have you.[5]

McAlmon I unfortunately read about a year ago. Altho he may make a bum out of Mark Twain, Dickens etc. I have never yet succeeded in re-reading anything by McAlmon.[6] On the other hand I remember all of McAlmon I've ever read. This is the truth, which you asked for.

Rose et Noir seemed unimportant if true and if not true what the hell. I hope he likes it in America.[7]

Blue Beard's Last Wife reminded me unpleasantly of all the Italian intellectuals I knew when I was a little boy. However if I saw Linati I would tell him it was a strange and amazing story beautifully told and losing, I am sure, much in the translation. All us wops lie to each other.[8]

Djuna's story excellent. Much better than the Perlmutter girls that it is about. Why didn't she make Radiguet a writer in the story?[9] I believe when you are writing stories about actual people, not the best thing to do, you should make them those people in everything except telephone addresses.

Think that is only justification for writing stories about actual people. It is what McAlmon always does and then he blurs them to make them unrecognizable and not being an artist he usually blurs them to the reader also. Still Djuna's is a hell of a good story.

I have read my own story twice. [*Moorhead notation*: "The Undefeated"] Disliked it when I read the proof. I thought it was a great story when I wrote it. Don't think I am getting vacillating or doubtful about my stuff and do not, for instance, think it is a hell of a lot better story than my well known contemporaries can write. But the hell of it is that I am not competition with my contemporaries but with the clock—which keeps on ticking—and if we figure out some way to stop our own particular clock all the other clocks keep on ticking. For instance, of the two I would much rather have written the story by Morley Callaghan.[10] Though, to him, the Bull fight story will be much the better story. Oh Christ I want to write so well and it makes me sore to think that at one time I thought I <u>was</u> writing so well and was evidently in a slump. Callaghan's story is as good as Dubliners.[11] Have not read Bill Williams yet.

Think you could tell Harriet Monroe to go to hell with fewer words. After all Harriet Monroe is just a faintly sensitized, dried up old bitch who runs a long dead magazine. She never has written a line of poetry and never could. If she wrote the Columbian Ode when the world's Fair opened and she likes to think of herself as having been a beautiful white starched young poetess—what the hell.[12] What the Hell? I only saw her once in my life and that was in Paris and if I hadn't been a little drunk I would have been so sorry for her that I couldn't eat my food.

As for Yeats he and Ezra and Anonymous are my favourite poets. If Yeats hasn't written swell poems then nobody else ever has or ever will. Naturally I think that thing you quoted from him is lousy but that is like judging Walter Johnson by one base on balls. I could never read Yeat's mystic stuff, his plays nor playlets nor any of that stuff. I thought his Memories—that ran in the Dial—were splendid.[13]

When you say you are the greatest living judge of poetry etc. that is just horse-shit. That is the sort of thing we ought to be called on when we say because we all have a tendency to get that way and outsiders don't know we are just getting a little noisy and discount things you really want them to believe. Maybe you are the best judge of poetry alive. But if you are—for Christ's sake never say it.[14] [*Moorhead notation*: As an American he ought to have understood E.W. better than this stupidity! E.M.]

Following out that principle I have to be retrained about yr. review of In Our Time but Christ I thought it was a swell review and I only hope I will be able to write the way you say I write. You are certainly getting to be a hell of a good writer of prose. Hadley wants to know where you found out about me and Jewish girls?[15] That has long been a thorn in the family side. You were very interesting on Carnevali.[16] Too much bag punching at the start of review of McAlmon's Distinguished Air. Think three of the stories in that book and Village are what Mc will have to show for credentials, with maybe two stories from A Hasty Bunch, if anybody ever reviews his stuff impartially.[17] Trouble with Mac is that he has been so mis-judged and slandered and made so many enemies, usually while drunk and vomitty, that he never gets any impartial criticism. Everybody who likes his stuff knows he has had such a lousy deal from the reviewers that they over-praise it and the others are worse in the opposite direction. Which doesn't do him any good.

When you say Mac is better than Mark Twain you are right in that Mark Twain wrote great, vast quantities of Hog Wash. He also wrote one, and one only very wonderful thing—Huck Finn. And if you will, now, read Huckleberry Finn, honest to God read it as I re-read it only about three months ago, not anything else by Mark Twain, but Huckleberry Finn, and the last few Chapters of it were just tacked on to finish it off by Howells or somebody. The story stops when Jim, the nigger, is captured and Huck finds himself alone and his nigger gone. That's the end.[18] Well you read Huckleberry Finn and if you really, honest to ourselves believe MacAlmon has ever written anything or everything together that deserves to be mentioned in the same room, house, city, continent or magazine with Huckleberry Finn I will stop writing because there will be no damn use to write if such a state of things can be. I am serious about this. I don't mind your making grand and enormous statements to help your friends but between us, privately, I would like to know how you stand on this. Because I feel pretty strongly about Huck Finn and that does not mean I don't consider Mc a very worthy performer, and if he did not have money, worthy of every sort of financial support.

Your list of unrecommended pubs and docs is grand. I'll forward all your mail when you start dodging the libel suits.[19] Forwarded that letter to Clarke day it came. Hope it does the business.[20]

I think comment at foot of Aldington's letter was in bad taste as he was doing his damndest, Brit. Reviewer's Damndest, to write a swell letter about Ezra, being perfectly impartial, for the good it would do. I admired his letter.[21]

Antheil supplement a swell idea. Best thing you can do for any artist. Only two things you can do for an artist. Give him money and Show his stuff. Those are the only two impersonal needs. Music reproduced beautifully.[22]

Bumby very proud of his picture in magazine. Says, "Vla Petit Jean dans la neige et papa." He hasn't learned about avec yet.[23]

Well I could go on and write like this for a couple of days and don't know what better compliment I could make This Quarter. It is a hell of a fine review. A hell of a fine review.

Although I am catholic have never had much admiration for martyrs or Saints. Mac is being made a martyr of, largely his own fault, no less largely the pressure of the world which is strong, and you are now engaged in making Mac a saint. One of the good things about the church, correct me if I'm wrong, is that they make a definite time limit before we can become Saints. To a real Saint that makes no bloody difference, any more than it makes a difference to a man, if he has really performed the act of valor, whether he is decorated or not. But it keeps out a lot of Roosevelts and Wilsons. Of course on the other hand it lets in people like Jeanne DV Arc who were the shit in life but developed wonderful publicity organizations after their death.[24] Still it's a good rule. And it seems to me a damned sight more important to give people an impartial square deal in criticism than to try and get them canonized here on earth.

And finally I don't think that good writing or good poetry has anything to do with our age at all—makes no bloody difference.

And this is my idea of Poetry—

> O western wind, when wilt thou blow
> That the small rain down can rain?
> Christ, that my love were in my arms
> And I in my bed again!

from somehwre around the 16th century[25]
   and Andy Marvell To His Coy Mistress somewhere in 17th century[26] and this from anonymous written godnose when

> As I was walking all alane
> I heard twa corbies making a mane:
> The tane unto the tither did say,
> 'Whar sall we gang and dine the day?'

> —-In behint yon auld fane dyke
> I wot there lies a new-slain knight;
> And naebody kens that he lies there
> But his hawk, his hound, and his lady fair.

> His hound is to the hunting gane,
> His hawk to fetch the wild-fowl hame,
> His lady's ta'en anither mate,
> So we may mak our dinner sweet.[27]

Hell you probably know the rest as well as I do. To me it's not a question of Keats and Shelley having been great and we having changed since then and needing another kind of greatness. I could never read Swinburne, Keats or Shelley. I tried it when I was a kid and simply felt embarrassed by their elaborate falseness. But of real poetry, true poetry, there has always been, rymed and unrymed, a very little in all ages and all countries—. That's another large statement. I don't know about all countries etc. All I can say is that I believe there has always been good poetry and with a little luck there will always be a little. But there won't be a hell of a lot.[28] And I think you're making hell's own strides as a poet. And I think Ethel Moorhead's portrait of Carnevali is fine. Now I know what Carnevali looks like.[29]

This is too much for now. You've done a damned fine job—both of you. Hadley sends her love and says she is crazy about your new poems. Best luck. yrs. always,

Ernest

Have been sick again. 5 days in bed. Throat swollen shut. Old stuff. Up tomorrow. Plays hell with my heart. Think will have throat operated on again in N.Y. It is simply a bludy nuisance. You're sick but you never write like it. If I'm in bed 2 days I get funereal as Job.

Ernest

JFK, TLS

Carlos Baker dates this letter as 2 January 1926 (*SL*, 186–90). However, EH dated the preceding letter to Ernest Walsh as 2 January 1926; at that time, he had not yet seen a copy of the second number of *This Quarter* (Autumn–Winter 1925–1926). As late as 9 January, Walsh himself had not yet received a copy either and wrote to EH that the publisher claimed to have sent it from Milan ten days earlier (JFK). Here, EH reports he received the magazine "this morning."

1 Moorhead wrote notes on this and other EH letters she and Walsh received, apparently sometime after Walsh died in October 1926 and before she sold them to a London dealer. In April 1930, the Scribner's Rare Book Department bought the letters to remove them from the market, and Maxwell Perkins shared them with EH (*TOTTC*, 143).

2 The first number of *This Quarter* (Spring 1925) included a series of poems titled "Maine Visit" by American author and editor Isidor Schneider (1896–1977) and the poems "Ireland" and "The Irish Lover" by Anthony Breen, identified in the issue's notes on contributors simply as "from Portarlington, Queen's County, Ireland" (263). The "late Mr. Eliot" probably refers to T. S. (Thomas Stearns) Eliot (1888–1965), whom EH often facetiously dubbed "Major Eliot" (*MF*, "Ezra Pound and His Bel Espirit"). Eliot's work never appeared in *This Quarter*.

3 William Carlos Williams (1883–1963), H.D. (Hilda Doolittle, 1886–1961), and Marianne Moore (1887–1972), American poets. Williams's "An Essay on Virginia" and H.D.'s play "Hippolytus Temporizes" had appeared in the first number of *This Quarter*. The second number featured Williams's essay "Jacataqua." Moore had won the 1924 *Dial* award of $2,000 and served as the magazine's editor from 1925 to 1929; she would not publish anything in *This Quarter*.

4 The "Prose" section of *This Quarter* no. 2 included "Flight" by Kay Boyle (1902–1992), "The Fate of Mrs. Lucier" by Raymond Knister (1899–1932), and "Incendiaries (Work in progress)" by Ethel Moorhead.

5 *This Quarter* no. 2 included James Joyce's "Extract from Work in Progress," an early fragment that would become Book 1, Chapter 7, of his novel *Finnegans Wake* (1939). Several segments of his "Work in Progress," begun in 1923, had already appeared in *Transatlantic Review, Contact Collection of Contemporary Writers, Criterion*, and *Navire d'Argent*. The River Liffey, which flows through Dublin, figures significantly across Joyce's work.

6 McAlmon's prose piece "Transcontinental (an extract)" appeared in *This Quarter* no. 2. Walsh not only compared McAlmon to Dickens and other "fathers of English literature" in his review of McAlmon's *Distinguished Air* (331), but elsewhere in the issue he proclaimed McAlmon "bigger and better than Mark Twain" (309).

7 "Rose et Noir," short story by American writer (and later film actor) Wilton Ratcliffe-Graff (1903–1969), concerns a failed American expatriate writer in Paris. According to the notes on contributors to *This Quarter* no. 2, "Wilton Ratcliffe-Graff sent his story from Paris but he has now returned to his native Hartford, Conn. U.S.A." (347). A ship passenger log shows he sailed for the United States from Cherbourg on the *Orita* on 30 May 1925.

8 "Bluebeard's Last Wife," a short story by Italian writer and translator Carlo Linati (1878–1949), was translated into English by Italian poet Emanuel Carnevali (1897–1942).

9 "The Little Girl Continues" by Djuna Barnes (1892–1982), American journalist, poet, playwright, and fiction writer, best remembered for her novel *Nightwood* (1936). The story's characters are based upon sisters Tylia and Bronia Perlmutter, Polish Jews who worked as artists' models in Paris and whom EH would recall in *MF* ("With Pascin at the Dôme"). Raymond Radiguet (1903–1923), French poet and novelist and a friend of Barnes, had planned to marry Bronia before his premature death from typhoid. In Barnes's story, "Monsieur X," the lover of one of the girls, is an actor who dies of fever.

10 Canadian writer Morley Callaghan (1903–1990) was working as a cub reporter at the *Toronto Daily Star* when he first met EH in 1923. EH had encouraged and critiqued the younger man's fiction writing, suggesting in March 1925 that he submit "a good story" to *This Quarter* (*Letters* vol. 2, 288–89). The second number included Callaghan's story "A Girl with Ambition," his first literary publication.

11 James Joyce's short-story collection *Dubliners* (London: Richards, 1914; New York: Huebsch, 1916).

12 Harriet Monroe (1860–1936) founded *Poetry: A Magazine of Verse* in 1912 and served as editor and publisher until her death. Six of EH's poems had appeared in the January 1923 issue. Monroe's "The Columbian Ode" was the official poem for the World's Columbian Exposition in Chicago in 1893. In *This Quarter* no. 2, Walsh published a scathing open letter to Monroe in response to what he saw as her condescending review of the inaugural number of *This Quarter* in the June 1925 issue of *Poetry*. In his "Editorial," he questioned *Poetry* magazine's selection of Ralph Cheever Dunning (1878–1930) and Leonora Speyer (1872–1956) as prize recipients, taking it as "a signal of the passing of the great days" of the magazine (291). In a third piece, Walsh criticized Monroe's own poetry together with that of Irish poet and playwright William Butler Yeats (1865–1939), referring to them as "Their Majesties" and finding their work stiff and outdated.

13 In his essay "Senator William Butler Yeats and Miss Harriet Monroe," Walsh quoted Yeats's poem "No Second Troy," calling it "as correct and polished as the King's Speech from the Throne. And as empty" (335). Yeats's "More Memories," the series of autobiographical pieces that EH calls "splendid," had appeared in the *Dial* from May to October 1922 and were included in his memoir *The Trembling of the Veil* (1922). The second number of *This Quarter* also included "Cantos XVII–XIX" by expatriate American poet Ezra Pound (1885–1972). Walter "Big Train" Johnson (1887–1946), right-handed pitcher for the Washington Senators from 1907 to 1927, would be inducted into the Baseball Hall of Fame in 1936.

14 In his laudatory review of Carnevali's *A Hurried Man* (Paris: Contact Editions, 1925), Walsh drew a distinction between critics and judges of literature, declaring, "I am not the best critic alive. I am a judge of what is being written in this particular period dating from 1895 to 1925. I understand just where this period belongs in relation to other periods and

all that kind of humbug analysis. I am the best judge of poetry in the English language" ("A Young Living Genius," 328).

15 Walsh enthusiastically reviewed *IOT*, with special praise for EH's distinctive style and his "use of *speech* as distinguished from *language*" ("Mr. Hemingway's Prose," 321). In his poem "Ernest Hemingway," Walsh wrote: "the King of Israel would have / Said *This kid knows a few things* and given him / Two plump dancing jewesses to lean on / While he ordered up a fat roasted calf / For in those days Kings preferred art to business" (67).

16 In "A Young Living Genius," Walsh described Carnevali's eight-year struggle as an immigrant in the United States and his hospitalization after returning to Italy with an illness "that would kill most men." Carnevali suffered from encephalitis lethargica, and until Walsh and Moorhead visited him at the hospital in Bazzano, he had not had a visitor in two years (323–24). After Walsh's death from tuberculosis in October 1926, Ethel Moorhead would recall the "wild" and "rich" friendship shared by Walsh and Carnevali, two men of ill health but "with fierce hearts" (*This Quarter* no. 3 [Spring 1927]: 8).

17 Walsh devoted roughly the first third of his review of McAlmon's *Distinguished Air* to excoriating the "scholarly and dull" style and judgment of self-important critics who were writing for the *Times Literary Supplement* and the *Mercury*, naming T. S. Eliot, G. K. Chesterton, and H. L. Mencken among other offenders. EH refers to McAlmon's 1924 novel *Village* and his story collection *A Hasty Bunch* (Lyon: Maurice Darantière, 1922).

18 EH would repeat his assessment of Twain's novel in the first chapter of *GHOA*, declaring, "All modern American literature comes from one book by Mark Twain called *Huckleberry Finn*" and expressing the same criticism of its ending. William Dean Howells (1837–1920), American novelist, playwright, and proponent of literary realism, whose best-known works include *The Rise of Silas Lapham* (1885). During his tenure as editor of the *Atlantic Monthly* (1871–1881), Howells published a number of works by Twain and the men were close friends. Howells read and critiqued the manuscript of *Adventures of Huckleberry Finn* before the novel's U.S. publication, on 10 February 1885.

19 *This Quarter* no. 2 featured a section titled "Hors D'Oeuvres," attributed to Heliogabalus (c. 203–222), Roman emperor who promoted sun worship, that pokes fun at French tastes. It concludes with "a list of unrecommended hotels and garages and other services," including tourist offices, banks, and doctors in French and Italian locations favored by American tourists, advising that "these places should be avoided like sin" (303).

20 English printer Herbert Clarke (1866–1931), who had been printing books in Paris since the turn of the century, produced the first number of *This Quarter* at his small press at 338, rue St. Honoré. In his 9 January 1926 letter to EH, Walsh had complained that Clarke was "trying to get more money after he has been paid twice over." Writing from Grasse, France, Walsh enclosed a letter to Clarke that he asked EH to mail from Austria in order to confuse Clarke as to his whereabouts. Walsh was also anxious to retrieve from Clarke all the mail he was holding (JFK).

21 *This Quarter* no. 2 printed a letter from English poet Richard Aldington (1892–1962) evaluating the strengths and weaknesses of Ezra Pound, to whom the first number of the magazine had been dedicated. In a footnote at the end of the letter, Walsh pokes fun at Aldington and referred readers to his own "open letter" to G. K. Chesterton on the following page, which asserts that English critics are better at extolling their own dead English authors than appreciating the achievements of American and all modern poets (311–15).

22 The second number of *This Quarter* included a twenty-four-page "Musical Supplement" reproducing musical scores from seven works by avant-garde American composer George Antheil (1900–1959), including his futuristic "Airplane Sonata" of 1922.

23 The "Personalities" section of *This Quarter* no. 2 featured a photo of EH with Bumby standing on his father's skis, taken in Schruns the previous winter. "Vla" is probably short for "voilà." Bumby's remark translates literally as "Look at Little John in the snow and Papa." *Avec*: with (French).

24 Theodore Roosevelt (1858–1919), twenty-sixth president of the United States (1901–1909). Woodrow Wilson (1856–1924), twenty-eighth president of the United States (1913–1921). Both presidents had been wartime leaders: Roosevelt as a military commander during the Spanish-American War (1898) and Wilson as Commander-in-Chief during WWI. Each was awarded a Nobel Peace Prize, Roosevelt in 1906 and Wilson in 1919. Jeanne d'Arc (c. 1412–1431), French military leader during the Hundred Years War against England, was burned at the stake for heresy. In 1920 she was canonized.

25 EH's version of "Western Wind," an anonymous sixteenth-century English lyric, first published in 1792. In Chapter 28 of *FTA*, Frederic Henry, thinking of Catherine Barkley, alludes to the poem: "Christ, that my love were in my arms and I in my bed again. That my love Catherine. That my sweet love Catherine down might rain. Blow her again to me."

26 "To His Coy Mistress" by English poet Andrew Marvell (1621–1678) was first published posthumously in 1681. In Chapter 23 of *FTA* Frederic Henry quotes from the poem: "But at my back I always hear / Time's wingèd chariot hurrying near."

27 "The Twa Corbies" ("The Two Carrion Crows"), ballad first collected by Sir Walter Scott (1771–1832) in 1802, although likely composed much earlier. Later that spring of 1926, EH would consider using "A New Slain Knight" (from the second stanza of "Twa Corbies") as a title for his next book of stories or for his next novel; he considered it again in 1949 as a title for his WWII novel, *Across the River and Into the Trees* (1950).

28 English poets John Keats (1795–1821), Percy Bysshe Shelley (1792–1822), and Algernon Charles Swinburne (1837–1909). In *This Quarter* no. 2, Walsh pronounced Carnevali "more important than Keats" because "He has lived in a more important age and known a larger world" (328).

29 Two dozen "New Poems" by Walsh appeared in *This Quarter* no. 2. Moorhead's line drawing portrait of Carnevali serves as the issue's frontispiece.

To Ernest Walsh, [mid-January 1926]

Dear Ernest—Please tell Ethel Moorhead for me that she can write. And to please keep on doing it.

And you, please, do not insult her by comparing her to McAlmon.[1] I <u>have</u> reread the McAlmon and McAlmon is the hero of all his works and a very superior hero and stalks through his works like God among the grasshoppers. And I find it very bad and very silly.

Yours very truly,

Ernest

Also, just for historical accuracy, I don't believe I would have pulled Bony's nose but instead would have soldiered very hard and tried to be

Prince of Moskova or Duc au Elchingen—but instead would have been shot in the ass probably at Ulm or Jena or much earlier as in all the wars I have ever been in.[2]

Also the French are very fine soldiers and one of the things I regret is that I did not soldier with them straight along instead of some people I have soldiered with. I am a rotten poet but once wrote a poem called March Militaire that ran in part—

> All armies are the same
> Publicity is fame
> Artillery makes the same old noise
> Valor is an attribute of boys.
>
> Packs drag the same on every back
> Good soldiers harden till they crack
> Old soldier's all have tired eyes,
> All soldiers hear the same old lies
> Dead bodies always have drawn flies
> Officers are always right
> Hot weather swells all dead alike
> Warm comfortable erections ease a hike

And much more youthful wisdom
    Think the end was

> And those who save their glorious nation
> Go home to bore the civil population.

Very bad poem probably but supposed to be like guys marching on a road. Interesting as only piece of writing done in 2½ years of la vie militaire.[3]

JFK, ALS

This letter reads like a postscript to the preceding letter to Walsh, in which EH acknowledged receipt of the second number of *This Quarter*. The conjectured date of [mid-January 1926] allows for delivery between Schruns and Grasse of this letter and of Walsh's replies, which EH answered on 1 February.

1 *This Quarter* no. 2 included Moorhead's thirty-nine-page fictional piece "Incendiaries (Work in progress)." In his review of McAlmon's *Distinguished Air*, Walsh identifies

Moorhead, McAlmon, and Carnevali as representative of "the school that writes by instinct and creates its own language" (334).

2 Walsh's poem "Ernest Hemingway" in *This Quarter* no. 2 describes EH as "a big guy from near Chicago" and declares, "Napoleon and him / Wouldn't have said much together / He'd have pulled Buonaparte's nose / And absolutely ruined french history" (67). Napoleon I (Napoleon Bonaparte, 1769–1821), emperor of the French from 1804 to 1815. "Prince of Moskova" and "Duc au Elchington" were titles conferred upon Michel Ney (1769–1815), one of Napoleon's commanders. During the Ulm Campaign (1805), the French Army outmaneuvered and captured the Austrian Army. The Battle of Jena-Auerstedt (1806) was a decisive French victory over Prussia. In Chapter 4 of *SAR*, Jake Barnes admires the statue of Ney in front of the café La Closerie des Lilas in Paris.

3 A shorter untitled poem consisting only of lines 1–4 and 7–9 of the version EH presents here is included in *Poems* with the editorial note "Paris, ca. 1922." A pencil manuscript draft of the shorter version survives at JFK (item 230a). EH overstates the duration of his "vie militaire" (military life): he enlisted in the Missouri Home Guard in the fall of 1917, shipped to Europe as a volunteer driver for the ARC Ambulance Service in May 1918, and returned from Italy to the United States in January 1919.

To Harold Monro, 19 January 1926

Harold Monro Esq.

The Poetry Book Shop.

35, Devonshire Street

Theobold Road, London W.C.

Dear Mr. Monro:

I regret very much not having sent you something for the Chapbook and look forward to receiving the copy which you are sending.

I was in Spain last year when I received the letter from the Chapbook, had no Ms. with me and by the time I was again in Paris I had lost the letter.

My permanent address is

Care of the Guaranty Trust Co. of N.Y.

1, Rue des Italiens

Paris.

Thank you for your letter. If you like I will send you a short story for the coming number. At present I have only some very long stories but when I write anything of a length at all suitable I will be very glad to send it to you.[1]

Yours sincerely,

Ernest Hemingway
Hotel Taube,
Schruns, Vorarlberg, Austria
January 19, 1926.

JFK, ALS

1 EH is responding to Monro's letter of 21 December 1925 (JFK) in which the editor of *The Chapbook* expressed regret that EH could not contribute to the 1925 issue and announced that the periodical would appear as an October annual in the future. However, *The Chapbook*, established by Monro in 1919, published its final issue in October 1925.

To Horace Liveright, [c. 19 January 1926]

Dear Mr. Liveright:

I have your letter of December 30th rejecting Torrents of Spring.[1] About two weeks ago I cabled you to deliver the manuscript of Torrents of Spring to Donald Ogden Stewart at the Yale Club. I hope you have done this.[2]

As Torrents of Spring is my second completed book and as I submitted it to you and as you did not exercise your option to publish it; according to my contract with you your option on my third book then lapses. This is quite clear and open and shut. There was nothing in the contract about what order books should be submitted, whether the second book was to be a collection of short stories, a satire, a humorous book or a novel. The contract said one of my next three books must be a full length novel. There was nothing in the contract which said that a full length novel must be the second book which I submitted to you. On the other hand the contract is quite explicit that if you do not exercise your option to publish the 2nd book within 60 days of the receipt of the manuscript your option lapses and if your option lapses on the 2nd book it lapses on the 3rd book. There can be no doubt on this point. ~~There is no obligation~~[3]

I did not submit The Torrents of Spring to you in the hope that you would turn it down. I consider it a good book and John Dos Passos, Louis Bromfield and Scott Fitzgerald, who are people of different tastes are enthusiastic about it.[4] Your turning it down was your own affair. You say that everyone in your office was opposed to it and I may perhaps remind you that your office also was opposed to In Our Time and turned it down after discussion. Later you reversed this decision yourself. Your office was also enthusiastic about a novel of Harold Loeb's called Doodab which I believe did not prove to be a wow even as a succés d'estime.[5] But how, because your office turns down my books, ~~as fast as I write them~~ you can expect to continue to hold an option on my future books, when that option has, by contract, lapsed I do not see.

I therefore regard myself free to give The Torrents of Spring and my future books to the publisher who offers me the best terms. I have already received offers for the Torrents of Spring and The Sun Also Rises, which I am still working on, from several publishers.[6] I have not approached these publishers. They have heard of the books from friends who have seen the manuscript and in whose judgement they place some confidence.

I am going to be writing for some time and you cannot expect me to have looked with enthusiasm to a continual rejection of whatever I write by your office force, partners and associates, because they do not believe it to be a guaranteed best seller. I know that publishers are not in business for their health but I also know that I will pay my keep to, and eventually make a great deal of money, for, any publisher. And I most assuredly have not given a right to Boni and Liveright to reject my books and still keep an option on any future big money makers that may come: all for $200.[7]

I will be very glad to read your answer to this letter and look forward to meeting you in N.Y. I expect to sail as soon as my new passport arrives. I hope within 10 days.

Will you please address me care of
    The Guaranty Trust Company of N.Y.
    1, Rue des Italiens
    Paris.

JFK, ALD

This is EH's draft reply to Liveright's cable and letter, both dated 30 December 1925, informing him that Boni & Liveright was rejecting TOS (cable at UDel, quoted in *Fiestas, Moveable Feasts and "Many Fetes"*: in their time/1920–1940: *An Exhibition at the University of Virginia Library, December 1977–March 1978* [Bloomfield Hills, Michigan, and Columbia,

South Carolina: Bruccoli Clark, 1977 (item 42)]; letter at UVA). A separate fragment of this letter's conclusion is presented next in this volume, followed by the final version of the letter, dated 19 January 1926, that EH actually sent to Liveright (UDel).

1 On 7 December 1925, EH sent Liveright the manuscript of *TOS*, a parody of the novel *Dark Laughter* by Sherwood Anderson (1876–1941) that Boni & Liveright had published in 1925. As EH told Pound in late November, he had written the "funny book" of "28,000 words in ten days"; by 3 December, it was in the hands of a typist (*Letters* vol. 2, 422, 428). When EH submitted the manuscript to Liveright, he mentioned he was not happy with the advertising of *IOT* (*Letters* vol. 2, 435). In his letter to Fitzgerald of 31 December 1925–1 January 1926, EH said he had expected Liveright to reject *TOS* ("as it makes a bum out of their present ace and best seller Anderson"), thus freeing EH to switch publishers, although he claimed he did not "have that in mind in any way" when he wrote the parody (*Letters* vol. 2, 458). In both his cable and letter of 30 December rejecting *TOS*, Liveright indicated that he was still looking forward to receiving the manuscript of *SAR*.

2 Writing to Fitzgerald on 31 December 1925, EH said that he would wire this instruction to Liveright the next morning; the cable itself has not been located (*Letters* vol. 2, 460). Stewart was a 1916 graduate of Yale University. The Yale Club, a private club for alumni, was built in New York City in 1897 at 17 Madison Square and relocated in 1915 to 50 Vanderbilt Avenue.

3 EH accurately summarizes the terms of his 17 March 1925 contract with Boni & Liveright for *IOT* (UDel; facsimile in Trogdon *Reference*, 49). As defined by that contract, *TOS* would have been EH's second book with Liveright.

4 Louis Bromfield (1896–1956), American novelist. In late 1925 Bromfield had alerted Alfred Harcourt (1881–1954), co-founder of the New York-based publishing firm Harcourt, Brace, & Company, that EH was thinking of changing publishers, thereby prompting Harcourt to express interest in both *TOS* and EH's next novel. In his 31 December letter to Fitzgerald, EH quoted a letter he had received from Bromfield, who related verbatim Harcourt's expression of interest in EH's work (*Letters* vol. 2, 459–60).

5 *Succès d'estime*, French phrase meaning a critical rather than popular or commercial success. Boni & Liveright published the novel *Doodab* by Harold Loeb (1891–1974) in 1925; both the reviews and sales were disappointing.

6 Three New York publishers had expressed interest: Alfred A. Knopf; Harcourt, Brace & Company; and Charles Scribner's Sons. EH reported to Fitzgerald on 31 December 1925 that Harcourt had "practically offered to take me sight unseen" (*Letters* vol. 2, 460). However, Scribner's was the most serious contender, Maxwell Perkins having already expressed, by wire to Fitzgerald on 8 January 1926, a readiness to publish both *TOS* and *SAR* (Trogdon *Racket*, 25).

7 The Boni & Liveright contract for *IOT* provided for an advance of $200.

To Horace Liveright, [c. 19 January 1926]

2 Liveright.

and waiting for the appearance of a best seller: all this for $200.

I will be very glad to read your answer to this letter and look forward to meeting you in New York. As soon as my new comes, now a week overdue, I am sailing. Will you please address me care of

The Guaranty Trust Co. of N.Y.

1, Rue des Italiens

JFK, TLccFrag

This draft fragment presents an alternative conclusion to EH's reply to Liveright, apparently abandoned as he composed the sent letter of 19 January 1926 that follows in this volume.

To Horace Liveright, 19 January 1926

Hotel Taube,

Schruns, (Vorarlberg)

Austria.

January 19, 1926.

Dear Mr. Liveright:

I have your letter of December 30 rejecting The Torrents of Spring. About two weeks ago I cabled you to deliver the manuscript of Torrents of Spring to Donald Ogden Stewart at the Yale Club. I hope you have done this.

As The Torrents of Spring is my second completed book and as I submitted it to you and as you did not excercise your option to publish it; according to my contract with you your option on my third book then lapses. This is quite clear. The contract is quite clear that if you do not excercise your option to publish the second book within sixty days of the receipt of the manuscript your option lapses and the contract further states that if your option lapses on the second book it lapses on the third book. There can be no doubt on this point.

There was nothing in the contract about what order books should be submitted in, whether the second book was to be a collection of short stories, a humourous book, or a novel. The contract said one of my next three books must be a full length novel. There was nothing in the contract which said that a full length novel must be the second book which I should submit to you. On the other hand the contract is quite explicit that your option on further books lapses if you reject my second book.

I submitted The Torrents of Spring to you in good faith. I consider it a good book and Scott Fitzgerald, Louis Bromfield, and John Dos Passos, men of widely divergent taste, are enthusiastic about it. You turned it down saying that everyone in your office was opposed to it. I can quite understand that as I remember that every one in your office, excepting, I believe, Mrs. Kauffman, was opposed to In Our Time and it was quite formally turned down after a discussion.[1] Your office was also quite enthusiastic about a novel by Harold Loeb called Doodab which did not, I believe, prove to be a wow even as a <u>succes d'estime</u>. But because it is <u>your office</u> that turns down my books, even though you reversed the decision on In Our Time, you can not expect to hold an option on my future books when the option has, by contract, lapsed.

I therefore regard myself as free to give The Torrents of Spring and my future books to the publisher who offers me the best terms.

As you know I expect to go on writing for some time. I know that publishers are not in the business for their health but I also know that I will pay my keep to, and eventually make a great deal of money for, any publisher. You surely do not expect me to have given a right to Boni and Liveright to reject my books as they appear while sitting back and waiting to cash in on the appearance of a best seller: surely not all this for $200.

As soon as my new passport, now a week overdue, arrives I am sailing for New York. I look forward to meeting you there and meantime may have an answer to this letter. Will you please address me care of The Guaranty Trust Co. of N.Y. 1, Rue des Italiens, Paris, France.

Yours very truly,
Ernest Hemingway.

UDel, TLS

Across the top and down the right side of the letter's first page is a penciled note, written partly in shorthand. A typewritten transcription in the form of an office memo filed with this letter at the University of Delaware Library reads: "February 10th, 1926. / Hemingway was in and absolutely proved that our contract specified if we rejected his second book we relinquished our option on the third book. He also proved that Torrents of Spring was a good and honest deliverage on his second book. The various people here in the office had nice chats with Hemingway who would be willing to take away from the publishers who have Torrents of Spring if we would reconsider our decision. In spite of some things that we said to him in Paris he would like to stay with us but our decision on Torrents of Spring is irrevocable. H. B. LIVERIGHT"

1 Beatrice Bakrow Kaufman (1895–1945), American editor, short-story writer, and playwright, was head of the editorial department for Boni & Liveright, having joined the firm in 1920; she was married to playwright and producer George S. Kaufman (1889–1961). The two were members of the Algonquin Round Table, a group of writers and critics known for their acerbic wit who regularly lunched at the Algonquin Hotel on 59 West 44th Street in New York City, beginning in 1919.

To Ernest Walsh, 1 February [1926]

[*PARIS, LE*] 1, Feb.

Dear Ernest—

Have had your grand letter and your small letter.[1] Carry the first around to read. The second, coming today, has worried me greatly. I do hope nothing bad has happened to you. I hope to hell it was just that you were in an Irish black mood.

I didnt mean my note to be uncheerful. Only to tell how much I enjoyed Ethel Moorheads stuff. Also I have re-discovered that The Undefeated is a grand story and I'm very proud I wrote it. Am sending you a long story of which I am very fond as soon as I can get back to Schruns and type it.[2] Sail Wed—3rd—on Mauretania. (2nd class) Will be in N.Y. 1 week.

Dont worry about me and MacAlmon. I'm really very fond of McAlmon and besides would never hit any one. Have never hit but 2 gents outside of boxing in my life. Then only because they wanted to hit me. I dont brawl.

Dont let's any of us die of disease.[3] Altho the more I think of it the more I think that any form of dying can be made pretty swell. One of the things that I really look forward to is dying—but want to be at least 85 when it happens. Life is pretty swell and let's only be sore at shits like the English sometimes are. I see your point about Aldington. Also about every thing else.

So Long and good luck, My best to Ethel Moorhead. I'd have loved to go by Grasse but have to get to N.Y and <u>back</u>.[4] Especially back. I miss Hadley and Bumby terribly and always drink too much when I'm not with them.

Yours,

Ernest

UVA, ALS; letterhead: VÉNÉTIA-HOTEL / 159, BOULEVARD DU MONTPARNASSE / PARIS-VI

EH was in Paris en route to New York to meet with publishers while Hadley and Bumby remained in Schruns. The Vénétia, where he was staying, was around the corner from the Hemingways' apartment at 113, rue Notre Dame des Champs, which they had sublet from mid-December to mid-March (EH to Mr. Choleston, 3 December 1925, *Letters* vol. 2, 424–25). In a letter to Hadley of 29 January, Pauline reported, "I've seen your husband E. Hemingway several times—sandwiched in like good red meat between thick slices of soggy bread. I think he looks swell, and he has been splendid to me" (JFK).

1 These letters from Walsh to EH remain unlocated.
2 Possibly a reference to "A Lack of Passion," which was inspired by EH's first experience at the Fiesta of San Fermín in Pamplona in 1923. He began writing the story in 1924, repeatedly postponing and then resuming writing until finally abandoning it in 1927.
3 In his letter to EH, Walsh may have written about his deteriorating health; he would die of tuberculosis that October.
4 Walsh and Moorhead were living in a rented villa in the South of France, near the village of Grasse, famed for its perfumes. They were joined in February 1926 by Kay Boyle, who had come to recuperate from a lung ailment, and she and Walsh soon became lovers. Boyle's sister Joan (1900–2004) worked at Paris *Vogue* with Pauline Pfeiffer; in her memoirs, Boyle recalled that when Joan and Pauline came to visit Grasse, Pauline received daily letters from EH, ostensibly about perfumes and lingerie that he wanted her to bring back for Hadley (Robert McAlmon and Kay Boyle, *Being Geniuses Together 1920–1930*, rev. edn. with supplementary chapters and an afterword by Kay Boyle [San Francisco: North Point Press, 1984], 175–76; 180, 183–84).

To Isabelle Simmons Godolphin, 10 February [1926]

[*New York,*] Wednesday, February 10—

7, a.m.

My Dear Izz—

Am in N.Y. for a week. Got in last night on the Mauretania. Hadley and Bumby are in Austria ski-ing. Hadley sends you all her love. I'm crazy to see you and Frisco.[1] When you get this will you call me up here at the Brevoort?[2] If I'm out leave your phone number and I'll call as soon as I come in. I was a little tight last night and was all for setting out to call upon you gents at somewhere around mid night but was dissuaded by wise and kind friends.

Best love,

Ernie

PUL, ALS; letterhead: Hotel Brevoort / ANCIENNEMENT BREVOORT HOUSE / Coin de la 5me Avenue et de la 8me Rue; postmark: NEW YORK / MADISON [*illegible*], FEB 10 / 11 AM / 1926

1 Nickname for Isabelle's husband, Francis R. B. Godolphin (1903–1974), whom she married in 1925. A 1924 Princeton graduate, he would join the faculty there in 1927, becoming a noted classics professor and, in 1945, Dean of the College.
2 Located on Fifth Avenue between East 8th and 9th Streets in Greenwich Village, the Brevoort was one of the oldest and best-known hotels in New York City, catering to an international clientele. Opened in 1854, it was razed in 1954.

To Jack Cowles, [c. 14 February 1926]

To Jack Cowles on Valentine's day. (This has no sexual segnificance)

Ernest Hemingway.

Biblioctopus, Inscription

EH wrote this inscription on the front free endpaper of a first edition of *IOT*, published by Boni & Liveright on 5 October 1925. Cowles, who lived in Greenwich Village and was known for his bootlegging connections, was among EH's companions during his visit to New York. EH's notation "Blood (2$ worth)" refers to the $2.00 price of the book. Within the volume, EH wrote in his corrections to changes that Liveright, fearing censorship, had made to the story "Mr. and Mrs. Elliot." On facing blank endpapers, EH wrote in his two poems that had appeared in the German magazine *Der Querschnitt*, "The Age Demanded" (February 1925) and "The Earnest Liberal's Lament" (November 1924).

To William B. Smith, Jr., and Harold Loeb, [18 February 1926]

Thursday.

Gents—

Yours Special to hand. I came alone, Men, accompanied only by my moral turpitude.

Youre right I gotta return on the 'veldt.[1] I would flash to Provincetown like a flash but for engagements with Publishers, Critics, and the like. Benchley is flashing Carol-less with me.[2] I will also be accompanied by Mrs. ̶M̶i̶s̶s̶ Dorothy Parker. We will try and get off a quip or so.[3] I'll tell Benchley how you feel about Arlen.[4] Don's in Hollywood. He hasnt written to me, nor to Bob, nor to Hadley, nor to Phil Barry, nor to the Murphys, nor to any body.[5]

Scribner's advance me $1500 on The Torrents of Spring (satire) and The Sun Also Rises (novel) They will pay 15% royalties on everything. No cut on the movies nor dramatics.[6] Have an option on only these 2 books / Say that they pleasing me is all the option they want. God but they are white people.

They will also buy stories for the magazine at from 200 to 250 depending on length.[7] Want all the stories I can give them. Will feature same.

I got loose from Liveright on account him turning down the satire. Scribners say they will back me solidly and loyally no matter how the books turn out financially. So now I dont have to worry. Only to work. Will try and write some swell ones. I'm not going to think any more about what is to happen to the stuff. Just work.

God I'd love to fortify the optic nerve with a flash at you men on your native heath. Give my best to Hutch Hapgood. We'll be over in the Autumn any way.

Hadley's in Schruns with Bumby. I'm going right back there. Stay til end of March. Then Paris for a couple of weeks. Then visit the Murphys at Antibes and go to Spain in May to stay through June, July, maybe August.

I have to get back to hang onto the dough I've picked up. In Our Time seems to have went well with the critics, writers etc. At least Neck and Neck with Doodab.[8] Us writers ought to stick together.

I'm crazy for you to see the funny one [*TOS*]. It's pretty tough but they're not cutting a word.

Gee I hope you hit them between the orbs at tale vending. I'm all admiration for the achievments of Kate [Smith].

Also [*EH drew arrow pointing to* "Kate" *in the previous sentence*] here's the best love of one Wemedge if you got any use for it or would like to have it mounted by a taxidermist and put over the fire place.

So long Boid.[9]

A screed to the boat would materially shorten the passage.

It's President Roosevelt sailing Feb 20th at Midnight from Hoboken. [*EH insertion*: My cabin is 116—] Just imagine pouring a man aboard at that hour in Hoboken.

Best on the sphere to youse lads.

Always.

E. Miller

Private Collection, ALS

1 EH would sail for Cherbourg on 20 February aboard the *President Roosevelt*.

2 Among EH's fellow passengers on the return to Europe was American humorist Robert Charles (Bob) Benchley (1889–1945). A founding member of the Algonquin Round Table, Benchley had been managing editor of *Vanity Fair* (1919–1920) and was drama critic for *Life* magazine (1920–1929). Benchley had been married since 1914 to Gertrude Darling (1889–1980), whom he had known since childhood. He was having an affair with Carol Goodner (1904–2001), whom he had met in 1923 when she was a telephone operator at the Biltmore Hotel and who had become a stage and screen actress.

3 Dorothy Parker (née Rothschild, 1893–1967), American poet, fiction writer, and columnist, began her career at *Vogue* (1916–1917) and was drama critic for *Vanity Fair* (1917–1920) before becoming a key contributor to the *New Yorker* from the time of its founding in 1925.

Renowned for her wit, she was a founding member, with Benchley, of the Algonquin Round Table. In 1926 she was still legally married to Wall Street broker Edwin Pond Parker II (1893–1933), whom she had wed in 1917. Although their marriage effectively ended in 1919, she insisted on being addressed as Mrs. Parker, even after their divorce in 1928.

4 Michael Arlen (1895–1956), English writer whose popular novel *The Green Hat* (London: Collins, 1924) was also produced as a play in 1925 in both London and New York.

5 Donald Ogden Stewart's career as screenwriter and playwright began with a job in Hollywood that year. Philip Barry (1896–1949), American playwright whose best-known works include *Holiday* (1928) and *The Philadelphia Story* (1939). He and his wife, Ellen Barry (née Semple, 1898–1995), owned a villa on the French Riviera near the Murphys' Villa America.

6 EH's contract with Scribner's for *TOS* and *SAR*, dated 15 February 1926, specified the advance and the royalty rates as EH reports here. While the contract did not specifically address screen or stage rights, it stipulated that profits from any publication of the works "in other than book form" were to be divided equally between author and publisher (PUL).

7 In a letter to EH of 1 February 1926, Perkins offered $250 for "Fifty Grand," which Fitzgerald had sent him, saying "everyone here was roused up by it." The amount was "more than we usually do pay for short stories," he noted, but said it would need to be cut by 1,500 words for publication in *Scribner's Magazine* (JFK; *TOTTC*, 34–35).

8 In his 1 February letter, Perkins had told EH, "You would be pleased if you heard what people said of 'In Our Time,' those people who are quick to catch on to notable publications. It is vastly admired and this admiration is bound to spread" (*TOTTC*, 35). Loeb's *Doodab*, also published by Boni & Liveright in 1925, had not been well received.

9 "Wemedge," a nickname for EH among his friends from summers in Michigan; "Boid" is one of EH's nicknames for Smith (a variant of yet another nickname, "Bird"). Smith later recalled that he and EH "were both great nicknamers" and that they would change endings of words: "Eating would become eatage, reading readage, walking walkage, etc. ... Hemingway's name became Hemage and then, somehow, Wemedge" (Bertram D. Sarason, *Hemingway and the Sun Set* [Washington, D.C.: NCR/Microcard Editions, 1972], 160).

To Isabelle Simmons Godolphin, [25 February 1926]

At Sea aboard the Roosevelt

My Dear Izz:

Greater shame hath no man but here are the bare shreds of my alibi.[1] I asked you to eat breakfast. You couldnt or wouldnt. All right. Then a lot of people came in, then I had to be at Ernest Boyds at eleven oclock.[2] Then he and I had three shakers of cocktails. Then I was late to lunch with Jack Cowles and Robby Rouse.[3] Then we drank ale. Went to a show with Robby. Had [t]o stop at O'Neils to get and return stuff and say goodbye.[4] Had toget liquor from Jack Cowles bootlegger from the trip. Had a dinner date at the

Merley at 7. Not packed up to theat point. Arrived at the Merley and fpund everybody cockeyed including myself.[5] Marc Connelly wanted us to go to his show but I said I had to pack.[6] Finally left about nine to go and pack. Meantime fell for a girl named Eleanor Wylie. Great love at first sight on both sides.[7] Went to the Brevoort and riding down from $'48th street got over Eleanor in the cool evening air. Found your message and while Rouse and I packed I called you up three times between 9.30 and 10. Went up to the theater where we were supposed to meet Connally or Conilly and found everybody coming out. So I didnt see the Wisdom Tooth but everybody says it was swell. Fell back in love with Eleanor Wylie and we stopped at several bootleggers enroute to Hoboken.[8] It now lacking twenty minutes of when the boat was to sail. My head cleared on the H[o]boken ferry, not fairy, and decided that what was Wylie to me? Finally the boat left and some of the seeing [o]ff party stole all Dorothy Parkers Scotch. It has been a swell trip: grand weather and we've had a swell time. This is the [f]irst I've written, letters, cables or anything at all. Now it is Thursday and we are due in Cherbourg on Sunday night. Figure [o]ut I had about a quart and a half [o]f Scotch exclusive of champagne and cocktails on Saturday. Also Ale. I wish youse guys had been along. To drink it if for no other reason

Anyway it was swell swell swell to see you and we'll see you again in the fall. I still love you, in spite of the hamperings of your married state and I think Francis is a grand guy and that you married damned well and on the other hand I only hope Bumby will marry as well as Francis did. Very best of everything to you both and let us have a letter. Hotel Taube, Schruns, Vorarlberg, Austria until the end of March and then Guaranty Trust Co of N.Y. 1 and 3, rue des Italiens, Paris.

Best Love,

Ernie ~~Ernest~~

P.S. I never did succeed in writing my family nor in cabling. So just deny any rumours that I was in N.Y. It was some impostor.

I Left a grand gold mounted waterman fountain pen, large size in my room, No. #344 at the Brevoort. I wonder if you could go over and get it and maybe send it by Hammy before they padlock the Brevoort.[9] Also I may have left other things haven't had the courage to look yet. The pen has a gold band around the part of the cap that screws down, it is a self filler and has a very hard sharp point. Is double size barrel. I know I left it so you might be very nasty to them if they say they havent got it.

Best always and thanks a lot.

Ernie

PUL, TLS

1 Allusion to John 15:13: "Greater love hath no man than this, that a man lay down his life for his friends." All biblical references are to the King James Version.

2 Ernest Boyd (1887–1946), Irish-born American writer, translator, and critic. A protégé of H. L. Mencken, he became a familiar figure on New York's literary scene in the early 1920s. By 1926 Boyd was a freelance contributor to several prominent American literary journals and had published translations and critical works on European and American literature including *Ireland's Literary Renaissance* (1916; rev. edn. 1922), *Portraits: Real and Imaginary* (1924), and the biography *H. L. Mencken* (1925).

3 Robert Rouse (1898–1980), Princeton graduate and one of the young bachelors who, with EH, had shared the Chicago apartment of Bill Smith's older brother, Y. K. (Yeremya Kenley) Smith (1887–1967), in 1920–1921. At the time of this letter Rouse was working for the Morgan Guaranty Trust Company in New York.

4 American businessman and poet David O'Neil (1874–1947), his wife Barbara Blackman O'Neil (b. c. 1880), and their children George (b. 1906), Horton (1907–1997), and Barbara (1910–1980) were then living in New York City. EH met the family, friends of Hadley's from St. Louis, after they moved to Europe in 1922. George had joined EH for skiing and bobsledding in Chamby, Switzerland, in the winter of 1922–1923 and for the festivities at Pamplona in 1924.

5 Perhaps the Hotel Merley at 308 West 23rd Street.

6 Marc Connelly (1890–1980), American playwright and producer, one of the founders of the *New Yorker* magazine in 1925, and a member of the Algonquin Round Table. His first play as an independent dramatist, his popular comedy *The Wisdom Tooth*, opened 15 February 1926 on Broadway at the Little Theatre. He would be awarded a Pulitzer Prize in 1930 for his play *Green Pastures*.

7 Elinor Wylie (1885–1928), American poet and novelist, was poetry editor of *Vanity Fair* (1923–1925) before becoming editor of *Literary Guild* and contributing editor to the *New Republic* in 1926. She published four collections of poetry and four novels between 1921 and her death in 1928. When EH met her, she was married to American poet William Rose Benét (1886–1950), her third husband.

8 The *Roosevelt* sailed from Hoboken, New Jersey, on the Hudson River across from Manhattan.

9 The expensive Waterman pen was a gift from Pauline. The brand was established in 1884 when Lewis Edson Waterman patented the first fountain pen designed to reliably regulate ink flow. "Hammy" is most likely Helen Hamilton (1902–1982), a mutual friend and neighbor in Oak Park and, with Simmons, a member of the Oak Park and River Forest High School (OPRFHS) class of 1917. On the day of EH's departure, the Brevoort Hotel was indicted for selling liquor and the management was given the choice between having the front door padlocked for six months or facing a court trial ("Famous N.Y. Hotel Ordered

Padlocked," Paris *Tribune*, 21 February 1926, 1; "First Padlock Move Against Hotel Here Aimed at Brevoort," *New York Times*, 21 February 1926, 1).

To Morley Callaghan, 5 March 1926

March 5, 1926

Hotel Taube,

Schruns,

Vorarlberg.

Austria.

Dear Cal—

I had to go to N.Y. before I read your novel and I havent read it yet.[1] But I have some good news for you. In N.Y. I shifted to Charles Scribners as publishers and got $1500 advance on my next book—sold several stories and got a grand contract. Thats not your news tho. I met Alfred Kreymbourg who is head reader for a new publishing house—formerly publishing Eleanor Glyn etc. They want to shoot with some good stuff and have some money to spend—[2] He asked me about young writers as did Herbert Gorman, Edmund Wilson, Paul Rosenfeld etc.[3] And I told them all you were—with John Hermann—the best prospect there was.[4] I also told them all that you wrote better than Herrman and that you were hot stuff and would go a long way. But dont get the big head and think about anything than how to write better or I will come to Toronto next time and kick your ass. Anyway I'll send your novel to Kreymbourg and he will be sure to give it the best reading it can get and will let you know. I hope they'll take it and they ought to give you a hundred or two hundred advance if they do. But the money is not the important angle. It is the stuff that is important and I hope to hell it is a good novel. I'll read it before I write Kreymbourg so I can tell him how good it is if I think it's that good.

Yes. Most reviewers are horses asses. There are more horses asses than horses and more reviewers than horses asses. Have had 162 reviews of In Our Time and the best ones come from the sticks. Guys like Rosenfeld are more interested in the way they themselves write than in what they are writing about. I thought it a very silly review.[5]

Was in N.Y. less than a week. I pocketed the dough and hurried back to where I could buy things with it. Didnt even let my family know I was in N.Y.

Best to you and to Greg and the good guys in Toronto[6]

Write me.

Yours always

Hem.

Private Collection, ALS; postmark: LUFTKURO[RT] / SCHRUNS / WINTERSPORTPLATZ, 6. III. 26

On the verso of the envelope, torn away in places, EH wrote, "I may send Ms. to you with suggestions about changes and a letter to Kre[ymbourg.] Remember in this business [*torn*] no hurry. I'm taking [*torn*] granted what you want [*torn*] is write well."

1 In his letter of 23 January [1926] (JFK), Callaghan asked if EH had received the manuscript of his novel, then called *Backwater*, that he had sent to EH's Paris address "about Dec. 1st" for feedback and help with placement. The letter, postmarked from Toronto on 27 January, had been forwarded from Paris to Schruns, where EH apparently found it upon his return on 4 March.

2 Alfred Kreymborg (1883–1966), American poet and editor of such modernist periodicals as *Glebe* (1913–1914), *Others* (1915–1919), and *Broom* (1921–1924), which he co-founded with Harold Loeb. Elinor Glyn (née Sutherland, 1864–1943), English writer of popular romantic novels and socialite, best known for her novel *Three Weeks* (1907), then considered scandalous, and for her role in developing and writing the 1927 film *It*.

3 Herbert Gorman (1893–1954), American writer, editor, and critic, had favorably reviewed *IOT* for the *New York World* (18 October 1925). Edmund Wilson (1895–1972), reviewing EH's first two books, *TSTP* and *iot*, in the October 1924 *Dial*, had been one of the first American critics to recognize EH's originality, identifying him, together with Gertrude Stein (1874–1946) and Sherwood Anderson, as part of a new school producing distinctively American prose. Paul Rosenfeld (1890–1946), prolific journalist and music critic for the *Dial*.

4 American writer John Herrmann (1900–1959), whose first novel, *What Happens*, was published in Paris by Robert McAlmon's Contact Editions in 1926.

5 In his review of *IOT* in the *New Republic*, Rosenfeld had praised EH's experimental style for its "tough, severe and satisfying beauty related equally to the world of machinery and the austerity of the red man" (25 November 1925, 22).

6 *Toronto Star* features editor Gregory Clark (1892–1977), whom EH met when he began writing for the newspaper in 1920.

To Louis and Mary Bromfield, [c. 8 March 1926]

Dear Louis and Mary—

Well what happened in N.Y—if I've really been to N.Y and havent just been cockeyed and will wake up to find it's all still to be gone through—was that as soon as I was definitely clear of Mr. Liveright or Horace—because we're Horace and Ernest now—I had a couple of drinks with Horace and told him how sorry I was etc and was up all that night because I couldnt sleep worrying about the Messers. Scribners and Harcourt. I tried to kid myself that I did not have to give Scribners the first look at Torrents but I would have been just a crook if I hadnt because last March I promised Maxwell Perkins that if I was ever free I would turn to them. So there wasnt anything else to do.[1] Max Perkins read it and thought it was grand and not at all censorable as Scott had cabled him and I agreed to let them have Torrents and The Sun Also Rises for a $1500 advance, 15% flat, no split on any outside rights except 2nd serial rights etc.[2] He wrote an awfully swell contract and was very damned nice.

I should have done the business man and tried to see what Harcourt Brace would do in opposition but I think that's all the advance I can expect on any business basis except that they want to back me over a long period of time whether the books sell or not and as they were doing that and never even asked to look at The Sun etc. I just told Perkins I would take it and went over and told Mr. Harcourt the news. I thought he, Alfred Harcourt, was one of the finest. I dont think you could be doing better in any way than going to them. I told him how much I had been sold on Harcourt Brace by you. But altho I could decide for Harcourt with my head I had the obligation to Scribners, not so much an obligation as a promise, if there is a distinction———and I wouldnt have any fun writing the stuff if I did something that made me feel crooked inside.

Anyway Mr. Harcourt said I could always come over there and he seemed to mean it. He said, also, that he admired Wescott's stuff and I told him I thought Wescott's stuff was fundamentally unsound.[3] Which I suppose I shouldnt have said. I felt sorry as soon as I said it. But I know so well what a literary fake his prose is and I was feeling so cockeyed honest about turning down the chance at Harcourt which my head told me was the thing to do that I said what I thot of Wescott before I thot to keep my mouth shut.

I called up Isabel Patterson twice but missed her. Saw John Farrar at the Coffee House one night.[4] I dont know whether he has always looked exactly like a woman—a woman in sheeps clothing—but he does now. He was very pleasant and we were always going to get together but somehow we never got together. But it was wonderful to have seen him.

Ernest Boyd was grand. I had met Madeleine Boyd before and she was grand too. Madeleine Boyd said she was handicapped in sending you the dirt because her great news source Bernadine Szold is in Paris and I told her I had met her and liked her.[5]

Met hells own amount of people. Bob Benchley came back with me. He couldnt get a sailing and they just gave him a contract saying they'd put him anywhere there was and there wasnt anywhere so he slept in one of the maid's rooms and the 4th day out he said it was funny but he felt just like the time he had crabs and the 6th day out he <u>had</u> crabs. You'll probably see him. He's cured now anyway. Dotty Parker came over too. She's going South for a while.

This is a rotten letter. Hadley says it's been Spring here all of February. It looked very beautiful yesterday and now ever since morning it's been snowing.

How are you both and how are things going? We'll be in Paris the end of this month or the first of April. I've told Hadley about your apartment. She's wild to see it. She doesn't believe it can be as wonderful as I say but she figures that dividing all that in two it is still worth a trip to Paris. The Gerald Murphys have asked us to Antibes in April but we may not go until August. That way we can see a lot of you in April and May—which can be the best months of the year in Paris. Before the inrush of visiting Elks.[6]

Hadley sends her love to you both. Dont say anything to anybody, will you, about my business arrangements with Scribners. I wanted to give you all the dope but dont want to spread it around.

You and Ford seem the most generally admired novelists in N.Y.[7] Manhattan Transfer is in its 4th printing.[8] Gatsby—done by owen Davis pretty darn close to the book—is a hit. I had to pay to get in. Would have paid to get out a couple of times but on the whole it is a good play. Understand it's been turned down by the movies as immoral.[9]

Don Stewart is still in Hollywood.

Everybody on the boat had at least 3 copies of Gents. Prefer Blondes. One of the dullest books I've ever read. It's sweeping the country like the Flu in

1918.[10] Maybe it will sweep the world. Well the world needs sweeping, maybe.

All people talk about in N.Y. is when they are going to come to Paris so I guess we're all not so badly off.

Do write and my very best to you both.

Affectionately,

Ernest Hemingway.

Bumby's talking all german now.

He's wonderfully well and strong.

Stanford, ALS

1 In February 1925, Perkins had written two letters to EH expressing interest in his work, but by the time EH received them, he already had accepted Boni & Liveright's offer to publish *IOT*. In a letter to Perkins of 15 April 1925, EH expressed appreciation for his interest and wrote, "if I am ever in a position to send you anything to consider I shall certainly do so" (*Letters* vol. 2, 318). Bromfield had recommended EH's work to publisher Alfred Harcourt. In a letter dated c. 30 December 1925, Fitzgerald wrote to Perkins that EH's "only hesitation" about coming to Scribner's was "that Harcourt might be less conservative in regard to certain somewhat broad scenes" (John Kuehl and Jackson Bryer, eds., *Dear Scott/Dear Max: The Fitzgerald-Perkins Correspondence* [New York: Scribner's, 1971], 128).

2 On 8 January 1926, Fitzgerald had cabled Perkins, "YOU CAN GET HEMINGWAYS FINISHED NOVEL PROVIDED YOU PUBLISH UNPROMISING SATIRE." Perkins responded the same day, "PUBLISH NOVEL AT FIFTEEN PERCENT AND ADVANCE IF DESIRED ALSO SATIRE UNLESS OBJECTIONABLE OTHER THAN FINANCIALLY" (*TOTTC*, 36).

3 Glenway Wescott (1901–1987), expatriate American writer and the model for the character Robert Prentiss in *SAR*. He published his first novel, *The Apple of the Eye* (1924), at the age of twenty-three, and he would receive the Harper Prize for Fiction for *The Grandmothers* (1927).

4 Isabel Mary Paterson (née Bowler, 1886–1961), Canadian-born journalist, author, and book columnist for the *New York Herald Tribune*. John Chipman Farrar (1896–1974), American writer, editor, and publisher. He joined the New York publishing firm of George H. Doran in 1921, serving as editor of *The Bookman*, the company's literary journal, from 1921 to 1927 and as editor of the company from 1925 to 1927. The Coffee House, a New York City social club originally called "The Foes of Finance Dinner Club," was founded in 1914 by Frank Crowninshield (1872–1947) and Rawlins L. Cottenet (1866–1951) in rebellion against the stuffy Knickerbocker Club, of which they were members. The Coffee House was located at the Hotel Seymour, 54 West 45th Street, from 1915 until 1982, when the club moved to 70 West 45th Street.

5 Madeleine Boyd (née Reynier, c. 1886–1972), French-born writer, translator, and literary agent; she and Ernest Boyd had married in 1913. Bernardine Szold (née Sholes, 1896–1982), American expatriate journalist who worked as a reporter for the *Chicago Evening*

Post and *New York Daily News* before moving to Europe in 1925 and becoming a Paris correspondent for the *New Yorker*.

6 The Benevolent & Protective Order of Elks, an American fraternal order established in 1868 and organized into local lodges. EH is likely remarking on the influx of Main Street Americans pouring into Paris, "straining for a glimpse of a real bohemian" as Reynolds puts it, noting that on 24 April 1926 alone, eleven ocean liners full of tourists departed from New York bound for France (*AH*, 21, 225).

7 Ford Madox Ford, (né Ford Hermann Hueffer, 1873–1939), English novelist and founder of the *Transatlantic Review* in 1924, for which EH served as subeditor beginning in February 1924. Ford's novel *No More Parades*, the second volume of his WWI tetralogy *Parade's End* (1924–1928), was published by Alfred and Charles Boni in 1925 to critical acclaim. Bromfield's novel *Possession* (New York: Stokes, 1925) had already gone into a seventh printing by early 1926 (Frederick A. Stokes Company advertisement, *New York Times*, 21 February 1926, BR 14).

8 *Manhattan Transfer* (New York: Harper & Brothers, 1925), an expressionistic montage-style depiction of life in New York City by John Dos Passos. In a recent review, Sinclair Lewis (1885–1951) had called it "a novel of the very first importance" and possibly "the foundation of a whole new school of novel-writing" ("Manhattan at Last!", *Saturday Review of Literature*, 5 December 1925, 361).

9 Owen Gould Davis (1874–1956) wrote a three-act stage version of F. Scott Fitzgerald's novel *The Great Gatsby* (New York: Scribner's, 1925) that ran for more than a hundred performances at Broadway's Ambassador Theatre between 2 February and 7 May 1926 and continued as a traveling production in several U.S. cities throughout 1926. The first *Gatsby* movie, a silent film by Famous Players-Lasky-Paramount Pictures, would be released on 8 November 1926; it played for two weeks at the Rivoli Theatre in New York but was not well received.

10 *"Gentlemen Prefer Blondes": The Illuminating Diary of a Professional Lady* by American writer Anita Loos (1888–1981). Originally serialized in *Harper's Bazar* (as the magazine's title was then spelled) and published by Boni & Liveright in 1925, the light-hearted novel was the second bestselling book of 1926. The 1918 influenza pandemic, the worst in recorded history, killed an estimated 50 million people worldwide.

To Maxwell Perkins, 10 March 1926

Hotel Taube,

Schruns, (Vorarlberg) Austria

March 10, 1926.

Dear Mr. Perkins:

I was sorry to hear that Colliers did not take the Fifty Grand story but not surprised and I will not be surprised if it comes back from the Post and Liberty.[1] It is quite hard in texture and there is no reason for them to take something that is not absolutely what they want and are used to until the name means something to them.

It was for that reason that it would have meant very much to me in various ways for the story to have been published in Scribners.

At present I can promise you The Sun Also Rises for fall publication. I have only five more chapters to do over and would then like to have another look through it before sending the Ms. over but I think you will probably have the Ms. some time in May. That should give me plenty of leeway on the proofs. I would perhaps get a better perspective on it that way. Anyway it is sure for fall and you can go ahead on that.

Bob Benchley and I had a grand trip on the Roosevelt. Perfect weather and a very good time. I've been working ever since. Scott and Zelda were in Paris and we had lunch and dinner before they left for Nice. They were looking well and Zelda's cure was very successful.[2]

I am very anxious to see the Torrents proofs and get them back to you. Dos Passos is arriving here tonight or tomorrow and we have planned to go to Munich and fly from there to a place between here and Innsbruck in the Silvretta. Neither the Gerald Murphys nor Dos can ski and that seems the simplest way of getting them up where the ski-ing is good now with the short time they have. All it needs is good weather.[3]

I will be very glad to be through with The Sun etc. and able to think about something else and write some stories.

From now on will you please use my permanent adress / Care The Guaranty Trust Co. of N.Y.

1, Rue des Italiens,

Paris—France.

As we will be going to Paris, Antibes, and Spain as soon as I have sent back the Torrents proofs.

With best regards,

Sincerely,

Ernest Hemingway.

PUL, TLS

1 In his letter of 19 February 1926 (PUL), Perkins told EH that *Collier's* had rejected the story and that he would submit it to the *Saturday Evening Post* and *Liberty*. Neither magazine accepted it.

2 F. Scott Fitzgerald, his wife Zelda (née Sayre, 1900–1948), and their daughter Frances Scott (Scottie) Fitzgerald (1921–1986) lived in Europe from May 1924 through December 1926. In early March 1926, they were living at Villa Paquita in Juan-les-Pins, about 16 miles southwest of Nice on the French Riviera. In January 1926, the Fitzgeralds had traveled to Salies-de-Béarn, a spa town in the French Pyrénées known for its thermal pools, in the hope of curing Zelda's colitis.

3 As EH later recalled, there were no ski lifts or funiculars then in Schruns: "Anything you ran down from, you had to climb up" (*MF*, "There Is Never Any End to Paris"). The plan to fly into the high mountains apparently never materialized. Instead, the Hemingways, Murphys, and Dos Passos moved from Schruns (c. 2,265 feet) to Gaschurn (c. 3,280 feet), a more remote village in the Montafon Valley closer to the Silvretta range, where they skied. The guest register of the Hotel zum Rössle-Post in Gaschurn shows that the party stayed there 12–17 March 1926 (Reynolds *AH*, ix, 224).

To Isidor Schneider, 23 March [1926]

March 23.

Schruns (Vorarlberg) Austria.

Dear Isidor,

Thanks so much for forwarding the mail and for sending the books. The books have not yet come but they will probably be here in a few days or else in Paris when we go up there. I will take the Frank to read in Spain. Would they like me to review it? Or would it just be enough to say that it was the only book taken by E Hemenngway the prominent boy writer on his recent extensive travels in Spain next summer?[1]

Imagine it being Virgin Spain. The country that lost its virginity the first of any. America did not lose its Virginity until the World's Series scandal in 1919.[2]

Waldo probably imagines it was Virgin until he planted his gigantic phallic tool in the innermost uterus of the Picos de Europas.[3] I'll tell you, I'll review it for you and you can say on the jacket—Waldo Frank is young full of ~~laughter~~ horse shit and he can't write. His stories anecdotes and historical misstatements are soft passionate bits of nothing. Although it lacks the depth and vitality of a book like Sherwood Anderson's Notebooks yet it is a worthy successor to Samuel Butler's Hudibras. In this volumne Frank takes his place with Borrow and Cervantes.[4] Tirso de Molina writes of Mr. Frank's new book in El Sol—I have never read anything like it. Lope da Vega in the N.Y. Sun—I haven't yet read it but all his friends say, "This is Heywood's Big Book.["][5]

I liked Dr. Transit very much.[6] So did Hadley. I cannot feel that the volumne will have a pronounced financial success but I want you to know that, as your publisher, I stand back of you. We back our authors to the limit. More than any other publisher in New York we play for the long chance. Steve Brodie was one of our authors. Look where Brodie is now.[7]

I've just done The Sun Also Rises all over again and am tired as hell. Been working a twelve hour day on it. I wrote Mr. Liveright once that I was tired when I finished it the first time. Now I wrote Mr. Schneider that I'm tired the second time. Today is wednesday and the end of the week we are going up to Paris.[8] I look forward to seeing Manuel Komroff very much and will try and look after him and see he gets comfortable.[9] We're going to stay in Paris until the middle of May and then go down to Spain for all summer. The Guaranty Trust address will always reach us.

I wrote to you and to Helen from the boat. Did you get it?[10] The one thing I never got in N.Y. was the In Our Times. Could you send one to

and one to—

Don Juan Quintana[11]	Don Rafael Hernandez[12]
Hotel Quintana	Galileo, 15
Pamplona	Madrid
Spain	Spain

I'll pay for them if they don't want to charge them to my royalty account. It's pretty important to me that those guys should get the book. I promised it last summer. They'll think I'm a damn liar and never wrote a book. My very best to Helen,

Yours always
Ernest

[*On verso EH typed his address and added the two final lines in pencil:*]
Permanent adress.
   C/ Guaranty Trust Co. of N.Y.
   1, Rue des Italiens,
   Paris France.

Please write

Regards to Jack Clapp and Maurice.[13]

Columbia, TLS with autograph postscript

1 Even after EH's break with Boni & Liveright, Schneider, the firm's publicity director, remained on good terms with EH and offered to send him recent Liveright publications as well as any other books he wanted. In his response to this letter, Schneider would explain that after a delay in mailing, the books were on the way ([8 April 1926], JFK). EH refers to *Virgin Spain: Scenes from the Spiritual Drama of a Great People* (New York: Boni & Liveright, 1926) by Waldo Frank (1889–1967), American novelist, magazine editor, and social historian. Written after Frank's visits to Spain in 1921, *Virgin Spain* and his subsequent works on Hispanic culture and inter-American relations gained the author wide recognition, especially in South America.

2 In a gambling scandal that marred the 1919 World Series, eight Chicago White Sox players were accused of throwing the series to the Cincinnati Reds. They were formally indicted on charges of conspiracy by a Chicago grand jury on 28 September 1920. Although acquitted in August 1921 on insufficient evidence, the players were banned for life from professional baseball.

3 EH would later refer to *Virgin Spain* as an example of "erectile writing," typical of an American school of writers who "sought to make all objects mystic through the slight distortion of vision that unrelieved turgidness presents" (*DIA*, Chapter 5). The Picos de Europa (literally "Peaks of Europe"), a mountain range in northern Spain characterized by limestone peaks rising to more than 8,500 feet and deep hollows, river gorges, and caves. *Pico* is also a vulgar Spanish term for penis.

4 *Sherwood Anderson's Notebook*, published by Boni & Liveright in 1926. In his response to this letter, Schneider called Anderson's memoir "a sad, feeble book" and suggested that Scribner's advertising should refer to it to show why *TOS* was needed. *Hudibras* (1663–1678), a mock heroic narrative poem by Samuel Butler (1613–1680). EH alludes to *The Bible in Spain* (1843) by English author George Henry Borrow (1803–1881), and *Don Quixote de la Mancha* (1605) by Miguel de Cervantes (1547–1616).

5 Tirso de Molina (1584–1648) and Félix Lope de Vega (1562–1635), Spanish dramatists. Heywood Broun (1888–1939), American journalist, novelist, and member of the Algonquin Round Table. EH alludes to a review of Broun's novel *Gandle Follows His Nose* (New York: Boni & Liveright, 1926) in the 22 October 1925 *Notre Dame Scholastic* that stated, "According to advance press notices, his best friends proclaim the work, 'Heywood's big book!'" (149).

6 Schneider's novel *Doctor Transit* (New York: Boni & Liveright, 1925).

7 Stephen Brodie (1861–1901), a New York City saloon keeper, achieved notoriety in 1886 for his claim to have jumped off the Brooklyn Bridge. He perpetuated his daredevil reputation with subsequent stunts, including his claim in 1889 to have gone over Niagara Falls. In Chapter 13 of *TOS*, Brodie is mentioned as someone who "had taken a chance."

8 In 1926, 23 March fell on a Tuesday. EH may have misdated the letter, or he may have continued writing the letter on Wednesday after starting it the day before. On 30 March, the Paris *Tribune* column "Latin Quarter Notes" would report EH's return to Paris the previous day "with an extra pound or two under his belt" (3).

9 Manuel Komroff (1890–1974), American writer and editor, served as Boni & Liveright's production manager and editor of the Modern Library series from 1921 until he moved to Paris in 1926 to pursue a career as a writer. In 1925 Boni & Liveright published his first book, *The Grace of Lambs: Stories.*

10 Schneider responded that he never received EH's letter from the boat. Schneider's wife, Helen Berlin Schneider (1903–1992), American writer and editor who later worked as writer and secretary for the American Communist Party newspaper, the *Daily Worker*, in the late 1930s.

11 Juan Quintana Urra (c. 1891–1974), bullfight aficionado and owner of the Hotel Quintana in Pamplona, which was commonly frequented by bullfighters. He would lose his hotel in the Spanish Civil War. A lifelong friend of EH, he served as the prototype for Montoya in *SAR.*

12 Rafael Hernández Ramírez (1889–1971), Spanish journalist and bullfight critic. Next to each man's address is a penciled checkmark and date "4/7/26," probably indicating that the books were sent to them on 7 April 1926.

13 John S. Clapp (1899–1990), sales representative for Boni & Liveright, and American author Maurice A. Hanline (1895–1964), who served as an assistant to Horace Liveright and as the firm's European representative.

To Edwin L. Peterson, Jr., 30 March [1926]

30 March.

Dear Mr. Peterson,

Thank you very much for your letter sending me the review of In Our Time. It makes me feel very good to have you like the book so much.[1]

About Anderson: I think he has written better than anyone has ever written in America. His last book—Dark Laughter—seemed awfully bad. He can write so very beautifully that if he had a good head he would be one of the very greatest writers who have ever lived. You see, the thing about a writer(s) like [*EH insertion*: for the grammarians→(such as)] Hardy, or Turgenieff, or the Tolstoi of War and Peace is that they were not only great artists but were intelligent.[2]

Words aren't enough.

You must have the ability to do what you want with words first—and such are as rare as .450 hitters in baseball—and then, to be a really great writer you must be intelligent.[3] Take Fielding as an example of the intelligent writer.[4] And how often do they come?

Anatole France, Hardy, Knut Hamsun—Conrad—with his blind spots—[5]

By intelligent I dont mean smart or cynical or surface sophisticated.

Anyway I've tried to get what I feel about sloppy thinking and borrowed thinking into this satire that Scribners are bringing out this Spring. It's called The Torrents of Spring. I hope you'll like it. In the fall I'm going to have a pretty long novel called The Sun Also Rises. Scribners are going to publish them all from now on.

Anyway I sent the photo so you could check up on the description.[6] Am going to Spain next month until Sept [*EH insertion:* Following the bull fights again.] and then coming over to the States for a year or so. Not New York.

Thanks again for sending the clipping.

With Best regards,
Ernest Hemingway.

permanent address.

    c/o Guaranty Trust Co. of N.Y.

    1, Rue des Italiens

    Paris

    France.

Lets hear from you and if you think that's all horse shit about Anderson say so

Newberry, ALS; letterhead: VÉNÉTIA-HOTEL / 159, BOULEVARD DU MONTPARNASSE / PARIS-VI

1 Peterson's letter and the enclosed review remain unlocated.

2 Thomas Hardy (1840–1928), English novelist, and Russian writers Ivan Sergeevich Turgenev (1818–1883) and Leo Tolstoy (né Lev Nikolaevich Tolstoy, 1828–1910). Tolstoy's *War and Peace* was first published in Russian in six volumes (1865–1869) and translated into English in 1886.

3 The only player ever to finish a full season with a batting average above .450 was Levi Samuel Meyerle (c. 1845–1921), who hit a .492 during the first season of major league baseball in 1871.

4 Henry Fielding (1707–1754), English author of the satirical 1742 novel *Joseph Andrews*. In writing *TOS*, EH had set out "to be an Am. Fielding," as he told Ezra Pound in a letter of [30 November 1925], and he regarded *TOS* as "the funniest book I've read since Joseph Andrews" (*Letters* vol. 2, 422). EH used a passage from the "Author's Preface" of *Joseph Andrews* as the epigraph of *TOS*.

5 Anatole France (né Jacques-Anatole-François Thibault, 1844–1924), French recipient of the 1921 Nobel Prize in Literature; Knut Hamsun (1859–1952), Norwegian recipient of the

1920 Nobel Prize in Literature; and Joseph Conrad (1857–1924), Polish-born English writer.
6 In his reply of 13 June 1926, Peterson thanked EH for "the snap of yourself" (JFK).

To Maxwell Perkins, 1 April [1926]

[*PARIS, LE*] 1, April.

Dear Mr. Perkins:

I have not yet received the proofs [of *TOS*] but expect them today or tomorrow and will try and get them off on the Aquitania on Sat April 3. The jacket looks very attractive.[1]

It is quite all right about Maude Adams. We will change Maude Adams to Lenore Ulrich or Ann Pennington—which should be funnier and will make the same joke without mentioning Miss Adams' name.[2]

Dos Passos was down in Austria with us and we had a good week of ski ing. I finished re-writing The Sun Also Rises and felt a desire to let down in a rather larger town than Schruns so we came up to Paris. The people who sub-let our flat are getting out by Easter so we will be moving in tomorrow or the next day.[3]

The Sun Also Rises will go to the typist to be re-typed and then I'll send it to you in a couple of weeks. It is some 330 typewritten pages in my typing which is without margin. Reading it over it seems quite exciting.

We are going to Spain on the 15th of May for 4 months. From now on my permanent address will be

Care—Guaranty Trust Co. of N.Y.

1, Rue des Italiens

Paris

France.

They are very good and accurate

I am sorry no one wanted the 50 Grand story. You have my authority to make any arrangement with Reynolds.[4] I am very anxious to write some stories again—and will try and write the shortest ones first. I would like to draw 600\underline{^{00}}$ from the balance of that advance.[5] Could you have it sent to me care of The Guaranty Trust Co. address?

Enclosed are a couple of pictures which may or may not be of use to the Publicity Department. There is also one of my boy for your own information. I will be fooling around with bull fighting during the latter part of June and the first three weeks of July but have no intention of The Sun Also Rises being a posthumous work.

Yours very sincerely,

Ernest Hemingway.

Thank you very much for the trouble you took about 50 Grand.

PUL, ALS; letterhead: VÉNÉTIA-HOTEL / 159, BOULEVARD DU MONTPARNASSE / PARIS-VI

1 In a letter to EH of 15 March 1926, Perkins wrote that he had sent off the proofs of *TOS* two days earlier, "without even having read the last of them" (PUL). He also enclosed "a proof of the wrap which is almost right." It included no blurbs about *TOS* but focused on EH. Perkins told EH, "all that ought to be said should be about you."

2 In his letter, Perkins had suggested removing the name of American actress Maude Adams (1872–1953) from *TOS* because of her "extreme sensitiveness" (PUL). Adams was best known for starring in J. M. Barrie's popular stage play *Peter Pan*, beginning with the first U.S. performance in 1905 and continuing through several Broadway revivals. EH changed the name to refer instead to Lenore Ulric (née Leonara Ulrich, 1892–1970), American stage and screen actress (who years later would play the role of Anita in the 1940 Broadway production of EH's *The Fifth Column*). However, EH retained the reference to *Peter Pan* in the passage in Chapter 5 of *TOS* describing a waitress: "Her face was lined and gray. She looks a little like that actress that died in Pittsburgh. What was her name? Lenore Ulric. In *Peter Pan*. That was it." Ann Pennington (1893–1971), American stage actress and singer.

3 A Mr. and Mrs. Choleston had sublet the apartment at 113, rue Notre-Dame-des-Champs since 12 December 1925 (*Letters* vol. 2, 424–25). In 1926, Easter Sunday fell on 4 April.

4 Like *Collier's Weekly* and *Liberty*, the *Saturday Evening Post* also turned down "Fifty Grand." Informing EH of this last rejection, Perkins had proposed in his letter that EH use the services of a literary agent, and had recommended letting Paul Revere Reynolds (1864–1944) attempt to place the story in return for a 10% commission.

5 Perkins would send EH $600 of the remaining $1,500 advance for *TOS* and *SAR* on 12 April 1926 (PUL).

To Herbert Gorman, [c. 4 April 1926]

113 Rue Notre Dame des Champs

Paris VI.

Easter

Dear Gorman—

I was glad to get your letter and went at once to Bill Bird of the Three Mountains Press, 19 Rue D'Antin—the address in case you want it ever. He said he would send you a copy of the Cantos. I hope the hell he does. He wrote down the address and said he would anyway.[1]

Have finished re-writing The Sun Also Rises and am having a swell time in town again. Have a box for all next week at the Six day Bike race.[2] As it took all next month's rent and food money to buy it I hope I'll be able to sell the Extra four seats. They are easy to sell though. Bring double and triple price if I wanted to scalp them. The trees are out and it is warm and fine.

Scribner's wrote they'd sent me the proofs of the satire so I imagine they've gone to you too.[3] I'll speak to them about it in my next letter. I hope you'll be able to let me have one of the books of poems but if it's so limited don't rob yourself. I'd like awfully to see it.[4]

Have seen no literary gents here as yet but see by the clippings that am a constant attendant at literary teas with Bercovici, Louis Bromfield, Edith Wharton, Seldes etc. Who is Bercovici? Is he the same one that used to write the Local Color stories?[5]

I'm sorry as hell that we'll be in Spain from the middle of May on. Will have some extra fun as I've gotten mixed up in the making of some bull fight films for S. American and European consumption. It will be fun because I like the actual making of the pictures and want to lay off writing for several months and am always in Spain in Summer anyway and this way will get my bull fights free.[6] Did you ever read the bull fight thing ["The Undefeated"] in This Quarter? I'm anxious to see your corrida piece. When are you going to send it?[7]

The getting off (from Hoboken) was very funny. I wish you'd been there. I was tighter than a hog's ass in fly time. But it seemed others were tight too.

I do hope you get the Cantos all right.

Come on over as soon as you can. Paris is very exciting after Schruns and very grown up and restful after New York. Give my best to [Edmund] Wilson if you see him.

Yours always,
Ernest Hemingway.

UVA, ALS

1 William Augustus (Bill) Bird (1889–1963), American journalist and director of the Continental branch of the Consolidated Press in Paris, whom EH had met while covering the Genoa Economic Conference in the spring of 1922. That summer Bird purchased a hand press and established the Three Mountains Press, named for the three hills of Paris: Montmartre, Montparnasse, and Montagne Sainte-Geneviève. Bird published Pound's *A Draft of XVI. Cantos* (1925), the first installment of *The Cantos*, a series of poems that comprised the major project of Pound's life. During EH's New York City visit in February 1926, Gorman had offered to review Pound's volume of cantos for the *New York Times*, but it was Gorman's review of *Personae: The Collected Poems of Ezra Pound* (New York: Boni & Liveright, 1926) that would appear in the *New York Times* on 23 January 1927.
2 In this indoor sport, which began in England in the late nineteenth century and quickly became popular on both sides of the Atlantic, individual cyclists or teams would race continuously for six days on banked wooden tracks; whoever covered the greatest distance won. The Paris race began on 5 April 1926 and featured U.S. champion cyclist Reggie McNamara (1887–1971), fresh from victory at a six-day race at Madison Square Garden in New York City that drew a crowd of 18,000 for the finish.
3 Gorman would not review *TOS*, but he would praise *SAR* in his review "Hemingway Keeps His Promise" (*New York World*, 14 November 1926).
4 Gorman's *Notations for a Chimaera* (New York: M.I.D. Einstein, 1926) was published in a deluxe limited edition of 100 copies.
5 Romanian-born Konrad Bercovici (1882–1961) was known in the 1920s for his local color stories of New York City's ethnic groups, published weekly in the *New York World*. His book *On New Shores* (1925) features vignettes of immigrant communities throughout the United States. American expatriate novelist Edith Wharton (1862–1937), author of *The House of Mirth* (1905) and *Ethan Frome* (1911), won a 1921 Pulitzer Prize for *The Age of Innocence* (1920). Gilbert Seldes (1893–1970) served as managing editor of the *Dial* 1921–1922 and as its drama critic 1920–1929; his best-known book was *The Seven Lively Arts* (1924).
6 Probably a reference to a movie that EH and his friend George O'Neil were working on in 1924, not known to have been completed. In a letter to his mother of 18 July 1924 describing the fiesta at Pamplona, EH wrote that O'Neil "had a movie machine and took 23 reels of films of the bull fights, amateur fights, dancing and religious processions." In August 1924 letters to Gertrude Stein and Alice B. Toklas, EH reported that the film was being developed in Paris by Man Ray, who pronounced it "one of the best movies he's ever seen" (*Letters* vol. 2, 133, 138, 144). EH also referred to the bullfighting film in his "Pamplona Letter" in the September 1924 *Transatlantic Review* (300). O'Neil's footage of the bullfights remains unlocated.
7 If Gorman published a piece about bullfighting, it remains unlocated.

To Ernest Walsh, 7 April 1926

113 Rue N.D des Champs.

Paris VI

April 7 1926

Dear Ernest—

How the hell are you anyway. I've heard not a damned thing since I wrote you just before leaving for America[1] We saw Pauline Pfeiffer the other day— She'd visited with you and said you were well. I wrote her at your address to pay her some money I borrowed going through Paris. She bought me some night gowns for Hadley. God Nose I havent been writing letters. Havent written Ezra [Pound] since December. He must think me a fine shit. I'll write him tomorrow. The Sun Also Rises is finally finished. Scribners are going to publish it and The Torrents of Spring. I got enough of an advance so that I scuttled back with it practically intact and after deducting the cost of the trip we can still go to Spain next month for 3 months. My writing is shaky from 9 hrs at the 6 day bike race with a fiasco—completo—of chianti and 2 btls. Volnay.[2] Maybe that wouldn't make your hand shake but it makes my hand shake. I'm healthy as hell and very fit. Going to write stories for the next 3 months. Every body in N.Y. was reading This Quarter—I saw it everywhere I went where there were any literary guys.

Paris is exciting as hell to be back in. I've been drinking a great deal of wine and feeling very damned good to have the book done. McAlmon is in town and is very nice and pleasant and we all get along swell.

Enclosed picture of Bumby and his old man. This is a rotten letter but if you write I'll write a good one. I cant write letters but have better luck answering them. I'm very anxious to write stories again. A novel goes on too long and I dont know anything else while I'm doing it and it raises too much hell.

So Long and good luck and write!

Yours always,
Ernest

JFK, ALS; postmark: PA[RIS] / Av. D'ORLEANS, 7 / AVRIL / 18³⁰ / 26

1 EH's letter to Walsh of 1 February.
2 Wines from the Chianti region of Italy were traditionally bottled in a *fiasco*, a round-bottomed bottle with a straw covering. Volnay, a red wine produced in the Burgundy region of France.

To Maxwell Perkins, 8 April 1926

April 8, 1926
113 Rue Notre Dame des Champs
Paris VI

Dear Mr. Perkins—

I am mailing you the proofs of Torrents by the "<u>Berengaria</u>" Sailing April tenth—[1] So you should have them with this letter. As you will see the Maude Adams is changed to Lenore Ulrich and I changed the Liveright. The original of the Marquis of Buque is the Marquess of Bute whose seat is at Cardiff Castle. On verifying the spelling of his name in Burke's Peerage, when I first wrote the story, I discovered that he had been Honorary Lieut. Col. of some British regiment so it seemed extremely unlikely that he had served as a private in Ford's regiment of Welch Fusiliers. So I made it quite an aprocryphal name. If anyone objects that there is no Marquis of Buque you can state for me that I'm aware of that. None of this is of any importance and I don't know why I should write it except that a Burke's costs 900 francs and weighs 5 pounds and therefore you like to get some good out of it other than the very fleeting pleasure of looking up your friends in the stud-book.[2]

The type the Torrents is set in is splendid. Will you send sheets or advance copies—however it is done—to

Herbert S. Gorman
  47 West 12th Street
    N.Y.C.
	Sheets or book

Ernest Boyd[3]—whose address you must have—"	
Edmund Wilson	Sheets or book
Robert Woolf[4] 46 Perry Street N.Y.C.	Woolf is stupid but well meaning. Book
———	
Burton Rascoe[5] c/o Johnson Features 1918 Broadway.	Sheets or book

Robert C. Benchley
Care of Life   Sheets or book

Donald Ogden Stewart
   Mark Twain Hotel   Book
     Hollywood
       California

Ezra Pound[6]
   Via Marsala, 12   book
     Rapallo Italy

Edward J. O'Brien[7]
c/o Messers. Jonathan Cape Ltd.   book.
   30 Bedford Square
   London W.C. 1.

William Rose Benét   <u>Sheets or book.</u>
c/o The Saturday Review of Literature.
   Paul Rosenfeld } I don't care about but you might send them review
   Waldo Frank   } copies if you have their addresses.[8]

James Joyce
   192 Rue de Grenelle   Book
     2 Square Robeac
       Paris France

Joseph Freeman[9]
care/ The New Masses   Sheets or book.
   39 West 8th Street
     N.Y. City

Ernest Walsh
Editor This Quarter
Chateau Simon

18 Route de Saint Valliers
   Grasse
    (A.M)   <u>Book</u>
      France

Don Rafael Hernandez y Ramirez De Alda
   Galileo, 15   <u>Book</u>
      Madrid, Spain.

Miss Isabel Patterson
   N.Y. Herald-Tribune   Sheets or book.
   N.Y. City

I'll try and think of some more. Herbert J. Seligman in The Sun, Hershel Brickell in the Post and LLoyd Morris in The Times all gave In Our Time long reviews. Also a man named Alan Tate in The Nation.[10] I'd like to send a copy to Elinor Wylie and one to Sinclair Lewis but I suppose I should write in those.[11] The others can go off and I can write in them when I see the people.

Your criticism of Dos Passos' book seems very sound. Twice I didnt think I would be able to finish it—or care about finishing it and each time when I started reading again it was much more interesting. The style is very tiring. Dos himself says now he thinks it was a mistake coupling the words.[12] We argued it. I was arguing on the basis that what you gain in a shade of meaning you lose by making a mechanical jolt which the reader gets when it's not intended. The ideal way would seem to write using all such tricks or mannerisms that help it to come smoother and then eliminate them before publishing. ~~It doesnt make any difference how it helps the author if it has an effect he doesn't work for or want on the reader.~~ I said all that last sentence once.

Thank you so much for sending Thomason's book.[13] It will be very interesting. He has a very fine soldierly quality that I admire greatly and I think it's a miracle that he is so articulate. It is always very fine to have somebody writing about something they know about. You get very tired of the writer, usually unhealthy, standing apalled at various spectacles.

The Sun A.R. gets back from the typist today and after I have another look at it will probably send it on a Wednesday boat.

I hope you get the proofs promptly. There is no need, of course, for page proofs. If you get the proofs within 10 days when will the book be out?

We're having a great time at the 6 day bike race this week. I've a box for the week and do all my work there. It's a great show.

Yours always,

Ernest Hemingway.

PUL, ALS

1 The *Berengaria* departed from Cherbourg on 10 April, arriving in New York City on 17 April 1926.
2 At the time, Sir John Crichton-Stuart (1881–1947), whose family seat was at Cardiff Castle in Wales, was the 4th Marquess of the County of Bute. In *TOS*, the fictional Marquis of Buque serves as a private in "Ford's regiment," which is billeted at his castle (Chapter 15). Ford Madox Ford served during WWI not with the Royal Welch Fusiliers (generally recruited from Mid-Wales and North Wales), but with the 9th Battalion of the Welch Regiment (generally recruited from southwest Wales). *Burke's Peerage*, genealogical and heraldic history first published in 1826 by John Burke (1786–1848).
3 Boyd's favorable review of *TOS* would appear in the 12 June 1926 issue of the *Independent*.
4 American novelist Robert Wolf (1895–1970) reviewed *IOT* for *New York Herald Tribune Books* on 14 February 1926, writing: "I know of no American writer with a more startling ear for colloquial conversation, or a more poetic sensitiveness to woods and hills. *In Our Time* has perhaps not enough energy to be a great book, but Ernest Hemingway has promise of genius" (3).
5 American writer and editor Burton Rascoe (1892–1957), whose syndicated column "A Bookman's Day Book" was a regular Sunday feature of the *New York Herald Tribune* from 1924 to 1928. Rascoe had called attention to *iot* in his column of 15 June 1924 and favorably reviewed *IOT* in the November 1925 issue of *Arts & Decoration*.
6 In a letter to the editor in the 5 October 1927 *New Republic*, Pound would refute a critical review of *TOS* by Robert Littell (1896–1963) that appeared in the 10 August 1927 issue, saying *TOS* "kicks the bunk out of a number of national imbecilities" (177a).
7 Edward J. O'Brien (1890–1941), editor of the annual *Best Short Stories* anthologies, who had included EH's "My Old Man" in the 1923 volume and dedicated it to "Ernest Hemenway." O'Brien would review *IOT*, rather than *TOS*, in the Autumn 1926 issue of *Now & Then*, the house magazine of British publisher Jonathan Cape, declaring, "It is obvious that [EH] has been influenced by Sherwood Anderson, and that he in turn has influenced Anderson. I regard him as the more significant writer of the two because he has succeeded in freeing himself completely from the sentimentality of American life and also from the fear of sentimentality" (30).
8 Rosenfeld's and Frank's names are crossed out in pencil, possibly by Perkins or someone else at Scribner's.
9 American radical writer Joseph Freeman (1897–1965), founding editor of the *New Masses* (1926–1948) and the *Partisan Review* (1934–2003).

10 *IOT* had been reviewed by American journalist and author Herbert J. Seligmann (1891–1984) in the *New York Sun* (17 October 1925) and by American journalist, book columnist, and editor Herschel Brickell (1889–1952) in the *New York Evening Post Literary Review* (17 October 1925). Neither Seligmann, Brickell, nor American writer and critic Lloyd Morris (1893–1954) is known to have written a signed review of *TOS*. Allen Tate (1899–1979), American poet and critic, had reviewed *IOT* in *The Nation* (10 February 1926), and his review of *TOS* would appear in *The Nation* (28 July 1926).

11 In a letter of 31 January 1927, Sinclair Lewis would tell EH that he had refused Liveright's request to praise *IOT* because he was already praising another Liveright author and did not want to become known as one of Liveright's "best little boosters." Telling EH "thus tardily" how much he liked his work, Lewis praised *SAR* as "one of the best books I have ever read" and said he knew of "no youngster" who had "a more superb chance to dominate Anglo-American letters" (JFK).

12 *Manhattan Transfer* (1925), the most recently published book by John Dos Passos, is written in an experimental expressionistic style, frequently employing such compound words as "orangerinds," "manuresmelling," and "leadentired."

13 *Fix Bayonets!* (New York: Scribner's, 1926), a collection of short stories by U. S. Marine Corps officer, writer, and artist John W. Thomason, Jr. (1893–1944).

To Maxwell Perkins, [c. 10 April 1926]

Sat. about 10 oclock

Dear Mr. Perkins.—

These are about 1/3 of the clippings— What Liveright had duplicates of. If you want others, more sincere from the hinterland, I'll send them.

Very Sincerely,

Ernest Hemingway.

P.S.

You might send an advance copy or galleys, to Ernest Boyd who said he would be very keen to see Torrents.

PUL, ALS

To F. Scott Fitzgerald, [16] April 1926

April 1926

Dear Scott—

Had a letter from Curtis Browne that Jonathan Cape wants to publish In Our Time and will pay 25 pounds advance and 10% and 3 D. a copy for

British Empire rights not including Canada. Liveright wouldnt sell them sheets—they are going to set it up themselves. Curtis Browne is going to be my Continental and British agents and say they are dickering with a German publisher that wants I.O.T.[1]

I've returned the proofs of Torrents to Scribners a week or so ago. It looks very good.[2]

Sun Also Rises is all done and back from the typists[.] 1085 francs total typing charges. So I guess I'll send it off. I've cut it to about 90,000 words.

May dedicate it like this—

To My Son

John Hadley Nicanor

This Collection of Instructive Anecdotes

I'm hoping to hell you'll like it. You'll see it in August. I think may be it is pretty interesting. [*EH insertion*: Later—You won't like it.]

Chink is in town for 2 weeks. He and I are going to walk from Saragossa across the Pyrenees by way of Andorra the end of July. I've had a rotten cold. Been being very social and am god damn tired of it. Do you know anything about the girl Don's marrying?[3] We go to Spain the 12th of May. Hadley's playing the piano very well. Where are you on your book? Write to me. Rousseau asks about you at the bank.[4] He had us to lunch. We went. Went 5 of the 6 days to the bike race. It was swell yest went with Chink and many generals etc to see Sandhurst play Saint Cyr.[5]

Yr. letter just to hand and Walsh's poem or coming in his pants ~~or Jazz Age gesture~~ or whatever you want to call it made me vomit again seen on the envelope. But unlike the dog which returns to his vomit I tore up the envelope—just as I tore out the original poem and just as threw away This Quarter after tearing out my story to keep it.[6]

Havent seen Archie MacLeish on acct his absense in Persia.[7] Seen Bromfield's once. Glad to see you're feeling bitter as understand that stimulates literary production.

Glad to hear you see further than Tarkington. Sorry to hear you see not as far as Hemingway. How far do the French women see?[8]

Very glad if you realize criticizm to be horse shit without horse shits pleasant smell nor use as fertilizer. Have not seen Bookman. Nevertheless I thank you for services rendered.[9] Havent seen the New Fiction except Gents Prefer which seemed 2nd rate Lardner and very dull. Perkins sent Thomason's book which seemed very juvenile. I'd thought it would be much better. There wasnt that much hand to hand fighting in 100 years of the Crusades. Have not seen Sherwood Anderson's note book though I believe I should in order to get a lot of new ideas.[10]

Fifty Grand is, I believe, in the hands of some agent. I could use the 250 I could have gotten by cutting it for Scribners. Am thoroly disgusted with writing but as there is nothing else I care as much for will continue writing.

Paul Nelson would be a good story for you to write if you knew anything about it[11]

I'm glad as hell you got the money for the movie rights of Gatsby. With that and Gatsby in person at the Ambassador you sh'd be able to write a pretty good novel with the franc around 30.[12] Maybe someday you'll get the Nobel Prize. Understand it's not yet been given to an American.[13] Am recommending to Mr. Walsh that he give you This Quarter's $2000 bucks and have just called in my attorney to make you my heir.[14] So Dont Worry About Money. Chink says he'll leave you Bellamont Forest too if you like.[15] Pauline Pfeiffer says you can have her job on Vogue. I've written Scribner to send all my royalty checks to you.

It makes no difference your telling G. Murphy about bull fighting statement except will be careful about making such statements. Was not referring to guts but to something else. Grace under pressure.[16] Guts never made any money for anybody except violin string manufacturers.

Your friend Ring [Lardner] is hampered by lack of intelligence, lack of any aesthetic appreciation, terrible repression and bitterness. Any one of those is a terrible load for any writer to carry no matter how talented. He is, of course, 100 times as intelligent as most U.S. writers.

Bumby has the whooping cough. Hadley has had a rotten cough now for over 6 weeks. I expect they give it back and forth to each other.

We go to Spain May 12. If Bumby is not well then I'll go on ahead and Hadley come later. We go to U.S.A. in End of Sept. Antibes in August. I'll have a copy of Sun etc there and w'd welcome your advising me on anything about it. Nobody's read any amount of it yet. If you are worried it is not a series of anecdotes—nor is it written very much like either Manhattan Transfer nor Dark Laughter. I have tried to follow the outline and spirit of The Great Gatsby, but feel I have failed somewhat because of never having been on Long Island. The hero, like Gatsby, is a Lake Superior Salmon Fisherman. (There are no salmon in Lake Superior) The action all takes place in Newport, R.I. and the heroine is a girl named Sophie Irene Loeb who kills her mother. The scene in which Sophie gives birth to twins in the death house at Sing Sing where she is waiting to be electrocuted for the murder of the father and sister of her, as then, unborn children I got from Dreiser but practically everything else in the book is either my own or yours. I know you'll be glad to see it. The Sun Also Rises comes from Sophie's statement as she is strapped into the chair as the current mounts.[17]

Well why not write?

> Regards to all yr. family
> Herbert J. Messkit.

PUL, ALS

1 Founded by American journalist Albert Curtis Brown (1866–1945) in New York and London in 1899, the literary agency Curtis Brown Ltd. served as European selling agent for Boni & Liveright. In a letter of 7 April 1926, L. E. Pollinger, manager of the agency's Department of American Books, informed EH that the firm of Jonathan Cape (1879–1960), established in London in 1921, had offered to publish a British edition of *IOT* (JFK). Curtis Brown subsequently represented EH's interests and successfully negotiated the contract with Cape. In a letter to EH of 13 April 1926, the manager of the agency's Foreign Department wrote that a German firm had applied for translation rights to *IOT* (JFK). The firm of Ernst Hermann Heinrich Rowohlt (1887–1960), founded in 1910, would be the primary publisher of German translations of EH's works, and in 1932 would publish *In Unserer Zeit*, the German translation of *IOT* by Annemarie Horschitz.

2 Acknowledging receipt of the proofs in his letter of 19 April 1926, Perkins would report that Scribner's "instantly proceeded toward the manufacture" and that publication of *TOS* was expected "by May 21st, at worst" (PUL). The actual publication date would be 28 May 1926.

3 Donald Ogden Stewart would marry Beatrice Ames (1902–1981) on 24 July 1926 in Montecito, California, and they would honeymoon in Europe. They would divorce in 1938.

4 Theodore Rousseau (1880–1953), an acquaintance of the Fitzgeralds, worked at the Guaranty Trust Company in Paris.

5 In a rugby match in Paris on 15 April, the Royal Military Academy at Sandhurst (the initial training center for British Army officers) defeated France's École Spéciale Militaire de Saint-Cyr by a score of 7 to 6. Chink Dorman-Smith attended Sandhurst 1912–1914,

graduating as a lieutenant, and returned as an instructor from 1924 to 1931. After this sentence EH switched from writing in pencil to writing in black ink.

6 Fitzgerald's letter remains unlocated. Later, in separate letters to Callaghan and Fitzgerald of September 1926, EH would use the same language to express his distaste for Walsh's poem "Ernest Hemingway," claiming it "made me vomit." The poem had appeared in the second number of *This Quarter* along with EH's story "The Undefeated."

7 American writer and poet Archibald MacLeish (1892–1982) visited Persia from March to June 1926 as part of a group sent by the League of Nations to investigate opium production.

8 Booth Tarkington (1869–1946), American author whose books *The Magnificent Ambersons* (1918) and *Alice Adams* (1921) each received a Pulitzer Prize. EH alludes to a comment by Harry Hansen in his review of Fitzgerald's *All the Sad Young Men* (1926), which had appeared in the *Chicago News* on 22 January 1926: "Fitzgerald sees a bit farther, just as he sees farther than Tarkington, and not quite so far as Ernest Hemingway" (193). EH also alludes to the dialog that appears on the title page of *iot*:
A GIRL IN CHICAGO: Tell us about the French women, Hank. What are they like?
BILL SMITH: How old are the French women, Hank?

9 Fitzgerald praised *IOT* at length in "How to Waste Material: A Note on My Generation," published in the May 1926 *Bookman*.

10 Ringgold (Ring) Wilmer Lardner (1885–1933), American humorist and short-story writer, had published several books by 1926, including *How to Write Short Stories* (1924). Lardner was a close friend of Fitzgerald, a fellow Scribner's author, and an early influence on the young EH, who had imitated Lardner's style in stories for his high school newspaper, the *Trapeze*. EH refers to *Gentlemen Prefer Blondes* (1925) by Anita Loos, John W. Thomason's *Fix Bayonets!* (1926), and *Sherwood Anderson's Notebook* (1926).

11 Paul Nelson (1895–1979), American artist and architect who graduated from Princeton in 1917, served as an aviator in France and Italy, and studied at the École des Beaux-Arts in Paris after the war. He and EH played tennis together in 1925. Writing to Bill Smith on 4 March 1925, EH described him as "a good guy—former society guy," a "former great drunk—married and reformed," and "one of the solidest backers" of EH's writing (*Letters* vol. 2, 264).

12 According to Fitzgerald's ledger, in 1926 he earned $13,500 (after commission) for the movie rights to *The Great Gatsby*, although the silent film released that November by Famous Players-Lasky-Paramount Pictures was a flop, running for only two weeks. The stage version of *Gatsby* that played on Broadway at the Ambassador Theatre from 2 February to 7 May generated $2,616.98, and the play's tour performances earned him $3,347.23 (Matthew J. Bruccoli, ed., *F. Scott Fitzgerald's Ledger: A Facsimile* [Washington, D.C.: NCR/Microcard Editions, 1972], 60).

13 In 1930 Sinclair Lewis, author of *Main Street* (1920) and *Babbitt* (1922), would become the first American to win the Nobel Prize in Literature, established by Swedish munitions manufacturer Alfred Nobel (1833–1896) and awarded since 1901. EH would receive the Nobel Prize in 1954, but Fitzgerald never did.

14 Reference to *This Quarter's* award of $2,000 that never materialized. Walsh had announced in the first number that the magazine had "received cheques towards the sum of two thousand dollars or five hundred pounds to be given to the contributor publishing the best work in the first four numbers of *THIS QUARTER*" (Spring 1925, 261). Walsh died after publication of the second number. Later, EH would write an unflattering sketch of Walsh, who purportedly had promised the award separately to both EH and Joyce, and possibly to Pound (*MF*, "The Man Who Was Marked for Death").

15 The Dorman-Smith family's estate near Coothill in County Cavan, Ireland, which Chink would inherit from his father in 1948 (Lavinia Graecen, *Chink: A Biography* [London: Macmillan, 1989], 5).

16 This is the first known written record of EH's use of this phrase. Dorothy Parker, in her *New Yorker* profile of EH ("The Artist's Reward," 30 November 1929, 28–31), would call it "Hemingway's definition of courage" and attribute that "grace under pressure" to Hemingway himself for having "never once compromised" as a writer.

17 EH's description of *SAR* is a pastiche of incongruous fictional and historic elements, including a reference to Jay Gatsby's humble origins (born James Gatz, he had worked as a clam digger and salmon fisherman on Lake Superior); the placement of Sophie Irene Loeb (1876–1929), a Russian Jewish immigrant, writer, and child welfare advocate, in fashionable Newport, Rhode Island; allusions to *An American Tragedy* (1925) by Theodore Dreiser (1871–1945); and a likely reference to the matricidal plot of an early version of Fitzgerald's novel-in-progress, which would become *Tender Is the Night* (1934). In Dreiser's novel, the protagonist is convicted of murdering his pregnant girlfriend and is executed by electrocution—the plot inspired by a murder case that resulted in a 1908 execution at Auburn Prison in upstate New York (not at Sing Sing, the maximum security state prison at Ossining, New York).

To Ezra Pound, [17 April 1926]

No I never got the Corriere Hemorrhage. But I'm all the lousy things you care to call me for not having written. Send the Corriere thing direct or outline the channels so I can trace it.[1] Bill Bird's gone to Spitzbergen.[2] Mac [McAlmon] is in London, Eng. There's nobody in town. I went to N.Y. in Jan. and came right back. Scribner's are bringing out the satire [*TOS*] that Liveright turned down as too tough.

Saw Gorman in N.Y. and he wanted to do a full page review of the Cantos in NY Times if he could get a review copy. I told Bill and he made a note of it.

    Herbert S. Gorman

    47 West 12th Street

    N.Y.C.

He wrote me about it after I got back and I gave his address to Bill. You might write Bill's Secretary and see if it ever went off. Boni and Liveright are supposed to be bringing out yr Selected works the middle of this month[3]

Marse Henry was in fine shape and we had a pleasant time.[4] I've written Scribners to send you an advance copy of the satire. Not for review. Not for anything except maybe pleasure.

Gorman wants to do a full page feature on you. He's never seen the Cantos. Wants to do them. He's a nice little fella.

We go to Spain 12th of May—until August. Go to Antibes in Aug and sailing along the coast. Where'll you be? Got a good chunk of money off Scribner's. They were very nice. Want to pooblish me from now on and I can say son of a bitch or shit or anything I need to say. Nicer than Mr. Liveright's bucket shop. I'm fertig[5] with Liveright—but on a friendly basis. Had no row. I was automatically clear as soon as he turned down the satire— The reason I never sent you a copy was because due to changing pooblishers they were all tied up.

How the hell are you anyway? Be sure and send the <u>Corriere</u> thing. Is it more Linati? What am I now? Commander of a sub marine? or flying again. Well all us aviators have got to stick together— How are the Fuorocisti?[6]

What's the dope on Walsh? He hasnt written me since I went to U.S.A.

Ford is America's Sweetheart as a writer. Literary coicles dazed by his Proustian Projects.[7] Have you read Violent Hunt's The Flurried Years? A large 400 or so page Vol. all about the Master—his dental arrangements— his phantom divorces—his incalculable genius etc. A good buy at any price.[8] The Master is returning here next Tues. their at home coincides with the rentree of Mascart at Cirque de Paris.[9] Saw Stella last night.[10] She says that Ford's latest—and greatest work—(in which you may remember the undefiled Teajens was to be actually at the front—) opens on Armistice Day. You may recall my prediction that Tcheegins would never actually face the Boche. Because if Ford had any confidence that he could handle combat he would, even with a forthrightly style, not have taken 2 vol's to get his hero back of the lines. Teijens will have fought all right in this Vol. God how he'll have fought we'll have flashbacks and glimpses of it.[11] Glenway Wescott will doubtless write the great novel of the war.[12] Tolstoi wrote it all anyway. and the 25 or 30 pages out of the great mass of crap of La Chartreuse de Parme.[13]

Be a good guy and write me the dope. Im a son of a bitch not to have written for so long. Love to Dorothy.[14] When is Walsh quartering again? Are you going to get the 2000? Is there a 2000? Is Carnevalli really anything beside sick? His stuff seems very Eytalian to me. Very Eytalian. All Eytalians crushed by life, women, beauty, War, pestilence etc. seem to write much the same.

My new theory is that all nations get just what they deserve—I.E. produce—

Italy = Mussolini—[15]

USA = Coolidge—[16]

Idaho = Sen. Borah + Ezra.[17]

England during war = Northcliffe—Mr. George[18]

England now = Mr. Baldwin.[19]

What survived in Ireland after all the shooting was—Tim Healy.[20]

What the hell. I see the passports are now a handier size. Also Spanish visa now $1.50 Austrian $2.00— all others coming down. So youre not living in vain.

Hadley sends her love.

yrs.

Hem.

Yale, ALS; postmark: PARIS / GARE D'AUSTERLITZ, 17 / AVRIL / 8[30] / 26

EH addressed the envelope to "The Honorable / Ezra Pound K.C.M.G. / Via Marsala, 12 / Rapallo / Italie." KCMG signifies the rank of Knight Commander of the Order of St. Michael and St. George, the second highest class of the British chivalric order, instituted in 1818 and awarded for extraordinary nonmilitary service in a foreign country.

1 In a letter to EH that remains unlocated, Pound apparently had referred to a piece in the Milan newspaper *Corriere della Sera*. Carlo Linati's review of *IOT*, "Racconti in verde e sole" (which loosely translates as "Outdoor Stories") appeared in its 4 March 1926 issue.

2 Bird was in Norway as a correspondent for the *New York Times* covering the polar expedition led by Richard E. Byrd (1888–1957) and based in Spitzbergen. On 9 May 1926, Byrd and Floyd Bennett (1890–1928) succeeded in flying over the Pole, as Bill Bird reported in his front page story headlined "BYRD FLIES TO NORTH POLE AND BACK; ROUND TRIP FROM KINGS BAY IN 15 HRS. 51 MIN.; CIRCLES TOP OF THE WORLD SEVERAL TIMES" under the byline William Bird (*New York Times*, 10 May 1926, 1).

3 Boni & Liveright would publish *Personae: The Collected Poems of Ezra Pound* on 22 December 1926.

4 Probably American painter Henry Strater (1896–1987), whom EH had known in Paris and Rapallo in 1922–1923 and who had returned to the United States with his family in March 1924. In his letter to Strater of [24 July 1926], EH refers to their having seen each other in New York.

5 *Fertig*: done, finished (German).

6 Carlo Linati was a regular columnist for *Corriere della Sera*, which on 10 July 1925 had published his article "Fuorusciti" ("Exiles"), praising the bold and playful innovations of American expatriate writers and citing as an example EH's poem "They All Made Peace— What Is Peace?" Linati's translation of EH's "Soldier's Home" had appeared as "Il ritorno del soldato" in the Milan magazine *Il Convegno: Rivista di Letteratura e di Arte* (30 June– 30 July 1925). In his introduction to the story, Linati mistakenly claimed that EH had been an aviator in Italy during WWI. In *SAR*, EH made Jake Barnes an aviator "flying on a joke front like the Italian" (Chapter 4).

7 EH compares Ford Madox Ford's tetralogy *Parade's End* (1924–1928) to the seven-novel sequence *À la recherche du temps perdu* (1913–1927) by Marcel Proust (1871–1922), translated as *Remembrance of Things Past* (1922–1931) by Charles Kenneth Scott Moncrieff (1889–1930).

8 Violet Hunt (1862–1942), English novelist and short-story writer. Her memoir *The Flurried Years* (London: Hurst & Blackett, 1926; published as *I Have This to Say: The Story of My Flurried Years* [New York: Boni & Liveright, 1926]) is a partial account of her relationship with Ford Madox Ford, with whom she lived from 1909 to 1918. Ford's wife, Elsie Martindale Hueffer (1876–1949), whom he had married in 1894, was a devout Roman Catholic and would not grant a divorce. The Boni & Liveright edition of Hunt's memoirs ran to 306 pages and was priced at $3.50.

9 French boxer Edouard Mascart (1902–1976) was the European featherweight champion at the time of his 20 April 1926 bout with English boxer Bugler Harry Lake (1902–1970) at the Cirque de Paris. Mascart knocked out Lake in the sixth round.

10 Australian artist Esther Gwendolyn (Stella) Bowen (1893–1947) met Ford Madox Ford in 1917, and the couple lived together from 1919 to 1928. They had one daughter, Esther Julia (Julie) Madox Ford (1920–1985).

11 EH refers to Ford's *A Man Could Stand Up* (London: Duckworth, 1926; New York: A. and C. Boni, 1926) and its protagonist Christopher Tietjens. The novel is the third volume of Ford's WWI tetralogy *Parade's End*.

12 EH's jab at Wescott's lack of war experience; born in 1901, Wescott was a student at the University of Chicago between 1917 and 1919.

13 *La Chartreuse de Parme* (1839) by French novelist Stendhal (né Marie-Henri Beyle, 1783– 1842); in 1925 Boni & Liveright published a translation by Charles Kenneth Scott Moncrieff titled *The Charterhouse of Parma*. EH had borrowed the new two-volume translation from Sylvia Beach's bookstore in December 1925 (Michael S. Reynolds, *Hemingway's First War: The Making of* A Farewell to Arms [Princeton, New Jersey: Princeton University Press, 1976], 154–55). In his introduction to *Men At War* (1942), EH would write, "The best account of actual human beings behaving during a world shaking event is Stendhal's picture of young Fabrizio at the battle of Waterloo," calling it "more like war and less like the nonsense written about it than any other writing could possibly be." Although Stendhal served with Napoleon and saw some of history's greatest battles, "all he ever wrote about war," according to EH, was that one long passage, which he included in his war anthology (xx).

14 Dorothy Shakespear Pound (1886–1973), an English artist who married Ezra Pound in April 1914. She was the daughter of Henry Hope Shakespear (1849–1923), a solicitor and a landscape painter, and of novelist Olivia Shakespear (1863–1938). Dorothy's work appeared in the Vorticist magazine *Blast* no. 2 (1915), and she illustrated works and designed book covers for various modernist writers.

15 Benito Mussolini (1883–1945) founded the Italian Fascist Party in 1919, became prime minister in 1922, and ruled Italy until 1943. Although Pound was an admirer of Mussolini, EH had expressed scorn for him as early as 1922 and 1923 in pieces for the *Toronto Star*,

including "Mussolini, Europe's Prize Bluffer, More Like Bottomley Than Napoleon" (*Toronto Daily Star*, 27 January 1923; *DLT*, 253–56).

16 Calvin Coolidge (1872–1933), thirtieth president of the United States (1923–1929), a taciturn Republican with a public image of frugality and honesty, whose conservative values enjoyed popularity during the prosperous 1920s. Isolationist in foreign policy, he believed in small government and a laissez-faire policy toward business, vetoing aid to farmers.

17 William Edgar Borah (1865–1940), flamboyant attorney and United States senator from Idaho (1907–1940), known for his isolationist foreign policies. He opposed the ratification of the Treaty of Versailles and U.S. membership in the League of Nations. Pound was a native of Hailey, Idaho.

18 Alfred Charles William Harmsworth, Viscount Northcliffe (1865–1922), journalist and newspaper magnate who served as director of British propaganda during WWI and wielded strong political influence as owner of more than one hundred newspapers and periodicals. During and after WWI, Northcliffe used the London *Times* to attack the policies of David Lloyd George (1863–1945), the British prime minister from 1916 to 1922.

19 Stanley Baldwin (1867–1947), Conservative Party leader who served three terms as prime minister of Great Britain (1923–1924, 1924–1929, and 1935–1937).

20 Timothy Michael Healy (1855–1931), Irish Nationalist leader and first governor-general of the Irish Free State, 1922–1928.

To Maxwell Perkins, 24 April 1926

113 Rue Notre Dame des Champs

Paris VI

April 24, 1926.

Dear Mr. Perkins:—

I am mailing you today The Sun Also Rises. It will probably be much better for you to have it so that you can go ahead on it and I can do additional working over in the proofs.[1] There are plenty of small mistakes for the person who reads it in Mss. to catch before it goes to the printer— misspelled words, punctuation etc. I want the Mss. back with the proofs.

The three quotations in the front I'd like to see set up. May cut out the last one.[2]

Jonathan Cape is publishing In Our Time. Setting it up and printing it themselves. Mr. Liveright refused, Curtis Brown write me, to sell them sheets some months ago. I have the contract today. They get the British Empire rights not including Canada and pay me 10% royalty. 25 pounds advance.[3]

Curtis Brown gave them the first refusal of both Torrents and The Sun A.R. Advances and terms for them to be arranged when and if published. This seemed just to me as they are setting up the In Our Time. Torrents would probably be useless in England and it would not seem fair for them to miss a chance at the novel.[4] I believe you said I had the British and foreign rights. I dont think Jonathan Cape is the best publishing house in England but they're not the worst.

I had a long letter from Scott [Fitzgerald] a few days ago saying he'd started his book, was seeing no one, not drinking and working hard. He said he'd gotten $15,000 for some movie rights and this, with other things, would probably see them through until Christmas. I felt very touched by his precarious financial situation and told him that if he was worried about money I would write you to send all my royalties direct to him at the Villa Paquita, Juan les Pins. A.M.

Am working on a couple of stories. La Navire D'Argent published a 15,000 word story of mine translated a couple of months ago and various frenchmen got very excited and made extravagant statements about it so now they all want them and I have a fine french market (in francs)[5] Am supposed to be the re-incarnation of Prosper Merimee whom I've never read but always supposed was pretty bad.[6] The good thing about being a popular French writer, like Mr. Merimee and myself, rather than an imported great American Name is that, I believe, the Great Names have to pay the translator which seems to me, if the law of supply and demand still operates, commercially unsound.

I was awfully sorry to be disappointed in Capt. Thomason's book [*Fix Bayonets*]. There were too many bayonets in it somehow. If you are writing a book that isnt romantic and has that as one of its greatest assets it is a shame to get awfully romantic about bayonets. The bayonet is a fine and romantic thing but the very fact of its being attached to a rifle which is such a fine and practical thing automatically restricts its use in the hands of any practical man also presumably armed with grenades to purely ornamental killing—with which I am not in sympathy. Most of it is fine and the writing is often splendid. There was just that little journalistic something that was disappointing. When you tell so much of the truth you cant afford to have anything not true because it spoils the taste. A little Arthur Guy Empey is awfully poisonous.[7] It makes you realize though what an awfully good book Through The Wheat was. I hear there is a good new war book called Toward The Flame. Have you read it? After I read War and Peace I decided there wasnt any need to write a war book and I'm still sticking to that.[8]

This is a long drooling letter but if it arrives at the same time as the Sun A.R. (the pig that you bought in a poke) you'll probably be so busy reading the pig that whatever this letter says will not be very important—nor is it.

Yours very truly

Ernest Hemingway.

PUL, ALS

1 In his letter of 12 April 1926, Perkins told EH that Scribner's had "prepared a cover, a wrap and our men will go out on the first of May with dummies. In fact, the book will be complete except for the text. That I shall await with great eagerness" (PUL).
2 EH is referring to the epigraphs for *SAR*. The first, "You are all a lost generation," he attributed to "Gertrude Stein in conversation." The second epigraph is quoted from Ecclesiastes (1:2, 4– 7), beginning "Vanity of vanities, saith the Preacher, vanity of vanities; all is vanity" and including the verse from which EH derived the title: "One generation passeth away, and another generation cometh; but the earth abideth forever . . . The sun also ariseth, and the sun goeth down, and hasteth to the place where he arose." A third epigraph, "For in much wisdom is much grief and he that increaseth knowledge increaseth sorrow" (Ecclesiastes 1:18), would be cut before publication (Frederic J. Svoboda, *Hemingway and "The Sun Also Rises": The Crafting of a Style* [Lawrence: University Press of Kansas, 1983], 108).
3 The Cape contract for *IOT* was dated 20 April 1926 (Jonathan Cape Archive, University of Reading).
4 In a letter of 31 August 1926, L. E. Pollinger of Curtis Brown would inform EH that Jonathan Cape rejected *TOS* because he thought that "the authors whom Hemingway parodies" in the book were not well enough known in England (JFK). However, EH would sign Cape's contract for *SAR*, dated 10 December 1926, and Cape would publish the British edition of the novel, titled *Fiesta*, on 9 June 1927.
5 "The Undefeated" had been published as "L'invincible" in the March 1926 issue of the magazine *Navire d'Argent* (*Silver Ship*), edited in Paris by Adrienne Monnier (1892–1955), owner of the bookshop La Maison des Amis des Livres (The House of Friends of Books) on the rue de l'Odeon. Monnier was a close friend and, until 1937, longtime domestic partner of Sylvia Beach (1887–1962), whose own English-language bookshop, Shakespeare and Company, was across the street from Monnier's. EH's story was translated into French by Georges Duplaix (1895–1985), best known for his children's books.
6 Prosper Mérimée (1803–1870), French author best known for his novella *Carmen* (1845– 1846), which served as the basis for Georges Bizet's opera of the same title, first performed in Paris in 1875.
7 Arthur Guy Empey (1883–1963), American author of *Over the Top: By an American Soldier Who Went* (1917), a bestselling autobiography of his experiences with the British Army during WWI. A charismatic personality, Empey joined celebrities at the 1917–1919 Liberty

bond rallies organized by the U.S. Army and found a place for himself in Hollywood, where he assisted with the production of a 1918 film version of his book. During the 1920s he set up a small film production company and wrote war stories for pulp magazines.
8 The WWI novel *Through the Wheat* (New York: Scribner's, 1923) by American author Thomas Boyd (1898-1935). *Toward the Flame* (New York: Doran, 1926), a war memoir by American author Hervey Allen (1889-1949).

To Ezra Pound, [c. 2 May 1926]

Dear Duce—[1]

2,000 what you ask. Well I don't know. Though I believe it was to be 2000 dollars to be given away. It always seemed to me a beautiful idea. Bill's gone to Spitzbergen to be with the polar flyers and will be gone for months. If you look at Spitzbergen on the map you'll be impressed. I doubt if Bill [Bird] will be back before July—may be end of June.

When actually do you plan to hit Paris?

Jo Nathan Cape is bringing out In Our Time in England. Not caring about England nor what the Englisch think, if they think, and I dont think it's ever been proved that they think, that great news has not excited me to such an extent that I've been forced to toss myself off among the coats—but I held out for 25 pounds and got it. It is an advantage, financially, not to care whether your stuff is published or not. I believe that the reason most authors can be so badly[2] treated is because they have this reprehensible desire to see their stuff published . . .. thinking it makes any difference either way wherther it is published or not. Except of course the question of eating and by now no man ought to be such a bloody damn fool as to expect to be able to live off of any sort of writing.

See by the paper Damrosch is going to do George.[3] Hope Geirge will be able to restrain himself from giving interviews telling how he taught Damrosch to conduct, if any, until after it comes off. Thus increasing the chances of it coming off.

BIG WHITMAN exhibit going on now.[4] Believe you like WHITMAN. Me, I've never been able to read Whitman. I'm sorry as hell not to be here when you come up. It's rained steadily and intermiddenly for a month.

Walsh don't write to me anymore. No word from Bill. I owe everybody else letters.

Chink was in town, and providentially for Ford, gave Ford the technical what it is that happens which is the crucial part of the final spasm of Teijens. The situation that drove teijens crazy. The noble teij takes over command of a battalion and finds there has been absolutely no provision made for communication with the battalions on either flank——this is a symbol of how badly everything was run in the war except teijens—and teijens ORGANIZES LIASON With the two battalions on either flank. The NORTH HEREFORDS and WEST HOLSTEINS. A feat never before attempted in the entire military history of the B.A. [British Army] But it drives Teijens mad. You've got to admit it is a tragic story. It opens on armistice day and Teijens, noble teijens, is mad. Then there is flash back to in front of Cambrai where teijens some months before is driven mad. It will rock the country. We got Ford to cut out a few things like the germans waiting to attack on acct the wind was not right for their clouds of gas——not used since 1915——and a few other bits of the real authentic stuff which we pursuaded the Good Soldier to eliminate.[5] The action takes place in 1918 during the Grt. British Retreat—which—a fact only now revealed would have been a colosal disaster but for teijens who stopped the entire thing—but, of course, at the cost of his reason. But still what's a man's reason vs. the chanell ports.

Well I'd better mail this. Answering yrs. re the maternity of Herbert Clarke, printer, wd say that I believe, or have heard, that his mother and Mr. Walsh's mother were sisters.[6]

Bill's secr[e]tary is Mrs. Rosen.

What Ford wanted from Chink was just what would a man [d]o to organize liaison or however you spell the missued but once respectable word. Write. Love to Dorothy.

HEM

Yale, AL/TL with typewritten signature

1 *Il Duce*: the Leader (Italian), the title commonly applied to Mussolini.
2 The letter is handwritten to this point; the remainder, which begins on a new page, is typewritten.

3 George Antheil and German-American conductor Walter Damrosch (1862–1950). At the time of this letter, the young Antheil was studying music in Paris while Damrosch was living in New York. On 30 April 1926, the *New York Times* reported that Damrosch had accepted Antheil's new *Symphonie en fa* (1925–1926) for a November performance by the New York Symphonic Society.

4 Sylvia Beach was holding an exhibition of manuscripts, letters, photographs, and early editions of American poet Walt Whitman (1819–1892), including items from her personal collection. EH had attended the 20 April opening at her Shakespeare and Company bookshop with Chink Dorman-Smith.

5 Dorman-Smith, a British Army career soldier, was advising Ford on the literary depiction of military matters involving the protagonist Tietjens in *A Man Could Stand Up* (1926), which Ford was preparing for publication. EH's reference to two breeds of cattle, Herefords and Holsteins, may allude to a scene in Chapter 4 of *No More Parades* (1925) in which Tietjens, organizing lines of troops, compares the scene to "getting cattle into condition for the slaughterhouse." EH refers to Ford by the title of his 1915 novel, *The Good Soldier*.

6 Clarke's mother, Ann Maria Clarke (née Whiteley, 1845–1919), and Walsh's mother, Sarah Lampson Walsh, were unrelated.

To Isidor Schneider, 4 May 1926

May 4, 1926.
c/o Guaranty Trust Co. of NY
1, Rue des Italiens
Paris—

Dear Isidor:

Thanks so much for the Virgin Spain and for shipping I.OT. to the various Dons.[1] It has rained here every day for 3 weeks and I will be glad to get away to Spain. I have finished a story and sent The Sun Also Rises off to Scribners a couple of weeks ago.[2] The Torrents book will be published the 21st of May. This will be a dull [*text obscured*] that is the way rainy weather [*text obscured*] How are you and Helen? [*text obscured*] [Komro]ff has been here and seems [*text obscured*] terribly that he should have [*text obscured*] weather because Paris needs sunlight more than any other town. [*text obscured*] [readin]g quite a few books but cannot remember what. I will send this but [*text obscured*] I will be discouraged from writing remembering how terribly dull it was last time I tried to write. Please write [*text obscured*] Guaranty Trust Co.

address. [*text obscured*] We go to Madrid to [*text obscured*] Hadley has just said that she knows what Spain will be like—that I will sit around and read newspapers. Maybe that is the way everywhere is like. [*text obscured*] yourself!

Ernest

Please say what you think of the Torrents book.[3]

Parke-Bernet Galleries catalog, New York, 9 November 1966, lot 135 (partially illustrated), ALS

This transcription derives from the auction catalog description and illustration of the letter (portions of which are obscured in the photograph by another letter laid atop it). Portions of the text not visible in the illustration, as well as any text conjectured by the editors, are indicated in square brackets. The catalog description and illustration are reproduced in facsimile in *Hemingway at Auction*, compiled by Matthew J. Bruccoli and C. E. Frazer Clark, Jr. (Detroit: Gale Research Company, 1973), 114–15. Although the letter sold, it remains unlocated. It is not found among EH's other letters to Schneider that were sold at the same auction and are now housed in Special Collections at the Columbia University Libraries.

1 In his 23 March 1926 letter, EH had asked Schneider to send copies of *IOT* to Don Juan Quintana and Don Rafael Hernández Ramírez.
2 The story was probably "An Alpine Idyll," which EH would enclose in his letter to Maxwell Perkins the following day.
3 According to the catalog description, "There are three footnotes, two asking for Schneider's opinion of *The Torrents of Spring* and [William Faulkner's] *Soldiers' Pay*, the other being Hemingway's comment on Capt. Thomason's book about fighting—apparently *Fix Bayonets*." *Soldiers' Pay* (New York: Boni & Liveright, 1926) was the first published novel by Faulkner (1897–1962).

To F. Scott Fitzgerald, 4 May [1926]

May 4.

Dear Scott—

Dont you write any more? How are you going?

I have finished a story—short—and am sending it to Scribners tomorrow. We go to Spain a week from Thursday. Maxwell Perkins writes that Torrents will be out at latest May 21st. I sent them The Sun etc. about 10 or 12 days ago. It's rained here every day for 3 weeks. I feel low as hell. Havent seen Bromfields, Edith Wharton, Comrade Bercovinci [Konrad Bercovici] or any other of the little literary colony for some time. Maybe there will be a literary colony in Madrid.

Dotty Parker, Les Seldes and Seward Collins—you remember, the man who shot Lincoln—all went to Spain and of course hated it.[1]

Murphys arrived yest. and it isn't Dos that's marrying. It's Don [Stewart]. If I said Dos it was a slip of the ink. I'll pour that ink out. Oh Jesus it is such foul weather and I feel too low to write. I wish to hell you had come up with Murphys— I've not had one man to talk to or bull shit with for months. In Spain of course I can't talk at all—am in for 3 mos. of listening and reading the papers.

Write to me. I dont even get letters[.] How are you feeling? Are you really working on your novel? Is it true that you are swiping my big death house scene? Is it true that you have become blind through alcoholic poisoning and had to have your pancreas removed? I have just given 200,000 francs to save the franc.[2] Harold Stearns is giving the same amount.

I am thinking of going out, in a few minutes, and getting very cock eyed drunk.

Love to yr. family,

Yrs.

Ernest

(Christ what a name)

PUL, ALS

1 "Les Seldes" (French for "the Seldes"), referring to Gilbert and Alice Seldes (née Hall, 1899–1954), who were married in 1923. EH facetiously confuses Seward Collins (1899–1952), American publisher of *The Bookman*, with William H. Seward (1801–1872), who served as U.S. secretary of state under Abraham Lincoln (1809–1865) and was himself shot and severely wounded when the president was assassinated. A prominent figure on the New York intellectual and social scene during the 1920s and 1930s, Collins was romantically involved with Dorothy Parker at the time.
2 The value of the franc had been falling due to fears that France would be unable to make payments on its war debt. A "save-the-franc" fund was established, with contributions coming in from around the world. The currency began to stabilize after Raymond Poincaré (1860–1934) became France's prime minister (for the third and last time) on 23 July 1926.

To Maxwell Perkins, 5 May 1926

May 5, 1926

Dear Mr. Perkins:—

The title will be The Sun Also <u>Rises</u>—I see nothing to be gained by using the archaic Ariseth of the King James version. ~~as the title is suggested by the quotation from Ecclesiastes rather than taken exactly.~~

I am enclosing a story ["An Alpine Idyll"] which I hope both you and the magazine will like. I'm glad Proffessor Copeland liked the In Our Time and I'm pleased about Galsworthy.[1] La Nouvelle Revue Française are going to publish 50 Grand in translation—but I think I wrote you that. Has there ever been any news of it from Reynolds?[2]

It has rained here for 21 days and I'm feeling very low with no excercise and consequent insomnia etc. Have started another story.[3] We go to Spain a week from today.

I hope you like this story. <u>Corriere della Sera</u> of Milano—which is the best and the biggest paper in Italy—has published a 2 column review of In Our Time.[4] I would send it to you—and will if you like—but have been keeping it to impress the wop bartender at the Bar Torino which is located just under the place we live in at Madrid.[5]

Thanks very much for the check for 600 dollars.

With best regards
Ernest Hemingway

PUL, ALS

1 Perkins reported in his letter to EH of 12 April 1926 that he had received "enthusiastic comments" from people to whom he had sent copies of *IOT*, including Charles Townsend Copeland (1860–1952), a professor at Harvard. English novelist John Galsworthy (1867–1933) "also was impressed," Perkins wrote, "although Scott [Fitzgerald] would regard that as far from a compliment" (PUL). Galsworthy would be awarded the Nobel Prize in Literature in 1932.
2 About six weeks had passed since Perkins gave "Fifty Grand" to literary agent Paul Reynolds for placement.
3 Possibly "The Killers," which EH worked on and may have completed in Madrid later that month. (For a detailed account of that story's composition history, see Smith, 138–39).
4 *Corriere della Sera* featured Linati's review of *IOT* on 4 March 1926.
5 EH usually stayed at the Pensión Aguilar at 37, Carrera de San Jerónimo, an inexpensive pension popular with bullfighters, near the Puerta del Sol in Madrid (Mandel *HDIA*,

53–54). The Bar Torino may have been part of the Buffet Italiano, a restaurant listed in a 1929 German Baedeker guide at the same address as the Pensión Aguilar (*Spanien und Portugal: Handbuch Für Reisende*, 5th edn. [Leipzig: Karl Baedeker, 1929], 55).

To Robert McAlmon, 13 May 1926

May 13. 1926

Dear Mac—

I'm enclosing the Callaghan Ms. You spoke of it one time at the Select. You'll know what you think of it when you read it.[1]

I read it 4 months ago and find I still remember it and that parts of it seem very actual. It seems as though the kid were working along the real line and naturally, in Canada, with anything but encouragement. Also I think that with the defects he's got a hell of a lot of stuff. [*EH notation in left margin*: I think the picture of the town and of the people and the petering out of everything is swell. The mannerisms don[t] matter.]

If you dont want to publish it will you send it to him with a letter at

Morley Callaghan

    35 Woolfrey Ave.

    Toronto

    Canada.

He's probably never read Dorothy Richardson so he doesnt know she wrote a book called Backwater—so he should be glad to change the title.[2]

He seems to me like a kid that is worth doing something about—if you like it. I'd be glad to go 50–50 with you on the cost of publishing it because I think once he gets published it will clear things up and he can go on and not worry about this stuff. I know thats the way it made me feel.

How the hell are you? I'm going to Madrid tonight.[3] Hadley's coming down in 10 days. Write me care

    Thos. Cook and Sons.

    Madrid.

You remember how gentil they are.[4]

Yours always,

Hem.

Big h[ors]eshit about you and George and me in this Mos Town and Country.[5]

Marks, ALS

1 The manuscript of Morley Callaghan's first novel, then called "Backwater." Le Select, along with Le Dôme and La Rotonde, is one of the cafés on the boulevard du Montparnasse mentioned by name in *SAR*.
2 McAlmon replied on 16 May (JFK) that his Contact Editions would publish Callaghan's novel only if the author could not find an American commercial publisher first. In 1928 Scribner's would publish the book as *Strange Fugitive*, the title apparently changed to avoid confusion with *Backwater* (London: Duckworth, 1916; New York: Knopf, 1917) by English novelist Dorothy Richardson (1873–1957).
3 EH's daily log of his May 1926 stay in Madrid indicates that he left Paris on the night train at 8:40 p.m. on 13 May and arrived in Madrid at 10:37 p.m. the next day (JFK).
4 The Thomas Cook travel agency, specializing in guided group travel since the mid-nineteenth century, was founded by Thomas Cook (1808–1892), who first organized rail excursions in England in 1841. EH may be punning on the French word "gentil" (kind, nice) and the English word "genteel."
5 *Town and Country* magazine featured a monthly column about life in Paris, "Letters of Elizabeth," by American painter, writer, and interior designer Elizabeth Eyre de Lanux (1894–1996). In a piece on Sylvia Beach's bookshop in the 1 May 1926 issue, she remarked that the group of McAlmon, George Antheil, and EH "is producing some of the best thinking and writing in English to-day" (58). Of EH she wrote, "His sentences are muscular contractions; there is no waste flesh about his thinking. He thinks quick and sharp and his words are as polished and compact as bullets" (114).

To F. Scott Fitzgerald, [c. 15 May 1926]

Dear Scott:

I was glad to hear from you and glad to note that you were on the "Waggon". Sorry my letter was snooty—I didnt mean it that way[.] You were saying how little you valued critical articles unless they were favourable for practical purposes and I was just agreeing. Thats was all the services rendered was about.[1] Youll be seeing Hadley today.[2] Wish the hell I were[.] Madrid is fine and cold and dry with a very high sky and lots of ~~fine~~ dust blowing down your nose—or up my nose. Corrida called off for today by the veterinaries who wouldn't pass the bulls (sic) because they were too small and sick. I was out when they turned them down and it was a collection of animals Harold Stearns could have killed while drunk with a jack knife.

Didnt Ford say I was the great writer of English?[3] Tomorrow they have a lad from Seville with a dose of clapp—a local boy (who was admired by Gilbert Seldes if that means anything to you) and one of the lousiest bull fighters on Earth—named Fortuna—and I might just as easily—a damn sight easier be seeing you at Juan les Pins.[4] I missed the big fight on the 13th—of course—todays called off—tomorrow's a lot of cruts and Monday maybe a good one.

Mencken is noble all right.[5] I wish to hell I had your letter to answer. Herschel Brickel is in Paris. He read Torrents and was crazy about it. If that means anything. He's a nice guy personally anyway.[6] Seldes is certainly nothing about Seldes. We met [*EH drew arrow to* "Seldes" *in previous line*] and a lot of other 2nd class passengers at Nöel Murphys where we were invited by 2 pneumatiques 2 telegrams and a personal call.[7] I hadnt seen so many 2nd class passengers since I crossed on the Mauretania.

I dont want to look up my Spanish friends because then Ill have to be talking Spanish, if I can talk Spanish, and going around and I'd like to work. Yeah you were right about generalities about Ring [Lardner]. All such are the bunk. You were wrong about Paul Nelson—way way wrong— I was referring to a very special exciting and dramatic story that you dont know. No scandal. Neither, however, was it the simple minded uneducated young writer having the wool pulled over his eyes by the smooth Irish chameleon as you suggested. That isnt snooty. Why the hell should we have to pull our punches writing?

Im glad as hell that your book is going and that it is so swell. That's not kidding. I'll be glad to hear from Max Perkins what they think of Sun etc. It is so obviously <u>not</u> a collection of instructive anecdotes and is such a hell of a sad story—and not one at all for a child to read—and the only instruction is how people go to hell— (Doesn't it sound terrible, I can hear you say) that I thought it was rather pleasant to dedicate it to Bumby— If you're right I wont put in the anecdote part—but Ill dedicate it to him for reasons that will be obvious when you read the book and also for another reason.[8] I've a carbon with me and you can read it at Juan les Sapins if there aren't proofs before then.[9]

The 2 bottle men drank <u>port</u> and the best were 3 [*Ditto marks*: bottle men] but I understand the bottles were small.[10]

Did you ever read the Encyclopaedia Brit. on Lawn Tennis in America? There are a hell of a lot more Salmon in Encyclopaedia Brit. than in Lake Superior. Besides it doesnt make any difference because look at Shakespere and the seacoast of Tchecoslovakia etc.[11] Nouvelle Revue Francaise is going to publish 50 Grand as <u>Cinquante Grosse Billetes</u> in July or Aug.[12]

No news here. Write me and I swear to God Ill write a good letter next time. I know this is lousy but I'm lonesome as hell

Best to Zelda. Hadley will greet you all fully.

Always your co-worker for the Clean Books Bill.[13]

Ernest M. Shit.

PUL, ALS

1 In his letter of [16] April 1926, EH had thanked Fitzgerald for "services rendered," referring to Fitzgerald's review of *IOT* in the May 1926 *Bookman*.

2 After EH left for Madrid on 13 May, Hadley traveled to Antibes with Bumby, who had been ill, to visit the Murphys at their Villa America, rather than leaving Bumby in Paris and joining EH in Spain as they originally planned. The Fitzgeralds were staying at Juan-les-Pins, near Antibes.

3 Reference to Ford's endorsement featured on the dust jacket of *IOT*: "The best writer in America at this moment (though for the moment he happens to be in Paris), the most conscientious, the most master of his craft, the most consummate, is Ernest Hemingway."

4 Algabeño (né José García Rodríguez, 1871–1947) from La Algaba, near Seville; Valencia II (né Victoriano Roger, 1898–1936) a native of Madrid; and Fortuna (né Diego Mazquiarán, 1895–1940), Spanish bullfighters. The three were scheduled to perform in Madrid on Sunday, 16 May, but that day's bullfight was canceled because of snow. In Chapter 19 of *DIA*, EH describes Fortuna as a flawed and uninteresting bullfighter.

5 H. L. (Henry Louis) Mencken (1880–1956), editor and columnist for the *Baltimore Sun*, literary editor of the *Smart Set*, and co-founder with George Jean Nathan (1882–1958) of the *American Mercury* in 1924. Mencken gained national renown while covering the July 1925 Scopes Monkey Trial, which focused on the legality of teaching evolution.

6 Herschel Brickell's commentary appeared regularly in such venues as the *New York Herald Tribune*, *New York Times Book Review*, and *Saturday Review of Literature*.

7 Nöel Haskins Murphy (1895–1952), New York debutante and trained singer who had performed with the Washington Square Players. In 1920 she married Frederic Timothy Murphy (1885–1924), Gerald Murphy's brother, and the couple moved to Paris. After Frederic died of health problems resulting from his WWI wounding, Nöel settled in Orgeval, about 20 miles west of Paris, where she entertained friends, who included Gertrude Stein and Alice B. Toklas.

8 In his previous letter to Fitzgerald, dated [16] April 1926, EH had tried out the wording for the *SAR* dedication: "To My Son / John Hadley Nicanor / This Collection of Instructive Anecdotes." The published dedication reads "This Book is for Hadley and for John Hadley Nicanor."

9 *Sapins*: fir trees (French); EH's wordplay on Juan-les-Pins.

10 In the absence of Fitzgerald's incoming letter, EH's reference is uncertain. According to a nineteenth-century history of drinking lore, "The usual allowance for a *moderate* man at dinner seems to have been two bottles of port. Men were known as two-bottle men, three and four-bottle men, and even in some instances *six-bottle* men" (John Bickerdyke, *The Curiosities of Ale and Beer: An Entertaining History* [London: Swan Sonnenschein, 1889; reprinted London: Spring Books, 1965], 292).

11 EH refers to the *Encyclopaedia Britannica*. In *The Great Gatsby*, the young James Gatz was a Lake Superior salmon fisherman. In Shakespeare's *The Winter's Tale*, Act 3 scene 3 is set on the sea coast of Bohemia—in reality, a landlocked area.

12 The story would appear as "Cinquante mille dollars" (literally, "Fifty thousand dollars") in the 1 August 1927 *Nouvelle Revue Française*.

13 In 1923 John S. Sumner (1876–1971) of the New York Society for the Suppression of Vice and New York Supreme Court justice John Ford (1862–1941) proposed a Clean Books League bill to the State legislature that would have promoted censorship in books; it was defeated, as were subsequent versions in 1924 and 1925.

To Lewis Galantière, 16 May 1926

May 16, 1926

Dear Lewis—

Brickel brought the proofs back and I left them with Hadley and Virginia Pfeiffer to deliver to you. The book should be out the 21st of May. I hope you'll like it.[1] My novel is called The Sun Also Rises and will be out this fall. I sent the ms. to Scribners about 3 weeks ago. Its been cut to about 90,000 words. I give you this dope because you asked for it the other night.

Madrid is cold as Medicine Hat[2]—but very clear and nice. Snowed a little yest. afternoon. The bull fight was called off yest. because the bulls (sic) were too small and sick. Today there is a rotten card— Tomorrow a good one Marcial Lalanda and Niño de la Palma.[3] I thought De Montherlant's book pretty lousy— The idea being of a little french boy (every effort is made that you realize the little french boy is De Mouthorgan) who goes down and makes bums out of the Spaniards at bull fighting—a thing which as yet has not happened.[4]

It is a very peurile book though there are some very interesting parts. It contains, of course, the usual stage Englishman (heavily damned on acct. of the Livre[5] at 155 francs) and other bids for popularity. Also a great deal of mysticism and horse shit. How would you like it if I would write a bull fight story in which I would be the hero. But of course De Motherland can't see that his having killed calves in an amateur bull fight is of absolutely no importance to bull fighting—about which, presumably, he's writing. Like poor André Maurois has the girl in his Bernard Quesnay arbitrarily talk English—drags it in by the heels—just because he knows English [*EH insertion*: and lots of English] and wrote Col. Bramble—Doc O'Grady etc. Oh well.[6] Have you heard my new poem on the great revival of Catholicism?

The Lord is my shepherd
I shall not want him for long.[7]

——‖——

Write me here to—Thos. Cook and Sons
    Avenida de Conde de Penalver
    Madrid
how you like Torrents
Best to Dorothy—Hadley's coming here via Barcelona—

Yours Always,
Ernest

Columbia, ALS

1 EH may have hoped that Galantière would review *TOS*, but any such review remains unlocated. Virginia Ruth Pfeiffer (1902–1973), called "Jinny" or "Jin," was Pauline's younger sister.
2 Small city in southeastern Alberta, Canada.
3 Marcial Lalanda del Pino (1903–1990), renowned Spanish bullfighter, who appears under his own name in *SAR*. Niño de la Palma (né Cayetano Ordóñez Aguilera, 1904–1961), Spanish bullfighter and prototype for Pedro Romero in *SAR*.
4 *Les Bestiaires: Roman* (Paris: Grasset, 1926), by French novelist Henry de Montherlant (1896–1972), would be translated as *The Bullfighters* (New York: Dial, 1927; London: Jonathan Cape, 1928). EH owned the French edition (Brasch and Sigman, 258).
5 Pound (French), in reference to the British currency.
6 André Maurois (né Émile Salomon Wilhelm Herzog, 1885–1967), French novelist and author of *Bernard Quesnay* (Paris: Gallimard, 1926); *Les Silences du Colonel Bramble* (Paris:

Grasset, 1918), translated as *The Silence of Colonel Bramble* (1919); and *Les Discours du Docteur O'Grady* (Paris: Grasset, 1922).

7 EH's "Neo-Thomist Poem" would be published (with the title misspelled "Nothoemist Poem") in the first issue of Pound's magazine, *The Exile* (Spring 1927). The poem alludes to Psalm 23:1: "The Lord is my shepherd; I shall not want."

To Maxwell Perkins, 20 May 1926

Madrid

May 20, 1926.

Dear Mr. Perkins—

I've heard nothing from you as yet about receiving The Sun A.R. mss. nor about the story I sent.[1] It takes three or four days for mail to come down here from Paris.

The weather has been very cold and the roads in Asturias are blocked by snow. La Voz reports the wolves as making considerable ravages in the livestock. From the quality of the two messes of bulls they have served up here it would seem though the ravages of the wolves had been conclusive.[2]

Enclosed is a letter I wish might be forwarded with a copy of Torrents to Sherwood Anderson care of Boni and Liveright.[3]

I add a list of reviewers that I believe I had not previously sent. [*Along left margin, perpendicular to list of reviewers, in hand other than EH's*: Sent 6/3/26]

David Merrill Anderson[4]

Balt. Eve. Sun.

———

Schuyler Ashley[5]

Kansas City Star

K.C. Mo.

———

Herbert J. Seligman[6]

N.Y. Eve. Sun.

———

Mary Plum[7]
Eve. Post. Chicago Ill.

———

Karsten Roedder[8]
Brooklyn Citizen.

———

Virginia Lyne Tunstall[9]
Pilot-Norfold Va.

———

Warren Tayler[10]
Nashville Tenn. Tennessean.

———

Frances Newman[11]
Journal Atlanta Ga.

———

Toledo, O. Times.[12]

———

Athene Farnsworth[13]
Salt Lake City, Utah, Telegram.

I may have sent these before, but find them copied out on a sheet of paper in my brief case and can't remember having sent them.

With best regards,
Ernest Hemingway.

The Guaranty Trust Co. adress in Paris will always find me.

PUL, TLS

1 Perkins's and EH's letters crossed each other in the mail; in his letter of 18 May 1926, Perkins reported having read the manuscript of *SAR*. He called it "a most extraordinary performance," and concluded, "I could not express my admiration too strongly" (PUL; *TOTTC*, 38). It would be almost another month before Perkins would respond to EH's submission of "An Alpine Idyll," rejecting the story in his letter to EH of 14 June 1926.

2 On 15 May 1926 the front page of Madrid's evening paper *La Voz* featured a report that in the intense cold, wolves had preyed on cattle and horses near the town of Molledo, south of Santander ("El Temporal / En Santander / FRIO. LOBOS" ["The Storm / In Santander / COLD. WOLVES"]).

3 See the following letter to Sherwood Anderson, dated 21 May 1926.

4 David M. Anderson, a book reviewer at the *Baltimore Evening Sun* whose short stories had appeared in 1925 in the *American Mercury* and in *Century Magazine*.

5 Schuyler Ashley (1897–1927), book reviewer for the *Kansas City Star*, had reviewed *IOT* for the newspaper's 12 December 1925 edition. He also likely wrote the unsigned review of *TOS*, titled "Hemingway Burlesques a Certain School of Fiction," that appeared in the *Star* in August 1926 and survives among EH's papers at JFK. Ashley's review of *SAR* would appear in the *Star* on 4 December 1926.

6 Seligmann's name is crossed out in pencil, probably because EH had already mentioned him as a potential reviewer in his letter of 8 April 1926.

7 Mary Plum's review of *IOT*, "A New Chicago Author," appeared in the *Chicago Post* on 27 November 1925. No review of *TOS* by her has been located.

8 Karsten Roedder (1901–1986), Norwegian-born American novelist and regular contributor to various periodicals, would review *TOS* in "The Book Parade" in the 6 June 1926 *Brooklyn Citizen*.

9 Virginia Hunter Lyne Tunstall (1892–1988), an American poet, is not known to have reviewed any EH work for the *Pilot* of Norfolk, Virginia.

10 A review of *IOT* by Warren Taylor (1903–1991), "Chiseled Prose Found in Fiction of Hemingway," appeared in the *Nashville Tennessean* on 10 January 1926. A review of *TOS*, "'Dark Laughter' Is Satirized in 'The Torrents of Spring,'" by Richard Sedgewick West, Jr. (1902–1968) would appear in the newspaper's 25 July 1926 edition.

11 Southern novelist and critic Frances Newman (1883–1928) had reviewed *IOT* for the 24 January 1926 *Atlanta Journal*. She is not known to have reviewed *TOS*.

12 An unsigned review of *SAR* would appear in the *Toledo Times* on 14 November 1926; it only briefly refers to *TOS* as "a tale which broadly satirizes certain recent literary tendencies" (JFK, EH Newspaper Clippings file).

13 Athene Henrietta Farnsworth (1896–1972), a writer for the *Salt Lake City Telegram*, and a high school teacher in Salt Lake City, Utah. No review of EH's work by Farnsworth has been located.

To Sherwood Anderson, 21 May 1926

Madrid

May 21, 1926

Dear Sherwood:

Last fall Dos Passos and Hadley and I ate lunch one noon and I had just loaned Dark Laughter to Dos. He'd read it and we talked about it. After lunch I wemt back to the house and started this Torrents of Spring thing and wrote it right straight through for seven days.

You said I was all wrong on Many Marriages and I told you what I thought about the Story Teller's Story.[1] All I think about the Dark Laughter is in this Torrents book. It is not meant to do any of the things I see the ad writers say it is, and the great race I had in mind in the sub-title was the white race.[2] It is a joke and it isn't meant to be mean, but it is absolutely sincere.

You see I feel that if among ourselves we have to pull our punches, if when a man like yourself who can write very great things writes something that seems to me, (who have never written anything great but am anyway a fellow craftsman) rotten, I ought to tell you so. Because if we have to pull our punches and if [*EH insertion*: when] somebody starts to slop they just go on slopping from then on with nothing but encouragement from their contemporaries—why we'll never produce anything but Great American Writers i.e. apprentice allowance claimed.

I guess this is a lousy snooty letter and it will seem like a lousy snooty book. That wasn't the way I wanted this letter to be—nor the book. Though I didn't care so much about the book because the book isn't personal and the tougher it is the better.

It looks, of course, as though I were lining up on the side of the smart jews like Ben Hecht and those other morning glories and that because you had always been swell to me and helped like the devil on the In our time I felt an irresistable need to push you in the face with true writer's gratitude.[3] But what I would like you to know, and of course that sounds like bragging, is— oh hell I can't say that either.

It goes sort of like this: 1 Because you are my friend I would not want to hurt you. 2 Because you are my friend has nothing to do with writing. 3 Because you are my friend I hurt you more. 4 Outside of personal feelings nothing that's any good can be hurt by satire.

Only, of course, it may not hurt you at all [*EH insertion*: I.E. make you feel badly.]. Because nobody likes to be called on anything—but you don't mind being called, it is simply annoying, it doesn't raise any hell with you, if you know the person doesn't know what they are talking about. So that's the way it may turn out. Anyway I think you'll think the book is funny—and that's what it is intended to be—

It is cold and raining here. I'm writing some stories and waiting for Hadley to come here next week. Where are you living now? We are coming over to the states in the fall and live in Piggott, Ark. It's nice country.[4] I haven't seen Gertrude Stein since last fall. Her Making of Americans is one of the very greatest books I've ever read.[5] We were in Austria all winter and I went a week to New York. I work pretty hard all the time and try and write better and sometimes I do and sometimes I don't.

Please let me hear from you whether you're sore or not. My regular adress is care

The Guaranty Trust Co. of N.Y.

1, Rue des Italiens,

Paris. France.

They'll always forward. We are going to be down in Spain all summer. Best always to you and to your wife from Hadley and me,[6]

Yours Always,

Ernest Hemingway.

Newberry, TLS

EH enclosed this letter with his 20 May 1926 letter to Perkins, asking that Perkins forward it to Anderson along with a copy of *TOS*.

1 Anderson's novel *Many Marriages* (1923) and his autobiographical *A Story Teller's Story* (1924) had been published in New York by B. W. Huebsch (1876–1964). EH had reviewed *A Story Teller's Story* for the March 1925 issue of *Ex Libris*, the magazine of the American Library in Paris, pronouncing it "a wonderful comeback after 'Many Marriages,'" which EH termed a "poor book" (quoted in Matthew Bruccoli, "A Lost Book Review: *A Story-Teller's Story*," *Fitzgerald-Hemingway Annual 1969* [Washington, D.C.: Microcard Editions, 1969], 71–75).
2 *TOS* is subtitled "A Romantic Novel in Honor of the Passing of a Great Race."
3 Ben Hecht (1894–1964), American journalist, novelist, screenwriter, and director, was the son of Russian Jewish immigrants. With American poet and novelist Maxwell Bodenheim (1892–1954), Hecht had founded the short-lived *Chicago Literary Times* (1923–1924) and in 1926 went to work in Hollywood. Although Hecht had strongly supported Anderson's early work, their relationship cooled, and he painted an unflattering portrait of Anderson in his novel *Erik Dorn* (1921). EH's reference to "morning glories," which bloom in the morning and fade later in the day, may be a comment on Hecht's support for Anderson or on Hecht's own literary accomplishments. "Morning glory" is also a colloquial term in horseracing (an interest EH and Anderson shared) for a horse that performs impressively during training but does poorly in races. Anderson had supported EH's early writing, and his praise was prominently featured on the dust jacket of *IOT*. In response to this letter, Anderson wrote, "About the little plug I put in for you with Liveright. I'm sorry I ever mentioned it. I've done the same for men I hated and I like you" ([June 1926], JFK).
4 Pauline Pfeiffer's family lived in Piggott, a town in northeast Arkansas near the Missouri border, having moved there from St. Louis in 1913 shortly after Pauline graduated from high school. Her father first purchased land in the area in 1902 and eventually owned more than 63,000 acres, subdividing it for tenant farmers.

5 EH met American expatriate writer Gertrude Stein (1874–1946) in Paris in 1922, and she became a literary mentor. He persuaded Ford Madox Ford to publish Stein's voluminous novel *The Making of Americans: Being a History of a Family's Progress* serially in the *Transatlantic Review*; seven installments appeared in the magazine before it folded in January 1925. In 1925, McAlmon's Paris press Contact Editions also published the book. EH broke with Stein in 1925.

6 From 1924 to 1932 Anderson was married to his third wife, Elizabeth Prall (1884–1976), who ran the Doubleday bookstore in New York City.

To Clarence Hemingway, 23 May [1926]

Care Thos. Cook' and Sons.
Madrid.
May 23.

Dear Dad:

I was so glad to hear from you about your splendid Smoky mountain trip and all the news.[1] We are planning to come to the States the end of September or beginning of October and will spend the winter in Piggott, Arkansas. That is the plan at present though nothing is definitely settled.

I made a flying trip to N.Y. while you were in Fla. stayed under seven days—just business— I wanted to come out but had to go back on the President Roosevelt and knew it would just complicate matters if we tried to hook up and make everybody feel bad if we didn't so I didn't let anybody know I was in town.

Shifted to Scribner's as publishers and have an excellent contract with them. They are bringing out a satire of mine The Torrents of Spring—this month— It's out now I believe. and a novel The Sun Also Rises—this fall. I am writing stories now that will be published in Scribner's magazine.

Hadley went with Bumby and his nurse to Antibes on the Riviera when I came down here to Madrid and she was to join me here today.[2] But Bumby has developed the whooping cough and she can't leave him so I am joining her on the Riviera in a few days and when Bumby is all right—we will return to Spain until August—which we are spending with some friends at Antibes.

I've been writing on some stories here. I'm glad you and mother had such a good trip and that everybody is all right. We will come to Chicago when we land and stay three or four days with you in Oak Park if you want us to. Hadley wants to see her people in Saint Louis too but I don't want to get stuck in a lot of entrtaining and that sort of stuff so I may stay in Oak Park while she goes down with Bumby and just pick her up for one day of facing the relatives before we shove to Piggott.[3] In Piggott I figure that I will be far enough away from people so they won't come and bother and I can work. I will be working on another novel and some gents when they are working on a novel may be social assetts but I am just about as pleasant to have around as a bear with sore toenails. Pauline Pfeiffer who was down in Austria with us and is going to Spain this summer lives in Piggott when she's in the states and is getting us a house there. I heard that you were upset about my wanting to winter at Windemere so decided not to bother you on that score.[4]

Having been to mass this morning I am now due at the bull fight this afternoon. Wish you were along.

Best love always to you and mother and the kids and Aunt Grace and Grandfather,[5]

Ernie

Thanks so much for the <u>many</u> fine sports magazines.

JFK, TLS with autograph postscript; postmark: MADRID / II, 24 MAY 26–3

1 The letter from Clarence to which EH is apparently responding remains unlocated.
2 Marie Rohrbach, the Hemingways' longtime housekeeper, also cared for Bumby. "A sturdy peasant from Mur-de-Bretagne," as Baker describes her, she lived in Paris with her husband, Henri, whom Bumby called "Ton Ton" (*Life*, 123).
3 Hadley Richardson had been born and raised in St. Louis. In April 1927, after she and EH divorced, she would travel to St. Louis with Bumby to spend time with her sister Florence (Fonnie) Wyman Usher (1889–1967).
4 Windemere was the Hemingway family's cottage on the shore of Walloon Lake, Michigan, where EH had spent part of every summer of his life through 1917.
5 EH's mother, Grace Hall Hemingway (1872–1951). The youngest three of his five siblings were still living in Oak Park: EH's sisters Carol (1911–2002) and Madelaine (1904–1995), who was also known as "Sunny" or "Nunbones," and his brother, Leicester (1915–1982). EH's aunt Grace Adelaide Hemingway (1881–1959), Clarence's younger sister, lived in her parents' Oak Park home and cared for them until their deaths. EH's paternal grandfather, Anson Tyler Hemingway (1844–1926), was a Civil War veteran who fought under Ulysses S. Grant at Vicksburg in 1863. He established a successful Oak Park real estate business and

was active in civic organizations, including the YMCA and the First Congregational Church.

To Rafael Hernández Ramírez, [c. 15 May–27 May 1926]

[*As quoted in catalog description:*]

To Don Rafael Hernandez, hoping that some day it will be translated into Spanish so that, if he has absolutely nothing else to do, he may read it. From his friend Ernest Hemingway.

Sotheby's catalog, Maurice F. Neville Collection Sale (Part One), New York, 13 April 2004, Lot 88, Inscription

According to the catalog description, EH wrote this inscription on the front free endpaper of a first edition copy of *IOT*. In his letter of 23 March 1926, EH had asked Isidor Schneider to send a copy of the book to Hernandez. EH likely inscribed the book during his stay in Madrid, 14–28 May 1926.

To Maxwell Perkins, 5 June 1926

Dear Mr. Perkins—

I was very glad to get your letter and hear that you liked The Sun a.r. Scott claims to too. We are here temporarily quarantined with whooping cough.[1] I went to Madrid and my wife came down here with the child and nurse expecting to join me in a week in Madrid. Himself developed the whoopings on arriving here [*EH insertion*: so after 3 weeks in Madrid I came on here,] and we will be here another three weeks and then take up our Spanish trip.

As to addresses

Care Guaranty Trust Co. of N.Y.

1, Rue des Italiens

Paris.

is the best permanent address. I will keep them informed by wire of my address in Spain and they have an excellent mail forwarding service.

Between July 6 and July 13—inclusive—I will be at the Hotel Quintana
    Pamplona
      (Navarra)
        SPAIN   if you should want to reach me by cable.

It would be better not to try and hit that address with mail.

That is the only address I am sure of but will keep the Guaranty Trust exactly informed. They will re-wire all cables and re-forward letters with no delay.

I believe that, in the proofs, I will start the book at what is now page 16 in the Mss. There is nothing in those first sixteen pages that does not come out, or is explained, or re-stated in the rest of the book—or is unnecessary to state. I think it will move much faster from the start that way. Scott agrees with me. He suggested various things in it to cut out—in those first chapters—which I have never liked—but I think it is better to just lop that off and he agrees.[2] He will probably write you what he thinks about it—the book in general. He said he was very excited by it.

As for the Henry James thing— I haven't the second part of the Ms. here—it is over at Scott's—so I can't recall the wording. But I believe that it is a reference to some accident that is generally known to have happened to Henry James in his youth.[3] To me Henry James is as historical a name as Byron, Keats, or any other great writer about whose life, personal and literary, books have been written.[4] I do not believe that the reference is sneering, or if it is, it is not the writer who is sneering as the writer does not appear in this book. Henry James is dead and left no descendants to be hurt, nor any wife, and therefore I feel that he is as dead as he will ever be. ~~The survival of persons who are a part~~ I wish I had the ms. here to see exactly what it said. If Henry James never had an accident of that sort I should think it would be libelous to say he had no matter how long he were dead. But if he did I do not see how it can affect him—now he is dead. As I recall Gorton and Barnes are talking humourously around the subject of Barnes' mutilation and to them Henry James is not a man to be insulted or protected from insult but simply an historical example. I remember there was something about an airplane and a bicycle—but that had nothing to do with James and was simply a non-sequitor. Scott said he saw nothing off-color about it.

Until the proofs come I do not want to think about the book as I am trying to write some stories and I want to see the proofs, when they come, from as new and removed a viewpoint as possible.

Up till now I have heard nothing about a story called—An Alpine Idyll—that I mailed to you sometime the first week in May.[5] Did you ever receive it? I have another copy which I will send if you did not. In Madrid I wrote three stories ranging from 1400 to 3,000 words.[6] I haven't had them re-typed and sent on as I was waiting word about The Alpine Idyll.

What is the news about Torrents? Have any copies been mailed to me as yet?

Could you send me a check for $200. in a registered letter to the Guaranty Trust Co. address?[7] It was very pleasant to get your letter and learn that you liked the book.

Yours very sincerely,
Ernest Hemingway.
Villa Paquita
Juan les Pins
(A.M)
June 5, 1926

PUL, TLS

1 EH is responding to Perkins's letter of 18 May 1926, in which Perkins expressed his admiration for *SAR* (PUL; *TOTTC*, 38). When Bumby was diagnosed with whooping cough and put under quarantine, the Fitzgeralds offered Hadley the use of the Villa Paquita, which they had leased for the summer but which was vacant after they moved to the larger Villa St. Louis nearby.

2 Soon after EH's arrival in Antibes, he and Fitzgerald discussed the version of *SAR* that EH had sent to Perkins. The next day, Fitzgerald wrote EH a ten-page letter objecting to the "elephantine facetiousness" of the opening section and suggesting revisions (JFK; Bruccoli *Fitz–Hem*, 64–68).

3 With regard to the implication in Chapter 12 of *SAR* that American writer Henry James (1843–1916) had been made impotent by an accident while riding a horse or a bicycle, Perkins had written to EH, "I swear I do not see how that can be printed" (18 May 1926, PUL; *TOTTC*, 38).

4 George Gordon, Lord Byron (1788–1824), English Romantic poet. On 20 July 1926, Perkins would reply that many people he knew, including four friends of Henry James who worked at Scribner's, would not share EH's perspective (PUL).
5 On 14 June 1926, Perkins would reject the story "An Alpine Idyll" as unsuitable for *Scribner's Magazine*. The magazine's editor, Robert Bridges (1858–1941), regarded the story as "too terrible, like certain stories by Chekov [sic] and Gorky" (PUL). Set in the Montafon valley near Schruns, the story describes a peasant who regularly hangs his lantern from the jaw of his wife's frozen corpse, which he has propped up in a wood shed until she can be buried after the spring thaw.
6 According to EH's log of his Madrid visit, he wrote "The Killers," "Today Is Friday," and "Ten Indians" on 20 May and "rewrote Indian story" on 21 May 1926 (JFK). However, as Baker notes, "EH had a start on them before going to Spain" (*SL*, 209); manuscript evidence indicates that only "Today Is Friday" was written entirely on that day (Smith, 154).
7 EH is requesting part of the $1,500 advance his contract provided for *TOS* and *SAR*. On 16 June 1926, Perkins would report that he had sent the check (PUL).

To Pierre Chautard, [c. 8 June 1926]

Monsieur:

I regret that any such incidents as you describe should have been produced. I am writing today, on your demand, asking the persons occupying the apartment at 113 Rue Notre Dame des Champs to vacate it by the 20th of June.

~~For several months, at your and your wife's suggestion, I have paid you~~

These persons were originally invited to occupy the apartment because your wife stated before witnesses, that she did not wish the apartment to be left vacant because of her fears and requested us to find tenants whenever we left the apartment vacant for a long period.[1]

For several months I have at your wife's and your own suggestion paid the rent of the apartment at 113 Rue Notre Dame des Champs in dollars. On May 8th I gave to you and you accepted as rent for the period May 8-June 8 a sum in dollars equal at the Cours du Jour to 750 francs. My wife, judging from this, the loyer having been augmented before with no annotation made on the agreement of loyer, informed Mlle Lincoln that the rent was 750 francs a month. You later remitted 100 francs of this loyer to me— insisting—against my wishes on doing this—as your <u>belle mere</u> were to occupy a part of the apartment. This occurred on the day I left for Spain. I did not see Mlle Lincoln and had no opportunity to inform her of this reduction. As soon as I learned, on returning to France, that my wife had no opportunity of informing her of this reduction I at once wrote and informed her myself.

The last time I found a [tenant ?] for the apartment, on your wife's ~~suggestion~~ demand that the apartment not be left vacant, I informed them that the rent was 650 francs altho you raised the rent to 700 francs on their entry—which rent I paid three months in advance in dollars.

Considering these facts, Monsieur, I believe you will agree that there has been no commerce of sou louage.[2]

Etc. etc.

Ernest Hemingway.

JFK, ALDS

This draft is accompanied at JFK by a four-page French translation in Hadley's hand, signed by EH with the notation in his hand "Mailed Recommandé June 8."

1 EH is replying to a letter from his landlord dated 4 June 1926 and written in French (JFK). During their absence, EH and Hadley had sublet their Paris apartment to a "Miss Lincoln." In his letter Chautard complained that Miss Lincoln's cleaning woman had caused an unpleasant scene one day when she found the apartment door locked. After the cleaning woman and her husband insulted and threatened Chautard and his wife, Chautard had pressed charges with the police. When Chautard insisted that Miss Lincoln fire the cleaning woman or move out, Miss Lincoln refused, asserting she had paid rent through 20 June and that EH had recommended the servant. Chautard threatened immediate eviction if EH did not ensure that Miss Lincoln would vacate the premises by 20 June. Chautard pointed out that EH had made a profit by charging Miss Lincoln more than he had paid to the Chautards for the month and that it was illegal to sublet without authorization from the Prefecture of the Seine.
2 *Cours du Jour*: daily exchange rate; *loyer*: rent; *belle-mère*: mother-in-law; *sous-louer*: to sublet (French).

To Isidor Schneider, 29 June [1926]

Juan les Pins
(A.M.)
France June 29

Dear Isidor:

Your letter was fine and it was grand of you to send the clippings. They seem pretty good on the whole.[1] I am sorry you did not like the book but maybe you will like The Sun etc. and if you don't like that maybe you will like the next one.[2] One very fine thing about life is that you don't have to like books when you don't like them.

I was in Spain for two or three weeks waiting around for Hadley to who or whom I'd sent our passport and who couldn't come and meet me because Bumby had the whooping cough. So finally I came down here and we've been swimming all the time and just eating and going on very long bike rides and sleeping every night at nine o clock. On the fourth of July we finally get off again for Pamplona which starts on the seventh. Then staying in Spain through July and August.

About not liking Torrents—it hasn't anything to do with anything like the In Our Time stories and I just wrote it for fun—and I wrote it in not ten days but exactly six days— I meant it for a satire and not a parody and some people it will be funny to and some people it won't. In Madrid I wrote three stories and I've worked them over and will work on them some more once we leave here. I read some of Waldo Frank's book—all of the dreadful chapter about the bull fight—and then I loaned it to Herschel Brickel.[3] We met him and his wife in Paris and they were very nice. I haven't read anything new by anyone[.] In Madrid I read Tom Jones and thought it was very fine but that there was too much of it and I read Hudson's Far Away and Long Ago and loved it very much.[4] The rest of the time I read Spanish, which as I do not read it well gives me a great deal of pleasure in reading about almost anything and never makes me angry with bad writing.

We saw Komroff quite a lot in Paris. He is very nice. So was Brickell. I didn't see anybody else. ~~Have been going through the usual spring rutting season.~~ Hudson writes the best of anyone, I think. I like Borrow very much though he does have the mind of a Y.M.C.A. gym instructor.[5]

Bycycle riding is very exciting to me. The roads are fine here, very smooth, and run alongside the sea and we ride 50 and sixty miles a day and stop at little towns for lunch and swim on the beaches when it is hot. It is very grand except when the wind is too strong. I didn't think I coukd do it with my leg but it works well. Only when there is a wind I can hadly move against it. Although Hadley, being much smaller, cuts through it better. We are both black as niggers and I have never been so healthy. Hadley is as thin and as fine as before we were ever married and had children—i.e. a child—one—male. But it will be very exciting to go back into Spain again where no one takes any excercise and where everyone stays up all night. Scribners say they are starting to get proof on The Sun Also Rises but won't send it to me until they have about half the book. We are coming home about the middle of September but will land probably in Texas—Galveston I think—and go up, to Piggott from there. Some time in the winter we'll come to N.Y. for a week. I won't have enough money to stop off going. Scribners seemed to like The Sun etc. but writing to Scott Fitzgerald (This confidential to you) they said that altho very enthusiastic it was a mixed pleasure on acct. of The Sun etc. being almost unpublishable.[6] So maybe it will be good after all. While we've been here I've forgotten all about it and all about writing and all about everything and just gotten healthier and healthier and hard as rocks and maybe when I start to write again the juice I have ahead now will last me awhile. I was tired as hell when we left Paris. It rained for 45 days.

This is a rotten letter and your letter was very good. I know the long poem will be good.[7] Don't worry about it. Worrying and feeling low are just luxuries that when we allow ourselves they make things easier for a little and then take it out. later. Never worry about anything. I give you this splendid advice because I always worry all the time about everything. So I know it must be good advice.

Write me to Thos Cook and Sons,
   Madrid,
   Spain.
We?ll be in Spain till along in August.
   My best to Helen. Please send the pictures.[8]

Ernest

Columbia, TLS

On the verso of this letter's second page is a list, likely in Schneider's hand, of forty-two titles, including several of the Liveright publications that EH would request in his letter to Schneider of [30 September 1926] and acknowledge receiving in his letter of [14 February 1927]. The list also includes works EH would request in a letter of 18 [April 1927], suggesting that Schneider assembled this list over time, adding to it and checking off what had been sent.

1   In his letter of [11 June 1926], Schneider enclosed clippings of two reviews of *TOS* (JFK). In "Hemingway's Parodies, An American Parody," Harry Hansen (1884–1977) calls EH "the most promising American author in Paris," but notes he is parodying Sherwood Anderson ("who turned handsprings and welcomed this newcomer to the ranks of America's great men") and concludes that EH is better at writing short stories than parodies (*New York World*, 30 May 1926, 4M). Ernest Boyd's more positive review, published in the 12 June 1926 *Independent*, termed the book "exceedingly witty" and the kind of parody that is "real criticism" ("Readers and Writers," 694).

2   Schneider wrote in his [11 June 1926] letter that he did not like *TOS*, although if someone else had written it, he "would have whooped it up." He deemed it "too faithful" to its subject and in spots "as dull as Anderson." However, he expected *SAR* to be "one of the biggest things done in America."

3   Schneider asked how EH liked Frank's *Virgin Spain* (1926), saying that while he himself "found portions in the middle not so bad," he regarded it as "an enormous dose of hokum as a whole."

4   *The History of Tom Jones, a Foundling* (1749), a lengthy novel by Henry Fielding originally published in six volumes. *Far Away and Long Ago: A History of My Early Life* (1918), memoir by British naturalist W. H. [William Henry] Hudson (1841–1922).

5   Schneider wrote that he liked George Borrow "in spite of his religion and his bully's way of writing" (JFK).

6   In a letter to Fitzgerald of 29 May 1926, Perkins had praised the vitality of *SAR* and its "marvelously concealed" art but termed it "almost unpublishable," partly because of its depiction of actual people, members of the "Lost Generation" with "disintegrated personalities." Topics such as the sexual impotence of the book's narrator and of Henry James presented "a problem," as did the "many words seldom if ever used before in print" (JFK).

7   Schneider had mentioned his difficulties with a narrative poem he had been writing for a year, saying "I ache all over from it and will feel like a man out of prison when the last line is down." The poem may have been "The Temptation of Anthony," which would appear in the September 1927 *American Caravan* along with EH's "An Alpine Idyll."

8   Schneider had promised to send snapshots of himself and his wife, Helen, "so that we can be properly introduced to Hadley."

To Sherwood Anderson, 1 July 1926

July 1, 1926

Dear Sherwood Anderson:

Your letter was fine (this is not the Master talking to his pupil) and what a horse's ass I must become as soon as I sit in front of a typewriter if those are the snooty kind of letters I've written you. But anyhow if I did write that way I won't write that way anymore.[1] I won't even try and headslip that one—but will take it on the nose by removing the if and putting in an as. But anyway I think you're quite right in saying the book will do you good (publicity) and I am sure it will hurt me with a lot of people. So what the hell. Because I had a grand time writing it for six days and thought it was funny and got five hundred dollars for it (previous writing earnings 200 dollars and no story ever yet sold in the states) and you being the middle weight champion and as such not having a glass jaw and me not having a glass jaw either—but now having or having had five hundred dollars I feel fine about it.[2]

But I'll counter your lead about the noble reporter in Cleveland by pointing out that I didn't tear up or burn this mss. to "protect" you and all I meant by the letter from Madrid was to say "Mr. Anderson I have read and admired you for a long time and I am now about to attempt to sock you on the jaw and here are my reasons and a copy of my apology which can be read aloud at my funeral."[3]

I'll be awfully glad to see Church. We will be back in Paris in August and will be there until we sail about the middle of September. It would be grand to come through Troutdale and we might do it.[4] I imagine though that we will land in Texas or New Orleans and go straight up to Piggott from there. We haven't any money and will save the R.R. fare from New York and get a cheaper boat that way. Later in the winter if you've not gone to Paris I'd love to bum up through and see you. It would be grand to see you again and we would love to come to Troutdale. It sound like lovely country.

Anyway so long and good luck and if you don't go over to Paris I'll see you some time before Christmas—and when I do I'll try and not lead with my chin and forget to duck—like in the last letter. Hadley sends you and your wife her best.

Best to you always,
Ernest Hemingway.

Newberry, TLS

1 Responding to EH's letter of 21 May 1926 (and to his other letters of the "last two or three years"), Anderson had expressed his surprise at EH's "patronizing," saying, "You always do

speak to me like a master to a pupil. It must be Paris—the literary life. You didn't seem like that when I knew you" ([June 1926], JFK).

2 Anderson wrote, "I think the Scribner book will help me and hurt you." He also said, "You speak so respectfully, tenderly, of giving me a punch ... I pack a little wallop myself. I've been middle weight champion. You seem to forget that."

3 Anderson wrote that EH reminded him of a reporter at the *Cleveland Plain Dealer*, who in a drunken state wrote an article but then, still drunk, came to Anderson crying to say that he had torn it up because he was certain it would have ended Anderson's writing career.

4 Anderson wrote that he was sending Ralph Withington Church (1900–1969), an American doctoral student of philosophy at Oxford, to visit EH in Paris. Anderson also invited the Hemingways to stop by on their way to Arkansas and visit him in Troutdale, Virginia, where he had bought a farm and planned to build a house.

To Pierre Chautard, [c. 21 July 1926]

Monsieur P. Chautard

113 Rue Notre Dame des Champs

Paris

Monsieur:

I have received today your insufficiantly addressed lettre recommandee— the said letter having gone through ~~great~~ delays difficulties to reach me due to the fact that banks and turist agencies do not forward letters without prenom or initials—and there being this summer several people named Hemingway in Europe.[1] I wrote and telegraphed Mlle Lincoln to deliver all keys to you on quitting the appartement and will write to her again demanding that she do this if she has not done so already.[2] Perhaps the keys have been delivered in your absense or to your wife.

I note that you rent the appartement a partir de l'8 Aott, non plus au trimestre, mais aux mois avec preavis de 15 jours et je vous envoizez un cheque de 700 francs pour la loyer 8 Aout–8 Septembre. Je note aussi votre intention de fixer le loyer depuis le 8 September a un somme plus elevé.

Agreer, Monsieur, mes sinceres salutations,[3]

JFK, ALD

This undated draft is written in a notebook in EH's hand. Also surviving at JFK is a complete French translation, dated "Jeudi, le 22 juillet, 1926" [Thursday, 22 July 1926], written in Hadley's hand and signed in EH's name. Although Hadley's French translation is cleaner than EH's draft, it, too, includes some cancellations and may be another draft of a letter actually sent.

1 *Lettre recommandée*: registered letter; *prénom*: first name (French). Chautard had sent his 8 July 1926 letter to "E. Hemingway, Villa Paquita, Juan les Pins." The envelope shows the letter was forwarded from Juan-les-Pins to Pamplona and San Sebastian. Postmarks indicate that it was forwarded on 20 July from San Sebastian to Madrid, where it finally reached EH (JFK).
2 Reporting that Mademoiselle Lincoln had left on 20 June, Chautard complained she had taken with her not only the apartment keys but four keys for the street door, two of which Chautard had especially made for the subtenant's friends.
3 Written in imperfect French, the conclusion of EH's letter translates: "I note that you rent the apartment starting 8 August, no longer quarterly, but monthly with a 15-day notice and I send you a check of 700 francs for the rent 8 August–8 September. I note also your intention to raise the rent after 8 September / Please accept, Sir, my sincere greetings." In his 8 July letter, Chautard had notified EH of, and asked him to confirm, a change in the terms of the lease exactly as EH describes here, except that Chautard specified an increase in the rent to 1,000 francs, starting 8 September. Chautard also acknowledged receipt of EH's check for the rent from 8 June to 8 August but noted that EH had sent 300 francs extra to be applied to the next payment.

To Pauline Pfeiffer, [c. 24 July 1926]

PAULINE PFEIFFER
8 RUE PICOT
PARIS
TODAYS STILL PFEIFFER DAY IN VALENCIA
LOVE HADLEY AND ERNEST

JFK, TN with typewritten signature

This note, typewritten sideways on lined notebook paper, is probably a cable draft. Reynolds reports that Pauline, who had returned to Paris after the Fiesta in Pamplona, received a telegram with this wording on 24 July, two days after her thirty-first birthday (*AH*, 50).

To Maxwell Perkins, 24 July 1926

Hotel Valencia—Valencia—Spain
July 24, 1926.

Dear Mr. Perkins:

Thanks so much for sending me the adventures of a Younger Son. I haven't received it yet but look forward to it with a great anticipation.[1] I imagine we are in accord about the use of certain words and I never use a word without first considering if it is replaceable. But in the proof I will go over it all very carefully. I have thought of one place where Mike when drunk and wanting to insult the bull fighter keeps saying—tell him bulls have no balls. That can be changed—and I believe with no appreciable loss to—bulls have no horns. But in the matter of the use of the word Bitch by Brett—I have never once used this word ornamentally nor except when it was absolutely necessary and I believe the few places where it is used must stand.[2] The whole problem is, it seems, that one should never use words which shock altogether out of their own value or connotation—such a word as for instance fart would stand out on a page, unless the whole matter were entirely rabelaisian, in such a manner that it would be entirely exaggerated and false and overdone in emphasis. Granted that it is a very old and classic English word for a breaking of wind. But you cannot use it. Altho I can think of a case where it might be used, under sufficiently tragic circumstances, as to be entirely acceptable. In a certain incident in the war of conversation among marching troops under shell fire.

I think that words—and I will cut anything I can—that are used in conversation in The Sun etc. are justified by the tragedy of the story. But of course I haven't seen it for some time and not at all in type.

The reason I haven't sent any more stories to the magazine is because Scott was so sure that it would buy anything that was publishable that my hopes got very high and after I'd tried both a long and a short story—and I suppose the stories aren't pleasant—and both were not publishable it made me feel very discouraged;[3] as I had counted on that as a certain source of income, and I suppose I have been foolish not to copy out more stories and send them. But I will when we get back to Paris the 10th of August. As yet no proofs have arrived.

I plan to go over The Sun etc. in Paris very carefully. By what date should you have the proofs returned?

As for our returning in the fall—the financial situation is so rotten—it being very tenuous and easily affected by whooping cough and the necessity of the Riviera and one thing and another—that I can see no prospect of it although I had hoped and counted on it tremendously. In several ways I have been long enough in Europe.

How did the Torrents go?

The Guaranty Trust is always a permanent address.

I hope you have been having a good summer. Spain is very dusty and hot but much the best country left in Europe.

Yours always,

Ernest Hemingway.

PUL, TLS

1 *Adventures of a Younger Son* (1831), by the English writer Edward John Trelawny (1792–1881), is an autobiographical account of Shelley, Byron, and the author. In his letter of 30 June 1926, Perkins wrote that he expected EH to like the book, "alive with grand material," but recanted in his letter of 20 July, saying, "I'm afraid I've misled you about The Younger Son. I see it gets to be theatrical" (PUL).

2 In a letter of 29 June 1926, Perkins wrote, "I think some words should be avoided so that we shall not divert people from the qualities of this book to the discussion of an utterly impertinent and extrinsic matter" (PUL). In a letter of 20 July 1926, Perkins singled out "a particular adjunct of the Bulls" mentioned by Mike Campbell "a number of times" and suggested replacing the words with blanks to avoid charges of indecency. In the first edition of *SAR*, Mike's statement to Romero in Chapter 16 was edited to read, "Tell him that bulls have no horns." In the 1954 edition and subsequent editions, "Tell him that bulls have no balls" would be restored to the text (Trogdon *Racket*, 41). Brett Ashley's use of the word "bitch" remained unchanged.

3 "Fifty Grand" and "An Alpine Idyll."

To Clarence Hemingway, 24 July 1926

Hotel Valencia

Valencia,

Spain

July 24, 1926

Dear Dad—

I certainly would have loved to be with you going up to Windemere.[1]
After being back in France until the fourth of July we are in Spain again.

Bumby had quite a siege of whooping cough but came out of it all right as the pictures show. They were taken on the beach at Juan les Pins on the Riviera where Hadley and I stayed from about the 25th of May until the 4th of July.[2] He is still there with his nurse whose husband has joined her for his vacation and they are then all going north to Paris the 3rd of August where we will join them shortly thereafter. From here we go to Antibes to visit some friends for a week before returning to Paris.[3]

Franklin Hemingway turned up in Madrid the day we were leaving it— last Wednesday—this is Saturday as I write.[4] His Princeton room-mate was with him and they are going back to the French border—driving across the Pyrenees and then coming down here next week to see something of the bull fights. I will show them around and see that they see whatever Spanish is going on. Several of my friends are bull fighting here during the big week of eight fights and I have already seen the bulls unloaded and they look as though they would make the boys sweat in a most healthy manner.[5]

As the Torrents was a satire on the way of thinking and writing of a writer you hadn't read and wouldn't like if you did read I couldn't expect it to rate very highly with either you or mother. Still I've gotten over a hundred very good and some exceedingly enthusiastic reviews. I hope it's selling. It's only been out a month or so but the reviews have been very satisfactory.[6]

Our plans and many things are very upset and I can't make any definite date for arriving in the states. But whenever we do and wherever you are, Florida, Canada, Wyoming or Massachusetts we will all have a good visit.

Catch some trout for me if there are any left. I'm glad you are missing the great heat wave in the middle west that I read about in the papers here. In Spain it often gets to 40 degrees centigrade and sometimes to 50 in the summer. But here we can swim and they know how to handle heat and the houses are built for it. The bull fights start tomorrow. Wish you could see one sometime. When they are good there is nothing to touch them. You being a surgeon would not mind seeing the horses deliver up their tripe [a]nymore than I do. Hadley sends you and Mother and all the kids her best love and my best to Leicester and especially old Nunbones to whom I am writing shortly, Best love from,

Ernie

PSU, TLS

1 EH's parents and youngest siblings, Carol and Leicester, were then at the family's summer cottage on Walloon Lake, Michigan. EH addressed the envelope to "Dr. C. E. Hemingway / R. F. D. No. 1 / Petoskey / Michigan / Estados Unidos."
2 A currency exchange receipt of 27 May 1926 shows EH was still in Madrid on 25 May (JFK). According to the daily log he kept during his travels between 13 and 30 May, he received the returned passport from Hadley on 27 May and left Madrid by train on the morning of 28 May, spending a night in Pamplona on his journey to Antibes. Two of the photos that EH enclosed are included in the plate section of this volume.
3 At the beginning of August, EH and Hadley would return to Antibes to join the Murphys, Archibald and Ada MacLeish, and the recently wed Donald Ogden Stewart and Beatrice Ames, who were on their honeymoon.
4 EH's first cousin Franklin White Hemingway (1904–1984), son of Clarence's brother Alfred Tyler Hemingway (1877–1922) and Fanny Arabell Hemingway (née White, 1876–1963) of Kansas City, Missouri. Franklin had just graduated from Princeton on 22 June. "Last Wednesday," 21 July, was EH's twenty-seventh birthday.
5 As EH wrote in "Dates of Bullfights" (*DIA*), the first fight of the feria at Valencia typically took place on July 25, with "seven to nine fights on successive days until and through August 2." In 1926 the feria ran from 25 July through 1 August (Tomás Orts-Ramos, *Toros y Toreros en 1926: Resumen Crítico-Estadístico de la Temporada Taurina* [Barcelona: Lux, 1926]).
6 After Scribner's publication of *TOS* on 28 May 1926, Perkins sent EH reviews on 14 June and 29 June. The reviews in the second set were, according to Perkins, "all favorable, some enthusiastic, and several good" (PUL). EH's parents did not specifically mention having read *TOS* in any located letters of that time; a year later Clarence would write, "I am proud of your progress and have read all your stories and books with great interest" (28 September 1927, JFK).

To Henry Strater, [24 July 1926]

Hotel Valencia, Valencia
Charleston! Charleston[1]

Dear Mike:

The pictures were swell and thanks for sending them. I am terribly sorry about your mother's death.[2] So is Hadley. She sends her love and her sympathy to you both. There is one thing about dying and that is that the good people do it. I have never yet known a shit to die altho if we live long enough it may happen.

You were awfully swell to me in N.Y. and don't think I don't remember it. We aren't coming through in the fall and if we do will go by Galveston, Texas,. Everything is all shot to hell in every direction but in the meantime there are eight bull fights here starting tomorrow. Gallo, Belmonte, Sanchez Mejias, Nino de la Palma and Villalta. Miuras, Villamartas, Concha y Sierras, Murubes, Perez Tabernos, Guadalests and Pablo Romeros.[3] Hadley and I are down here together. Pamplona was grand. We were gypped out of Ondarroa[4] by Bumby getting the whoop cough and getting himself and Hadley and eventually me, coming from Madrid, quarantined on the Rivieria in a former Villa of Scott Fitzgerald's at Juan les Pins (Alpes Maritmes).

There isn't any news that's fit to print.[5] I'm awfully glad you like the Torrents book and will have the novel [*SAR*] fired to you by Scribners this fall just as soon as it's out. We've just been conge-ed in Paris and have to go up and get things cleaned out by the 8th of August.[6] Please remember Hadley to the Von Schlegell's[7] and all our love to you and Maggie and the kids.[8]

Write me care of the Guaranty in Paris. I do hope you were able to do something for your father—though it must be an awfully hopeless business to lose someone you've been in love with and made your life with. It's one of the swell things especially reserved for all of us. So Long, Mike, and write—

Yours always,

Hem

PUL, TLS

On the envelope of the 12 June 1926 letter from Strater to which he responds here, EH wrote, "Answered July 24" (JFK).

1 In a joking echo of the repeated "Valencia" in his return address, EH quotes the refrain of the popular song "Charleston" (1923): "Charleston! Charleston! Made in Carolina."
2 In his 12 June letter, Strater said that he was sending EH reproductions of a couple of his paintings and that his mother, Adeline Sutphen Helme Strater (1859–1926), had died unexpectedly on 28 March following surgery. Strater wrote he was "trying to get Father started on a fresh tack, otherwise he will not last long" (JFK). His father, Charles Godfrey Strater (1856–1937), who changed his middle name from Gottfried with the start of WWI, made his fortune as co-founder with his two brothers of the Strater Brothers Tobacco

Company in Louisville, Kentucky. Strater's parents married in 1883 (Michael Culver, "Sparring in the Dark: The Art and Life of Henry Strater," unpublished manuscript, n.p.).

3 EH names Spanish bullfighters El Gallo ("The Rooster," nickname for Rafael Gómez Ortega, 1882–1960), Juan Belmonte García (1892–1962), and Ignacio Sánchez Mejías (1891–1934) as well as Niño de la Palma (Cayetano Ordóñez Aguilera) and Nicanor Villalta Serris (1897–1980). Miura, Villamarta, Concha y Sierra, Murube, Pérez Tabanero, Guadalest, and Pablo Romero are breeds of bulls, which generally carry the family name of the respective breeder.

4 Ondarroa, a medieval fishing port town on the Bay of Biscay in the Basque country of northern Spain.

5 Reference to the slogan of the *New York Times*: "All the News That's Fit to Print," which has appeared on the front page of every issue of the newspaper since 10 February 1897.

6 *Congé*: a notice to leave, a dismissal (French).

7 Strater mentioned in his letter that the von Schlegells were in Ogunquit, Maine, that summer, writing, "He is a prince. The missus seems nice too." Gustav William von Schlegell (1877–1950), a painter who taught at the Art Students League in New York City, summered with his family at Ogunquit, where he was a member of the Ogunquit Art Colony. He was married to Alice Anderson von Schlegell (b. c. 1892), also an artist; their son David (1920–1992) became a renowned painter and sculptor.

8 Strater's wife, Margaret (Maggie) Yarnall Conner Strater (1895–1971), an artist who attended Vassar College and the Pennsylvania Academy of Fine Arts. Married in 1920, the couple had two children at the time of this letter, David Eli (1921–2002) and Martha (1925–1995). They would have two more sons, Michael Henry (1929–1984) and Nicholas Appleby (1931–2003), before divorcing in 1942.

To John M. Stahl, 26 July 1926

Permanent address
Guaranty Trust Co. of N.Y.
1, Rue des Italiens
Paris—France
Hotel Valencia, Valencia, Spain.
July 26, 1926.

John M. Stahl Esq.
President The Allied Arts Association,
Chicago, Illinois.
Dear Mr. Stahl:

Thank you very much for you pleasant invitation in the name of the Allied Arts Association.[1] At present I do not know when I will be home again but when I come to America I shall surely be in Chicago and it would be a very great pleasure to either lunch or dine with you.

Whenever I know when I will be in Chicago I will drop you a letter and you might fix a date.

With best regards,
Very truly,
Ernest Hemingway.

Knox, TLS

1 The Allied Arts Association of Chicago was founded in 1923 by Stahl, who also served as its president. Its mission was "to encourage the beginners in art and increase recognition of those that had 'arrived'" (Stahl, *Growing with the West: The Story of a Busy, Quiet Life* [London: Longmans, Green, 1930], 447–48). The association held eight to ten dinners honoring chosen artists every year.

To Ezra Pound, [7 August 1926]

Dear Mister Pound:

Yours to hand and a copy of the dribble [*TOS*] was sent to yr Eytalian address by the Messers. Scribners. I am again oreja-less but in good health and planning to arrive in the Paris of the guidebooks on abt. Aug 12 or 14 and hope to Gawd you'll be there.[1]

Stick around.

My salutations to your mother in law—my love to your wife—and my humble American obeisances to Mr. and Mrs. Eliot of the New Criterion—[2]

It will be very fine to see you again.

Hem—

Yale, ALS; letterhead: VILLA AMERICA / TEL. 3.57 CAP D'ANTIBES A-M.

EH is responding to Pound's letter of 31 July [1926], mailed from Paris and forwarded to EH at Villa America; its envelope bears EH's note, "Answered Aug 7" (JFK).

1 *Oreja*: ear (Spanish). Pound had asked if EH had "yet got the oreja," referring to the bull's ear traditionally presented to the successful matador as a token of honor. He had also teased that EH was "cowardly shrinking from Le Paris musical seezun in the safe precincts of the bull ring" (JFK). A production of Pound's own musical composition, "Paroles de Villon," featuring Olga Rudge (1895–1996) as violinist, had been performed at Salle Pleyel in Paris

on 29 June 1926. Pound and Rudge were lovers, and she had given birth to his daughter, Maria Rudge, on 9 July 1925. Pound had also asked EH when he was going to "make yr. pip squeak again heard on the Bullyvards?" (JFK).

2 Pound reported that he, his mother-in-law (Olivia Shakespear), his wife (Dorothy Shakespear), and T. S. Eliot had all read George Antheil's copy of *TOS* "with relief & amusement" (JFK). EH evokes the title of his own short story "Mr. and Mrs. Elliot" (*IOT*) in his reference to T. S. Eliot (1888–1965), who was then married to dancer Vivienne Haigh-Wood (1888–1947). Eliot was editor of the London literary quarterly *Criterion* from its founding in 1922 until it ceased publication in 1939. The periodical appeared as the *New Criterion* between January 1926 and January 1927.

To Genevieve Taggard, [7 August 1926]

> Guaranty Trust Co. of N.Y.
> 1, Rue des Italiens
> Paris[1]

Dear Miss Taggart:

Your letter of May 20 to the Am Ex Co. came today.[2] Words For the Chisel came just before we went to Spain. I took it along in spite of the Seltzers—and it was a very fine book and was read and twice re-read in Spain which is a lot more than you can do with most books.[3] You know all about how good your poetry is so it would be silly and impertinent for me to try and tell you.

I'm sorry about the New Masses and what poetry did I ever promise to send for when? And are you sure it was me?[4]

Spain was very pleasant and not at all Virgin Spain and now France looks very french and even frenchified. We're going back to Paris in a week. I hope you have had a good summer and written poetry. I wrote R. Woolf from Valencia.[5]

> With best wishes
> Ernest Hemingway.

NYPL, ALS; letterhead: VILLA AMERICA / TEL. 3.57 CAP D'ANTIBES A-M.

1 EH crossed out the Murphys' stationery letterhead and wrote this return address underneath.

2 Taggard had sent her letter of 20 May 1926 to the American Express Company in Paris, from where it was forwarded to 74, rue du Cardinal Lemoine, the address of EH and

Hadley's first Paris apartment (1922–1923). On the verso of the envelope EH wrote, "Answered Aug 7, 1926" (JFK).

3 EH refers to Taggard's poetry collection *Words for the Chisel* (New York: Knopf, 1926). In her letter she explained, "I sent you a copy of my book mistakenly inscribed to Thomas & Adele Seltzer. Don't mind it please. They got your copy!" Thomas Seltzer (1875–1943), journalist and first editor of *The Masses* (published 1911–1917), opened his own publishing company in New York in 1919 and brought out Taggard's first volume of poetry, *For Eager Lovers*, in 1922.

4 The first issue of *New Masses* appeared in May 1926, with Taggard named on the masthead as one of more than three dozen contributing editors. In her 20 May letter, Taggard had written to EH, "There is a new mysticism a new affectation & a new religion in the New Masses—have you seen it? You've never sent me the poetry I asked for— I have to send the stuff to press the 10th of June, so I guess its too late."

5 Robert Wolf, Taggard's husband, whom she married in 1921 and with whom she had a daughter that year.

To Edith Finch, 18 August 1926

Guaranty Trust CO. of N.Y.
1, Rue des Italiens.
Paris.
August 18, 1926

Dear Miss Finch:

Thank you very much for sending the Descriptions of Literature. I think it is one of the best things of Miss Stein's that I have ever read and I am very pleased to send you something to appear in the same series.[1]

I am enclosing a story that I hope you will like. I think it is the best story that I have. There are only two things that I would like to ask you to do; first that the story be printed on consecutive pages—as it would be very bad for the continuity of something taking place in such a short time to be printed with the pages broken up as was the case in your printing of Miss Stein's essay on Literature. Secondly that it be copyrighted in my name and marked All Rights Reserved.[2]

With best wishes for the success of your pamphlets,
Very sincerely,
Ernest Hemingway.

This is the only Mss. of Today Is Friday that I have so I would like to have it back, or a copy of it, (If you could have one made) as I will be including it in a book in about a year. When do you plan on publishing the next two pamphlets?

Yale, TLS with autograph postscript

1 In a letter of 14 August 1926, on Gertrude Stein's recommendation, Finch offered EH 400 francs to contribute an essay to a new pamphlet series by The As Stable Publications, edited and published in New Jersey by Finch; George Platt Lynes (1907–1955), American portrait and fashion photographer; and Adlai Harbeck (1908–1981), a close friend of Lynes. The series planned to publish both unknown and known writers. As an example, Finch enclosed Stein's essay "Descriptions of Literature," the featured work of the second in the series (JFK).
2 EH's story "Today Is Friday" was published as Number 4 of the pamphlet series in November 1926 under the terms he stipulated. The corrected typescript that he enclosed survives at the Beinecke Library at Yale University. The story would be included in *MWW*, published in October 1927.

To Maxwell Perkins, 21 August 1926

69 Rue Froidevaux,[1]
Paris, France.
August 21, 1926.

Dear Mr. Perkins:

The proofs came ten days ago while we were at the Cap D'Antibes on our way home from Spain and I have been over them very carefully with the points you outlined in mind.[2]

1st—I have commenced with Cohn—I believe the book loses by eliminating this first part but it would have been pointless to include it with the Belloc eliminated—and I think that would be altogether pointless with Belloc's name out.[3]

2nd—Roger Prescott is now Roger Prentiss. I believe I went to school with a Roger Prentiss but at least he was not Glenway [Wescott].

3rd—Hergesheimer now changed to something else.[4]

4th—Henry James now called either Henry or Whatsisname—whichever seems best to you.[5]

5th—I do not believe that the blanks left in the Irony and pity song can be objectionable—anybody knowing what words to put in might as well put them in. In case they are offensive the word "pretty" can be inserted.

6th—The bulls now without appendages.

I've tried to reduce profanity but I reduced so much profanity when writing the book that I'm afraid not much could come out. Perhaps we will have to consider it simply as a profane book and hope that the next book will be less profane—or perhaps more sacred.[6]

In today's mail there is an invitation to broadcast Torrents of Spring from the Sears Robebuck radio station W L S accompanied by a short talk and the information that "it gives common people a real thrill, to be remembered always, to hear the voice of a well known, admired author". (And who do you think that would be)[7] The other letter was from the Missouri Historical Society asking for a copy of Torrents to be preserved along with the most complete collection of the books of all Missouri authors, which it seems a very strange thing to suddenly be.

In this same mail I am sending you a story—The Killers—which has been typed by the well known, admired author himself on a six year old Corona.[8] So if the magazine does not want it you might send it to the Sears Roebuck broadcasting station care of Mr. John M. Stahl and maybe he would like to have it to show to a lot of the common people.

I also find, in yesterday's mail, that I owe Henry Romeike, Inc. 220 West 19th Street, N.Y., sixteen dollars for clippings, and as I have no dollars and Mr. Romeike, who is I believe by his own admittance the original Romeike, is very lovely about sending clippings, I wonder if you could have this sixteen dollars sent to him and charged to what must be rapidly becoming my account. If this were done it might be well to tell Mr. the original Romeike that the money is coming from me and that he may continue to send clippings to the same place.[9]

Zelda was looking very well and very lovely when I saw her last week. Scott was working hard. Don Stewart has arrived with a very new and awfully nice and good looking wife.

I hope you've had a good summer. We had a grand time in Spain. I'm working very hard now—plan to mail the proof the end of the week and will send another story.

With best regards,
Ernest Hemingway.

PUL, TLS

1 Upon returning to Paris from Antibes, EH and Hadley set up separate households. EH accepted Gerald Murphy's offer to stay in his studio at 69, rue Froidevaux, and Hadley rented rooms for herself and Bumby at the Hôtel Beauvoir at 43, avenue de l'Observatoire.

2 In his letter of 20 July, Perkins wrote that he had sent galley proofs of *SAR* to EH in care of the Guaranty Trust Company Paris (PUL; *TOTTC*, 41–43).

3 Perkins wrote that he did not object to EH's proposal of cutting the beginning of the novel; as a result, *SAR* opens with the introduction of Robert Cohn. However, Perkins warned of the dangers of libel and suppression. He regarded the reference to Hilaire Belloc (1870–1953), French-born English writer, as "the most dangerous" and suggested disguising Belloc's name in some way. EH cut the anecdote about Belloc from *SAR* but years later would refer to Belloc by name in the "Ford Madox Ford and the Devil's Disciple" chapter of *MF*.

4 Perkins had objected to a reference in which H. L. Mencken is reported to have called the popular American novelist Joseph Hergesheimer (1880–1954) a "garter snapper," fearing it might damage the two men's friendship. EH would change the name Hergesheimer to Hoffenheimer (Chapter 6).

5 See EH to Perkins, 5 June 1926. The reference to "Henry James's bicycle" would become "Henry's bicycle" in Chapter 12.

6 In Chapter 12 of *SAR*, Bill Gorton sings a bawdy lyric that begins, "Irony and Pity. When you're feeling . . . Oh, Give them Irony and Give them Pity." Perkins suggested EH should "not so plainly indicate the second line" (with its implied rhyme of "shitty") by using blanks, but rather "leave it as if Barnes did not hear it well, for Gorton was humming." For a detailed discussion of the phrase, see Scott Donaldson, "'Irony and Pity': Anatole France Got It Up," in *Fitzgerald–Hemingway Annual 1978*, ed. Matthew J. Bruccoli and C. E. Frazer Clark (Detroit: Gale Group, 1979), 331–34. Referring to the phrase "bulls have no balls," Perkins also recommended that "a particular adjunct of the Bulls, referred to a number of times by Mike, be not spelled out, but covered by a blank" and generally urged EH to reduce profanity "so far as you rightly can" (PUL; *TOTTC*, 41–43).

7 Chicago radio station WLS (for "World's Largest Store") was established by the Sears Roebuck Company in 1924 for the benefit of area farmers. Owing in part to the influence of economist and farmer John M. Stahl, who founded the Society of Midland Authors, WLS became known as a reliable source of cultural information.

8 Hadley had given EH his first typewriter, a Corona number 3, for his twenty-second birthday on 21 July 1921.

9 Henry Romeike (1853–1903), Prussian-born American businessman. Romeike started a successful newspaper clipping service in New York City in 1885, supplying customers with newspaper articles mentioning their name or business. In 1914, Henry's brother Albert started his own company, prompting Henry's son Georges Romeike to include with the clippings paper slips reading "Be Sure It's Henry. Other Romeikes May Disappoint." In 1926, the tagline was changed to "No connection with any other ROMEIKE."

To Hadley Richardson Hemingway, [23 August 1926]

3 pm
Monday

Dear Niggy—

I've gotten the mail and will leave it at your house.

Waxen

You have 2 letters. I left a note for you at your house too and am leaving some money.

JFK, ALS

The envelope, which bears no postage, is addressed to "Hadley R. Hemingway / c/o Guaranty Trust Co. of N.Y." The verso of the envelope is stamped "GUARANTY TRUST CO. OF NEW YORK / PARIS, RECEIVED / AUG 23 / CUSTOMER'S MAIL." On the envelope flap, EH wrote the following train schedule information:

| 7^{am} | | 11.25 | Gare d- L'est. | 8.35. |
| 1.35 | | 8.17 | Couchettes. | 16.20. |

To Maxwell Perkins, 26 August [1926]

August 26.

Dear Mr. Perkins—

I am sending the proofs tomorrow on the Mauretania so you should have them in a week now.[1]

You did not send a proof of the quotations in the front or of the dedication and I have forgotten exactly what they were. For the quotations I want the quotation from Gertrude Stein which I believe was "You are all a lost generation" there may have been more to it—it's to go as it was on the Mss. and the quotation from Ecclesiastes.

The dedication is to be—TO HADLEY RICHARDSON HEMINGWAY AND TO JOHN HADLEY NICANOR HEMINGWAY

THIS BOOK IS TO HADLEY FOR HADLEY AND FOR JOHN HADLEY NICANOR.[2]

I may have changed a few more things and made more cuts before mailing the proofs but you will have seen all that by now. I believe that the book is really better starting as it does now directly with Cohn and omitting any preliminary warming up. After all if I'm trying to write books without any extra words I might as well stick to it. Now that it is finally out of my hands and there ~~When do you think~~ is no chance of doing anything to make it any better I feel rather cheerful now about The Sun. Hope you feel the same way.

A letter from Scott today said he was working very hard with the front door barred and all the blind[s] down and expected to sail for N.Y. on December 10th from Genoa.[3]

If the Irony and pity ditty bothers there are a couple of things you could do—reduce the size of the dashes and omit periods after them. Or just run it all in together. No dashes and no periods. Do whatever you like with it. I don't care what happens to that as long as the words are not changed and nothing inserted.

The other things I believe are all fixed up. We've eliminated Belloc, changed Hergesheimer's name, made Henry James Henry, made Roger Prescott into Roger Prentiss and unfitted the bulls for a reproductive function.

Now I'll get this off so there won't be any further holding up. When do you expect that The Sun will be out? And how did Torrents go? You might send me a check for 200 dollars if you would.[4] It is grand to have The Sun etc. finally off and to be able to start on something else without things to do on the book coming in and smashing up the production of anything else. I'd like to forget it now for a long time. It is a great mistake to put real people in a book and one I'll never make, I hope, again.

With best regards,
Yours very truly,
Ernest Hemingway.

PUL, TLS

1 The corrected proofs of *SAR* left Cherbourg aboard the *Mauretania* on 27 August 1926 and arrived in New York on 3 September. In his reply to EH of 8 September, Perkins would write that the proofs had been "so lightly corrected as to put us in an excellent position to put it through." Regarding the revisions EH had made, Perkins wrote, "Certainly you have done all that we could have asked,—and I hated to ask as much as I did" (PUL).
2 This is the version of the dedication that would appear in *SAR*.
3 The Fitzgeralds would sail from Genoa aboard the *Conte Biancamano* on 10 December, arriving in New York on 20 December 1926.
4 In a letter to EH of 9 September 1926, Perkins would report that *TOS* had sold nearly 1,400 copies and that a $200 check was enclosed (PUL).

To John Gunther, [2 September 1926]

Dear Gunther:

I'm sorry that I can't lunch today—but I'd love to tomorrow at the same time.

If you cant tomorrow drop me a pneu and name any day next week.[1]

Best always,

Ernest Hemingway.

Alexander Autographs catalog, 19 November 2002 (illustrated), ALS; postmarks: PARIS / AV. D'ORLEANS, 2 du 9 / 26; PARIS / R. GLUCK, 2 DU 9 / 26

This single-page letter was folded over and addressed on the verso to "Monsieur / John Gunther / Chicago Daily News / 10, B^ld des Capucines / Paris E.V." (*en ville*: within the city). Above this address, EH wrote and double-underlined the word "Pneumatique," indicating that the letter was sent via Pneumatic Post, the pressurized tube system that operated in Paris from 1866 to 1984, quickly conveying mail in canisters from one post office to another.

1 EH is responding to Gunther's pneumatique of Wednesday, 1 September 1926, sent to him at Murphy's studio and inviting him "to come down to lunch tomorrow—Thursday—here at the office at 12:45—" (JFK). Replying to this letter from EH in another pneumatique sent the same day [Thursday, 2 September], Gunther regretted he could not make it "tomorrow," "Friday for lunch, as you suggest" and proposed they meet Monday or Tuesday (JFK). However, on Monday, 6 September, Gunther regretted again because he had to leave town (JFK).

To Morley Callaghan, [4 September 1926]

Dear Morley:

Thanks for sending me the Sat. Night and for writing it. Only for God's sake don't write book reviews unless you need to do it to have the money. This doesn't mean I don't appreciate the review a hell of a lot.[1] But dont get mixed up in that sort of thing. You cant run with the hares and hunt too.

About theology—I can't argue and never have been very interested and anyway wouldn't argue with an international debater.[2]

About yr novel—good. You are playing things just right.[3]

About pictures—haven't got any. Will send one if I have

Ernest Walsh is, I believe, getting out a new Number right away—this may mean anytime the rest of this year. Walsh, now it seems, altho I nhaven't had any correspondence with him except to tell him that his poem on me made me vomit—now no longer regards me as the bright luminary of literature but as a might have been who sold out to make money by writing funny books. He is attacking me on that ground I understand in a coming number of the New Masses and in This Quarter. The affections of the Irish.[4]

Sent the proofs of the Sun etc. off to Scribner last week. Hope yoou'll find it a real novel. It is around 80,000 words long, has people and places in it and starts and finishes. The hero of the story is not the author. All the women in the story get screwed with the exception of a girl called Edna who is not in the story long enough. It is not about sex. Maybe it will be a real novel. Let us maybe hope so anyway. I'll be very happy to hear what you think about it and will write Scribners to send you a review copy so you won't have to buy it.

You must be getting a hell of a literary authority to be able to put over that Sat Night business.

I've been feeling like hell for quite a while in almost every way and working and re-workign over The Sun etc.—three times re-writing—going over in proof etc. until I hate it's guts—and of course couldn't get anything else going because of that coming back into it and interrupting all the time. Written three new stories. Will have time between now and this time next year to write some stories for a book of Sht stories to come out a year from this fall. So far have The Undefeated—the bull fight one from this quarter) A long fight story called Fifty Grand and another long bull story called A Lack of Passion each about 15,000 words and three short ones. It won't take many more for a book.[5] Have a swell novel to write and will start on it maybe soon. The old insomnia put me pretty well bug house for a while but once read over the Studebaker Theater in Chicago that all passes art alone endures and hope it's true.[6]

Thanks again for the review Cal.

Let me hear from you always—and get back to work. Naturally it gets a hell of a lot harder to write as you learn more about it but the product is appreciated, eventually, in proportion. You are right that Ford is a poisonous influence. Remember that what makes a style, true style, is knowing what you want to say and then saying it clearly. It is sloppy thinking or woozy thinking that makes woozy writing. Old Ford is on the very personal and very woozy side and naturally the old ego gets in and gums everything up. His way of writing is as affected as the worst of Stevenson. Not that treasure island isn't a grand book[7]

You will come through all right. You better because you are my only white hope and I'm liable to beat the shit out of you if I see you quitting.[8]

Yours always

Hem

Private Collection, TLS; postmark: PARIS / AV. DE L'OBSERVATOIRE, 20* / 4–9 / 26

1 In his letter of 12 August [1926], Callaghan sent EH a clipping of his review of *IOT* and *TOS* published in the Canadian paper *Saturday Night* on 7 August 1927 (JFK). "Hemingway is writing the best short stories coming from an American today," Callaghan declared in his review, calling EH "a fine naturalist" who "cuts down the material to essentials and leaves it starkly authentic" (7). Callaghan also applauded *TOS* as "a robust and lively satire on the affectations of some modern writers" ("Introducing Ernest Hemingway," 7–8).

2 Callaghan wrote in his 12 August letter that he had "a real amateur interest in theological questions and some skill in disputation after the fashion of the Schoolmen" and said he was looking forward to "any number of beautiful discussions" with EH.

3 Callaghan told EH that McAlmon was prepared to publish his novel in the spring, but that in the meantime Callaghan was going to send his manuscript to about half a dozen publishers and had already sent it to Boni & Liveright. McAlmon himself, in a letter to EH of 18 May, had said he planned to advise Callaghan to send his novel to a U.S. publisher, and that if it was rejected, McAlmon would publish it (JFK).

4 The third number of *This Quarter*, published after Walsh's death on 16 October 1926, included no attack on EH. However, the October 1926 issue of *New Masses* would feature Walsh's negative review of *TOS*, "The Cheapest Book I Ever Read."

5 "A Lack of Passion," abandoned by EH in 1927, was finally published in 1990, edited by Susan F. Beegel from EH's corrected typescript at JFK, with accompanying pieces concerning its background and surviving manuscript variants ("'A Lack of Passion': Its Background, Sources and Composition History" and "The 'Lack of Passion' Papers," *Hemingway Review* 9, no. 2 [Spring 1990]: 50–93). The "three short ones" are probably "An Alpine Idyll," "The Killers," and "A Canary for One," all of which would be included in *MWW*.

6 Opened in 1885 as a showroom for the Studebaker Carriage Company, the building at 410 South Michigan Avenue was renovated in 1898 to include theaters and art studios and was renamed the Fine Arts Building. Carved in marble over the entrance are the words "ALL PASSES—ART ALONE ENDURES," derived from "L'Art" ("*Tout passe— L'art robuste /*

Seul a l'éternité") by French writer Pierre Jules Théophile Gautier (1811–1872), from his 1852 poetry collection *Émaux et Camées [Enamels and Cameos]*.

7 Callaghan confessed in his letter that he had not written anything "for some months." He could no longer write without feeling self-conscious about his style and did not want to become like Ford Madox Ford who, he felt, "thinks of himself almost every sentence he writes." Robert Louis Stevenson (1850–1894), Scottish author of *Treasure Island* (1883).

8 After Arthur John "Jack" Johnson (1878–1946) became the first African American to win the heavyweight boxing title, the term "Great White Hope" was given to many of his white opponents, including James J. "The Boilermaker" Jeffries (1875–1953), who came out of retirement to fight Johnson in "the Battle of the Century" on 4 July 1910. Johnson's victory sparked race riots across the country; he would reign as champion from 1908 to 1915.

To Maxwell Perkins, 7 September 1926

69 Rue Froidevaux, Paris, France
September 7, 1926.

Dear Mr. Perkins:

The proofs of The Sun etc. went off on the Mauretania almost two weeks ago so I did not answer your cable about sending them in completed galleys. By now you doubtless have them and have gone ahead.

Today I have your letter of August 23 from the country.

As a matter of fact I am not now discouraged, although I may have been when I wrote you from Valencia, and I don't think there is any question about artistic integrities.[1] It has always been much more exciting to write than to be paid for it and if I can keep on writing we may eventually all make some money. In the meantime the thing would seem to be to write and I am now trying to sell, give away or in some way clear out all the stories I have ahead to clear the way for some more.

O'Brien has written today for permission to publish The Undefeated, a story that I do not know if you ever saw, in his 1926 volumne.[2] I suppose that all becomes publicity. It might help The Sun Also Rises as the Undefeated has something to do with bulls and neither of the two mention any of the embarrassing appendages.

Yours always,
Ernest Hemingway

PUL, TLS

1 Responding to EH's letter of 24 July 1926, in which EH expressed discouragement over *Scribner's Magazine*'s rejection of his stories, Perkins wrote on 23 August, "I don't think you ought to be discouraged, except financially. You may not realize how highly you are regarded, how seriously, by those whose opinion as a rule prevails in the end" (JFK).
2 "The Undefeated" would be included in Edward J. O'Brien's *The Best Short Stories of 1926* (New York: Dodd, Mead, 1926), selected from among stories published in American magazines between October 1925 and August 1926.

To Sherwood Anderson, [c. 7 September 1926]

Dear Sherwood—

Thanks for the swell letter. Troutdale sounds very fine and I envy you the fall. It must be awfully grand. I am so homesick for America evry fall that I get into awful shape. Piggott is shot to hell now along with a lot of other things. As it was one of the two things that I wanted to do really badly.

Saw the New Masses—Gene Jolas showed it to me with his poems in it— and it seems to be some sort of a house organ.[1] I've sent the proof of my first novel—called The Sun Also Rises off to Scribners. I hope to hell you will like it. It isn't smarty anyway but it's Christ's own distance from the kind of novel I want to write and hope I'll learn how to write. But the only way seems to be to write them and in the end maybe they average up.

You can put enough weight on a horse so he can't have a chance of winning and in America (and Americans are always in America—no matter whether they call it Paris or Paname) we all carry enough weight to kill a horse—let alone have him run under it. I've been living this side of bughouse with the old insomnia for about eight months now. And it's something you can take with you to any country but I'm glad that I was built on the tough side and maybe it will all work out.[2]

I still feel badly about having ever written to you in an ex cathedra or ex-catheter—they have catheters as well as cathedrals over here—manner but I think that is just that the young have to be very sure always, because the show is really very tough and it is winning all the time and unless you know everything when you're twenty five you don't stand a chance of knowing anything at all when it's had time to shake down and you're thirty five. And we've all got to know something. Maybe.

This is a lousy letter but I wish to hell I was in Troutdale. Anyhow we'll be here when you come in November and it will be grand to see you again.[3]

As ever,

Ernest

Newberry, TLS

1 Eugene Jolas (1894–1952), American journalist, poet, translator, and editor, moved to Paris after WWI and wrote for the Paris *Tribune*. The fourth issue of the *New Masses* (August 1926) featured his sequence of six poems, "From a Newspaper Office." The majority of the pieces in the August 1926 issue of the leftist journal were written by those listed on its masthead, including founding editors Michael Gold (né Itzok Isaac Granich, c. 1894–1967) and James Rorty (1890–1973) as well as Dos Passos, a member of the executive board.

2 *Paname*: French slang for Paris. In his previous letter, Anderson suggested that EH was tougher than most: "What I always felt in you is a sense of vitality—the ability to take it. Most so called artists havn't enough juice to get through the first few years" ([August 1926], JFK).

3 Anderson wrote that if he and his wife could afford to visit Paris, they would arrive in late November and stay until March.

To F. Scott Fitzgerald, [after 8 September 1926]

69 Rue Froidevaux

Paris 14.

Dear Old Fitz—

Glad to hear again from the Master. How goes the work, Fitz? Glad to hear it. Glad to hear it. Keep it up old boy. I had exactly the same experience myself when I started writing. Then one day I met George Horace Lorimer in the Petit Chaumiere and from then on things simply slipped along.[1]

How the hell are you anyway? I decided to give away all my stories when I got here so as to clear away all the stuff I was counting on selling and that would force me to write some more. So I gave Today Is Friday to some pamphlet organization that had written asking for an essay to be published with a drawing by Cocteau[2] and sent the Alpine Idyll to the New Masses which is the most peurile and shitty house organ I've ever seen—they also having requested a contribution—and just to see what the alibi would be sent The Killers—which I'd just finished to Scribners. So right away back I get a cable from Max Perkins saying Killers grand bridges writing offer Sun proofs received Perkins.[3]

So even cynical little boys like Ernest get pleasant surprises. Only now I only wait to hear of the sudden death of Bridges, the losing of his job by Perkins and the suspension of Scribner's magazine. Otherwise may get published.

Since then have completed a new story, yest. and am starting another one.[4] Thanks a lot for the letter from Reynolds and for your sterling attitude on the censorship question.[5] All France is proud of you. Don't listen to any of the subversive element of Juan les Pins, exemplified by the police or other bureaucratic classes, that may try to nullify this. The author of Gatsby le Magnifique will be backed by at least as many people as went to bat for Dreyfuss. Don't let them jail you. Just don't let them. The real France is backing you.[6]

Hadley and I are still living apart. I am thinking of riding down to Marseilles on my bike in Oct. and living in Marseilles for a month or so and working. Will ride over and see you when you get the book finished.[7] Our life is all gone to hell which seems to be the one thing you can count on a good life to do. Needless to say Hadley has been grand and everything has been completely my fault in every way. That's the truth, not a polite gesture. Still having been in hell now since around last Christmas with plenty of insomnia to light the way around so I could study the terrain I get sort of used to it and even fond of it and probably would take pleasure in showing people around. As we make our hell we certainly should like it.

I cut The Sun to start with Cohn—cut all that first part. made a number of minor cuts and did quite a lot of re-writing and tightening up. Cut and in the proof it read like a good book. Christ knows I want to write them a hell of a lot better but it seemed to move along and to be pretty sound and solid. I hope to hell you'll like it and I think maybe you will.

Have a swell hunch for a new novel. I'm calling it the World's Fair. You'll like the title.[8]

Give my love to Zelda and tell her how sorry we were not to see you when we came around to say goodbye. I haven't been drinking, haven't been in a bar, haven't been at the Dingo, Dome nor Select.[9] Haven't seen anybody.

Not going to see anybody. Trying unusual experiment of a writer writing. That also will probably turn out to be vanity. Starting on long semi-permanent bike trip to last as long as the good weather lasts as soon as my present piles go down. Then will get a lot of work done, all the stories I want to write, probably working in Marseilles. Then we'll see.

The world is so full of a number of things I'm sure we should all be as happy as kings.[10] How happy are kings?

Stevenson.

Yrs always,

Ernest

Walsh, author of the Soldier drugfiend bullbaiter poem is attacking me to the extent of several columns in the next This Quarter charging Hemingway has sold out to the vested interests.[11] I wrote him a postcard saying his poem made me vomit when This Q. came out. Now it seems from a flawless knight of LITERATURE I have become a hack writer in the pay of SCRIBNERS earning these vast sums. I saw a copy of this which he is circulating largely in carbons before publication. Gentlemen I give you the Irish.

Write if you fell like it. I get lonesome.

PUL, TLS

This letter is dated c. 7 September 1926 in Baker's *SL* (216). However, at the time of this letter, EH had received the 8 September 1926 cable from Perkins informing him of Scribner's acceptance of "The Killers" and "since then" had completed one story and begun another. He had not yet received the letter of 8 September 1926 from the editor of *New Masses* rejecting "An Alpine Idyll" (JFK).

1 EH is apparently responding to notes Fitzgerald wrote on two letters he had received and then forwarded to EH. At the end of a 12 August 1926 letter from literary agent Harold Ober (1881–1959) expressing interest in EH's work, Fitzgerald added a note to EH claiming he was "on the wagon + working like hell," signing it "Ernestine Murphy" (PUL; Bruccoli *Fitz-Hem*, 71). On the verso of a 17 August 1926 letter from Perkins, Fitzgerald wrote to EH, "Working like hell. Are you?" (JFK). While the *Saturday Evening Post*, edited by George Horace Lorimer (1869–1937), had rejected EH's submissions, it served as Fitzgerald's primary outlet for his stories and paid him top prices. Under Lorimer's editorship (1899–1936), the *Post* reached a peak circulation of nearly three million, making it then the most widely read magazine in the United States. La Petite Chaumière was a bar in Paris known for its homosexual clientele. EH refers to it unfavorably in the "Birth of a New School" chapter of *MF*.

2 A drawing by French artist, filmmaker, and author Jean Cocteau (1889–1963) appeared on the front cover of the fourth number of the pamphlet series by The As Stable Publications that featured EH's "Today Is Friday," a story in the form of a one-act play.

3 On 8 September, Perkins had sent EH both a cable and a letter accepting "The Killers" for publication in *Scribner's Magazine* (PUL). The formal acceptance letter from Robert Bridges is dated 15 September 1926. EH would receive $200 for the story, his first to appear in *Scribner's Magazine* (March 1927).

4 Smith identifies the "new story" that EH completed the previous day as "A Canary for One" and the second as "In Another Country" (159). For an in-depth discussion of the stages of Hemingway's work on this story, see Scott Donaldson's "Preparing for the End: Hemingway's Revisions of 'A Canary for One'," *Studies in American Fiction* 6 (Autumn 1978): 203–11.

5 EH refers to Ober's 12 August letter to Fitzgerald, in which Ober said that although he had not been able to place "Fifty Grand," he hoped to see more of EH's work. Regarding the "censorship question" of *SAR*, Fitzgerald told Perkins in a letter dated by Turnbull as c. 10 August 1926, "The only censorable thing I found in Ernest's book was the 'balls' conversation. I didn't find the James thing objectionable but then he seems to me to have been dead fifty years" (Andrew Turnbull, ed., *The Letters of F. Scott Fitzgerald* [New York: Scribner's, 1963], 207).

6 EH refers to the title of the French version of *The Great Gatsby*, translated by Victor Llona (1886–1953) and published in Paris by Simon Kra in 1926. Alfred Dreyfus (1859–1935), a French Jewish army officer, was convicted of treason in 1894 for allegedly selling military secrets to the German government. Over the next decade, the Dreyfus Affair would split the French public into two camps. Initially, those with anti-Semitic, nationalist sentiments supported the verdict, but later, following an 1899 retrial, many came to Dreyfus's defense and accused the French government and army of plotting against him. In 1906 a civil court of appeals overturned the guilty verdict and Dreyfus was freed, but the army would not declare his innocence until 1995.

7 In a letter of [23 December 1926], Fitzgerald would express regret that EH did not come to Marseilles (JFK; Bruccoli *Fitz–Hem*, 79). The Fitzgeralds had been staying at Juan-les-Pins, about 120 miles from Marseilles.

8 "The World's Fair" was an early working title for the novel that would later become Fitzgerald's *Tender Is the Night* (1934).

9 EH later recalled meeting Fitzgerald for the first time at the Dingo bar on the rue Delambre, off the boulevard Montparnasse (*MF*, "Scott Fitzgerald"). The Dingo is mentioned by name in *SAR*, as are Le Dôme and Le Select, cafés on the boulevard du Montparnasse.

10 EH quotes in its entirety the one-sentence poem "Happy Thought" by Robert Louis Stevenson, included in his 1885 collection *A Child's Garden of Verses*.

11 The first line of Walsh's poem "Ernest Hemingway," published in *This Quarter* no. 2, reads: "Papa soldier pugilist bullfighter."

To Ezra Pound, [c. after 10 September 1926]

Dear Ezra:

Foyot's gave me the news. It's great and I hope everything's all right.[1]

Maybe you wont be back in time to get this but anyway I will go to Lavigne's (Toulousian Nigger) for lunch.[2] Come on up there if you're not lunching. I'll be there from 12 on.

Suppose as I dont know how things are we'd better not make any dates.

You can reach me at 69 Froidevaux. Hadley at Hotel Beauvoir 43 Avenue de L'Observatoire. Let us know anything to do.

I'll be at the Lilas tomorrow morning from 10 on if you want to come for 2nd breakfast, walking or talking. If you want to see me tonight send me a pneu.[3]

All our love to Dorothy Also the Father.

Hem

Yale, ALS

1 Ezra and Dorothy Pound stayed at the Hotel Foyot at 33, rue de Tournon, Paris, during the summer of 1926. She had become pregnant by another man while traveling in Egypt unaccompanied by Pound. The "news" likely refers to the birth of Omar Shakespear Pound (1926–2010) on 10 September. Hemingway, not Pound, took her by taxi to the American Hospital in Neuilly outside of Paris for the delivery, and the next day Pound signed papers identifying himself as the boy's father.
2 Le Nègre de Toulouse, an inexpensive restaurant at 157–59, boulevard du Montparnasse, where EH and Hadley often dined. Paris records verify that Lavigne was its proprietor between 1924 and 1929 (Gerry Brenner, *A Comprehensive Companion to Hemingway's* A Moveable Feast: *Annotation to Interpretation* [Lewiston, New York: Edwin Mellen Press, 2000], 283). The restaurant is mentioned in *SAR* (Chapters 3, 4, and 8) and *MF* ("With Pascin at the Dôme").
3 La Closerie des Lilas, at 171, boulevard du Montparnasse, where EH had written portions of *SAR*. The café appears in the novel (Chapters 4, 6, 8) and in *MF*, most prominently in "Evan Shipman at the Lilas." *Pneu*: abbreviation for "pneumatique."

To Maxwell Perkins, [c. 28 September 1926]

Dear Mr. Perkins:

I am awfully pleased about The Killers and will send you some more. Everything you say about the arrangement of the title page etc. of The Sun seems to me be very good. Unless you have already done it, in which case it doesn't matter, there is no necessity of changing the Roger Prentiss to

Robert as I verified the name of the kid I was at school with and found it was Prentiss as a first name.[1]

I was just joking about profanity in the next book.[2] I have a grand novel to write when I get some tranquility in the head again. There will be no real people in it as there unfortunately were in The Sun etc. That is a thing that I'll never do again. You see last year after Pamplona Don Stewart went to Vichy and took a five weeks cure for his liver and kidneys and I unfortunately cleansed mine out in writing The Sun Also Rises.[3] But this is all only for you and me to know. In addition to Mr. Prescott you may have recognized Harold Stearns in the gentleman who was always going off by himself like a cat and I'm afraid Ford may be in it and a number of other people[4] and I am to assist in some major capacity at the marriage of Brett and Mike next month, the divorce having finally been obtained.[5] That is I imagine I will assist if the book has not already appeared. All of which is very depressing.

JFK, TL

This is apparently a draft of the following letter to Perkins, dated 28 September 1926. It includes a paragraph about *SAR* that EH omitted from the final letter.

1 In addition to telling EH that *Scribner's Magazine* had accepted "The Killers," Perkins in his letter of 8 September 1926 outlined design plans for the title page, epigraphs, and dedication of *SAR* (PUL).

2 In his 21 August letter to Perkins, EH said that they might simply have to consider *SAR* a profane book and "hope that the next book will be less profane—or perhaps more sacred." In his 8 September reply, Perkins reassured EH, "As for profanity in the next book, I would not worry about that" (PUL).

3 Vichy, fashionable spa town in the Auvergne region of France known for the curative properties of its mineral waters. In his autobiography, *By a Stroke of Luck!* (1975), Stewart recalled that after the 1925 fiesta, it also occurred to him that the events of Pamplona "might make interesting material for a novel"; however, while EH had started work on *SAR*, Stewart had joined the Murphys at Antibes, "bought a bottle of sun-tan lotion and relaxed on the beach" (144). Stewart made no mention of going to Vichy.

4 Stearns is the prototype for the dissipated Harvey Stone in *SAR* (Chapter 6), and Ford Madox Ford is thinly disguised as Henry Braddocks (Chapter 3).

5 The characters Brett Ashley and Mike Campbell are based upon Duff Twysden (née Mary Duff Stirling Smurthwaite, 1893–1938) and her fiancé Patrick (Pat) Stirling Guthrie (1895–1932), who were part of EH's entourage at the 1925 Fiesta of San Fermín in Pamplona. In *SAR*, Brett is awaiting a divorce and has plans to marry Mike. In actuality, Duff was divorced from Sir Roger Thomas Twysden (1894–1934) in 1926, but she and Guthrie separated in 1927; she would marry American painter Clinton King (1901–1979) on 21 August 1928.

To Maxwell Perkins, 28 September 1926

Dear Mr. Perkins:

It was very pleasant about The Killers and I will surely send you some more stories. All that you say about the arrangement of the title page etc. of the Sun seems very good and I am sure that it will look well as you arrange it.

Unless it is done already, in which case it doesn't matter, there is no need to change Roger to Robert Prentiss. I verified the name of the kid I went to school with and found Prentiss was his first name.

When do you expect The Sun to be out? I had a letter from Curtis Brown saying they were sending copies of Cape's edition of In Our Time and had written Scribners for corrected proofs of The Sun to show to Cape.[1] It seems to me that he should take it.

Manuel Komroff, who edited the Marco Polo book, and sometimes writes excellent stories read Fifty Grand and when I told him why it had never been published offered to try and cut it 1500 words for me. He's taken it out in the country with him and when it comes back it may be a good magazine stoy and I could publish it in the original when I have a book of stories out. But if I don't like it I won't send it. I think Mr. Bridges might like to see some of Komroff's stories. Some of his eastern stories are very fine and very short.[2]

I will write Mr. Bridges a letter but am hurrying this off to catch the Majestic.[3]

Yours always,

Ernest Hemingway

69 Rue Froidevaux

28 September 1926

PUL, TLS

1 In a letter of 22 September 1926, the Curtis Brown literary agency had informed EH they were sending him three copies of Cape's British edition of *IOT* (JFK). The agency had earlier informed EH that because Cape was "very anxious" to read *SAR*, they had requested corrected proofs from Scribner's (31 August 1926, JFK).
2 Komroff's edition of *The Travels of Marco Polo*, a revised version of the 1818 translation by William Marsden (1754–1836), was published by Boni & Liveright in 1926. "*Marco Polo*"

was among the titles listed on the verso of EH's 29 June [1926] letter to Isidor Schneider. Komroff's first book, *The Grace of Lambs: Stories,* had been published in 1925 by Boni & Liveright. In a letter to Hadley of 16 September 1926, Komroff wrote that "Fifty Grand" was "by far the best prize fight story" he had ever read and that he was optimistic he could condense it "without changing hardly a word" (JFK).

3 The *Majestic,* owned by the White Star Line, was then the world's largest transatlantic ocean liner. The ship would leave Cherbourg on 29 September and arrive in New York on 5 October 1926.

To Isidor Schneider, [30 September 1926]

Dear Isidor—

Thanks for your grand letter with the pictures and for sending me the book. I did not get the letter until just now as Cook's held it in Madrid or I would have cabled you. But I do hope so that now there is nothing to worry about about Helen. It would be too damned awful to have anything happen to you two.[1]

The world is so tough and can do so many things to us and break us in so many ways that it seems as though it were cheating when it uses accident or disease.[2] But I hope so that now Helen is all right and you can both look ahead without the kind of things that sometimes you can forget only for a little while when you are first waked up in the morning and think things are like they always were.

Hadley and I have been having some hell too—but all you can do about hell is last through it. If you can last through it. And you have to. Or at least I always will I guess because I am very prejudiced against suicide because somehow I would not like to even run a chance of having to spend the rest of the time with a lot of the sort of people who commit suicide. Altho of course that doesn't hold true because there are some swell ones. The real reason for not committing suicide is because you always know how swell life gets again after the hell is over. So you have to resolve in advance to last out the time when you don't believe that.

So this sounds like a nice cheerful letter doesn't it. But really it is and if you two are all right I feel all right.

Scribner's have had the final proofs of The Sun etc. for about three weeks now so you know better than I when it will be out. I hope you'll like it but [i]t is all right if you don't because if I am any good and can last, and will last, sooner or later I'll have one you will like. If you'll give me your house address I'll write to Scribner's to send you an advance copy to that address. Something they might not do to the Boni and Liveright address. I have six stories toward the next book. One, the bull fight one, you read. That isn't a part of The Sun although I saw in some clipping that it was. There is a long fight story that they wanted to publish if I'd cut it a little and I couldn't cut it. and four shorter ones.³ Now I'll write stories for a while and like to very much. Scribner's are publishing a story called The Killers pretty soon. They sent a check for 200 dollars for it. That is the first story I've ever sold in America. They were going to give me 250 for the fight story and it made me sore as hell that I couldn't cut it. But each word hung on each other word.

You were awfully damned good to me to send the books. Tropic death hasn't come yet. Some of Waldo Frank's book was good but it was really shit. Soldier's Pay I couldn't finish. But unless you get books like that and try and read them you are fooled into thinking they are maybe very fine. Tropic Death sounds good. In Our Time is out in England now. If you'd like one of the English edition I'll send it.

If you'll send me The Red and Black and Harry Kemp's new book and a Sentimental Journey and Ezra's poems when you get time and let me pay for them I will be very happy.⁴ I borrowed the catalogue from Titus's bookshop.⁵ Also <u>Avowals</u> by Mr. Moore, not Miss Moore, and the Brillat-Savarin book.⁶ And let me pay for them because that way I can ask and buy books that I wouldn't ever be able to af[f]ord any other way.

You can send them directly here to 69 rue Froidevaux Paris XIV which is where I am living now. The permanent Paris address is care The Guaranty Trust Co. of N.Y., 1, rue des Italiens, Paris. I am afraid you sent some things to the American Express Co. and they got lost because I had a notice from them that some things—packages—had been held one week for me and then returned. They are bastards.

The Guaranty is very careful and reforwards everything. But 69 Rue Froidevaux is where I'll be living until January. Coming to America, which was the only thing I really wanted to do, has all blown up to hell. It was my fault too. But that never makes things any better. I don't mind bad things that happen when they are other people's fault.

When I think it over maybe you had better send everything to The Guaranty Trust Co. address because maybe I will ride down to Marseilles on my bike and work there for a month or so and it would be very exciting to have books come there and the Guaranty Trust would forward them.

So Long Isidor and I hope that Helen is well and that everything is all right. And please write me. All my love to Helen.

Yours always,

Ernest

Columbia, TLS

1 EH is responding to a six-page letter Schneider sent him from New York on 5 August 1926, c/o Thomas Cook & Sons, Madrid; at Madrid it was stamped on 20 August 1926 and forwarded to the Villa America, Cap d'Antibes. The envelope bears EH's note "Answered Sept 30." Schneider had enclosed a snapshot of his wife, Helen, taken in Bermuda and a photo postcard of the couple taken in New York. He reported that Helen was sick and that he had been "nursing and consoling her" (JFK).

2 EH's wording anticipates one of the key passages of *FTA*: "If people bring so much courage to this world the world has to kill them to break them, so of course it kills them. The world breaks every one and afterward many are strong at the broken places" (Chapter 34).

3 "The Undefeated," "Fifty Grand," "An Alpine Idyll," "Today Is Friday," "The Killers," and "A Canary for One." All six stories would be included in his 1927 collection *MWW*.

4 The books EH names were 1926 Boni & Liveright publications: *Tropic Death*, a short-story collection by Caribbean writer Eric Walrond (1898–1966); *Virgin Spain* by Waldo Frank; *Soldiers' Pay* by William Faulkner; *The Red and the Black*, a translation by Charles Kenneth Scott Moncrieff of Stendhal's 1830 novel *Le Rouge et le Noir*; *More Miles: An Autobiographical Novel* by American poet and playwright Harry Kemp (1883–1960); *A Sentimental Journey through France and Italy*, originally published in 1768, by British novelist Laurence Sterne (1713–1768); and Ezra Pound's *Personae: The Collected Poems*.

5 In 1924 Edward Titus (1870–1952) opened a bookshop at 4, rue Delambre named At the Sign of the Black Manikin, described by Hugh Ford as "what in France is called a *librairie*, a sort of rare book room and gallery combined" (*Published in Paris: American and British Writers, Printers, and Publishers in Paris, 1920–1939* [New York: Macmillan, 1975], 120).

6 In 1926 Boni & Liveright published a new edition of the 1919 novel *Avowals* by Irish writer George Moore (not the American poet Marianne Moore, as EH notes) and a translation of the landmark text on gastronomy by French lawyer and epicure Jean Anthelme Brillat-Savarin (1755–1826), first published in 1825 as *Physiologie du goût; ou, Méditation de gastronomie transcendante*. The Boni & Liveright edition, titled *The Physiology of Taste; or, Meditations on Transcendental Gastronomy*, included a foreword by Frank Crowninshield.

To Robert Bridges, 30 September 1926

Dear Mr. Bridges:

Thank you very much for the check for The Killers. I shall look for the proof at my permanent Paris address—care The Guaranty Trust Company of N.Y., 1, Rue des Italiens.

I don't know whether you know Manuel Komroff's stories but I am suggesting to him that he send you some. He edited Marsden's translation of Marco Polo and has travelled over a great part of Marco Polo's route and writes stories of the east that are often very excellent—and always very short. Edward O'Brien is dedicating his next anthology to him although I do not believe this is as yet known.[1]

Very truly yours,
Ernest Hemingway.
69 Rue Froidevaux
Paris XIV
Sept 30, 1926.

PUL, TLS

1 *The Best Short Stories of 1926*, dedicated to Komroff, would be published in December. In his introduction (dated "London. September 25, 1926"), O'Brien wrote that Komroff's "tales" have "the vitality of improvisation and the ripeness of well-cultivated art" (x).

To T. S. Eliot, [c. after 16 October 1926]

Dear Mr. Eliot:—

It is much too late but I would like to apologise to you for an insulting statement I made about you in an article in the Transatlantic Review for September 1924. I was looking at the Bound Volumnes of the Transatlantic today and saw the article and it made me feel remorse for being more violent and ignorant than usual even.

I felt very badly when Conrad died. I had read all his books; at that time it was very difficult for me to read and I could always read his novels, and I felt very badly that there would be no more of them. Why, because I was sorry Conrad was dead, I should insult you in an article which I was writing at the request of Mr. Ford, who was waiting in the next room for it to be finished, I can only lay to that violence which you may have observed at ~~the cheaper~~ certain funerals and wakes.[1]

It now occurs to me that I may have insulted you in an article written also by request (of the late Mr. Walsh this time) to the greater glory of Mr. Pound.[2] I fortunately have not this here so that re-reading it can not further depress me this afternoon. I hope, if you ever saw it, you will lay it to this same violence.

I hope to have gotten out of this violence so that it would now be possible to speak well of the dead without insulting the living and praise a friend without insulting his friends and contemporaries.

~~At any rate it makes me feel much better to have written this to you~~ It is quite possible that you never read either of these ~~famous~~ articles but ~~can only wish I never had~~ if you should have ~~It is~~ ~~It gives me a certain satisfaction to apologise to you and~~ I hope by making ~~it~~ [*EH insertion*: this apology] as short, although complete, as possible that it will not bore you—

Yours very truly,
Ernest Hemingway.

JFK, ALDS

The conjectured letter date is based on EH's reference to "the late Mr. Walsh." *This Quarter* editor Ernest Walsh died on 16 October 1926.

1 Joseph Conrad died on 3 August 1924. In his essay for the September 1924 *Transatlantic Review*, EH had written that if he could resurrect Conrad "by grinding Mr. Eliot into a fine dry powder and sprinkling that powder over Mr. Conrad's grave," he "would leave for London early tomorrow morning with a sausage grinder" ("Conrad, Optimist and Moralist," 341–42).

2 In the first issue of *This Quarter* (Spring 1925), dedicated to Ezra Pound, EH had called Pound "a major poet" and Eliot, by contrast, "a minor poet": "All of Eliot's poems are perfect and there are very few of them. He has a very fine talent and he is very careful of it. He never takes chances with it" ("Homage to Ezra," 222).

To Ezra Pound, [c. 12–18 October 1926]

[*Archibald MacLeish writes:*]
Here for example you have Santos[1]

AMacLeish

[*EH writes:*]
Mas Santos que Cantos y No hay derecho Senores.[2]
~~In the bull fights~~
Sorry I wasnt home. How are your absci?

Hem

Yale, A Postcard S; verso: photograph captioned "ZARAGOZA. Muro exterior de La Seo" [Exterior wall of La Seo Cathedral]; postmark: [ZARA]GOZA

Traveling from Paris by overnight train, EH and MacLeish arrived in Zaragoza on 12 October, the first day of the weeklong fiesta of Pilar, the patron saint of the province of Aragón, celebrating the appearance of the Virgin of Pilar to Saint James. Festivities included marching bands, parades, masses, strolling folk musicians, a religious procession, and an evening concert (Mandel *HDIA*, 473; Reynolds *AH*, 68–71). Ticket stubs at JFK indicate that EH and MacLeish attended bullfights on 14 and 17 October, thus seeing at least two of the four bullfights of the fiesta, which EH later described as "the last important *feria* of the season"

(*DIA*, "Dates of Bullfights"). This postcard, mailed from Spain, is addressed to Pound at the Hotel Foyot in Paris but was forwarded to him in Rapallo.

1 *Santos*: saints (Spanish). Pictured on the postcard is La Seo (the Cathedral of San Salvador), one of Zaragoza's two imposing cathedrals. In addition to numerous representations of saints, La Seo houses relics of three: San Valero (patron saint of Zaragoza), San Vicente, and San Lorenzo.
2 EH is probably punning on the Spanish *cantos*, meaning songs or religious chants, in reference to Pound's *Cantos*. The sentence loosely translates as "More saints than songs, and that's not fair, gentlemen" (Spanish).

To Clarence Hemingway, 22 October 1926

35, Rue de Fleurus[1]

Paris VI

Oct 22, 1926

Dear Dad:

I am dreadfully sorry to learn of Grandfather's death. It makes me very sad not to have seen him again before he died but it is good he died so happily and peacefully.[2]

Our own plans have been entirely upset. The only thing certain is that we can not now come to the States this fall or winter. It is a great disappointment when we had counted so on seeing you.

As for my war trophies I hope you can put them all in a trunk or box and store them if you sell the house as I value them very much for Bumby.[3]

Both Bumby and Hadley are well and we all send you and Mother our love and deepest sympathy on Grandfather's death.

Best love to all

Ernie

I am so sorry not to have written more this summer and fall but have been held up by not knowing whether we should be able to come or not. I hoped until the last that we should as it was what I wanted to do more than anything else could possibly be.

Aunt Mary never let us know when she was in Paris. Or else we were still in Spain.

She may have tried for us through the American Express—but that has ceased to be our address for over two years. I felt terribly not to see her. We entertained Franklin [White Hemingway] in Spain.[4]

Thank you and mother for your birthday letters. I hope I answered them—but I havent my files and I'm not sure.

I hope you had a good birthday and a fine wedding anniversary.[5]

Love to all the kids

Ernie

JFK, ALS; postmark: PARIS·S / [R.] DE VAUGI[R]ARD, 19 / 22–10 / 26

On the front of the envelope, EH wrote "Via Paqueboat / "Berengaria" / Cherbourg 23 Oct. 23." At the end of this letter, Clarence wrote "Rec'd / Nov. 2nd 1926."

1 The address of Hadley's new apartment, on the same street where Gertrude Stein and Alice B. Toklas lived. On the envelope flap, EH wrote his mailing address: "Guaranty Trust Co. of New York, 1, Rue des Italiens, Paris—France." He had not yet told his parents that he and Hadley had separated.

2 In his letter of 7 October 1926, Clarence wrote that his father, Anson Tyler Hemingway, had died that morning "with no suffering, slept away. The day before he had written several letters and paid up all his bills" (JFK).

3 In a letter of 21 September 1926, Clarence wrote that they expected to sell the "big house" any day and wondered what EH wanted his parents to do with "your war trophies and other things we have here" (JFK). In his 7 October letter, Clarence reported, "The home has not yet been sold and we are still hoping to get to Florid this winter" (JFK). Although Reynolds assumes this refers to the family home at 600 North Kenilworth Avenue (*AH*, 72–3), Baker reports that Clarence hoped to sell his deceased parents' nearby home on Oak Park Avenue (*Life*, 593). In his letter to EH of 18 December 1926, Clarence himself would clarify the reference, writing, "I think there is a Sale made of the Old Homestead," adding the inter-linear notation "400 N. OP. Ave." and commenting that he was eager to settle his father's estate before more taxes were due (JFK).

4 In his letter of 14 August 1926, Clarence wrote that EH's aunt Mary Hemingway (née Mary Eliza Williams, 1875–1974), wife of Clarence's brother Willoughby Hemingway (1874–1932), would be visiting Paris with their two children, Isabel (1908–2009) and Winifred (1916–2007) (JFK). In his 24 July 1926 letter to his father, EH had mentioned seeing his cousin Franklin White Hemingway in Madrid. In his 7 November 1926 response to this letter, Clarence would confirm that Aunt Mary had tried to find EH in Paris through American Express, but noted EH was probably in Spain at the time (JFK).

5 Clarence had turned fifty-five on 4 September. He and Grace had marked their thirtieth wedding anniversary on 1 October.

To Maxwell Perkins, 25 October 1926

October 25, 1926

Dear Mr. Perkins:

Thank you so much for paying the Romeike bill. I sent back the Killers proofs as soon as I received them. Scott writes occassionally from Juan les Pins. The bad weather has commenced now after a very wonderful autumn—the finest I ever remember in France.

Enclosed is a story.[1] I will try and send another soon—am working on them now. Nothing ever came of Komroff's cutting Fifty Grand.

The Sun should be out soon now I imagine. I'll be curious to see the reviews. Don Stewart has bet me 100 to 60 dollars that it will sell over 4,000 copies by the first of February so I stand to make 100 dollars more and if it really starts to sell, sixty dollars will not be much.[2] Also bought a 100 pesata lotery ticket in the Christmas Spanish lotery with a grand prize of 15 million pesetas so you see I have many irons in the fire.

With best wishes,

Very truly,

Ernest Hemingway

PUL, TLS

1 EH enclosed "A Canary for One," which Bridges, on behalf of *Scribner's Magazine*, accepted on 11 November 1926, paying $150 (JFK). The story would appear in the April 1927 *Scribner's Magazine* and in *MWW*, published in the fall of 1927.
2 *SAR* was first published by Scribner's on 22 October 1926 with an initial first print run of 5,090 copies and sold for $2.00. To meet demand, it would be reprinted in November 1926, in December 1926, in January 1927, and twice in February 1927 (Grissom, 58–59). By 4 February 1927 Perkins would be able to tell EH, "The book goes right on. It must now have passed twelve thousand" (PUL).

To Paul Nelson, [c. 28 October 1926]

69 rue Froidevaux

Thursday morning.

Dear Paul—

I find I have to go out this afternoon but I'll try and drop in on you before dinner this evening. If you're not there maybe you could leave word when you usually will be home. It was swell to see you again but you're looking pretty thin. I've felt a son of a bitch about not coming around but I felt so damn badly I did not want to see anybody

Hem.

JFK, TLS

On the envelope which bears no stamp or postmark, EH typed "<u>PNEUMATIQUE</u>." It is addressed to "Monsieur Paul NELSON / 70 bis rue Notre Dame des Champs," the address of Ezra and Dorothy Pound before they moved to Rapallo in 1924.

To Ezra Pound, [c. 31 October 1926]

Dear Ezra—

That will be fine. I don't get though whether you want stuff sent now to see if there is enuff and good enuff stuff to warrant yr. starting or just to know that there is stuff. As far as I'm concerned there is stuff.[1]

Also will be glad to write articles for said review as ferinstance On Ernest Walsh, Deceased. or any other topical subjects.

Christ knows there ought to be some review and there is at present no review of any sort.

Glad to hear no painting and hope no music.[2]

Who is going to put up the money and any other details? Don't be shy. I don't care who puts up money. Only like always to know.— Anything I've got or will have is yrs.

Hem.

Yale, TLS

1 EH is responding to Pound's letter of 28 October 1926, in which Pound asked if EH had "anything unsaleable and too good to be hidden in the Queerschnitt," as he was considering starting a literary review on his own. "I orter know by noo yearz whether there is enough stuff lying round apart from my own reserve, to make it worth while," Pound wrote (JFK).

Four issues of *The Exile* would be published in 1927–1928, with Pound serving as editor, publisher, and chief financial backer.

2 Pound had written that his review would include "NO art," but in his 3 November response to this letter he was not ready to assure EH "an abs. on-musical review" (JFK). Walsh's *This Quarter* had included reproductions of paintings, with a supplement of musical scores by George Antheil in the second number.

To Ezra Pound, [c. 6 November 1926]

Signor Duce—

Pay me the compliment of imagining that Miss OxP X does <u>not</u> write.[1]

As for distribution you should use both Titus and Sylvia. The problem is simple. Nobody goes into Titus's that would buy magazines. Sylvia on the other hand will probably do all she can to avoid selling them but a certain number will be sold by underlings. Titus on the other hand will sell them. Use them both. (If anybody comes in that would read a mag. containing both of us.)

Glad to hear yr. entering court of equity with clean hands. You might as well spend yr. money that way as on building bigger bassoons.[2]

If I get any money, and I may, will shove it yr. way. There is a chance, it seems, that my latest Oppiss may sweep America. Also hold 100 peseta ticket in Christmas Lottery)Spanish) first prize 15 MILLION pesteas— many others down to a MIllion. At any rate put me down for a contributing membership on a basis of no art, practically no music, no women writers who have not contributed at least 1,000 francs to all male contributing members and then let them be able to be blackballed by one vote. Or else let us publish the writings of RICH CONTRIBUTORS OR WOMEN including NATALIE BARNEY &MISS COWSHED with the little addenda— COUMMUNICATED after them like the true to life news item ads in the HERALD.[3]

Was in Spain—at Saragossa—wrote you a postal card. Mac Leish is a hell of a good guy and has written some good ones. Started late. He is not a mis-tic and will contribute. He is no croesus, reports were exaggerated, but a good spender and will kick through.[4] He also is against WOMEN WRITERS. Write him you are going to start a review wit no women poets

133

allowed to contribute, that you are paying for it, that there are to be NO DONORS, OR BACKERS, or privileged gents and that so far you and I are the only backers and ask him if he wants to get aboard—then wait for the check. [*EH crossed out the remainder of this paragraph and the next one with a large x and pencilled in the left margin*: this unimportant.] Might mention will not be a musical review. He thinks you are the greatest poet that ever lived and the cantos the swellest poems but he also does not give a shit about moosical criticism as a form of prose.

How would you like me to devote my life, in public, to proving what a lovely bull fighter young Cagancho[5] is and proving it in technical terms nobody could understand—and maybe he'll go bad like all the other boy wonders anyway. Fine you say. Fine I say too. Bull fighting is certainly as good an art as music. I see your point. Maybe we'll have a little bull fight criticism too. All the gents their hobbies.

Don't say you can't write a letter to MacLeish. Not an appeal. A letter. Noboddy writes letters any easier than you.[6]

As for writers. There are no writers. Some might however appear.

Bill Williams has always been the same except he gets a little duller. He writes well but it is getting very worn and shiny.

Mac Almon, without money, would never have been published anywhere by anybody except for Village and about 3 maybe 4 stories. Make him give you good ones. Don't publish shit because written by McAlmon.[7]

Let's have no friendship in this fucking review.

Next time will send some stuff. Have to copy it.

I am not sorry Walsh is dead. Except in the sense of being sorry for anybody dead. And I have known too many good guys die to be able to sweat much from the eyes about the death of a shit.

It is horse ass folly to think you can get good stuff ahead for three numbers. If you get good stuff, really good stuff, for one number other and better stuff will come. There never was in the world good stuff ahead enough for three numbers of anything.

On the other hand [*EH insertion*: referring Paris Herald,] Walsh got a swell obituary on front page of Tribune which noboddy grudged him. What difference does an obituary make to anybody?[8]

Ford ran a review for a year and did not print one single good story—the
only ones that looked even externally good were rewritten in the office—
only good story he ran of mine was Indian woman having a baby.[9]

Ford cares nothing for printing good stories. He cares for editing a
magazine of significance, vague [*EH pencilled arrow pointing from* "vague"
to "significance"], but dull and middle-westish. Says he brought out great
group of middle west writers, right off the prairies. One of them a,
Asch, a russian jew from Paris and N.Y., another Djuna who's never been
west of Albany, another Carlos Drake fils of the biggest hotel owner in
America[10]—and all time spent by Ford kissing asses of people with money
and insulting others with a little less money to prove we never kiss the ass
of anyone.

R.I.P. [*Heavy pencil cancellation obscuring rest of typewritten line*]

Let's insult nobody and kiss nobody's ass and not publish the ladies
and maybe print literature—the production of which can be stimulated
by there being some place it can go. We can blague each other in the
back of the magazine. Us on one another and things in general would
make better reading than a humourless near celt like Walsh razzing
things in general and Walsh's razzing was all I could ever read in That
monumental review. There was so much shit surrounding your cantos
that they were like say over-manuered tulip bulbs. I mean shit writ by
others.

You'll never see a guaranteed sale of 200 copies unless somebody
gurantees to take 200 copies and pay for '3m and that makes ten guys at
twenty copies apiece and twenty copies apiece is 10 bucks a shot or 40 a year
if it's a quarterly.[11] So far that is a lot of money for me unless I hit on the
book or lottery—but if I make any money at all can easily spot you forty
bucks or 50 bucks. However I have now absolutely no money except the
money I make writing and The Sun etc. has to sell 3500 copies before I
touche another sou—that being the amount of sales I've already covered
with advances. I get 200 bucks a story from Scribner's and from the last nine
month's product have sold one story ["The Killers"]. I won't write stories to
order for Scribners or anybody else and so it is only the occassional one, the
let us say sport, that can be sold.

However this last book may go well. At present I have 110 dollars ahead to live on indefinitely. The franc has taken this opportunity to go under thirty. There is now no cheap money anywhere in Europe. Which is bad.

This is not an hard luck story. It is simply to outline the actual financial situation of one of yr. reviews big financial backers. I will never be so broke as not to be able to contribute ten bucks toward a number IF we can get some good stuff. Which is how you feel about the review situation maybe.

I think fifty copies might be consumed in Paris.

Transatlantic with all the poohbah never sold over 350. You could get rid of others by subscription and in N.Y. etc. where they sell but where you never get the money from. Subscriptions are the only way of getting money. That and sale from places like Titus and Sylia's. The overhead eats it all up any other way. I am sure Scribner's would not touch it. Even though I aint seen it. At my safest am regarded by Scribner's a little as nice old lady regards her trained rattle snake[12] that may be atavistic. Have put all of worst side forward. Write. Will be in and out here for next 3 mos. Then a long way away.

Hem

Love to Dorothy—

Yale, TL/ALS

1 Probably a reference to Pauline Pfeiffer. The typescript is unclear: EH may have intended to overstrike the letters O and P with three small x's, or vice versa. In his letter to EH of 3 November 1926, Pound said he was "not personaly in favour of having lady writers" in his new journal, "not unless Miss Fife herself writes" (JFK).

2 Pound had asked EH's "candid opinium" as to possible distributors for the journal in Paris: bookstore owners Edward Titus (At the Sign of the Black Manikin), Sylvia Beach (Shakespeare and Company), or both. Saying he was "too old to APPEAL" for funding, Pound was prepared to fund the review himself to maintain independence. Pound had noisily been learning to play the bassoon, as EH later recalled in *MF* ("Birth of a New School").

3 Natalie Barney (1876–1972), American expatriate writer, wealthy heiress and central figure in the lesbian community of the Left Bank, was well known for the literary salon she held at her home on rue Jacob. "MISS COWSHED," apparently a reference to one or more of the other women writers on the expatriate scene, may be a play on the last name of Djuna Barnes; a rhyming reference to Ethel Moorhead, co-editor and financial backer of *This Quarter*; or an allusion to Gertrude Stein, who used the expression "to have a cow" to mean sexual pleasure in her recently published work *A Book Concluding With As a Wife Has a Cow: A Love Story* (Paris: Éditions de la Galerie Simon, 1926).

4 In his 3 November letter, Pound had suggested that EH let MacLeish know of the planned review, saying, "The rich bastards has got to pay their way" and adding, "If you hadn't tole

me he wuz rich, I shd. prob. have axd. you if he had any mss." However, Pound recalled that *Poetry* magazine had described MacLeish as "a mistick or sumfink" and commented "I aint long on misticks." Croesus, last king of Lydia in western Asia Minor (c. 560–546 B.C.), was legendary for his wealth.

5 Cagancho, fighting name of Spanish bullfighter Joaquín Rodríguez Ortega (1903–1984).

6 In a six-page letter to MacLeish of 19 November 1926, Pound would outline his hopes and plans for the new literary journal (JFK). MacLeish would donate $100 to support *The Exile*.

7 In his 3 November letter to EH, Pound mentioned William Carlos Williams and Robert McAlmon as potential contributors for the review.

8 Pound commented in his letter to EH, "I am sorry Mr Walshh is dead, and he shudn't have writ that article about you, but thats no reason for a little goat turd like Moss, to keep a two inch obit. out of the Herald." American expatriate Arthur Moss (1899–1969), founder and co-editor with Florence Gilliam of the little magazine *Gargoyle* (1921–1922), wrote a column of gossip and commentary about the Left Bank literary scene called "Over the River" for the Paris *Herald*. While the *Herald* apparently did not run an obituary for Walsh, the 26 October 1926 Paris *Tribune* featured a laudatory front-page article by Eugene Jolas headlined "Ernest Walsh, Poet and Editor, Dies in Monte Carlo At Age of Thirty-One."

9 EH's "Indian Camp" appeared under the heading "Works in Progress" in the April 1924 issue of Ford's *Transatlantic Review*.

10 Nathan Asch (1902–1964), Djuna Barnes, and Carlos Drake (1900–1992) were among the American expatriate writers whose work had appeared in the *Transatlantic Review*. Carlos Drake was the son of Tracy C. Drake (1864–1939), who with his brother John B. Drake (1872–1964) had built the luxurious Blackstone (1910) and Drake (1920) hotels in Chicago. *Fils*: son (French).

11 Pound wrote to EH that he planned to print 500 copies of the first issue of *The Exile* and was hoping for "a guaranteed, or at least probable sale of 200 copies." Five hundred copies of the first issue would be printed in spring 1927 by Maurice Darantière in Dijon, France; 270 of those would be sent to the United States, where 250 prepaid orders had been placed.

12 From this point the remainder of the letter is handwritten.

To Pauline Pfeiffer, 12 [November 1926]

October 12[1]

Dearest Pfife—

I have not heard anything since your letter October 26 when you were feeling so low except the one cable—communication stopped. When I wrote the last letter, that you will get some time the middle of next week—I did not know that you were in such terrible shape, nor even that you had begun to feel so badly and to worry. So that my letter will probably seem very little understanding and quite heartless. If I had only gotten your letter about how terribly you were feeling I could have written you about that—but it came just after the cable and after I'd sent my last letter.[2]

I've felt absolutely done for and gone to pieces Pfife and I might as well write it out now and maybe get rid of it that way. It was certain that your mother would feel badly about your marrying some one who was divorced, about breaking up a home, about getting into a mess—and it is certain too that silent disapproval is the most deadly and something that you can do nothing about. I was sure that part of it would go badly. Your mother naturally could not feel any other way. Jin showed me a letter she wrote, your mother, on November First saying that when you first came back you were looking well and quite happy and that now all that last week—the week during which I didn't hear from you—you were gone to pieces with nerves and in very bad shape.[3] That you were really quite alone in Piggott with your own thoughts and that your own thoughts were <u>naturally</u> not pleasant. So it looks as though you were being put through a fairly complete hell—which may—because you are not strong and very run down, break you. And then we're broken and what good did that do? So I have that to think about all day and all night—and the worry is like a band of some sort across the inside of the top of my head—and there isn't anything else. All I can think is that you that are all I have and that I love more than all that is and have given up everything for and betrayed everything for and killed off everything for are being destroyed and your nerves and your spirit broken all the time day and night and that I can't do anything about it because you won't let me.

I know that when my letter came you had to decide one way or another and I know you took the harder thing and the thing you thought was right and I admire your courage—but I don't know at all that it was what we would have done if we could have talked it over together and all the time day and night I've just felt that it was fatal and that we were being smashed.

You see when you went to Piggott you said that you were going to tell your mother and that if she didn't like it you would leave—or that she would have to come around to it—because it was us against the world and that we had to do our own thing and that you were going to rest and not worry and get he[a]lthy and strong above all not worry— Well and how did all that work out?

Now I can look back on the days when I had just straigt lonesomeness and waiting for you—but knowing that everything was all right and that it was just waiting—and they seem unbelievabely happy. Because now you have given yourself and your heart as a hostage to your mother too and the whole thing seems so absolutely hopeless. You were always going to cable if you went more than three days without writing—but there wasn't any cable—and your last letter was written the twenty sixth and Jinny got a letter from your mother yesterday that was written November First. And I didn't get anything. So I don't know whether you've given me up—or even then— before you got the letter about the new time—weren't trying to give me up and Pfife the time goes so slowly and so horribly and so flatly that I feel as though I would have to scream out and in the nights it is simply unbelievably terrible.

And all the time when you won't get letters and me instead of us being so happy and having all the world just being made into the figure representing sin and I get the horrors and hear you saying, "I won't go on with it. I won't. I can't do it. I just can't do it any longer."

So that's what I think about. Because if all the other promises were broken how can I rely on that one?

All day long I think of things to say to you and things to tell you and I start to clip things out of the paper and I think how simple it would be and how there was never anything, any difficulties that we got up by ourselves that we could not settle together,—only I'm absolutely tied.

I know that you did the extra three months because you thought that was what Hadley wanted—and also because at the time you were in such a state that sacrifice seemed like the thing to do. And of course al that Hadley wanted was to delay the divorce—anything to delay the divorce—she didn't want to just smash us both up—she won't admit it but she knows we're the same person—sometimes she has admitted it—but instead of giving her the delay that is practically the only thing left in the world that she wants we railroad her toward divorce and smash ourselves both up at the same time.

That makes nice thinking too.

So now no matter how bad it gets, I can't send the wire about <u>Hurry</u> because that is [a]utomatically shut off because you made the choice— evidently it was better to run a chance of smashing—or smash—than see each other and delay the divorce— So I can't do anything that might ever delay it.[4] And I'm not sure I'm not going to smash, Pfife.

Only I won't of course. Only when you see me maybe think or wonder is this what I went through it all about and that's what it will be.

Because anybody can be smashed and evidently we are to be smashed by choice—our own free choice—in a grievous matter, with deliberation and full consent.

So I know this is a lousy terribly cheap self pitying letter just wallowing in bathos etc. etc. etc. and etc. and so it is. Oh Christ I feel terribly. Just terribly Pfife.

And then where will be at the end when Hadley won't divorce or stalls again on the advice of friends.

As long as I had you I could stand anything and get through anything— and now I haven't got you and you've taken yourself deliberately away and I know you are sick and ill in the head and miserable Pfife and I can't stand it.

Last fall I said perfectly calmly and not bluffingly [a]nd during one of the good times that if this wasn't cleared up by christmas I [w]ould kill myself—because that would mean it wasn't going to clear up—and I've learned about blowing up from you Pfife and I can't stand it—and evidently all I can do is to remove the sin out of your life and avoid Hadley the necessity of divorce—and compliment ~~you both~~ Hadley—by killing myself. So then later I promised that I wouldn't do it or think about it under any circumstances until you came back. But now it is getting all out of control again and you have broken your promises and I should think that would let me out. Only nothing ever lets you out. But I'm not a saint, nor built like one, and I'd rather die now while there is still something left of the world than to go on and have every part of it flattened out and destroyed and made hollow before I die.

But I won't and I won't think about it and maybe you'll come back and maybe there will be something left of you and maybe we'll have a little guts and not try self sacrifices in the middle of surgical operations and maybe we'll come through and maybe an[d] maybe and maybe and maybe.

And all I want is you Pfife and oh dear god I want you so. And I'm ashamed of this letter and I hate it. But I had to get this poison out and I've just been stewed in it and not hearing and all the mail boats that get in with nothing on them and then that horrible awful letter from your mother yesterday in which you were getting your just punishment. I'm perfectly willing to go to hell after I'm dead rather than now. But not both. Altho now it looks like both. But it won't be. And please forgive this letter Pfife. It is everything contemptible. But that is the way I get when I'm too long away from you. Its only 84 days more now. And between now and next Friday I should surely get a letter and Jin has wired to hear how you are—and I pray for you hours every night and every morning when I wake up. I pray so for you to sleep and to hold tight and not to worry and oh Pfife I love you love you love you so—and I'm your all shot to hell

Ernest

JFK, TLS

1 Internal evidence establishes that EH misdated the letter and most likely wrote it on 12 November.

2 Having sailed from Boulogne on the *Pennland* on 24 September, Pauline was back at her parents' home in Piggott, Arkansas. She had left France after Hadley said she would agree to a divorce if EH and Pauline would stay apart for three months and were still in love at the end of the separation. In a letter to EH of 25–26 October 1926, Pauline had reported feeling "awfully low," partly because her mother, a staunch Roman Catholic, was distressed over Pauline's involvement with a married man (JFK). EH's "last letter" to Pauline remains unlocated, as does the "one cable" he received. However it is likely one she sent on 3 November; in a letter to EH that he had not yet received (dated "Oct. 2" but apparently written on 2 November), Pauline wrote, "I am wiring tomorrow NO COMMUNICATION BEGINNING NOW STOP WRITE TERMINATION DATE CUBISTS" (JFK). In that letter she referred to a "misunderstanding about the three months" that had prompted Hadley to request a month's extension of the separation agreement, and Pauline summarized the revised agreement: "We go three months beginning the 3rd of November without communication, but the letters already started may count, and so maybe the time doesn't start until those are all received, so that's why I have to know the date of the end of the three months. Then, as close to that date as possible Hadley gets the divorce." Surviving among EH's papers at JFK is an undated note in Hadley's hand that reads, "November 3rd to Feb. 3rd leave of absence without communication between Ernest M. Hemingway and Pauline Pfeiffer—Signed Hadley Richardson Hemingway." (The note is included in the plate section of this volume).

3 Pauline's sister, Jinny Pfeiffer, then in Paris, functioned as a go-between during the couple's separation.

4 In her letter of 2 [November], Pauline had mentioned their agreed-upon code words for an emergency cable: "Of course, if either of us gets shot, there is the cable HURRY and COMING."

To Ezra Pound, [c. 14 November 1926]

Dear Herr Gott—[1]

Glad to hear it's tericiary—hence judge it must be worse than a bad cold already.[2]

Re me on bulls—offer to write about bulls or their baiters was sarcasm— feeling that you must feel about bulls much as I do abt. electric pianos.[3]

YRpo[i]nt about Lil Review and stuff gotten ahead in those days well taken. Shall we say there were giants in those days. Or shall we say the giants had no publication facilities in those days while now the publication facilities have no giants.[4]

The only excuse, beside an organ for vituperation and the tri-annual publication of yr. cantos, for this review is if there is conceivably stuff being written by unknown guys who are presumably so disgusted by the shit being shovelled in every literary direction that they have not come out into their holes—preferring to work than to publish.

Are there such guys?

Once upon a time there were a few guys something like that. But now the facility for publication is so enormous and the stuff to be published so very weak and shitty—so that the ass burns in farting—that I don't know whether there is any good stuff. There must be stuff.—I know damn well there is—but <u>who</u> do you <u>know</u> that's writing <u>anything</u> worth publishing?

To bring that stuff out should be the function of a review.

The L.R. did not get you for it's first issue—

My own selfish interest in said rev. is to have a place to blow off into and a place to write stuff for sin trampas ni cartones[5]—knowing that there is some place where you can pooblish the stuff you ought to write and want to write with no thought about even any possibility that it would ever sell to Scribner's or other wolf chasers—.

As for McAlmon—that disappointed half assed fairy English jew ass licking stage husband literary figure—you won't have to keep the peace between us because I will keep a long way away from the above gt. British writer.[6]

Walsh fortunately is dead.

Twice when I've kidded abt. bulls you've taken me seriously. Leave us get bulls straight. I have never regarded bulls as anything but animals. I have never been a lover of animals. I have never heard of Mithra—lacking a classical education.[7] I have been very interested in bulls because people make large sums of money by killing them and bulls are the only animals bred to kill humans—a thing I always enjoyed doing myself and take an intelligent interest in. The technique of the bulls killing the gents and the gents killing the bulls I have and still am <u>greatly</u> interested in. You will recognize this as legitimate interest your having some interest in techniques yerself and remembering that gents have certain things that serve to occupy the mind which cannot always be focussed on production of literature, support of families, etc.

I shd. suggest that we might insult—

ALL FAIRIES.

The Dead Mr. Walsh.

The Living Carnavalli.

(What the hell has death or sickness got to do with it)[8]

I wd. be glad to write on the technique of making a man into the a martyred president without the necessity of killing him with a few observations on Ricciotti Garibaldi and an enquiry into the authenticity of attentats or making Lincolns overnight.[9] But fear you won't want that.

I would be glad to insult Gertrude Stein but would prefer to do it through a more widely circulated medium. Altho it might be more effective if coming from well inside.

I wd. consider insulting Coolidge a waste of time and at best poor amateur insulting on acct. neither of us having seen or known coolidge.[10]

[*EH insertion*: Cant think of people I hate at moment but] Would be glad however to insult anybody you pick out that I know.[11] To damn people properly you <u>must</u> have the dope on them[.] Imagine what a wonderful job of insulting Walsh could have done if he had known as much about me as I knew about him. He, poor guy, had to work with only a whos who sketch to go on.[12]

Let's have no windy insulting. Let's have facts.

Yrs.

Hem

Yale, TL/ALS

1 Literally, "Dear Mr. God," a pun on *der Herrgott*, a German expression for God or the Lord.

2 In a letter to EH dated "8 or 9 Nov." [1926], Pound wrote that the planned journal "wont be quarterly, it will be tertiary (that'll give em something to look up in the censor's dept.)" (JFK).

3 In the same letter, Pound wrote that he disliked animal stories ("The bathos of the bull etc.") and said, "hope we do not offend. But I feel about bulls and Blasco Ibanez, rather as you do about bassoons." EH likely alludes to Antheil's *Ballet Mécanique*, which had premiered in Paris on 19 June 1926. As reported on the front page of the Paris *Tribune* the following day, "The composer was at the mechanical piano, which controlled also a number of fans, propellers, xylophones, and other articles for producing sound." In response to the noisy displeasure of the audience, Pound had stood and shouted, "Silence, imbeciles!," using the "French inflection, though the audience was anything but French" ("George Antheil's Ballet Stirs Huge Audience to Plaudits and Catcalls," Paris *Tribune*, 20 June 1926, 1).

4 Pound wrote to EH that in 1917, when he was foreign editor of the *Little Review*, he "hadn't stuff to FILL three numbers" but planned "a FEECHURE, to make each of the first three or four numbers different from the other, and give each one a augment or kick." Pound felt it imperative that before going to press or announcing publication of his new review, he must have "THREE ITEMS OF INTEREST," one for each number, to "justify existence of yet anodder goddtamn review."

5 *Sin trampa ni cartón*: without tricks or fakery (Spanish, generally used in the singular form, rather than the plural form EH employs here).

6 Pound wrote in his letter that "Keepink the peace between you and MCA. will be a cinch" compared to other "diplomatic relations" he had mediated between writers. McAlmon, who was homosexual, was married from 1921 to 1927 to the poet Bryher (née Annie Winifred Ellerman, 1894–1983), daughter of English shipping magnate and financier Sir John Reeves Ellerman (1862–1933). Ellerman had provided the funding for McAlmon's Contact Press in Paris (which published EH's first book, *TSTP*, in 1923). Bryher had been involved since 1918 in a lesbian relationship with American poet H.D. (Hilda Doolittle, 1886–1961). McAlmon later described his marriage to Bryher as "legal only, unromantic and strictly an agreement" because as an unmarried woman she could not be away from home and travel freely (Robert McAlmon and Kay Boyle, *Being Geniuses Together 1920–1930*, rev. edn. with supplementary chapters and an afterword by Kay Boyle [San Francisco: North Point Press, 1984], 45). Bryher identified herself as Jewish.

7 Pound had remarked that he preferred "stories about Sweeds and Americans to stories about exotics, Mithraic ritual, etc.," referring to Mithraism, a Persian cult associated with bull sacrifice that spread throughout the Roman Empire in the second century A.D.

8 Pound had written, "Who the hell CAN we insult."

9 *Attentats*: assassination attempts (French). EH is referring to the attempted assassination of Benito Mussolini during a parade in Bologna on 31 October 1926 by teenaged anarchist Anteo Zamboni (1911–1926), who was killed by Fascists in the crowd. The next day, the Paris *Tribune* observed that "Signor Mussolini's miraculous escapes from death have had the effect of increasing his popularity among the Italian people, over whom he now exercises his powers as dictator with the entire country's ardent approval" ("Lynch Youth After Attempt to Slay Duce / Enraged Fascists Kill Assailant Who Fires on Mussolini," 1 November 1926, 1). Ricciotti Garibaldi, Jr. (1881–1951), a grandson of Italian patriot Giuseppe Garibaldi (1807–1882) and a suspected leader of the anti-Fascist movement, was arrested in Nice on 4 November 1926 by French Secret Service agents and confessed to being an *agent provocateur* for the Italian National Fascist Party.

10 In his 3 November letter, Pound advised EH, "if you feel like writing a life of Calidge Colvin or doing some other IMPRACTIcable or unpractical half sheet of verse, like the Peace Conference; dont sqush the impulse jess cause there aint no where to go" (JFK). Pound was referring to EH's poem about the 1922 Lausanne Peace Conference, "They All Make Peace—What is Peace" (published in the Spring 1923 *Little Review*).

11 From this point the remainder of the letter is handwritten, except for the typewritten "Yrs."

12 EH had sent Walsh a biographical sketch of himself that appeared in the first number of *This Quarter* among the notes on contributors (EH to Walsh, 29 January 1925 and [c. 30 January 1925]; *Letters* vol. 2, 230–34).

To Maxwell Perkins, 16 November 1926

November 16–1926

Dear Mr. Perkins:

Thanks so much for sending the reviews and advertisements.[1] The portrait, Bloomshield's drawing, looks much as I had imagined Jake Barnes; it looks very much like a writer who had been saddened by the loss or atrophy of certain non replaceable parts. It is a pity it couldn't have been Barnes instead of Hemingway. Still it is fine to have at last succeeded in looking like a writer. The ads and the blurb seem excellent.[2]

I wish that I could do as you suggest about inserting some of the matter about Brett. It doubtless would be of value to anyone reading the stuff for the first time and there is some very good dope on Brett. On the other hand any sort of a foreword or preface would seem to me to break up the unity of the book and altho it does not show there is a certain rhythm in all that book that if it were broken would be very much missed. It was a complete unit with all that first stuff including the Belloc episode—I could cut it where I did and have it stay a unit—but the hard luck we had with Fifty Grand shows the difficulty of cutting that sort of stuff and further tinkering wouldnt help, I'm afraid.[3]

I am terribly sorry because I would like very much to do it for you but I think we'll find maybe, in the end, that what I lose by not compromising now we may all cash in on later. I know that you would not ask me to put that back in unless you really liked it and I know it would be good in many ways—but I think in the end perhaps we would both lose by it. You see I would like, if you wanted, to write books for Scribner's to publish, for many years and would like them to be good books—better all the time— sometimes they might not be so good—but as well as I could write and perhaps with luck learning to write better all the time—and learning how things work and what the whole thing is about—and not getting bitter— So if this one doesn't sell maybe sometime one will— I'm very sure one will if they really are good—and if I learn to make them a lot better—but I'll never be able to do that and will just get caught in the machine if I start worrying about that—or considering it [*EH insertion*: the selling]. Altho God knows I need the money at this present time and I would so like to see the book really go because you have been so very decent to me.

The other thing is that Brett Ashley is a real person and as long as there were no changes in the way other real people James, Belloc, Hergesheimer etc. were handled I did not mind what happened to <u>my</u> people—but since they (the others) were protected I might as well leave out that stuff so long as it is not actually necessary. That was the only stuff in the book that was not imaginary—the Brett biography.

I see that Mr. Bill Benet is very disappointed to find me lifting a character from Michael Arland and that is rather funny as I have never read a word of Arland but went around, after the war, with Lady Duff Twisden, Nancy Cunard, Mary Beerbohm and Iris Tree who took Arland or Arlen up as a deserving Armenian youth and let him in on a few things and then dropped him as soon as he became annoyingly Armenian and less deserving—but not before he had gotten a little way behind the scenes into various people's lives.[4]

So now it is pretty amusing to have known a girl and drawn her so close to life that it makes me feel very badly—except that I don't imagine she would ever read anything—and watch her go to hell completely—and assist at the depart—and then feeling pretty damned badly about it all learn that you had with boyish enthusiasm lifted a character from the un-read writings of some little Armenian sucker after London names.

What do you suppose it is—that Benet imagines that nobody ever really had a title? Was it the title that offended him? Or do people only have titles in books written for servant girls? But as I haven't read Arland I don't know—and now I'm afraid to—because maybe it is like Arland. That would be awfully funny.

Maybe Arland would write a couple of chapters and it would sell millions. Perhaps Benet could get ahold of him for us.

Komroff finally cut only a couple of hundred words out of Fifty Grand. Maybe you could run it some time between serials or if Mr. Phelps were sick and copy was short. You might offer Mr. Phelps from me that if he will condense and give me the space I'll pay him whatever it's worth a page where I overlap into him. Or I'll split the price of the story with him. I'd like to have that story published sometimes before boxing is abolished. Or magazines abolished.[5]

Everything I publish over here is stolen by Samuel Roth who has never had my permission to publish one word and and pirates everything that appears here as fast as it comes out and has never paid me a cent. I've seen the advertisements in the Nation and New Republic of his Two Worlds Monthly.[6]

Joyce is all broken up about it. Roth has stolen his Ulysses without permission, never paid Joyce a cent, is publishing Ulysses in monthly installments and expurgating it. I saw Joyce today and he has just received a copy of an interview Roth gave to some N.Y. paper in which he declares that he is publishing Ulysses with Joyce's consent, that he has a financial arrangement with Joyce greatly to Joyce's advantage which he cannot at present divulge and that Joyce has made large sums selling the book under cover in America. Joyce is in absolute despair. The work of thirteen years of his life being stolen from him by a man who not content with that trys to blacken Joyce's character—and not content with stealing a man's life work and lieing about it then garbles it.[7]

Kenneth Simpson who is in the district attorney's office has promised to nail Roth as soon as he gets back to N.Y. Joyce meantime is trying to get an injunction against Roth.[8]

It is horrible and discouraging business and does not make one love the Jews any better. I feel badly about his stealing my stories—but that is a small matter compared to his theft of Joyce's entire book—but it does seem as though reputable publications like The Nation should refuse to accept his, Roth's, advertising. Isn't there some national organization that can blacklist the advertising of crooks?

Life seems quite complicated today.

Next week I am planning to ride down to the Riviera with a friend who has to take a car down there and I'll see Scott. He's sailing the 12th of December, I believe.

I still have a check for 200 dollars that I haven't cashed because the franc has been too high—but it looks as though it were going to stay there. I hope the Sun will sell so that I may get some more from you when I need it—it seems as though it should—it's pretty interesting and there seems to be a difference of opinion about it—I've always heard that was good. The Times review I had to read to the end before I found whether they really liked it or not. Aiken seemed to like it. Archie MacLeish tells me he's a good critic— Aiken I mean. Maybe that will encourage some of the other boys to like it. It's funny to write a book that seems as tragic as that and have them take it for a jazz superficial story. If you went any deeper inside they couldn't read it because they would be crying all the time. Life's all very funny[9] today— and this typewriter seems to have run away with its-self

Yours

Ernest Hemingway

PUL, TLS

1 In a letter to EH of 30 October 1926, Perkins wrote that *SAR* had been out for a week and that the "first real reviews" were "admirable" (PUL; *TOTTC*, 46–47). He sent copies of two he considered most important, both published on 31 October 1926. The *New York Times Book Review* called *SAR* "unquestionably one of the events of an unusually rich year in

literature" ("Marital Tragedy," 7). American poet Conrad Aiken (1889–1973), in *New York Herald Tribune Books*, called EH "in many respects the most exciting of contemporary American writers of fiction" and pronounced the dialogue "brilliant" ("Expatriates," 4).

2　A portrait drawing of EH by American artist John Blomshield (1895–c. 1952) was featured on the back of the dust jacket for *SAR* and in advertisements. The illustrated ad in *Publishers' Weekly* (30 October 1926) proclaimed, "And with this book Mr. Hemingway's sun also will rise, for this is a novel able to command the sharpest attention even in a season so crowded with good fiction" (1745). The portrait also accompanied Aiken's review in *New York Herald Tribune Books*.

3　Perkins had proposed that EH could, if he so wished, write "a foreword or prologue, or whatever it might be called" for subsequent editions of *SAR*, presenting information on the novel's central character Brett Ashley that was lost when EH decided to omit the book's original opening.

4　In his column "The Phoenix Nest" for the *Saturday Review of Literature*, William Rose Benét commented, "Brett, Lady Ashley, came as something of a shock. She had strayed out of 'The Green Hat.' We couldn't see what she was doing in Hemingway's novel" (30 October 1926, 268). Michael Arlen had based the character Iris in his 1925 novel, *The Green Hat*, on Nancy Cunard (1896–1965), English author, publisher, and heiress to the Cunard shipping line fortune. Brett Ashley in *SAR* was based on Lady Duff Twysden, the Englishwoman whom EH met in Paris in 1925. Agnes Mary Beerbohm (c. 1866–1949), English dress designer and sister of the English caricaturist and critic Henry Maximilian (Max) Beerbohm (1872–1956). Iris Tree (1897–1968), English poet and actress. Michael Arlen was of Armenian descent.

5　Perkins had encouraged EH to send Scribner's some stories, "possibly 'Fifty Grand' curtailed," but he acknowledged that Manuel Komroff, who had offered to cut the story, would find that he had "tackled something considerable." William Lyon Phelps (1865–1943), American writer and professor of English at Yale University, wrote a column for *Scribner's Magazine* titled "As I Like It."

6　Samuel Roth (1893–1974), publisher of the American literary magazines *Two Worlds* (1925–1927) and *Two Worlds Monthly* (1926–1927). In his response, Perkins would explain that because EH's stories had originally appeared in magazines published abroad, they were "uncopyrightable" in the United States (26 November 1926, PUL). However, although Roth had placed advertisements naming EH as among the writers whose work would be published in upcoming volumes of *Two Worlds Monthly*, none of EH's stories ever appeared in the magazine.

7　Sylvia Beach's bookstore, Shakespeare and Company, had published James Joyce's *Ulysses* in 1922, but its publication and distribution were banned in the United States. In 1926 Samuel Roth began the unauthorized serialization of *Ulysses*, in twelve installments, in *Two Worlds Monthly* and also sold copies of the novel for which Joyce received no royalties. In his 26 November letter to EH, Perkins would write that he believed there was nothing "to prevent a man who is that kind of man, from taking uncopyrighted material, and apparently Joyce is uncopyrighted." However, a number of authors, including EH, would sign a petition titled "A Protest against Pirating 'Ulysses'" that appeared in *New York Herald Tribune Books* (6 March 1927, 21). Joyce would bring a suit against Roth, and Roth would cease publication of *Ulysses* in the fall of 1927.

8　Kenneth Simpson (1895–1941) served as Assistant United States Attorney of the Southern District of New York, 1925–1929. Joyce would file suit against Roth, though he would not receive any damages. Late in 1928, New York State Supreme Court Justice Richard

H. Mitchell would issue an injunction to prohibit Roth from publishing any of Joyce's work without consent, but by then *Two Worlds Monthly* had ceased publication.
9 EH typed to the bottom of the page and from this point completed the letter by hand, squeezing in another line in the bottom margin and writing sideways up the right margin.

To Hadley Richardson Hemingway, 18 November [1926]

Thursday morning.
November 18

My dearest Hadley—

I am terribly sorry that I did not get your letter until after I had seen you—and because I did not know what decisions you had made nor what was in your mind—hurt you again and again by talking about something that you had so wisely concluded we should not discuss but only write about.

I think your letter like everything that you have ever done is very brave and altogether unselfish and generous.[1]

During the past week I found out, and the horror of it was very great, how Pauline and I without me[a]ning to had constantly exerted a pressure on you to divorce me—a pressure that came from a sort of hurried panic fear that we should lose one another—that naturally you were suspicious of and re-acted against as a basis for two people to marry on. Your reactions have always been right and I have always trusted them and believed in them as well as in your head.

I think that perhaps when Pauline and I realized how cruel we had been to you in that way and that we could not expect to found any basis of happiness on such a continued cruelty—and re-alized that we could go on any length of time that would suit you without each other rather than have you consent to a divorce that you did not really feel was inevitable, or desireable,— I think that when you felt that, and I hope you believe it was sincere, it maybe have helped to remove your natural and right re-action against setting two people free to marry each other who did not seem to deserve each other or anything else.—[2]

Now, if you wish to divorce me, I will start at once finding out the details and about lawyers. I will start that at any rate—as you ask in your letter— and will write you what I learn.

If you donVt want to start now or until after Pauline comes back—or later please do what you wish.

If it is an inevitable step I think we will all feel better and things can start to clear once it is started. That is, please dear Hadley, not me trying to influence you—or speed up my own affairs. It is only that we seem like two boxers who are groggy and floating and staggering around and yet will not put over a knock-out punch: which would terminate the combat and let the process of healing and recovering start.[3]

Another thing—I do not know your plans about America—but I do not think you should be hurried through a divorce in order to get to America which may not be what you want when you get there.

What you could do is—start the dvorce—and go to America and have a look around and see how you like it and exactly what the situation is in the interval which must elapse between the starting of the divorce and the three or four months which must elapse before it would be necessary for you to appear again in the divorce. I think the process is that a huissier would serve me with a demand to return to you—which if I refused would be followed by a second service some months later—then we would both have to appear for a formal refusal to reconcile—ten minutes or five minutes—before a juge d'instruction or something like that and then you would be given a decree of divorce.[4]

If you wished to go to America I am sure you could do it without great expense and it would be a very good way of seeing how things are over there—both on the coast and in N.Y.—you might take one of the very comfortable dollar line boats which would take you from Marseilles and land you in California—by the canal. And return to Paris by way of N.Y. which would give you a good chance to see both places. Would change les idees and give you the dope on

In any event, no matter what you do, I am writing to Scribners that all royalties from The Sun Also Rises should be paid to you. These will not commence until after 3,000 copies have been sold—we spent the advance on that sale together—but from then on will mount rapidly at 30 cents a copy on each book. And from the way Max Perkins writes about future printings etc. and the way they are advertising it might, if it should go, be a very good sum.

In any event you can absolutely count on all the royalties from Cape—I am instructing my agent that these also should be paid to you— Cape has offered to bring the book out between January and March—pay on publication the royalties on all advance sales and a royalty of 10% of the first 3,000 copies, rising to 15% up to 5,000 copies and after that 20%. Which are very generous royalties on a book that might have a great sale in England.

I want you please not to make any objection to this—it is the onlt thing that I who have done so many things to hurt you can do to help you—and you must let me do it.[5]

There is no question of my suffering from any lack of money as I know that I could borrow money from Scott [Fitzgerald], Archie [MacLeish], or the Murphies—all of whom are wealthy people—or that I could accept money from Pauline whose Uncle Gus seems always wanting to give it to her.[6] I need in the mantime the financial pressure of starting clean—and the income from those books belongs to you by every right—you supported me while they were being written and helped me write them— I would never have written any of them In Our Time, Torrents or The Sun if I had not married you and had your loyal and self-sacrificing and always stimulating and loving—and actual cash support backing.

I would include In Our Time, and Torrents but I believe the one is on the deficit side still and the other not likely to m[a]ke money.

But I am making a will and writing to my agents and my publishers that in case of my death the income from all my books, past and future, is to go to Bumby where you can hold it in trust for him.

I must see that you get these Sun royalties Hadley and will you please just take it as a gift without any protestations or bitterness. Because it is really your right and due and it would make terribly happy if instead you would be very generous and take it as a gift.

With that to count on—it cannot be less than several hundred dollars— you can make the American trip and not worry about money. During your absense I would give Bumby the benefit of whatever benefit a papa is. I would also be on my honor that Pauline would not see Bumby in case she should be here any of that time—so you would not have to worry about that. If it would be a thing you would worry about.

Our conversation confused certain phases of your letter. You say the three months absense thing is officially terminated. If it would make any difference to you I am sure Pauline and I would be glad, I am sure, to complete the three months apart from each other. If it makes no difference I imagine she might come back in January or when she wished. Please let me know about this and if you want me to communicate the facts of our letters to Pauline.

I am sorry this is so long and there are doubtless many things I have left out. I'll see a lot of Bumby—and I think perhaps the luckiest thing Bumby will ever have is to have you for a mother. And I won't tell you how I admire your straight thinking, your head, your heart and your very lovely hands and I pray God always that he will make up to you the very great hurt that I have done you—who are the best and truest and loveliest person that I have ever known.

Ernest

JFK, TLS

1 EH is responding to Hadley's letter of 16 November 1926, in which she announced that "the three months separation is officially off" and declared, "I am <u>not</u> responsible for your future welfare—it is in your hands and those of God (a pretty <u>good</u> scout and a <u>swell</u> friend)." Therefore, she felt free to seek the divorce he had requested. She asked EH to check into the legalities but, "for the sake of peace" and to spare Bumby, requested that he "put all discussion and arrangement of these matters into letters." She also invited him to come see Bumby as much as he wished, "so that he will know you are his real papa" (JFK).

2 In her letter to EH of 29 October [1926], Pauline worried that she and EH "didn't give Hadley a chance," saying, "We were so cock-eyed crazy about each other, and so very scared we might loose each other—at least I was—that Hadley got locked out" (JFK). In an undated letter to Hadley, Pauline urged her not to feel obligated to give EH a divorce after the three months' separation from Pauline, but to "act only when you are so inclined," free of "any coercion from hastily given promises" ([October 1926], JFK).

3 Hadley would reply the next day, "Haven't I yet made it quite plain that I <u>want</u> to start proceedings for a divorce from you—right away?" If EH felt any hesitation, she said, she would start things herself (19 November 1926, JFK).

4 EH would file for divorce on 8 December 1926, and on 27 January 1927 Hadley received the preliminary judgment, giving her custody of Bumby. By French law, the divorce decree was final for Hadley on 14 April and for EH on 21 April 1927 (Reynolds *AH*, xi, 243). On 16 April, Hadley and Bumby would sail for the United States on the *Berengaria* for a six-month stay that included a visit to Oak Park. *Huissier*: bailiff; *juge d'instruction*: examining magistrate (French).

5 Cape had outlined the terms for the British edition of *SAR* in his offer of 9 November 1926, which was forwarded to EH by the Curtis Brown agency in a letter of 11 November 1926 (JFK). In her 19 November response to EH, Hadley wrote that she still needed to think over money matters. Meanwhile, she thanked him for his gift of the royalties for *SAR*, which she found "very acceptable" and could think of no reason to refuse "just now."

6 Gustavus Adolphus Pfeiffer (1872–1953), Pauline's paternal uncle.

To Gerald and Sara Murphy, [c. late November 1926]

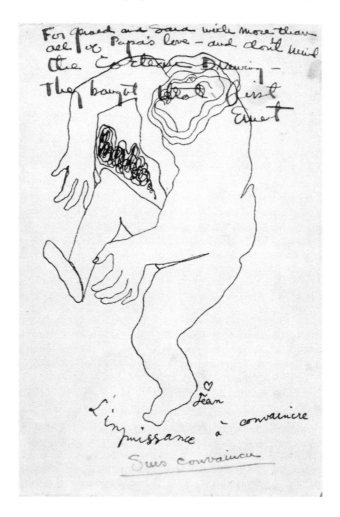

[EH *inscription on cover of "Today is Friday" pamphlet*:]

For Gerald and Sara with more than all of Papa's love—and don't mind the Cocteau Drawing— They bought that first[1]

Ernest.

[*EH letter written on the last blank page and on the inside back cover of the pamphlet*:]

Dear gents—

Thanks for the review. Archie read me a grand letter from Sara to Ada.[2] I will write you a fine letter soon—but today it is raining.

I am very comfortable at 69 (rue Froidevaux he hastens to add) and about as happy as the average empty tomato can.

Archie and I went to Zaragoza and had a fine trip. He took away from me—with a couple of books and his fine legal mind—the Popes, Caesar and Shakespeare (all Fairies) and the Holy Grail (Just a goddam lie or legend) and gave me in exchange A Great Yale Football Team (They'd just beaten Dartmouth).

Well we got home and the next Sunday I read the paper and Holy Cross or some place like that had beaten Yale 33–6. So I wrote Archie a pneu and said I was sending back his great Yale Team including their great new quarterback and would he return me by return post all the Popes, Caesar, Shakespeare and The Holy Grail.[3]

But so far I havent got them back.

However I love you both very much and like to think about you and will be shall we say <u>pleased</u> to see you—

It is swell that Gerald is working so well and I will be pretty excited to see the stuff—

When do you come back? My love to Patrick Baeth and Honoria.[4] Bumby and I lived together for 10 days while Hadley was on a trip and one day when I bought him an harmonica and a glace and he was holding the one and eating the other at the café he said, "La Vie est beau avec Papa."[5]

[*EH notations on the back cover of the pamphlet*:]

Papa's in gentle company. Maybe it's a Fairy's house organ.[6]

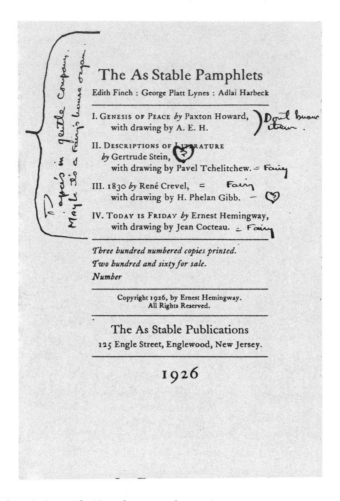

The As Stable Pamphlets

Edith Finch : George Platt Lynes : Adlai Harbeck

I. GENESIS OF PEACE *by* Paxton Howard, with drawing by A. E. H.

II. DESCRIPTIONS OF LITERATURE *by* Gertrude Stein, with drawing by Pavel Tchelitchew.

III. 1830 *by* René Crevel, with drawing by H. Phelan Gibb.

IV. TODAY IS FRIDAY *by* Ernest Hemingway, with drawing by Jean Cocteau.

Three hundred numbered copies printed.
Two hundred and sixty for sale.
Number

Copyright 1926, by Ernest Hemingway.
All Rights Reserved.

The As Stable Publications
125 Engle Street, Englewood, New Jersey.

1926

phYale, Inscription with AL and autograph notations

EH's *Today Is Friday* was published in November 1926 by The As Stable Publications of Englewood, New Jersey, in a limited edition of 300 numbered copies. EH inscribed the front cover of no. 47 to Gerald and Sara Murphy and penned a letter on the last blank page and the inside back cover. He also wrote quips and notations on the front cover and on the back cover list of the first four pamphlets in the series.

1 In her letter to EH of 14 August 1926 inviting his contribution for pamphlet number 4 of the series, Edith Finch explained that they had already acquired Jean Cocteau's drawing and hoped to pair it with an essay by EH (JFK). Beneath Cocteau's drawing on the front cover, with his imprinted signature "Jean" and the caption "L'impuissance à convaincre"

("The powerlessness to convince" [French]), EH wrote, "Suis convaincu" ("I am convinced" [French]).

2 Ada Taylor Hitchcock MacLeish (1892–1984) had met Archibald MacLeish in 1910 when she was a student at Westover, a girls' preparatory school in Connecticut founded by MacLeish's aunt. The couple married in 1916 and from 1923 to 1928 lived in Paris, where she took voice lessons.

3 MacLeish was a 1915 graduate of Yale. On 16 October 1926 the Yale football team beat Dartmouth by 14–7. On 30 October 1926, Army defeated Yale 33–0 in its first victory over Yale in fifteen years. No record has been located of a 1926 football game between Yale and Holy Cross, a small Jesuit college in Worcester, Massachusetts. Yale's quarterback at the time was Phil Wolfe Bunnell (1903–1991).

4 The Murphy children: Patrick Francis (1920–1937), Baoth Wiborg (1919–1935), and Honoria Adeline (1917–1998).

5 EH had stayed in Hadley's apartment to care for Bumby during her November trip to Chartres with Winifred Mowrer (1883–1977), whose husband, Paul Scott Mowrer (1887–1971), visited them there. According to Gioia Diliberto, Paul Mowrer invited EH to dine with him in Paris while the women were away and asked EH if, in fact, his marriage was over, not mentioning that "he was falling in love with Hadley, and he wanted to make sure she was free" (*Hadley* [New York: Tickner & Fields, 1992], 241). Hadley and Paul Mowrer would marry in 1933 after a relationship of several years. *Glace*: ice cream; *La vie est belle avec Papa*: Life is beautiful with Papa (French).

6 As a student at the Berkshire School in Sheffield, Massachusetts (class of 1925), George Platt Lynes had launched The As Stable Pamphlets with the help of classmate Adlai E. Harbeck, publishing a story by another classmate, Paxton Howard, as the first in the series. Visiting Paris in 1925, Lynes met Stein and elicited her contribution for the second pamphlet. After returning from Paris to his parents' home in Englewood, New Jersey, where his father was an Episcopal clergyman, Lynes secured the financial backing of Edith Finch to establish The As Stable Publications. Pavel Tchelitchew (1898–1957), Russian painter; René Crevel (1900–1935), French Dadaist and surrealist writer; and Henry William Phelan Gibb (1870–1948), English Fauve painter, whose work was featured in the second and third pamphlets, were all friends of Stein.

To Maxwell Perkins, 19 November 1926

November 19, 1926

Dear Mr. Perkins:

I don't know whether the magazine would care for any humorous stuff. Anyway here is a piece and if they should not want it will you use your judgement about turning it over to Edmund Wilson care of The New Republic—who has written saying they will pay me $50 for a page of 1200 words on more or less anything—or perhaps to Reynolds who wrote Scott they would like something more of mine——and who might be able to get me some money for it.[1]

Thank you for the Transcript review. They did very nobly by us all. It was refreshing to see someone have some doubts that I took the Gertrude Stein thing very seriously[2]—I meant to play off against that splendid bombast (Gertrude's assumption of prophetic roles) (Nobody knows about the generation that follows them and certainly has no right to Judge.)—the quotation from Eccles.—one generation passeth and another generation cometh but the earth abideth forever—The sun also Ariseth. What I would like you to do in any further printings is to lop off the Vanity of vanities, saith the preacher, vanity of vanities; all is vanity—What profit hath a man of all his labour which he taketh under the sun?—delete all that. And start the quotation with and use only the 4th, 5th 6th and 7th verses of Ecclesiastes. That is starting with One generation passeth away——and finishing with unto the place from whence the rivers come thither they return again.[3]

That makes it much clearer. The point of the book to me was that the earth abideth forever—having a great deal of fondness and admiration for the earth and not a hell of a lot for my generation and caring little about Vanities. I only hesitated at the start to cut the writing of a better writer— but it seems necessary. I didn't mean the book to be a hollow or bitter satire but a damn tragedy with the earth abiding for ever as the hero.

Also have discovered that most people don't think in words—as they do in everybody's writing now—and so in Sun A.R. the critics miss their interior monologues and aren't happy—or disappointed. I cut out 40,000 words of the stuff that would have made them happy out of the first Mss—it would have made them happy but it would have rung as false 10 years from now as Bromfield.

The Sun Also rises could have been and should have been a better book— but first Don Stewart was taking a cure for his liver in Vichy while I wrote the first draft of S.A.R. instead—and secondly I figure it is better to write about what you can write about and try and make it come off than have epoch making canvasses etc.—and you figure what age the novelists had that wrote the really great novels. There can be the tour de force by a kid like The Red Badge of Courage—but in general they were pretty well along and they knew a few things—and in the time they were learning and going through it they learned how to write by writing.[4]

Well I'd better stop before I start getting like a critic myself which would be pretty bad. I hope you like this funny one anyway.

With Best regards

Ernest Hemingway

PUL, TLS

1 EH's parody of *My Life* (1922–1927) by Frank Harris (né James Thomas Harris, 1856–1931), would be published in the 12 February 1927 *New Yorker* as "My Own Life: [After reading the second volume of Frank Harris' 'My Life.']." In 1926 Harris had been prosecuted in France in connection with the second volume of his racy memoir, published privately in Nice in 1925 ("Harris Prosecuted in France for Book," *New York Times*, 10 August 1926, 8). EH's published piece includes sections titled "How I Broke with John Wilkes Booth," "The True Story of My Break with Gertrude Stein," "How I Broke with My Children," and "How I Broke with Benchley." An early draft includes the unpublished sections "How I Broke with My Wife," "How I Broke with F. Scott Fitzgerald," and "How I Broke with Donald Ogden Stewart" (item 593a, JFK). Filed with the published version at JFK is the check stub for $75 from the *New Yorker* (Item 593, JFK).

2 The *Boston Evening Transcript* review signed "K.J.W." (6 November 1926) called *SAR* "a beautiful and searching novel" and concluded that the characters depicted "are not a lost generation, Miss Stein to the contrary" (2).

3 In his reply of 1 December 1926, Perkins told EH that Scribner's had made the change he wanted (PUL; *TOTTC*, 52). The revision was made in the plates of the fourth printing of *SAR* (January 1927), omitting the verse regarding vanity from Ecclesiastes 1: 2 (Grissom, 58–59).

4 *The Red Badge of Courage: An Episode of the American Civil War*, popular and critically acclaimed novel by Stephen Crane (1871–1900), was syndicated in 1894 and published in book form in October 1895, shortly before his twenty-fourth birthday.

To Ezra Pound, [c. 20 November 1926]

Respectabillissimo—

Time perhaps ripe for less controversy and more production of material. Therefore enclose very short poem and very superior poem of Archie's.[1]

Returning however to controversy.

Not that I would like to expose you, nor ever would to the bastone of the saviours of civilization—but what makes you think a gent can't be au courant abt the state of affairs in the unforchnit country when everyone who knows or cares anything abt. same is expelled into France where they arrive fresh all the time with the DOPE. Not to mention the agents of the govt. its-self—chief of police of Rome—Ricciotti and Co. who come here to prepare the complots that put the grt. man among the living martyrs.[2]

If you actually and honest to God or what have you admire or respect the gent and his works all I can say is SHIT and if I ever start to see any leanings in that direction, obvious ones, (like say N.C.MacCormick's and the late Mrs. Butler's)[3] yr. secret ones being your own business—I will take practical steps by denouncing you here in Paris as a dangerous anti-fascist and we can amuse one another by counting the hours before you get beaten up inspite of your probity—which in such a fine country as it must be would undoubtedly save you.

But, in fact, I won't do any of this and I will not mention politics again in a letter. Only don't you ever call me on Dago politics. Yes I know the lire is stabilized and all about the improvements in the TRAIN SERVICE.[4]

In re Giants in those days—The crusaders—the leading ones—averaged abt. 5 feet 8 according to the measurements of their armor.[5]

The New Masses would seem to afford facilities for publication due to the open armed way in which they received Walsh's undocumented attack on me—but they are really hermetically sealed to shall we call it literature and to anything funny. They just took the Walsh thing on acct. of hating me because they thought I was trying to destroy something that they have all copied so far that it is too late for them to learn another way of doing it. Also they thought I was making money. A widespread delusion. They are just a house-organ of parlour, i.e. subsidized by the rich, revolution. You've got no hope there.

Abt. Mac. No, not about Mac. Let us not discuss turds on this so lovely rainy morning.

When DID Rodker have anything fit to print of his own?[6]

initial contribution follows:

Neo-Thomist Poem by Ernest Hemingway

The Lord is my shepherd I shall not want him for long.

> Yrs.
>
> Hem

Yale, TLS

This letter apparently crossed in the mail with Pound's letter to EH of 20 November [1926], in which he had enclosed a long letter for MacLeish, dated 19 November 1926, encouraging MacLeish to contribute to his new literary review (JFK).

1 In his 22 November [1926] response to this letter, Pound would accept EH's very short "Neo-Thomist Poem" for publication in the opening number of *The Exile* (Spring 1927) but regretted having to turn down MacLeish's poem, saying he could not see "any way of expurgating it for inclusion without destroying its point" and did not expect it would get "past the post office or the Brit. customs" (JFK). MacLeish's poem may have been his satiric twelve-line attack on Edmund Wilson's literary taste and masculinity, characterized by Scott Donaldson as "a scurrilous piece of doggerel" (*Archibald MacLeish: An American Life* [Boston: Houghton Mifflin, 1992], 171). No work by MacLeish would appear in *The Exile*.
2 In his 18 November response to EH's earlier letter [c. 14 November 1926] regarding Ricciotti Garibaldi's arrest, Pound had declared, "Not being the stuff of which martyrs are made, I shall exclude your views on eyetalian politics (especially as you aren't very up to date on conditions here . . .)" (JFK).
3 American sculptor Nancy Cox-McCormack (1885–1967), a friend of the Pounds, had opened a studio in Rome in 1922 and in 1923 was commissioned to create a bust of Mussolini, which was exhibited at the 1924 Spring Salon in Paris. The "late Mrs. Butler" is a reference to Alice Carter Butler (1873–1924), a writer and the mother of Dorothy Butler (b. c. 1896). In 1922 Dorothy had accompanied EH and Hadley on a walking tour in Germany with her then fiancé Lewis Galantière, to whom she was married from 1924 to 1928. Alice Carter Butler's flattering profile of the Italian dictator, "A Close-Up of Mussolini," appeared in the *Chicago Tribune Sunday Magazine*, Paris, 15 June 1923, and was reprinted posthumously in *A. C. B.: A Life in Armor*, edited by Dorothy Butler and George H. Butler (Chicago: Covici, 1925), 273–80.
4 The claim that Mussolini made the trains run on time was a commonplace promoted by government propaganda.
5 Regarding EH's assessment of present-day writers in his c. 14 November letter, Pound replied on 18 November: "I pussnly. dont consider that the gi-yants in them days wuz any giganter than at present."
6 In his 18 November letter to EH, Pound told EH that English writer John Rodker (1894–1955) claimed to have "nothing fit to print of his own" in Pound's new review. Nonetheless, *The Exile* would include segments of Rodker's novella *Adolphe 1920* in its first three issues (Spring 1927, Autumn 1927, and Spring 1928).

To Maxwell Perkins, 22 November 1926

November 22, 1926

Dear Mr. Perkins:

Enclosed is a story for the magazine that I think you will like. I am going to write a couple more about the old days in Italy and will send them as soon as they are done. For some reason that time seems very real now.[1] I hope you like this one and that Mr. Bridges will to—tell him I'll find another word for whores if it is objectionable—it's not needed in the story.[2]

Yours always,

Ernest Hemingway.

Perhaps they will verify the spelling of the one Italian phrase—I could never spell Italian and have no dictionary.[3]

PUL, TLS

1 EH enclosed the typescript of "In Another Country" and soon went on to write two more WWI stories set in Italy, "Now I Lay Me" and "A Simple Enquiry." On 1 December 1926 Perkins would acknowledge receiving "In Another Country," and on 4 December 1926 Bridges accepted it for *Scribner's Magazine*, where it would appear, together with "A Canary for One" under the heading "Two Stories," in April 1927. Both stories would be included in *MWW*.
2 Surviving typescripts of "In Another Country" include the sentence, "The girls at the Cova were very patriotic, and I found that the most patriotic people in Italy were the whores— and I believe they are still patriotic" (JFK, items 492 and 492a). In the published story, the word "whores" is replaced by "café girls."
3 EH supplies his intended Italian phrasing in the following letter to Perkins, written on the same day.

To Maxwell Perkins, 22 November 1926

Nov 22–1926

Dear Mr. Perkins:

Referring to the story In Another Country the Italian should read "A basso gli ufficiali!"[1] I have forgotten my Italian or so mixed it with Spanish that I could not remember how to spell "bacco" for the very good reason that there is no such word.

I sent the story off today by Leviathan.[2]

Yours always

Hemingway.

PUL, ALS

1 "*Abbasso gli ufficiali!*": "Down with the officers!" (Italian).
2 The *Leviathan* arrived in New York on 29 November.

To Maxwell Perkins, 23 November 1926

Dear Mr. Perkins—

Yesterday on the Leviathan I sent you a story called—In Another Country for the magazine. Enclosed is a letter from College Humor which Don Stewart tells me pays vast sums.[1] You might send this to [Paul] Reynolds with the funny thing I sent a week or so ago—unless it has gone somewhere else or something has happened to it. He could send it to College Humor.[2]

I am awfully sorry to bother you about this and would not do so if I had Reynold's address—or if I had not wanted first to give the Magazine a chance at the funny one.

I wonder if College Humor would buy Fifty Grand. Reynolds might send them that. I think that's a good hunch.

I am writing on another Italian story.[3]

The letter from Mr. Bridges about the Canary story has just come and your two enclosures of ads. They look very handsome.[4]

I took my son, who is three years old, to the café the other afternoon to get an icecream and while he was eating it and holding his harmonica in the other hand he looked all around and said, "Ah la vie est beau avec papa!"

Yours always,

Ernest Hemingway

Nov 23-1926

PUL, TLS

1 *College Humor*, a Chicago-based magazine founded in 1923 by H. N. (Harold Norling) Swanson (1899–1991), who served as its editor until 1931. At the suggestion of EH's high school friend Morris McNeil Musselman (1899–1952), Swanson had written to EH inviting him to submit a sketch, essay, or piece of fiction to the magazine (9 November 1926, PUL). Stewart's novel *Mr. and Mrs. Haddock in Paris, France* (New York: Harper & Brothers, 1926), was serialized in *College Humor* between April and July 1926.
2 In a letter of 3 December 1926, Perkins would confirm that he sent the "Harris sketches" (EH's parody of Frank Harris's memoirs) to *College Humor*. He expressed some doubt that the magazine would accept the piece and recommended *Vanity Fair* and the *New Yorker* as more appropriate and better paying outlets (PUL).
3 Probably "Now I Lay Me."
4 In a letter of 11 November 1926, Robert Bridges accepted "A Canary for One" for publication in *Scribner's Magazine*. The enclosures may have been the advertisement for *SAR* in the

New York Herald Tribune, of which Perkins had sent EH a marked-up proof (11 November 1926, JFK), and the large advertisement for newspapers and *Publishers' Weekly* that Perkins had sent him earlier (30 October 1926, PUL).

To F. Scott Fitzgerald, [c. 1 December 1926]

Dear Scott:

Ive been trying every week to get down to see you before you leave— Mike Ward was getting a car to drive down but first he was sick—then the cars were always full; then the guy who was to take his place in the bank was sick and that brings us to this Wednesday which was today and the last time we were to start.[1]

How are you and how have you been—? Have you worked and how is the novel. I'll bet it will be a damned good novel once you settled down to writing it—and you must have had plenty of time at Juan les Pins for writing lately.

I've had a grand spell of working; sold another story to Scribners— making two—and have sent them another that I am sure they will buy—a hell of a good story about Milan during the war—and just finished a better one that I should be typing now. Have two other stories that I know can't sell so am not sending them out—but that will go well in a book.[2]

This is a bloody borrowed typewriter—my own busted.[3] I see by an ad in the World that The Sun etc. is in 2nd printing and Heywood Broun in the same paper Nov. 19 a full col. on it etc.[4] Reviews have been good although the boys seem divided as to who or whom I copied the most from you or Michael Arlen so I am very grateful to both of you—and especially you, Scott, because I like you and I don't know Arland and have besides heard that he is an Armenian and it would seem a little premat[u]re to be grateful to any Armenian.[5] But I am certainly grateful to you and I am asking Scribners to insert as a subtitle in everything after the eighth printing

THE SUN ALSO RISES (LIKE YOUR COCK IF YOU HAVE ONE)

A greater Gatsby

(Written with the friendship of F. Scott FitzGerald (Prophet of THE JAZZ AGE)

God I wish I could see you. You are the only guy in or out of Europe I can say as much for (or against) but I certainly would like to see you. I haven't enough money to come down on the train and so have been at the mercy of these non leaving free motors. The bad weather has made biking impossible. I started once that way but had a hell of a spill and luxe-ed my epaule.[6] How the hell are you anyway.

What does 2nd printing mean in numbers?[7] Book was published Oct. 22 that was in the ad of Nov. 19. Max Perkins wrote the first of Nov. that the advance orders hadn't been much but that re-orders were coming in. He didn't mention any figures. Has he written to you?

College Humor has written asking me to write them essays, pieces, shit or long fiction and I turned the letter over to Max to give to Reynolds. Sometimes I have funny stuff and I think Reynolds might be willing to sell it as somebody told me Cowedge Humour paid large prices. They said they were reviewing Sun Also etc, in January issue. Hope it goes better at Princeton than the Lampoon.[8]

As for personal life of the noted, notedby who, author, Hadley is divorcing me. Have turned over to her all existing finances and all received and future royalties from Sun. Cape and Heinemann have both made offers for British rights.[9] Do you think Reynolds might sell it to the Movies or some such place. I'm going to take a cut on those if there are any. Have been eating one meal a day and if I get tired enough sleeping—working like hell lately—find starting life poorer than any time since I was 14 with an earning capacity of what stories I sell to Scribners very interesting. I suppose everybody's life goes to hell and anyway have been very healthy and, lately, able to use the head again. If anybody in N.Y. asks about me don't tell them a god damned thing. I would tell you all about things but don't seem able to write about them and am not very good at talking about them. Anyway so many people seem to talk so well about one's affairs that there doesn't seem ever any necessity to speak about them oneself.

Anyway I'm now all through with the general bumping off phase and will only bump off now under certain special circumstances which I ~~hope will~~ don't think will arrise. Have refra[i]ned from any half turnings on of the gas or slitting of the wrists with sterilized safety razor blades.[10] Am continuing my life in original role of son of a bitch sans peur et sans rapproche.[11] The only thing in life I've ever had any luck being decent about is money so am very splendid and punctilious about that. Also I have been sucked in by ambition to do some very good work now no matter how everything comes out. I think some of the stuff now is good. Have learned a lot.

It is now time to cut this off and mail it.

Write to me and tell me all the dirt. What do you hear from N.Y.? Where are you going to live? How are Zelda? and Scotty? Bumby and Hadley are damned well. I had Bumby for ten days while Hadley wzs on a trip and one morning I took him to a cafe and got him a glace and a new harmonica and holding the harmonica and eating the glace he said, "La vie est beau avec papa." He is very fond of me and when I ask him what does papa do, hoping to hear him say Papa is a great writer like the clippings. He says Papa does nothing. So then I taught him to say, "Bumby will support Papa," so he says that all the time. What will Bumby do? Bumby will support papa en espagne avec les taureaux.[12]

Love to you all

Ernest.

PUL, TLS

Carlos Baker dates this letter as c. 24 November (*SL*, 231–33). The later date of [c. 1 December 1926] allows for EH's receipt of Maxwell Perkins's letter of 22 November with enclosed clippings from the *New York World* of 19 November. This date also accommodates the timing of Heinemann's expressed interest in Hemingway's work in late November.

1 T. H. (Mike) Ward worked at the travel desk of the Guaranty Trust bank in Paris and in 1924 introduced EH to six-day bicycle racing at the Vélodrome d'Hiver, as EH later recounted ("The End of an Avocation," *MF*). On 10 May 1927 Ward would serve as witness, along with Virginia Pfeiffer, at the wedding of EH and Pauline.

2 In a letter to EH of 4 December 1926, Bridges would accept "In Another Country" for *Scribner's Magazine*, having earlier accepted "The Killers" and "A Canary for One." The "better" story EH said he just finished was "Now I Lay Me," and the two he did not expect to sell were "A Pursuit Race" and "A Simple Enquiry," both published for the first time in *MWW* in October 1927 (Smith, 172).

3 Pauline had written to EH on 11 October 1926 that she would be bringing him a new typewriter when she returned to France. Reynolds notes that EH's broken typewriter had been a gift from Hadley six years earlier (*AH*, 75).

4 In his letter to EH of 22 November 1926 (PUL), Perkins enclosed an ad from the *New York World* and a review by Heywood Broun (1888–1939), whose column "It Seems to Me" appeared in the paper from 1921 to 1939. In his 19 November 1926 column, Broun had

written of *SAR*, "the truthfulness of the book should be evident to all. And its beauty should not be missed by many" (17).

5 Echoing William Rose Benét's claim in the 30 October *Saturday Review of Literature*, the author of an unsigned review of *SAR* in *Time* declared that EH had taken "his widow from Michael Arlen's *The Green Hat*" (1 November 1926, 48), and Burton Rascoe pronounced that the characters in EH's novel were "real" except Brett, who "stepped into 'The Sun Also Rises' out of 'The Green Hat'" ("Diversity in the Younger Set," *New York Sun*, 6 November 1926, 10). Conrad Aiken remarked that EH "has learned something from Mr. Anderson, and something, perhaps, from Mr. Fitzgerald's 'Great Gatsby'; he may even have extracted a grain or two of ore from Miss Gertrude Stein—which is in itself no inconsiderable feat" ("Expatriates," *New York Herald Tribune Books*, 31 October 1926, 4).

6 EH is playing on the French verb *disloquer*, to dislocate. In proper French the phrase would be, *Je me suis disloqué l'épaule*: I dislocated my shoulder.

7 There were three printings of *SAR* in 1926: the first (5,090 copies) on 9 October; the second (1,970) on 24 November, and the third (2,290) on 29 November (Grissom, 58–59).

8 *College Humor* editor H. N. Swanson had told EH in his 9 November 1926 letter that a "generous review" of *SAR* would appear in the magazine's January 1927 issue (PUL). However, in the "Book Looks" column of that issue, reviewer Kerry Scott wrote that EH "keeps pushing a great many readers in the face by an attitude that says, 'You wouldn't be interested in this anyway'" and concluded, "They are going to take him at his word and stay away from the book in great numbers" (*College Humor*, January 1927, 85). EH probably alludes to the *Harvard Lampoon*, Harvard University's humor magazine, established in 1876. Fitzgerald had attended Princeton University but did not complete a degree.

9 Founded in 1890 by William Heinemann (1863–1920), the London publishing company bearing his name gained considerable success by pioneering six shilling novels and attracting such authors as Henry James, Rudyard Kipling, and H. G. Wells. After Heinemann's death, the New York publisher Doubleday acquired a controlling interest in the firm. Doubleday managing director Charles S. Evans expressed Heinemann's interest in *SAR* and entered negotiations for the British rights with the Curtis Brown agency late in 1926.

10 For EH's description of his earlier suicidal feelings, see his letter of 12 [November 1926] to Pauline.

11 *Sans peur et sans reproche*: without fear and beyond reproach (French). The phrase is most famously associated with French knight Pierre Terrail, Seigneur de Bayard (1473–1524), known as "*le chevalier sans peur et sans reproche*" and as a paragon of chivalric values.

12 *En espagne avec les taureaux*: In Spain with the bulls (French).

To Clarence and Grace Hall Hemingway, [1 December 1926]

Dear Dad and Mother—

Thank you both for your fine letters. I am so glad to hear of mother's success in painting. I felt terribly not to get back this fall and to miss the hunting with Dad but things did not come out.[1] Don't worry about Bumby's health as he lives not in a studio but in a comfortable, light, well heated apartment on the sixth floor with a lovely view and all modern comforts. He recovered completely from his who[o]ping cough, plays in the parc—the Luxembourg Gardens—and is tremendously husky and strong. He talks French and good German and some english and says very intelligent things. It is me that works in the studio where nobody has the address and can't bother me.[2]

The reviews of my novel have been splendid and I see by an ad in the N.Y. World of November 19 that it is in its second printing. The Boston Transcript gave it two columns and the N.Y. Times, World and Tribune all good reviews. It is being published in England shortly. In Our Time has been published there and had a very good press. I'll save some of the reviews that Scribner's send me and send them to you if you'd like to see them.[3]

Have a story in December Scribner's magazine I believe. Either Dcember or January. One in the following number too. Have read the proof on both of them but am not altogether sure what numbers they are appearing in.[4]

I have a fine new picture of Bumby to send you for Christmas. Man Ray who took the one of me you liked did it.[5] Bumby says he is going to go to Spain with papa next year and sleep with the bulls. He prteneded to have drunk some cleaning fluid and when Hadley told him that if he drunk it it would kill him and he would go to heaven with the baby jesus. Bumby said in french that that was true and if the baby Jesus drunk the cleaning fluid it would kill the baby Jesus too.[6] I taught him all his prayers in English but he doesn't take them very seriously yet and when I took him to church one Sunday he said it was very fine because the church was full of lions. He goes down six flights every morning and brings up the paper all alone.

Best love to you both, to Carol, Leicester, Sunny, Marce, and Ura and all their husbands, lovers, and projeny.[7]

Ernie

JFK, TL/ALS; postmark: PARI[S] [S], 18 / 1 −1[2] / 2[6]

1 EH is responding to his mother's letter of 31 October 1926 and his father's of 7 November 1926 (JFK). Grace reported on her September exhibit of landscape and marine paintings, including *The Blacksmith Shop*, at the Carroll L. Bragg Real Estate Office in Oak Park. Grace's primary artistic expression turned from music to painting in the 1920s, when she began taking art classes at the Chicago Art Institute and elsewhere and painting several

hours a day. In his letter Clarence expressed his disappointment that EH did not visit Oak Park that fall. He had planned to take EH and his younger son Leicester on a hunting trip to Southern Illinois, where EH's uncle Frank Bristow Hines (1859–1933) "was to find the best Coon and Fox hounds in the country."

2 "Are you all camping in the studio?" Grace had asked, wondering if the place was heated and worrying that Bumby might be vulnerable to tuberculosis, which she had heard was "rampant" in Paris. While EH lived in Murphy's studio, Hadley and Bumby were living in an apartment at 35, rue de Fleurus near the Luxembourg Gardens. EH had not yet told his parents that he and Hadley had separated.

3 The British edition of *IOT* was published by Jonathan Cape on 23 September 1926; *Fiesta*, the British edition of *SAR*, would be published by Cape on 9 June 1927.

4 "The Killers" would appear in the March 1927 issue of *Scribner's Magazine* and both "In Another Country" and "A Canary for One" in the April 1927 issue.

5 American expatriate photographer Man Ray (né Emmanuel Radnitsky, 1890–1976) moved to Paris and opened a studio in 1921. Grace had used a photograph of EH taken by Man Ray in Paris in 1923 as the model for an oil portrait that she painted in the spring of 1925 (reproduced in the plate section of *Letters* vol. 2).

6 The letter is typewritten to this point; the remainder is handwritten.

7 In his 7 November letter, Clarence briefly mentioned all five of EH's siblings. Fifteen-year-old Carol was "doing especially well in High School." Eleven-year old Leicester was "growing fast into manhood. He is a real chum for me and enjoys the out of doors the same as you and I do." Sunny was "still single and may be for a time," although she and her twenty-year-old boyfriend "sure are devoted to each other"; Clarence described him as "rather the type you would call a radical and a real guy," but said he would likely "make it go all right" when he was a bit older. "Good word from both Marcelline and Ursula and their daughters and husbands," Clarence reported. The eldest sibling, Marcelline (1898–1963), married Sterling Skillman Sanford (1893–1990) on 2 January 1923 and had a daughter, Carol Hemingway Sanford (1924–2013). EH's sister Ursula (1902–1966), nicknamed "Ura," married Jasper Jay Jepson (1903–1973) on 12 September 1925; their daughter, Gayle (1926—1998), was born on 14 August 1926.

To Pauline Pfeiffer, [c. 2–3 December 1926]

Unless promised vogue or want work Newyork would welcome Boulogne after January first stop been and am condition hurry

If promised vogue or want work newyork stay otherwise welcome boulogne after january first virginia working sorbonne[1] stop am grave condition hurry doubtless passing like art
Cubists[2]

JFK, TCD

Before Hadley called off the extended separation agreement that would have ended on 3 February, Pauline reported in her letter to EH of 2 [November 1926] that she had been offered a six-week job at *Vogue* in New York City beginning the day after Christmas, which would "carry me through to the sailing date, and help the mind, and make us some money" (JFK). She added, "if either of us gets shot, there is the cable HURRY and COMING, and New York is a lot nearer to you than here"—referring to their code words to signal that EH could no longer bear the separation and Pauline should take the first ship back to France regardless of the agreement. EH likely drafted this cable in response to Pauline's letter of [c. 15 November 1926], which he received in a pneumatique from Jinny Pfeiffer on 2 December 1926. In that letter to EH, written just after learning that Hadley had terminated the separation agreement, Pauline explained she was "thick in negociations with Vogue for the six weeks ending February 1" and wondered if it would be better for her to take the job or to return to France sooner. Pauline asked that EH cable her upon receipt of her letter if he felt strongly one way or another. In the following two letters to Pauline of [2 December 1926] and [3 December 1926], EH expresses uncertainty as to whether he should send her such a cable.

1 La Sorbonne, historic name for the University of Paris. EH's comment may have been prompted by Pauline's letter to her sister of [c. 15 November 1926], which Jinny forwarded to EH on 2 December along with Pauline's letter to him. Pauline warned Jinny that the family disapproved of her "drifting in Paris, not doing ANYTHING, not even studying" and were considering "taking away the independence" (JFK).

2 "Cubists" is a code signature that EH and Pauline used in cables.

To Pauline Pfeiffer, [2 December 1926]

Thursday night at midnight

Today was lawyer day but the lawyer put it off until tomorrow.[1] However there was a pneumatique tonight enclosing your letters to Jinny and to me—from Jinny.

I dont know what to wire about working—because it seems as though you wanted to do it—but I don't know if they even agreed to the 100-a week.[2] If time doesnt make any difference you might as well stay in NY and work until Feb. 1 as to come over after Xmas. It—time—seems somehow to make a lot of difference to me—due to being just horribly cock-eyed lonesome—and feeling about it—time—as I felt when you went away—

Had the horrors last night and am going to try and stay up through tonight on acct. last night was plenty.

The Homeric—I believe—gets in Saturday and that means may be I'll get a letter with some more dope on it—if you write—.[3] I suppose should cable but by now surely you've accepted Vogue or not—if you have it means you want to do it. And if you want to do it you do it.

As far as the money angle is I should think N.Y. would eat up 75 or so a week in overhead and I can get 200 a story from Scribners—and could write them if we could have say a little tranquility and I get out of this damned depression of loneliness.

All this last week I would have sent the cable about hurry except that I knew you had your Christmas plans, family, me the MacLeishes etc. People in the lives.[4]

Have put off starting anything lengthy on acct. of constant changes, emotional gauntlets etc. that would bust it up. But now am going to start a play. Have an awfully swell play to do.[5] Maybe wait till you come back—because it would be terribly exciting to do when you were here so I could find out about it at the time from you—and someone to feel swell with when day's work over instead of gradual and regular evening coming on of despair. Sounds very melodramatic about [*Ditto mark*: despair] but it comes about five o'clock like a fog coming up from a river bottom

JFK, AL

This appears to be an abandoned start to the longer, typewritten letter EH wrote the next day, which follows in this volume.

1 Hadley was represented in the divorce proceedings by a lawyer named E. Burkhardt. The French divorce papers, dated 8 December 1926, signed by EH and by Burkhardt on Hadley's behalf, survive at JFK.

2 In the letter to EH that Jinny forwarded to him on 2 December, Pauline reported that *Vogue* had offered her no more than $85 a week for the six-week job, but she had countered that she could not take it for less than $100. She asked EH to cable her if he felt strongly as to whether she should take the job or return to France sooner ([15 November 1926], JFK).

3 The *Homeric*, of the White Star Line, left New York City on 27 November and would arrive in Cherbourg on Saturday, 4 December 1926.

4 Pauline had made plans to spend Christmas with her family in New York, visiting her brother and sister-in-law, Karl Gustavus Pfeiffer (1900–1981) and Matilda Schmitt Pfeiffer (1904–2002). EH had made plans to go with Archibald and Ada MacLeish to Gstaad, Switzerland, for a skiing vacation starting 25 December.

5 In 1920 EH and his high school friend Morris Musselman had collaborated on a comedy, *Hokum: A Play in Three Acts*, which was copyrighted by Musselman on 4 June 1921 and first published in 1978 in a limited edition, with an introduction by William Young (Wellesley Hills, Massachusetts: Sans Souci Press). In a letter to EH of 2 June 1926, Musselman reported on his latest efforts as a playwright and said he wished EH were in Chicago so they could collaborate on a play. Musselman's letter to EH of 8 November 1926 indicates that they had corresponded about the possibility. Musselman wrote, "your basic idea has floored me," and he proposed they write a play together: "Then we'll sell it and draw down 500 bucks a week royalty apiece" (JFK).

To Pauline Pfeiffer, [3 December 1926]

Dearest Pfife your letter to me through jinny and the air mail came last night—Thursday December 2—and either tonight or tomorrow will s[e]nd this cable—maybe wait[i]ng until tomorrow for the week end rates—maybe sending tonight from the Bourse.[1] Jinny is coming here at seven. Was to spend yesterday with the lawyer but he put it off until this afternoon.

I've been in pretty terrible shape now for a while and would have wired hurry except I knew you had your Christmas planned and the family and the MacLeishes taken rooms and sleeper for me etc. People in the lives.

Doesn't take any particular form outside of the horrors at night and a black depression. You see Pfife I think that when two people love each other terri[b]ly much and need each other in every way and then go away from each other it works almost as bad as an abortion. It isn't as though there were a war or it were a whaling voyage or any case of force majeur[2]—where something you could not do anything against ran it—but where you could buck against that thing; the daily routine of a war or the work of a long trip with nothing to do about it. But the deliberate keeping apart when all you have is each other does something bad to you and lately it has shot me all to hell inside. I know, or anyhow I feel, that I could be faithful to you with my body and my mind and my spirit for as long as I had any of them—and I know now too that because being the same guy and yet a whole something started with my body that had gotten to be an integral part of everything that being alone and just lonesome all sorts of things seem to damn up and the balance of it all be thrown off and it attacks the spirit and it isn't so good for the head either. You lie all night half funny in the head and pray and pray and pray you won't go crazy. And I can't believe it does any good and I do believe it does hell's own amount of harm.

And you had yours too—and I felt so terribly about that—and now you are swll and fine and practical in the head (like we both used to be) and I will be again because I'm not a depressed rat naturally. And I've sense enough to know when I think all the time I want to die that I'm just a fool because what I think about as wanting to die is just to have oblivion until I can have Pfeiffer. But I know it will be s[w]ell and to let you know that I am feeling swell and that the world is grand and that I feel good inside and not just dry like a piece of cuttle fish bone like they feed canaries but really fine I'll wire you EXCELLENT—and that means that you just read this letter as by somebody else and know that I'm fine in the head and inside.

I love you so Pfife and I want a letter from you—just about loving each other and no facts bulletins nor anything timely—because it has been a terrible long time since I had a letter like that nor one that wasn't written to catch a mail in ten minutes and what I miss worse is not having any intimacy with you—nor any feeling of us against the others. I knew it was swell and practical and I admired the mechanics and performance of it [*EH insertion*: the air mail] in every way but when I got your first letter after the cable—the first time I'd heard from you and was to make contact again—open in a letter from Jinny I just felt like hell.³ So would you maybe write me a letter like that sometime when [t]hre isn't anything else to say and ordinarily you wouldn't have been writing a letter—if you should ever feel that way—in which our loving each other will sound like something pleasant and stick in maybe a few references to the future as being something pretty good. All the letters before your bad time sounded as though you loved me more than anything in the world and when one came I used to be just cock-eyed happy. Then since there was just the grand last letter but it seemed as though there wasn't any joy any more—just loyalty and I was afraid maybe you had really given me up as you said you had had to and were just going through wih it now——and oh everything else bughouse. And I would like a letter like they used to be before you felt so badly

JFK, TL

1 This is apparently EH's second attempt to respond to the letter from Pauline of [15 November 1926] that he received in a pneumatique from her sister on 2 December 1926. Pauline had sent the letters to EH and Jinny by air mail to New York in order to catch the *Majestic*, bound for France, reporting in her letter to EH, "I went down this morning to see about air mail, if it was routed from St. Louis to New York, and I asked the mail clerk if he knew anything about air mail and he said he thought it went by airplane. So that's what I have to go on, and it may miss the boat" (JFK). The post office at 4, Place de la Bourse was one of two in Paris that were open all night for telegrams (Baedeker's *Paris*, 28).

2 *Force majeure*: literally, "superior force" (French); an unavoidable circumstance or "act of God."
3 In the letter to EH that Jinny forwarded to him on 2 December, Pauline wrote that she was "cockeyed happy" to have received Jinny's telegram the night before saying "THREE MONTHS TERMINATED AT HADLEYS REQUEST SHE STARTING IMMEDIATELY OWN REASONS STOP COMMUNICATION RESUMED STOP."

To Louis and Mary Bromfield, 6 December 1926

December 6, 1926

Dear Louis and Mary—

It was awfully exciting to hear you both liked the book. I'm terribly sorry I can't come to dinner either Thursday or Friday this week—going down to Chartres—sounds like going to Hoboken—but I'd love to dine with you any night next week except Monday or Tuesday. It will be great to see you both again. If you want me next week—or any other time—drop me a note to the bank. I'll be in and out of town until Christmas.[1]

I see by the reviews that Early Autumn—a grand title—is exterminating the remaining New Englanders.[2] That's splendid. I got discouraged on the reviews myself when I discovered through them that I'd taken Brett or whatever her name was out of The Green Hat. If you have a copy of the Green Hat I'd like to read it. Maybe I could get some more characters without having to ruin my liver drinking with them.

Yours always,

Ernest Hemingway

OSU, TLS

1 EH is responding to separate letters from Mary and Louis Bromfield expressing their enthusiasm for *SAR* (JFK). In her letter of 2 December [1926], Mary had invited EH to dinner "next Thursday" (9 December). In her reply to this letter from EH, she changed the dinner date to the following Wednesday (15 December). Archibald MacLeish would reminisce in a letter to EH the following summer about good times they had shared, including bicycling to the cathedral town of Chartres, about 60 miles southwest of Paris (19 June [1927], JFK).
2 Louis Bromfield's novel *Early Autumn: A Story of a Lady* (New York: Stokes, 1926) won a Pulitzer Prize in 1927.

To Maxwell Perkins, 6 December 1926

December 6, 1926

Dear Mr. Perkins:

Thanks so much for the reviews and the information about the Sun's prospects.[1] As for the movie rights please get the best you can i.e. the most money—I do not go to the movies and would not care what changes they made.[2] That is their gain or loss—I don't write movies. Although if they would film Pamplona they could make a wonderful picture.

All that racing of the bulls through the streets and the people running ahe[a]d and into the ring, amateurs being tossed, the bulls charging into the crowd etc. really happens every morning between the 7th and 12th of July and they could get some wonderful stuff. We made a movie from inside the ring one year with a German portable camera—the sort that takes full size movies; you have only to load it and press down a button to keep it shooting—no cranking—and had the rush of people coming into the ring, coming faster and faster and then finally falling all over themselves and piling up and the bulls jamming over them and right into the camera. It was a wonderful thing but so short that it wasn't of any commercial value. Have another one of Don Stewart being tossed in the amateur fight and one of me bull fighting. When I come over to the states will bring them and we can run them off sometime.[3]

About the stories—I have ten stories now—Two long ones The Undefeated—a bull fight story of between 12 and 15,000 words; and Fifty Grand. Eight others will average around three thousand words or so. I don't know whether that is enough for a book. In any event do you think it would be wise to have another book out so soon as Spring—rather than wait until early fall?[4] In Our Time came out last November—Torrents in the early summer—The Sun in Oct.[5] Don't you think we might give them a rest? Or isn't that how it's done?

I will keep the bull fight book going and might do the first part and get it out of the way up to date. It will have illustrations—drawings and photographs—and I think should have some colored reproductions. It is a long one to write because it is not to be just a history and text book or apologia for bull fighting—but instead, if possible, bull fighting its-self.[6] As it's a thing that nobody knows about in English I'd like to take it first from altogether outside—how I happened to be interested in it, how it seemed before I saw it—how it was when I didn't understand it my [o]wn experience with it, how it reacts on other—the gradual finding out about it and try and build it up from the outside and then go all the way inside with chapters on everything. It might be interesting to people because nobody knows anything about it—and it really is terribly interesting—being a matter of life and death—and anything that a young peasant or bootblack can make 80,000 dollars a year in before he is twenty three does something ~~of interest~~ to people. I think a really true book if it were fairly well written about the one thing that has, with the exception of [t]he ritual of the church, come down to us intact from the old days would have a certain permanent value. But it has to be solid and true and have all the dope and be interesting—and it won't be ready for a long time. But you can figure on it for the future if you like.

I think [th]e next thing to figure on is a book of stories—and I think it's very important that it should be awfully good and not hurried. Because if The Sun sh[o]uld have some success there will be a lot of people with the knife out very eager to see me slipping—and the best way to handle that is not to slip. Then I'd like to write another novel when things get straightened out and my head gets tranquil. In the meantime I might as well write stories for a while. I had a note from Scott that he was leaving for Genoa—so I imagine you may see him before you get this letter.[7]

My own typewriter is broken and this borrowed one has so many wretched individual traits that my mind is half occupied all the time I'm writing with the malignancy of the machine and I haven't been able to re-write the other story I was going to send you or do anything new.[8] I'll enclose the proofs of the little canary story with this and perhaps you will turn them over to Mr. Bridges with my compliments.

Yours always,
Ernest Hemingway.

PUL, TLS

Written across the top of the first page in a hand other than EH's is the note, "March No. out Feby."

1 In his letter of 22 November 1926, Perkins reported that reviews of *SAR* "continue to be excellent" and "the prospects are at present altogether favorable" (PUL). He enclosed copies of the review by Ernest Boyd in the 20 November 1926 *Independent* that called the novel's technique "fascinating," as well as Heywood Broun's piece in the 19 November 1926 *New York World*.

2 In the same letter, Perkins wrote that two "movie people" had inquired about *SAR*, but while there were certainly possibilities, "they would require, I should think, such a revision to make a movie story, that you might hesitate" (PUL). It would take several years until an agreement was reached. In 1932 RKO Radio Pictures Inc. would purchase the rights to "the world motion picture, silent and sound" for $13,200 (RKO voucher, 5 July 1932, PUL; Scribner's to Maurice Speiser, 7 July 1932, PUL). However, the material was deemed too sexual for film production at that time, and a movie version of *SAR* would not appear until 1957.

3 EH refers to filming that took place at the Pamplona fiesta in July 1924. "George O'Neill had a movie machine and took 23 reels of films of the bull fights, amateur fights, dancing and religious processions," he had reported in a letter to his mother of 18 July 1924 (*Letters* vol. 2, 133). He wrote to Gertrude Stein and Alice B. Toklas on 9 August 1924, "Our Movie of Pamplona Man Ray says is one of the best movies he's ever seen" (*Letters* vol. 2, 137). In a later letter he told them that Man Ray was enlarging some of the movies, including one of EH executing a pass with a cape ([c. 22–27 August 1924], *Letters* vol. 2, 144). EH also mentioned film of the bullfights in his "Pamplona Letter" for the September 1924 *Transatlantic Review*. The movie footage remains unlocated.

4 In his 22 November letter, Perkins raised the question of EH's next book, suggesting that if EH had enough stories, they might plan for a March 1927 publication date (PUL). In his 18 December 1926 response to this letter, Perkins would suggest fall publication for a book of stories so as not to "divert attention" from *SAR*, which he expected to "sell steadily throughout the spring season" (PUL).

5 Liveright published *IOT* on 5 October 1925; Scribner's published *TOS* on 28 May 1926 and *SAR* on 22 October 1926.

6 In his 22 November letter, Perkins expressed interest in the "large book on bull fighting" that EH had once mentioned. Perkins assumed EH "meant to make its preparation a matter of years" but encouraged him to keep it in mind as a future project. As EH described it in a 12 January 1925 letter to Miriam Hapgood, he envisioned "a real long book—two volumes maybe—everything about the Bull ring." He expected to work on it for five or six years, so that it would be "scientific and accurate and also have the story of the different trips to Spain and travelling with the bull fighters and the actual life in the profession" (*Letters* vol. 2, 214). EH began writing the book in a concentrated way in 1930, and in 1932 Scribner's would publish it as *DIA*, a 532-page volume with more than sixty photographs.

7 In an undated note from Villa St. Louis, Juan-les-Pins, Fitzgerald wrote that he and Zelda were leaving for New York via Genoa and urged EH to let him know "if there is anything you need done here or in America" ([December 1926], JFK; Bruccoli *Fitz-Hem*, 78). Sailing from Genoa on the *Conte Biancamano* on Friday, 10 December, the Fitzgeralds arrived in New York on Monday, 20 December.

8 Probably "Now I Lay Me" (Smith, 172–73).

To Maxwell Perkins, 7 December 1926

December 7, 1926

Dear Mr. Perkins;

Today your letter of Nov.26 came. I don't think the book could have been better made nor finer looking.

One thing I would like—four copies only were sent me—and I would like a few more as I had to buy it here at 70 francs a copy to send over to Curtis Brown for his negotiations with Heinemann etc.

I have set a trap for Roth by letting a local N.J. printer get out a few hundred copies of a thing of mine called Today Is Friday—which Roth will be very liable to lift for one of his publications. This I have had copyrighted and have just received the certificate of copyright registration from Washington. We may be able to bag him with that.

About the drawing—it really makes no difference.[1] At the time I hated to have my family think that I really looked like that. They feel, I understand, very humiliated because of "the way I write." A copy of The Literary Digest Book Review Magazine from my father has underlined in blue and red pencil the following—The Penn Publishing Company, of Philadelphia, which reports a <u>constantly increasing sale</u> for the books of Temple Bailey, wrote in part— "Our feeling is that there is a strong reaction against the sex novel, and even the highbrow realistic novel——and that (later on) the clean, romantic, or stirring adventure tale will always <u>command the wider public</u>." But the drawing may have pleased them. And it seems to reproduce very well.

What you say about The Green Hat is quite true. My contact with Arlen was through Scott's talking about him and his stuff when we once drove Scott's car from Lyons to Paris.[2] I remember telling Scott who the people were that had taken Arlen up—and even getting quite irritated about Arlen—Don Stewart talked about him too. I took it for granted that the Green Hat must be a cheap book when I heard that the heroine killed herself—because the one very essential fact about all those people that Arlen knew was that none of them had the guts to kill themselves. So I guess it was really protesting about that sort of twaddle that I made Brett so damned accurate that practically nobody seemed to believe in her. Maybe they do now though. Anyway it was very funny.

There really is, to me anyway, very great glamour in life—and places and all sorts of things and I would like sometime to get it into the stuff. People aren't all as bad as Ring Lardner finds them—or as hollowed out and exhausted emotionally as some of The Sun generation. I've known some very wonderful people who even though they were going directly toward the grave (which is what makes any story a tragedy if carried out until the end) managed to put up a very fine performance enroute. Impotence is a pretty dull subject compared with war or love or the old lucha por la vida.[3]

I do hope though that The Sun will sell a tremendous lot because while the subject is dull the book isn't. Then maybe sometime, and with that impetus to go on, we'll have a novel where the subject won't be dull and try and keep the good qualities of this one. Only, of course, you don't have subjects—Louis Bromfield has subjects—but just write them and if God is good to you they come out well. But it would always be much better to write than to talk about writing.

My son looks forward very much to the Christmas book and told his mother very excitedly—Max Perkins va me donner un jolie cadeau! When she asked him what it was he said it was a very beautiful big book not written by papa.[4]

Yours always
Ernest Hemingway.

PUL, TLS

1 In his letter to EH of 26 November 1926 (PUL), Perkins lamented that Samuel Roth could not be stopped from reprinting EH's stories that had first appeared in magazines published abroad, but asked if EH had any objection to Roth's using Blomshield's portrait drawing of EH that appeared on the rear dust jacket of *SAR* and in some of Scribner's advertisements. If so, Scribner's would change the drawing in the next printing. On the rear jacket of the seventh printing in February 1927, the Blomshield portrait was replaced by a photograph of EH wearing a hat and overcoat (Grissom, 57).
2 In mid-May 1925 EH and Fitzgerald took the train to Lyon to retrieve the car that Fitzgerald and Zelda had abandoned there while en route from Italy to Paris in late April 1925. EH would provide a memorable account of the trip in the "Scott Fitzgerald" chapter of *MF*.
3 *Lucha por la vida*: struggle for life (Spanish).
4 Perkins promised in his 26 November letter to send Bumby "a Christmas present—one of the biggest books ever published. I believe he will like the pictures." EH reports Bumby as

saying (in imperfect French), "Max Perkins is going to give me a pretty gift!" The book may have been *Winnie the Pooh*, written by A. A. Milne (1882–1956) and illustrated by E. H. Shepard (1879–1976), which was an immediate success when it was published on 14 October 1926 (London: Methuen; New York: E. P. Dutton).

To Pauline Pfeiffer, [10 December 1926]

PAULINE PFEIFFER

PIGGOTT

ARKANSAS

BEARS ~~ABOUT~~ without CABLES[1]

[*Nom et domicile de l'Expéditeur*] Hemingway 69 Rue Froidevaux

JFK, ACDS; letterhead: WESTERN UNION CABLEGRAM / SIÈGE SOCIAL EN FRANCE: 2, RUE DES ITALIENS, PARIS

1 In her letter of 10 December [1926], Pauline would reply, "I just got your cable BEARS WITHOUT CABLE, and I feel terrible." She had delayed cabling EH because she had been waiting to receive a second story from EH after he sent her a copy of "In Another Country" (JFK). She also wrote she would be sending him a cable saying "WAS AWAITING NOT YET ARRIVED SECOND STORY BUT SHOULDNT HAVE STOP COUNTRY OREJAS EASY STOP CUBISTS ABOUT STARTED." The cable EH actually received, stamped "Paris 10–12," survives at JFK, but is missing the final words "ABOUT STARTED."

To Maxwell Perkins, 15 December [1926]

Dec 15—

Dear Mr. Perkins—

I have your letters of Dec 1 and 3 and writing this in a hurry to catch the Paris.[1]

I am interested in the Brady-Wiman offer. Both theatrical and movie rights—however—is a large order. What terms are they prepared to make if they are serious?

For the movie rights I think you should <u>ask</u> a good sized sum. There seems to be no real basis or reason for the sums paid by movie people for books. It seems very fantastic and I do not know what sums of <u>actual cash</u> are involved.

I should <u>ask</u> $30,000 of movie people—<u>as a minimum</u>—and take whatever you can get in <u>cash</u>.[2]

As for the stories— It would mean a lot to me to have them published in the magazine.[3] Selling the stories is now practically my only source of income and, as yet, I have not had a single story published in an American Magazine. Once the cork is drawn other magazines will buy them too. It seems ridiculous that a story like <u>50 Grand</u> cant be sold.

Edward O'Brien took me out to lunch yesterday and said he thought it was the best story I'd written so far.[4] Only I cant get it published.

So if the magazine publishes some stories I feel it would increase my chances of selling others. Other magazine editors might think if Scribners Magazine wont publish his stories—(granted that the stories arent exactly what they're used to or expect) why should we take a chance?

I understand perfectly why you should not want to announce them and then have a book on the way in the Spring. But if the Sun holds up I should think early fall would be be plenty of time for a book of stories.[5]

Anyway, in a way, short stories are, as a form, are designed for publication in a magazine. Where each one stands alone and the reader isn't jolted in his reaction by having a new one by the same author, just over the page. However I have great confidence in your judgement and am willing to do whatever you think best there.

Do what you think best about the movie, stage etc. rights. Or if it is too much of a problem of negotiation and you want a good bargainer why not place that in the hands of Reynolds?[6]

Yours always

Ernest Hemingway.

PUL, ALS

On the recto of Scribner's envelope, addressed to EH in care of the Guaranty Trust Company in Paris and postmarked from New York on 4 December 1926, EH wrote: "Friday nights Friday aft / 3–4 pm / Sherwood. / <u>Bumby's tree</u> / Thursday / Noon—⑫ / Evan to go out to Vincennes / Friday AM / get winter coat, / Hadley's pants — / Dinner shoes and / sweat shirt / from 113 with / Evan."

1 The Compagnie Générale Transatlantique steamship *Paris*, which operated from 1921 to 1939, departed from Le Havre on 15 December and arrived in New York on 22 December.

2 Theatrical producer Dwight Deere Wiman (1895–1951), of Brady and Wiman, Inc. of New York, wrote to Perkins on 2 December 1926 offering to purchase the dramatic and movie rights for *SAR* (with terms to be discussed) and asking Perkins to find out if EH was interested. Enclosing Wiman's letter in his own letter to EH of 3 December 1926, Perkins called it a sincere offer but also warned that a theatrical production "would imply very serious modifications of the story" and that he regarded theater people as "the most eccentric and vacillating in the world next to the movie people. You can never count on anything until you have a signed contract,—I might almost say, a check" (PUL). Nothing would come of the Brady–Wiman offer.

3 In his 3 December letter Perkins explained the importance of timing a book of stories. Scribner's did not want to publish a story collection in tandem with publication of the same stories in *Scribner's Magazine*.

4 In a letter of 9 August 1927 (PUL), O'Brien would ask Scribner's for permission to include "Fifty Grand" in *The Best Short Stories of 1927*, but Perkins would turn down his request.

5 EH and Perkins had arrived at the same conclusion. In a letter of 18 December 1926 that crossed with this one in the mail, Perkins informed EH that it would be most strategic to publish the next book of stories in the fall and that Scribner's was ready to do that (PUL).

6 Ann Watkins (née Angeline Whiton, 1885–1967) of A. Watkins, Inc., rather than Paul Reynolds, would be the agent to negotiate the *SAR* movie rights contract of 5 July 1932 between EH and RKO.

To Maxwell Perkins, 21 December 1926

[PARIS] December 21 *[19]*26

Dear Mr. Perkins:

Thanks for the figures on the Sun. I do hope it will go on again after the New Year and think it may as there seems to be much divergence of opinion etc. which must mean discussion.[1] John Bishop showed me a letter from Edmund Wilson last night in which Wilson was very enthusiastic saying he thought it best novel by any one of my generation—but that plenty of others didn't and what did he, Bishop, think. Maybe Wilson will write something about it. I'm awfully glad he liked it.[2]

I think it is a splendid idea of Bridges about running the three stories together— They are all short—none of them long enough to make much of a row alone—but all 3 complement one another and would make a fine group.[3] And perhaps cheer up Dos, Allen Tate and the other boys who fear I'm on the toboggan.[4] I take it for granted then he's buying In Another Country—and if he wants to send it I could use the check.

Thank you ever so much for the Christmas book for Bumby. And a very merry holiday time

Ernest Hemingway.

Dos Passos sent me a carbon of his review.[5] I think it was fine about his not liking the book and wanting it to be better but a poor criticism that Pamplona in the book wasnt as good as Pamplona in real life—because I think it was maybe pretty exciting to people who'd never been there—and that was who it was written for. It would be easy to write about it for Dos and make it very exciting—because he's been there. But written for him it wouldnt mean anything to the quite abstract reader that one tries to write for—

I suppose by now you have seen Scott [Fitzgerald]. Please give him my best greetings.

I am leaveing Paris on Christmas night—perhaps for several months—but letters to the bank will always be forwarded promptly. They relay cables too.

Cape took The Sun with a 50 pound advance—10-15-20-royalties and Spring publication.[6]

I have been writing some more stories. I have given my wife all the Sun royalties—both British and American—and I hope they will be considerable. I dont know when the royalty checks come out. When one does I wish you could consider the advance on Torrents as $500 and that paid on the Sun as $1000 and let the check go on when the earnings commence after the $1000 is paid off.

I dont imagine that Torrents earned $500 but you can deduct the difference from my next book.

When the royalty check comes due you may send it to Hadley R. Hemingway—Guaranty Trust Co. of N.Y. One Rue des Italiens. Paris.

I imagine, now that they seem to be rowing about it that the Sun may go very well. The chief criticism seems to be that the people are so unattractive—which seems very funny as criticism when you consider the attractiveness of the people in, say, Ulysses, the Old Testament, Judge Fielding and other people some of the critics like. I wonder where these thoroughly attractive people hang out and how they behave when they're drunk and what do <u>they</u> think about nights. Oh hell. There's at least one highly moral hotel keeper in the book. That's my contention and I'll stick to it. And an exemplary Englishman named Harris.

And why not make a Jew a bounder in literature as well as in life? Do Jews always have to be so splendid in writing?

I think maybe next book we can save money on the clippings.

Critics, this is still Mr. Tate—have a habit of hanging attributes on you themselves—and then when they find you're not that way accusing you of sailing under false colours— Mr Tate feels so badly that I'm not as hard-boiled as he had publicly announced. As a matter of fact I have not been at all hard boiled since July 8 1918—on the night of which I discovered that that also was Vanity.[7]

PUL, ALS; letterhead: THE CHICAGO DAILY NEWS / 10, BOULEVARD DES CAPUCINES / PLACE DE L'OPÉRA / VISTORS' WRITING ROOM.

1 In his letter to EH of 10 December 1926, Perkins reported that 4,471 copies of *SAR* had sold to date and provided the print numbers: a first printing of 6,000 copies plus second and third printings of 2,000 each. He cautioned, however, that these three printings did not reflect sales numbers and that it was difficult to predict exactly how the Christmas season would affect sales in the new year (PUL).

2 American poet and critic John Peale Bishop (1892–1944) and Edmund Wilson had attended Princeton with F. Scott Fitzgerald. Wilson, who had favorably reviewed *TSTP* and *iot* in the October 1924 *Dial*, would review *SAR* together with *MWW* in the 27 December 1927 *New Republic*, lauding EH for his "remarkable effects, effects unlike anything else one remembers" by which "we are made to feel, behind the appetite for the physical world, the falsity or the tragedy of a moral situation" ("The Sportsman's Tragedy," 103). Later, in his landmark essay "Ernest Hemingway: Bourdon Gauge of Morale," Wilson would describe the novel's protagonist, Jake Barnes, as one "who keeps up standards of conduct" and lives by a "code" that "supplies a dependable moral backbone" amidst social chaos (*Atlantic Monthly* [July 1939]: 38). Bishop would later describe the Hemingway of the 1920s and of *SAR* as a Byronic figure who offered his generation "an attitude with which to meet the disorders of the post-war decade" ("Homage to Hemingway," *New Republic*, 11 November 1936, 39).

3 In his letter to EH of 4 December 1926 accepting "In Another Country," Bridges mentioned the possibility of publishing EH's three stories in a "single group," and in his 10 December letter, Perkins said he favored that idea. However, in his letter of 18 December, which crossed in the mail with this one, Perkins reported that Bridges had decided to publish "The Killers" separately in the March 1927 number of *Scribner's Magazine*, while the other two stories were planned for "an early number thereafter" (PUL).

4 Both John Dos Passos and Allen Tate had written mixed reviews of *SAR*. Although Dos Passos praised it as an "extraordinarily well written book," he faulted it for being not the epic of a lost generation, but rather "a cock and bull story about a lot of summer tourists

getting drunk and making fools of themselves at a picturesque Iberian folk-festival" ("A Lost Generation," *New Masses* [December 1926]: 26). Tate recognized it as "a book that will be talked about, praised, perhaps imitated" but "not hard-boiled enough, in the artistic sense" and marked by sentimentality and flawed characterization ("Hard Boiled," *The Nation*, 15 December 1926, 642–44).

5 In his letter to EH of [10 November 1926], Dos Passos expressed regret over his "damn priggish mealy mouthed review" of *SAR* for the *New Masses*. He enclosed a carbon copy of the review's typescript with his handwritten note, "I've sworn off writing reviews, after this" (JFK).

6 EH's contract with Jonathan Cape for *Fiesta*, dated 10 December 1926, specified "A royalty of Ten per cent (10%) of the published price of all copies sold up to Three Thousand (3,000), Fifteen per cent (15% of the published price of all copies sold above Three Thousand (3,000) up to Five Thousand (5,000) and a royalty of Twenty per cent (20%) of the published price of all copies sold thereafter" (Jonathan Cape Archive, University of Reading).

7 The date of EH's wounding during WWI. As a volunteer with the ARC Ambulance Service, he was seriously injured by an Austrian mortar explosion and machine gun fire while distributing cigarettes and candy to Italian troops at Fossalta on the Piave River. He was hospitalized in Milan through the fall of 1918 before returning home to Oak Park in January 1919. EH alludes to the biblical passage from which he had drawn the epigraph to *SAR*, beginning "Vanity of vanities, saith the preacher, vanity of vanities; all is vanity" (Ecclesiastes 1:2).

To Louis Bromfield, [c. mid-December 1926]

Dear Louis—

I didnt realize until getting home how badly we had gipped you on taxis—going both ways from the opposite ends of Paris and never even putting the hand in the pockets—

So am enclosing 25 francs 29 to apply on this matter praying you to accept it in order that my conscience will cease troubling me— My conscience troubling keeping me from writing which keeps me from earning money— So you will be making me money by accepting this bill which has, as well as monetary value a certain historical value as bearing a much admired portrait of the Father of Our Country—

We had a fine time

Ernest

OSU, ALS

The conjectured letter date range is based partly on notes from Louis and Mary Bromfield (including one dated 2 December and another postmarked 8 December 1926; JFK), inviting

EH to dinner on 9 and 15 December at their home at 25, boulevard Flandrin, on the far western edge of Paris in the 16th arrondissement. The exchange rate for December 1926 aligns with EH's comment that the enclosed dollar bill (bearing the likeness of first U.S. president George Washington) was worth 25.29 French francs.

To Robert Bridges, 1 January 1927

January 1, 1927

Dear Mr. Bridges:

Thank you very much for the check for "In Another Country."[1] I think it would be a very good idea, as you suggest, to run the three short stories you now have in one group. As you say "The Killers" would go well alone— but the three together, I believe, would complement one another very well.

With best wishes for a happy New Year.

Yours very truly,
Ernest Hemingway.

PUL, ALS; letterhead: GRAND HOTEL ALPINA / GSTAAD-SUISSE / OBERLAND BERNOIS

1 On 7 December 1926, Scribner's had sent EH a $200 check "in full payment for all serial rights" to "In Another Country," with a request for acknowledgment of receipt (JFK).

To Ezra Pound, [2 January 1927]

Dear ~~Trotsky~~ Poundsonoff:[1]

So you joined The Revolution—New Masses. I.E. all well salaried style— and then they knocked you to glorify that other noble brother of the Proletariat the late Rev. Walsh.[2]

Listen and papa will tell you why Messers. Rorty, Freeman, Mike Gold etc etc. want a revolution. Because they hope that under some new order they would be men of talent.

That's all. Also they all are well paid.

Your remarks on the story very good.

I wish it were better. Scribner's and your Comrade Rorty turned it down (as too <u>horrid</u> or <u>hawid</u>). If I get a better one I'll give it to you. Meantime you got that one.[3] It's no Gorda in the lottery but you wont get any better stories from yr. other boy writers.[4] Will write you a better one if I can.

Did you refuse to sign the Joyce petition on purpose? It's no bloody importance about the L.R. because you cant come into a court of Equity without clean hands and as L.R. was suppressed for Ulysses etc that bitches them on that.[5]

P. S. FUCK the New Masses and their Revolution. In case you'd mistaken my sentiments.

The boys I.E. Comrade M. [MacLeish] myself and others felt badly you wouldnt sign.

Or doesnt the New Masses back any, however hopeless efforts to protect the P.B. "artist."[6]

Comrade MacLeish is here. I am here as Comrade M's guest.

Comrade MacLeish seemed put out that you should think he took some town in Persia that it took him 4 months to get to out of yr. works or the Anabasis or one of those other great books I haven't read.[7]

I consoled the comrade by telling him you were often full of shit but that out of that nettle, shit, we pluck this pearl, wisdom.[8]

Nobody else knows <u>anything</u> and there is nothing for the boys like criticism. If you hadn't become a classic at the age of was it 23—people would still read you. But the trouble with classics is that people dont read them they just refer to them. Mr. Bird pointed that out I believe.[9]

I myself cannot become a classic because 1st I dont know grammar 2nd I havent read any of the other classics and so cant form my work and life on same (you will note that <u>all</u> <u>contemporary</u> classics are like former classics. It is only the ones that dont arrive so fast that ever differ somewhat in structure or content and 3rdly—but I find I am writing shit myself and so will close—Your devoted Comrade.

Hemovitch.

Yale, ALS; letterhead: GRAND / HOTEL ALPINA / GSTAAD-SUISSE / OBERLAND BERNOIS; postmark: GSTAAD / (BERN), 2.1.27.10

1 Leon Trotsky (né Lev Davidovich Bronstein, 1879–1940), a leader in the October 1917 Russian Revolution, vied with Joseph Stalin for leadership of the Communist Party after the death of Vladimir Lenin in 1924. After losing his seat on the Politboro in October 1926, Trotsky would be expelled from the Party in late 1927 and exiled from the Soviet Union in 1929. Trotsky's book *Literature and Revolution* (published by the Soviet government in 1924 and translated to English in 1925) addresses the place of art in a revolutionary society. EH would later own the 1930 Scribner's translation of Trotsky's *My Life* and *The Revolution Betrayed* (1937) (Reynolds *Reading*, 193). EH seems to be making up a Russian-sounding name for Pound, perhaps playing on "Romanov," the name of the Russian dynasty that was overthrown in the 1917 revolution.

2 Pound's letter to the editors of the *New Masses* appeared in the December 1926 issue under the heading "Pound Joins the Revolution!" (3). That issue also included "A Note on Ernest Walsh" by Michael Gold. While eulogizing Walsh's "rugged and sane and courageous writing," Gold asserted that he had been held back by "the professional esthetic group in which he came to live" and was hurt by Pound's "chamber-passion" of fault-finding, which struck Walsh like "a cannon shooting butterflies" (26). In his letter to EH of 21 December 1926, Pound wrote, "I see by the noo masses that I am joined the revolution on one page, that I haff champer-bassions on another (I spose dot means I dont in the park), and that you have no something or other by Mr Dose Passouts" (JFK), referring to Dos Passos's review of *SAR*.

3 EH had sent Pound "An Alpine Idyll" for possible inclusion in *The Exile*. Pound responded in his 21 December letter that it was a "good story" but too "licherary." He promised to include it in his new journal but wanted EH to revise it. After *Scribner's Magazine* had turned down the story as "too terrible," *New Masses* editor James Rorty also rejected the story, calling it a "stark shocker" (8 September 1926, JFK). It would never appear in *The Exile*.

4 *Gordo*: the fat one (Spanish), the term commonly applied to the "fat" or "big" prize of Spain's annual pre-Christmas lottery.

5 EH was among 162 authors who signed a letter dated Paris, 2 February 1927, objecting to Samuel Roth's unauthorized publication of Joyce's *Ulysses*. In his letter to EH of 2 December [1926], Pound enclosed a clipping of a full-page ad in the 13 November 1926 *Saturday Review of Literature* announcing the publication of *Ulysses* in Roth's *Two Worlds Monthly*. In a letter of 19 November 1926, Pound advised Joyce on the best strategies for stopping Roth, but in another letter to Joyce of 25 December 1926, Pound explained he did not sign the protest because he considered it misdirected, the fault lying not with Roth, but with "the infamous state of the American law which not only tolerates robbery but encourages unscrupulous adventurers to rob authors living outside the American borders, and with the whole American people which sanction the state of the laws" (*The Selected Letters of Ezra Pound: 1907–1941*, ed. D. D. Paige [New York: New Directions, 1971], 206). "L. R." refers to the *Little Review*, edited by Margaret Anderson and Jane Heap, whose authorized serialization of *Ulysses*, begun in 1918, came to a halt in 1920 when the editors faced obscenity charges. They were convicted and fined in 1921.

6 P.B., perhaps "Poor Bloody."

7 Among the poems MacLeish had sent to Pound was apparently "You, Andrew Marvell," which mentions Ecbatana, the ancient Persian city that Pound depicted (in Canto IV and Canto V) as a paradigm of human order. In response to Pound's criticism that his work was derivative and that he should find another city that had not been preempted by him, MacLeish wrote to Pound in a letter of 29 December [1926] that he used Ecbatana "because

I have twice lived in the city and carry certain sensations which seem to me related to it" (Winnick, 192). In his anthology *Men at War* (1942), EH would include "The March to the Sea (400 B.C.)," an excerpt from Book IV of the *Anabasis*, the eyewitness account by the Greek military leader and writer Xenophon described in EH's headnote as "the epic story of the retreat of ten thousand stranded Greek soldiers from the heart of Persia back home to Greece" (354).

8 In Shakespeare's *Henry IV, Part One*, Hotspur remarks about someone who warns of the danger of his rebellion, "I tell you, my lord fool, out of this nettle danger we pluck this flower / safety.—" (2.4.7–9). All citations of the work of William Shakespeare are taken from *The Norton Shakespeare: Based on the Oxford Edition, 3rd Edition*, ed. Stephen Greenblatt et al. (New York: W. W. Norton, 2015).

9 Most likely Bill Bird, whose Three Mountains Press published Pound's first volume of *Cantos* in 1925 as well as EH's *in our time* (1924) and other limited editions of modernist works.

To Isidor Schneider, [c. 18–20] January [1927]

Hotel Rossli

Gstaad

Suisse

Jan 18–19–20?

Dear Isidor:

It was fine to hear from you again. I was afraid you disliked The Sun etc. too much to ever write again. It is better to write. Your criticism about the "plot" is good. Of course I didn't mean to have any plot and didn't mean for it to be tricky but there it is as you saw. In the hospital in Milan there was a ward of men who were wounded in their genito-urinary organs and I often thought about them and ones I knew and I began to make up what would happen to such a man—I took the girl and the man and went on and that was the story. It was a dull story and I meant it to be dull. Of course I don't believe the shit the critics write about it and I don't blame you for feeling badly about it. It has many many faults and the only part I liked was the Spanish part and some of that I liked very much. Where I think your criticism is weak is in saying that you think people shouldn't drink t[o]o much, should like beautiful things etc. because I think that has nothing to do with it. Those people are the way they are and because they have been smashed they are hollow and dull—<u>but that is the way they are</u>.[1] They are not my people nor the way I am and I don't like <u>anybody</u> in the book except a few incidental characters—but I don't dislike them. They are hollow and many people have written about hollow people and tried to make them attractive and I didn't. I left them the way they are and that is always a fault. When I saw a copy of the book and tried to read it I disliked it intensely. I have given all the royalties etc. and the British rights to Hadley. The last I heard—in December it was not quite 10,000. I expect I'll read next year in the criticisms about how having all this money has affected me so you might as well know for your own information, because you would like me to be a good writer, that Hadley and I lived on the advance—which at 15% meant a sale of 3,000 copies—all last summer in Spain and when we got in a jam and separated I made over to Hadley all my royalties, income etc. and have lived since on three stories I've sold to Scribner's and which they seem in no bloody hurry to publish. The Killers, they write, will come out in March. Two others in the same number a month later. One called In Another Country I think you will like. I hope the damn Sun etc. will sell on and make Hadley a lot of money. I will give her your and Helen's love when I write her tonight. She has been ski-ing in Haute Savoie and I have been down here.[2]

I will send you a check—or dollars in bills—as soon as the books come. They will be grand down here. You did not mention in your letter how much they were. I am very excited about them coming.[3]

I had a long 15,000 word story for The American Caravan called A Lack of Passion—it was another bull fight story. When I went over it to send to them I didn't think it was good enough. Now I will send them a short story called An Alpine Idyll. Scribner's have it in N.Y. I will cable Scribner's to send it to Kreymbourg. Kreymbourg cabled me for something today.[4]

Am living here for $1.50 a day with wonderful food and fine ski-ing. I have a good sunny room with a reading light and a comfortable place to work.

I'm glad you didn't publish the review because after all we are writers and it is up to the critics to find out what is wrong without our helping them.[5] I wrote for twelve years with all my friends telling me it was shit and then when it is at all shitty they all say how fine it is—there is no need for us to help them out any. They will turn quickly enough and us damn performers have no business showing them where all the gaps in one another's armour lie.

Besides nothing that anybody says makes any difference about stuff. Except us to each other. You see by the time they can see there is something rotten and diagnose it we would all be past hope. So I think it is better to write to one another. Because we will never be pleased and we know what is wrong in time.

I saw Sherwood [Anderson] in Paris and we had a fine time together twice.

Everybody misses Manuel.[6]

Please give my love to Helen.

Best to you always and thank you so much for sending the books and for writing.

Yours always,

Ernest

Scribner's wanted a book of stories for next Spring. I have ten stories—two of them very long—but don't want to publish another book until next fall. Scribner's have been damned good and have been perfect about everything.

Columbia, TLS

1 In his last letter, Schneider told EH that he disliked *SAR*, particularly "the trick of the plot," saying "the love of the unsexed man for a loose-sexed woman turned out to be neither tragedy nor comedy for me." Schneider also commented that he "couldn't like, or dislike the people in the book. I just didn't care about them, except the bull fighter" ([November 1926], JFK).

2 In January 1927, Hadley joined Winifred and Paul Scott Mowrer for a skiing vacation in Haute-Savoie, in the eastern French Alps.

3 Schneider wrote that he was sending the books EH had requested in his letter of [30 September 1926], with a 60% discount off the list price.

4 In letters of 1 July 1926 and 24 November 1926, Paul Rosenfeld, editor of the *American Caravan*, had invited EH to contribute something to the first volume, scheduled for publication in the fall of 1927. Rosenfeld and co-editors Van Wyck Brooks, Lewis Mumford, and Alfred Kreymborg solicited experimental pieces of fiction and poetry that were "neglected and inhibited by the publishing trade" (1 July 1926, JFK). The cable from Kreymborg has not been located.

5 Schneider told EH he "felt so worked up" over *SAR* that he had written and submitted a review of it to the *Saturday Review of Literature* but was glad the magazine had rejected it.

6 In a letter to EH of 29 December 1926, Manuel Komroff reported that he had returned safely to New York (PUL).

To Maxwell Perkins, 20 January 1927

Hotel Rossli

Gstaad

Switzerland.

January 20, 1927

Dear Mr. Perkins:

Enclosed are two notes from Rex Lardner and Manuel Komroff.
I wrote to Mr. Lardner today telling him I was writing you to
please send him Fifty Grand. When they send it back maybe some one
in the office could send it to the Editor of the Atlantic Monthly.
Then when it comes back from there I think we might put it in dry
dock.[1]

Fifty Grand should bring an enormous price to try and get back some of
the postage.

I have had letters and now a cable from gents conducting the American
Caravan. This it seems is not only a book but a worthy American venture.
When they first wrote me last summer I promised Paul Rosenfelt a long bull
fight story called A Lack Of Passion. I thought it was a very good story but
when I came to re-write it decided it was no bloody good at all and that re-
writing wouldn't save it. So now I don't know what to send them. Perhaps
the Alpine Idyll would do. I may cable you tomorrow to turn it over to
Kreymbourg at 77 Irving Place. I would like to send them a longer thing but
think we ought to keep the Fifty Grand for the next book and haven't any
other long stories on hand.

Sherwood Anderson is in Paris and we had two fine afternoons together.
He said a very funny thing about the Editors of the New Masses: they, he
said, wanted a revolution because they hoped that under some new system
of government they would be men of talent. He was not at all sore about
Torrents and we had a fine time. He spoke fondly of Scribner's as having
paid him $750 for a story in the Christmas number. If that is exact I will try
and get something epoch making for Mr. Bridges for next Christmas. It
would be grand sometime to write a story that was neither too long nor too
short and full of either the Christmas Spirit or Love Interest. The Nouvelle

Revue Francaise wants to bring out The Sun etc. in French but I am stalling them to bring out a book of stories first.[2]

With best regards to yourself and to Scott when you see him,

Yours always,

Ernest Hemingway.

PUL, TLS

1 In his letter to EH of 4 December 1926, Reginald "Rex" Lardner (1881–1941), associate editor at *Cosmopolitan* and older brother of Ring Lardner, wrote, "We were all so fascinated by 'THE SUN ALSO RISES' that we should be very glad to talk over with you the possibilities of your doing something for Cosmopolitan magazine, or perhaps one of the other of our periodicals" (PUL). The International Magazine Company also owned *Harper's Bazar* (later *Harper's Bazaar*) and *Good Housekeeping*. Komroff, in his letter of 29 December 1926, recommended that EH send "Fifty Grand" to the *Atlantic Monthly*. Komroff had told one of its editors that "it was the best prize-fight story I have ever read," and the editor was "anxious to see it" (PUL). The *Atlantic Monthly* would publish "Fifty Grand" in its July 1927 issue.
2 In 1928 Éditions de la Nouvelle Revue Française, the in-house publishing company of the literary periodical *La Nouvelle Revue Française*, would publish a limited edition of 110 copies of *Cinquante mille dollars* (*Fifty Grand*), a collection of six of EH's stories translated into French by Georges Duplaix under the pseudonym Ott de Weymer. The book would be reissued twice in 1928 under the imprint of Éditions Gallimard, which in 1933 would also publish *Le soleil se lève aussi*, the French translation by Maurice Edgar Coindreau (1892–1990) of *SAR*.

To Maxwell Perkins, 20 January 1927

GSTAAD 18
LCD MAXWELL PERKINS SCRIBNERS NEWYORK
PLEASE SED ALPINE IDYLL TO KREYMBOURG 46 BANK STREET
FOR AMERICAN CARAVAN HEMINGWAY[1]

PUL, Cable; destination receipt stamp: JAN 20 1927

1 On 21 January 1927 Perkins wrote to Kreymborg that he was sending him "An Alpine Idyll" at EH's request (PUL). The *American Caravan* would include the story in its first volume, published in September 1927, the month before it also appeared in *MWW*.

To Ezra Pound, [after 20 January 1927]

Dear Ezra—

Your quite right. The bloody story ["An Alpine Idyll"] wasn't good enough. Yet not a bad story. Kreymbourg and co. have been cabling me for something for their American Caravan which is not only a book of pieces by gents but in addition a worthy American venture. I figured this was just about the class to be included in a worthy american cause venture etc. and have cabled Scribner's to turn it over to your old pal Kremmy at his Caravan address.

My head, sic, is commencing to function again and I ought to have something for you pronto. Have also promised something for Princest Backhouseiano by the First of Feb. But there won't be anything.[1]

Mr. Paul and Mr. Jolas aint going to get anything. Naturally I told them I'd give them something.[2] Learned that in Spain. Always accept invitations. Never come unless you feel like it. Knocks hell out of splendid frankness as a policy.

No matter who or whom, for all I know of grammar whom is the feminine of who, the literary journalists Messers Paul and Peter Jolas get for their first number a review can't be run without intelligence. Mr. Jolas is a moron. Mr. Paul is better but has no taste. Let them blow up hoisted by their own peeturds.[3]

Ford was not intelligent but highly resceptive and a great knack for editing. These gents sont pas serieuse.[4]

If you wanto do something for me give me a title for a book of stories— not out till next fall—have the stories but they have to have a name to make up a dummy and start selling them this spring.[5] Sun Also rises now in fifth large printing. First printing 5,000 others 2,500 apiece. I suppose if it sells a couple of hundred thousand the stories ought to sell a couple of thousand even if they won't read them. Don't think anything any good except a couple but am writing a little better. Lanterncorpse story not a good sample.[6] It's better now. Scribners don't know it but am going to make them publish old Up In Michigan story with the fucking in it. If they won't I won't publish book at all.[7] Aint going to be great best selling litrary figure for nothing. So long as I don't get the money might as well get the fun. What do you think?

Have been laid up with my throat again. Any spirit messages from brother Walsh? Understand various ladies on pilgrimages to America to raise money for Monument to great dead poet of Machine Age.[8] Didn't anybody ever die before? Christ I've known so much better guys than that that we didn't even have time to bury. Stunk too. Had to bury 'em finally.

My love to Dorothy.

yrs. HEM.

Yale, TL with typewritten signature

1 "Backhouse" is a slang term for an outhouse or privy. EH refers to the Princess of Bassiano, Marguerite Chapin Caetani (1880–1963), founder of the Paris literary review *Commerce* (1924–1932) and cousin to T. S. Eliot. She was married to Italian composer Roffredo Caetani (1871–1961), Prince of Bassiano and Duke of Sermoneta. On 1 January 1927 MacLeish had written to her from Gstaad to say he had "been after Hemingway" and that EH had promised "a good story for February first if not before" (Winnick, 193). EH would send her "A Pursuit Race" (by way of MacLeish) for publication in *Commerce*, but she would reject it in a letter of 17 February [1927] (JFK).
2 Elliot Paul (1891–1958) and Eugene Jolas, American expatriate journalists and founding editors of the influential literary journal *transition*, which would appear in twenty-seven numbers between April 1927 and spring 1938. Publishing an international cast of contemporary writers, including James Joyce, Gertrude Stein, Hart Crane, Dylan Thomas, Franz Kafka, and Samuel Beckett, the magazine often ran over two hundred pages and already in 1927 had attracted more than one thousand subscribers. EH's "Hills Like White Elephants" would appear in the August 1927 issue.
3 EH alludes to Shakespeare's *Hamlet*: "For 'tis the sport to have the engineer / Hoist with his own petard" (3.4.185.5–6).
4 *Ne sont pas sérieux*: are not serious (French).
5 EH refers to a printed and bound promotional version of a forthcoming book, containing blank pages or brief extracts.
6 Reference to "An Alpine Idyll," in which a peasant hangs his lantern from the open mouth of his wife's frozen corpse.
7 "Up in Michigan" appeared in EH's first book, *Three Stories and Ten Poems*, published in Paris by McAlmon's Contact Editions in 1923, but the story would not be reprinted until 1938, in *The Fifth Column and First Forty-nine Stories*.
8 "There is a great deal of talk these days about MACHINE-AGE and the end of art and literature," Walsh had remarked in "Mr. Hemingway's Prose," his laudatory review of *IOT* in the second number of *This Quarter*. However, with the emergence of Hemingway's work, he wrote, "Now the good days are beginning" (320–21).

To Director, Spar- und Leihkasse in Thun, 1 February [1927]

Hotel Rossli,

Gstaad, Suisse.

February 1, 1926

The Director,

Spar und Leihkasse in Thun,

Thun, Suisse.

Dear Sir:

Since writing you in regard to a $500. draft which which was changed into french francs at a lower rate than I had declared I would accept the manager of your Gstaad Branch has called on the telephone to inform me that the draft is at my disposition in his office. I am sure that his informing me it was too late to recover the draft was purely a misunderstanding.

I am, therefore, very sorry to have troubled you with my other letter of today and hope that you will not regard it in any way as a complaint against your manager here.

Yours very truly,

JFK, TL

As EH was not in Gstaad in February 1926, he mistyped the year.

To the *New Yorker*, [c. 4 February 1927]

Newyorker

West 45th Street

Newyork

unless publishing manuscript without alterations or deletions please deliver edmund wilson new republic Hemingway[1]

JFK, TCD with typewritten signature

1 EH is responding to a letter of 14 January 1927 from Katharine S. Angell of the *New Yorker*, accepting "How I Broke with John Wilkes Booth" for publication (JFK). Although EH had intended it for the *New Republic*, where Edmund Wilson was then an associate editor,

Perkins had sent the piece to the *New Yorker*, expecting it could pay more. Enclosing a check for $75.00, Angell expressed enthusiasm and encouraged EH to submit additional satirical pieces. She also noted that the magazine might have to make one or two slight alterations, "but they will be very slight and if you were near at hand we should, of course, send you the proof and give you a chance to protest" (JFK). In response to the cable that EH drafted here, the *New Yorker* cabled back, "MANUSCRIPT TO BE PUBLISHED WITHOUT DELETION AND ALTERATION" (7 February 1927, JFK). The *New Yorker* would, however, retitle the story without securing EH's permission, and publish it as "My Own Life" in the 12 February 1927 issue.

To Chard Powers Smith, [c. 5 February 1927]

My Dear Smith:

I received your letter several weeks ago but did not wish to answer it hastily. It is very interesting to find you identifying yourself with characters in In Our Time and I hope it may induce you to purchase several copies of the book which, on my next visit to Paris, I will be very glad to inscribe for you or for any of your friends.[1]

Your letter too, in spite of certain defects in construction, seemed a very interesting example of a letter written to some one you were sure was out of town. I noted too, how, unable to rely absolutely on this premise (my absence) you brought in a hope-for-better-things note at the end; very nicely designed to remove the danger from the first part. May I congratulate you on the improvement of your prose style?

Your application of the term "contemptible worm" to myself was very flattering.[2] I feel you must be an authority on anything contemptible and will not attempt to dispute your classification. I remember the feeling of contempt I had for you on meeting you and regreted it intensely as a very cheap emotion and one very bad for literary production. I feel we are in accord on this. However this feeling, contempt, has persisted, greatly to my regret, and has, in fact, increased the more I have heard of you and your adventures in America. I am sure I am a contemptible worm to you, because you have told me, and I feel very humble beside you; because to me, my dear Smith, you are a very contemptible mountain.

It will be a great pleasure to see you again in Paris and somewhat of a pleasure to knock you down a few times, or perhaps once, depending on your talent for getting up; although I am sure I should feel very sorry afterwards. I doubt however if you will still be in Paris in March when I return and if you are I have no doubt you will be carrying numbers of pistols, sword canes or other things commensurate with your truly mountainous character.

You must believe, my dear Smith, that this letter does not end on anything but a note of sincere and hearty contempt for you, your past, your present and your future—and—lest you should have been deceived in an earlier paragraph—for the prose style of your letters.

Your admiring friend,

Ernest Hemingway

JFK, TLS

The conjectured date is based on this letter's distinctive physical similarity to the following letter, which EH dated 5 February. Both are typed in red ink on the same dark cream-colored paper, with EH's insertions and cancellations in pencil. No accompanying envelope has been located among EH's papers at JFK. He may not have sent the letter.

1 In a letter to EH of [1 January 1927] (JFK), Smith had objected to the depiction of his wife in the story "Mr. and Mrs. Elliott" (which EH had originally titled "Mr. and Mrs. Smith" but changed before its publication). The story appeared in the *Little Review* (Autumn–Winter 1924–1925) and, with numerous revisions, in *IOT* (1925). The story satirizes the marital and sexual problems of an inexperienced couple and their unsuccessful attempts to conceive a child; by the end, the wife shares her bed with her girlfriend while the husband stays in a separate room, and they are "all quite happy" (*IOT*). In actuality, Mrs. Smith had died in childbirth in Naples on 11 March 1924, the month before Hemingway wrote his story (Smith, 76).

2 Smith had expressed his "contempt" for EH, calling him "a worm who attempted a cad's trick and failed to pull it off."

To Clarence and Grace Hall Hemingway, 5 February [1927]

Hotel Rossli Gstaad—Suisse

Feb 5

permanent address

Guaranty Trust Co of NY.

1, Rue des Italiens

Paris

Dear Mother:

[*Above the typewritten salutation to his mother, EH pencilled* "Dear Dad and Mother." *In the left margin, EH wrote* "Starting out" *with an arrow pointing to the typewritten* "Dear Mother:"]

Thank you very much for sending me the catalogue of the Marshal Field exhibit with the reproduction of your painting of the Blacksmith Shop in it. It looks very lovely and I should have liked to see the original.[1]

I did not answer when you wrote about the Sun etc. book as I could not help being angry and it is very foolish to write angry letters; and more than foolish to do so to ones mother. It is quite natural for you not to like the book and I regret your reading any book that causes you pain or disgust.[2]

On the other hand I am in no way ashamed of the book, except in as I may have failed in accurately portraying the people I wrote of, or in making them really come alive to the reader. I am sure the book is unpleasant. But it is not <u>all</u> unpleasant and I am sure is no more unpleasant than the real inner lives of some of our best Oak Park families. You must remember that in such a book all the worst of the people's lives is displayed while at home there is a very lovely side for the public and the sort of thing of which I have had some experience in observing behind closed doors. Besides you, as an artist, know that a writer should not be forced to defend his choice of a subject but should be criticized on how he has treated that subject. The people I wrote of were certainly burned out, hollow and smashed—and that is the way I have attempted to show them. I am only ashamed of the book in whatever way it fails to really give the people I wished to present. I have a long life to write other books and the subjects will not always be the same— except as they will all, I hope, be human beings.

And if the good ladies of the book study club under the guidance of Miss Butcher, who is <u>not</u> an intelligent reviewer—I would have felt very silly had she praised the book—agree unanimously that I am prostituting a great talent etc. for the lowest ends—why the good ladies are talking about something of which they know nothing and saying very foolish things.

As for Hadley, Bumby and myself—altho Hadley and I have not been living in the same house for some time (we have lived apart since last Sept and by now Hadley may have divorced me.) we are the very best of friends.[3]

She and Bumby are both well, healthy and happy and all the profits and
royalties of The Sun Also Rises, by my order, are being paid directly to
Hadley, both from America and England. The book has gone into, by the
last ads I saw in January, 5 printings, (15,000) copies, and is still going
strongly. It is published in England in the Spring under the title of Fiesta.
Hadley is coming to America in the Spring so you can see Bumby on the
profits of Sun Also Rises. I am not taking one cent of the royalties, which are
already runing into several thousand dollars, have been drinking nothing
but my usual wine or beer with meals, have been leading a very monastic life
and trying to write as well as I am able. We have different ideas about what
constitutes good writing—that is simply a fundamental disagreement—but
you really are deceiving yourself if you allow any Fanny Butchers to tell you
that I am pandering to sensationalism etc. etc. I get letters from Vanity Fair,
Cosmopolitan etc. asking me for stories, articles, and serials, but am
publishing nothing for six months or a year (a few stories sold to Scribners
the end of last year and one funny article out) because I know that now is a
very crucial time ~~in my career~~ and that it is much more important for me to
write in tranquility, trying to write as well as I can, with no eye on any
market, nor any thought of what the stuff will bring, or even if it can ever be
published—than to fall into the money making trap which handles
American writers like the cornhusking machine handled my noted
relative's thumb[4]

I'm sending this letter to both of you because I know you have been
worried about me and I am always sorry to cause you worry. But you must
not do that—because, although my life may smash up in many different
ways I will always do all that I can for the people I love (I don't write home a
lot because I haven't time and because, writing, I find it very hard to write
letters and have to restrict correspondence to the letters I have to write—
and my real friends know that I am just as fond of them whether I write or
not) that I have never been a drunk nor even a steady drinker (You will hear
legends that I am—they are tacked on everyone that ever wrote about
people who drink) and that all I want is tranquility and a chance to write.
You may never like any thing I write—and then suddenly you might like
something very much. But you must believe that I am sincere in what I

write. Dad has been very loyal and while you, mother, have not been loyal at all I absolutely understand that it is because you believed you owed it to yourself to correct me in a path which seemed to you disastrous.

So maybe we can drop that all. I am sure that, in the course of my life, you will find much cause to feel that I have disgraced you if you believe everything you hear. On the other hand with a little shot of loyalty as anaesthetic you may be able to get through all my obvious disreputability and find, in the end, that I have not disgraced you at all.

Anyhow, Best love to you both,

Ernie

JFK, TLS

This letter is typewritten in red ink with pencilled return address and notations. At the top of the first page, Clarence wrote in red crayon pencil, "Feby 5. 1927."

1 With her letter of 21 January 1927, Grace sent EH the catalog for the Chicago No Jury Society of Artists Exhibition, held 10–22 January 1927 in the Galleries of Marshall Field & Company. Two of her paintings were in the show, *Anastacia Island* (priced at $275) and *The Blacksmith Shop at Horton Bay* (priced at $375), and the catalog included a photograph of the latter (Clarke Historical Library, Mount Pleasant, Michigan). Grace mentioned that her work had also been accepted into the 31st Annual Exhibition of Chicago Artists, opening on 3 February. She was "getting big prices" for her paintings ("$200 per"), which she considered "very gratifying with only two years study and experience" (JFK).

2 In her letter to EH of 4 December 1926, Grace had criticized *SAR* as "one of the filthiest books of the year" and enclosed a clipping of a negative review by Fanny Butcher (1888–1987) titled "Hemingway Seems out of Focus in 'The Sun Also Rises'" that appeared in the 27 November 1926 *Chicago Daily Tribune* and that was reprinted in the Paris edition on 19 December 1926 (JFK). Clarence, in his letter to EH of 13 December 1926 (JFK), said he hoped his son would apply his "wonderfull ability" to "a different sort of subject matter" in the future. He enclosed a positive review by Schuyler Ashley (1897–1927) that had appeared in the 4 December 1926 *Kansas City Star*, recognizing *SAR* as an accurate depiction of the expatriate generation ("Hemingway Leads Young Ineffectuals Through Europe," 8).

3 In his 13 December letter, Clarence said he had heard gossip about "a serious domestic trouble" and implored his son, "please write to me the truth, so I can deny the awfull rumors, that you and Hadley have had a break" (JFK). In her 20 February 1927 response to this letter from EH, Grace would write, "Im sorry to hear that your marriage has gone on the rocks,—but most marriages might to[o]—I hold very modern and heretical views on marriage—but keep them under my hat" (JFK).

4 EH's uncle Willoughby Hemingway had lost his right index finger "in a boyhood accident with a cornsheller," Baker reports, noting that he nevertheless went on to become a successful missionary surgeon in China (*Life*, 13).

To Ezra Pound, [13 February 1927]

Sunday

Dear Cosmo—[1]

I shd think a major pote who refuseed to follow Amy into the drear wastes wd have, at least, the pooblic on his side—even tho it were all a mistake.[2]

Personally have not seen the Times N.Y. or Lunnon.[3] Have sent again for Suns but believe the messers Scribners prefer to sell them than to give them away. they don't want to send them to me nor to my friends. They have sent me a wrapper—admirably conceived—beautifully executed (fuck this typewriter)[4] for the 5th printing—lacking a copy of the noble work I have placed the wrapper around your own vol.[5] It doesn't fit but looks lovely. Don't believe anything you hear abt. the Sun. It is a rather interesting book with some pretty good conversation and the startling innovation that all the fucking takes place off the stage as in Shakespeare.

You may twit Horace [Liveright]. He said, you know, he wanted only classics or best sellers. I didn't look like either to him.

Head has gotten going well again lately. Written two <u>good</u> stories. Will write some more. gord willing. Anyway will send you best I can do. One of these I sent to Barseiano—an act of charity to accept only 200 smackers from La Barse but a promise a promise. Noblesse oblige. Princesse oblige.[6]

McFadden a shit himself. One of the biggest.[7] Covici is publisher of Dorhty Butler's Memoirs of her MOTHER. Called A Life In Armour—not Armours.[8] Your a hopeful bastard. Remember words of Goya Y no hay remedio. probly misspelled.[9]

Hickock and I are demarring in H's motor propelled veehcle for Rimini and San Marino on or abt. March 20. Should encounter enroute or at Milan on way or way back or at Rapallo. I gotta be back in Paris April 4.[10] Have for long time cherished idea of becoming good author before great author—have quite a way to go to become first. Never favoured springing full panoplied from womb of Jove ala F. M. F.[11] Get's to be too great a strain maintaining initial perfection. Perfection shit. Wrote Toorents of Springs to avoid necessity of looking in mirror to observe whether halo on straight. Thus disappointing many.

Mr. Walsh died of it.

Daresay remark about hem another gt. am. writer came from McAlpin. MacAlpin you know started originally to write to make the Sat Eve Post. Disgusted with their lack of appreciation of good literature he went in for Art. Ah had art only gone in for McAl— One can become interested in a brick maker who makes bricks without straw if the guy lives next door or is in the fambly—but. May have been Williams. Williams a form of McAlpin— a higher form.[12]

Send on all the dirt. Hotel Rossli until the end of the month.

Love to Dorothy

Hem

Yale, TLS

1 EH's play on Cosimo de' Medici (1389–1464), patriarch of the Florentine Medici dynasty and a patron of arts and letters. He is mentioned in several of Pound's Cantos.

2 EH is responding to Pound's remarks regarding his aesthetic disagreements with American poet Amy Lowell (1874–1925). In his letter of 11 February 1927, Pound asked, "what shd. a 'major poet' (your phrase, mon cher, now current apparently in them states) what shd. a maj., capt. or man at arms pote, do in case of admiring reviewer who says laudatorily that said MaJ, 'does not always follow Amy Lowell into the bleak (or something or other) field of rhymelessness'" (JFK). Pound quotes an anonymous reviewer of his *Collected Poems* who praised Pound by saying, "the poet has not always followed Amy Lowell through the bleak realms of rhymelessness" ("Cargo of Ezra Pound's Verse Assembled in Stately Bulk," *Philadelphia Record*, 15 January 1927; quoted in *Ezra Pound: The Contemporary Reviews*, ed. Betsy Erkkila [Cambridge: Cambridge University Press, 2011], 159). Pound established the Imagist movement in 1912 with H.D. (Hilda Doolittle) and Richard Aldington and had included a poem by Lowell in *Des Imagistes* (1914). After Pound turned his attention to Vorticism and Lowell became the chief proponent of Imagism, editing three annual anthologies of Imagist poetry (1915–1917), Pound would dismiss the movement as "Amygisme." In 1926, Lowell was awarded a posthumous Pulitzer Prize for her poetry collection *What's O'Clock?* (Boston: Houghton Mifflin, 1925).

3 Pound wrote to EH, "I haff just a HALF PAGE of the Times seen (N.Y. not London) mit your fotograft" (JFK). Scribner's half-page ad for *SAR*, featuring a full-length photograph of EH, appeared in the 23 January 1927 *New York Times*. Herbert Gorman's review of Pound's *Personae* appeared in the same issue of the newspaper.

4 Like other letters EH wrote from Gstaad, this is typewritten in red with portions of a few characters appearing in black. EH apparently was using a standard black and red ribbon, with the typewriter ribbon holder stuck so that the keys struck primarily the red-inked portion. Only the top portion of the characters in the word "admirably" is visible on the page.

5 EH refers to the dust jacket of the fifth printing of *SAR*, released in February 1927. While the front and rear cover illustrations were unchanged, the wrapper of the fifth printing was the first to include on the spine a list of the dates of all printings of the novel—a practice

that would continue in subsequent printings. EH probably refers to Pound's recently published poetry collection, *Personae*.

6 EH had not yet received the 17 February letter from Marguerite Caetani, Princess of Bassiano, turning down "A Pursuit Race," the story he had submitted to her literary review, *Commerce* (JFK).

7 Bernarr Macfadden (né Bernard McFadden, 1868–1955), American publisher, physical fitness advocate, and an admirer of Mussolini. Macfadden Publications underwrote a number of magazines focusing on health, diet, and exercise, including *Physical Culture* and *True Story*. In his 11 February letter, Pound had written, "By the way, what about, and what is McFadden? Can he be headed onto the s,o,bs. or is he too much of that ctgry. himself."

8 In the same letter, Pound asked, "Know anything about Covici, of KIKago? said to want to modernize the semiWest." Pascal Covici (1888–1964), Romanian-American publisher. Following the dissolution of his first publishing partnership, Covici McGee (1922–1925), he had begun to publish under his own imprint. EH refers to Dorothy Butler's *A. C. B.: A Life in Armor*, a memorial volume of her mother Alice Carter Butler's personal correspondence and notes (Chicago: Covici, 1925).

9 An etching depicting execution victims, from the series *Desastres de la Guerra* (*Disasters of War*) by Spanish artist Francisco José de Goya y Lucientes (1746–1828), bears the caption "*Y no hai remedio*" ("And there's no help for it").

10 *Démarrer*: to start up (French). EH joined Guy Hickok (1888–1951), head of the Paris bureau of the *Brooklyn Daily Eagle*, on a road trip through northern Italy in Hickok's old Ford coupe from 15 March to 26 March 1927. Starting at Genoa, they visited Ezra and Dorothy Pound in Rapallo before traveling through La Spezia, Pisa, Florence, San Marino, Rimini, Forlì, Bologna, Parma, and back to Genoa. EH's piece on the trip, "Italy, 1927," would appear in the 18 May 1927 *New Republic* and later that fall, titled "Che Ti Dice La Patria?," in *MWW*. EH wanted to return to Paris for the six-day bicycle races starting on 4 April.

11 According to the myth of the Roman goddess Minerva's birth, she sprang fully formed and clothed in armor from the head of Jupiter (Jove). F. M. F. is Ford Madox Ford.

12 In his letter of 11 February, Pound had written, "I want enough text to disprove the assertion, made recently to me, that H. is just another great american author. That flank I can still protect." In response to EH's speculation here as to who might have made the remark, Pound would reply in a letter of 15 February [1927], "NO. Your woild is too small it wuz not McA. nor anyone you have MET, who passed the remarks on yr. greatness being american" (JFK). Robert McAlmon and William Carlos Williams were close friends and co-founders of the little magazine *Contact*, publishing four issues in 1920–1921 and a fifth in 1923.

To Maxwell Perkins, [c. 14 February 1927]

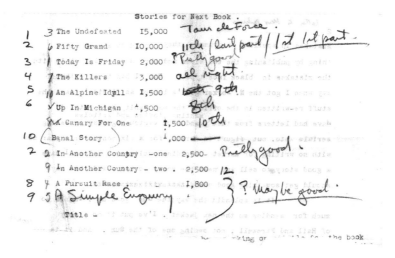

[*On verso*:]

2

mistakes in spelling or grammar they could do a very funny thing by publishing the two wires and the thing as I sent it with the mistakes in black face type. But I had to wire that way when I got the N.Yorker girl's letter as I didn't want the stuff re-written in the office the way Vanity Fair etc. do.[1] Have had letters from them, wanting stories and articles[2] and from various agents requesting serials etc. but figure on working for six months or a year now with no writing for market—avoiding publication unless I have a good story to sell and need the money to eat—and that way should get something good ahead.

It is splendid the way the Sun goes up. Thanks so much for sending me the new jacket. I've put it on a copy of Hail and Farewell, not owning one of the Sun, and it is[3]

[*remainder of page torn away*]

JFK, TLFrag

This fragment, apparently a draft of EH's following letter to Perkins of 14 February [1927], is typewritten in red ink on both sides of a single sheet of paper, the bottom half torn away. In a letter of 14 January 1927, Perkins had written to EH, "Remember that it won't be so very long before we shall be planning for the book of short stories. So you ought to have it in mind, and think about it, and what you will put into it, and the order, and that sort of thing" (PUL). The two columns of handwritten numbers to the left of the typewritten story titles and approximate word counts, together with EH's penciled notes to the right of them, reflect EH's planning of the selections and sequence of stories to be included in *MWW*.

1 Reference to EH's cable to the *New Yorker* of [c. 4 February 1927] in response to Katherine Angell's letter of 14 January 1927, in which she mentioned that the editors might make "slight alterations" to the piece it was accepting for publication (JFK).

2 In a letter of 6 January 1927, Lewis Galantière, on behalf of *Vanity Fair*, invited EH to submit stories "which could be read by the intelligent people who are reading The Sun Also Rises." EH was free to "write about pretty nearly anything . . . except abortion and allied subjects, maybe." In a letter of 7 March 1927, Galantière would add that the magazine was ready to pay EH $150 dollars upon acceptance of a story, with an increase for subsequent contributions (JFK).

3 In his last three letters, Perkins recorded a steady increase in the number of *SAR* copies sold. On 14 January 1927 he wrote that sales had "not yet quite reached eight thousand"; by 25 January 1927 the number was "almost to the point of ten thousand" and "rising steadily"; and on 28 January 1927 the number was "close upon eleven thousand" (PUL). George Moore's trilogy "*Hail and Farewell!*" (*Ave*, 1911; *Salve*, 1912; and *Vale*, 1914) was published in a two-volume edition in the United States in 1925 (New York: Appleton-Century-Crofts). EH would later name *Hail and Farewell!* among the books necessary for a writer to have read ("Monologue to the Maestro: A High Seas Letter," *Esquire*, October 1935; *BL*, 218).

To Maxwell Perkins, 14 February [1927]

Hotel Rossli, Gstaad, Suisse.

February 14.

Dear Mr. Perkins:

Thank you for the good news about the increasing elevation of the Sun.

I went to the local photographer and had a picture taken which will be ready for tonight to be mailed with this.

As for biographical material—I once at a man named Ernest Walsh's request made out a biography of about 150 words for his magazine and within a year he was using that 150 words as a basis to attack me on in The New Masses for having widely advertised and capitalized my war record (sic).[1] He happily died shortly after. Really though I would rather not have any biography and let the readers and the critics make up their own lies.

As for the book of stories for the fall—I have been working very hard and concentrating on a title etc. Want to call it

~~Women Without~~

Men Without Women

and it will have	The Undefeated	15,000	In all of these, almost, the softening feminine influence through training, discipline, death or other causes, being absent.
	Fifty Grand	10,000	
	The Killers	3,000	
	Today Is Friday	2,000	
	An Alpine Idyll	1,500	
	In Another Country	2,500	
	A Pursuit Race	1,800	
	Banal Story	1,000	
	A Simple Enquiry	1,200	
	Up In Michigan	1,600.	
etc.		40,000 words.[2]	

The number of words is approximate but fairly accurate I think[.] Will have some other stories probably. (Please pardon this ribbon)[3] My head is going well again and I am writing some stories that seem pretty good.

Am staying here and ski-ing and working on alternate days—the best snow in four years—until the snow goes. After that plans are un-made.

The way the stories are listed is not the order they will be in in the book. I just wanted to give you an idea of what you would have so they could go ahead with it. You have seen most of the stories so you will know about what it is like. The Undefeated is the long bull fight story from O'Brien's story book.[4] You may have seen it. A Pursuit Race and A Simple Enquiry are two I've just done. One is about the advance man for a burlesque show who is caught up by the show in Kansas City. The other is a little story about the war in Italy. Up In Michigan I'm anxious to print—it is a good story and Liveright cut it out of In Our Time. That was the reason I did not want to stay there. I think it is publisheable and it might set Mr. Tate's mind at rest as to my always avoiding any direct relation between men and women because of being afraid to face it or not knowing about it.[5] Anyway when I get to Paris in March I will get them all in shape—you have the Fifty Grand—and send them over. Is that about right for length? Is Scott still Holywooding?[6]

With best regards,
Ernest Hemingway.

The 5th Printing jacket is very handsome. Lacking a Sun I have placed it on G. Moore's Hail and Farewell—the fine 2nd Vol.

PUL, TLS with autograph postscript

1 EH had sent a biographical sketch to Walsh on 29 January 1925 for inclusion in the first issue of *This Quarter* (Spring 1925) (*Letters* vol. 2, 231). In his review of *TOS* in the October 1926 *New Masses*, Walsh wrote, "Mr. Hemingway was then twenty-seven years old and even at that time everybody knew he was born in Oak Park, Illinois, and wounded on the Italian front" ("The Cheapest Book I Ever Read," 27). Perkins, in his letter of 28 January 1927, had requested "a sort of biographical sketch." He explained, "Papers are glad to print almost anything we send about you, and we are very hard put to it. I even took one or two incidents out of your letters" (PUL).
2 This is EH's first mention to Perkins of the title *Men Without Women*. In his reply of 28 February 1927, Perkins would call it a "splendid title." Although he thought forty thousand words was "rather short," he considered it preferable to EH's feeling "forced into writing more against your inclination" (PUL).
3 At this point, the typewriter ink color changes from black to red for the remainder of the letter.
4 Edward J. O'Brien's anthology, *The Best Short Stories of 1926*.
5 EH refers to Allen Tate's review, "Hard Boiled," *The Nation* (15 December 1926).
6 In a letter to EH of 4 February 1927, Perkins reported that F. Scott Fitzgerald had "disappeared into the golden west dazzled by the gold exhibited to him by a motion picture magnate" (PUL).

To Isidor Schneider, 14 February 1927

February 14, 1927
Gstaad, Suisse.

Dear Isidor—

I am enclosing a check for nine dollars for the books. The ones that I got were the Ezra, Sentimental Journey, Tramping on Life (my god what a vol) Rouge et Noir, and Avowals.[1] Hope the check works out all right.

It has been a fine winter here and my head is going good again and have written some good stories.

How is everything?

Thanks ever so much for sending the books. I believe that Boni and Liveright have the Am. Express Co. as my permanent address.

Could you correct that to Guaranty Trust Co. of N.Y., 1, rue des Italiens, Paris—France?

Do you know if the In Our Time is out of print yet?

Hadley is coming over to N.Y. in the spring—abt. the first of April—first part of April—and I would like very much for her to see you and Helen.

My love to Helen and all good wishes.

Yours always,

Ernest

[*On verso:*]

Dear Issy—

Found I had no checks and so am sending odd collection of only available cash. 20 francs Swiss should make $4. but I'll send you more dollars from Paris and you can keep the other on acct.

Ernest

So sorry this has been delayed!!

Columbia, TLS with autograph postscript

1 All but one of these are books EH asked Schneider to send him in his [30 September 1926] letter, except Kemp's *Tramping on Life: An Autobiographical Narrative* (New York: Boni & Liveright, 1922). EH had actually requested "Harry Kemp's new book" (*More Miles: An Autobiographical Novel* [New York: Liveright, 1926]). Born in Youngstown, Ohio, the "hobo poet" Harry Kemp left home at sixteen and traveled extensively, riding the rails and stowing away on a ship. He lived in Greenwich Village and Provincetown, joining the Provincetown Players in 1916, and spent time in Paris in the 1920s.

To John Dos Passos, 16 February [1927]

Dear Dos—

Mexico sounds grand. I wish to hell you would have wired me last fall. I was all ready to shove.[1]

What the hell do you write a play for if it doesn't go or if you've got enough jack?[2] (Or did you get the jack to write the Play?) Lay off. What is the use of trying to screw if you are dry. Lay off and it always comes back. Lay off and don't try and do a damn thing and let the juice come back. You've done too bloody much writing and you are stale as hell on it. For christ sake you've published six books that I know about and I don't know how many behind my back.[3] You ought to go to grass and not when you ought not to be writing a damn thing be working on a bloody play.[4]

I know how you feel about folks being all shot to hell and they get all shot to hell.[5] But ones come up and aren't shot to hell until they get shot to hell— and some last a long time. Some recover. And really I think more than themselves it is a blind god damned idiocy of fate that gyps them. When it's that we can look at it. It's only when they are doing it themselves that it is too lousy to watch. Anyway I wish to hell I'd gone to Mexico with you.

Have been ski-ing ever since Christmas (Now Feb16). When you get up high enough—anywhere above 2,000 meters it doesn't make any difference what country you're in. Snow above that level very international. Been having a swell Madlener haus life.[6]

Hadley is in swell shape. Bumby too. I sent her your love when I wrote her yest. She is getting big money off the Sun etc. which is out-selling Bromfield's, Fitzferald's, and Co. I get letters from Vanity Fair, New Yorker, Cosmopolitan etc. asking for articles, stories, serials, etc. and so far haven't answered any. Aint goint to sell anything for six months or a year or maybe more—sold a few stories to Scribner's last fall (3) and Scr[i]bner's sold a funny thing to N.Yorker and that will be all for 1927. Got enough stories for a book for next fall. Going to work when I feel like it and not dry fuck when I don't feel like it. Been working lately like in the old days and put the result away in the trunk. Publication is the fucking damn evil. I shdn't ever have published the stories in In Our Time. Nor written Torrents except for us guys to read at the time and then put it away. Sh'd never have published Sun etc.

You are right about sticking people's names in. You shdn't do it.[7] I only did it at the time to kid sticking people's names in. That was why I tried to make out the writer an imbecile in the notes to the reader in Torrents. That was my idea of a writer. Anyway it's bad.

The bull fights sound rotten. Bull fighting is all gone too but every once in a while you get a good one when the boys forget themselves—and then there are always good young kids coming up that are fine before they get killed or really scared.

Did you see N.Y.Daily News, now with larger circulation than Sat Ve Post now has come out for censorship of the press saying someone must put a stop to this filth that is debauching the youth of N.Y. and country?[8]

I wish to hell I was in Mexico or you up here ski-ing. What are you going to do when you leave Mexico?

Hem

That was a swell affiche against the Kewpies.[9]

UVA, TLS with autograph postscript

1 Dos Passos traveled in Mexico from December 1926 to March 1927 and wrote several articles describing life there for the *New Masses*. In a seven-page letter of [c. 15 January 1927], he wrote that EH had "better come to Mexico. Its morbid staying so long in Europe" (JFK).

2 In his letter Dos Passos reported that he was "up shit creek from every point of view—except financial" and that he was having a hard time writing a play. "I've got plenty of plans for writing but I can't get down to them because I haven't any confidence in what I write about."

3 Dos Passos had by then published seven books: *Three Soldiers* (1921), *One Man's Initiation— 1917* (1922), *Rosinante to the Road Again* (1922), *A Pushcart at the Curb* (1922), *Streets of Night* (1923), *Manhattan Transfer* (1925), and *The Garbage Man* (1926).

4 To "go to grass" in this sense is derived from the farming practice of resting the soil by letting grass grow in a field rather than planting a crop.

5 Dos Passos had written, "But honestly Hem, things are in a bad way. I dont mean things I mean folks. Just folks are in a terrible bad way. All except Mexicans."

6 EH alludes to the good times they had shared at the Madlener Haus, the mountain hut in the Silvretta range where they had stayed during their skiing vacation in Austria a year earlier.

7 In his letter Dos Passos had explained at length why he regarded "all the tendency to write about friends" as "rotten" and objected to EH's inclusion of "various people's maiden names" in *TOS*.

8 An editorial published on 31 January 1927 in the *New York Daily News* called for a clean-up of the press, admitting culpability, together with other newspapers, for going "so far beyond the line of decency as to seem insane" in its sensational news coverage (citing the "Peaches– Daddy Browning trial" of January 1927, in which the teenaged wife of a middle-aged New York real estate mogul sought a separation just months after their well-publicized wedding). "Unless the minds of the children of New York are to be drenched in obscenity it seems to us that a censorship of the press as well as of the theater must come," the editorial declared ("Censorship of the Press—Well, Why Not?", 13).

9 *Affiche*: a public notice, placard, advertisement (French). Illustrations of "Kewpies," cupid-like winged infants, by Rose Cecil O'Neill (1874–1944), first appeared in the *Ladies' Home Journal* in 1909 and inspired an array of commercial products, including Kewpie dolls. O'Neill employed images of her Kewpies in posters advocating women's suffrage and published several books featuring Kewpies. The context of EH's comment is unclear.

To Maxwell Perkins, 19 February [1927]

Gstaad, Feb 19.

Dear Mr. Perkins,

Your letters of the 4th and 7th of February came today.

I wrote about a week ago giving an outline of the stories for the book and a title. Men Without Women may have struck you as a punk title and if it did please cable me and I'll try and work for another one. I don't know anything about titles here in Gstaad. You wrote once you wanted one by March—that was why I hurried it.

Have now had requests for articles stories or serials from New Yorker, Vanity Fair, Harper's Bazaar, Hearst's etc. This all looks so much like the fast smooth flowing shutes that I've watched so many of my ancestors and contemporaries disappear over that I've decided not to sell or send out anything for a year—unless I have to sell a story to eat. In that event I'll send them to you and the magazine can have the first crack. Really I should have an agent, if for no other reason to take this story selling business off your hands. Do you know of one who would try and sell the stuff and yet would not write me letters trying to get me to do serials etc.? It would be fine to have someone who would do that so I would never hear anything about the stuff after I sent it away unless I got a check for it. That way at the end of each two months I could clean the stuff out of my trunk, go over it and send what was good to the agent.

Any arrangement you would make for me with such an agent would be all right. Curtis Brown my London agents take 10 per cent. Has there been any more news about movie rights for the Sun? Am about broke.[1]

As to the biographical material attached to the wood-cut from Hank Strater's portrait—I was attached to the Italian infantry for a time as a very minor sort of camp follower—I was a long way from being a football star at school—and only have one child.[2] I was wounded and have four Italian decorations [*EH insertion*: La Medaglia d'argento al valore militare and Croce di guerra (3)] but all of them were given me not for valourous deeds but simply because I was an American attached to the Italian army. At least one of the Croce di Guerra was given me by mistake and the citation mentions an action on Monte Maggio—transport of wounded under heavy bombardment—which I did not participate in—being 300 kilometers away in the hospital at the time.[3] For these reasons anyone reading war record or other personal publicity coming from Scribner's and knowing the facts would think I had furnished you with the information and simply regard me as a faker or a liar or a fool.

For instance today I read something by Burton Rascoe in which I earned my way through college as a boxing instructor![4] As I never went to college and have never told a living person that I went to college that just was amusing as fantasy rascoe. But if Scribner's repeated it—people would think I had put it out and those that knew me would think I was mad.

I know I should have given you some sort of biographical material but the only reason I didn't was because I hate all that ~~personal stuff~~ so that I thought if I didn't furnish it there would not be any. So it would be a great favor to me if we could lay off the Biography—or if the first paragraph on this sheet could go out in the publicity sheets so it would correct the other. I don't care anything about stories that start out-side; but I feel anything we put out ought to be true. And anytime if I break a leg or have my jewels stolen or get elected to the Academie Francaise or killed in the bull ring or drink myself to death I'll inform you officially. From the way the lies spring up I think they'll handle the other publicity. And anything we don't put out we are not responsible for.

Scribner's have been so very fine to me that I hate to speak about this biography stuff. I know you will understand and realize that it is simply a sensitive point. I'll send all the pictures you want.

Of course the whole thing that is wrong is this damned clipping system. No living person should read as much stuff about themselves as they get through those cursed clippings. I ought to stop them but I don't because they are practically all the mail I get—and living in the country or by ones-self the mail becomes such an event. But I am going to have to stop them. So will you stop them? I think Scribner's are paying for them. They have not sent me a bill in a long time.

Hope Scott gets back safely from the coast. They seem to have absorbed Don Stewart pretty well out there.[5]

Hope the Atlantic does not take Fifty Grand. Don't imagine they will. It will be good to keep it intact for the book. Thanks so much for sending the Idyll to Kreymbourg. I liked the piece in the Scribner Bookstore very much.[6]

With best regards,

Yours always,

Ernest Hemingway.

PUL, TLS

1 Thanking EH in a letter of 6 February 1927 for having sent her a check for 5,100 francs, Hadley noted that only 5,000 francs cleared, leaving a balance of 44 francs in his account, or about $2.00 (JFK; Reynolds *AH*, 238).

2 "I am sorry about the publicity,—particularly about the two children, for I knew that there was but the one boy," Perkins would reply on 2 March 1927. There were three publicity men at Scribner's who were "particularly wild" over *SAR* and "ravenous for any kind of advertising material." Perkins assured EH that "there will be no more of this gossip whatever" (PUL).

3 EH refers to the two Italian military decorations he received, the Medaglia d'Argento al Valore Militare (Silver Medal of Military Valor) and the Croce al Merito di Guerra (War Cross of Merit).

4 EH had received from his clipping service an article by Burton Rascoe titled "Sketches of 'Little Old New York'" (*Middletown New York Journal*, 14 February 1927; JFK, EH Newspaper Clippings File). In this syndicated column, Rascoe mentioned a rumored amateur boxing match between EH and Charles MacArthur and claimed that EH was a prizefighter who had boxed his way through college. MacArthur (1895–1956), American journalist, playwright, and screenwriter, began his writing career in Hemingway's home town as a reporter for the *Oak Leaves* and in the 1920s was a member of the Algonquin Round Table group.

5 Both Fitzgerald and Stewart were in Hollywood at the time.

6 In his letter of 4 February 1927 Perkins wrote, "I am sending herewith a copy of the Scribner Bookstore because it contains a comment on 'The Sun Also' which I thought good" (PUL). The author of the favorable piece on *SAR* was Byron Vinson Dexter (1900–1973), a 1923 Princeton graduate and Scribner's staff member who edited *Scribner Bookstore News*, a periodical pamphlet that presented a selected list of current books from all publishers.

To Isabelle Simmons Godolphin, 5 March [1927]

Hotel Eiger—Wengen—

March 5

Dearest Izz: I certainly have been a kike bastard not to have written—but everything was so bum I couldnt write— And you know what a punk correspondent I am even when things are swell.[1] But now nothing is bum.

You were awfully damned swell to write me and I still feel the same way about you that I've always felt. I love you very very much and treat you like a bastard.

I dont know what you heard and imagine the boys could work up some pretty good stories about Hadley and myself. I havent issued any statements and never was good at denying things but for your <u>own</u> information here's the dope. We got in a jam about me loving somebody else—naturally I didnt want to do anything about it—having been in that splendid womanic state for years but Hadley said I should— Then she fell in love with some one—swell guy—by now maybe guys—[2] She can tell you all about it. She's coming to N.Y. April 16 and crazy to see you. She's swell and Bumby too. Hadley's going to stay in U.S. for 6 months. We're on swell terms. She's in grand shape and very happy. I gave her all the royalties from Sun Also Rises—both Am and Eng. Should be a lot—

Bumby's down here at <u>Wengen</u> (where you were once) for ten days with Pauline and her sister Jinny and me. We were at Gstaad and then came here to use the railroad to get high ski ing. Were up at 2800 meters yest. with a 3 hr. run down.

I'm swell now. I'm cockeyed about Pauline and going to get married in May— Hadley's happy and having a swell time and as long as she's all right I'm happy.

Pauline thinks you are a swell girl from hearing about you from me and you'd like her as much as you'd ever like anybody.

I've condensed a lot. None of this is for Oak Park consumption. I dont care what the hell they think out there—

I'm terribly glad you and Frisco liked the book.[3]

I'm working on short stories again. Have a book ready for next fall.

I wanted to write right away when I got your letter but then everything was in a jam and I felt too like hell to write. But now everything is very very good and everybody feeling swell.

Wish I was in N.Y. for a while to see youse guys. It's probably dull but the country is nice around Princeton and it ought to be lovely in the Spring. It's like Cortina here now. Wasn't that a grand time?[4] We were going down there now but figured it was too long a trip for Bumby. Aw hell I dont know what to write— Your letter was so fine and you're so fine. But dont worry Izz— I'm all right. <u>Not</u> drinking myself to death. Had my damn life busted on me—but through <u>nobody's</u> fault but my own. And now got a swell new life started. Know hell's own amount of girls but only 3 altogether swell girls—You and Hadley and Pauline.

My head's working well again. Sleeping again. Can write and feeling swell. Hadley can give you any dope. She loves you too.

Well Izz this is as bum and bummer letter than I usually write. I'll write you a good one sometime. The damn ~~In Our T~~ Sun Also etc is coming out in England next month and Pauline is reading the proofs. There it's called Fiesta—[5]

Sure we'll see youse if you come over next summer. When do you come? For how long? Keep me accurately informed! We go to Spain in July. Could you come down there? Swell bull fights. I felt terribly to miss Hammie last summer.[6]

Have a story in March Scribners and I think in April too.

Not pooblishing much. Saving 'em up.

And how are you?

And how is Francis? And how is everything?

Write a letter with all the dope.

Bumby is swell. He came down with me in a wagon lit and woke up at every station to look out of the window. He would say "Il faut voir tous qui passe dans un train papa!"

When we woke up in Suisse he said, "La Suisse est vraiment magnifique papa!"[7] So now I'm teaching him English and he goes around to everyone saying "I spik Englich." I took him out on the skis this morning. You'll be cockeyed about him. I gave Hadley your address and she's going to write you when she gets to N.Y. and come out or you come in.

Anyway forgive me for not writing and give my best to Francis and always love to you— Deny anything you hear about me in Oak Park.

Yours Always

Ernie.

Guaranty Trust Co of NY, 1 Rue des Italiens is a permanent address—

PUL, ALS

1 EH is responding to Godolphin's letter of [5 November 1926] (JFK).
2 EH most likely is referring to Paul Mowrer, Paris correspondent and foreign editor for the *Chicago Daily News*, who would become Hadley's second husband. In the fall of 1926, Mowrer became romantically interested in Hadley, and although Hadley was not then ready for a serious relationship, she began spending a good deal of time with him and his wife, Winifred, who did not object (Gioia Diliberto, *Hadley* [New York: Ticknor & Fields, 1992], 239).
3 In her letter, Isabelle wrote that she and her husband, Francis (nicknamed "Frisco"), had "just finished the novel" and thought it "absolutely the nuts!!" (JFK).
4 Isabelle had joined EH and Hadley at Cortina d'Ampezzo, a ski resort in the Dolomite Mountains of northern Italy, in the spring of 1923.
5 *Fiesta* would be published by Jonathan Cape on 9 June 1927.
6 Probably a reference to Helen Hamilton, a mutual friend from Oak Park and a classmate of Isabelle in the OPRFHS class of 1920.
7 *Wagon lit*: sleeping car (French). Bumby was saying, "One must see everything that passes by a train, Papa" and "Switzerland is truly magnificent, Papa."

To Edward J. O'Brien, [11 March 1927]

Dear Edward—

I appreciate enormously your getting me invited to the pen club dinner and I know how valuable it would be for me to have been able to come.[1] But I couldn't because (1) I haven't any money [*EH insertion*: (or clothes) distinguished writers ought to own dinner clothes] for a trip to London. (2) I have to be herein Paris from April 4–10 for the six day bike race. Have arranged to see it from the inside with MacNamara and Marcillac.[2]

Have a story in March Scribners and a couple, announced, in the same mag. for April. Been working hard and have some pretty good stories ahead but figure on working as much as I can and publishing as little as possible for the next year or so. Too many offers. As soon as anybody asks me for a story I can't write it. Have to pretend there aren't any magazines nor any chance of publication.

Please give my best regards to Miss Wilson.[3] It was fine seeing you again in Paris. I saw Sherwood [Anderson] a couple of times but he was looking more like Mother Hubbard than ever.[4]

Just got back here yesterday from the mts. Have to go down to Italy next week to see about all the monkey business and get back just in time for the bike races.[5] Let me know if you come over.

With best regards,

Ernest Hemingway

c/o Guaranty Trust Co. of N.Y.

1 rue de Italiens

Paris

UMD, TLS

1 Founded in London in 1921 by British novelist C. A. (Catherine Amy) Dawson Scott, the international P.E.N. Club (originally an acronym for Poets, Playwrights, Editors, Essayists, and Novelists) began as a dinner club to foster friendly interactions among writers. By 1927 P.E.N. had established organizations in seventeen countries. On 17 February 1927 Sylvia Beach cabled EH in Gstaad to relay the invitation O'Brien had wired from London: "Received following telegram will you be guest of honor as most distinguished American writer penclub dinner london April fifth club cannot pay your expenses o'brien" (PUL). EH declined, and James Joyce would be guest of honor at the 5 April dinner.
2 Reginald "Reggie" McNamara (1887–1971), Australian-born American bicycle racer known as the "Iron Man," and Gabriel Marcillac (1904–1984), French bicycle racer. McNamara would win the event.
3 Florence Roma Muir Wilson (1891–1930), English novelist, biographer, and editor who published under the pen name Romer Wilson. Her third novel, *The Death of Society* (1921), received the Hawthornden Prize in 1921. She and O'Brien had married in 1923 and later moved to Switzerland, where Florence died of tuberculosis shortly after her thirty-eighth birthday.
4 In *GHOA*, EH would declare of American writers, "At a certain age the men writers change into Old Mother Hubbard. The women writers become Joan of Arc without the fighting" (Chapter 1).
5 Probably a joking reference to Serge Voronoff (1866–1951), Russian-born French surgeon famed for his technique of grafting tissue from monkey testicles onto the testicles of aging men for purportedly rejuvenating benefits. To ensure a steady supply of glands, he owned and ran a monkey farm in Ventimiglia on the Italian Riviera, which EH would mention in his [23 March 1927] letter to Isidor Schneider.

To Ezra Pound, [22 March 1927]

Tuesday Night

Good crossing—

Forli last night.

Gave your card to Sigismundo and the Elephanti.[1] Heading North. Visited San Marino today—tea-ed with minister of foreign affairs.[2]

Hem

Yale, A Postcard S; verso: image captioned "Rimini— Tempio Malatestiano"; postmark: RIMINI / FORLI, 23.3 27 20

EH and Guy Hickok had visited the Pounds in Rapallo on their two-week road trip through northern Italy.

1 Renaissance patron of the arts Sigismondo Malatesta (1417–1468), Lord of Rimini and subject of Pound's "Malatesta Cantos" (VIII–XI) in *A Draft of XVI. Cantos* (Paris: Three Mountains Press, 1925). The picture postcard features a graytone image of the Tempio Malatestiano in Rimini, where Sigismondo Malatesta is buried. "Elephanti" refers to the elephant symbol of the Malatestas, a motif that appears on the family coat of arms and as a motif throughout the temple.
2 EH may be referring facetiously to the recent announcement by the tiny independent Republic of San Marino, neutral during WWI, that it had concluded peace with Germany ("San Marino is at Peace / Republic Denies That It Is Still at War with Germany," *New York Times*, 11 January 1927, 9). Alternatively, EH may be making a joking reference to prime minister Benito Mussolini, who at the time also served as Italy's minister of foreign affairs.

To Isidor Schneider, [23 March 1927]

Dear Isidor— Your letter was forwarded down here.[1] Guy Hickock and I have come down here from Paris in a ford—crossing the Appenines and passing Voronoff's monkey farm at Ventimiglia.[2] Starting back tomorrow. I'll write from Paris. I'm terribly glad you liked The Killers and hope you'll like the other ones. That's great about InOur Time in 2nd printing—hope I'll get a royalty statement. Am broke again. I sent Caravan a story ["An Alpine Idyll"] that thought was good but no one else did. This is a fine town dominated by a great dead man named Sigismundo Malatesta. Been up at the Republic of San Marino seeing a priest I knew during the war.[3] Your Spring catalogue looks fine.[4] Hadley sails for N.Y. April 16 on the Berengeria.

This seems full of news. Have been very excited all day reading in Corriere della Sera about the fall of Shanghai.[5] Your people are very fine. Best to you and Helen always

Ernest.

Columbia, T Postcard with typewritten signature; letterhead on verso: Grand Hotel
Aquila D'Oro / Corso d'Augusto / Rimini; postmark: FORLI

Because the canceled postage stamp is missing, only the portion of the postmark that reads
"FORLI," imprinted on the card itself, remains.

1 EH is responding to Schneider's letter of [8 March 1927] in which he called "The Killers" a
  "wonderful story" and informed EH that Boni & Liveright's second printing of *IOT* was "in
  the works" (JFK).
2 EH also mentioned passing Voronoff's monkey farm in his [11 March 1927] letter to
  O'Brien.
3 This previously unpublished letter supports the claim of biographers who report that on his
  Italian trip, EH met Italian priest Don Giuseppe Bianchi, who had anointed him after his
  wounding at Fossalta in 1918; however, those accounts have placed the meeting in Rapallo
  (Baker *Life*, 183; Mellow, 346; Jeffrey Meyers, *Hemingway: A Biography* [New York: Harper
  & Row, 1985], 184–85, 594–95). Although EH told Ernest Walsh that he had received
  "extreme unction" during the war (letter of 2 January 1926), Pauline apparently believed EH
  had been baptized. In a letter she sent to him in Italy, she asked him to try to bring back
  "conclusive proof" of his baptism so they could be married in the Catholic Church,
  suggesting "maybe you could find the priest who baptized you" (17 March 1927, JFK).
4 Schneider had sent EH Boni & Liveright's new catalog and offered to send him more books
  ([8 March 1927], JFK).
5 An armed uprising of Chinese laborers organized by the Communist Party of China had
  paralyzed Shanghai on 21 March 1927, as reported in the Italian newspaper *Corriere della
  Sera* on 22 and 23 March 1927.

To F. Scott Fitzgerald, 31 March [1927]

March 31—toujours care of the
Guaranty Trust co.

Dear Scott*

And you are my devoted friend too. You do more and work harder and
oh shit I'd get maudlin about how damned swell you are. My god I'd like to
see you. I got the two letters from the Roosevelt Hotel and the cable about
Vanity Fair this week. In principle I'd decided to not write any articles
stories to order serials etc. because I don't work very easily and can't throw
it off but only throw it out and then it's used up and gone. But you thought
up a swell subject that wouldn't be any form of jacking off for me to write on
at all. You're a hell of a good guy. Wrote something for them yest. morning
in bed. Will look at it tomorrow and then fic it up and send it on. Some crap
about bull fights. I think it's interesting maybe.[1]

How the hell have you been? How nearly done is the book really?[2] How do you feel?

Hadley and Bumby are sailing for N.Y. April 16. Bumby was down in Switzerland with me for a while and was grand. I'm to have him vacations according french law and whenever I want him according to Hadley. She is in grand shape, very happy and very much in love. None of this to tell anybody. I told Scribners to turn all the Sun royalties over to her directly. Did the same with Cape. It comes out in England this month. I went over the proofs so they didn't re-write and garble it like In Our Time.[3] Have a couple of stories you'll see in April Scribners. Have written four since. Max perkins will have told you the Atlantic took fifty grand. Don't know whether they plan to print it on special easily inflammable paper with punctures along the edge so it will detach so that subscribers can detach it and hurl it into the fire without marring their files of the Atlantic. [*Typewritten upside down at bottom of first page*: They were too gentlemanly to mention money.[4] As yet I've heard nothing about money for it. Do the Atlantic pay?]

Isn't it fine about Mencken. Well well well pitcher that. That last is the Sinclair Lewis influence. That's the way his characters talk.[5] You can write this book you're working on at random without even keeping track or remembering which characters are whom and still not be in danger of any competition from the other boys. Don [Stewart] has taken to automatic writing and his wife assures him it is better and finer than ever. Bloomfield's next book is about a preacher (unlike Somerset Maugham or S. Lewis) Bloomfield will probably make him a decayed old new england preacher named Cabot Cabot Cabot and naturally he talks only with God—to rhyme with Cod.[6] But sooner or later I can see that the decayed French aristocracy will come into the book and they will all be named the Marquis Deidre de Chanel and will be people whom Louis Bromfield the most brilliant and utterly master of his craft of all the younger generation of decayed french aristocracy novelists will have studied first hand himself at the Ritz and Ciros—doubtless at great expense to his friends.[7] I went out there to dinner one night and they had a lot of vin ordinaire and cats kept jumping on the table and running off with what little fish there was and then shitting on the floor. Bloomfield, in the effort to make me feel at home did everything but put his feet on the table. I thought to show I felt at home perhaps I had better piss in the finger bowls. We talked about what fine books we each wrote and how we did it. Personally I do mine on a Corona Number 4. And when I wash it my dear I simply can't do a thing with it.

Have been broke now for a couple of months.[8] Happily at present it coincides with Lent. I will have piled up so much credit above that will be able to get you, Zelda and [*Typewritten on two lines of the paper that EH apparently reused for this letter, leaving extra space between the lines of the letter to avoid typing over the following text*: (We sat at a table in the shade of the station) this the start of something or other] Scotty all out of purgatory with no more strain than a bad cold. Pat has left Duff and taken to living with Lorna Lindsay or linslay. A guy named Loeb was in town and was going to shoot me so I sent word around that I would be found unarmed sitting in front of Lipp's brasserie from two to four on saturday and Sunday afternoon and everybody who wished to shoot me was to come and do it then or else for christ sake to stop talking about it. No bullets whistled. There was a story around that I had gone to switserland to avoid being shot by demented characters out of my books.[9]

Pauline is fine and back from America.[10] I've been in love with her for so damned long that it certainly is fine to see a little something of her.

Haven't been in the quarter nor seen anyone—Murphie's came through enroute to Central Europe with the MacLeish's. Had a card from Gerald from Berlin giving me conge on his studio where I've been living for May 1st. Someone else is going to use it for something else.[11] It was swell of them to let me use it and a hell of a lot better than under, say, the bridges. They have been swell. Also MacLeishes.

If you don't mind, though, you are the best damn friend I have.[12] And not just—oh hell—I can't write this but I feel very strongly on the subject.

Give my love to Zelda and remember Mr. Hemingway to Scotty.

Yours always,
Ernest

What about The Sun also and the movies? Any chance?

PUL, TLS

EH typed this three-page letter on two sheets of bond paper, with the first two pages written on both sides of a single sheet. The third page continues on a reused sheet of paper bearing what appears to be typewritten first notes for the story "Hills Like White Elephants": "(We sat at a table in the shade of the station) this is the start of something or other."

1 EH is responding to letters that Fitzgerald wrote on letterhead stationery of the Hotel Roosevelt in Washington, D.C., and signed as a "Devoted Friend" ([March 1927] and [14 March 1927], JFK; Bruccoli *Fitz–Hem*, 81–82). EH is also responding to Fitzgerald's cable of 27 March 1927: "VANITY FAIR OFFERS TWO HUNDRED DEFINITELY FOR ARTICLE / WHY SPANIARDS ARE SWELL OR THAT IDEA / ANSWER BY LETTER" (JFK; Bruccoli *Fitz–Hem*, 236). EH may have begun working on the piece that would appear as "The Real Spaniard," with unauthorized revisions by the editor Arthur Moss, in the October 1927 *Boulevardier*.

2 Fitzgerald would respond, "My novel to be finished July 1st" (18 April 1927, JFK; Bruccoli *Fitz–Hem*, 86), but he would not complete *Tender Is the Night* until 1933.

3 Grissom notes that the first printing of Cape's English edition of *IOT* varies from the first Boni & Liveright printing "in some 136 readings of which 44 are substantive" (39).

4 In his cable of 9 March 1927, Perkins informed EH that the *Atlantic Monthly* had accepted "Fifty Grand" (PUL), and in a letter of 23 March 1927 the magazine's editor, Ellery Sedgwick (1872–1960), directly informed EH of the acceptance (JFK). Although Perkins had encouraged Sedgwick to "take up the matter of price" with Hemingway (9 March 1927, PUL), Sedgwick did not raise that topic in his letter.

5 In his [March 1927] letter to EH, Fitzgerald reported having lunched with H. L. Mencken in Baltimore the previous day: "Got him to say he'd pay you $250 for anything of yours he could use. So there's another market." In responding to the news, EH mocks the folksy speech of Sinclair Lewis's characters. EH had needled Mencken in print in both of his novels. *TOS* is dedicated to "H. L. MENCKEN AND S. STANWOOD MENCKEN IN ADMIRATION," referring to Solomon Stanwood Menken (1870–1954), a founder of the isolationist National Security League, who embodied values that Mencken scorned. In *SAR*, Bill Gorton holds up a chicken drumstick and jokes, "Don't eat that, Lady—that's Mencken" (Chapter 12). Mencken had reviewed neither *IOT* nor *SAR*, but a brief unsigned notice in the August 1925 issue of his magazine *American Mercury* dismissed EH's *iot* as "the sort of brave, bold stuff that all atheistic young newspaper reporters write" (quoted in Bruccoli *Fitz–Hem*, 82).

6 Mocking the proliferation of preacher figures in contemporary fiction, EH likely alludes to "Rain" by William Somerset Maugham (1874–1965), a short story depicting a married missionary's involvement with a prostitute that was made into a popular play, which ran on Broadway from 1 September 1924 into March 1926. EH also alludes to the alcoholic and womanizing preacher in Sinclair Lewis's novel *Elmer Gantry*, which had just been published by Harcourt on 10 March 1927 to great fanfare, was the Book-of-the-Month Club's March selection, and was promptly banned in Boston, boosting public interest. Louis Bromfield's wife Mary was descended from the Appletons, an old New England family whose society background provided inspiration for his 1926 novel *Early Autumn*. "Cabot Cabot Cabot" refers to the Bostonian Cabot family, featured in John Collins Bossidy's 1910 doggerel "Boston Toast": "Here's to dear old Boston / Home of the bean and the cod / Where the Lowells speak only to Cabots / And the Cabots speak only to God."

7 After traveling to France on vacation in 1925, the Bromfields decided to stay. They first lived in Paris, then leased the Presbytère de St. Étienne in the medieval town of Senlis, about 30 miles north of Paris, where they became known for their lavish entertaining. EH

alludes to the Marquise de Sevillac, a figure in Bromfield's novel *Possession* (1925), who was the last of her family and continued to hold court in her house on the outskirts of Paris even as the revolution approached. EH also makes reference to Paris fashion designer Coco Chanel (née Gabrielle Chanel, 1883–1971), who opened her first shop in 1910. Located in the Place Vendôme, the Ritz is listed first among "Hotels de Luxe" in the 1924 *Baedeker Guide to Paris*. Ciro's, at 6, rue Daunou, is named among "Restaurants of the Highest Class" (Baedeker's *Paris*, 2, 15).

8 In a letter postmarked 18 April 1927, Fitzgerald would reply, "I hate to think of your being hard up. Please use this if it would help" (JFK; *Fitz–Hem*, 85), enclosing a check for $100, misdated as 16 April 1926 and made payable to "Ernest Hemmingway." EH endorsed the check by signing his name on the back of it twice, both incorrectly and correctly. In his letter of [c. 15 September 1927], EH would belatedly acknowledge receipt of the check.

9 Pat Guthrie left Duff Twysden for American writer and expatriate Margaret "Lorna" Lindsley (1889–1956), best known for her 1943 memoir, *War is People* (New York: Houghton Mifflin). Harold Loeb was unflatteringly portrayed as Robert Cohn in *SAR*. EH recalls the Brasserie Lipp on the Boulevard Saint-Germain in the "Hunger Was Good Discipline" chapter of *MF*.

10 Pauline had returned to Cherbourg on 8 January 1927.

11 *Congé*: a notice to vacate (French). In a letter to EH of 19 March [1927], Murphy wrote confidentially that he was planning to collaborate on a film project with French painter Fernand Léger (1881–1955), so starting the week of 1 May the studio at 69, rue Froidevaux had to be as empty as possible (JFK; quoted in L. Miller, 26).

12 In his letter of [23 December 1926], written aboard the *Conte Biancamano* bound for New York, Fitzgerald told EH, "I can't tell you how much your friendship has meant to me during this year and a half—it is the brightest thing in our trip to Europe for me" (JFK; Bruccoli *Fitz–Hem*, 78).

To Edward W. Titus, [c. March 1927]

Dear Titus:

I pursuaded your assistant to let me me take a copy of <u>Revolt In The Desert</u> by Col. Lawrence—claiming I was a friend of yours and that it would be all right.[1] If it isnt it's not her fault and I'll buy the book.

Hemingway.

IndU, ALS; letterhead: EDWARD W. TITUS, / THE ENGLISH BOOK SHOP/ 4, RUE DELAMBRE / PARIS (XIVᵉ)

EH apparently pencilled this note at Titus's bookshop and left it there for him.

1 *Revolt in the Desert* (London: Jonathan Cape, 1927; New York: Doran, 1927), a memoir by English military officer T. E. (Thomas Edward) Lawrence (1888–1935), also known as Lawrence of Arabia. After its publication in London on 10 March 1927 and in New York nineteen days later, the book received excellent reviews and became a bestseller.

To Madelaine Hemingway, [12 April 1927]

Dear Nunbones:

I've been going to write every day but have had to get things straight to know what dope to give you. Even now they're not straight—but cant put off writing any longer.[1]

This is <u>private</u> and <u>confidential</u>—no one knows it but you and it's not to be repeated to <u>anyone</u>—surtout la famille.[2] I expect to marry Pauline Pfeiffer—who is a swell girl and that's not just my own biased opinion—either in May or June. She and I'll then go South somewhere and then to Spain.[3] If we were still in France—or if you came in May or early June—I'd come down and meet you and start you around. It will be cock-eyed swell to see you.

Anyway Pauline's sister—Jinny—who is also a swell girl—will be on tap for you to bum around with. She thought you and she could maybe take a motor trip—She has a tin can <u>Citroen</u>[4]—down to the Riviera where you could swim etc.

You would like her and she is 25 and as crazy as you are. But talks French and drives a car swell. When did you plan to come over? As soon as you know definitely cable me care of Guaranty Trust Co. Paris[.] Cable address is simply

> Ernest Hemingway
> GARRITUS
> PARIS

Because Jinny wants to know so as to plan for the summer.

Cable when you plan to arrive and for how long and I'll make all our plans conform as much as possible.

You understand the difficulty of me inviting you on a honeymoon, and also difficulty of delaying same.

But in every other respect will fix things up.

You are a swell kid and I'll love to see you.

If you come later on in the summer—when I'm in Spain—would love to see you there but may not be able to raise money to come up to Paris to meet boat.

Am poor as hell—gave all Sun Also Rises profits to Hadley. She is swell—happy and with plenty of money. All that happened with us was we got in a jam.

You'll have a swell time—whether you come early or late—but let me know when and for how long—bring all the jack you can and cross as cheaply as possible—if you run out of Jacksonian I can always let you take some.[5]

Love to the family and to dear old Nunbones.

If you come in the middle of the summer and could come down to Spain and be with us it would be swell.

It would be swell if you could come in May or June.

I dont think we'll go to Spain much before July. When we're married we'll probably go right down to Riviera.

You could drive down with Jin and stay some place near.

If you come before I'm married I'll show you around Paris. Otherwise Jinny will.

But if you're coming Kid let us know right away when and for how long.

I'll see that the vintners are put on a 12 hr. day until your arrival. So that things will be prepared.

Best love—

Ernie

If I hadnt been getting married I would have wanted you to come over and live with me this summer—you were swell to think of it and we could have had a grand time.

As it is we'll have a grand time too.

Cable as soon as you've the dope.[6]

PSU, ALS; postmark: PARIS–XIV / AV. D'ORLEANS, 12 / AVRIL / 27

On the envelope EH wrote in pencil, "Par / Paquebot / 'France' / Havre 14 avril" and "Personal." He addressed it to his sister care of "Dr. RS Barker DS.," the Oak Park dentist for whom she worked and whose address she had provided in her letter of 26 February 1927, in case he wanted to reply "confidentially" (JFK).

1 EH is responding to his sister Sunny's letter of 26 February 1926, in which she had asked if she could come visit him in Paris that summer (JFK). EH probably hoped to know the exact dates of his wedding and honeymoon before answering, but French laws made prediction difficult. The date of the divorce decree was 14 April 1927, but according to a letter from Hadley of 17 February [1927], EH was "not free to remarry until between the 20th and 30th of April" because her lawyer still had "to put things right after the decree" (JFK). EH may not yet have known he would be free to remarry after 21 April, when "his part of the divorce" would be final (Reynolds *AH*, 122, 243).

2 Especially the family (French).

3 Following their wedding on 10 May 1927, EH and Pauline would honeymoon for about
   three weeks at Le Grau-du-Roi, a small fishing port in Southern France. They would return
   to Paris by 7 June and then spend July and August in Spain.
4 The Citroën, manufactured in France beginning in 1919, was the first mass-produced,
   mass-marketed automobile in Europe.
5 EH's embellishment of the slang term "jack" for money; likely also a play on the name of
   President Andrew Jackson (1767–1845), whose portrait has appeared on U.S. paper currency of various denominations since 1869.
6 On the back of the envelope in which EH sent his letter, Sunny drafted in pencil her cable
   response: "Cant come— / Folks object / Money gone / Writing." The telegram she sent, with
   identical wording, would arrive in Paris on 7 May 1927 (JFK).

To Hugh Walpole, 14 April 1927

Dear Mr. Walpole—

Thank you very much for writing to me about the book. It was very
exciting to get your letter and I cannot tell you how much I appreciated it.

Cape is going to bring the book out in England as Fiesta. He seems a little
afraid of it and to be handling it very gingerly. It will be amusing to see what
happens to it in England. Cape has announced it as dealing with the doings
of a little group of young Americans in Paris than which I can imagine
nothing that one would be more eager to avoid reading about.

It was funny to get your letter from the Muehlbach hotel in KansasCity
where I used to sleep in the bath tub of the press room when it was too late
to go home after working Saturday nights on the Star[1]—~~it was in the same
press room~~ and it was very damned nice of you to write because I have not
felt so cheerful about it—it not seeming such a bloody masterpiece but
really a failure where nothing came out the way it really should except about
an hour and a half of the fiesta and a part of the fishing trip. You work very
hard and then afterwards (after the thrill is gone) it seems so very awful and
the thrill all comes back to have some one that you respect really like it.

If you ever come to Paris I would like awfully to meet you. My bank has
my address and will always forward anythin[g.]

Yours sincerely,
Ernest Hemingway
Paris,
April 14, 1927

Guaranty Trust Co. of N.Y.

1, rue des Italiens

Paris.

phNYPL-Berg, TLS

A note on the folder holding this photocopied letter at the New York Public Library indicates that the original was stolen by Lee Israel (1939–2015), author of several biographies of famous women during the 1970s and 1980s. With access to library collections, Israel turned to stealing and selling original letters written by luminaries before she began forging letters in the name of Dorothy Parker, Lillian Hellman, and others, which she sold to collectors. After being caught by the FBI, Israel published *Can You Ever Forgive Me? Memoirs of a Literary Forger* (New York: Simon & Schuster, 2008).

1 EH worked as a cub reporter for the *Kansas City Star* from October 1917 to May 1918. Walpole, who was on a lecture tour of the United States from October 1926 to April 1927, delivered his lecture "Life and the Creative Spirit" in Kansas City on 31 January 1927.

To Maxwell Perkins, 16 April 1927

April 16, 1927.

Dear Mr. Perkins;

This note will be brought or sent to you by my wife. It is to her that the royalties on the Sun are due, I haven't the contract here so I don't know just when but I have told her you would be able to give her an advance on royalties due—say a thousand dollars. Also perhaps you can tell her when the royalties are due and how it is going. And she will tell you where they can be paid, and give you any news of me.[1]

At any rate it will give me great pleasure for you to meet one another [*EH insertion*: It occurs to me now that perhaps you have met already,] and as the boat train is very nearly leaving this note will be no longer. I enjoyed meeting Dexter very much, He's gone on down to Italy.[2] Atlantic paid 8883.25 francs for <u>Fifty Grand</u>. It was a great job selling it there. I'm working on some more stories.

Yours always,

Ernest Hemingway.

Perhaps you can let Scott know that Mrs. Hemingway is in town[.] I haven't his address.[3]

PUL, TLS with autograph postscript

1 After her visit with Perkins, Hadley would report from New York that *SAR* was "still going very well with some slight decrease in sales," detailing the numbers: 18,363 sold in the United States, plus 188 sold abroad. Total royalties due her were $5,537.10 minus EH's advance of $1,000, leaving $4,537.10. Of that, she told EH, "I drew a thousand (thanks!)" (30 April 1927, JFK).
2 Byron Dexter, a member of the Scribner's staff, was "very anxious" to meet EH, Perkins wrote in an 18 March 1927 letter of introduction that Dexter delivered to EH in Paris that spring. Perkins reminded EH that he had recently sent a copy of Dexter's article on *SAR* in the *Scribner Bookstore* and wrote that Dexter's "appreciation" of the novel "was of great value in the presentation of the book" (PUL).
3 The Fitzgeralds had recently moved to Ellerslie Mansion in Edgemoor, Delaware.

To Isidor Schneider, 18 [April 1927]

May 18

Dear Isidor:

I have been going over the catalogue again—maybe you would send me

The Physiology of Taste—Brillat Savarin.

On Love—Stendhal.

White Buildings—Hart Crane

The Mad Proffessor—Suderman

Poorhouse Sweney—Ed Sweney

Loeb's Book.

Napoleon—Emil Ludwig—[1]

and anything else you like yourself. Did you ever get the money I sent last time? I was sorry it was such a messed lot of currency. From Paris I can send dollars. It will be swell to see the Am. Caravan with your stuff.[2] Hadley and Bumby sailed Saturday on the Berengeria— I gave her your address[.] She wants to meet you and Helen. You'll like her but she is shy about looking anyone up. Manuel [Komroff] will probably bring her around. Her address in N.Y. is care of the Guaranty Trust Co.

Had an awfull trip in Italy. I wrote you from Rimini was terribly pleased you liked The Killers. Have 2 more in April Scribners.

Been writing again lately[.] The Spring is lovely.

Transition is all right. Jolas is serious but not very sound taste. They published a good poem by Evan Shipman.[3] I'll look for yours.

Thanks like hell for the books. But for you I couldn't buy books. You can send them to Guaranty Trust Co. of N.Y. same address.

Love to Helen and best luck

Ernest

Columbia, ALS

EH's reference to Hadley and Bumby's departure for the United States suggests he misdated the letter; they sailed on the *Berengaria* on Saturday, 16 April 1927. EH wrote this letter in blue crayon on both sides of a sheet of paper, crossing out typewritten text on the verso: in the top left corner, "Ernest M. Hemingway / 1, rue des Italiens / Paris, France"; and a few lines lower, in the center of the page, "ITALY 1927" / The road of the pass." These are the opening words of EH's piece about his March 1927 trip to Italy with Guy Hickok, published in the May *New Republic* as "Italy, 1927" and in *MWW* as "Che Ti Dice La Patria?"

1 In his letter of [30 September 1926], EH had already asked Schneider for Brillat-Savarin's *The Physiology of Taste*. *On Love* (Boni & Liveright, 1927), a translation by Vyvyan Beresford Holland (1886–1967) of Stendhal's *De l'Amour* (1822). *White Buildings* (Boni & Liveright, 1926), Hart Crane's first book of poems. *The Mad Professor* (which would be published by Boni & Liveright in 1928), a translation by Isabel Leighton and Otto P. Schinnerer of the 1926 novel *Der tolle Professor: Ein Roman aus der Bismarckzeit* by German author Hermann Sudermann (1857–1928). *Poorhouse Sweeney: Life in a County Poorhouse* (Boni & Liveright, 1927), by American writer Ed Sweeney, with a foreword by Theodore Dreiser. *The Professors Like Vodka* (Boni & Liveright, 1927) by Harold Loeb. *Napoleon* (Boni & Liveright, 1926), Eden and Cedar Paul's translation of the popular biography of the same title (Rowohlt, 1926) by German author Emil Ludwig (1881–1948).
2 Schneider's poem "The Temptation of Anthony" appeared in *The American Caravan: A Yearbook of American Literature* (New York: Macaulay, 1927) alongside "An Alpine Idyll."
3 Shipman's poem "Cry Heard in the Night" appeared in *transition* no. 1 (April 1927).

To Maxwell Perkins, [c. 25 April 1927]

Dear Mr. Perkins—

I'm awfully sorry not to have sent the mss. I didn't realize how far into Spring it was getting. I want to go over all the stories and should have them off inside of three weeks.[1] I'll do it as soon as I can. There should be two or three more to add to the ones I scheduled and I think you can count on it being a full sized book. If it is possible I would like to be able to add some stories during the early part of the summer. I don't know where I got the idea that I could do this, probably a misunderstanding of something you said about being able to get the Sun stuff in until August. I had two quite long stories I was planning to re-do entirely in June and July and a couple of more I was working on. Anyway I'll go over what there is—send it on—and the others the minute they are ready. I had, unexpectedly, to make a trip down to Italy after some stuff, which I couldn't get, and it knocked out my entire schedule of working.

Could you send me an advance of $650 or $700 against Men Without Women?[2] If this is not reasonable please tell me. What I want is to have a certain amount of money in hand to buy a letter of credit to carry me through this summer in Spain. I want to leave here in three weeks for a summer of hard working. Most of the things which have been smashing up work have been cleared up and I'm awfully anxious to give the head a chance to function.

I noticed the correction in the magazine about Killers not being first story in an Am. magazine. Don't think it was a mis-statement. Little Review coming out quarterly, semi-annually or anually hardly comes under magazine as Mr. Bridges understands it. I'd forgotten about the Little Review. What I was impressed by was the fact that Killers was the first story I'd ever been paid for in America.[3] Atlantic paid 8883.25 francs for Fifty Grand. Approximately 365 dollars[.] I think it was awfully sporting of them to take it. They're certainly taking chances with me and Al Smith.[4]

Do give my best to Scott. I want awfully to come and see them in the new decor. Should get over very soon if there is ever enough cash on hand. Thing to do now seems to be to get in a summer's work

With best wishes,

Yours Always

Ernest Hemingway

PUL, TLS

The letter date is conjectured relative to Perkins's letter to EH of 13 April 1927, to which EH is here responding, and to Perkins's 9 May 1927 reply to this letter from EH.

1 In his letter of 13 April 1927, Perkins had urged EH to send along the copy for *MWW*, remarking "we could now with great advantage use the manuscript itself. I hope you will therefore send it as soon as you can" (PUL).
2 Perkins would send a check for $750 on 9 May (PUL).

3 When "The Killers" appeared in the March 1927 issue of *Scribner's Magazine*, an announcement in the magazine's "Behind the Scenes" section claimed it was "the first short story by Ernest Hemingway ever to be published in an American magazine" (2; in Hanneman, 145). Perkins would tell EH in his letter of 9 May 1927 that the *Little Review*, having published "Banal Story" in its Spring–Summer 1926 issue, understandably objected to that boast, thus prompting *Scribner's Magazine* to publish a correction (PUL).

4 Alfred Emanuel "Al" Smith (1873–1944), governor of New York 1923–1928 and Democratic presidential candidate in 1928, who would lose the election to Herbert Hoover (1874–1964). The April 1927 *Atlantic Monthly* featured "An Open Letter to the Honorable Alfred E. Smith" by Episcopalian attorney Charles C. Marshall (1860–1938), questioning whether Smith's Roman Catholicism was reconcilable with his political ambitions. Smith's rejoinder, "Catholic and Patriot," was published in the May 1927 issue.

To Maxwell Perkins, 4 May 1927

May 4. (1927

Dear Mr. Perkins:

Enclosed is the copy on hand for Men Without Women.

The Stories go in this order

The Undefeated—

Today Is Friday—

In Another Country

The Killers   } you have these

A Canary For One

Pursuit Race—

An Alpine Idyll—

A Simple Enquiry—

Banal Story } will send this week.

Fifty Grand.

You better this any way you wish. I've just drawn it up tentatively.

Within three weeks at the latest I plan to send you two more stories— Italy 1927 and After The Fourth—these I am re-writing now.[1] I hope by the middle of June or so to have three more—A Lack Of Passion (Not absolutely sure on this) a long bull fight story—which I am re-writing—and a couple more. Those should make a full sized book I imagine. Will you let me know until what date I can get stories in for the book?[2] I have been unable to decide about Up In Michigan. Want a little more time to look at the revised version.

I should be going pretty well next month and would like awfully to have a couple of more good ones.

I think there is nothing in the stories to bother any one except a couple of words in Pursuit Race and if I find any way of re-placing those in the proofs I will.[3] You know I never want to shock with a word if another will do—especially if the one word will shock beyond it's context—but if there is nothing to be done sometimes that is all there is to be done.

Any suggestion you would make about the order of the stories I would greatly appreciate. It is not at all finally fixed if you think it can be bettered. I hope you'll like the ones you haven't already read.

I have not sent copies of The Killers, Canary, or In Another Country as you can take them from the March and April Scribner's.

There will probably be quite a good deal more material if there is time to get it in. I want the book to be full 2.00 size but there is no use sending stories that would just be filler. Though I need some quiet ones to come in between the others. Hope to have something good next month.

I am leaving Paris to start working next Tuesday the 10th[4] but the Guaranty Trust will have my addre[s]s and always forward anything. I'll send anything as soon as it is ready and perhaps you will give me a final date. and let me know how the book shapes up on length with what you have. There will be two more stories within the month and can be others. The two will add another 6,000 words.

With very best regards,
Ernest Hemingway

I have another called A Banal Story which appeared in the Little Review and which I had forgotten and have not yet gotten a copy of—(have written) but remember Edmund Wilson writing that he liked it very much. Probably will find others.

This copy of FiftyGrand is the one Komroff cut. I have marked all the cuts
<u>stet</u> so will you mark it for them to pay no attention to the pencilled cuts and
set it up as it was originally typed.

PUL, TLS

1 For publication in *MWW*, EH would rename both stories. "Italy, 1927" appeared as "Che Ti
   Dice La Patria?" and the previously unpublished "After the Fourth" appeared as "Ten
   Indians."
2 On 16 May 1927 Perkins would respond, "we have now forty-eight thousand words, and ten
   stories. This amounts to about fifty thousand words in the case of a novel, because of the
   space taken up between stories." If EH would send the "long bull fight story—'A Lack of
   Passion'" and "two or three others," Perkins thought it would be "a very impressive
   collection, even in a physical sense." Scribner's gave a deadline of 1 July for these last stories
   (PUL).
3 Perkins would object to "those two words" or rather to the "one word used twice, and it is
   the one word of all others in English that looks the worst in print." The unmentionable
   word was "shit," which appears in an early manuscript version explicitly as part of EH's pun
   on "sheet" (Smith, 180–81).
4 On 10 May EH and Pauline Pfeiffer would be married in Paris, with a civil ceremony in the
   town hall of the 14th arrondissement followed by a Roman Catholic ceremony at the Église
   St. Honoré d'Eylau in Place Victor Hugo.

To Pierre Chautard, [5 May 1927]

Cher Monsieur Chautard—

Voulez vous trouver ci dessus un cheque pour 900 francs pour la loyer 8
Mai–8 Juin 1927. Je deja demenage quelque peu dimanche dernier et je
pense a prndre mes autre effects auusi-tot que possible. Je vais ecrire a
Marie de venir prendre mes effects et nettoyer l'appartement. Comme ca
vous pouver utiliser la grand chambre pour votre belle mere quand pous
voulez.

Dear Mosnieur Chautard—

Enclosed please find check for 900 francs for the rent 8 Mai–8 Juin 1927.[1]

I have already moved out most of my things and will write Marie
[Rohrbach] to remove my other effects and clean up the apartment so you
may use the big room for your mother in law as soon as you wish.

JFK, TL

The date of this letter is mentioned by Chautard in his reply of 7 May 1927 (JFK). On the verso of this letter is an undated typewritten note from Pauline to EH that begins, "I got mixed up on where we were to meet." She wrote that the time was "a quarter to eight," and she would be waiting for him at Brasserie Lipp. Her sister Jinny had decided to eat at home.

1 EH had maintained the lease for the apartment at 113, rue Notre-Dame-des-Champs following his separation from Hadley. He and Pauline had since negotiated the lease for an apartment at 6, rue Férou and paid three months' advance rent starting on 1 April (Reynolds *AH*, 121). On 7 May 1927 Chautard, the landlord of the old apartment, acknowledged receipt of EH's notice of termination effective 8 June 1927 and of EH's check for 900 French francs (JFK).

To Madelaine Hemingway, [6 May 1927]

Plan arrive middle June Stay with me Paris then Pamplona together early July all Expenses paid. Counting on you absolutely

Ernie

Come

JFK, ACDS

Written on the verso of Sunny's letter to him dated 23 April 1927, this is apparently EH's draft of the cable he sent in reply on 6 May, as he notes in the following letter. Sunny had assured EH that she was not going to tell the family that he was marrying Pauline, but said that in light of his marriage plans and for financial reasons, she would not be able to visit him that year. At the end of the letter she added, "P.S. accept this as the last decision. I can't make it this year" (JFK).

To Madelaine Hemingway, 6 May [1927]

—May 6—

Address Care Guaranty Trust Co. of NY.

1, Rue des Italiens

Paris

Dear Nunbones—

I got your letter this morning and sent you a wire to come the middle of June stay in Paris with me, at my expense naturally, and go to Pamplona for the Fiesta with me with all expenses paid.

Why you old bum—you must have thought I was tighter than the parents. While I have a sou it's at your disposal.[1]

We have a swell place to live here—got it since I wrote you—plenty of room for you to put up.[2] We'll be back in Paris by the first of June the way things are planned now— Anyway will be here when you come.

I'll meet you at the boat train—you get on it when you step off the boat—put you up in the house and you wont have anything to pay for grub or lodging all the time your here— Then after two weeks or so in Paris you and I will go down to Pamplona and take in the Fiesta for a week. I'll pay for everything.

Pauline has a great friend coming over, Clara Dunn, and she can bum with Clara while we go to Pamplona.[3]

Pauline is crazy about your coming and helped me figure out the wire so dont think you are horning in on anything. Not a bloody bit.

If you have some dough, fine, but if not you can absolutely count on me for food and lodging in Paris and the trip to Pamplona.

I want to go to Pamplona like very hell myself—Pauline cant go this year because I was there with Hadley last year and we dont want to go together until next year and you will be a god send to me.[4]

Pamplona starts the 6th of July and is over the 13th and after that you could go back up to Paris [*EH insertion*: I'd look after everything—getting you a place to stay and putting you on boat train] or—with your dough intact take a trip on the Riviera with Jinny.

This is the best chance you'll <u>ever</u> have to take a trip with your brother so tighten up the old belt and come along. I dont know how long you planned to come for but have planned for a month—and until the 13th of July you wont have to spend a cent if you dont want. I'll handle all Paris expenses, railroad fare to Pamplona, bull fight tickets and hotel expenses. Everything. ~~Toda.~~[5] Wines, beers and cigars and your railway fare and expenses back to the boat if your hard up. Come students 3rd class to save money on boat.

I feel like hell about delaying so long writing but it was because I didnt know what the hell about anything.

Now come along and we'll nail any gloating by the family. And you'll be the first one of all the kids to see Europe—and I'll have a grand time showing it to you.

Youve got to come. I turned over all the Sun Also money to Hadley, British and American. She's in swell financial shape. I'm getting an advance on my next book and sold a story to Atlantic Monthly for $365 and 3 to Scribners.

Pauline and I are in <u>good</u> shape on dough now and it would make me cockeyed happy to help you to have a really swell trip. You wont have <u>anything</u> to worry about youll be completely looked after.

If you got here after the middle of June between the 15th and 22–25 it would still give you a good 2 weeks in Paris. In this new place there is plenty of room for you and even if there wasnt I could get you a room in a hotel just across the street (on me) and you could eat with us. So finis mit all this final non coming decision stuff because you must come— It will be swell to have you and I need you to go to Pamplona with me.

We'll show the bastards whether you can make it or not.

<u>Not a word to anyone about</u> anything I've written you. I know it's hard on the family not to have dope on my private affairs—but they have never merited my confidence nor backed me—and fond of them as I am I cant carry the extra weight of home criticism. I'll tell them in good time.

Youll be crazy about Pamplona and can see all the Sun Also Rises stuff.

You'll like Pauline— Maybe youll like me. Dont worry about butting in on us because you wont be—we both want you and will fix it so you are comfortable. And dont be a fat head and worry about expense. You wont have to spend a seed from the time you hit Paris until you go home if you dont want to—and there will be no embarrassement of not keeping up your end with other girls but instead be visiting your own brother who loves you and has invited you.

Now come on. I hope ~~by now~~ before you get this you will have wired what date to expect you.

Imagine the family not slipping you a hundred or so. What do they want to do. Have it buried with them?

It's really worked out swell because no other time would we have a chance to take a swell trip like Pamplona just us together.

Dont worry about bumming because you're not—youre invited all expenses paid as a royal guest—if you have some dough to kick in—fine— but you dont need to and arent expected to and maybe you can use it instead to buy some clothes here.

You were fine not to denounce me as a piece of limburger—but I didn't know how much dough you had or anything. But just remember that Marce was the direct inheritor of the family genius for not loosening on scheckels and not your devoted Bro.

Ernie

See you in June. If you pull any final decision stuff I'm through with you. Come now while I'm still above the sod.[6] Cant guaranty that'll be longer than this summer.

PSU, ALS; postmark: PARIS-6 / R DE VAUGIRARD, 20* / 6–5 / 27

On the envelope EH wrote: "via Paquebot / 'BERENGERIA' / partant cherbourg / 7 Mai." He addressed the envelope to "Miss Madelaine Hemingway. / c/o Dr. R. S. Barber D.D.S. / 104 N. Oak Park Ave. / Oak Park / Illinois / Etats Unis," and wrote <u>Personal</u> to the left of the address.

1 *Sou*: a French coin, here used idiomatically to mean a penny or a cent.
2 Pauline and EH's Paris apartment at 6, rue Férou, near the church of Saint-Sulpice.
3 Clara Dunn (1890–1979), a classmate of Pauline's at the University of Missouri. Pauline had lived with Clara while working for the *New York Morning Telegraph* and made her first trip to Europe with Clara in 1922. During the summer of 1927 Virginia Pfeiffer and Clara also became close friends. EH would come to disdain Clara's influence on Pauline; in Chapter 10 of *GHOA*, the narrator remarks, "I hate Clara Dunn."
4 Pauline did not join EH in Pamplona except perhaps for the last day of the fiesta on 12 July. Instead, Waldo Peirce joined him in Pamplona that year. In a letter of 12 July 1927, Peirce wrote his mother, "Hemingway left last night for San Sebastian to meet his wife." As Peirce explained, EH wanted to keep his second marriage secret because the Spanish did not approve of divorce, and therefore EH was "coming back with his wife incognito" (quoted in William Gallagher, "Waldo Peirce and Ernest Hemingway: Mirror Images," *Hemingway Review* 23, no. 1 [Fall 2003]: 31).
5 Everything (Spanish).
6 Sunny's wired response to EH's cable of 6 May would arrive in Paris on 7 May 1927, the day after EH posted this letter. The telegram read: "CANT COME FOLKS OBJECT MONEY GONE WRITING = SUNNY" (JFK).

To Waverley Root, [c. mid- to late May 1927]

Hotel Bellevue

Grau du Roi

Dear Mr. Root—

I'm awfully sorry not to be in town but am down here at the wrong end of the Camargue from Paris. Hope to be back in Paris in July and would enjoy seeing you.[1]

About the town; If you're at the rue Saint Jacques there is a good place to eat at the Café restaurant de la Observatoire near you at the corner of the B$^{\underline{d}}$ Port Royal and the Avenue de L'observatoire.[2] Right across the street is the Closerie de Lilas which is a good place to drink. The B$^{\underline{d}}$ Port Royal becomes the B$^{\underline{d}}$ Montparnasse at that point and if you follow it for a couple of hundred yards it wont make any difference if you speak French or not—but after you pass the Dome and the Rotonde and the Select you come to several small restaurants where you can eat well cheaply. They're all within walking distance of where you live—but of course maybe you're in a pension.

I hope you're having a fine time and remember me to Johnny Herrmann if you write him.

Yours always.

Ernest Hemingway.

There is a friend of John's called Robert Wolf in town—if you'd like to see him. His address is care of

the Guaranty Trust Co.

1, rue des Italiens.

UMD, ALS

1 Le Grau-du-Roi, the small sea port on the Mediterranean where EH and Pauline spent their honeymoon, is located at the western edge of the Camargue, a large wetlands area of the Rhône river delta south of Arles.
2 L'Observatoire de Paris, the Royal Observatory of Paris, built 1667–1672 during the reign of Louis XIV, was a short walk from EH and Hadley's old apartment over the sawmill.

To Maxwell Perkins, 27 May [1927]

Grau du Roi (Gard)
May 27—

Dear Mr. Perkins—

Here are two more stories for the book.[1] I didn't get a copy of the Little Review with the Banal Story in it—as I recall it wasn't much but I remember Edmund Wilson writing that he liked it so it might be worth getting hold of in N.Y. It was the number of the L.R. which came out last summer.

Did you see some pieces in the New Republic for, I imagine, the week of May 5?[2] If you think it advisable we could include them at the end of the book. How did it look as to length? They were three sketches called Italy 1927 and were more on the story side than anything else. I would put on a different title in the proofs. I think they would go rather well.

So that makes three more things to go in and if they are set up (if it's not too late) I can arrange their order in the galleys.

I have your letter with the check for $750. Thank you very much. Dexter was very nice. He is still in Paris and I'll see him when I go up there next week. I'm working pretty well now.

Donald Freide, who is one of the partners in Boni and Liveright, came to see me in Paris. He was very worked up about getting me to come back to his firm saying that I would never have been allowed to leave if he had been there etc. He said he had made the trip especially to see me etc. and wanted me to sign a contract giving me an advance of $3,000. on any novels, $1,000 on any book of short stories or essays, 15% royalties, no cuts on byproducts and I forget what else. His argument was that Boni and Liveright had published In Our Time when no one else would and that I had only been allowed to leave because he wasn't there.[3]

I told him that I could not discuss the matter as I was absolutely satisfied where I was, that I thought Scribners had advertised the Sun splendidly and had supported it and pushed it [t]hrough a time before it began to sell when many publishers would have dropped it, and that I had only left Boni and Liveright when they turned down the Torrents which you took without ever having seen the mss. of The Sun. As for the In Our Time, I told him I was sure you would have published it as I found a letter from you, written a long time previously, waiting for me on returning to Paris after accepting Liveright's cabled offer.

Freide also offered to try and buy the Torrents and the Sun from yourselves and bring them all out later in a uniform edition. He said Scribners had offered to buy the In Our Time but that Liveright had no intention of selling it and were now bringing out a new edition. I don't know whether there is anything to that story except the new edition part which I heard some time ago was coming out.

I write you this for your own information so you will not get any garbled versions or think I am dickering with other publishers. The Cosmopolitan people came over here a few weeks ago but I told them before they could talk money that it was useless as I was absolutely satisfied. Freide, however, had his mind made up that he had to make this offer and I could not avoid it.

This is a fine place below Aigues Mortes on the Camargue and the Mediterranean with a long beach and a fine fishing port. Am going back next week to Paris for a month and then down to Spain until the $750 runs out. Am healthy and working well and it ought to be a good summer.

Hugh Walpole writes me on May 16th that he is saying something in the English Nation of that week which sounds to me extravagant but which, if you encounter the Nation, might make good advertising.[4] I hope you have a fine summer and that these stories are not too late.

Yours always,
Ernest Hemingway.

PUL, TLS

1 Probably "Ten Indians" and "Now I Lay Me," earlier titled "In Another Country—two."
2 "Italy, 1927" appeared in the 18 May 1927 *New Republic.*
3 Donald Friede (1901–1965), publisher and literary agent who had become a vice president at Boni & Liveright in 1925. In response to EH's account of his former publisher's renewed interest and offer, Perkins would respond, "The Liveright incident is definitely closed and so I should like to say that the terms they offered you are the terms we will give you any time" (8 June 1927, PUL).
4 Walpole's letter of 16 May most likely was his reply to EH's letter of 14 April 1927. In his article "Contemporary American Letters," which appeared in the 4 June 1927 issue of the *Nation and Athenaeum,* Walpole called EH "the most interesting figure in American letters in the last ten years" and described "The Killers" as "one of the best short stories in the American language" (303).

To Hugh Walpole, [c. 27 May 1927]

Dear Walpole—

Couldn't you come over to Paris the end of June? July we'll be in Spain and August too I'm afraid. Then the end of June you could still hear a little French talked on the boulevards and that's supposed to be a great rarity and attraction during the annual invasion of my coutrymen. Perhaps you would come down to Spain. I'll be in Valencia the end of July from the 25th till the second of August and then somewhere in the north through August. Pamplona comes the 6th through the 12th of July and after planning to stay away it has become quite impossible not to go. I find myself waking up in the morning feeling very happy because it is getting time to go to Pamplona— so I imagine that anything that makes one feel happy in the morning I'll have not to miss.

We can't put you up but if you let me know any time you are coming I can get you a room at Foyots which is very near and we can feed you

JFK, TL

This is an early draft of the letter of [c. 27 June 1927] that EH, probably delayed by sickness, sent in reply to Walpole's letter of 16 May.

To Pierre Chautard, 7 June 1927

June 7, 1927.

Dear Monsieur Chautard:

Enclosed please find check for [900?] francs for the apartment rent June 8— July 8 1927[1]

Thank you for forwarding my mail care of the Guaranty Trust Co.

Yours very truly,
Ernest Hemingway
Care of Guaranty Trust Co.
1, rue des Italiens
Paris E.V.

Because I am leaving Paris I shall not keep the apartment any longer. You may rent it <u>immediately</u> if you wish—the keys have already been delivered to you—and I have had it cleaned and put in order. You checked over the furnishings with me yourself—the other things had been taken downstairs Both while we were in the apartment and in our absence. The kitchen, and toilet had been used in our absence while I was paying full rent.

I am giving you one months notice instead of two weeks in order that you may rent the apartment <u>at once</u>—thus giving you a month's rent free which you may apply on any possible deterioration of the original furnishings due to use.

With Best wishes to you and to Madame Chautard

Very Sincerely, Ernest Hemingway.

My permanent address will be Care Guaranty Trust Co. of <u>N.Y.</u>

JFK, ALS

1 For Hadley and EH's former apartment at 113, rue Notre-Dame-des-Champs.

To Pierre Chautard, [after 7 June 1927]

Cher Monsieur Chautard:

Je regrette d'avoir ecrit a vous en anglais mais j'etiez tres pressé et je ai cru que mon lettre etait assez claire—que vous pouviez louer immediatement l'appartement meme que je vous a deja payer le loyer 8 Juin-8 Juillet. Comme ca vous aviez le montant de ce loyer pour employer comme vous voudriez.

J'ai toujours plusiers livres chez vous que vous seriez bien gentil de garder pour moi jusqua que je peux venir pour les prendre. Comme il sont deja instaleé dans votre ~~caisse pour livers~~ bibliotheque j'éspere que il ne sont pas trop genant.

Voulez vous acceptez ~~pour vous et pour Madame Chautard mes meilleures~~ mes meilleures salutations

[*Translation follows:*]

Dear Mr Chautard:

I regret having written to you in English but I was in a great hurry and I believed that my letter was clear enough—that you could rent the apartment immediately even though I had already paid the rent from June 8ᵗʰ till July 8ᵗʰ.[1] That way, you had the amount of this rent to use as you wished.

I still have several books at your place that you would be quite kind to keep for me until I can come and get them. Since they are already placed on your bookshelf I hope that they are not too much of an inconvenience.

Would you accept ~~you and Mrs Chautard my best~~ my best greetings

JFK, ALD

1 EH is referring to the preceding letter of 7 June 1927 that he wrote to Chautard in English.

To Mary Pfeiffer, [c. after 7 June 1927]

[*EH autograph notation*: Continuation.]

It was very fine of you to send Pauline and me such a letter for the day we were married and I wish I could tell you how much we both appreciated it.[1] We've had a grand trip and been working pretty hard, getting off a book for this fall and Pauline getting the apartment in shape and running smoothly and the end of the month we're going down to Spain for the summer. Uncle Gus sent us a copy of the marriage publicity page that went out to the living relatives so if this is a short and quiet note it doesn't mean that Uncle Gus and I are not contemplating putting up a string of Transatlantic Bull rings where lectures can be given about who knew Mussolini when and other topics by Mr. and Mrs. Hemingway the brilliant young writers. We went to lunch at the Anglo-American press association and Guy Hickock, of the Brooklyn Eagle, who sat with us figured out that Uncle Gus must be a relative of mine and knowing that any relative must feel very badly about any books that I'd write tried to make him believe that at one time I had been a practical newspaper man thinking that might encourage him.[2]

But if you can forget the broadcast and not mind the stuff I write, or not read it if you don't like it, then if I've made Pauline a good husband for ten or fifteen years I would feel easier about not being a better prospective son in law. We're really having a grand time and working is going awfully well.

Jinny is seeing a lot of Clara and consequently, very consequently, Mrs. Dunn,[3] who doesn't come to our house so much on account of the lack of a corps of beautifully trained servants and three flights of stairs, and Jinny while disliking Mrs. Dunn is getting, through imitating her, to talk very much like her and can let her voice rise and fall as though she too had the blood of English Kings in her veins. Clara seems awfully tired and worn but I think is picking up.

The only practical use I might be is to tell you something about your daughters from time to time. Pauline is in grand condition and weighs 114 eats all we can pay for at any time, sleeps well goes to church on Sunday, has a fine Livret de Famille Chretien, probably misspelled,[4] given her by the first vicar which she is to present and have stamped every time any of her children are baptized, rode 68 kilometers on the bicycle without getting tired, is now in the other room copying a story after having gotten breakfast and cleaned things up and seems very happy.

Jinny is picking up after the strain of marrying off sisters in a foreign country, weighs 110, also goes to mass on Sunday, also keeps ember days,[5] in fact having reminded us of it when there were pork chops for lunch [*EH insertion*: and it hadnt been announced at church] spends a lot of time chaperoning Mrs. Dunn who believes that if she will only speak English loud and clear enough any french person will understand if they really want to, and also seems happy. She worked tremendously hard over Pauline's wedding and fixing up this place.

We've also met Leonard Kluftinger who seems to be a grand boy and as square as a square peg in a round world.[6]

This isn't a good letter but if it is going to go on tomorrow's mail boat it has to stop now. I can't tell you how much I appreciated the welcome you gave me and I'll try very hard to live up to it.

Ernest

PUL, TLSFrag

At the top of the page is EH's handwritten notation "Continuation"; any earlier portion of the letter has not been located.

1 Pauline's parents had sent their best wishes and a monetary gift when she and EH were married. Mary had written, "For many months I have been asking Our Heavenly Father to make the crooked ways straight and your life's pathway one of peace and happiness, and this morning I feel a quiet assurance that my prayers have not been in vain." Although it seemed "strange" to her not to have attended the wedding, she wrote: "My dear Ernest if you are all that those who know you best, believe you to be, we are glad to give our heart's treasure into your keeping" ([10 May 1927], PUL).

2 The Anglo-American Press Association of Paris was founded on 16 December 1907 by correspondents of the *London Chronicle* and *Chicago Daily News*, who shared offices. Weekly lunches were established in 1914, featuring speeches by public officials from around the world, who sometimes would speak to attending reporters off the record.

3 Lillie Rogers Dunn (1859–c. 1948), Clara's mother.

4 *Livret de famille chrétien*: Christian family record book (French).

5 Three days of fasting, abstinence, and prayer prescribed by the Roman Catholic Church four times a year, corresponding roughly to the beginnings of the four seasons and cycles of the liturgical calendar.

6 German-born Leonhard Kluftinger (b. 1896) ran the Berlin operations of the Pfeiffers' pharmaceutical business, Gödecke & Co. The Kluftingers were maternal relations of the Pfeiffer family.

To Maxwell Perkins, 10 June [1927]

June 10—

Dear Mr. Perkins—

I am enclosing another story for the book—HILLS LIKE WHITE ELEPHANTS. Leaving out the Banal Story—which is not really a story and in spite of Wilson hardly worth re-printing—that makes 13 stories—if we need to print it for the length I'm willing.[1] Am simply neutral about it. I think [y]ou'll like this last new one. That will make 6 unpublished stories and [T]oday Is Friday which only appeared in some 350 copy pamphlet form.[2]

I am enclosing an approximate order for the table of contents. I arranged the bulk of the stories as you did in the Contents you sent—feeling you must have some reason for that arrangement. If you want to shift any of these others you may. It is very hard for me to arrange them when I haven't the stories here to see.

I have entitled the Italy, 1927—Che Ti Dice La Patria? which I think will be better than Italy 1927 as it may not always be 1927. It could be translated what do you hear from home or what doth the fatherland say to thee or etc. But I don't think we have to translate it and it is very good and pure Italian to sock the erudite with. I don't think one foreign title on a story will mar the contents. You said you had lifted it from the New Republic—there is I believe only one mistake—in the last paragraph ROMAGNA was misspelled.[3]

About the little bull—he is very long in the legs and thin through the withers and has a faintly lesbian look which might be very attractive in a cow but would never get a bull anywhere. I am enclosing some sample bulls.[4] The defect of our present bull seems to be that while his sex is clearly indicated nobody, from the general shape of his body and build, would believe it. In the post-card entitled Gran Par de Banderillas[5] there is a bull in approximately the same position as the one in the proofs—you see the difference in the thickness of the body, the heavy quality and the shortness of the legs of the fighting bull. If it isn't too late or too much trouble and if you still want the bull I think the artist could get up one a little more on the Spanish side after studying these pictures. The characteristics of the Spanish fighting bull are exemplified by the big hump of muscle that comes above his shoulders, the angle and regular curve of his horns, the short legs and the width through the chest and the barrel.

But the jacket is not my province and I only offer these suggestions in case it is not yet completed. I think he's a good idea and if it's too late to do any correcting it is all right.

Now if this is to go off on the Aquitania tomorrow I must go over the HILLS story and recopy the table of contents.

I am sorry about the Lack of Passion being held up—but it is no good having it bum and I think this will make quite a lot of stories. If I should have luck and get it done I will send it before the end of the month. I've had a bad time with it.

Am returning the memorandum.[6] Thank you very much for sending it.

Yours always
Ernest Hemingway.

I'll see about the two words in the Pursuit Race in the proof—should be able to fix them.

[Enclosed typewritten list on half sheet of paper, with numbers and three story titles ("An Alpine Idyll," "Banal Story," and "Lack of Passion") handwritten in pencil:]

1	The Undefeated.	14,200
4	Fifty Grand	13,000
7	The Killers	4,500
2	In Another Country	2600
3	Pursuit Race	2000
5	A Canary For One	2200
6	A Simple Enquiry	1400
8	Ten Indians	2800
9	An Alpine Idyll	2700
10	Now I Lay Me	3800
11	Hills Like White Elephants	2250
12	Today Is Friday	1500
14	Banal Story	647
13	Che Ti Dice La Patria?	3900
15	Lack of Passion	

[EH handwritten notation to the right of the list:] You may be able to get a better order.[7] Without having the stories is hard to arrange them by titles and remembering them. I wish I could see them.

Change this order if you wish. Today is Friday might be better at the end. If you think the Italian title is no good or objectionable please tell me.

PUL, TLS

1 "Banal Story" would be included in *MWW*. Edmund Wilson would later call the story a "prose poem," citing it as an example of EH's skill as "an admirable miniaturist in prose" ("Ernest Hemingway: Bourdon Gauge of Morale," *Atlantic Monthly* [July 1939]: 39).
2 By the time Scribner's published *MWW* on 14 October 1927, ten of the fourteen stories had already appeared in print. "A Simple Enquiry," "Ten Indians," "A Pursuit Race," and "Now I Lay Me" were previously unpublished.
3 In his letter to EH of 16 May 1927, Perkins said he had clipped the story out of the *New Republic* but assumed that EH would send him another copy with possible changes (PUL). In the magazine publication of the story, "Romagna" was misspelled as "Romogna."

4 In his letter of 27 May 1927, Perkins enclosed "some front matter" prepared for the forth-coming *MWW*, including the title page and dust jacket featuring a drawing of a "little bull," which Perkins thought "appropriate to a book called 'Men Without Women' and particularly to one that had one magnificent bull fight story in it, and will probably have another" (PUL). EH enclosed with this letter two photographic postcards depicting bullfighting scenes and a color illustration clipped from a Spanish magazine showing a group of bulls being herded into a bullring. On the verso of the clipping is EH's handwritten notation: "File/Bulls."

5 A great pair of banderillas (Spanish). Banderillas are flagged dowels "with a harpoon-shaped steel point placed in pairs in the withers of the bull in the second act of the bullfight" (*DIA*, Glossary). The photograph on the postcard depicts a matador leaning close to a charging bull to place the banderillas.

6 Scribner's "Memorandum of Agreement," the contract for the publication of *MWW*, dated 27 May 1927, which required EH's signature (PUL). The agreement provided EH with a 15% royalty on the retail price of all copies sold and stated that EH acknowledged having received an advance of $750.

7 With the exception of "Lack of Passion," all of the listed stories appear in *MWW* but in a different order.

To Mildred Temple, [16 June 1927]

Thursday afternoon.

Dear Miss Temple,

I did not get your wire until I went to the bank Wednesday morning but at once wired that I would be at 6 rue Ferou all this week.

As it was Wednesday already and you spoke of flying over on Wednesday I did not know if it was still practicable for you and so did not set some other meeting place than here where I am working. Since then Harper's Bazaar have been sending off a two year old address and complicating things in general.[1]

The only address I have in Paris is care of the Guaranty Trust Company and I do not give them the address of the place I may be staying when I'm in town as calls from visiting firemen, no matter how welcome, make work impossible. But when out of town they forward all mail and cables. I'm working now before getting away to Spain and will be here until about the 25th of June. I'll be very glad to see you any time here at the rue Ferou or if you drop me a note to meet you anywhere you wish.

Yours very truly,
Ernest Hemingway.

JFK, TLS

The conjectured date of this letter is based on EH's reference to having received Mildred Temple's wire on a Wednesday, this reply of "Thursday afternoon," and his 24 June 1927 letter to Maxwell Perkins mentioning that he had met Temple in Paris the previous week. The letter's typewritten envelope, addressed to Mildred Temple in London, gives EH's return address as "Guaranty Trust Company of N.Y. / 1, rue des Italiens / Paris." The envelope bears no postage stamps or postmark.

1 *Harper's Bazar* (the spelling changed to "*Bazaar*" in November 1929) was among the publications of the International Magazine Company, for which Temple acted as European editorial representative.

To Maxwell Perkins, 24 June [1927]

June 24

Dear Mr. Perkins,

I am enclosing a copy of a letter which arrived with a check for 25,483.40 francs enclosed yesterday morning. Also enclosing a draft of the letter I am sending returning the check.[1]

Mildred Temple is the new Hearst representative over here. She flew over last week with a copy of this letter except that the serial price was 10,000 and the movie rights 15,000 and it did not contain the clause about no cutting.[2] They came up over the week end. I had said I didnt think I'd do it anyway but certainly not on the original terms.

I was pretty badly tempted as it is a splendid chance to sell stories but I really think that the pressure would be too strong and too subtle in regard to the novel. It is a hell of a job for me to write anyway and with the pressure of a possible 42,000 dollars if it turned out to be what they wanted—somehow it seemed like too much extraweight to take on at this time in my career.

This is the sort of thing I would like to have eventually—but I can't see it doing me any good now—and I have never seen an American writer survive it. Then eventually something else may smash me and I never get it. But that's covered by the expression—What the hell.

Only it seems bad luck to have it come now and lose it instead of having it it 15 years—or even ten years—when it could not harm one.

Of course I would not sign anything without consulting you about the serial thing. All my instinct is against it—granted that I were strong enough not to have it affect me it would be splendid—but has anybody ever survived that sort of thing?

So will you please advise me about the serializing business—practically—from the publishing standpoint—and also as my friend.[3]

In considering it please throw the money end out. We both take it for granted that the money would be a fine thing to have but for the next ten years it must be a side issue. I always took you at your word about the question of advances etc.— I have plenty of money now to last several months.

I really think that eventually I might have a book which might sell a great deal—or one which, on being completed, might serialize well. But now doesn't seem like the time to get into what seems to me to be the greased shutes.

Your letter was awfully nice about the Liveright thing. I only mentioned it so that you wouldn't hear any different versions or rumours.

As for horse and eagle offal I don't know what to do. Could we leave a dash? S—— might be all right.[4]

Walpole's review was in the June 4 Nation. Cape has gotten the Sun out in the cheapest form possible is advertsing it as an amusing story of the sort of thing young Americans are doing in the Latin quarter today and is trying hard to sell it as a hammock book. On that basis it is getting and will get panned. I feel disgusted with Cape and always have been.

They cut the In Our Time, changed many words, anglicized it to make walked along the ties read walked along the <u>sleepers</u>—etc. etc.[5]

This must make the boat so I'll close. There is no need to cable about the serialization thing—a letter would be better. Please tell me all you think. I don't even know whether it is supposed to be good or bad for the sale of a book.[6]

There wont be another story by the first of July except by a miracle. I was sick for ten days with an infected cut (all cleared up now) but looked serious for a while.

Yours always.
Ernest Hemingway.

Go to Spain on the 5th through September. Guaranty Trust will forward Proofs and mail and I will be <u>very</u> prompt with them.

PUL, TL/ALS

1 EH enclosed a letter dated 22 June 1927 from the International Magazine Company signed by Mildred Temple (PUL) that detailed an offer and would have functioned as a contract had EH signed it. As EH mentions, this was a revised version of a less generous offer dated 15 June 1927 (JFK). The check, equivalent to $1,000, was for the requested option to purchase the first British and American serial rights for specified future work by EH. By the time EH wrote this letter, he had already written the letter to Mildred Temple returning the contract offer of both dates along with the $1,000 check for the requested option.

2 In its more generous offer of 22 June 1927, the International Magazine Company requested the option to buy British and American serial rights for the next ten stories and one novel. EH was to receive $1,000 for each of the first five stories, $1,250 for each of the next five stories and $1,500 for the film rights for each story. The offer for the novel's serial rights increased from $10,000 (offered in the earlier agreement of June 15) to $12,000 and for the novel's film rights from $15,000 to $30,000. Also, two clauses were added—one granting EH prior approval of any editing or cutting, and the second stipulating that none of the contracted material could appear in book form until after the magazine publication.

3 Perkins would respond, "As for serialization, I think if you can possibly manage it, it is better to write without any thought of it; but when the novel is finished, if you can make a good serial arrangement, you ought to do it" (14 July 1927, PUL).

4 In the story "A Pursuit Race," the line in question reads, "If you love horses you'll get horse-shit and if you love eagles you'll get eagle-shit." In *MWW*, the offensive words appear as "horse-s—" and "eagle-s—."

5 As examples of Cape's numerous changes to *IOT*, in "A Very Short Story," "They had a joke about friend or enema" was changed to "They had a joke about friend or enemy," and "he contracted gonorrhea" became "he contracted a disease." In "The Battler," the word "ties," in reference to railroad tracks, was changed to the British term "sleepers."

6 The letter is typewritten to this point; the remainder is handwritten.

To Mildred Temple, 24 June 1927

June 24, 1927.

Dear Miss Temple,

I am returning the check and the two contract forms with this letter. This is not because they are unsatisfactory, they are thoroughly so and I appreciate very much Mr. Long's offer and the way you presented it, but after you left and I thought things over I realized that it would be impossible to enter into any agreement for serialization without first condulting

Scribner's and getting their approval and permission. So I am writing them tonight to go on the mail boat tomorrow.[1]

You presented the whole thing so attractively that I am very disappointed not to be able to sign the papers and if you are in the habit of sending back checks for 25,000 francs that only need endorsement you know how cheerful that makes you feel.

If Scribner's decide that serialization would not fit in with their publishing plans there is nothing that we can do. In some ways, for my own good, I think it would be better to write on the novel with no idea of eventual serialization in mind. I have worked so far with no sort of contract and while this is a very good contract, with a thoroughly satisfactory price and all advantages given me (and I can't tell you how much I appreciate it) perhaps it would be better for me to go on working without one.

At any rate I am satisfied with the prices and with your whole handling of the matter and, if you like, I will send you some stories for Mr. Long when I have them, and I give you my word that I will not enter into any negociations with any one else for serializing the novel. When it is done if I decide to serialize it Mr. Long can have if he wishes at the price stated in the offer, $12,000 with the $30,000 movie option.

I write this so that you will see that I am not trying to hold things up in order to get a better offer somewhere else on the strength of this one. There are only two difficulties in the way of signing the contract. The first that I would not wish to serialize against Scribner's wishes. The second that, after consideration, I do not want to take an advance which might even unconsciously affect the writing of a novel because of the necessity for submitting it for serialization.

It was awfully pleasant meeting you and Mrs. Hemingway and I both hope we will see you in Paris again sometime. We are leaving for Spain the fifth of July and will be there through September. The Guaranty Trust Company here will always forward my mail and I have your address. I hope we will see you over here again some time in the fall.

With best regards,
Very truly,
Ernest Hemingway.

PUL, TLS

This letter was enclosed in EH's letter to Perkins of the same date.

1 EH was returning the check and the two contracts, dated 15 June 1927 and 22 June 1927, that Temple had sent him. Ray Long, the company's editor in chief, had approved the terms of the higher offer.

To Jonathan Cape, 27 June 1927

June 27, 1927

Dear Mr. Cape:—

Thank you for your letter enclosing the clippings. Perhaps it would be better in the future to address me care of my bankers, The Guaranty Trust Company of N.Y. 1, rue des Italiens as mail addressed there is always forwarded while communications addressed to book shops may go some months without being delivered.[1] Curtis Brown have always had the Guaranty Trust Company as my address and I am sure would have been glad to furnish you with it.

As for the clippings; they are what one would expect in regard to a book advertised as dealing with "the life of the younger generation of Americans living in Paris today, traveling in France and through Spain, here shown with remarkable fidelity."[2] I cannot imagine a British critic approaching such an advertised recital with anything but distaste and lack of interest. Perhaps you can tell me why the fact that many of the characters, and two of the principal figures, are British is so carefully withheld from any possible reader.

Of the binding, jacket and numerous typographical errors perhaps it would be better not to speak. I can only say that I appreciate greatly your not having bowdlerized the text as was done with In Our Time. Perhaps though, had that been done, the book might have received a heartier critical reception.

Thank you again for your letter and for the clippings. No copies have, as yet, arrived from Curtis Brown. I do not, however, await them with enthusiasm.

Yours very truly,

JFK, TL

1 In a letter of 17 June 1927, Cape wrote that he had left a copy of *Fiesta* with Sylvia Beach and
   that he was sending copies of the few reviews that had appeared since the book's publication
   on 9 June (JFK).
2 EH is quoting from the dust jacket flap of *Fiesta*. The blurb continues, "It is a vivid book,
   relentless in its character-drawing. Here is an author to be reckoned with."

To Hugh Walpole, [c. 27 June 1927]

Dear Walpole:—

You were awfully good to write and I feel very badly that I'll not be here
the end of July nor August. I've just been writing a letter to Cape in which I
have been trying to write English in order to keep him in his place and so if
any English gets into this lay it to Cape and his thorough bloodiness. In a
letter to Cape you say (one says) cuttings for clippings, bankers for bank,
and thank you for your letter instead of go to hell.

Anyway it was very sporting of you to write the thing in the Nation
especially now that it seems that all the book was was a dreary meddly of
maudlin boringness conveying no impression of reality in which the
younger generation of Americans drink more than is humanly and
physically possible for a British critic to contemplate. Oh that wearisome,
drenching deluge of drink! (The Sunday Observer)[1]

It seems that I have been sick (ill) with something that killed Mrs.
Harriman (Lady Sir Alfred Mond) (approximately) [*EH insertion*: or worse]
in two days but have recovered and feel very badly at not having written to
you.[2] My only comfort at dying in only an approximate state of grace would
be that the gentleman in the Sunday Observer, would no more be bothered
with that wearisome drenching deluge. However if you would come down
to Spain we'll be at Valencia from the 25th of July until the second of August
then Madrid for a few days then Bilbao through the middle of August and
then almost anywhere until the Feria at Sevilla the end of September. If you
will be over here and should be going south I would love to see you and will
write exactly where we will be. I'm leaving here the fifth and will be back in
October.

The Guaranty Trust Company is a permanent address but we live at 6 rue Ferou. I can't imagine coming over to London except to kill Cape and hide him in a big trunk of some sort in the classic manner but would be afraid I'd not have time to leave the country as I'm sure Cape's presence in the trunk would be betrayed instantly by a strong odour.

Do let me know if there is any chance of your coming to Spain, or even near Spain; in which case I'd make arrangements for crossing the border.

Yours very truly,

Ernest Hemingway.

NYPL-Berg, TLS

This is the final, sent version of EH's draft of [c. 27 May 1927].

1 In the 4 June 1927 *Nation and Athenaeum*, Walpole described EH's recent novel as "most remarkable" ("Contemporary American Letters," 303). EH refers to the negative review of *Fiesta* by English critic Gerald Gould (1885–1936) in the 12 June 1927 *Observer*, describing the characters as "so consistently soaking themselves with alcohol as to lose all human interest." Gould wrote, "O that wearisome, drenching deluge of drink! Cocktails for coxcombs and highballs for highbrows. Why does Mr. Hemingway, who *can* draw flesh-and-blood, waste his time on these bibulous shadows?" ("New Novels," 8).
2 On 25 June 1926, American actress, musician, and dancer Alice Laidley Harriman (1903–1926) had died of blood poisoning at the American Hospital in Paris. She had married John Harriman, an American in the railroad business, in 1922. Alfred Moritz Mond (1868–1930), English industrialist and politician.

To Barklie McKee Henry, 14 July 1927

July 14 1927

Dear Buzz:

I've wanted like hell to write to you and carried your letter around all winter and Spring—and once had carried it a week of course never did. So you dont have to call me one because I know I am.[1]

It is grand that you are on the Youth's Companion and as soon as Bumby can read I'll put him in your hands.[2] He is 4 this fall—if I've the dates right. Is out in California with Hadley. Skied with me last winter and will again this. He says Papa est en Espagne couche avec les taureaux![3]

Am down here after Pamplona getting a swim before going on to
Valencia. Have 8000 Kilometers of r.r. fare and hope to see several places.
Wish you could come over again. How are Barbara and your family? I sent
you a wire when your first child was born but haven't read of any others in
the Spanish Austrian or French papers so I dont know to what extent youve
become a father.[4]

It was swell of you to speak about my stuff to Mr. Sedgewick and I think it
was cockeyed sporting of them to publish the story. I was terribly pleased
you liked it. Will have it in a book along with 12 others this fall.[5] I'll write
Scribner's to send you one.

I havent seen Jo for a long time but saw old Steff this Spring.[6] Dos Passos has
been down in Mexico. He's working on the theatre now—whatever that
means. I've never had any little theatre movements myself but then you can
never tell with the kind of food a man eats in N.Y. But Dos is a grand bird.

Pamplona was grand this year. I wish you and Barbara could come some
year. I cant write about it and dont seem to be able to write about anything.
But dont mind what a lousy letter this is because I want to write to you so
much that it is like these meetings you have with people after a long time
away when you cant say anything.

The Guaranty Trust Co. is my only permanent address but they always
forward.

Wanted to come home last fall like hell but couldnt but will this fall,
winter or Spring and I'll send the wire and we'll go on a party and then can
climb up on the top of the tall buildings and pee on the surrounding
countryside for auld lang syne— But you may be were drunk at the time and
don't remember what the roof of 113 [Notre-Dame-des-Champs] used to
be used for. Anyway So Long Buzz and all good luck and my very best to
Barbara and I hope I see you soon.

Ernie.

Your letters were most highly cockeyed fine reading and anytime you want
to write I'm your public and will write back even though past performances
look bad. (I never got the cable) But it was damned swell of you to send it.

PUL, ALS; letterhead: HOTEL BIARRITZ / SAN SEBASTIAN

1 In a letter to EH of 29 June 1927, Henry mentioned that he had sent a congratulatory telegram on the publication of *IOT* as well as a "terrifically long letter" back in February 1927 but had received no answers—perhaps because they were addressed to EH's former residence at 113, rue Notre-Dame-des-Champs (JFK).
2 Henry was then managing editor of the popular American magazine *Youth's Companion*, which EH read as a child. Originally established as a religious publication for children, it was published from 1827 until 1929, when it merged with *American Boy*.
3 *Papa est en Espagne couchant avec les taureaux*: Papa is in Spain sleeping with the bulls (French).
4 Barbara Whitney (1903–1982), daughter of sculptor Gertrude Vanderbilt Whitney and a member of one of America's wealthiest families. She and Barklie Henry married in 1924, and their daughter, Gertrude Whitney Henry (1925–2009), was born the following year on 25 March. The couple also had a son, William B. Henry; information concerning his date of birth has not been located.
5 In his 29 June letter, Henry wrote that he had recommended EH's work to Ellery Sedgwick of the *Atlantic Monthly* and congratulated EH on the publication of "Fifty Grand" in that "high brow magazine"—particularly because such magazines "number a great many old ladies among their readers. So far as I know, you are about the only writer who has gotten away with it."
6 American sculptor Jo Davidson (1882–1952) and American journalist Lincoln Steffens (1866–1936), both of whom EH had met while working as a journalist in April 1922 at the Genoa Economic Conference. Henry had written, "I haven't seen Joe Davidson for the past fifty years."

To Waldo Peirce, 22 July 1927

Hotel Inglés
Valencia
July 22 1927

Muy Caballero Mio:

I sweat all over the first sheet and had to start over. You certainly had a hell of a time getting home. It sounded like a fine place though. Thanks for the dough. I feel that I let you in on a lot more expense than you figured on and then Jimmy-ed you out of more.[1] Will try and make it up sometime.

It has been hell hot now for three days. Wish you were here to sweat. I can out sweat all the big local sweaters and they are going to bring in outside competition and have me sweat derrier grosse motos.[2] I owe you 50 pesetas on Wills. Do I owe you anything on Sharkey? Never bet on a Lithuanian if he can talk.[3]

Had three tickets in the lotery yest 5 pesetas a decimo[4] and won on all three in the evening list—still won on one in the morning paper—but it is the worst printed paper so am waiting for the official list.

Yesterday they desencajconada-ed 58 bulls for the Feria. All in the ring a corrida at a time as per the picture. The Pablo Romeros—and Concha and Sierras are the best—6 of the last bigger than Miuras when we were boys.[5]

How the hell are you now?

I sent Jimmy a wire and he sent over the glasses I'd left in the car.

Meditteranean feels like a pee-ed in bath tub.

Pauline sends her best[.] And all mine to you and Ivy.[6] Write anytime you feel like it.

The drawings for Bumby were damned lovely.[7] I sent them off. He'll be awfully happy. Thanks like hell.

We're here until July 31st at Hotel Inglés—then go to Madrid for 3 or 4 days— Then La Coruña—7–8–9 August—then Bilbao 21–22–23–24— Then don't know. Let's hear from you. This is a shitty letter but its so damned hot. This is fine dusty town.

Yrs always Ernest.

Colby, ALS

1 EH is replying to Peirce's letter postmarked 16 July 1927 in which Peirce described his arduous return journey from Pamplona to meet his wife in a remote location near Arcachon, France, on the Bay of Biscay. Referring to their trip to Pamplona, Peirce thanked EH for "taking me down there & financing me à la Rothschild" and assured him that upon his return to Paris, he would deposit 400 pesetas to EH's account at the Guaranty Trust Co. "Jimmy-ed" probably refers to the unidentified mutual acquaintance named Jimmy who is mentioned later in the letter.

2 *Derrière des grosses motos*: behind some big motorbikes (French).

3 American heavyweight boxers Harry Wills (1889–1958) and Jack Sharkey (né Joseph Paul Zukauskas, 1902–1994), a son of Lithuanian immigrants. Wills was knocked out by Spanish fighter Paulino Uzcudun (1899–1985) at Ebbets Field in Brooklyn on 13 July 1927, and Sharkey was knocked out by Jack Dempsey (né William Harrison Dempsey, 1895–1983) at Yankee Stadium on 21 July 1927.

4 *Décimo*: a tenth (Spanish), here meaning a tenth-part share of a lottery ticket.

5 *Desencajonar*: to release a bull from the *cajon*, or travel container (Spanish). Bulls are transported in large *cajones* from the ranch to the bullring, where they are released into the ring's corrals. EH refers to pedigreed bulls bred since the nineteenth century by the Spanish bull breeder families of Pablo Romero, Concha y Sierra, and Miura (Mandel *HDIA*, 328–29, 99–101, and 282–86).

6 Peirce had married American actress Ivy Troutman (1883–1979), his second wife, in 1920.

7 Peirce wrote that he was sending EH "some more drawings for Bumby," which were to "round out the ballade of Don Ernesto El Kid." Peirce's 1927 scrapbook, "Don Ernesto en Pamplona," a bound manuscript poem in Spanish illustrated with ink and chalk drawings, is in the Collection of Waldo Peirce Materials, Colby College Special Collections, Waterville, Maine.

To William B. Smith, Jr., 28 July [1927]

Hotel Ingles—Valencia

write to the

Guaranty—Paris.

July 28

Dear Smith,

Glad to hear you earned three squares a day propelling gloves Smith because that way you will be able to defend the enditer from detractors of his veracity when you read that he earned three squares a day bull fighting in the French and Italian armies. A man does not have to put out that shit. The blurb and publicity writers invent it. I have made it a point not to ever furnish a paragraph of biographical material. Consequently the invented and legendary crap is something formidable. I occasionally write to Scribner's to nail some lie such as me having been a lt.col. bull fighting in the Italian Army in 1912 against the moors but since have stopped the clippings don't even see the shit so much any more.

Wouldn't it be wonderful if there should be oil in them hills? I'll bet Bert is the last man to lease and will only offer some of his property after the oil merchants have pulled up and left the country. Lease a little Smith but hold onto the bulk in case there should be oil.[1] No signs of Deak down here. Had half expected him. He said in Paris he might come down.[2] Bull fighting's been desastrous.

Belmonte cogida badly, Marcial Lalanda cogida with a nine inch deep wound from a splintered horn in the groin leaving the femoral uncovered and cutting the safena vein. Villalta with the typhoid. Nino cogida yesterday—only a slight wound. Aguero cut in the foot with the sword. Simao da veiga—th[e] portuguese kill them on horse-back merchant with his shoulder out of joint. The whole, season gone to hell. The writers sole appearance in the unsquared circle not a success—even with the horns blunted. Nino also a bridegroom of one week. Today they have Miuras with Valencia II substituting for Lalanda, the convalescent Villata who added a cubit to his neck during the illness, and the newly wed Nino.[3] Don Stewart's reported to have nearly died of the Erysipelas.[4] The writer has worms. Apparently a whole colon full of them. Why I never had these splendid little sportsmen when I was trout fishing so that a simple crap would have attracted th[e] finnied ones for miles I do not know. The maker moves in a mysterious way his wonders to perform and at present he has filled the writer with worms.[5] The smallest but liveliest variety. I am eating the loca[l] vermifuge but it only seems to act as an aperatif for them.[6] A sponn plunged up the anus would bring out a round dozen of the liveliest at any time. As yet I haven't plunged a spoon only offer that as a conjecture.

Last night at carpage time the little fellows seemed weary and no longer moved with the old merry abandon but this morning after the appearance of several cadavers which encouraged the writer greatly and made him cry Vermifuga! Vermifuga! a brace of lively citizens made their appearance and now the writer writes in a state of wormy despair. I don't know what novelty the grave will hold.

At any rate write Smith and slip me the dope. We might hit statewards in the fall. Where will you be? [Ne]edless to say the writer does not envisage placing the foot on [th]e home soil without a visit with the writee. Where will you be located?

I would like to tangle with a few finny ones. Are there any [f]inny ones left in U.S. Where? Do you use bait or dry flies?

How dry flies?

Yours,

Wemedge.

Pleaze say nothing to <u>anyone</u> about proposed visit to Native Land.

PUL, TL with typewritten signature; postmark: SUCURSAL 7-ALCANCE / NORTE-VALENCIA, 28 JUL 27. 8 T

EH addressed the envelope to Smith at "15 Cottage Street / Provincetown / Massachusetts / Estados Unidos." The letter was forwarded to Smith at 1711 Tribune Tower, Chicago, Illinois, with a forwarding postmark of 16 August 1927.

1 In letters to EH of 19 May 1927 and 15 June 1927, Smith mentioned speculation about oil in the land surrounding Horton Bay, Michigan, including farmland owned by Smith and his sister Kate. Smith had already been approached by someone wanting to lease the land but did not trust him (JFK). William Bert (b. c. 1871) was a farmer in the area (William H. Ohle, *How It Was in Horton Bay, Charlevoix County, Michigan* [Boyne City, Michigan: William H. Ohle, 1989], 67–68).

2 "Deak" may be a nickname for John Sherwood Foley (1897–1984), a brother of Kate Smith's friend Edith Jeanette Foley (b. 1894). In his 19 May letter, Smith wrote that he was going to "meet Deac who is here for a spell prior to a trip abroad. He intends to look youse upwards."

3 Spanish bullfighters Juan Belmonte García, Marcial Lalanda, Nicanor Villalta, Niño de la Palma, Martín Agüero Ereño (1902–1977), and Victoriano Roger "Valencia II." *Cogida*: the tossing of a person by the animal, from *coger*, meaning "to catch" (Spanish). As EH explains in *DIA*, "if the bull catches he tosses" (Glossary). Seven bullfighters were hurt in late July 1927 at the Valencia fair, which EH attended on 26, 27, 28, and 29 July. Among those were Juan Belmonte, Marcial Lalanda, and Niño de la Palma (Mandel *HDIA*, 234, 261, 318–19). Portuguese bullfighter Simão da Veiga, Jr. (1903–1959) fought on horseback, in the Portuguese tradition of *rejoneo*. Da Veiga was such a masterful rider that EH would later include him in the glossary to *DIA* in the "*jaca torera*" entry. Niño de la Palma (Cayetano Ordóñez) had recently married the gypsy singer Consuelo Araujo (1904–1978).

4 In his memoir *By a Stroke of Luck!*, Stewart recalls he almost died from erysipelas, a skin infection, in the spring of 1927, but was saved by "a new experimental serum. I had no idea how close to death I was, but Bea had been told that there wasn't much hope" (158–59).

5 Allusion to the opening lines of "Light Shining Out of Darkness" by English poet William Cowper (1731–1800): "God moves in a mysterious way / His wonders to perform." The hymn was written in 1772 and published in 1779.

6 Vermifuge, a medicine to expel worms from the intestines.

To Barklie McKee Henry, [c. 9–13 August 1927]

Dear Buz,

Am here in La Coruna waiting for proof.[1] Sounds like a murder or suspicion of adultery but really only proof from Scribner's—which now ought to be here and I hope to God it comes. Need to read some bloody thing I've written in order to convince myself that ever have written anything in order to eventually write something else. Maybe you know the feeling.

Thanks like hell for the letter that came today. I think it was very damned sporting of Owen Wister—who seems as much of a classic as Homer— except that have never read Homer—not even Homer Croy.[2] It was awfully nice of him to like the stuff. I can quite understand his not liking the In Our Time because that was so much on the side of your and my generation that we couldn't expect anybody much older to get it. If there is anything. Anyway I was awfully pleased with what he wrote you. I'd love to meet him.

You're a damned good egg to write me and tell me stuff that is cheerful. I stopped the bloody clippings last winter when they began to get too potent but now without any news I realize that I do like to hear how things go and when people like them. Hearing once in a while is useful and swell—but the clippings coming all the time are poisonous.

This is a grand town as far out in the old Atlantic as Europe can get, fine wide streets with no sidewalks nor gutters and the first good food I've had all summer. The country is a lot like Newfoundland and it only clears between rains but the rain is natural and you don't seem to get wet. Going fishing next week. Somewhere between here and Santiago in the mountains. Am figuring on coming over to the states this fall. Don't say anything about it to anybody. But I hope we can get together. Do you know any place where there would be some sort of fishing—any kind—and some partridges or ducks to shoot—the mosquitoes gone—and pretty good food—within twelve or fifteen hours of New York? I don't know any place in the east at all but would like to go up in the woods for a month or so and then come into town and bum around a while and keep the old ear from going stale and see a few fights and then go back to Paris and work. Do you know a place to go and about what it would cost? I mean board per week if it's a camp. I'm homesick to be back but don't want to see a lot of literary gents.

Anyway write me—it's always grand to hear from you. My very best to Barbara. Bumby now writes he can speak English comme[3] Papa. He's going to spend the winter ski-ing with me. Think I'll meet him in N.Y. in September.

Yours always,

Ernie

PUL, TLS

1 EH refers to the proofs for *MWW*.
2 In his letter of 25 July 1927, Henry quoted at length Owen Wister's praise for EH's work, excerpted from a letter Henry had received from Wister (1860–1938), "one of the deans of American Letters" and a family friend (JFK). Although Wister had not liked *IOT* initially, he wrote, "I must now eat humble pie. His recent tale in the Atlantic ["Fifty Grand"] and the book, 'The Sun Also Rises' are both perfectly extraordinary. I don't know any young writer whose style and gift seem to me to approach him. Were I thirty, that's the way I should wish to write." Homer Croy (1883–1965), Midwestern humorist and screenwriter, best known for the novels *West of the Water Tower* (1923) and *They Had to See Paris* (1926).
3 *Comme*: like (French).

To Harry Hansen, 16 August [1927]

[As published in Schulson Autographs catalog:]
Dear Mr. Hansen:

I'm awfully sorry not to be in Paris—but why don't you come down here? This is a long way the best town in Europe and I'll try and see you had a good time.[1] Come on down and bring Mr. Crowninshield's beverage with you, but if you can't will you write to this address?[2] It's really not so impracticable coming down here—you can get a train to Vigo—it's only 2 hrs. from there on a bus and you can sail home from Vigo if you want to. It's a grand town and lovely country. Am working here until the middle of September. Would be awful pleasant to see you if you've nothing better to do.

Ernest Hemingway.

Schulson Autographs catalog, 15 November 2006, ALS

1 According to the catalog description, this two-page letter was written from Hotel Suizo, Santiago de Compostela, Spain. The city's Cathedral of Santiago, constructed between the eleventh and the thirteenth centuries and housing the tomb of St. James, is the destination of the Camino de Santiago, a network of centuries-old pilgrimage routes.
2 Frank Crowninshield, editor of *Vanity Fair* from 1914 to 1936. EH's reference is uncertain.

To Maxwell Perkins, 17 August [1927]

Acknowlegement   to ~~Atlantic Monthly~~
~~Scribner's Magazine~~

Some of these stories were first published in The Atlantic Monthly, Scribner's Magazine, This Quarter, The Little Review, Transition, La Nouvelle Revue Francaise, Der Querschnitt and The New Republic.

Santiago de Campostela.
August 17

Dear Mr. Perkins:

The proofs came yesterday and I have done them today. They were delayed by the french customs. Your letters and the front matter mailed the same time came over a week ago.

I think the enclosed order is very good.[1] I have typed out the names of the magazines the stories were published in above. You will know the form of acknowledgement to make. As short and inconspicuous as possible. Today Is Friday was published by something called the As Stable Publications but copyrighted in my name and all rights reserved. It was limited to, I think, 150 copies. I don't imagine an acknowledgement is necessary. Six of the stories have never been published.

In the list of books would it be possible to include In Our Time? Or are books only listed when published by the same publisher?[2]

I was sorry about the Lack of Passion but it was about one third the size of a novel and after a lot of re-working it would not come right.

Will try and add something to the proof tomorrow—but don't suppose one small story more or less makes much difference.

The dedication is—

To Jinny, after a hard winter.[3]

I was awfully sorry not to see you when you were in London but perhaps we will get together this fall or in the spring at the latest. I must write Scott? Is he still at Brandywine Hundreds and is his novel finished.

About the little bull in the cut—I'm sorry I ever interfered with him because what he has gained in masculinity he seems to have lost in energy and horns.[4] If there is time perhaps the artist could look at the pictures again. But if it would hold things up please do not bother. No one reading English would care much how a bull looked anyway—but this present seems to have not so much muscle in his neck as a hump on his back like a buffalo. But do not let me delay things with this tauro-culture. I don't have to pass on any more of them. Any way you have it fixed will be all right—or if it left out.

I'm mailing the proofs now with this. Registering them—which will delay them slightly—but insure the stamps being stolen off and them dropped in some galician rio.

Thanks ever so much for the Fifty Grand clippings and the bookstore booklet. I'm glad to see the sun still advertised. How many has it sold by now?

It was funny about the % 50 Grand coming out just at the time of this epidemic of fouls in N.Y. fights.[5] The Nouvelle Revue Francaise published it in August as Cinquante Mille Dollars—a very imposing sum to a french audience with the dollar at 25 even. It had a certain success I think due to the number of dollars mentioned.

Yours always,
Ernest Hemingway.

This is a wonderful town—the loveliest I've ever been in in Spain and am working pretty well. Good trout fishing back in the hills between here and La Coruna.

[Enclosed typewritten list, with the first two lines and the numbers handwritten in pencil:]

Contents
Men Without Women

1 The Undefeated

2 In Another Country

3 Hills Like White Elephants

4 The Killers

5 La Patria

6 Fifty Grand

7 A Simple Enquiry

8 Ten Indians

9 A Canary for One

10 An Alpine Idyll

11 A Pursuit Race

12 Today is Friday

13 Banal Story

14 Now I Lay Me

[Typewritten in left margin, perpendicular to the other text on the page:]

Dedication

To Jinny, after a hard winter.

PUL, TLS

1 On a separate half sheet of paper EH typed a list of the fourteen stories in the order in which they would actually appear in *MWW*.
2 In the front matter of the first edition of *MWW*, the list of "Books by Ernest Hemingway" would include *IOT* (published by Boni & Liveright) along with EH's three Scribner's titles.
3 EH would change his mind about dedicating *MWW* to Pauline's sister Jinny, as he would cable Perkins on 6 September 1927. He would explain his reasons in his 1 October 1927 letter to his mother-in-law, Mary Pfeiffer.
4 The illustration of the bull for the title page and dust jacket of *MWW* had been altered in response to EH's letter to Perkins of 10 June [1927].
5 "Fifty Grand" is about a boxer who throws a fight by hitting his opponent below the belt. Following the controversial finish to the 21 July 1927 championship bout at Yankee Stadium between Jack Dempsey and Jack Sharkey, New York City saw a string of contentious results in July and August of 1927, leading to public outcry for better refereeing.

To Waldo Peirce, [c. 20 August 1927]

Hotel Suizo

Santiago de Campostela

Spain

Dear Waldo:

Never head from you after we left Valencia. What the hell? Or did you write to Cook's at Madrid.[1] I went around there and left forwarding directions but nothing ever came. We went up to Madrid—then La Coruña then here.

This is the cockeyedest swell place I've ever been in in my life. Not a foreigner—good Pension for 10 pesetas—good rooms—wonderful goddamned wonderful town and fine hilly country— Galicia— Good trout streams in every direction—wild country. Weve been out fishing twice— Didnt get many on acct not knowing their habits but saw, the last time, some hellish big ones. Would run 3–4 pounds. Got 4 on flies day before yesterday— Cooked them up with a mess of frogs legs.

This town is better looking and sweller buildings than Toledo even. 2 hrs. ½ on the bus from either La Coruña or Vigo. No railway from Coruna but one from Vigo.

We'll probably stay down here another week or 10 days and then work north.

Bull fights all shot to hell— Belmonte, Marcial Lalanda, Nino, Cagancho, all cogida.

Eight cogidas yesterday.

Dont think we'll go back to Madrid— Sick of City and no exercise— From here we'll go up to Hendaye or some place where you can swim and send for the bikes. How about the place where Ivy was? This is a hell of a swell place. Only trouble is it rains a lot. But suppose it does that everywhere this summer. How are you and how did the pictures come out? Are you working? I've just finished the proofs on the next damn book.[2] I think you'd like this damn place if you'd like to come down—it's got 46 Churches all with bells— If you'd come down wire me.[3] The food's good here at the hotel and no <u>chinchas</u>.[4] If you'd be coming down we'd stick here a couple of weeks more any way. It's a swell place to work.

Yours always,

Ernest

Love to Ivy

Colby, ALS

1 EH and Pauline traveled from Valencia to Madrid on or near 1 August. Thomas Cook, the travel agency.
2 EH returned the proofs for *MWW* to Perkins on 17 August.
3 Peirce replied in a letter of 12 September [1927] that EH's letter from Santiago had missed him and was forwarded several times. Had he received the letter earlier, Peirce wrote, he would have joined EH in Galicia (JFK).
4 *Chinches*: bedbugs (Spanish).

To William B. Smith, Jr., 21 August [1927]

Write care of The Guaranty.

This place is in Galicia—August 21.

Smith—

Yours with enclosures to hand. Answering yours as to where Dempsey could hurt sharkey with a punch between the solar plexus and the belt—[1]

Anyehwre on either side under the ribs Smith. More birds are knocked out by body punches that land on the liver—which lobes downthere under

1 Hadley Hemingway and Pauline Pfeiffer at Schruns, Austria, where Pauline joined the Hemingways on their winter vacation, December 1925–January 1926.

2 Pauline Pfeiffer and Ernest Hemingway, Schruns, December 1925–January 1926.

3 Hadley and Ernest with son Bumby, Schruns, March 1926. Returning from a trip to New York to meet with publishers, Ernest had lingered in Paris to carry on his affair with Pauline. He later wrote that when he saw his wife and son standing beside the track as his train pulled into Schruns, "I wished I had died before I loved anyone but her."

4 Maxwell Perkins, Hemingway's editor at Scribner's from the time they met in February 1926 until Perkins's death in 1947.

5 Skiing the Silvretta range in Austria, Frau Lent, Hemingway, John Dos Passos, and Gerald Murphy, March 1926.

6 Gerald and Sara Murphy, on the beach near their Villa America at Cap d'Antibes, summer 1926. Photo © Estate of Honoria Murphy Donnelly/Licensed by VAGA, New York, NY.

7 Zelda and F. Scott Fitzgerald with their daughter, Scottie, at Juan-les-Pins, where they spent the summer of 1926.

8 and 9 Bumby with Ernest and with Hadley on the beach at Juan-les-Pins, where the Hemingways stayed from late May to early July 1926. Ernest enclosed both photos in a letter to his father of 24 July 1926.

10 Gerald and Sara Murphy, Pauline, Ernest, and Hadley at the fiesta in
Pamplona, July 1926, a month before Ernest and Hadley separated.

11 Before Hadley would grant Ernest a divorce to marry Pauline, she stipulated
that the two remain apart for three months without communication. Hadley
called off the separation agreement in mid-November 1926, saying she wished to
proceed with the divorce.

12 Ernest with Virginia Pfeiffer, Pauline's sister, Gstaad, Switzerland, February 1927.

13 Hemingway sent this photo to Maxwell Perkins with the caption, "This to re-assure you if you hear reports of another of your authors dying of drink." Gstaad, February 1927.

14 Ernest and Pauline at the time of their wedding in Paris on 10 May 1927.

15 Bumby at the Hemingway family home in Oak Park, Illinois, during a visit to the United States with Hadley. The caption, in Grace Hemingway's hand, reads, "Bumby with First Gun & U.S. Flag. May. 1927."

16 Near Pamplona, July 1927. Hemingway enclosed this photo in a letter of 1 October 1927 to his new mother-in-law, Mary Pfeiffer, describing it as "me carressing what the photographer hopes would be a bull–but what is very [o]bviously a very tired and resigned old steer."

17 At Shakespeare and Company, Paris: employee Myrsine Moschos, her sister Hélène, Sylvia Beach, and Hemingway, March 1928. Hemingway inscribed the photo to Beach and, with a line pointing to his bandaged head, wrote, "E. Hemingway. His mark." He had been injured when a bathroom skylight crashed and gouged his forehead.

18 Portrait by Helen
Breaker, Paris, March 1928.

19 Pauline, Hotel Ambos
Mundos, Havana, April
1928.

20 Clarence and Ernest Hemingway in a chance meeting in Key West, 10 April 1928. Father and son had not seen each other since Christmas 1923.

21 Ernest's uncle Willoughby Hemingway, Ernest, Grace Hall Hemingway, and Pauline (seven months pregnant), 10 April 1928. The new Model A Ford was a wedding gift from Pauline's Uncle Gus Pfeiffer, delivered to the couple in Key West.

22 Hemingway's handwritten caption on the back of the photo reads, "Native Fisherman (Sea Indian) holding ferocious barracuda." Spring 1928.

23 Hemingway, Bill Smith, and Captain Bra Saunders, Key West, spring 1928.

24 Ernest and Waldo Peirce with their catch, May 1928. Photo inscribed to Sylvia Beach.

25 John Dos Passos, Hemingway, Captain Bra Saunders, and unidentified companion, Dry Tortugas, May 1928. From the scrapbook of Waldo Peirce, Colby College.

I can't seem to think of a way
To say what I'd like most to say
To my very dear son,
Whose book is just done,
Except give him my love
and "HOORAY."

26 Clarence Hemingway enclosed this poem in a letter to Ernest of 23 October 1928, congratulating him on completing the manuscript of *A Farewell to Arms*.

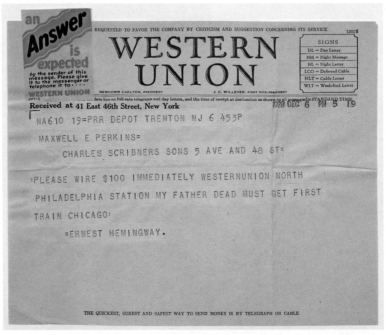

27 En route by train from New York City to Key West with his son, Hemingway received the cabled news of his father's death. Needing money to travel immediately to Chicago, he wired Maxwell Perkins. At Philadelphia, he left Bumby in the care of a Pullman porter to continue to Key West. Ernest did not yet know that Clarence Hemingway had committed suicide, shooting himself at home that morning, 6 December 1928.

28 Patrick Hemingway, born in Kansas City, 28 June 1928.

29 Ernest and Bumby, Key West, early 1929.

30 Portrait of Hemingway by Waldo Peirce, 1928.

the ribs than anywhere else. Anybody punch can be dangerous if it lands flushed and the gut muscle is relaxed.

When you saw Sharkey taking them in the gut the muscles were taught and they were not k.o. punches.

But the solar plexus as the place where a boxer has to be ko-ed by a body punch was invented by the box writers. Anywhere on the body can drop a man if it hits hard enough.

Whether Dempsey fouled him or not I can't have an opinion on even from the pictures nor the critics. The intelligent critics like McGeehan don't know enough about fights and despise the whole game sothat they are prjudiced by their intelligence—and the birds that have seen thousands are as dumb as Sparrow Robertson.[2]

It would seem to be down on the volumnes for Dempsey to win as a bigger drawing card than Sharkey for Rickard's gate in Chicago.[3] And since the series between the Sox and the Reds few of the things leading to the biggest gates have been passed up in professional sport.[4]

What dope have you on the Paolino fight? It is hard to judge from here where the only available news seems to a certain extent prejudiced shall we say— There being a booklet on sale here called Paolino Is Invincible! and all the comentaries taking that tone. It would seem however that that the lad was jobbed at least as to the bending in of Delaney's coquille if that's true. I don't believe a goddam word in the Spanish papers—but if Paolino had lasted seven rounds with Delaney I should think he would have a chance to win as gawd knows he is tough—and it seems can sock again. I imagine Delaney must have just made a monkey out of him at the start—left handing him to death. But if he could why didn't he knock him out. I think the Virile Vasco must have something—perhaps he is like Jeff.[5]

This is a swell town—Santiago de Campostela—clean and nice like Pamplona and cockeyed beautiful with a wonderful cathedral swell old buildings and grand hilly country around. Hundreds of streams. So far we have only tried two of them. Got two trout the first time. Four the next and two again. Fishing flies exclusively now and miss lots of strikes. The last ones we got were very nice size and chunky. Saw one that would run a good three pounds. The small streams are ruined by the natives who poke the trout out with poles into wicker baskets that they hold over the holes. The big streams are like the Sturgeon—lots of trout—and big ones—but temperamental. they hit a McGinty fine though and strike well when the sun goes under.[6] We go about forty minutes out of town on an Autobus that goes on the road to La Coruna and then itvis about half an hour to the big stream. It's about the size of the Sturge and I hope to take some big ones. I know damn well we c[o]uld get some at night—there are lots of holes ten and twelve feet deep—but in August fishing in the middle of a day they are pretty wise.

A man can pick up a mess of frog's legs along the stream any time and Pauline and I cook up the trout and the frog's legs and drink a bottle of vino tinto—the frawgs strike at a fly dangled two feet away from them. The enditer found himself and wife on the stream figuring on eating fish and frogs and without other provisiones except lard and salt and no knife! The teeth were brought into play to start the first frog but due to the strong taste of same additional frogs were separated from their limbs by whamming them hard against the foot holding them by the limbs—until something broke. Once something breaks on a frog I can handle it. The trout—four of them—were cleaned with a Yale lock key.

No word from Deak [Foley]. He claimed he was coming to Spain and I told him to leave me know through the Guaranteed Trustful.

What is the oil dope.[7] How are you vending? You have outvended anyone I ever heard of. I've done the proofs of the next book and sent them of to Scribenheims. I doubt if fairy's sell to many fairies as I have never heard of a fairy buying anything. Howver I shouldn't wonder if your agent was a fairy. Most vivadores of the writing business—agents etc. that I have encountered have seemed to have a little fairy in the home or office. Leave that not discourage you Smith—if he sells the yarns and slips you the monetary return let who will have their will with his anus nights.

I am glad as hell you are getting one hundred of the handsome ones for a story now. That is more than we could make digging potatoes Smith—even by the old negro method.[8]

Writing is a wonderful thing. Speaking of writing write the writer all about the Bay, Chicago, etc. etc. Belmonte, Marcial, Nino, and everybody else have been cogida and the bull season bitched.

Write. Immer[9]

Miller

PUL, TL with typewritten signature; postmark: SANTIAGO / (60), 23 AGO 27 7 T

The envelope is typewritten and addressed to "William B. Smith Jr. / care Y. K. Smith / 715 Rush Street / Chicago / Illinois / Estados Unidos del America," with the typewritten instruction "Please Forward." The letter was forwarded to Smith at Villa Maria in Long Beach, Indiana, with a forwarding postmark from Chicago of 5 September 1927.

1 EH is apparently responding to a letter from Smith that remains unlocated. Surviving among EH's papers at JFK are Smith's letters of 15 June and 13 August 1927, but neither mentions the 21 July heavyweight boxing title bout between Dempsey and Sharkey that EH discusses here, which Dempsey won by knockout.

2 William O'Connell McGeehan (1879–1933), American sportswriter with the *New York Herald Tribune* and Scottish-born American sportswriter William Harrison "Sparrow" Robertson (1859–1941) with the *New York Herald*, Paris Edition.

3 George Lewis "Tex" Rickard (1870–1929), American boxing promoter and enthusiast. Between 1921 and 1927, Rickard promoted a series of heavyweight title fights featuring Jack Dempsey, each bout earning more than a million dollars in gate receipts. The 22 September 1927 rematch between Dempsey and Gene Tunney would bring in a record gate receipt of more than $2.6 million.

4 EH refers to the infamous "Black Sox" scandal of 1919 in which eight members of the Chicago White Sox were accused of conspiring with gamblers to throw the World Series baseball championship to the Cincinnati Reds.

5 Paulino Uzcudun, known as "the Basque Woodchopper," lost to Jack Delaney (1900–1948) on 11 August 1927, disqualified by a low blow. After the fight, Delaney's protective cup was found to be bent, a condition that Uzcudun's supporters claimed existed before the fight began. *Vasco*: Basque (Spanish).

6 EH and Smith had frequently fished together on the Sturgeon and Black rivers in Michigan. The McGinty fly, resembling a bumblebee or wasp, was widely used at the time in fly-fishing for trout.

7 In his 13 August 1927 letter, Smith complained he had heard nothing more about the oil prospects near Horton Bay. "They may be drilling wells right & left, or they may not have started" (JFK).

8 During their youth, Smith and his siblings, Y.K. and Kate, had spent summers with their maternal aunt and guardian, Laura M. Charles (c. 1855–1924), at her farm near Horton Bay, where their friendship with EH began. In a letter to Smith of 6 December [1924], EH remembered the "swell times" they had on the farm, "potato digging and the whole damn thing" (*Letters* vol. 2, 185–86).

9 Always (German).

To Ezra Pound, 23 August [1927]

Hotel Suizo

Santiago

Galicia

Spain

Aug 23.

Dear Ezra:

Send me No 2 so it will inspire peristallic action for No 3.[1] Will always try and fill any honoured seat.

(The above seems to have gotten beyond original intention!)

Saw old Ford 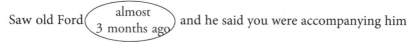 and he said you were accompanying him to N.Y. on a lecture tour this fall. ? ? ? What the hell? Ford said New York only city to live in. Yes, quite, Paris very charming to run over to etc. He'd seen my people (I.E.) my family. That's more than I'd do![2]

All bulls drowned by the rain.

Have been living quietly here—Santiago de Campostela—Saint Jacques de Campostelle fine place.

Archibald is in New England—even at that I cant feel that either New England nor the New Criterion are so god damned new.

I have written Hickock urging him to come down here for the early fall drinking season which starts on September 1st. This is really a hell of a fine place.

How are you and how is Dorothy and how is the Youthful Exile—have you taught him to say "Shit on Coolidge," yet? I sent Bumby to America equipped with many such useful phrases.[3]

Will be here for 10 days or so more but due to the postal speed and the lack of r.r. to anywhere but Vigo better send it to Guaranty Trust Co. of N.Y. 1 rue des Italiens Paris who will forward.

Yrs. Immer

Hem.

Yale, ALS

1 The second and third numbers of *The Exile* were dated Autumn 1927 and Spring 1928.
2 Ford Madox Ford proposed that Pound join him in October and November 1927 for a
lecture tour with stops in New York and Chicago, and he even set up speaking and writing
assignments to pay for Pound's trip. While Pound called Ford's efforts "most noble," he
refused to visit the United States (Pound to Ford, ALS, 23 June [1927], in *Pound/Ford: The
Story of a Literary Friendship*, ed. Brita Lindberg-Seyersted [New York: A New Directions
Book, 1982], 89–90). Ford had visited Clarence and Grace Hemingway in Oak Park in
February 1927. In a letter to EH of 20 February 1927, his mother reported, "We enjoyed
your friend Mr. Ford Madox Ford very much. Hope he was not too bored with us . . . Mr.
Ford is a dear" (JFK).
3 The "Youthful Exile" is Omar Shakespear, Pound's son through marriage, who was almost a
year old by this time. Omar lived primarily with his maternal grandmother in England, and
Pound rarely saw him.

To Archibald MacLeish, 29 August [1927]

Aug. 29—

Santiago de Campostela

Dear Archie—

Yours of aug. 13 to handand contents noted. You are very sound about G.
and I agree with you perfectly.[1] As for Mrs. Bullet knowing all about me the
bitch where in hell does she get that stuff.[2] I went to their house once and
refused many an inviation and didn't ask them to ours—and believe that is
the best way to make half kikes know all about you. I did know her when her
hair was blonde but that was in Constantinople and besides the wench sic
was surrounded by naval officers.[3]

We will go ski-ing we certainly will. We were thinking about it yesterday.
By God ski-ing is lovely.[4]

Speaking of the bull fights old Marcial tore-ared yesterday—his first
apperance since the goring we told you about in Valencia about the 27th of
July. That is fast work. However Villalta, all of him including his neck was
caught by the bull last Thursday in Bilboa and the horn entered in the
scrotum and the furthest point it reached was the navel. Due to the peculiar
formation of the horn they couldn't get Villalta off and he was given 5
complete revolutions by theanimal and carried all around—pretty good for
a bull with such a big chap as Villalta. But the papers say, dentro de la

gravidad, that he will live all right and this morning's Tuesday's paper says he can now urinate. The horn really went all the way to the naval or navel but did not puncture the intestines for which all agree that Villalta was a lucky felllow. However arrangements are being made to get him a new peritoneum if possible.[5]

We leave here Thursday—grand fishing yesterday—caught four only but all big ones—two enormous bastards and had a fine time— These trouts having been converted to Christianity by the apostle St. James know a thing or two by now. They are pursued by dinamitors, seiners, basket workers armed with pike poles and spears—and to catch tme on a dry fly you have to fool them.

Hickock writes that the Paris police are very pleased at being able to guard TWO American institutions—The Guaranty Trust and the Consulate with onle ONE million police.[6]

All rioting has been censured out of the Spanish papers.

We go north to Palencia—then to Hendaye and then to Paris the end of September—it will be cockeyed swell to ski next winter and we will do it for a couple of months maybe. Let's stay up at Saanenmoser—[7]

How are you working? I saw the bloody Atlantic with me as a bull fighter in Ferench and Spanish armies. Shit from the city of Gov. Fuller.[8]

Pauline sends her love to youse both and papa aussi—yrs for you gents to hurry back— Ada's letter was grand.

Pappy

We've sent Jinny [Pfeiffer] three wires and two letters without being able to locate her. She was reported off for portugal.

LOC, TLS; postmark: SANTIAGO / CORUNA, 29 AGO 27

On the envelope flap, EH wrote "Well look how stupid Papa was." Postmarks and notations on the envelope indicate that the letter followed a circuitous route before reaching MacLeish. EH had mistakenly addressed the envelope to MacLeish in Plainfield, Massachussetts, although MacLeish was staying in Ashfield. A notation on the envelope reads "Try / N. J." A forwarding postmark reads: PLAINFIELD, MA, SEP 16 / 1927. EH's typewritten return address (Guaranty Trust Company in Paris) is crossed out in ink, and in a European script is written "c/o Shakespeare & Co." along with the bookstore's Paris address.

1 In his letter to EH of 13 August [1927], MacLeish wrote about Gerald Murphy: "I always knew and so told you that Gerald would get over whatever was eating him the moment he

saw you. I didn't know for sure that you'd get over your irritation with Gerald ditto. These damn school girl quarrels of Geralds are the things that make it so hard for me to believe in his affection. Relationships built on your personality and my personality just aren't relationships" (JFK).

2 EH refers to Louise Bryant Bullitt (née Mohan, 1885–1936). A well-known journalist, short-term member of the Provincetown Players, and lover of Eugene O'Neill, Louise Bryant was married to the Communist journalist and activist John Reed from 1916 to 1920. She married American foreign correspondent and diplomat William Christian Bullitt (1891–1967) in 1923. In his 13 August letter, MacLeish reported that Mrs. Bullitt "says she knows ALL about Pappy" and questioned how that could be, since MacLeish understood that "Pappy knew her very slightly and respected him for it."

3 EH was in Constantinople from late September to late October 1922 covering the Greco-Turkish War for the *Toronto Star* while also filing reports with Hearst's International News Service with the byline "John Hadley." Louise Bryant was also in Constantinople in 1922 reporting on the war for the International News Service. EH alludes to *The Jew of Malta* (c. 1589–1590), by Christopher Marlowe (1564–1593). Replying to a charge of fornication, the Jew Barabas says, "but that was in another country, and besides the wench is dead" (Act 4 scene 1, lines 43–44). EH alludes to the line in the title of his short story "In Another Country" and in Chapter 8 of *SAR*, when Jake Barnes introduces Bill Gorton to Brett Ashley as a taxidermist: "'That was in another country,' Bill said, 'and besides all the animals were dead.'"

4 In his letter MacLeish asked, "When do we go to Switzerland?" (JFK). That winter, the Hemingways and MacLeishes would spend another skiing vacation in Gstaad, Switzerland, where they had been the year before.

5 Villalta was injured at Bilbao on 25 August, according to the 1927 bullfighting yearbook *Toros y Toreros. Dentro de la gravedad*: notwithstanding the seriousness of the situation (Spanish).

6 The execution in Boston of Italian anarchists Nicola Sacco (1891–1927) and Bartolomeo Vanzetti (1888–1927) on 23 August 1927 ignited worldwide protests against the American government, and police officers had been injured during a riot in Paris. EH alludes to the reported declaration by Maurice Bokanowski (1879–1928), French Minister of Commerce and Aviation: "A million French comrades-in-arms are ready to protect members of the American Legion from possible outbreaks in France during the coming convention" ("Bokanowski Assures Legion of Protection," *New York Times*, 28 August 1927, 3).

7 Saanenmöser, a ski resort near Gstaad in the Bernese Oberland region of Switzerland.

8 A short note about EH appeared in the "Contributors' Column" of the July 1927 issue of the *Atlantic Monthly*, which also printed his short story "Fifty Grand." The column reported that, in his "remarkable career," EH had been "an amateur boxer, newspaper man, bull-fighter (in Spain), and soldier of fortune. In the war, he fought with the French and Italian armies" (140). Alvan Tufts Fuller (1879–1958), Republican governor of Massachusetts from 1925 to 1929, received considerable criticism for his handling of the Sacco–Vanzetti case.

To Edward J. O'Brien, 31 August [1927]

Santiago de Campostela
August 31.

Dear Edward,

I feel badly about Scribner's withholding the Fifty Grand but it comes out this way. They are bringing out the book of stories late in the fall—there are only two long stories in the book—The Undefeated and Fifty Grand. No one would buy the book for any other stories—the twelve other short ones are the kind that drive away the purchasers and after this wire—enclosed—I don't know what I can do with them when I've already taken and spent an advance of $750 on the book. It would have to sell pretty well anyway to earn that.[1]

I just had a royalty statement from Cape claiming they had only sold 124 copies of In Our Time and that I owed them Pounds 20/18/0 on an advance of 25 pounds! Liveright claims I still owe them on the first In Our Time.[2]

I'm sure Scribner's would have been glad for you to have the Fifty G. if the Undefeated had not already been published in the Best Short Stories—if the 50 G. is too, they haven't anything to shoot with. If I was not in the position of having sold it to them and they being my only source of income I could tell them to go to hell.

Of course I could anyway. I told you in Paris you could have it—as you can have anything I have—only I wish you'd ask me for something else.

I'm awfully glad if you liked the Sun etc. I'd like to read Lawson and it's a shame he's dead. But it seems a habit that all the good writers have. Maybe I can get Cape to loan me a vol. instead of giving me an advance on another book.[3] It's because of Cape and Liveright that I think so much of Scribner's and hate to go against them.

Either The Killers or In Another Country that Scribner's published wd make good stories if you wanted them and I don't think Scribner's would have any objection. I see why they want to hang onto the Fifty G. They wanted an absolutely unpublished long story for the book—and then at the last minute the Atlantic took it. I told them I would have another long bull fight story—A Lack of Passion—about 18,000 words—and worked and worked over the damn thing and couldn't get it right and so wouldn't let them have it. So they were figuring on The Undefeated and 50 Grand and are afraid they won't have anything new if you take the 50 G. too.

You have done more for me than anyone and I owe you more—but I don't think when you see how it shapes up on the book you would ask for that particular story. But anyhow I am very complimented by your asking for it and this is certainly a fine example of how not to write letters. But throw out anything that does not sound right because I am sure if we could talk we would agree.

Yours always,
Ernest Hemingway

The Guaranty Trust is permanent address

Either Killers or In Another Country are <u>better</u> stories than Fifty Grand— I'll force Scribners on them if they object—but I see their point on 50 g.

UMD, TLS

1 In a letter to Scribner's of 9 August 1927, O'Brien had requested permission to reprint "Fifty Grand" in *The Best Short Stories of 1927*, which was scheduled for publication in November 1927 (PUL). A cable from Scribner's to EH dated 24 August stated "Withholding Fifty Grand from O'Brien book because appearance there this fall would reduce importance of your book" (PUL). In a letter to O'Brien of 1 September 1927, Perkins would echo EH's explanation that Scribner's could not give its permission because "Fifty Grand," together with "The Undefeated" (already published in *The Best Short Stories of 1926*), constituted almost half of the forthcoming *MWW*, which was scheduled for publication in October (PUL).
2 Cape's British edition of *IOT* was published in London on 23 September 1926. Boni & Liveright had published the first American edition on 5 October 1925.
3 Australian poet and short-story writer Henry Lawson (1867–1922). In 1927 Jonathan Cape published a two-volume edition of Lawson's short stories, *While the Billy Boils*, for The Traveller's Library series. In EH's posthumously published novel *Islands in the Stream* (1970), the character Roger Davis stays up late reading Thomas Hudson's copy of Lawson's stories.

To Maxwell Perkins, 31 August [1927]

Santiago—Aug. 31

Dear Mr. Perkins—

The proofs were sent off August 17th. Hope you have them by now.

I had your wire about witholding 50 grand from the O'Brien book and quite agree with you.[1] I hated like hell for O'Brien to ask for that—he has been a very good friend to me and done more for my liturary careeah than anyone except yourself and Ellery Sedgwick who seems something like Santa Claus in the days when we believed in Santa Claus. I have just had a note from him asking me to use my influence with Scribner's to get permission—he had not yet had a refusal from you but feared one—and I have just answered that I can't do it because I see your point in not wanting it—one of the only two long stories in the book—published anywhere else.

So be very firm and refuse to let it be published no matter what you hear my public or private attitude is.

On the other hand I suggested to O'Brien that he ask for either the Killers or In Another Country if he wanted a story. I don't think printing either of those would hurt the book any. They are neither as "important" quotes as 50 Grand but are probably in the long run better stories.

That is all about O'Brien. Except that I feel badly about turning him down—but worse about his asking. Although there is no reason why a person should not ask for a thing, I suppose. O'Brien published a story called My Old Man of mine when it had never been published in a magazine, violating all his rules, it had been turned down by every magazine except Scribner's and The Atlantic and dedicated the Short Story book to me. The only reason the dedication did not help more was that the name was mis-spelled Hemenway—also on the story—and no one believed I wrote it.[2] He worked on Liveright to make him publish In Our Time, got Cape to publish it in London, obtained me various offers of great wealth from Hearst and an invitation to be the distinguished American guest of the Pen Club for at London last Spring. Fortunately I was unable to attend due to the presence of the English Channel or some other valid excuse. So I hate to turn O'Brien down—but at the same time I can't take the bread out of all our mouths and give it to O'Brien. But if he asks for anything else in the book I would like him to have it because he is not all this but a very good friend too.

Leave tomorrow morning for Palencia. There is one train leaving at six a.m. and getting there at five minutes past midnight and another at 3.59 in the afternoon getting there at 3.27 the next morning. A little beyond Palencia a train can be boarded which goes to Hendaye. These are the only connections for getting north. It is because of the difficulty of facing one or the other of these two trains that I've been so long in Galicia.

Could you tell me what The Sun has done up to date? Mrs. Hemingway will be in New York for three or four days before sailing on the Lancastria Oct.22 and may wish to draw some of the royalties due. If there are any— and if they have not been paid.

My own experience with the literary life has not as yet included receiving royalties—but I hope by keeping down advances to some day have this take place.

Yours always,

Ernest Hemingway.

I sent the proofs first class registered. It was very hard convincing them in the post office that there was anything in the world worth that many Spanish stamps.

PUL, TLS

1 Perkins's cable to EH of 24 August 1927 reads: "Withholding Fifty Grand from O'Brien book because appearance there this fall would reduce importance of your book" (PUL).
2 "My Old Man" appeared for the first time in *The Best Short Stories of 1923* (Boston: Small, Maynard, 1924).

To Maxwell Perkins, 6 September 1927

TW84 HENDAYE 22
LCD MAXWELL PERKINS CHARLES SCRIBNERS SONS NY
PROOFS MAILED AUGUST SEVENTEENTH PLEASE CHANGE
DEDICATION TO READ QUOTES TO EVAN SHIPMAN QUOTES
HEMINGWAY
5TH AVE 48

PUL, Cable; destination receipt stamp: SEP 6–1927

EH's cable, sent from Hendaye, refers to the proofs and the new dedication for *MWW*.

To Maxwell Perkins, [7 September 1927]

TW27 HENDAYE 13
LCD MAXWELL PERKINS SCRIBNERS PUBLISHERS NY
WOULD APPRECIATE PERMITTING OBRIEN REPRINT KILLERS
HEMINGWAY
597 5Th

PUL, Cable; destination receipt stamp: SEP8–1927

The cable, which survives in the Scribner's files, bears the notation in Perkins's hand "Proof received."

To Edward J. O'Brien, 7 September 1927

September 7, 1927
Hendaye—Hotel Barron

Dear Edward,

Thanks awfully for your wire. I got it and your letter forwarded here yesterday and this morning wired Scribners—WOULD APPRECIATE YOUR PERMITTING OBRIEN REPRINT KILLERS[1]

So imagine that was all right anyway even without the wire. I'm awfully glad you took the Killers. And I feel very badly you had so much trouble, cables etc.

I wish the hell you'd been at Santiago. It's the grandest town I've ever lived in—hell of a way to get to though unless you go in by sea from Vigo or Coruna—the twenty two hours traveling from Venta de Banos keeps most of the boys away. This place has a fine beach about two miles long and a Spanish summer population that thinks they are living on the cheap franc—which by the same token ruins me. You ought to be here to talk Basque.

I don't see how Scribner's could hold out on the Killers. I gave them seven or so stories without trying to sell them so they could have plenty of new stuff in it and I wrote Perkins from Santiago the same time I wrote you asking him to let you have any you asked for—suggesting the Killers or In Another Country. I'll send off the formal letter to Dodd Mead at the same time as this.[2]

Caught some pretty good trout outside of Santiago fishing a McGinty fly. They'd been fished for since before the Apostle converted the gallegans to Christianity and of late years the Christian Gallegans have been fishing with dynamite, poison, chloride of lime and one thing and another so that I had to use a twelve foot leader and make the McGinty act very Irish. But caught four big sons of bitches the night before I wrote you and then went out to the same stream at dusk the next night but the rain had roiled the water and they wouldn't rise.

Galicia's supposed to be the rainiest part of Europe but it only rained about four times all of August and the streams were very low and clear. I've got some damned disease or condition that swells the hands and feet and makes them itch like chilblains—my hands itched so last night that I couldn't sleep. Suppose I might try crossing them with silver.[3] Bought a bottle of chutney today and it was over half raisins. Put up by Liptons.[4] That seems to be all the news. Going back to San Sebastian Sunday to see Belmonte and try to smuggle a fine picture out of the country. Left it in San Sebastian while I crossed back and forth a few times to see what is the most practical way for a gentleman to leave Spain without annoyance.

You are a fine guy and you don't owe me anything for cables.

Yours always

Ernest

UMD, TLS

1 In both a cable and letter to Scribner's of 5 September 1927, O'Brien requested permission to include "The Killers" in *The Best Short Stories of 1927* (PUL). O'Brien's cable to EH and the forwarded letter that EH mentions here have not been located.

2 O'Brien's publisher was Dodd, Mead & Company of New York.

3 At the time, nitrate of silver was commonly considered to be a cure for chilblains.

4 Although best known as a purveyor of tea, Scottish entrepreneur Sir Thomas J. Lipton (1848–1931) began his career in the retail grocery business in Glasgow.

To George Norton Northrop, 8 September 1927

Hendaye—France

September 8, 1927

Dear Mr. Northrop,

I was very sorry not to have gotten your note enclosing Scott's card until it was too late to answer, even by wire, before you sailed. And I was much sorrier not to have been able to dine with you. It was very good of you to ask me and I hope that we may meet some time, in Paris again, or in Chicago. When you come to Paris again you must let me know beforehand and dine with us.

I hope that you had a good summer and that the weather was not too bad— Spain was very hot or very rainy and it seems very quiet and muggy to be back in France again.

Please remember me to Scott when you write him. I owe him a letter and many other things.

Yours very truly,

Ernest Hemingway.

James Cummins Bookseller, New York, catalog 121, lot 32 (illustrated), TLS

Northrop and his wife, Catharine (née Clerihew, 1888–1971), sailed from Cherbourg on 25 August 1927 aboard the *Antonia*, arriving in Quebec on 3 September. In his letter to F. Scott Fitzgerald of [c. 15 September 1927], EH would mention having received Northrop's note with Fitzgerald's calling card enclosed just as Northrop was leaving Europe.

To Eric Pinker, 13 September 1927

HENDAYE PLAGE 773 48 13 18$^{\underline{H}}$

REEXPEDIE DE PARIS 45 P$^{\underline{CV}}$ 125

=ERIC S PINKER 78 BROOH ST GOSVENOR SQUARE LONDRES 11

=YOUR LETTER RECEVED TODAY AM RETURNING TO PARIS SEPTEMBRE TWENTITH STOP VERY GLAD RECEIVE PROPOSITION[1] STOP ADDRESS HOTEL BARRON HENDAYEPLAGE BASSESPYRENEES STOP PERMANENT PARIS ADDRESS CARE

GUARANTY TRUST COMPANY OF NEW YORK ENEST
HEMINGWAY=

NYPL-Berg, Cable; destination receipt stamp: W.STRAND / 13SEP27 / FOR
MORNING DELIVERY

1 A reference to Heinemann's offer, discussed in more detail in EH's letters to Eric Pinker, 23
September 1927, and to Charles Scribner, 1 October 1927.

To Clarence Hemingway, 9–14 September [1927]

Hotel Barron
Hendaye Plage
(Basses Pyrenees)
September 9–14

Dear Dad:

Thanks very much for your letter and for forwarding the letter to Uncle
Tyley. I had a good letter from him yesterday.[1]

You cannot know how badly I feel about having caused you and Mother
so much shame and suffering—but I could not write you about all of my and
Hadley's troubles even if it were the thing to do.[2] It takes two weeks for a
letter to cross the Atlantic and I have tried not to transfer all the hell I have
been through to anyone by letter. I love Hadley and I love Bumby— Hadley
and I split up— I did not desert her nor was I committing adultery with
anyone. I was living in the apartment with Bumby—looking after him while
Hadley was away on a trip and it was when she came back from this trip that
she decided she wanted the definite divorce. We arranged everything and
there was no scandal and no disgrace. Our trouble had been going on for a
long time. It was entirely my fault and it is no ones business. I have nothing
but love admiration and respect for Hadley and while we are busted up I
have not in anyway lost Bumby. He lived with me in Switzerland after the
divorce and he is coming back in November and will spend this winter with
me in the mountains.

You are fortunate enough to have only been in love with one woman in your life. For over a year I had been in love with two people and had been absolutely faithful to Hadley. When Hadley decided that we had better get a divorce the girl with whom I was in love was in America. I had not heard from her for almost two months. In her last letter she had said that we must not think of each other but of Hadley.

You refer to "Love Pirates," "persons who break up your home etc," and you know that I am hot tempered but I know that it is easy to wish people in Hell when you know nothing of them.[3] I have seen, suffered and been through enough so that I do not wish any one in Hell. It is because I do not want you to suffer with ideas of shame and disgrace that I now write all this.

We have not seen much of each other for a long time and in the meantime our lives have been going on and there has been a year of tragedy in mine and I know you can appreciate how difficult and almost impossible it is for me to write about it.

After we were divorced if Hadley would have wanted me I would have gone back to her. She said that things were better as they were and that we were both better off. I will never stop loving Hadley nor Bumby nor will I cease to look after them. I will never stop loving Pauline Pfeiffer to whom I am married. I have now responsibility toward three people instead of one. Please understand this and know that it doesnt make it easier to write about it.

I do understand how hard it is for you to have to make explanations and answer questions and not hear from me. I am a rotten correspondant and it is almost impossible for me to write about my private affairs. Without seeking it—through the success of my books—all the profits of which I have turned over to Hadley—both in America England, Germany and the Scandanavian countries—because of all this there is a great deal of talk. I pay no attention to any of it and neither must you. I have had come back to me stories people have told about me of every fantastic and scandalous sort— all without foundation. These sorts of stories spring up about all writers—ball players—popular evangelists or any public performers. But it is through the desire to keep my own private life to myself—to give no explanations to anybody—and not to be a public performer personally that I have unwittingly caused you great anxiety. The only way I could keep my private life to myself was to keep it to myself—and I did owe you and Mother a statement on it. But I cant write about it all this time.[4]

I know you dont like the sort of thing I write but that is the difference in our taste and all the critics are not Fanny Butcher. I <u>know</u> that I am not disgracing you in my writing but rather doing something that some day you will be proud of. I cant do it all at once. I feel that eventually my life will not be a disgrace to you either. It also takes a long time to unfold.

You would be so much happier and I would too if you could have confidence in me. When people ask about me say that Ernie never tells us anything about his private life or even where he is but only writes that he is working hard. Dont feel responsible for what I write or what I do. I take the responsibility, I make the mistakes and I take the punishments.

You could if you wanted be even proud of me sometimes—not for what I do for I have not had much success in doing good—but for my work.[5] My work is much more important to me than anything in the world except the happiness of three people and you cannot know how it makes me feel for Mother to be ashamed of what I know as sure as you know that there is a God in heaven is <u>not to be ashamed</u> of.

This seems to go on and on so I'd better stop. Naturally I felt badly about Sunny not coming. I was quite lonely for her and would have given her a fine instructive and pleasant trip and she would have seen many things she won't see with a party.[6]

I'm awfully happy you liked Bumby.[7] He is my very dear and I hope because of my own mistakes and errors to be even a better and wiser father to him and help him avoid things— But I doubt if anyone can teach anyone else much. Anyway he is a fine boy and I hope inside of eight years we can all three go fishing together and you'll see that we are not such tragic figures. Leicester sounds like a fine kid. I have sent off the proofs of my new book [*MWW*]. It has 14 stories and will be out this Fall.

We are going to Paris next week and I am starting a novel and will work very hard until Christmas vacation.[8] I love you very much and love Mother too and I'm sorry this is such a long letter—it probably doesnt explain anything but you're the only person I've written six pages to since I learned to use a pen and ink. I remember Mother saying once that she would rather see me in my grave than something—I forget what—smoking cigarettes perhaps. (If it's of any interest I dont smoke. Havent for almost 3 years. Altho you probably will hear stories that I smoke like a furnace) Many times last winter I would have been very content with anything so simple as being in my grave but there were always enough people who would rather not see me in my grave to whom I owed certain responsibilities to make me keep on going. I just mention this so no one will mention seeing me in my grave— glad to do anything else to oblige.

I wish you'd let Mother read this letter. She wrote me a fine letter last Spring and I'm afraid I never answered it.[9] The reason I havent made either of you a confidant was because I was so upset about Mother accusing me of pandering to the lowest tastes etc in my writing that I shut up like a hermit crab— I knew that if we couldnt see eye to eye on the writing which I knew was no pandering what use was there of going into my life which looked much worse to an outsider.[10]

But anyway I hope you have the dope you both want in this letter—and I'll write often if we can lay off of literary criticism and personalities.

Yours lovingly,
Ernie.

JFK, ALS; postmark: HENDAYE PLAGE / B[SE] PYRENEES, 14–9 / 27

1 EH's great-uncle Benjamin Tyley Hancock (1848–1933), brother of EH's maternal grand-mother, Caroline Hancock Hall (1843–1895). EH is responding to a letter of 8 August 1927 from his father, who wrote, "Yours of July 21st rec'd and Enclosure for Uncle B T. Hancock forwarded by registered mail" (JFK). Neither EH's 21 July letter nor the enclosed letter has been located. However, Uncle Tyley's response to EH of 23 August 1927 reveals that EH had sent him "a kind letter" with an enclosure that "brought the tears": "I fell on my knees and prayed that you might be rewarded for so great a kindness" (JFK).
2 In his letter of 8 August EH's father wrote, "Oh Ernest how could you leave Hadley and Bumby? . . . Your dear mother & I have been heart broken over your conduct." Clarence was upset that EH had ignored his repeated pleas for the complete truth but "wrote Sunny what we had never known." Clarence complained that the rest of the family had to hear of EH and Hadley's divorce through public announcements in Detroit, Boyne City, and Chicago newspapers.
3 Clarence wrote in his letter, "I wish all the 'Love Pirates' were in Hell. Our family has never had such an incident before and trust you may still make your get-away from that individual who split your home."

4　In a letter of 28 September 1927, Clarence would reply: "I am so pleased to hear from you and accept your good letter with all the details in Confidence— No more mention of this matter" (JFK).

5　"I am proud of your progress and have read all your stories and books with great interest. I will look forward to the new book," Clarence would respond on 28 September.

6　In his 8 August letter Clarence wrote, "I assure you that your parents did not refuse Sunny the privelage to go abroad. She had too small amn't of money for a round trip and had excellent advice from those who love her."

7　In the same letter Clarence wrote, "I fell in love with Bumby and am so proud of him and you his father." Clarence and Grace met their grandson for the first time when Hadley and Bumby visited Oak Park on 25–26 May 1927 on their way to California to visit relatives of Hadley's.

8　EH is referring to the novel he started that fall, tentatively titled "A New Slain Knight" (Reynolds *AH*, 145–46). Although it was never completed, two scenes were published as "A Train Trip" and "The Porter" in *CSS*.

9　EH probably refers to Grace's long letter of 20 February 1927 (JFK) replying to his letter of 5 February [1927]. She also sent him a short letter dated 6 March 1927, written on a program for the Fourth Annual Exhibition by the Chicago Society of Artists, which included two of her paintings. In that note, she said she had read "The Killers" in *Scribner's Magazine* and deemed it "well written."

10　EH may be recalling Grace's letter of 4 December 1926, in which she said of *SAR*, "Surely you have other words in your vocabulary besides 'damn' and 'bitch'— Every page fills me with a sick loathing" (JFK).

To Maxwell Perkins, 15 September [1927]

Hotel Barron—Hendaye Plage

(Basse Pyrenees)

Frankreich[1]

September 15.

Dear Mr. Perkins—

That was a grand picture and caption and I hope that very clever youngster from Washington, Paris and "roundabout" has every success with the new volumne.[2] I bought a two week old World at the Gare in Hendaye and was made happy to learn who had the Harper Prize for 1927–8 and at the same time saw in the Chicago Tribune that Louis Bromfield was the American Fielding. So that made a big literary day.[3]

What about all these prizes? I am now writing a novel myself so am very interested. As far as I know Harpers have been announcing The Grandmother's for over a year so it seems to have fallen out very happily that it should be given a prize by the House its-self immediately on publication.

Couldn't we all chip in and get up say The New World Symphony Prize for 1927-8-9 and give it to Scott's new novel as an incentive that he finish it?[4] I'm sure mine would go faster and further if it were only assured of the Herman R. Scribner Memorial Prize for 1929 and in the meantime I could borrow money on the prize.

With the various litero-menstrual clubs (Book of the Month) The Something or other Guild and these prizes the whole things seems to be getting pretty filthy.[5] Any time a sum over one thousand dollars is found under the pillow in the literary, ball playing, popular evangelistic or other world crookedness seems to result.

Before I had your wire about O'Brien I had a very nice letter from him saying he would never have asked for the 50G. if he had had any idea how things were and would appreciate very much having the Killers. I didn't think you'd mind letting him have it as it was short, only one out of 14 others, was published in the magazine, and was in no sense the piece de resistance whatever that may be of the book. I figured that as long as we have a product that but for the grace of God and yourself and the way things happen to be we couldn't get published at all—or that if published any number of gents would be glad to jump on—and may yet; having such a product I think it is no loss to take whatever opportunities present to make it seems classic and unsuppressable such as O'Brien, Scribner's magazine, The Atlantic etc. Because there must be at home other people besides my own family who do not care for the stuff and would be glad to suppress it— and these people have been in power once and at home we have a dangerous habit of making laws which later they say they can do nothing about—and these people may be in power again and we may have such laws.

You asked about the novel[6] and as it seems that the more they are spoken of the slower they progress—except in the case of the gents who dictate them—I don't know anything to say except that 99/9/10 remains to be written but that I am going on the six hour a day regime in Paris next week with nobody having the address and that as Glenway says in the World "frankly I desire immortality" but am afraid that usually you have to die to prove you have it and would prefer to commence by trying to write a good novel. Would suggest to Glenway that if he desires immortality hard enough he might bump himself off while he's still going good because there is a certain type of young man which or whom if he dies young enough is always a source of interest to certain people.

This may seem a very wise letter but that is because of a dangerous facility in writing English which gives such a sense of security that it leads to positiveness after the humility of having talked a language all summer in which there is a great deal of outspoken repartee and in which I know only one word for - - - - as we say in Men Without Women.

Yours always,

Ernest Hemingway.

Have in this same mail several letters (two) from girls who think The Sun Also Rises is a wonderful book, so vivid and interesting with descriptions of real places and mustn't I have had a vivid and interesting life myself and would I send a short account of it and a picture. One of them hopes to be a writer herself and her name is Ernestine and you can see what a bond that would be between us. There have been a number of these splendid letters written to lead up to such a sort of literary friendship that people would have with, say, Barrie.[7] On the principle that the customer is always right I answer them—but in order not to lead the customer astray try and answer them as I hope John Greenleaf Whittier would.[8] If you have any pictures of white bearded New England gentlemen about the office that would be suitable for mailing you might have them autographed and held in readiness.

PUL, TLS

1 France (German).
2 With his letter of 31 August 1927, Perkins enclosed a newspaper clipping with a picture of Glenway Wescott incorrectly captioned, "Nancy Hoyt, that very clever youngster from Washington, Paris, and 'roundabout,' who has a new novel, 'The Unkind Star.'" Perkins wrote, "I thought that in view of certain opinions which you once expressed to me, the enclosed picture taken with its caption would amuse" (PUL). Nancy Hoyt (1902–1974), author of *Unkind Star* (New York: Knopf, 1927), was the sister of Elinor Hoyt Wylie.
3 *Gare*: train station (French). Harper & Brothers published Wescott's novel *The Grandmothers* on 25 August 1927. On 21 August, prior to its publication, the *New York Times* announced that the novel had been awarded the Harper Prize for 1927–1928. In her

positive review of Louis Bromfield's *A Good Woman* in the *Chicago Tribune* (30 July 1927), Fanny Butcher called Bromfield "the Henry Fielding of his day" (6).

4 EH alludes to the New World Symphony, or Symphony No. 9 in E Minor (1893), by Czech composer Antonín Dvořák (1841–1904).

5 The Book of the Month Club, founded in 1926, and the Literary Guild, founded in 1927, popular subscription book clubs whose members received through the mail special editions of new books selected by panels of literary experts.

6 In his response of 14 October 1927, Perkins would emphasize that *Scribner's Magazine* was very interested in serializing EH's next novel, explaining, "since all the other magazines have said something, I thought if we did not, you might possibly not realize the strength of our interest" (PUL).

7 J. M. (James Matthew) Barrie (1860–1937), Scottish novelist and playwright, whose first of several books featuring the character Peter Pan was *The Little White Bird; or, Adventures in Kensington Gardens* (1902). His acclaimed play, *Peter Pan; or, the Boy Who Would Not Grow Up*, premiered in London in 1904.

8 John Greenleaf Whittier (1807–1892), Massachusetts-born poet whose Quaker background is reflected in his poetry about religion, devotion, nature, and country life. His poems were published to popular acclaim, placing him among the canonical "Fireside poets" of his era.

To F. Scott Fitzgerald, [c. 15 September 1927]

Dear Scott,

I got your check cashed it like a son of a bitch without writing and never wrote.[1] All of which if you study your bank account I don't have to tell you. But don't think of me as having become an Hecht or a Bodenheim or one of those literary gents that thinks writing books gives a gent licence to larceny etc. because I am now writing and I will pay you the one hundred bucks as soon as the new monumental work entitled Men Without Women comes out. Not later than October let us both hope.

How the hell are you? What do you think of Men Without Women as a title? I could get no title, Fitz, run through Ecclesiastics though I did. Perkins, perhaps you've met him, wanted a title for the book. Perkins's an odd chap, I thought, what a quaint conceit! He wants a title for the book[.] Oddly enough he did. So, I being up in Gstaad at the time went around to all the book stores trying to buy a bible in order to get a title. But all the sons of bitches had to sell were little carved brown wood bears. So for a time I thought of dubbing the [b]ook The Little Carved Wood Bear and then listening to the critics explanations. Fortunately there happened to be a church of England clergyman in town who was leaving the next day and Pauline borrowed a bible off him after promising to return it that night because it was the bible he was ordained with. Well, Fitz, I looked all through that bible, it was in very fine print and stumbling on that great book Ecclesiastics, I read it aloud to all who would listen. Soon I was alone and began cursing the bloody bible because there were no titles in it—although I found the source of practically every good title you ever heard of. But the boys, principally Kipling, had been there before me and swiped all the good ones[2] so I called the book Men Without Women hoping it would have a large sale among the fairies and old Vassar Girls.[3]

If you think that paragraph is dull revert to the first paragraph where I promised to pay you back the hundred dollars. There's gold in that paragraph, Fitz.

How is your novel? Have you finished it? When is coming out? I know you will be glad to hear that I am calling my new novel The World's Fair.[4] So is Brommy as I call dear Louis [Bromfield]. Did you see how Fanny Butcher the woman with the Veal Brains called Brommy the American Fielding. Jesus Christ. It was this that moved me to write again. Due to climate, temperature, up-bringing, lack of experience education, and tripas[5] there isn't and won't be any American Fielding but I am resolved that son of a bitch—oh hell. It is funny though for a guy to set out to be the American Galsworthy and be dubbed the American Fielding.

I myself, Fitz, have had the splendid experience of being regarded as the tightest man in the world on acct. of never loosening up and spending any of my Sun Also Rises takings while having lived for five months on yr. 100 and $750 I got from Maxwell Perkins in the meantime having turned down large sums of dough from Hearsts including sending back a check for $1000 bucks sent as an advance on a contract for 10 stories at 1000 the first five 1250 the second five—15,000 for the serial etc. Doubtless it would seem more practical to an impartial observer for me to have taken a thousand off Hearst rather than a hundred off of Fitzgerald and I darsesay it would. The only trouble is that I <u>cant</u> absolutely <u>cant</u> write a damned thing under contract.

However am now going to write a swell novel—will not talk about it on acct. the greater ease of talking about it than writing it and consequent danger of doing same.

Got a sheet to fill out from Who's Who and my life has been so fuckingly complicated that I was only able to answer two of the questions and did not know but what they might be used against me.[6]

Hadley and Bumby are fine and have been out on the Pacific slopes where you were too so you know what the hell they are like.[7] Hadley plans to sail from N.Y. on the Lancastria Oct. 22 will be in N.Y. for three or four days beforehand—her address is care of the Guaranty Trust N.Y. If youn were around town and could see her I know she would be cockeyed pleased and I would appreciate it.

Pauline is fine. We were going to come over to the states thism fall but as I am starting working well I better keep on and get the stuff done and then come over in the Spring. Where will you be. Please Scott forgive me for being such a turd about not not writing or acknowleging the check. I had a note from [Northrop] in Santiago enclosing a card of yours—it came just as he was sailing. So I wrot him in Chicago.

Love to Zelda and Scotty—write me all the dirt. The Murphies have been in Antibes all summer I think. Have heard nothing from Don Stewart since he left last fall. Nothing from Benchley. Letters from Dos pretty often. MacLeishes are in America. Pat Guthrie after Duff got her divorce wouldn't marry her because she had lost her looks and now lives with Lorna Lindsley who saved him from jail on a bad check and who can let him go to jail at any time. Duff is on the town. She kidnapped her kid from England and has no money to keep him—all her small amt. of income goes to keep the kid and nurse in south of france in reduced style of titled youngsters.[8] I ran into her one night—she wasn't sore about the Sun—said the only thing was she never had slept with the bloody bull fighter. That was only night I was in the quarter for a year. Been in Spain since first of July—just bumming went all over Galicia.

What the hell. Please write. I would like to hear all about Liteary Affairs—wish I could see you and talk.

Yours
Ernest

PUL, TLS

1 EH is responding to Fitzgerald's letter of [18 April 1927], in which Fitzgerald said he hated to think of EH being "hard up" and enclosed a check for $100 (JFK; Bruccoli *Fitz–Hem*, 85–86).

2 The title of *Many Inventions* (1893) by English novelist Rudyard Kipling (1865–1936) is drawn from Ecclesiastes 7:29: "Lo, this only have I found, that God hath made man upright; but they have sought out many inventions." Kipling's poem "Boots" (1903) takes its refrain "There's no discharge in the war!" from Ecclesiastes 8:8. EH had drawn from Ecclesiastes for the title and epigraph of *SAR*.

3 Vassar College in Poughkeepsie, New York, founded in 1861, developed a reputation as a center for progressive studies and for the independence and self-reliance of its exclusively female student body.

4 Fitzgerald was still working on what would much later become the novel *Tender Is the Night* (1934). "The World's Fair" was among several early working titles Fitzgerald tentatively adopted.

5 *Tripas*: guts (Spanish).

6 EH would be listed for the first time as an author in *Who's Who in America* in vol. 15, 1928–1929. (See Trogdon *Reference*, 84, for a facsimile of the biographical data form that EH completed for the publication.)

7 Hadley and Bumby traveled to Carmel, California, for a vacation with Hadley's sister and brother-in-law, Fonnie and Roland Usher, and their four children. Fitzgerald had been in Hollywood earlier that year working with United Artists on a screenplay for "Lipstick," which never went into production.

8 Anthony Roger Duncan Twysden (1918–1946) was the son of Duff Twysden and Sir Roger Twysden, tenth baronet and an officer in the Royal Navy. During his parents' stormy marriage, Anthony was raised by Sir Roger's family, although Duff frequently took him to Paris or to visit her grandmother in Scotland. After the couple divorced in 1926, Sir Roger was awarded custody of Anthony (Bernice Kert, *The Hemingway Women* [New York: W. W. Norton, 1983], 157, 196).

To [Unknown], [c. after 20 September 1927]

You ~~made~~ accepted 400 pesetas for all expenses except French customs

You made price of 400 pesetas in advance for all charges except French customs for delivery of our furniture to domicile 6 Rue Ferou Paris Stop Hold your receipt number 804 for payment this sum Stop Furniture ~~billed~~ arrived here billed collect Stop Please ~~advise~~ wire Reucheraye at once this furniture ~~paide~~ shipped ~~expenses~~ charges paid in advance or accept consequences.

JFK, ACD

The cable draft probably refers to the shipping of furniture EH and Pauline bought in Spain for their new apartment in Paris.

To Eric Pinker, 23 September 1927

September 23, 1927
6, rue Ferou
Paris—France.

Dear Mr. Pinker,

I am very glad to accept Heinemann's offer. The offer of 100 pounds advance on the book of stories seems satsfactory and I believe 150 pounds should be all right as advance on the novel.[1] I do not know what Fiesta has done as I have had no correspondence of any sort with Cape since ~~early~~ June. I have been very dissatisfied with Cape ever since he published the first book but there is no need of going into that. My next book will be a volumne of short stories called Men Without Women which Scribner's are publishing next month. Will cable Scribner's to send revised proofs to Heinemann. At present I am working on a novel which should be ready for publication next fall.

I did not wire you because of the phrase in your first letter that you assumed that I had not an agent. Messers Curtis Brown have been my London agents. I wired you from Hendaye hoping to see you in Paris so that I might explain my situation— I have been very dis-satisfied with Cape— not the usual business of the author wanting more advertising etc.—but rather dis-satisfaction with typographical errors, ~~bodlerizing~~ changing of text without submitting proof, addressing letters to me, not care of my bank, but to various American book shops in Paris and one thing and another. My relations with Curtis Brown have been very pleasant but not entirely satisfactory.

I do not know the etiquette of the matter as I have had no experience with agents. I deal directly with Scribner's in America. I do not wish to place you in any sort of false position and would esteem it a great favor if you would write me under what conditions I can treat with you in this matter. In other words—under what conditions you can act as my agent in this matter. I have not communicated with Curtis Brown in any way since receiving your ~~first letter~~ letter and naturally will not until I hear from you.

About a fortnight ago I wrote Curtis Brown, in answer to a letter from them urging me to send proofs of my new book to Cape who was very anxious to see them, saying that I was not inclined to send proofs to Cape unless I was under option to as I was very dis-satisfied with him. I told them I did not have Cape's contract with me in the south and asked if they would inform me if I were under any option and to please write me their opinion of the whole matter. As yet I have had no answer to this letter. I did, however, on receiving your letter look up my contract with Cape and find he has no option on any books beyond Fiesta which he has already published.

That is where the matter stands. I am quite free to negociate with any British publisher and am very glad to accept Heinemann's offer made through yourself. Whether I am free to deal with you or whether I must first have severed any other relations is what I wish you would tell me. I am quite ignorant in the matter and would not like, through ignorance (which is, of course, no excuse) to act in any way which might have the appearance of bad faith. I will not communicate with anyone on this matter until I hear from you.

My permanent address is care of The Guaranty Trust Company of New York, 1 rue des Italiens. My personal address is 6 rue Ferou, Paris VI where I will be until after Christmas.

Yours very truly,
Ernest Hemingway.

To Eric S. Pinker Esq.

NYPL-Berg, TLS

1 In his letter to Charles Scribner of 1 October 1927, EH would summarize the details of the offer by Heinemann Publishing for British rights to his future work.

To Eric Pinker, 26 September 1927

PARIS 22798 29 24 12^{H}15=
=BOOKISHLY LONDON[1]
=WROTE YESTERDAY ACCEPTING HEINEMANNS OFFER FOR
BRITISH RIGHTS STOP THEIR OFFER FOR AMERICAN RIGHTS

RIDICUHOUS STOP SUN ALSO RISES WAS NEVER OFFERED TO
ANYONE BUT SCRIBNERS

HEMINGWAY=

NYPL-Berg, Cable; destination receipt stamp: CENTRAL TELEGRAPH OFFICE,
SP 26 / 27

1 The Pinker agency's cable address.

To Charles Scribner's Sons, 30 September 1927

TW 82 PARIS 12
LCD SCRIBNERS NY
PLEASE SEND REVISED PROOFS TO HEINEMANN S LONDON
HEMINGWAY
CHAS SCRIBNER S SONS 5TH AVE AND 48TH ST

PUL, Cable; destination receipt stamp: SEP 30 1927

To Charles Scribner, 1 October 1927

Paris

October First, 1927

Dear Mr. Scribner,

Thank you very much for sending the proofs and for sending them to me
rather than to Cape.[1] I have had rather continuous dis-satisfaction with
Cape and have decided to accept an offer for British rights made by
Heinemann's. So I wired yesterday asking that revised proofs please be sent
to Heinemann.

It is very pleasant that you like the new book and I hope that it will go
well. I am working very hard now on a novel and it seems to be going along.

Heinemann's offer 150 pounds advance on a novel or 100 pounds on a
book of short stories; on account of a royalty of 12½% on the first 2,000

copies, 15% on the next 3,000, 20% on the next 5,000 and 25% thereafter, the contract to carry an option on the next two books.

Mr. Eric Pinker cabled me another offer from Heinemann's for the American rights and followed it with a letter saying he was leaving with Heinemann's manager for New York the next day; that he was aware that Doubleday Page had turned down The Sun Also Rises but that he understood they now regretted this very much! This offer was for 400 pounds advance; the letter confirming it said royalty terms would have to be arranged.[2]

I cabled Pinker that the offer for American rights was ridiculous and that The Sun Also Rises had never been offered to anybody but Scribners. I only mention this in case you should have heard any reports that I was carrying on any negociations with Doubleday Page and Co. There has been nothing except Pinker's cable and letter to me and the answer I cabled.

The situation in England seems to be that the agents—nominally the author's agent and in that capacity taking 10% from his royalties—are in reality the agents of the different publishers. My first offer from Cape came through Curtis Brown who thus received percentage on all my dealings with Cape and throughout have spent their time explaining to me Cape's standpoint instead of acting as my agents with Cape. Mr. Pinker would seem to be the agent for Heinemann's.

As I now have two British, one each of Danish, Swedish, French and German publishers, apparently two agents in England, another agent in Germany (all volunteers all unsolicited and all collecting a percentage) at least two agents in France (both volunteers) and all these splendid people engaged in sending cables which have to be answered at some cost and the utter disruption of a morning's work—I would be very happy if some business man or woman would take over the whole mess.[3] So far Heinemann's contract has not arrived but Pinker's write they are sending it in a few days.

Yours very truly,
Ernest Hemingway.

To Charles Scribner, Jr.

PUL, TLS

1 The proofs of *MWW* intended for the British edition.
2 Late in 1926 the publishing house William Heinemann Limited (under the financial control of Doubleday, Page & Company) had expressed interest in publishing the British edition of *SAR*. However, in a letter of 1 December 1926 Heinemann's managing director Charles S. Evans (1883–1944) withdrew the offer after learning that Cape was already EH's publisher in England (JFK). In his 17 October 1927 response to this letter from EH, Charles Scribner would clarify that it was also Evans who went to New York with Eric Pinker and stopped by Scribner's office just after Scribner read this letter. "We were naturally annoyed at Pinker's offer for Doubleday Page," Scribner wrote, "as it is not good manners, to say the least, for publishers who have always enjoyed the pleasantest relations to approach one another's authors, unless the author had first decided to make a break." However, according to Scribner, Evans claimed "he had nothing to do with it and that he had felt personally" that EH's books "were rather too 'frank' for Doubleday" (PUL). As Scribner would tell Evans in a letter of 14 October 1927, "You can't blame us for having been a little annoyed" to hear from Hemingway "that he had been offered £400 advance on the American rights by Double, Page" (PUL).
3 EH refers to British publishers Cape and Heinemann; Swedish publisher Holger Schildt, who would publish a translation of *SAR* in 1929; French publisher Éditions de la Nouvelle Revue Française, which had published "Fifty Grand"; and German publisher Rowohlt. EH's agents in England were Curtis Brown and the James B. Pinker & Son Literary Agency. His German agent since July 1926 had been Edgar A. Mowrer (1892–1977) (brother of Paul Mowrer) with the Berlin Office of the *Chicago Daily News*, who in the summer of 1927 had placed three of EH's stories in the *Frankfurter Zeitung*. Responding to EH's outcry for someone to "take over the whole mess," Charles Scribner would join Perkins and Fitzgerald in recommending Paul Reynolds as a literary agent (17 October 1927, PUL).

To Grace Hall Hemingway, 1 October [1927]

October First.

Dear Mother,

That catalogue of your show looks very exciting. I think the reproduction of the painting of Anastasia Island is very lovely and I would love to see the original. I would rather see the whole show than anything that there will be in Paris this fall. It makes me very homesick to read the titles.[1] Am working very hard on a novel and going well. If you have any reproductions I would greatly appreciate them. I am very fond of and proud of the picture of the Bay you sent.

Yours lovingly and with many congratulations,

Ernie

If you would like me to send you the catalogue of the Salon or any reproductions of anything of the sort from here that you might be interested in I would be very glad to.[2]

PSU, TLS with autograph postscript; postmark: PARIS-25 / R. DANTON, 22$\frac{30}{}$ / 1 · X / 1927

1 EH refers to a catalog titled "Exhibition of Landscapes by Grace Hall Hemingway" (JFK). In her letter to EH of [9 October 1927], Grace would enclose a newspaper clipping titled "Art Exhibition Receives Ovation" from the 7 October 1927 *Oak Parker* reporting that more than 550 persons visited the Hemingway home at 600 North Kenilworth Avenue between 1 and 5 October to view the first public exhibit of Grace's paintings. The article describes visitors' enthusiastic response to Grace's hospitality and to the seventy-eight paintings shown, mostly "landscapes, natural ones untampered by a futurist's conception so much in evidence these days" (JFK). Titled paintings included *Playground of the Winds, One Misty Morning,* and *Birches at Sunset.* In a letter of 14 October 1927, Grace would report selling *Anastasia Island* for $375 (JFK).
2 It is unclear as to which of the Paris art salons EH is referring to here; in his letter to his mother of [c. November 1927], he would identify the major salons more specifically. In her letter to EH of 14 October 1927, Grace would reply, "Yes (indeed) I would appreciate catalogs & especially reproductions—Everything of that sort helps" (JFK).

To Mary Pfeiffer, 1 October 1927

October 1, 1927.

Dear Mrs. Pfeiffer,

We have been back now for a couple of weeks, the apartment is even better than we remembered it and I've been working very hard on a novel. Uncle Henry and Aunt Annie have been here all this week and are leaving this afternoon for Berlin. We took them out to dinner one night and they seemed very well, to have good appetites, and to have had a fine trip. You suggested that out of my wide experience I might be able to suggest something to Uncle Henry about disposing of his millions and I thought it was a fine compliment but my wide experience has never included the disposal of anything over 150 dollars a week, and that not for long. Besides the subject did not come up but I was prepared to offer any aid I could.[1]

Pauline is very well and runs the house beautifully. I'm enclosing a picture of her on the beach at San Sebastien and one of me carressing what the photographer hopes would be a bull—but what is very abviously a very tired and resigned old steer. The only value of this photo is that it was while it was being taken that the great discovery was made that holding the horn of an animal you can feel him or her chew even in the tip of the horn. No one seems as impressed as me by this discovery but I feel that some day it may be very valuable.[2]

Virginia's summer with the Dunn's brought her down to 45 kilos or 99 pounds and that is a little light for marrying off. We hope very much she will go to the mountains with us and get in the fine healthy shape she was in last spring. I don't think it was awfully healthy for her at 25 to be so much with Clara at 37 whose movements were in turn limited to those of Mrs. Dunn's age 68. In the end it seemed Mrs. Dunn who became younger and when we met them in San Sebastien after the summer Mrs. Dunn was looking much younger and very well, Clara was looking much better than when she came over and Virginia was looking very badly. But please do not quote me on this because we would like Jinny to get very strong and healthy and good looking and I donot think the prospect would be as attractive to her if it were presented as something medicinal.

About the dedication that Pauline wrote you about— I cabled Scribners to dedicate the book to Evan Shipman instead. He is a young poet who is having a hard time getting any recognition at all for his stuff which is really, I think, very very good. It seemed, after thinking it over, that in view of all last year and one thing and another the book being called Men Without Women and containing the fight stories etc. it would be better taste to dedicate it to a man. I would like to have given Jinny some sort of thing that she would like but thought it might possibly be an embarrassment

Virginia has been with Uncle Henry and Aunt Annie nearly all the time of their stay here, has taken them on long trips in the little car and has given them a grand time. I think they have enjoyed their stay very much.

I see how the Church would not feel like interfering with the Tunney-Dempsey business on the grounds stated since the Army-Navy football game was held in the same stadium since the congress and it is at least as rough as five prizefights.[3] Also Tunney is a good catholic and was publicly congratulated by Archbishop Hayes, I think it was, when he beat Dempsey before.[4] I understand perfectly your not liking fights nor liking much to read about them. The only reason I write about them is because I know about them and have to write about the things I know. As I get older perhaps I'll know about more things and among some of the stories there will be subjects you will like better.[5]

We would love to come to Piggott sometime soon but really do not know when. This novel is going very well so far and I think will keep me going every day until January to get the first draft done. Then we will go to the mountains and ski and rinse out the head on the inside if possible and then start re-writing in a couple of months. Whether to go to America before or after that is finished is sort of a problem. You see when you are not working for anyone, but only in your head, and not writing down something that has happened but making it all up entirely you get careful about going to new places while the work is going on because if one morning the head doesn't work and you can't make anything up you are through. So it is hard to promise but we would like to come over in the Spring.

This is a long letter and doesn't seem to be stopping and I guess the best thing to do would be to take it out of the typewriter.

Best regards to you and to Mr. Pfeiffer,[6] and thanks very much for your letter.

Yours always,

Ernest

PUL, TLS

1 Henry Pfeiffer, Jr. (1857–1939) and Annie Merner Pfeiffer (1860–1946), Pauline Pfeiffer's paternal uncle and his wife. Henry, the eldest of the ten siblings of his generation, was Gus Pfeiffer's business partner in the Pfeiffer Chemical Company. Henry would ultimately donate more than fifteen million dollars to a number of philanthropic organizations, schools, and hospitals.

2 The photograph EH describes of himself and the steer (with EH holding his beret on the animal's head) is reproduced in the plate section of this volume.

3 In her letter to EH of 7 September [1927], Mary Pfeiffer reported: "The Chicago Federation of Churches is bitterly opposing the staging of the Tunney–Dempsey fight that is scheduled for the stadium on Soldiers Field, and they are trying to arouse the Catholics to regester an

objection as it is to be on the same grounds that the Eucharistic Congress was held but our hierarchy is not easily stampeded and seldom rushes impulsively into anything" (JFK). The 28th International Eucharistic Congress of the Roman Catholic Church was held in Chicago on 21–23 June 1926 at Soldier Field, which was also the site of the 27 November 1926 national championship football game between Army and Navy. The game ended in a 21–21 tie, with the championship awarded to Navy. The heavyweight title rematch between Gene Tunney and Jack Dempsey was held at Soldier Field on 23 September 1927 before a crowd of 104,000.

4 On 2 October 1926 Cardinal Patrick Joseph Hayes (1867–1938), who served as Archbishop of New York from 1919 until his death, had congratulated Tunney on his victory over Dempsey in the 23 September 1926 title fight in Philadelphia.

5 In her 7 September letter, Mary Pfeiffer told EH, "I like the way you write but don't always care for your subjects: Bull and prize fights for instance. I always avoid the latter in the movies whenever I can but am always running into them. They seem very popular however."

6 Paul Mark Pfeiffer (1867–1944), Pauline's father, a successful businessman and philanthropist in Piggott, Arkansas.

To Georgia Lingafelt, 3 October 1927

Oct. 3 1927

Dear Miss Lingafelt;

Thanks very much for you letter. The books have been Three Stories and Ten Poems, Contact Press, 1923—350 copies out of print. In Our Time, Three Mountains Press, 1924, 150 I think. Way out of print. In Our Time, Boni and Liveright 1925, 1000 copies as near as I can figure although they may have given away some more—but anyway out of print. They claim to be issuing a new edition. Then Scribner's published The Torrents of Spring in the spring of 1926 in an unrestrained edition and The Sun Also Rises came out in the fall of the same year with, I believe, an attempt made to print and sell as many as possible. Scribner's are publishing something called Men Without Women this fall. That seems to be all. If you ever get any of these rare edition I would appreciate hearing about it as I own one copy of Three Stories and Ten poems and would be very happy if it became valuable in order that I might have something to leave to my children. The other books do not seem able to have been kept in the house.[1]

~~But since your enquiry I am arranging to place the 3stories and 10 poems under glass if there turns out to be any glass.~~ [*EH marginal notation with arrow pointing to cancelled text*: unsuccessful joke!]

Yours very truly,
Ernest Hemingway.

UVA, TLS; postmark: PARIS 110 / R. DE RENNES, 2 / OCTO /15 H / 27

The typewritten envelope, addressed to "Miss Georgia Lingafelt / The Walden Book Shop / 311 Plymouth Court / CHICAGO / ILLINOIS / ETATS UNIS," bears EH's handwritten notation "not for sale." EH either misdated the letter, or the postmark date is incorrect by a day.

1 Only 300 copies of *TSTP* were printed in 1923 and 170 copies of *iot* in 1924. The first Boni & Liveright printing of *IOT* in 1925 consisted of 1,335 copies, followed by a second printing of 500 copies in March 1927.

To Frederick Wicken, 7 October 1927

6 rue Ferou
Paris, France.
October 7, 1927.

F.L. Wicken Esq.
James B. Pinker Sons,
London.
Dear Sir;

I have received no draft of an agreement from Heinemann at this date and since their second offer seemed to wish the British rights contingent upon obtaining the American rights and as, at this time, I have no desire to involve the British r[i]ghts in any way with any American publisher I believe it is best to call the negociations off. There will therefore be no need for you to draw up an agreement with Heinemann's.

I appreciate very much Mr. Eric Pinker's attentions in this matter and I hope you will inform him of my decision if he is still in New York.

Yours very truly,
Ernest Hemingway.

NYPL-Berg, TLS

To Charles Scribner, 7 October 1927

Paris,
October 7, 1927

Dear Mr. Scribner,

As I have as yet received no draft of the agreement with Heinemann and as I am afraid that their British offer may have been made (on account of the second cable) with some idea of obtaining the American rights I have written today to Pinker's to call off all the negociations. I have seen Cape, straightened out my differences with him and will continue with him at least through this next book.

This note is only to keep you informed of the English situation. I am very sorry to have bothered you to send proofs to Heinemann's and I would appreciate it greatly if a set of corrected proofs, or an advance copy of the books if it is out, might be sent to Jonathan Cape.[1]

Yours very truly,
Ernest Hemingway.

Charles S. Scribner Jr.
Charles Scribner's Sons
New York.

PUL, TLS

1 Charles Scribner would reply in a letter of 17 October 1927 that two copies of *MWW* had been sent to Cape (PUL).

To Archibald MacLeish, 8–9 October [1927]

Oct. 8

Dear Archie— If I praise your damn poetry any more you'll think I'm a fairy or a critic but I thought your poem in the Caravan (which by the way smelled like a caravan that had been forced to shit in a closed room) was wonderful. It was a grand lovely poem and if you want to make Papa happy write like that and then dedicate to me.[1] I should say, Mac, that you can now write about life and death without getting life and deathy if that means anything to you. You are certainly going bloody good if your published works are any indication of anything and I shd only hope that you continue to be discouraged unappreciated etc. because you are now making a bum out of all the living poets of my perusal and many dead ones. Let us now leave the subject because I am afraid you will think I like you because you are such a fine poet. To hell with your poetry MacLeish.

Papa has been working like a sonof a bitch and has nine—count them but don't read them—chapters done. Is going well. reaping the results of the long layoff.

Been back three weeks or so, haven't been in bed later than 10 o'clock— seen nobody—working all the time. Day before yesterday Pauline and I rode to Versailles and back without getting off the bikes. This may be hard on Pauline but I am training to surprise Archie. You must promise not to get on a bike until you come back and then I'll say I haven't too and we will go out to ride and I'll say let's ride op the cote du Picardie, Archie and you'll say no Hem that's too hard. Shit I'll say that's not hard. And then we will start and I hope to kill you off a third of the way up. We rode up the Cote du Behobie this summer four kilometers long and climbing christ nose how many meters without getting off the bikes.[2] First time tried it had to get off 5 times and was dead. Well now you see where I get at training to surprise Archie. Bragging ruins the whole thing. Thats what braggibg does and then when we start to ride of course you will laver me the same as ever. There is no damn justice. Love to Ada Mimi and Kenny[3] from Papa, Pauline and Jinny.

Next Day

We certainly will go ski-ing. We'd like to go to Sweizzimen or however you spell it—on the other side of the Saanenmoser. Has a swell bob run down to it—fine little town, closer to the ski-ing, cheaper and more like a village. It's the terminus of the M.O.B.[4] Wonderful food. Pauline and I tried it. It's not quite an hour from Gstaad. Hurry up back.[5] I've got to start work now—Pauline's gone downtown and when she comes back we're going to ride to Versailles for lunch—that's the kind of competition you are going to run into. O don't you care for competetive sports, Mac. All right we'll have intra-murals.

Papa.

LOC, TLS

1 MacLeish's poem "Fragment of a Biography," published in the 1927 *American Caravan* (374–76), was dedicated to EH.
2 The distance from Paris to Versailles is approximately 25 kilometers or 16 miles, while La Côte Picarde (the coast of Picardie) is roughly 200 kilometers, or 125 miles, north-northwest of Paris. The hilly region of Béhobie outside Hendaye rises eastward from the coastal region into the Pyrénées.
3 Archibald and Ada's children, Mary Hillard MacLeish (1922–2012) and Kenneth MacLeish (1917–1977).
4 Zweisimmen and Saanenmöser, ski resorts in southwest-central Switzerland. M.O.B., the Montreux–Berner Oberland Bahn [Railway].
5 In his letter to EH of 18 September [1927], MacLeish reported that he and Ada would return to Paris in November (JFK).

To Frederick Wicken, 10 October 1927

6 rue Ferou
Paris
October 10, 1927

FC. Wicken Esq.
James B. Pinker and Sons
London.
Dear Sir:

I received your wire and a letter which I imagine contains the Heinemann agreement this morning. Thank you very much for writing. I am very sorry to have put you to so much trouble in this matter—but when two weeks passed without hearing anything further from Heinemann after they had changed their offer to include both British and American rights I decided to continue with my present publisher—at least through the book of stories (Men without Women[)] while making no contract beyond that.

I regret greatly there being any misunderstanding and appreciate your care in the matter and appreciate very much the Messers. Heinemann's offer.

Yours very truly,
Ernest Hemingway.

NYPL-Berg, ALS

To Burton Emmett, 15 October 1927

October 15 1927

6 rue Férou

Paris VI

Dear Mr. Emmett—

Thank you very much for your letter— I've been looking through the book case and find that I havent any files of The TransAtlantic Review in which I published various things—so cant give dates (should be a file at Pub. Library or I'll try and look it up over here if you like)— Nor can any copies of This Quarter be found—but remember Big Two Hearted River was published in the first number of that review and The Undefeated in the second—whenever they came out.[1] The Undefeated—a long bull fight story— was previously published in Der Querschnitt published by Propyläen Verlag— Berlin in the June and July numbers 1925.[2]

I had several poems in English in Der Querschnitt during 1924–1925–but cant remember dates.[3] A story called Hills Like White Elephants in Aug 1927 number of Transition— Had some sort of piece in Double Dealer of May 1922 called <u>A Divine Gesture</u>—and that's as far back as I remember.[4] Was not a literary gent in highschool and did not go to college. Fifty Grand was published in French in La Nouvelle Revue Francaise in Aug. 1927— L'Invincible came out in La Navere D'Argent for March 1926— Have published in the Frankfurter Zeitung, Il Convegno (of Milan) etc. but dont know dates. Dont think anybody else does either. Only one story (Soldiers Home) was in Il Convegno— But you dont care about translations I imagine and that seems to be all I have any dope on.[5] However The Undefeated was published in German before it ever appeared in English.

About the Manuscripts—I have no idea what they are worth—those things are only worth what people will pay for them— I have the handwritten Ms. of nearly everything in In Our Time—and almost all the stories of this new book—also Mss. of The Sun Also Rises— Would rather not sell more than one or two of the In Our Time as, if they are of any value, they will constitute shall we say the unique patrimony of my son Bumby.

It is damned nice of you to like the stuff and to have liked it so long ago—if you've liked the rest of it I think you'll like the Men without Women book—hope so anyway. I'm sorry I couldnt give you any more definite dope on the early stuff but outside of This Quarter—The Little Review—The Transatlantic and the series of obscene poems in Der Querschnitt I've published nothing in English until the magazine stories you mention of this year. If you want a couple or one of the I.OT. manuscripts perhaps you'd say what they would be worth to you. I dont like to put a price on them as it seems snooty and at the same time I have a hunch they may be worth something pretty good someday—if I dont go bad or turn out to be a false alarm—

Yours always

Ernest Hemingway.

The booklet—even with 10 pages missing was very impressive—

UNC, ALS; postmark: PARIS-25 / R. DANTON, 22 $\frac{30}{}$ / 25 X / 1927

EH addressed the envelope to "Burton Emmett Esq. / 40 East 34th Street / New York City / N.Y. / Etats Unis." The letter to which EH is responding has not been located.

1 EH's publications in the *Transatlantic Review* were: "Indian Camp" (titled "Work in Progress"; April 1924), "And to the United States" (titled "New York Letter"; May–June 1924); "And Out of America" (August 1924), "Joseph Conrad" (October 1924), "Pamplona Letter" (September 1924), "The Doctor and the Doctor's Wife" (November 1924), and "Cross Country Snow" (December 1924). The first number of *This Quarter* (Spring 1925) included EH's "Homage to Ezra" as well as "Big Two-Hearted River." The second number (Autumn–Winter 1925–1926) included "The Undefeated."

2 *Der Querschnitt*, a German magazine that often featured English and American expatriate authors, published a two-part serialization of "The Undefeated," translated by B. Bessmertny as "Stierkampf," in the Summer (June) 1925 issue and the July 1925 issue. Founded in Berlin in 1920 by publisher and art gallery owner Alfred Flechtheim, *Der Querschnitt* was the "brilliant German counterpoint of *The Dial*," characterized by its "cosmopolitan taste" and "espousal of the vanguard" (Nicholas Joost, *Ernest Hemingway and the Little Magazines* [Barre, Massachusetts: Barre Publishers, 1968], 131–32).

3 *Der Querschnitt* published EH's poems "The Soul of Spain with McAlmon and Bird the Publishers" (Part 1) and "The Earnest Liberal's Lament" (Autumn 1924); "Part Two of the Soul of Spain with McAlmon and Bird the Publishers" and "The Lady Poets with Foot Notes" (November 1924); and "The Age Demanded" (February 1925).

4 EH's fable "A Divine Gesture" appeared in the May 1922 *Double Dealer*, a little magazine published in New Orleans (1921–1926), and his poem "Ultimately" appeared a month later. As Hanneman notes, the *Double Dealer* was the first American magazine to contain a contribution by EH, other than his high school literary magazine, *Tabula* (135).

5 German translations of "Indian Camp," "The Battler," and "The End of Something" were published in the *Frankfurter Zeitung* as "Indianisches Lager" (10 April 1927), "Der Boxer" (17 April 1927), and "Das Ende von Etwas" (22 May 1927). Carlo Linati's Italian translation of "Soldier's Home" appeared as "Il ritorno del soldato" in the 30 June–30 July 1925 issue of the Milan magazine *Il Convegno: Rivista di Letteratura e di Arte*.

To Blanche Colton Williams, 18 October 1927

COPY

Paris, October 18, 1927.

Blanche Colton Williams
Chairman of The O. Henry Memorial Committee[1]
605 West 113th Street
New York

Dear Madam,

Thank you very much for your letter asking permission to reprint The Killers. I am very happy and proud that the committee should think so highly of the story and I am sorry that I cannot give the permission as that is in the hands of Charles Scribner's Sons.[2] Will you please communicate with Mr. Maxwell E. Perkins of Scribners at Fifth Avenue and Forty-Eighth street? I have sent him your letter and if he gives his permission I will be very happy to give mine. If he is willing for the story to be re-printed it will not be necessary for any further delay as you may consider his permission as mine. If he consents and you wish a formal letter of permission for your files I will be very glad to write it.

Yours very truly,
(Signed) Ernest Hemingway
Care The Guaranty Trust Co. of N.Y.
1, rue des Italiens
Paris—France

PUL, typewritten transcription of EH letter

1 American short-story writer William Sydney Porter (1862–1910) wrote under the pen name O. Henry. After his death, friends and colleagues formed the O. Henry Memorial to recognize contemporary American short-story writers. The prize was first awarded in 1919, and the first annual volume of *O. Henry Memorial Award Prize Stories* was published by Doubleday.

2 Williams informed EH in a letter of 26 September 1927 that the committee had placed "The Killers" on the list of stories (written by American authors and published for the first time in American magazines between October 1926 and September 1927) from which the first ($500) and second ($250) prize winners would be selected. She requested permission to reprint the story in volume 9 of the *O. Henry Memorial Award Prize Stories*, forthcoming from Doubleday, Page & Company (PUL). She also wrote to *Scribner's Magazine* editor Robert Bridges requesting "formal permission" to reprint the story (26 September 1927, PUL).

To Maxwell Perkins, 19 October 1927

October 19, 27

Dear Mr. Perkins,

When is the Men without Women coming out?[1] I've been expecting to hear something about it and wondered if it were delayed. The enclosed letter I am turning over to you. I had a cable asking me if I would permit the O.Henry book to reprint the killers and answered it ASK SCRIBNERS.[2]

Now comes this letter which seems to more or less promise the prize if they can do that without definitely promising it. Of course everyone may get a letter like this.[3]

Whether they reprint it or not is up to you. I hate to lose the money—but do not know when their book comes out. If it does not come out until late since it is the same story that O'Brien has it may not do any more harm to let them have it too. But you will know about that.

I would only consent to its being reprinted if it were to get a prize as I have no admiration for the collection—as a matter of fact it's pretty lousy. (This between ourselves) But as my earnings from shall we say literature have been 860 francs since I sold the Fifty Grand sometime last Spring I would be glad of the prize money.

However the decision rests with you. I do not want to do anything to hurt the Men without Women in any way and I do not want to give anything to the O.Henry Doubleday Doran people for nothing. So there is no question of even letting them print it unless you think the letter promises a 1st or 2nd prize. The fact that they omit to mention the third prize which is not a tempter would seem to mean that they will come through. But of course everyone may receive that letter. I will write Blanche C. Williams that the matter is entirely in your hands and that you will communicate with her.

Have been working every day on the novel—have about 30,000 words done.[4] It seems to be going well. Hope to get it done some time in the winter—then ski for a couple of months and re-write it, perhaps, in America. After the first draft is done I would like to write some stories. Would you mind telling Mr. Daschiell, who wrote me, that I hope to have some stories around February or March.[5]

What news of Scott? I wish he would write. I owe him $100. which I would like to pay as soon as the Men without Women makes it. I hope it will sell.

Decided to stick with Cape through the Men Without Women anyway. He promises to be good. I had decided to go over to Heinemann's but they amended their offer to include American rights and as I'd accepted the first one (for British rights) and ten days passed without getting any sort of an agreement or further word from Heinemann's I decided to stay on with Cape. As soon as I'd promised Cape I'd stay Heinemann's contract came over and they very upset about losing me. All damned annoying when you are writing a novel and don't want any business of any sort. I've spent more money than I've made answering cables. It's gotten now so I won't open any letter or cable until the end of the day and the day's work finished. Always excepting your own letters none of which have come.

Yours always,
Ernest Hemingway.

PUL, TLS

1 *MWW* was published by Scribner's on 14 October 1927.
2 EH presumably enclosed Blanche Colton Williams's letter of 26 September 1927 (PUL). Her letter to Robert Bridges of 18 October 1927 confirms that she received EH's "cryptogram," as she called the two-word cable (PUL).
3 Williams thanked Robert Bridges for his "non-publication of the second prize award" and confirmed in her letter of 1 November 1927 to Perkins that EH's story had been awarded the $250 prize (PUL). In a letter of 6 January 1928, she would officially notify EH that "The Killers" had been awarded "the prize of $250 for the second best story written" and that the story would appear in the ninth volume of the *O. Henry Memorial Award Prize Stories*, to be published by Doubleday, Doran, & Company on 19 January 1928 (JFK).
4 A reference to the novel EH would not complete.
5 Alfred S. Dashiell (1901–1970), American writer and associate editor at *Scribner's Magazine*. In his letter of 14 October 1927, Perkins mentioned that Dashiell had expressed "the Magazine's urgent desire for a story" (PUL).

To Ezra Pound, [c. 19 October 1927]

6 rue Férou
Paris VI

Dear Ezra:

Have been reading works of yr. good friend Wyndham in which it appears that principal fault of mine is Blood Lust—destruction of Bulls—Men—Women doubtless too and no doubt Dogs—(See Bitches) It appears that I've been urged on to this by you you son of a bitch. Who forced poor old Hem into these Bloody deeds through yr Influence. (and you always protesting against my youthful violence) Well well.[1]

Shit Shit.

I'm also it seems a Fascist! It makes funny reading.

Maybe youve not seen the publication. But imagine he sends it to you.

You it seems are a parasite.[2] Wyndham a true genius and original artist. The poor bird got a god knows how many page piece (Essay) entitled Paleface out of a book called The Torrents of Spring. Then he says that perhaps it is a good sign that I am beginning to see the light (His Light) on Anderson etc. There wasnt an idea in the whole thing that wasnt in Torrents. Only we dont explain them. We are not erudite.

Will he be able to keep it up? I hope so but fear the old spiroclite (or spyroclight however you spell the little fellows) after speeding up the brain and production will finally lead to a decline of some sort. Or has he never had syph?[3] If not we may get a lot more numbers of The Enemy because I prefer it to his friend Anita Loos[.] There is nothing makes such good reading as[4]

JFK, ALFrag

The date of this letter, probably abandoned, is conjectured relative to the publication date of Wyndham Lewis's journal *The Enemy* no. 2 (September 1927) and a record showing that EH checked out Lewis's book *Time and Western Man* (1927) from Shakespeare and Company's lending library on 18 October 1927, returning it the next day (PUL). The journal included Lewis's essay "Paleface," while the book reprinted his essay "The Revolutionary Simpleton," which had appeared in the first issue of *The Enemy* (January 1927).

1 EH refers sarcastically to English painter, writer, and literary critic Wyndham Lewis (1882–1957) as Pound's "good friend" because in his recent writing Lewis had attacked Pound, the early mentor and friend with whom Lewis co-founded the revolutionary magazine *BLAST* in 1914. EH alludes to Lewis's essay "Paleface," published in the second number of *The Enemy: A Review of Art and Literature*, the journal Lewis founded, edited, and illustrated, which ran for three issues (1927–1929). Lewis praised *TOS* as an amusing satire and declared EH had "very ably caricatured" Sherwood Anderson's "incurable romanticism." However, he questioned the central place of bullfighters, boxers, and physical action in EH's fiction. "The insatiable taste for violence—for sangre y arena, for blood and sand, blood and

iron, and all the other accompaniments of the profuse discharge of human blood" struck him as a form of "romantic brutality." He suggested that this "Fascist and marinettian (futurist) appetite for violence . . . has been encouraged in him" by Ezra Pound (27–28). EH would recall Lewis unfavorably in the chapter of his memoirs titled "Ezra Pound and His Bel Esprit" (*MF*).

2 In his essay "The Revolutionary Simpleton," published in the first number of *The Enemy*, Lewis compared Gertrude Stein to Anita Loos and said Ezra Pound was "the most gentlemanly, discriminating, parasite I have ever had" (89).

3 Syphilis is caused by the spirochete *Treponema pallidum*.

4 The letter fragment ends here.

To Clarence Hemingway, 20 October [1927]

October 20—

Dear Dad,

Thanks for your fine letter with the pictures. That was the first news I had of Aunt Grace's marriage. Would like to write and congratulate her.[1] We have been having fine October weather and I am working hard on my book—have about 30,000 words done. Bumby and Hadley got in a week ago. I met them at Havre and Bumby has been living with us while Hadley is fixing up the fine new apartment I located for her.[2] Bumby speaks English very well now and it is wonderful to have him back. I was very glad to hear all the news about you all. Everybody here is well and happy. Am not writing a longer letter, nor writing much of anything now, as working on the novel keeps me sucked pretty well dry.

Hope to get it done around Christmas time or the middle of January.

Best love to all the family,

Ernie

JFK, TLS

1 In a letter of 28 September 1927, EH's father enclosed several family photos, including snapshots of Bumby taken in May 1927 when he and Hadley visited Oak Park. (One is reproduced in the plate section of this volume.) Another family photo included Chester Livingston (1880–1961), who married Clarence's sister Grace Adelaide Hemingway (1881–1959) on 14 May 1927. The couple lived in Honolulu, Hawaii, Clarence told EH (JFK).

2 Hadley and Bumby returned to France earlier than planned, sailing from New York aboard the *Tuscania* on 8 October 1927 and landing in Le Havre on 16 October. Hadley's new apartment in Paris was at 98, boulevard Auguste Blanqui.

To Wyndham Lewis, 24 October 1927

c/o Guaranty Trust Co. of N.Y

1, rue des Italiens

Paris

October 24, 1927

Dear Mr. Lewis,

I've just received your letter sent to Cape on June 30—and by him forwarded to Titus's book shop. The Guaranty Trust Company is my only permanent address and God knows what impelled Cape to address me care of Herr Titus.

At any rate I'm very sorry not to have received the letter. There is not much chance of my getting over to London but if you ever come to Paris I would be very happy if we could meet again. I will be here until Christmas.

I was very glad you liked The Torrents of Spring and thought you destroyed the Red and Black Enthusiasm very finely in Paleface. That terrible shit about the nobility of any gent belonging to another race than our own (whatever it is) was worth checking. Lawrence, you know, was Anderson's God in the old days—and you can trace his effect all through A's stuff after he commenced reading him.[1] But of course in his autobiography "A Story Teller's Story," he never mentions him. In that, you find, he was formed through contemplation of the cathedral of Chartres! Accompanied, of course, by Jewish Gentlemen.[2]

As for my own stuff—I'm sorry there has been so much blood shed. I think it will decrease. The real reason for it (the bloodiness) was, I think, that I have been working for a precision of language and to get it at the start have had to treat of things where simple actions occurred—the simplest— and which I had seen the most of—was one form and another of killing. I imagine, though, that the blood letting will decrease.

Yours always,

Ernest Hemingway.

Cornell, ALS

---

1 In his essay "Paleface; or Love? What Ho! Smelling Strangeness," published in the second number of *The Enemy* (September 1927), Lewis accuses Sherwood Anderson and D. H.

Lawrence of romanticizing "anybody and everybody who is not a *pur sang* White, of the original american-european stock" (10). Lewis identifies Anderson's *Dark Laughter* as an example of such tendencies, while he applauds *TOS* as a parody of Anderson's novel.

2 In his memoir, *A Story Teller's Story* (New York: Viking, 1924), Anderson recalls his visit to the cathedral with American journalist Paul Rosenfeld (1890–1946), with whom Anderson had traveled to Paris in 1921. According to Irving Howe, the two were also accompanied by Louis Galantière, whom Anderson had known in Chicago, who "guided the visitors through Paris and to the Cathedral of Chartres before which Anderson stood deeply impressed" (*Sherwood Anderson: A Biographical and Critical Study* [Stanford: Stanford University Press, 1951], 131). Rosenfeld was Jewish; Galantière was of French-German-Jewish parentage, according to EH's piece "And to the United States" (*Transatlantic Review*, May 1924, 355).

To Maxwell Perkins, [c. 26 October 1927]

Dear Mr. Perkins:

Thanks for your letter and the clipping. I'm very ~~upset~~ worried about Scott and wish I were over there and could try and get him in some sort of shape. But I wont mention your having written.

About serialization—let's not think about it until the 1st draft is done. Thanks just the same.[1]

The Virginia Woolf review was damned irritating— She belongs to a group of Bloomsbury people who are all over 40 and have taken on themselves the burden of being modern and all very promising and saviours of letters.[2] When they are all busy at it they dislike what they consider the intrusion of anybody much under 40 into the business though God knows one doesn't wish to intrude. They live for their Literary Reputations and believe the best way to keep them is to try and slur off or impute the honesty of anyone coming up.

Of course where they are right is that literary reputations in ones life time are plants than can be nurtured—and blighted and they do their best to nurture theirs and their friends and throw off on the others. Well god be with them though I would have enjoyed taking the clothes off Virginia Woolf this noon and ~~forcing~~ permitting her to ~~do a Lady Godiva~~ walk down the Avenue de L'Opera letting everyone, truth, reality, whatever she liked— pass her close each time.

The deliberate twisting of the blurb [*EH insertion*: see col 4 page 8] was what angered me—that and the imputation that I faked and cheated etc.[3] I was glad I did not get it when I was having one of those hellish depressions when you feel you can never write again.

I wonder if you would save the clippings—quite a bunch of them—and then could send them over around Christmas time and I'd read them down in Switzerland— I'm working hard and the damned things are irritating and make you self conscious—especially the ones that misunderstand either on purpose or through dumbness. When a thing is misunderstood you want to explain and that going on in the head is bad for working.

Do you want another picture or pictures? Drawings from imagination or other drawings by gents called Louis Lozowick are too damned much. Where was [*Ditto marks*: Louis Lozowick] supposed to have drawn that?[4] It's only merit is that it looks a little like John [Peale] Bishop.

The other critical sportsman misses "Lady Brett that little wanton, so irritatingly childlike in her faith, so engagingly reprehensible in her morals." Well, well. Did you ever read "that amazing narrative of English and American after-the-war strays running up and down France and Spain in wistful wildness"—[5] That's a book you shouldn't miss.

Yours always
Ernest Hemingway.

The books havent come but I look forward to them.[6]

PUL, ALS

Although Baker dates this letter as c. 1 November 1927 (*SL*, 264–65), EH, worried about F. Scott Fitzgerald, apparently had not yet received Perkins's cable of 29 October 1927, reporting "Scott now fine" (29 October 1927, PUL). EH is responding to a letter from Perkins of 14 October 1927 (PUL); Perkins replied in a letter of 10 November 1926 (PUL).

1 Perkins had enclosed in his letter of 14 October 1927 a clipping of Percy Hutchison's review of *MWW*, "Mr Hemingway Shows Himself a Master Craftsman in the Short Story," which had appeared in the *New York Times Book Review* on 16 October 1927. He also enclosed clippings of the ad used on the day of publication, with EH's picture, and two follow-up ads. Perkins wrote that he had visited the Fitzgeralds at Ellerslie Mansion and reported that Scott was "in bad shape . . . terribly nervous, even to an alarming degree . . . as if he might have a breakdown nervously." He also wrote that it would be "a grand thing" if EH's novel-in-progress could be serialized in *Scribner's Magazine* (14 October 1927, PUL; *TOTTC*, 66–67).

2 A review of *MWW* by Virginia Woolf (1882–1941), titled "An Essay in Criticism," was published in the 9 October 1927 *New York Herald Tribune Books*. In his letter, Perkins called it "an enraging review, first because it appeared a week too soon" and second because Woolf "spent a large part of her time in talking about the function of criticism instead of functioning as a critic" (*TOTTC*, 66). Woolf was a key figure of the coterie of writers, artists, and philosophers who met informally for discussion in the Bloomsbury district of London between 1907 and 1930. Others associated with the Bloomsbury Group include novelist E. M. Forster, biographer Lytton Strachey, art critic Clive Bell, and painters Vanessa Bell and Duncan Grant.

3 "As the publisher puts it ... 'the softening feminine influence is absent—either through training, discipline, death, or situation,'" Woolf writes, but she counters that "the greatest writers lay no stress upon sex one way or another." She remarks that D. H. Lawrence and James Joyce "partly spoil their books for women readers by their display of self-conscious virility; and Mr. Hemingway, but much less violently, follows suit."

4 Louis Lozowick (1892–1973), Russian-born American artist known for his lithographs of cityscapes, geometric structures, and scenes of the common working man. A portrait drawing of EH by Lozowick is featured prominently on the front page of the *New York Herald Tribune Books* section of 9 October 1927 alongside Woolf's review of *MWW*.

5 EH quotes almost verbatim from Percy Hutchison's review.

6 Perkins wrote that he was sending EH six copies of *MWW*.

To Blanche Colton Williams, 29 October 1927

COPY

POSTAL TELEGRAPH—COMMERICAL CABLES

CABLE 1055P

PARIS OCT 29/27

WLT BLANCHE COLTON WILLIAMS

605 W 113 ST NEWYORK

　　MY LETTER MENTIONED MAXWELL PERKINS OF SCRIBNERS PUBLISHERS AS ONLY PERSON COMPETENT GIVE PERMISSION REPRINT KILLERS STOP HIS PERMISSION ESSENTIAL STOP BRIDGES ONLY SPEAKS FOR MAGAZINE STOP THANKS YOUR LETTER

　　HEMINGWAY . . . .

PUL, TCcc

In a letter to Williams of 28 September 1927, replying to her request of 26 September, Robert Bridges granted permission to reprint "The Killers" in the book of *O. Henry Memorial Award Prize Stories* but made it conditional upon EH's consent, and he advised her to contact EH about foreign rights to the story (PUL). In a letter to Perkins of 1 November, Williams would explain that she had already initiated the process of reprinting "The Killers" without Perkins's permission on the assumption that Bridges's permission alone was sufficient (PUL).

To The Editor of the *Chicago Tribune* (Paris Edition), [c. October 1927]

To The Editor of The Tribune,

Sir,

On returning to Paris an article has been brought to my attention in The Boulvardier signed with my name but containing several very humorous bits which were not written by the original author.[1]

I am always very happy myself to have any little changes or alterations made in anything I write by either the editor or the publisher and, indeed, often solicit this. But as I am unable to afford to write for The Boulevardier— which solicits manuscripts through promising to pay its contributors the lowest rates in the world—this article was very kindly written for me by my wife. [*EH cancellation of next two lines*] and

JFK, TLD

This typewritten draft stops in mid-sentence after two heavily crossed out lines. Although Reynolds notes that a final version of this letter titled "To the Editor of the Tribune" appeared in the Paris *Tribune* in mid-October and may be found in the form of a clipping at the JFK Library, the clipping has not been located (*AH*, 148, 247). EH's letter has not been located in microfilms of the Paris *Tribune*, and neither Hanneman nor Bruccoli and Baughman list it as a published item.

1 EH's article "The Real Spaniard" appeared, with unauthorized revisions by editor Arthur Moss, in *Boulevardier* 1, no. 8 (October 1927).

To Frank Curtin, 1 November 1927

c/o Guaranty Trust Co. of N.Y.

1, rue des Italiens

Paris

Nov. 1, 1927

Dear Mr. Curtin:

If your stationery hadn't said Frank A. Curtin, lawyer, at the top I would have had to send back the check for 5 dollars. But as this is the first time I have ever received money from a lawyer I'd better keep it. The autographs arent worth a damn thing and I'm awfully happy to write them for you. In fact for 5 dollars I'd be glad to rewrite any parts of the books you'd mention—or put in what the reviewers all seem to want—more female characters.[1]

About the Torrents—I never could figure out what happened to it— I was very fond of it—but nobody else seemed to like it except yourself. I dont think Scribner's have anything against it except the fact that it only sold 1200 copies. Which is 200 more than In Our Time sold.[2]

That damn Boulevardier piece was rewritten (part of it) in their office by a gent who felt he could improve on it and at the same time remove what he felt were seditious libels of one sort and another. The references to Paolino Uzcudun, Tex Rickard etc. were not mine. but replaced what was in originally— Naturally I was pretty sore but was down in Spain and couldnt do anything—[3]

But I'm not getting any where at ~~attempting to~~ finding something worth 5.$\underline{^{00}}$ to send you— It certainly was damned sporting of you to send that check— I've got two copies of the first book I ever published—out of print for 4 years—one of which you might be glad to have. I think it's supposed to be worth [that] and if you'd like to have it I'll send it along. I'd be glad to get Scribners to send over a copy of Men Without Women and endorse it to you but you may have that one already—if you havent let me know and Id do that.

Thanks awfully for your letter. I'll try and see Nolan.[4]

With all Best wishes
Yours always,
Ernest Hemingway

[*On separate page:*]
   To Frank Curtin
   from Ernest Hemingway
      Paris 1927

To Frank Curtin

from Ernest Hemingway.
Paris 1927

To Frank Curtin
from Ernest Hemingway.
Paris 1927

To Frank Curtin from the only other admirer of The Torrents of Spring
Ernest Hemingway. Paris 1927

Meeker, ALS

1 In his letter of 15 October 1927, Curtin strongly praised EH's work, particularly *TOS*, and
  asked EH to send him four inscription slips that he could insert in his volumes of EH's work
  (UTulsa).
2 Calling *TOS* "the most amusingly entertaining book of all books," Curtin wrote it was his
  favorite of EH's works and lamented that it had not been better publicized.
3 EH refers to the changes made without his permission to his piece "The Real Spaniard"
  before its publication in the *Boulevardier* (October 1927).
4 In his letter, Curtin wrote that Harry G. Nolan, a friend in Paris who had sent him the copy
  of the *Boulevardier* number, was, like himself, "a Hemingway enthusiast having recently
  read The Sun Also Rises at one sitting before going to bed one morning" and hoped to get
  EH to autograph his book.

To William B. Smith, Jr., 1 November [1927]

6 rue Ferou—Paris VI

Nov.1

Smith—

The writer has been playing the role of son of a bitch with you again Smith
due to nonwritage—but it has been due to working on a novel which has
emptied the writer like a sink or watercloset every day and made screeding
near an impossibility. I received your accts of Tunney Demp with great
interest.[1] The writer does not know how the wise money went but himself had
1,000 francs on gentle Gene. A huge horseman placed 10,000 at Harry's N.Y.
B. to be covered—He wagering on the Mannassa Maulier at evens.[2] I took a
thousand and induced Jinny to take 300. Since have seen the movie including
the slow motions of Tunney's K.D. and he certainly looked hurt.[3] But believe

he can whip D. every start. He is fast. He seemed to miss 3000 right hand drives due to Dempsey ducking them. Dempsey certainly was afraid of the polysyllabic right. He seemed pretty bloody cautious all the way through. I will put 10,000 on Gene if they ever meet again and I ever meet with 10,000. How have you been boid and how was the farm and the oil situation?

Pauline and I plan to come to Ameriky in the Spring—say may—say June at the latest—and will not consider the trip complete without a gathering and foregathering with youse men. Greet the sister for me. Why should not you and I take a fyshing trip after trout? Somewhere where they have them. The North Shore, Nova Scotchee, Newfumbland or something like that? If this Men Without Women sells I will be seeded as only drew 750 advance. Am working on the bloody novel and will be inhuman bondage to same most of the bloody winter—then will lay off and rewrite in America. Let's for God's sake get some good fishing. What I had this summer brought back the old taste and made me horney after trout. The only trouble is the blackflies and moscuitoes in the early season. There is supposed to be wonderful trout fishing in Wyoming in the Snake River and tributary streams starting in Oct. What about surf fishing? Have you any dope on that? Would it be worth while to go down to the keys of Florida and play the tarpons etc. around May? Get the dope Smith. If I come seeded I will come SEEDED. I am laying in trout tackle over here. Used two dozen and a half McGinty's this summer. Didn't play them with anything but a fly finally and laid into some hellers. Galicia is bloody good fishing but the season in Spring. There is no closed season and the dynamiters, the netters, the seiners, the cloride of lime users and the spearers and shooters and basketwork users do not help the trout. But it is so damn wild and so many many streams that we had some bloody good fishing at that.

I want to fish somewhere where the fisher is in actual danger from the number and ferocity of the finnied artivles and where a man would hesitate before going into [t]he stream nude if any of his organs were exposed.

Will you be on hand for such sport? Or will I have to fish with Coolige. Save what money you can. I may of course be penniless. If on the other hand I should be seeded I should expect to behave as a seeded male should. Not as they do.

The goddam Men Without Women may flop. Have you ever seen it? Screed an old friend and if I don't write as should the heart is still correctly situated but the goddam business of writing on a novel—fifteen chaps done— basterdises a male in every way. Yrs. for the wise money.

Hemingway (E Miller)

[*Typewritten upside down at bottom of page:*]

Pauline is fine and sends her best. Hadley is back and in fine shape. Bumby also. They have nailed fine unfurnished apt. [R]e-regards to Miss Katherine.

PUL, TL with typewritten signature

1 EH is referring to the controversial "long count fight," in which Gene Tunney defeated Jack Dempsey on 22 September 1927 at Soldier Field in Chicago. In his letter of 25 September 1927, Smith gave a detailed account of the fight and enclosed some photographs. "Both were in good shape, Jack especially," he reported, but he also acknowledged, "From where I sat in Soldier's field I could only get a general idea, all the infighting got by me of course" (JFK).
2 Founded by American jockey Tod Sloan in 1911, Harry's New York Bar at 5, rue Daunou was popular among American expatriates in Paris. "Manassa Mauler," a nickname for Dempsey, who was born in Manassa, Colorado.
3 K.D.: Knock down in round seven which results in the "long count," lasting at least fourteen seconds. EH refers to the film recording of the Dempsey–Tunney rematch. Thanks in part to the fight's controversial refereeing, the film was in high demand, quickly raising a national debate about the U.S. ban on such films. Bootlegged copies spread widely until one month after the fight, when federal judges began to rule in favor of legalizing fight films.

To F. Scott Fitzgerald, [c. 2 November 1927]

Dear Scott,

Yes I read that shall we say fucking Rascoe who hadn't read a damn thing in the book but knew it contained 50 G. and so reviewed it on that alone and dismissed the unread stories with a few well placed kisses of Miss Wescott's sphincter muscle.[1] Also read Virginia Woolf also read a poor fish in the Times who missed that lovely little wanton Lady Ashley—that's all have read so far and hope to God I read no more. These goddam reviews are sent to me by "friends" any review saying the stuff is a pile of shit I get at least 2,000 copies of. After I'd stopped Scribner's sending them because when one single damn one comes it throws me all off to hell when all I want is to be let alone to write. Glad to see F. Adamski has found it is easy to do and that anybody and especially he, Adamski, can do it much better.[2]

Have about 50,000 words done on a novel and due to these bloody damn reviews coming in and the piles and one thing and another have been knocked to hell on working all this week—going to Berlin tonight for a week and forget about the whole bloody business. Got a wire from Max Perkins yesterday that the book had sold 7,000 plus and as I only drew down $750 advance that means after paying off what I still owe on the Torrents that I'll have a thousand bucks maybe so Pauline and I are going for a week and see the Six Days, Flechtheim, Rowahlt ny German publisher and drink a little beer.[3] I suppose it may sell a thousand or so more though Imagine that the 7,000 was largely advance sale on acct. of The Sun and probably the last advance sale I'll ever get. Am thinking of quitting publishing any stuff for the next 10 or 15 years as soon as I get my debts paid up. To hell with the whole goddam business. I'm writing Max to send you a check for 100 bucks. I'm sorry as hell you've been nervous—it is a hell of a business but imagine that laying off liqor and smoking these coughless carloads will fix it up / Do you sleep all right?[4] I've been sleeping fine ever since last spring and working better than ever but am in a hell of a temper today after reading that shit ass Adamski talking about my swashbuckling affectations of style— that sonof a bitch when—oh shit no use talking about a turd like that that falls for a book like Dusty Answer[5]

What do you think about quitting either writing or publishing? The only reason I publish the damn stuff is because that is the only way to get rid of it and not think it is any good. There is certainly no other way to show up the shit to yourself. I didn't care anything about that 10 Indians story either and ouldn't have published it except they wanted enough for a book—did like White Elephants and In Another Country—I suppose that last is a swashbuckling affectation too.[6]

[*On verso of second page, typewritten upside down relative to the text on the other side:*]
Dear Scott,

I wish the hell you would come over.

JFK, TL

EH is responding to Fitzgerald's letter of [25 October 1927] (JFK; Bruccoli *Fitz–Hem*, 89–90). EH apparently abandoned this letter and put it away unsent. Written on two sheets of paper, it was folded in quarters, with EH's handwritten notation on an outer quadrant: "LETTER TO SCOTT."

1 Burton Rascoe (1892–1957), American journalist and literary critic, reviewed *MWW* in the September 1927 issue of *The Bookman* along with Wescott's *The Grandmothers* (1927), Conrad Aikens's *Blue Voyage* (1927), and H. G. Wells's *Meanwhile* (1927). Rascoe's comment on EH's collection consists of only one paragraph that discusses "Fifty Grand" and briefly mentions "The Killers." In his letter of [25 October 1927], Fitzgerald wondered if EH had read the "pre-review by that cocksucker Rascoe who obviously had only read three stories but wanted to be up to the minute."

2 American newspaper columnist Franklin Pierce Adams (1881–1960) had recently parodied EH in his satirical column "The Conning Tower" for the *New York Tribune*. Fitzgerald enclosed the clipping in his letter of 25 October.

3 Perkins reported a sale of "seven thousand plus" copies of *MWW* in a cable of 29 October 1927 (PUL). EH refers to the six-day bicycle race in Berlin (the Berliner Tage-Rennen) held 3–9 November 1927. Alfred Flechtheim (1878–1937), German art dealer and publisher who founded *Der Querschnitt*, the magazine that introduced EH's early work in translation to the German market. Flechtheim also owned the Galerie Flechtheim in Berlin and represented avant-garde artists including Pablo Picasso, Georges Braque, Paul Klee, and George Grosz.

4 In a letter of [24 November] EH would ask Perkins to send Fitzgerald a check for the $100 EH owed Fitzgerald. In his letter, Fitzgerald had written, "No work this summer but lots this fall. Hope to finish the novel by 1st December. Have got nervous as hell lately—purely physical but scared me somewhat—to the point of putting me on the wagon and smoking denicotinized cigarettes."

5 *Dusty Answer* (London: Chatto & Windus, 1927), best-selling novel by English writer Rosamond Lehmann (1901–1990), controversial for its depiction of teenage lesbian infatuation.

6 Fitzgerald reported that both he and Zelda liked *MWW*. Zelda's favorite was "Hills Like White Elephants." "Ten Indians" was the only one Fitzgerald didn't care for, and he was glad that "Up in Michigan" was omitted from the collection. Those two stories, he thought, "probably belong to an earlier & almost exhausted vein."

To Gerald and Sara Murphy, [c. 5 November 1927]

Belmonte wasnt killed Thank God except in the French Papers.[1] We are coming home in a week bringing handsome Rentenmarks for everyone.[2] Have been lecturing here on "Amerikan Womanhood."[3] You may have heard of it. Lectures a great Success. Thunderous Applause. All Customers Satisfied. Have contrakts to Lecture all over the World. Know you will be Happy. Ernest.

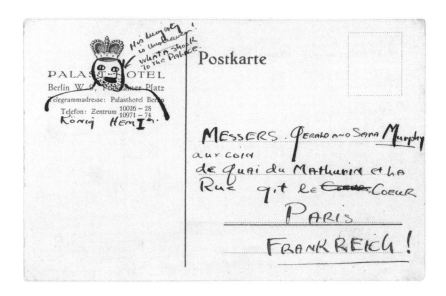

JFK, A Postcard S; letterhead on verso: PALAST HOTEL / Berlin W. 9, Potsdamer
Platz

On the address side of the postcard, EH drew a stubble-faced caricature of himself wearing the
crown emblem in the printed letterhead. He captioned the drawing "König Hem Ier" and to
the side wrote, "His majesty is unshaven! What a shock to the Palace."

1 Performing in Barcelona on 30 October 1927, Belmonte was gored in the groin by his first
   bull of the afternoon, sustaining a wound that required more than a month to heal. He
   would not return to the ring until 1934.
2 Rentenmarks, a temporary German currency issued in November 1923 to help stabilize
   inflation. Backed by agricultural and industrial assets rather than gold, the Rentenmark
   replaced the previous currency, the Papiermark. In August 1924 the Reichsmark, backed by
   gold, began to replace the Rentenmark. Both currencies were in use until 1948.
3 Louis Bromfield had embarked upon a cross-country lecture tour throughout the United
   States that autumn following the publication of *A Good Woman* (New York: Frederick
   A. Stokes, 1927).

To Mrs. Williams, 16 November 1927

Paris, November 16, 1927

Dear Mrs. Williams,

   I am afraid the girl in the White Elephant story was going to have a
baby— But I do not want you to lose any money over it. So perhaps she

wasn't. Though I rather think she was and hope, as literary godfather, that it turned out a fine healthy child.[1]

Anyway I am very happy that you and your husband liked the book. Thank you very much for writing about it.

Yours very truly

Ernest Hemingway.

c/o Guaranty Trust Co. of NY.

1, rue des Italiens

Paris, France.

Heritage Auctions, 2006 October Grand Format Autographs Auction no. 629, lot 25858 (illustrated), ALS

1 Although the word "abortion" is never mentioned in "Hills Like White Elephants" (*MWW*), the story centers on a couple's disagreement about whether or not to end a pregnancy.

To Maxwell Perkins, [24 November] 1927

Thanksgiving Day—1927

Dear Mr. Perkins:

Thanks very much for your two letters—the cable—and the check. It is fine that Men Without is doing so well. I'm trying to save the money to come to America in the early Spring—so may not cash the check in order to keep its full strength. I find that I live, automatically, on exactly the amount of money that I have—seem to get the same results for 100 a month as 1000— So I will try and save the 1000 intact—but doubt if I can. Thank you ever so much for sending it.[1]

Evan Shipman is the boy you know. I think his father is a poor lot too but Evan has unlimited guts (He's a bloody fool though) and has written some really superb poetry— He's led a life though like one of the Karamazov boys— I administered his financial affairs for him for a while—washed him off when he would get beaten up, carried him out on my shoulders of one bad bar room fight—he only weighs about 100 pounds—although he is six feet tall—lungs weak or something and in a perpetual state of gonorrhea (not his lungs) but with all those before mentioned attributes (which are not pugilistic assetts) he gets into the damnedest fights.[2] I've seen him through some extraordinary things which are better told than written— But he is an <u>excellent</u> kid and I think will be a great poet (He can't spell unfortunately) but he can translate beautifully from the French— I dedicated the damn book to him to show anyone interested that I looked on him as something serious and not just a bum. Also I am very fond of him and thought it might please him—if he ever saw it. He's working in a racing stable in America now. Trying to get enough money to come back here. Also he owes me a little money and I thought if he saw the dedication it would show him his credit was still good over here. His father, I believe, borrowed (without security) a good part of the money he came into when he was 21— All this is only between ourselves.

I dont know how wise his father was to let him run. A Boy is pretty much of a problem either way. I suppose if a kid is a poet though he might as well burn fast because god knows most middle aged or elderly poets are a sad thing to see.

I dont say I think he's a fine poet in the interest of getting him published because I think there's nothing <u>worse</u> for a kid than to publish him—unless not being published goes too long and starts to make him bitter. But Evan's not bitter.

The slips from Brooks are enclosed. I'd like to write a play if I could and if it didnt entail going to the theater to see other plays first. But I'm afraid it would.[3] I'd enjoy much more having some competent playwright do for (or to) some book of mine what Owen Davis did for or to the Great Gatsby and me stay 3000 miles away and collect royalties. You have to know a lot to write plays and I know nothing about it. Still it would be fun to try. Could you send me, or would Brooks send me, his play? I'll give him as many copies of Men Without Women as he wants in exchange. Please thank him very much for sending them to the theatrical gents—I appreciate it—and would like them charged to me.

Could you send $100^{00} to Scott and charge to my royalty acct? I have no dollar account and owe Scott that sum.[4]

I believe great authors like Miss Woolf write their own blurbs—
Mr. Dreiser does—also Waldo Frank— The comparisons of the great
masters with Dreiser were written by Dreiser— It must be fine to be hailed
as great and to have the satisfaction of knowing you started the hailing
yourself.[5]

The skiing should be good. There have been great snow falls in the alps
already and the Simplon and Gothard passes are blocked.[6] I was afraid after
no summer there might be no winter—but it has begun already.

I have 17 chapters done on novel and only a third or so through— I am
putting it in the third person now— Got tired of the limitations of the
bloody 1st person—always thinking in one person's head etc. and the
changing is difficult but I think will improve it very very much. It is easy to
write in 1st person—too easy— Today is Thanksgiving day and am using
that as an excuse not to work.

This is a very long letter. I will send a batch of pictures. Hope you get the
skating.[7]

I wish you could come over and ski some year. We will be coming to the
states in March or April and stay through the fall. Will try and get to N.Y.—
Maybe before sailing in the fall. Maybe Scott would team up and we could
lecture on American Womanhood like Louis Bromfield.[8] Maybe you would
come too and we could all lecture on Am. Womanhood. Maybe Flo
Zeigfield would loan some specimens of Am. Womanhood and it could be
an illustrated Lecture.[9]

Yours always,
Ernest Hemingway.

We had Meyer to lunch. He's very nice. I think he wants to stay over a
while yet but will be happy to go back to Scribners.[10]

PUL, ALS

1 In a cable of 29 October, Perkins wrote that *MWW* was getting "enormous praise" and had
   sold "seven thousand plus" copies (PUL). Two days later he sent a $1,000 royalty check,
   and wrote that *MWW* had earned "$400 odd beyond this $1000, after deducting the $750
   advanced" (31 October 1927, PUL; *TOTTC*, 67). By 10 November 1927, Perkins reported
   that sales were "barely short of 9,000 copies" (PUL).

2 In his letter of 10 November 1927, Perkins asked if Evan Shipman was the son of Louis Shipman, "once editor of Life." "If so," Perkins explained, he had always been interested in Evan "on account of his escapades, such as running away from school and working on a railroad, a newspaper, etc. He seemed to be his own man." Perkins added, "I thought not much of his father" (PUL). Louis Evan Shipman (1869–1933), American writer, playwright, and scriptwriter, was the editor of *Life* magazine from 1922 to 1924. He bought a home in the countryside outside Paris in the fall of 1925, where he lived until his death. EH alludes to *The Brothers Karamazov* (1879–1880) by Fyodor Dostoevsky (1821–1881). Much of the book's plot revolves around the rivalry between a dissolute landowner and his sons, one of whom is known for his debauched manner of living.

3 In a letter of 31 October 1927, Perkins had sent EH several slips to autograph for American playwright George S. Brooks (1895–1961), who said he wanted "to paste these into copies of 'Men without Women' and to give them to these theatrical gentlemen, one of whose names is on each slip." Perkins recommended Brooks on the basis of his play *Spread Eagle*, published by Scribner's and staged in New York City at the Martin Beck Theatre in 1927 (PUL).

4 In his reply of 8 December, Perkins would agree to send the check to Fitzgerald (PUL).

5 In reply to EH's letter [c. 26 October 1927] criticizing Virginia Woolf's review of *MWW*, Perkins had written that Woolf's comments based on the book's blurb were "outrageous" because "the author has nothing whatever to do with the blurb" and that Woolf should have complained about the publisher rather than the author (10 November 1927, PUL). All three writers EH mentions had books recently published: Woolf, *Mrs. Dalloway* (1925), Dreiser, *An American Tragedy* (1925), and Frank, *Virgin Spain* (1926).

6 Both the Simplon Pass and the Saint Gotthard Pass link southern Switzerland to northern Italy.

7 Perkins wrote that he anticipated a cold, dry winter with "grand skating."

8 On 16 October 1927 an editorial in the *New York Times* announced that the "age of chivalry, which has been comatose ever since women began asserting their rights forcibly, died outright when Louis Bromfield, playwright and Pulitzer Prize novelist, went on his current lecture tour" (6). In his lectures on the American woman, Bromfield maintained, "It is astonishing how American men worship their women. A tremendous, press-agented holiness has been developed. The American woman is unfair. She gives very little" (quoted in *New York Times* editorial, 6).

9 Florenz Ziegfeld (1867–1932), Chicago-born theatrical impresario. Dubbed the "glorifier of the American girl," he produced the *Ziegfeld Follies*, a series of revues staged on Broadway from 1907 to 1931 and featuring scantily clad women in musical and dance numbers.

10 Wallace Meyer (1892–1985), employee of Charles Scribner's Sons. In his 17 October letter, Perkins wrote: "Wallace Meyer, the man who advertised 'The Sun Also' is now in Europe—we hope temporarily. As he is a great admirer of you, he may look you up. I hope he does.— But he is a reticent chap, and may not" (PUL). Meyer would become EH's editor after Perkins's death in 1947 and senior editor of the firm in 1957.

To Wyndham Lewis, [17 or 24 November 1927]

Thursday 6.30 pm

Dear Mr. Lewis—

I'm awfully sorry not to have gotten your note until about an hour ago.[1] Could you eat lunch with me tomorrow, Friday? I will wait for you here at 6 rue Férou—from 12 until one oclock and we could have a drink and go out and eat somewhere.

You probably know the rue Férou—facing the Luxembourg Museum—[2] Hope it's not out of your way[.] If it would be more convenient to you to meet somewhere else will you send me word here?

I'm awfully damned sorry not to have been at the bank this noon.

Ernest Hemingway.

Cornell, ALS

1 In an undated letter, Lewis wrote to EH, "Can you meet for lunch tomorrow (Thursday) or the next day? Will you meet me at the Guaranty Trust at 12, noon?" (JFK).
2 The Luxembourg Museum (Musée du Luxembourg) is located at 19, rue de Vaugirard in Paris. In his memoirs, EH would recall studying Cézanne's landscape paintings at the museum to learn techniques he could use in his writing ("Hunger Was Good Discipline," *MF*).

To James George Leippert, November 1927

6 rue Férou

Paris

November (?) 1927

Dear Mr. Leippert—

Thank you ever so much for writing about the book. Living over here and rarely seeing anybody that reads my stuff it feels very good to hear from some one directly that they like it.

If you really want to write I dont know any advice to give you except to write and keep on writing. And not to be discouraged if the stuff is no good— Because it would be a very bad sign if it was anything else for a long time. It doesnt matter where you go or what you do as long as you really see what's going on and listen and Keep your eyes open.[1]

Best luck anyway and thanks again for writing.

Yours always,
Ernest Hemingway

Christie's catalog, New York, 15 November 2011, lot 73 (illustrated), ALS

1 This sentence appears to have been squeezed in later by EH as a final word of advice.

To Grace Hall Hemingway, [c. November 1927]

Dear Mother;

Thanks for your letters. I have been enquiring around and find that most all of the American artists who live or study here go to America to have their shows.[1] Those who show here hire a galerie for a period of 7 to 10 days— [*EH insertion*: which is, I believe, quite expensive.] or Exhibiting at the salons is done by submitting the pictures to a Jury—which throws out a large percentage of them. There are nearly 20,000 artists living in Paris. Some 2 or 3,000 I believe exhibit at the two annual Salons—the Spring and the Fall. There are also the Salon des Independants and another at the Palais de Bois.[2]

There are also many street exhibitions— In which two or three hundred artists—many very good ones—expose their pictures along the street on temporary stands and boxes on a Saturday afternoon and Sunday. Competition is terribly keen— There are about six painters for every picture buyer. There are also in France many of what are called "Sunday Painters"—men and women who can only paint during the week end or in their spare time—and yet who paint very well.

Most of the painters I know are dead Broke and their only hope is to be able to live for a small amount while they paint so they can save up to go to America and have a show. The prices that you get for your pictures already is more than the Luxembourg Museum is able to pay for the pictures it buys by living artists. The works of many great dead artists are sold at the auctions for much less— So you would seem to be in the land of opportunity already.

There have been expositions by American artists here—(joint shows)—but they are usually members of a group or people who share amg themselves the cost of the show. I am sending you a catalogue for the salon. It will doubtless contain the requirements for admission. The next Salon is in the Spring. I believe too that American artists exhibit at the American Woman's Club but I take it you want something more high sounding.[3]

If you wanted to send over a couple of canvasses I would be very glad to enter them for you in any show they might be allowed to enter—but I could not be held responsible for loss or damage to such valuable paintings.[4]

But when you see lines of really excellent paintings exhibited along the Boulevard Raspail for three and four blocks by good artists—who would give anything for an exhibition and are selling their paintings at from 100 to 500 francs—($4 to $20) you must realize what competition is here.

I buy pictures myself and paid 750 francs for a painting which is now listed and reproduced in all the books on Modern art. It is true it is now worth over 10,000 but it was the highest priced picture at the show when I bought it.[5] Bertram Hartmann who is well known in America could not get a show here in Paris—he only sold some 3 pictures in a year—$50 was the top price—which I paid. He is now back in N.Y. doing Batiks.[6]

You seem to have had the most phenomenal success I have ever heard about and I would advise you to keep after it in a country where there is so much money.

Glad you liked the advertisements of my book. I have not seen them. I imagine Fanny Butcher will have another Splendid Review.

To return to pictures—

The system over here is for an artist to sell through a dealer who sells the pictures at a very cheap price—almost a nominal price—if they have any real value they will be resold and the law of supply and demand operates. Thus an artist sells all his pictures to the dealer at a fixed price—as the public value goes up the dealer gives him a better price. But the idea is to get rid of the pictures and give them a chance to acquire a <u>real</u> not a fictitious (placed by the artist) value. Thus the artist may sell 200 pictures quite cheaply and for the 201st get as much as for all the others put together. But all good painters here start getting practically nothing for their pictures. But when they start to get big money it is a real market—their pictures have a staple value like commodities listed in a market. In America ~~you seem to be~~ it seems painters put big prices on pictures and sell a few rather than selling them all, doing more and letting the paintings get a real value—what people are willing to pay at auction.

This probably does not interest you— However, Cezanne's, which were sold 20 years ago for 10 and 20 dollars are now worth 50 to 100 thousand dollars— Picassos have increased in almost the same proportion in the past 5 years. Matisse too. The latter two probably painters you consider to be "nuts[.]"[7] Well this is too long already.

> Best luck,
>
> Yours,
>
> Ernie

[*On verso of outermost sheet of letter when folded:*]

> Love to Dad and the Kids.
>
> Ernie

PSU, ALS

This letter most likely was forwarded from Oak Park to California, where Grace was visiting her brother, Leicester Hall, and making sketches for her paintings. The envelope of her reply, dated 16 December 1927, is postmarked Glendale, California.

1 In her letter of 14 October 1927, EH's mother reported on her growing success as a painter and asked, "Is there any chance for me to get a picture exhibited in Paris?" (JFK).
2 The annual exhibition of the Société Nationale des Beaux-Arts, known as the Spring Salon, was initiated by the Académie des Beaux-Arts in 1774 to promote academic art and featured only juried entries. The Société des Artistes Indépendants was founded in 1884 as an nonjuried showcase for artists whose works were rejected by the traditional Salon. Formed in 1903 as a progressive alternative, the Salon d'Automne (Autumn Salon) was more open than the Spring Salon to exhibiting contemporary and avant-garde art. The 1924 Baedeker guide to Paris notes that the Salon des Tuileries, founded in 1923 by dissident members of the Société Nationale des Beaux-Arts, was first held in summer 1924 at the Palais de Bois, adjoining the Porte Maillot (36).
3 The American Women's Club, located on the Rue Boissière, served as a social club for American expatriate women. It is mentioned in Chapter 8 of *SAR*.

4 In her letter of 16 December 1927, Grace would reply, "I am glad of your advice and will take the chance you offer when I return to Chicago, the middle of February" (JFK).

5 It is unclear as to which of his paintings EH is referring. He had purchased Miró's *La Ferme* (*The Farm*) for 3,500 francs in 1925. He may simply be trying to temper his mother's expectations as to how much she might earn for her paintings in Paris.

6 C. Bertram Hartman (1882–1960), American artist and illustrator for such magazines as *The Dial* and *Judge*. During the winter of 1924–1925, Hartman and his wife, Gusta (neé Frank, b. c. 1885), had stayed at the Hotel Taube in Schruns, Austria, at the same time as EH and Hadley. According to Reynolds, that winter "Hadley took back to Paris as her own" two village scenes Hartman had painted while at Schruns (*PY*, 261).

7 Paul Cézanne (1839–1906), Pablo Picasso (1881–1973), Henri Matisse (1869–1954).

To Harry Crosby, [2 December 1927]

6 rue Férou

Paris

Dear Crosby—

I lost your note like a damn fool and didnt have the address. Finally got it from Sylvia Beach.[1] Hope this isnt too late. I'll come over about 3 oclock if that's all right. Bumby, my kid, has been to the Cluny twice this week and circus once and I'm afraid of making him blasé by taking him again. Why dont you try and get ahold of MacLeish He's at 8 rue Emile Augier— (Passy). I might bring him if I see him. Let's go in time to see Rico and Alex—they are Spanish and damned funny.[2] Thanks so much for asking me to go.

yrs always,

Ernest Hemingway.

Would love to see the lions
Do you know Peterson?

SIU, ALS; postmark: Paris, 27 / 2 du 12

1 EH addressed this carte pneumatique to Harry Crosby / 19 Rue de Lille / Paris / E.V.–
2 Musée de Cluny (National Museum of the Middle Ages), located at 6, place Paul-Painlevé. Spanish clowns Enrico Briatore (c. 1881–1965) and his uncle Alexandro (Alejandro) Briatore (c. 1870–1960) performed throughout Europe.

To Isabelle Simmons Godolphin, 5 December [1927]

<u>Merry Christmas</u>
Dec ⑤

Dearest Izz—

Congratulations on the hussy—if you want a godfather or anything count on the child's Uncle Ernie.[1] Youre a fine girl and thanks for the fine letter. I'd have answered before but have been working like hell and other times failing to work like hell which is even harder. Have twenty chapetrs done however and reading it over [it] seems all right part [o]f the time and other times what I have nicknamed horse manure. We go to Swiss in a week. Wish you and yr. immediate family were along—will go to Gstaad byond Chamby where we had the swell times. How is Frisco? Say Parent Heil to him for me and wish him luck. All fathers need luck. You're a fine girl though and I'm awfully glad about the baby. I've now found the letter and can comment more intelligently. Have looked up and now do not have to refer to the child, baby etc. can say Jean. Congratulations on Jean. What are your plans for this infant? Do you think she would like to marry Bumby? Bumby will not have much money and will also have to support his elderly male parent but if you don't mind that a marriage might be arranged. [O]r if you think Bumby is too old and sophisticated for Jean we will have lots more children that she might like to marry—or if she doesn't want to marry—and some don't—maybe we could get her to come and work for us and help bumby support us and thus take her off your hands, give her a fine moral influence, and teach her to read proof and then later she could go back to youse and maybe support youse. Who knows?

Anyway it was swell to hear from you and write again. How is Hammy [Helen Hamilton]? How are you yourself? Has my mother painted yr portrait yet? I read an interview with her she sent me in which she said she laughed at these young novelists and felt the pendulum was swinging back to normal—whatever the hell that means except that she is ashamed over her son Ernie and wishes he were Glenway Wescott or some highly respectable Fairy Prince with an English accent and a taste for grandmothers.[2]

Write me a swell long letter full of news about Oak Park? How bad are my mother's pictures? What has become of Katherine Meyer? Avery Balch? Mr. MacDaniel's and all the wild young people— What are my sisters like? Be good to them if you can. I think Carol would be a good kid— They all imagine me as with my toe and fingernails grown into cleft hoofs and horns coming out from the forehead.[3]

We are coming to U.S. in the Spring by way of somewher[e] besides N.Y. and will see youse surely before leaving in the fall. Will be down at Gstaad now for a monthor two or so. Am sick as a ——— with my throat as always this time of year—want to get down there and get helthy. Nearly died last Spring. If I ever kick out will leave a letter telling Bumby to marry Jean if satisfactory financial arrangements can be made [*long cross out*] started to make a fine joke but thought that any letter sent to Oak Pa[r]k ought to be read aloud to all our relatives. I still love you—read that aloud at your own discretion. Got married in the Spring—see Hadley every once in a while. She's grand shape. Sends her love to you. So does Pauline. Bumby also. /He's going down to Swiss with us. Best to Francis and to your Family and Simmy, Chuck and Lucy May and to you always,[4]

Ernie

Best to Hammy another swell girl

Glad you liked the stories—

Address in Gstaad—Hotel Rössli Switzerland but better send to Guaranty Trust in Paris as might move around

Merry Christmas again!

Live at 6 rue Férou

Don't say anything about me being married

PUL, TLS with autograph postscript

1 Isabelle and Francis Godolphin's daughter, Katherine Jeanne Godolphin, was born in November 1927. Jeanne later married Steven G. Kurtz (1926-2008), noted historian and principal of Exeter Academy.

2 Carlos Baker quotes an article by Bertha Fenberg in the *Oak Park News* of 8 November 1927 about Grace's paintings, headlined "Launches New Career After Raising Family," as saying that one might expect the mother of Ernest Hemingway to be "something of a harsh realist,

but this very jolly woman laughs at the pessimism of 'these young writers' and expresses the sane belief that the pendulum is swinging back to normal" (*Life*, 188, 596). EH alludes to Wescott's *The Grandmothers* (New York: Harper, 1927).

3 Catherine M. Meyer (c. 1901–1930), a member of the OPRFHS high school class of 1918, had lived at 601 N. Kenilworth Avenue down the street from the Hemingways. Avery Balch (1901–1983), also a graduate of OPRFHS, grew up at 611 N. Kenilworth Avenue, across the street from the Hemingway family home. OPRFHS Principal Marion Ross McDaniel (1875–1939) lived at 733 N. Kenilworth Avenue. It would be summer 1928 before Godolphin responded, "The news of the town run this way (by request) . . . Avery Balch—married Esther . . . Cat Meyer had nervous breakdown—been in sanatorium for 6 mos. . . . Hemingways—Madame paints and paints and paints. Dr. still running out at 8 in the morning in the old Ford on emergency case (I judge)—Carol & Sunny good gals—Carol looks like her brother Ernest" ([5 August 1928], JFK).

4 Isabelle's siblings: "Simmy," Howard L. Simmons, Jr. (1903–1962); "Chuck," Charles E. Simmons (1908–2000); and Lucy May Simmons (1906–1930).

To Vincent C. Donovan, [early December 1927]

Dear Father Vincent C. Donovan;

Thank you very much for writing me. I would like to have the book and would prize it greatly. It was very good of you to offer it and I would like to send you a copy of the last book of stories.[1]

I wish I had saved Don's life—but the only life saving was in the Chicago newspapers. Don will tell you he was in no real danger.[2] It was a ~~tough~~ rough Spanish game but no rougher than boxing or professional football. ~~Mr. Cameron Rodgers I know only very slightly~~

Don wrote in August that he was coming over in November but since then we have heard nothing of him. Now I hear that he is going to have a child and it is worth missing him if it's true.[3]

Mr. Cameron Rodgers I know only slightly; he was here this fall and I met him several times with friends, Eddy Tilyou (of Coney Island) a grand boy whom you may know and Waldo Pierce; but we never spoke of the Church.[4] I have been a Catholic for many years ~~and I think he must have been misinformed—although~~ (although I fell away very badly and did not go to communion for [nearly ?] 8 years) However I have gone regularly to mass for the last two years and definitely set my house in order within the year[.] However I have always had more faith than intelligence or knowlege and I have never wanted to be known as a Catholic writer because I know the importance of setting an example—and I have never set a good example.

~~I remember Don and I talking talking with Don about three or four years ago at a time when he was very upset about things and he saying there were only two solutions to things Hollywood or the Catholic Church. He meaning complete vulgarity or some mystical~~

~~But~~

~~I am trying to lead a good life in the church and am very happy and my only unhappinesses come from writing~~

Also I am a very dumb Catholic and I have so much faith that I hate to examine into it—but I am trying to lead a good life and to write well and truly—and it is easier to do the first than the second.

You were very good to write to me and I appreciate it greatly and hope we can meet in N.Y. sometime. In the meantime I would welcome the book— ~~or be glad to buy it here.~~ and will value it highly. Give my very best regards to Don and thank you again for writing

Yours very truly,

Ernest Hemingway.

JFK, ALDS

The date of this penciled draft is conjectured relative to Donovan's incoming letter of 24 November [1927] from New York, to which EH is responding, and Donovan's reply of 26 December 1927 (JFK), allowing time for transatlantic mail service. In his 26 December letter, Donovan mentioned that EH's letter had arrived "a week ago today." The letter EH actually sent remains unlocated.

1 In his letter of 24 November, Father Donovan offered to send EH a copy of his book *The Path to Peace* (JFK). In a letter of 30 January [1928], EH would ask Maxwell Perkins to send Donovan a copy of *MWW*.
2 Father Donovan wrote to EH that he had first heard of him while reading a Chicago newspaper article several years earlier describing how EH had saved Donovan's friend Donald Ogden Stewart from being gored by a bull in Pamplona. In a front-page story headlined "Bull Gores 2 Yanks Acting as Toreadores," the *Chicago Daily Tribune* reported on 29 July 1924 that "the bull rushed Stewart, lifted him on his horns, tossed him over, threw him into the air ... Hemingway rushed to rescue his comrade and was also gored." That account, together with *SAR* and some of EH's stories, had "so favorably impressed" the clergyman "with a note of sincerity and substantiality most often lacking in younger modern writers" that he hoped to meet EH one day.

3 Donald Ogden Stewart's first son, Ames, would be born on 21 May 1928.
4 Cameron Rogers, (1900–1971), American poet and nonfiction writer whose books included *The Magnificent Idler: The Story of Walt Whitman* (1926), *Gallant Ladies* (1928), and *The Legend of Calvin Coolidge* (1928). Rogers had told Father Donovan that EH had become a Catholic within the past year, and in his letter of 24 November Donovan expressed an interest in "the psychology of conversion." Edward Francis Tilyou (1896–1944) was the son of George C. Tilyou (1862–1914), who founded Steeplechase Park on Coney Island; after his father's death, Edward took over and modernized the amusement park.

To F. Scott Fitzgerald, 18 and [c. 20] December 1927

Dear Scott—

The enclosed scraps—if pieced together—will form a fine letter containing all the news; which I wrote—tore up—as too bloody dull to send but havent pep or anything else enough to write over. Wish the hell I could see you nobody to talk about writing or the literary situation with. why the hell dont you write yr. novel?

Best to Zelda and Scotty.

Max Perkins says M. Without W. is selling like a book by Fitzgerald (you know the guy who wrote Omar Kayam)[1]

We are coming to America in March or April—land at San Antonio Texas if its on the coast.

At moment of writing I have

1 Blindness—

2 Piles

3 A bad case of grippe

4 A toothache—

Mery Christmas to all and to all a Happy New Year like this one wasnt—

Yr. affect disciple in the literary game

HEm

[*Here follow the "scraps" that EH mentions above, taped back into one page, with upper left portion missing:*]

Hotel Rossli

Gstaad—Suisse

Dec 18

[*tear*] letter about six wee[k] [*tear*] [too ~~is~~] lousy to send. Glad you [*tear*] How the hell are you anyway? I started a novel early in the fall and had 20 chapters done—about 55–60,000 words then got sick (nothing) just grippy in the head so I couldnt write—then came down here with Bumby and Pauline to get healthy—and at Montreux on the way down Bumby when I picked him up in the night to put him on the pot stuck one of his fingers in my right eye and the nail went in and cut the pupil—just a little place like this ∩ — like a fishscale or something. But it was my one good eye and I've been in bed and shot to hell in one way or another ever since[.] So that's all the news except its been 30 below zero here.

This is no letter because I cant see yet but I'm sorry as [*letter ends*]

PUL, ALS

1 *Rubáiyát of Omar Khayyám the Astronomer-Poet of Persia*, a popular collection of Persian poems translated and published by English poet Edward FitzGerald (1809–1883) in 1859.

To Clarence and Grace Hall Hemingway, [c. 25 December 1927]

C160 CABLE GSTAAD 16 LCD
DR AND MRS HEMINGWAY AND FAMILY.
600 KENILWORTH OAKPARK (ILL).
MERRY CHRISTMAS FROM,
ERNIE AND BUMBY.

PSU, Cable; letterhead: HOLIDAY GREETING / WESTERN UNION

To William McFarland, [c. late December 1927]

Dear Mr. McFartland,

I have received your letter which I have been unable to understand. One sentence however is quite clear—"If none of these what is your attempt?"[1]

If none of these my attempt is to write stories and sometimes novels placing one word after another, hoping always that they will make sense, and that they will be stories or novels. You will, perhaps, yourself be able to define these terms; i.e. stories and novels, and tell in what they consist. I believe that there has sometimes been a lack of agreement on these definitions.

Wishing you the best success in your thesis and warning you in a friendly manner against becoming a writer, except perhaps a critic, I am yours very truly,

JFK, TLD

This is a draft of the following letter.

1 In a letter of 13 December 1927, McFarland identified himself as a student at the University of Michigan in Ann Arbor working on a thesis discussing thirty-five of the foremost contemporary novelists writing in English, titled "The Relationship of the Novel and Society." He asked EH, "Would you say your writing is affected by society?" McFarland also wondered if EH attempted "to picture, criticize, or improve society? (Realism, Satire, Utopianism.)" (JFK).

To William McFarland, [c. late December 1927]

Dear Mr. McFarland;

The questions which you ask can not be answered on the back of the sheet of paper you enclosed, if they can be answered at all, since they seem not to be questions but invitations to a discussion. You should enclose a definition of "society". A man would be an horse's ass to suppose that novels are not formed by people or people (society) affected by novels. Why not take up something less obvious and silly.

Yours very truly,

P.S. If a note from me would in any way help to intensify a desire on your part to become a writer yourself, someday, please do not consider this a note in that direction.

JFK, TL

With his 13 December 1927 letter to EH, McFarland had provided a stamped return envelope, which does not survive with his letter at JFK. It is uncertain whether EH mailed this response.

To F. Scott Fitzgerald, [late December 1927]

Dear Scott—

Always glad to hear from a brother pederast. You ask for the news. Well I have quit the writing game and gone into the pimping game.[1] They have been purifying Paris and running all the former and well known pimps out and it has left a big lack and a fine opportunity both of which I am trying to fill. I have lined up a fine lot of "girls" les girls" a french word and when you and the Mrs. Come over in the Spring I will be able to offer you some very interesting reductions.

Old Brommy has certainly swept the women's clubs. It was a sure thing that he would encounter my mother. "Mother of Four Takes Up Painting at 52" and he did.[2]

He told her he was certain he had recogn[i]zed her although he couldn't place her because Ernest was his best friend and how wouldn't he know Ernest's mother. Now my mother has a new cause to weep because I don't write like Brommy.

Are you keeping little Scotty off of the hop any better?[3] We hear many happy anecdotes over here about how she jammed H.L.Menken with her own little needle the last time he visited at the Mansions and that that was how the American Mercury came to be written.

Teddy Chandler the boy whom if I am not mistaken once killed your mother is over here. Also Bill Bullitt or Bull Billet a big Jew from Yale and fellow novel writer.[4] Pat Guthrie who once lived with Duff Twizden is now being kept by Lorna Lindsley who is looking even fresher and lovlier. None of these people I ever see but will be glad to loook them up for you.

My son Bumby is following in his father's footsteps and makes up stories. Hearsts have offered him 182,000 bits for a serial about Lesbians who were wounded in the war and it was so hard to have children that they all took to drink and running all over Europe and Asia just a wanton crew of wastrels. I have introduced him to a lot of them and he is writing hard and I am helping him a little now and then with the spelling and Pauline reads aloud to him your stories out of the Post so he will get an idea of the style which is going to be the same as that of the latest poems by MacLeish only trimmed with Persian Lamb. Bumby is calling the thing

lesbos Lesbos LESBOS

I see a few people except Mike Ward the ex Banker who had an amazing adventure the other night in the Club Daunou where he hit a man standing at the bar because he said something about me that he, Mike, did not hear but didn't like the sound of. He asked the man if he was a friend of mine and when the man said no Mike hit him. Later it turned out that the man had not mentioned me at all but Mike said that the man was no friend of mine he could tell.

You ought to have loyal friends like that Fitz.

There was no money in Spanish fly so I gave up. the Spanish Fly game. My eye is all right now and we are hoping it will snow. Jinny has been here since the 1st of December hopingit will snow too. We have only been hoping since the 14th of December. I have a sore throat and am in bed. I gues you will agree we got Lindberg a nice lot of publicity. Would you like me to be publicity man for either Scotty or Zelda. You are right about the spanish wine skin and I find it very comfortable but it has nothing so unhemanish as a zipper.[5] I have to watch myself that way and deny myself many ofthe little comforts like toilet paper, semi-colons, and soles to my shoes. Any time I use any of those people begin to shout that old Hem is just a fairy after all and no He man ha ha. On acct. being so laid up so long started a fine beard which ia now almost rabbinical. May keep it until come to the states but doubt it.

Write me all the news and views. Love to Zelda and little Scotty if you can keep her off of the stuff long enough for her to understand the message. You shouldn't let that child have Heroin Scott. I've thought it over from every angle and it can't be good for her. I know that you have to keep up appearances and I know the way things are nowadays but nobody can convince me that it really does a child of that age any good.

Write again. Now I don't owe you anything besides undying gratitude a and say 180 bottles of champagne I can write free-er.

yrs. always,

Ernest.

PUL, TL with typewritten signature

Although Baker dates this letter c. 15 December 1927, the conjectured date of [late December 1927] is based on the consideration that EH is responding to a letter Fitzgerald wrote and sent between c. 10 and 23 December ([December 1927], JFK). EH also mentions here that his eye, injured by Bumby on 13 December, "is all right now."

1 In his letter, Fitzgerald described writing short stories for the *Saturday Evening Post* in terms of prostitution, saying, "I am now their pet exhibit and go down on them to the tune of 32,000 bits per felony" (JFK; Bruccoli *Fitz–Hem*, 92–93).
2 Fitzgerald had commented that Louis Bromfield was "sweeping the west" on his lecture tour. EH's mother attended Bromfield's lecture at the Nineteenth Century Club meeting in Oak Park on 10 October 1927 and told EH in a letter of 14 October 1927 that she had introduced herself to Bromfield after his talk and he said that EH was one of his best friends (JFK). Grace Hall Hemingway had been the subject of an article headlined "Mother of Four Becomes Artist! Wins Notice for Portraits at 52," a copy of which survives in the Newspaper Clippings file at JFK (*Lynchburg* [Virginia] *Advance*, 30 November 1927). Grace had six children.
3 "Hop," slang for heroin.
4 Theodore Chanler (1902–1961), American composer. Chanler was a friend of Gerald and Sara Murphy and provided inspiration for the Francis Melarky character in an early version of Fitzgerald's *Tender Is the Night* (1934) that revolved around a case of matricide. William Bullitt, a 1912 Yale graduate, was the author of the 1926 novel *It's Not Done* (Harcourt).
5 Fitzgerald had written, "I hear you were seen running through Portugal in used B.V.Ds, chewing ground glass and collecting material for a story about Boule players; that you were publicity man for Lindberg; that you have finished a novel a hundred thousand words long consisting entirely of the word 'balls' used in new groupings; that you have been naturalized a Spaniard, dress always in a wine-skin with 'zipper' vent and are engaged in bootlegging Spanish Fly between St. Sebastian and Biaritz where your agents sprinkle it on the floor of the Casino. I hope I have been misinformed but, alas! It all has too true a ring." Charles Augustus Lindbergh (1902–1974) accomplished the first solo flight over the Atlantic Ocean, taking off from Roosevelt Field on Long Island, New York, on 20 May 1927 and landing at Le Bourget Field near Paris on the following day.

To Ezra Pound, [5 January 1928]

Dear Mr. Pound,

The enclosed cutting from the Paris Times will be, I hope, introduction enough. May I congratulate you—or aint it true. Jeesus and a relative of Longfellow too.[1] Why have you held that out on your old friend hem all these years? Well this is very good news. Hope you can plug up the old fistula now and enjoy the 2000 bucks.[2]

I had not written before because I was under the impression that you had lied to me. You told me that you were a friend of Wyndham Lewis (the critic and philosopher)

Lewis, as you know, has always been one of my idols and when I read in his magazine The Enema what he had to say about you I felt that you must have lied. That you could be no friend of Lewis. That all the time that I had thought you were helping Lewis and going to bat for him that you were probably knifing him.

Needless to say I await with eager anticipation an attack on you by Mr. Eliot—surely any bastard that you have helped as much as you have Major Eliot must be able to produce something that would rank with the better gladiatorial shows when he starts to knife you.[3]

I certainly am happy as a bastard that you got the prize. Even if it is delayed. May Thayer have nothing but tender arseholes for a year.[4] And to think of the prize being given to a man with such a perfect alibi as Fistula. You won't mind my cabling a story to the effect that you had suffered from this complaint for some time (with the dates and certificati medicale) and consequently could never have been buggared by Herr Thayer nor any of his friends and hence are in reality the First Genuine Receipant of the Dial Prize on a basis of Merito Litterario et Non Fallatio ni Assholio ni Kissassio.

As for that rival of the Satevepost the Exile I can't write about the Presidechul Candidoots for it as yet in any manner it or they being a subjeck on which I know nothing and hence hope to follow my unique au monde programme of not writing about it (i.e. subjecks on which I kno nothing)[5]

I am however going to our native country in March—entering by way of easy stages, Havana, Keye West etc. and working north to attend the Republican Nashnul convenchun at Kansas City in July. I would be very happy and proud to attend this convention as the Special Correspondent of The Exile if you would furnish me with credentials and will report it extensively to any extent you wish. I will be glad to report it in any way you wish and writing in any manner that does not involve work (i.e. the manner of Gertrude [Stein] or any other of our great writers) Would this offer of one of the Great Pens of our Age (see the clippings) placed at your disposal and at that of your publication be at all interesting?[6]

Have turned down contract of 1,500 bucks a story 15,000 for serialization of novel etc. etc. in order to be entirely free to write for your publication. I should expect the remuneration I have been accustomed to receive from you—i.e. the carefully unexpressed opinion that most of what I write is shit. I have found this to be of great value to me.

When will youse be coming out after July?[7] Should I take the Timely or the Imperishable note?

Let me know. Best to Dorothy—where is Omar? Watch out when you pick him up because Bumby poked his finger in my eye and the nail cut the pupil and in consequence I am now nearly as blind (harry Greb having poked his thimb in the other eye at an earlier and more active stage of my career) as the Irish Milton.[8]

Hoever if I can't see the convention I can hear enough to write you a good piece. Besides the eye is jelling nicely and is much better.

Send me an Exile. Don't be tight just because you now have 2,000 dollars. I know the rich have an obligation to be tight but fight it off. Send me an exile. If necessary end me your own number. Unless of course it contains fragments of an unpublished work by let us say John Rodker. In which event send me one when you get one.

Am here for a while. It has snowed according to the papers everywhere in yarrup but still not yet in Swisserland. Du[ri]ng the blind spell have had James, your old boy friend Henry, read aloud—The Awkward Age—Is it supposed to be good? It sounds like the most peurile, drool. Leave me know. My impression is that he knew NOTHING about people. Unless he is much better than in the Awkward Age he will not outlast Wm. Dean Howells.[9]

I can see that he had developed an easy way of writing. Anything else?

Gld to hear from you. You were quite right about a certain guy we once discussed.

yrs. Hem

Hotel Rossli—Gstaad—Suisse.

[*Typewritten upside down at bottom of page:*]

Enclosed please find congratulations

Yale, TL with typewritten signature; postmark: GSTAAD / (BERN), 5.1.28·16

1 An article in the 25 December 1927 *New York Times* announced that Pound had won the 1927 Dial Award for distinguished service to American letters, reporting he was related on his mother's side to the American poet Henry Wadsworth Longfellow (1807–1882). EH addressed this letter's envelope to "The Right Honorable DialPrizeman / Sig. Egg. EZRA POUND." The *Paris Times* (unaffiliated with the *New York Times*) was an independent afternoon newspaper that was published between 1924 and 1929, which catered to English-speaking expatriates, competing with the morning Paris edition of the *Chicago Tribune*. Responding in a letter of 7 January 1928, Pound noted that EH had neglected to enclose the "alledged clipping" (JFK).

2 In his letter to EH of 26 December [1927], Pound reported that he had been hospitalized with "bullfighter's complaint" but could "now again sit perpen diciler" (JFK). The Dial Award carried a prize of $2,000.

3 Pound had provided substantial moral and material support to T. S. Eliot (1888–1965), whose landmark poem *The Waste Land* (1922) was edited by Pound. Eliot had dedicated the poem to Pound, "*il miglior fabbro*" (the better craftsman[Italian]).

4 Scofield Thayer (1890–1982), editor and co-owner of *The Dial* from 1918 to 1929. Pound had submitted six poems by EH to *The Dial* in 1922. When all were rejected, EH developed a lifelong grudge against both Thayer and *The Dial.*

5 Pound had invited EH to "do a whoozoo of presidenshul candydates" for the fourth number of *The Exile.*

6 On 17 March 1928 EH and Pauline would return to the United States, sailing on the *Orita* from La Rochelle, France, to Havana. They went on to Key West, where they stayed until they left for Piggott and then Kansas City for the birth of their first child. EH would briefly attend the 1928 Republican National Convention, held 12–15 June in Kansas City, but did not write about it for Pound's magazine. Pound would reply in his 7 January letter, "Yes, by all moans cover Repub. convention. Brevity, pungency, and the inconvenient fax."

7 EH refers to the next number of *The Exile*, which would be dated Autumn 1928 and published in New York by Covici Friede.

8 American boxer Edward Henry Greb (1894–1926), the "Human Windmill," won the 1922 light heavyweight title. English poet John Milton (1608–1674), author of *Paradise Lost* (1667), went blind in his forties. The "Irish Milton" refers to Dublin-born author James Joyce, whose eyesight was failing.

9 Henry James's novel *The Awkward Age* (1899).

To Waldo Peirce, [c. 7 January 1928]

Muy senor mio—

That was a fine letter from Spain. Jailed for Judy. Under a dictatorship the only thing that isn't feo to kiss in public is the ass of the dictator. Remember that chico when travelling in Italy and the Peninsula.[1] That was a fine thing about Aiken kicking the goal after Joyce made the touchdown—. Let us hope Conrad put the pigskin over the crossbar.[2] Where in hell are you now?

I was in bed for ten days with one thing and another and it snowed all over God's Europe except here in Suisse. Bumby poked his finger in my one good eye and the nail cut the pupil— I'd picked him up at night in Mntreux to put him on the pot— Had a hell of a time. Harry Greb stuxk his thumb in the other eye at an earlier and more active period of my life. The puil is alll nicely jelled now and during the interval have also vanquished piles and the grippe. Pauline has been fine and has read Henry James (The Awkward Age) out loud and knowing nothing about James it seems to me to be the shit. He seems to need to bring in a drawing room whenever he is scared he will have to think what the characters do the rest of the time and the men all without any exception talk and think like fairies except a couple of caricatures of brutal "outsiders". You have read more and better ones than this doubtless but he seems an enormous fake in this. What ho? Was he a fake? He had obviously developed a fine very easy way for himself to write and great knowlege of drawing room but did he have anything else? Let me hear from you on this.

Why don't you come down here? It is a healthy damn life once the snow comes and if you can keep Bumby's finger out of your eye and is snowing now outside to beat hell. We are thinking of moving from here to Zweissimen where there are less Bloodies and better beer.[3] This place costs 12 swiss francs a day pension and is the cheapest pub in town with the best food. But for a man with as many families as me that is too much and think Zweissimen will be cheaper and they have good Munich beer and fine ski-ing. Pauline and Jinny have gone over this afternoon to look at rooms.

The Christmas cards were beautiful—the one of Col Baalam the chaste and the lewd and the one for us. They are damned lovely.[4] Would you like me to write anything for you. It is a son of a bitching thing the way you work like a bastard for your friends at your trade and what can they do for you.

Would you like a copy of

> The Earnest Liberal's Lament
> > I know monks masturbate at night
> > > That pet cats screw
> > > That some girls bite
> > > And Yet
> > > Oh Lord What can I do to set things right?

This dedicated to Oswald Garrison Villard and the editors of New Republic.[5]

If Pauline were here she would write something on this letter as she wanted to write you. She and Jinny and I would be happy as hell if you could come down. Also Bumby. He has fought every kid in town and learned German since coming down here. I asked him what he was going to do when he grew up and he said he was going to make whiskey for papa.

Love to Ivy. Do you know Pat and Whitney's address?[6] It is still snowing and looks like the real thing. Come on down. I have a three and a half week's beard and if you came down there would be two of them in town. Bumby is willing to grow a beard but can't make it. I don't know any news—is there any. Best to Saunders.[7]

best always,

Ernest

Colby, TLS

1 In a fourteen-page letter to EH dated 28 December 1927 and sent from Barcelona, Peirce reported on his dalliance with a married woman named Julie, for which he was thrown in jail (JFK). *Feo*: ugly; *chico*: kid, a nickname EH often used in addressing Peirce (Spanish).

2 In his letter, Ivy, Peirce criticized Conrad Aiken's recently published novel *Blue Voyage* (1927) saying, "A feeling for a novel does not make a novel—vaguely Joyce—Conrad trying to kick the goal after James scores the touch down."

3 "Bloodies" likely refers to the English tourists who frequented Gstaad.

4 Peirce wrote that he hoped his Christmas cards had arrived and mentioned that he sent his "wanton" card to T. S. Eliot along with a short poem and "a little jingle on Gerty [Stein]." In

the book of Numbers, Balaam is hired by Balak, King of the Moabs, to curse the Israelites, but God stops him and forces him to bless them instead.

5 EH's poem appeared in the Autumn 1924 issue of the German magazine *Der Querschnitt.* Oswald Garrison Villard (1872–1949), American journalist and staff member of the *New Republic* and editor and owner of *The Nation* from 1918 to 1932. Both magazines supported liberal causes.

6 American painter Patrick Morgan (1904–1982) and Whitney Cromwell (1904–1930), son of New York Stock Exchange president Seymour Cromwell, who was studying art in Paris.

7 Peirce mentioned in his letter that he was heading to "Nice for a day or so—to see Sanders at Cagnes [Cagnes-sur-Mer]" on the French Riviera. The identity of Sanders has not been determined.

To Ezra Pound, 9 January [1928]

January 9

Dear Ezra—

Enclosed are the clippings.

I was so excited about yr. getting this 2000 that I forgot to enclose.[1]

I did not imply that you suggested reading Awkward Age—only asked if you thought it was any good. I have no copy of yr. outline of Henry on hand. At the time I first read your strictures on various literary gents I had not read the gents referred to and could not be expected to retain them (the criticisms). We are not all educated at the same time.[2]

As matter of fack my letter was intended to be Kidding—(always dangerous with, say, MacLeish or Co.) but usually not between me and you.

Re Mr. Lewis I should say that it shd. not be difficult to be a philospher if one sticks to large enough subjects—The West—The East—Time etc.[3]

~~I believe Mr. Eliot would be very careful~~[4]

Wd. rather not refer to Mr. Eliot—whose honesty I have yet to be convinced of. He has written recently a very touching little poem about The Magi[5]

Mr. Thayer—according to his ex-wife—also Ex wife of Ethelred Estelle Cummings—has been in asylum for some time.[6] That may delay his sending the check but is there not Mr. Watson?[7]

The Paris Times clipping sounds as though Mr. Pierre Loving (or Letschitzky) had seen a copy of the Dial.[8]

There is a Rt. Rev. staying at this hotel the Rt Rev. Plowden-Warden and his wife Mrs. the [*Ditto marks*: Rt Rev. Plowden-Warden] was observed in surprized study of my mail this morning. I shall be forced to keep the whisky bottle off the table and replace it with the New Prayer book.[9] Is Mr. McAlmon now writing for you in French? I have long admired his spoken use of the French tongue and if he is now writing in it I would be glad to send a check for latest Exile. yrs. <u>Hem</u>

Regret siezure of Exiles[.] Couldnt Mr. Eliot as British Citizen get them releazed?[10]

Bumby had <u>not</u> read the Tribune. However the Doc says the eye will be O.K. I lost the use of the other through progressive atrophy of the optic nerve and was a little worried.[11]

Yale, ALS

1 Presumably the clippings from the *Paris Times* that EH mentioned but forgot to enclose in his [c. 5 January 1928] letter to Pound. EH again refers to Pound's $2,000 Dial Award.

2 In response to EH's derogatory comments about the Henry James novel in his previous letter, Pound had replied, "I never suggested that you read the Awkward Age. I made a nice little map of Henry, the high spots and the low spots, but ov course no one cd. be expected to follow the map, and THEN argue" (7 January 1928, JFK).

3 Alluding to Wyndham Lewis's *Time and Western Man* (1927), Pound wrote in his 7 January letter, "When gents become phylosophers and write about 'Time and Man' and similar subjeks the strongest ties of friendship are put to excessive strain."

4 Pound would reply, "Your deleted line re/ the eminent critic seems perfectly sound. I expect he has been" ([11 January 1928], JFK).

5 Pound wrote on 7 January, "I onnerstan Mr Eliot has also written an essay." Not having read it yet, Pound speculated, "I suspect Mr Eliot wd. be more incicive that W.L. if he started funeral services." Eliot's "Journey of the Magi," later part of his "Ariel" poems, was issued by British publisher Faber & Gwyer in August 1927.

6 Scofield Thayer and Elaine Eliot Orr (1896–1974) were married in 1916. With her husband's approval, Elaine embarked upon an affair two years later with American poet E. E. (Edward Estlin) Cummings (1894–1962) and in 1919 bore his daughter. Elaine and Scofield divorced in 1921. She married Cummings in March 1924 and he legally adopted his daughter, who retained the name Nancy Thayer (1919–2006). In December 1924, Cummings and Elaine were divorced. After a nervous breakdown in 1926, Thayer was hospitalized and subsequently resigned as editor of *The Dial*. He lived the rest of his life either in sanatoriums or under the care of guardians.

7 Dr. James Sibley Watson, Jr. (1894–1982), co-owner and publisher of *The Dial*.

8 Pierre Loving (c. 1893–1950), American journalist, editor, translator, and poet who worked both in France and the United States. In the absence of the clipping from the *Paris Times*, which does not survive with this letter, EH's reference to Letschitsky is unclear.

9 Pound's letter of 7 January was addressed to "The Rt. Rev. Ernesto HEMINGWAY / Hotel Rossli / GSTAAD / SVIZZERA" (JFK). "Right reverend" is the form of address for a bishop in the Anglican and Episcopal churches. EH is referring to the Book of Common Prayer, used in Anglican Church services. Revised versions proposed in 1927 and 1928 were adopted in services in England despite not being officially approved by Parliament. The U.S. Episcopal Church adopted the revision in 1928.

10 Pound reported that according to his publisher, Covici, agents in London had seized 500 copies of *The Exile* "on grounds of moral tone" and refused to circulate them. T. S. Eliot had become a British citizen in November 1927.

11 Pound made a convoluted joke in his letter after hearing that Bumby had scratched EH's eye, but expressed his "genuine condolences."

To Maxwell Perkins, 15 January [1928]

Jan 15, 1927

Dear Mr. Perkins—

I'm sorry not to have written acknowledging the Illuminated bull and the clippings— Thanks ever so much for sending them—especially the bull which has been universally admired.[1]

Have you heard anything of the O. Henry people's award? (I have not and their letter was so worded that they could avoid actually coming through with the prize if they wanted.

The reason I did not write you, or in fact write anything at all, was a bad cut in the pupil of my right (and only good) eye which is all healed now. The eye still aches though if I read or write. Was quite blind with it for a couple of weeks.

Since the 15th of December there has been 3 days of skiing here—The winter completely open. Our only two good snow falls have been followed by rain making breakable crust which is the most dangerous and nastiest thing to ski in there is. Archie MacLeish and I ski-ied down from the top of The Saanersloch Fluh—ordinarily a beautiful long run—and I took ten of the worst spills imaginable.[2] Even running straight the crust would break and the tip of the ski go under and catch to throw you. I was wearing goggles to protect my eye and once fell so hard and buried my head so deeply that the glass was smashed out of both of them. I have a tin knee and dislike falling intensely and never go in for it—but weighing 208 pounds I was just

what the breakable crust was hoping for. Dont know why I wrote this—
except there is nothing to write except the cursed weather.

How I got the eye cut was altogether unromantic—picked up my son out
of bed in Montreux in the hotel to have him perform an important function;
he put up his hand; one finger went in my eye and the finger nail cut a neat
half moon in the pupil.

That seems all the news except that we're coming to America in 2 months—
but not to N.Y until the fall.

Hope the Men Without still sells—thought for a while it wd. be last book
I'd have. Being blind even for a little while scares you—especially if you dont
write just out of yr. head but with all the senses you have on tap. Figured I
could probably write by touch on the typewriter—but stuff written on the
[*Ditto marks*: typewriter] is not much good—and nothing I write is any
good until it's rewritten several times and how would you re-write if you
couldnt see? Thought I might get a job hearing for Dexter.[3]

The new Magazine sounds very impressive—what would they pay for
pieces?[4] I saw a copy the other day and it looked very handsome but the
Swiss wanted a dollar for it so I thought I would have to try and contribute
something and get it for nothing.

A gentleman named Burton Emmett sent me a check for $500 to buy
some manuscripts of stories The Killers—Fifty G. etc. Have had various
other offers. But have given most of these Mss. away during the great
tissue towel famine. Dont however tell anyone this as if my eye started to
go bad it might be a good provision against the future to start making
manuscripts. At present there would seem to be more money in
Manuscripts than in Stories. I should think Scott's original Mss. would
bring thousands for the spelling alone. I wonder if Mr. Emmett prefers
Mss. of mine before or after I put in the grammar? But I am afraid to joke
with these Mss. buyers for fear they wont want them. Think I'll write back
and say they are all in the British Museum except The Sun Also Rises
which is in the Prado.

Yrs. always,

Ernest Hemingway.

What are the sales of The Sun—if it isnt too much trouble.

PUL, ALS

1 In his letter of 30 November 1927 Perkins enclosed, "with some trepidation," a copy of the *MWW* ad that had appeared in the *New York Times Book Review* on 27 November. The ad included a small picture of a bull distinguished by a halo around its penis, described by Perkins as "the curious incandescence of his most hellish feature" (JFK).
2 The Saanersloch Fluh ski run (peak elevation c. 6,400 feet) near Gstaad, Switzerland.
3 Byron Dexter, the Scribner's staff member who visited EH in Paris in the spring of 1927, was hard of hearing. In a letter to EH of 9 May 1927, Perkins noted that he meant to warn EH of the "difficulty of talking to him" (PUL).
4 *Scribner's Magazine* had been redesigned and given a new look. An announcement of the changes, enclosed by Perkins in his letter to EH of 8 December 1927, also promised readers that "one of its features will be Ernest Hemingway" (PUL).

To Henry Goodman, 16 January 1928

COPY

Switzerland, Jan.16, 1928.

Dear Mr. Goodman,

Thank you very much for your letter.

For the guidance of your classes: The way in which I wrote a story called The Undefeated was as follows:

I got the idea of writing it while on an AE bus in Paris just as it was passing the Bon Marche (a large department store on the Bd Raspail). I was standing on the back platform of the bus and was in a great hurry to get home to start writing before I would lose it. I wrote all during lunch and until I was tired. Rach succeeding day I went out of the house to a cafe in the morning and wrote on the story. It took several days to finish it. I do not remember the names of the cafes.[1]

I wrote a story called The Killers in Madrid. I started it when I woke up after lunch and worked on it until supper. At supper I was very tired and drank a bottle of wine and read La Voz, El Heraldo, Informaciones, El Debate so as not to think about the story.[2] After supper I went out for a walk. I saw no one I knew and went back to bed. The next morning I wrote a story called Today Is Friday. I forget what we had for lunch. That afternoon it snowed.[3]

My other stories have mostly been written in bed in the morning. If the above is not practical for the pupils perhaps they could substitute Fifth Avenue bus for AE bus, Saks for the Bon Marche, Drug Store for cafe— I believe there would be little difference except that they might not be permitted to write in a drug store.[4]

Yours very truly

(Signed) Ernest Hemingway

JFK, typewritten transcription of EH letter

1 EH had written "The Undefeated" in the fall of 1924.
2 During the early twentieth century each of these Madrid newspapers had a distinct political agenda. *La Voz* presented the liberal perspective, *El Heraldo* was moderate and conservative, *Informaciones* would soon lean toward promoting Nazism and anti-Semitism, and *El Debate* represented the voice of Spanish Catholicism.
3 According to the daily log EH kept during his stay in Madrid in May 1926, he wrote not only "The Killers" but also "Today Is Friday" and "Ten Indians" on 20 May 1926 and on the next day, he rewrote the "Indian Story" (JFK). (For details of the stories' composition history, see Smith, 138–39, 154, 197–98.)
4 In Paris the AE bus route began at the Opéra on the Right Bank, crossed to the Left Bank, and ended at the Porte d'Orléans on the southern edge of the city. The route passed Le Bon Marché, on the rue de Sèvres, the largest department store on the Left Bank and the oldest in Paris, designed by Gustave Eiffel and opened in 1852. In New York City, the elegant Saks Fifth Avenue department store at Fifth Avenue and 48th Street opened in 1924.

To Mildred Longstreth, 17 January 1928

Dear Miss Longstreth:

Thank you ever so much for writing me about the story. I'm awfully glad that you liked it and that you liked bull fights. But if you've seen good bull-fights you know how much better they are than stories about them—so knowing how much better the bull fight is than the story I'm very happy you got a kick out of both.

Yours very truly,

Ernest Hemingway

Gstaad—Suisse

Jan 17, 1928

Knox, ALS; postmark: GSTAAD / (BERN), 16.1.28 16

There is a discrepancy between the postmark date of 16 January and the date of "Jan 17, 1928" that EH wrote at the end of this letter.

To Glen Walton Blodgett, 28 January 1928

> Hotel Rossli
> Gstaad
> Suisse
> January 28 1928

Dear Mr. Blodgett;

Thank you for your letter. If I should ever be in Washington it would give me great pleasure and be of great interest to me to see your collection. It is very good of you to wish to include me in it.

I am afraid I cannot remember accurately anything from my stories to write but do remember one which started—

We were all drunk. The whole battery was drunk going along the road in the dark.[1]——

> Ernest Hemingway

I hope that will do. I am returning the stamp.

HSOPRF, ALS; postmark: GSTAAD / (BERN), 27. 1·28 [illegible]

EH addressed the envelope to "Glen Walton Blodgett Esq. / 1322 Rhode Island Ave. N.W. / Washington / D.C. / Etats Unis." EH either misdated the letter or the postmark date is incorrect by one day.

1 Chapter I of *iot* (1924) and *IOT* (1925) begins, "Everybody was drunk. The whole battery was drunk going along the road in the dark."

To James Joyce, 30 January 1928

> Hotel Rossli
> Gstaad
> Switzerland
> Jan 30, 1928

Dear Joyce,

I appreciated very very much your writing to Ivan Goll about the Rhein Verlag for me. He wrote me at once but I have had to wait trying to arrange things in Germany—an agent having already signed me up for at least one book with a Berlin publisher.[1] Have written Goll I would see him in Paris next month and hope by then it will be straightened out.

I hope you and all your family are well. Mac Leish's father died and he left for America to be back late in February. Mrs. Pierce is down here.[2] My family are leaving for Paris tomorrow and I'm taking a trip on skis to Lenk and Adelboden and back and then we'll go up to Paris.[3] Except for two weeks the weather has not been wintry nor dry and we've not had more than ten days of ski ing. My little boy, when I picked him up to put him on the pot at night at Montreux coming in here poked his finger in my eye and the nail cut the pupil. For ten days I had a very little taste of how things might be with you. It hurt like hell even with the cocaine wash the doctor gave me to take the pain out but is all right now.

I hope you are well and that everything goes well with you.

Yours always,

Ernest Hemingway.

SUNYB, ALS

1 Yvan [Ivan] Goll (né Isaac Lang, 1891–1950), artist, poet, and translator, was born in France, bilingual in French and German, and at this time the Paris agent for Rhein Verlag, the Swiss publisher of the German translation of *Ulysses* (1927). EH's German agent was Edgar Mowrer, brother of Paul Mowrer. The German publisher Rowohlt Verlag would publish a translation of *SAR* by Annemarie Horschitz (née Rosenthal, later Horschitz-Horst, 1899–1970) under the title *Fiesta* in 1928.
2 Andrew MacLeish (1838–1928), Archibald's father, died on 14 January 1928. Archibald MacLeish sailed from France for the United States on 25 January and was away for five weeks. Waldo Peirce's wife, Ivy, spent time in Paris in 1928.
3 An entry in Pauline's passport dated 31 January 1928 by the French Consulate of Bern, Switzerland, confirms she returned that day to Paris, presumably accompanied by Jinny and Bumby (JFK).

To Sylvia Beach, [30 January 1928]

Dear Sylvia—

Thanks awfully for sending me the Nation and the Vanity F—it was damned nice of you—we have had a fine time but little snow—none until Jan 15—lately it's been good. Pauline, Jany, and Bumby are going back to Paris tomorrow and I'm leaving on a 3 or 4 day ski trip to Lenk, Adelboden etc. over the mts. Then back.

I delayed writing Goll of the Rhein Verlag until I could hear from my German agent who had a contract made with some other German publisher for one book ("Sun Also Rises")

He, the agent, has gone to Amerika but I have written for a copy of the contract so I will know how soon I am free. Wrote Goll I would see him in Paris.

It was very very nice of Joyce to write him about me.

Merry Xmas and Happy New Year to you and Adrianne from all of us though late.

Love
Hemingway.

PUL, ALS; postmark: GSTAAD / (BERN), 1.II.28.14

The conjectured letter date is based on EH's reference to his planned ski trip and Pauline's return to Paris the next day, details he also mentioned in other letters clearly dated 30 January 1928.

To Maxwell Perkins, 30 January [1928]

Jan 30

Dear Mr. Perkins—

Thanks for your letter of Jan 18 with the statistics.[1]

Morley Callaghan had a novel which he then called Backwater—which I remember reading in Austria 2 or 3 years ago and still remember very vividly. [*EH insertion*: which is quite a test!][2] You might look at it. Maybe you have by now. I wish he would get published because he has been writing good stuff now for 3 years—good enough to be published—and I think it will be discouraging for him to go too long. It is bad to get published too quickly—but deadly to wait too long.

Am leaving tomorrow morning across the mountains from here on skis to Lenk and Adelboden—3 days—then back. Then to Paris to (work on the novel)—then leaving in March for US. to [*EH drew arrow pointing back to* "work on the novel"]

I would like it very much if you could have a copy of Men Without sent to Rev. Father Vincent C. Donovan

    Priory of Saint Vincent Ferrer

    869 Lexington Ave

    N.Y.C.

Thanks ever so much for the 3 copies of each of the last books which arrived here.

This is very hurried as am packing for the trip

Yours always—

Ernest Hemingway.

PUL, ALS

1 In his letter to EH of 18 January 1928, Perkins reported, "'Men without Women' to date is 15,701 copies in just about three months, and it progresses well. That of 'The Sun Also Rises' since August first is 3,070 copies. 'Torrents of Spring' has not held up much,—the number for that is 86 copies" (PUL).

2 Perkins wrote to EH that he read and enjoyed one of Morley Callaghan's stories and had just received a phone call from him. Scribner's would publish Callaghan's first novel, *Strange Fugitive*, in 1928.

To Guy Hickok, [c. 5 February 1928]

Dear Guy— Who in hell's Tumor's were they taking out? Yr. letter arrived just at lunch but was eating chili con carne and fortunately it (the letter) did not deal with the removal of gall stones.[1]

Arrived to find all the pipes bursted—really only—two—an elbow over the living room and 4 metres over bed room—But figure that without you and the concierge all would have been crevéd[2]

JFK, ALFrag

1 In a letter to EH of 2 February [1928], Hickok described a medical procedure he had witnessed as a news reporter: "Oh Boy! Tumor as big as your two fists . . . Hung the woman up by the feet and took it out with the cork screw. White inside like homard [lobster (French)]. Never again eat homard without wondering if its a fibrous tumor" (JFK). Hickok's letter, postmarked from Paris on 2 February 1928, was forwarded from Gstaad to EH's Paris address on 3 February (JFK).
2 *Crevé*: burst (French). Upon returning to Paris, EH discovered the burst pipes in the apartment at 6, rue Férou.

To Madelaine Hemingway, [c. 10 February 1928]

Dear Nunbones—

Yours received of recent date. Glad the wire and cooky arrived.[1] The enclosed checks evidently didnt but will now— Slip them to the kids and please mail the other to Uncle Tyley and Ura— I havent their addresses on tap.[2] The cake was intended for the paternal. I subscribed to an a[rt]ist magazine for the noted painter.[3]

Glad you liked the volumne of Sh stories. Dont let any doubts of the reality of our snake killings attack you nor of you kissing Volney Sheppard good night.[4]

I suppose the maternal parent after denouncing and loathing my writing all through the period when she might have encouraged me will finally—but why go on. on getting out of Oak Park and influence of Fanny Butcher she'll find its better thought of. I am leaving this town, Paris, for Foreign Parts, Spain, Cuba, the Carribbean and eventually points North the end of the month. Had a swell time in Switzerland with Bumby for two months. He is in grand shape— I asked him what he wanted to do when he grew up and he said grow whiskey for Papa.

Dont shock the family with such a career. Have been laid up with various diseases. [*Ditto marks*: Have] written 20 chapters on a new novel. About half through.

How goes the Dental game?[5] How is Ura? How is she getting along.[6] What news of Carol and Leicester? It's possible that I'll see youse guys this summer or fall.

I imagine Mother will take up writing sooner or later—she wont want to leave any of the arts unconquered. How is Dad on the Arts?[7] Has any pressure been brought on him to go in more seriously for the cornet? How is Leicester on the Arts? Have they tried to make a bass viol player out of him?[8]

I know I would never probably have been a writer but for the periods of enforced mental inactivity when supposed to be practicing in the music room.

Hope you can read this writing. I wrote those ~~damned~~ checks the night before going to Switzerland and on the way cut my one good eye and was laid up with all kinds of pain and blind as a ~~bastard~~ bat till nearly Xmas—10 days or so. Then it was too late to send them but it suddenly occurred to me that youse might welcome the cash as a Washington's Birthday memorial or as a means of observing Lent so here they are.[9] Tell Leicester and Carol that they do not require Thank you letters. As a recall a thank you letter detracted 82% from the free enjoyment of any gift. I have not yet become a great gratitude lover and hope to avoid that form of familial atavism. See what big woids he can use. And never even went to Business College.

Well Nunbones you ignorant kike you certainly passed up a fine visit to the old cathedral towns of Arogon and Navarre with your archeological male relative. I would have taken damned good care of you and you would have met some fine gents and ridden across the Pyrenees on a bike and caught trout and seen the bulls ~~operate~~ take the appendixes out of the horses.

I suppose the family pictured me as in a plot to sap your moral and physical well being while I simply had a swell trip planned. ~~You know you ou~~ oh well I was pretty sore but not any longer so we may take a trip yet—but dont wait until you are Aunt Grace's age to do it[10]

Love to all and thanks for a grand letter.

Yr affect. Bro.
Stein

PSU, ALS

EH is responding to a letter from his sister Sunny dated 6 January 1928 and postmarked from Oak Park on 31 January (JFK).

1 In her letter Sunny wrote, "The cable tickled Dad—aussie moi" [*moi aussi*: me too (French)], probably referring to the Christmas cable EH had sent from Gstaad. She reported receiving "the Swiss pastry," although it was "a little smashed."

2 In her reply of 5 March 1928, Sunny would report that she gave his checks to Carol, Leicester, and Uncle Tyley (who happened to be there for lunch), mailed Ursula's check to her home in Minneapolis, and used her own check to buy "one of the best looking evening dresses I ever saw" (JFK).

3 EH purchased a subscription for his mother to *L'ART VIVANT* [*Living Art*] at a price of 140 francs from the Paris branch of Brentano's Booksellers (Brentano's to EH, 20 December 1927, JFK).

4 In her 6 January letter, Sunny had reminisced, "we really did used to go out snake hunting in the prairie and I used to go kiss somebody Shepherd good night. There's no lying about that." Volney Shepard (1899–1979) grew up in Oak Park a few blocks from the Hemingways' home; in 1912 he and EH had performed together in "Robin Hood" at Holmes Elementary School ("Pupils Dramatize Robin Hood," *Oak Leaves*, 23 March 1912, 18).

5 Sunny reported she had "a good position with a Dentist here," and writing on stationery of the Optimist Club of Oak Park, she identified the club's president, Dr. Felix S. Tittle, as her employer.

6 Concerning their sister Ursula, Sunny would reply on 5 March, "You ask about Ura. She's apparently in great shape although ever since her child came through she's been having troubles with her innermost essentials."

7 In her 6 January letter Sunny commented, "We had a pretty good christmas this year with our conceited artist relative in Cal." By the time Sunny answered this letter on 5 March, Grace was back from California and "all the time fussing around." Sunny reported getting along "swell" with their father "but not a bit of it with the mater." Their Oak Park home had been taken over by "one oil canvas after another," she reported. "You would be surprised & shocked to see what the dump looks like."

8 Sunny would reply on 5 March that Leicester was "the violinist of the clan. Quite the white-livered-violinist. He has a way of hiding behind his mother's skirts in many respects, but as he is her pride and joy (because he's so much like her) he runs the joint."

9 George Washington's birthday, 22 February, was established as a federal holiday in 1879. Ash Wednesday, the first day of Lent, fell on 22 February in 1928.

10 In May 1927 their paternal aunt Grace Adelaide Hemingway had married for the first time at the age of forty-six and moved with her husband to Hawaii.

To Maxwell Perkins, 12 February [1928]

Feb 12

Dear Mr. Perkins—

Your letter of Feb 3 came today. I'm glad the book still goes so well—hope it keeps on steadily—it ought to do something to lay the story about people never buying short stories—[1]

We hit bad weather on the ski trip and had one tough day.[2] Got my new passport and came back to Paris to find all water pipes burst—no heat for a week—caught a cold and grippe in the head ~~but~~ have been trying to work every morning but ~~it has the usual quality of~~ all my production seems to be from the nose.

In the past twelve months have had the grippe 3 times, nearly passed out from anthrax—cut up my one good eye—etc. This probably due to having led a quiet non-alcoholic—non smoking life.

We leave the end of the month for Florida via Vego, Canaries, Havana, Key West. I'll need some money pretty soon but will write for it then. Wrote a story a few days ago to warm up to get back into stride before re-starting the book and thought it might do for the magazine but it is no bloody good.

I read the Roark Bradford story— It was awfully weak and watered beside An Occurrence at Owl Creek Bridge—the Bierce story you mentioned. He reversed the Bierce story and put on a happy ending. But I could see he got a lot of kick out of writing it—and I'm glad he got the $500. As an award the O Henry prize is a pretty damned doubtful honor and it ought to go to whom it will make happy.[3]

The best story I've read in a hell of a time was the Owen Wister story in O'Brien's book.[4] It wasnt a story but really part of a novel but part of it was wonderfully good and all very very good and a lesson to our generation in how to write.

The eye seems all right but still aches to read.

Otherwise no news.

Scott sent me an announcement of a debate between the Messers Bromfield and Wescott—[5]

Did you hear it? <u>What</u> did they debate?

Will you be coming down to Florida in April and May or Arkansas in June or Kansas City in June and July? Or where might we meet? I am going to the Rep Nat. Convention if they have it in Kansas City. Evan Shipman is going to get married.[6]

> Yours always.
> Hemingway

PUL, ALS

1 In his letter to EH of 3 February 1928, Perkins reported that almost 18,000 copies of *MWW* had been sold (PUL).
2 A reference to EH's ski trip from Gstaad to Lenk and Adelboden, starting on 31 January.
3 "Child of God" by American writer Roark Bradford (1896–1948), published by *Harper's Monthly* in April 1927, received the O. Henry Award as the best story of 1927 while EH's "The Killers" took second prize. The story "An Occurrence at Owl Creek Bridge," by American writer Ambrose Bierce (1842–c. 1914), first appeared in the *San Francisco Examiner* on 13 July 1890. Bierce's story centers on the hanging of a white Confederate sympathizer, while Bradford's describes the hanging of a black man. In Bierce's story, the narrative of the protagonist's escape is revealed to be illusory, whereas Bradford's story concludes with the hanged man returning to earth as a ghost to deliver a message of forgiveness to his executioners.
4 Owen Wister's story "The Right Honorable the Strawberries" appeared in Edward J. O'Brien's *The Best Short Stories of 1927* along with EH's "The Killers."
5 In his letter to EH of [December 1927], Fitzgerald enclosed an announcement of a radio program featuring Louis Bromfield and Glenway Wescott, to be broadcast on New York City station WJZ at 7:30 p.m. on 17 January 1928 (JFK; Bruccoli *Fitz–Hem*, 238). The program was advertised as "a 'friendly argument' on the modern novel."
6 Harriet Mann (1902–1994), a friend of Shipman's sister Mary (b. 1908), had arrived in Paris in autumn 1927 to study with the mystic spiritual leader George Ivanovich Gurdjieff (c. 1866–1949) and decided to look up Shipman. The couple embarked on a "tumultuous affair," to the disapproval of Shipman's father. After Harriet broke off the relationship, Evan sailed for the United States in early June 1928 (O'Rourke, 61–62).

To Ezra Pound, [c. 15 February 1928]

Dear Ezra—

The Jan. Dial to hand and contents noted. The Rev. Eliot confesses well but criticizes cagily— Why do they all fear Wyndham?[1]

I wd appreciate yr. giving me the outline of the good and bad Henry. If it's to be found in Instigations or some such tell me where and I'll get it and copy it.[2]

It now looks as though Rep. Natl Convention wd not be in K.C. In that event I wont attend. I was combining a visit to KC. with the convention. I got no reason to visit Cleveland.[3]

Have arrived home to find the pipes all bursted.

I did not see the former Mrs. Scofield Estlin personally.[4] MacLeish saw her at Murphys. MacLeish has gone to America to see where they've just buried his father. Necessary experience for a man of letters. I agree with Ford that it would be folly or sacrilege or whatever it is to seek for the holy person of the sacred emperor in a low tea house—or, I believe, in a Scotsman.[5]

It seems that none of us are <u>Modern</u> except Mr Eliot—Mrs. Woolf and all Bloomsbury.

Does he, Mr Eliot feel, that being sucked in by all the shit as it comes along Thomism, Steinism, Wyndism, East and Westism etc. makes Modern— What is Modern—of our own time. Do we have to swallow delicately (always ready to regurgitate and replace with something newer) all the current shit to be of our own time?

Glad to hear you have never made a mistake in picking winners. I myself had always hoped that Mr Dunning would prove to be a mistake but then, of course, it was me that Mr. Dunning threw the opium (and milk bottle) at [*page corner torn away*] may have prejudiced my hopes.[6]

Yrs.

Hem.

JFK, ALS

1 In his essay "Isolated Superiority" in the January 1928 *Dial*, T. S. Eliot suggested that Wyndham Lewis, in his magazine *The Enemy*, had treated Pound's *Cantos* "rather roughly." Eliot praised Pound's work as a unique and superior model for contemporary poets and suggested that Lewis, being a philosopher, had no ear for poetic rhythm.

2 In his letter of [11 January 1928], Pound offered to send EH a list of recommended volumes by Henry James (JFK). EH refers to *Instigations of Ezra Pound, together with an Essay on the Chinese Written Character by Ernest Fenollosa* (New York: Boni & Liveright, 1920).

3 The *New York Times* had reported that the convention might be moved to Cleveland, Ohio ("Kansas City May Lose Republican Convention; Hall and Housing Both Declared Inadequate," 5 February 1928, 1). Following assurances made by local Republicans, the newspaper subsequently reported the convention would remain in Kansas City.

4 EH conflates the names of Elaine Orr's first and second ex-husbands, Scofield Thayer and E. E. (Edward Estlin) Cummings. In his letter of [11 January 1928] Pound had wondered, "What's the ex-ex-wife like?" (JFK).

5 Archibald MacLeish's father, Andrew MacLeish, was buried at Graceland Cemetery in Chicago on 16 January 1928. EH quotes loosely from *The Wallet of Kai Lung* (London: Grant Richards, 1900) by Ernest Bramah (1868–1942): "It is a mark of insincerity of purpose to spend one's time in looking for the sacred Emperor in the low-class tea-shops" (6). MacLeish's father, a Scottish immigrant, became a successful entrepreneur in the United States, serving as director of the Chicago department store Carson, Pirie, Scott and as a trustee of the University of Chicago.

6 Before Pound left Paris for Italy in 1924, he befriended and supported American poet Ralph Cheever Dunning (1877–1930), who was addicted to opium. At one point, Pound gave EH a jar of opium for delivery to Dunning. In a moment of delirium, Dunning threw the jar and

then a milk bottle at EH. EH describes the incident in a letter of 22 October 1924 to Pound (*Letters* vol. 2, 167–68) and recounts it in the "Agent of Evil" chapter of *MF*.

To Jonathan Cape, [c. 2 March 1928]

Capajon
Westcent
Londres
You acknowleged receipt men without women october twentyseventh stop surely four months ample time investigate libelous aspect and advise me without necessity changing jewish to irish names without consulting author and ruining story Hemingway[1]

JFK, TCD with typwritten signature

1 In the American edition of *MWW*, the boxer Jack Brennan in "Fifty Grand" refers to boxer Kid Lewis as "that kike!" Ted "Kid" Lewis (né Gershon Mendelhoff, 1894–1970), Jewish boxer born in London, became Britain's youngest boxing champion at the age of seventeen and held several British, European, and world titles between 1913 and 1924. For the English edition of *MWW*, Cape had changed the name of Kid Lewis to "OBrien" but in response to EH's objection, wired on 5 March 1928 that he had "DECIDED TO DESTROY EDITION PRINTED AND TO REPRINT SUBSTITUTING RICHIE LEWIS FOR OBRIEN" (JFK).

To Jane Heap, 5 March [1928]

Dear Jane—

Enclosed please find a piece for the Final Number of yr. esteemed weekly.

I hope this will meet with your qualifications that it should not be literature.[1]

I have been working on this day and night since your letter came and wd. greatly enjoy your acknowleging receipt of same and whether you will use same as there is a great demand for my work by the Atlantic Monthly and kindred periodicals and wd. not like to disappoint there editors when I have a piece so immenently or emminently saleable.

Yrs. always,
Hem

[*Enclosure:*]

Valentine for a Mr. Lee Wilson Dodd and Any of His Friends who Want it.[2]

Sing a song of critics
pockets full of lye
four and twenty critics
hope that you will die
hope that you will peter out
hope that you will fail
so they can be the first one
be the first to hail
any happy weakening or sign of quick decay
(All are very much alike, weariness too great,
sordid small catastrophies, stacks the cards on fate,
very vulgar people, annals of the callous,
dope fiends, soldiers, prostitutes,
men without a gallus*)
If you do not like them lads
one thing you can do
stick them up your . . . . . lads
My Valentine to you.[3]

UWMil, TL with typwritten signature

1 EH is responding to Heap's invitation of 15 February 1928 to send "anything you choose just so it isn't what they call literachoor" for the final number of the *Little Review* (JFK). EH's letter and the enclosed poem, titled "Valentine," would appear in the magazine's May 1929 issue, the last to be published.
2 Lee Wilson Dodd (1879–1933), American lawyer, author, and critic whose negative review of *MWW*, titled "Simple Annals of the Callous," appeared in the 19 November 1927 *Saturday Review of Literature*. While Dodd was "amazed by" and "genuinely" admired the "lean virtuosity" of EH's work, he objected to "the narrowness of his range." "In the callous little world of Mr. Hemingway I feel cribbed, cabined, confined," he wrote (322–23).
3 *Gallus*: cock (Latin), a reference to the war wound of Jake Barnes, the protagonist of *SAR*. The published poem reflects the editorial instructions hand-marked in EH's original type-script, on which a word he typed was heavily cancelled in pencil and replaced by five dots.

To the Editor of the *New York Herald* (Paris Edition), 11 March [1928]

Paris March 8 11.

To The Editor of The New York Herald:[1]

The Herald's Mailbag today is headed A Unanimous Verdict. May I trouble the unanimity of this verdict by joining with Sisley Huddleston in his dislike of the new Herald type? I am enclosing several Herald Mailbags clipped on different days in which the letters of the enthusiastic congratulators are printed in blurred type. This is not a matter of personal like or dislike. It will be quite easy to see if the letters are blurred or not.[2] Doubtless on the paper used in New York the type prints very well or it would not have been approved by the occulists. But on the glazed paper on which the Paris edition is printed it does not have the same effect, an examination by anyone will show numerous letters blurred in every column—and I cannot believe that is good for the eyes. As for the numerous kidders of Mr. Huddleston; Mr. Huddleston holds his own opinions, he looks at the type himself instead of taking an oculists word for how it looks in New York—and he does not need to write for The Mailbag in order to see his name in the paper.

Ernest Hemingway

JFK, TLD with typewritten signature

This is a draft of the letter that follows in this volume.

1 American journalist and short-story writer Whit Burnett (1899–1973) served as city editor of the Paris edition of the *New York Herald* in 1927 and 1928.
2 After the newspaper's recent adoption of a new typeface, Ionic type No. 5, English writer and journalist Sisley Huddleston (1883–1952) complained in a letter to the editor that appeared in the regular column "Letters from the Herald's Mailbag" on 6 March 1928: "There must be many readers like myself who are displeased with the new type. Yet you have only received compliments" (4). By 11 March 1928, readers' praise for the new type and scorn for Huddleston's view was reflected in that day's "Mailbag" column heading: "A Unanimous Verdict." Surviving with this draft and the following letter are three clippings from the *Herald* on which EH circled examples of blurred type.

To the Editor of the *New York Herald* (Paris Edition), 11 March 1928

Paris, March 11, 1928

To The Editor of The New York Herald:

The Herald's Mailbag today is headed A Unanimous Verdict. May I trouble the unanimity of this verdict by joining with Mr. Sisley Huddleston in his dislike of the new Herald type? I am enclosing several Herald Mailbags, clipped on different days, in which the letters of the unanimous and enthusiastic congratulators are printed in blurred type. This is not a matter of personal like or dislike. It will be quite easy, by looking at them, to see whether the letters marked with a circle are blurred or not. Doubtless, on the paper used in New York, the type prints very well or it would not have been approved by the occulists. But on the glazed paper on which the Paris edition is printed it does not have the same effect. An examination by anyone will show numerous letters blurred in every column—and I cannot believe that does any active good to the eyes. Personally I will continue to read the Herald no matter what type it is printed in but there has been a good deal of promiscuous kidding of Mr. Huddleston going on and I mention this matter only for the benefit of Mr. Huddleston's kidders. I did not, like one of your correspondents, meet Mr. Huddleston at a studio party but I do know him well enough to feel sure that—(1) he looks at the type himself instead of taking an oculist's (or collection of oculist's) word for how it looks in New York and (2) he does not need to write for The Mailbag in order to see his name in the paper.

Ernest Hemingway[1]
Ernest Hemingway
12, rue de L'Odeon
3 Enclosures

JFK, TLS

This letter, the preceding draft, and the three newspaper clippings survive at JFK, along with an envelope addressed to "The Editor of the New York Herald / 38 rue du Louvre / Paris / e.v." but bearing no postage stamps or postmark. EH may not have sent the letter; no record of its publication in the newspaper has been located.

To Gustavus Pfeiffer, 16 March 1928

6 rue Férou

Paris

March 16, 1928.

Dear Uncle Gus—

I have hunted through all my old trunks here at the apartment to find the manuscript of Fifty Grand and The Undefeated so I could send them to you. But have found 8 or 10 other MSS. but not those. Evidently they are in storage with my 4 trunks of old letters and Mss.

So I am enclosing the manuscript of The Killers, the first typescript of The Undefeated and the only part I have found of Fifty Grand—the part I eliminated in publishing it.[1]

I hope you will hold these as hostages—they are for you too—until I can find the manuscripts you want when we return in the fall. I put in 6 hours or so going through old stuff in order to "make delivery" but havent found them yet and am sure they are in storage. (I never placed any value on them and so did not keep absolute track of them in all my very varied stuff)

Am also enclosing copy of the letter I sent to Burton Emmett.[2] You have been very good to us and I hope that some time I may justify your confidence. Anyway it was splendid to see you and we hope you will have a very good trip and that everything will go as you wish it.

Always yours.

Ernest Hemingway.

JFK, ALS

1 Apparently EH enclosed the original opening of "Fifty Grand," which Fitzgerald had encouraged him to omit (Bruccoli *Fitz–Hem*, 53–54). Later, EH regretted following Fitzgerald's advice. On the first page of the typescript of the original opening, EH wrote "1st 3 pages of story mutilated by Scott Fitzgerald" ("Fifty Grand" Typescript, item 388, JFK). For a close study of this topic, see Susan Beegel, "'Mutilated by Scott Fitzgerald?': The

Revision of Hemingway's 'Fifty Grand'," in *Hemingway's Craft of Omission: Four Manuscript Examples* (Ann Arbor: UMI Research Press, 1988), 13–30.

2 With this autograph letter to his uncle Gus, EH enclosed a carbon copy of the following typewritten letter, also dated 16 March 1928, to Burton Emmett (1871–1935), a collector of literary manuscripts. On the verso of the copy enclosed here, EH added this handwritten note: "My typewriter is packed and left[.] This one doesn't go so well. EH" His letter to Emmett bears several cancellations made by typing the letter *x* over other characters, along with handwritten corrections and insertions.

To Burton Emmett, 16 March 1928

March 16, 1928

Dear Mr. Emmett,

Thank you very much for your letter and for the check for $500 which I am returning with this letter.

I appreciate exceedingly your sending me the check but I have already disposed of the Mss. of Fifty Grand and The Undefeated as a gift to my Uncle Mr. G. A. Pfeiffer, whom, I believe, you have met. None of these Mss. have any real value, aside from the value which you were so good as to tell me were placed on them by the dealers, and I would not like to put a price on them or bzzgain with you in regard to them. After all a Mss. is very much of a by-product for the man who writes it and it would be a very bad thing for the man writing it to think of it in terms of saleability. So I think the best plan would be for me to give Mss. to my friends, to many of whom I cannot afford to give other gifts, and if they sell them (as I will advise them) they will then be able to be purchased by you at the current market price—the only one which has any real value. Mr. Pfeiffer will probably not sell them but I have other friends who will.

Also if the Mss. should ever have any value it would, perhaps, be a good idea to leave some of it to my children (there being small chance that I will leave them anything else). So, all around, it looks as though I had better not sell any. But I greatly appreciate your offer and if you really want one of the short stories for your collection I would be very glad to send you one.

Yours very truly,
Ernest Hemingway.
6 rue Ferou, Paris, France.

UNC, TLS; postmark: PARIS 113 / [*illegible*], 11* / 17–3 / 28

The surviving envelope bears postmarks showing that the letter, addressed to "Burton Emmett Esq." at 40 East 34th Street in New York City, was sent by registered mail from Paris on 17 March 1928, received at the post office in New York on 27 March, and sent on to Emmett on 28 March.

To Evan Shipman, [before 17 March 1928]

Dear Evan—

Pauline said you said 500 f. might do—wd be glad to let you have more but we are going to America, I owe $300 which have to pay this mo. etc.

I paid 140 f. worth of saucers and checks at Select and left 100 f. for you there for you to get when in bad shape so as not to make a horses ass out of yourself by not eating etc.

That makes 750 f.

Cancel the old 800— That is all off—you dont owe me any except this 750.

The best way would be, maybe, to try and pay back 100 or 200 when you get your monthly cash. I dont need it direly or anything but it's a good idea to pay some back on acct. a gent should only borrow with the idea of paying back at a definite time. Otherwise the whole economic system goes bad. You gotta work out some sort of a Dawes Plan—if you've got any sort of a regular monthly income you can do it.[1] I'm sorry I missed you yest. Pauline said you and she agreed Greco was a fairy on the strength of Saint Sebastien etc. I think it was Saint Sebastien was the fairy not Greco. His portraits of Comte de Orgaz and old Miguel Covarrubias dont look like Fairy painting.[2] Besides if he was a fairy they wd never have let him get unfashionable and he was up till 1908

Channick, AL

Although the date of this letter is uncertain, it was written before EH and Pauline sailed for the United States on 17 March 1928.

1 Charles Gates Dawes (1865–1951), American financier and U.S. vice president (1925–1929) under Calvin Coolidge. The Dawes Plan was adopted in August 1924 to address the

problem of post-WWI German reparations and to help Germany stabilize and strengthen its economy; it included a repayable loan of 800 million German marks. For this work, Dawes received the 1925 Nobel Peace Prize (awarded in 1926 and shared with British statesman Sir Joseph Austen Chamberlain [1863–1937]).

2 Cretan-born Spanish painter El Greco (né Domenikos Theotokopoulos, 1541–1614). EH may be referring to El Greco's first life-size nude painting, *St. Sebastian* (1577–1578), depicting the saint bound to a tree and penetrated by an arrow, or to his later *St. Sebastian* (1610–1614) at the Prado in Madrid. EH also refers to *The Burial of the Count of Orgaz* (1586–1588) and the portraits *Diego de Covarrubias y Leiva* (c. 1600) and *Antonio de Covarrubias* (c. 1600).

To Maxwell Perkins, 17 March [1928]

March 17

Dear Mr. Perkins—

Guy Hickock showed me a cable today from Scribners asking about my good health and I hope you werent worried. I was tired of recounting accidents so was not going to mention it. However it was the sky light in the toilet—a friend had pulled the cord that raised it instead of pulling the chain of the toilet—and cracked the glass so that when I tried to hook up the cord (going into the bathroom at 2 A.M. and seeing it dangling) the whole thing fell. We stopped the hemmorage with 30 thicknesses of toilet paper (a magnificent absorbent which I've now used twice for that purpose in pretty much emergencies) and a tourniquet of kitchen towel and a stick of kindling wood. The first two tourniquets wouldnt stop it due to being too short—(face towels) And I was rather worried as we had no telephone no chance of getting a doctor at 2 A.M. and there were two little arteries cut. But the third held it very well and we went out to Neuilly to Am. Hospital where they fixed it up, tying the arteries, putting in three stitches underneath and six to close it. No after effects but a damned nuisance.[1]

Maybe this will be the last. Scribner's could have made money this year insuring me.

Anyway the purpose of this letter is to tell you that I've finally had some pictures taken by Helen Breaker—who is sending them to you.[2] She is an old friend who has lost all her money and started in photography and I thought the pictures being reproduced might help her to get some reputation. I think photography is a lousy thing and that it has gone steadily backward since the Daguerrotypes but I ~~hope~~ promised that whenever her pictures are used they will be credited to her—HELEN BREAKER.—Paris. A person would have to be an old friend, stone deaf and to have lost all their money before I would have pictures taken by them. That has nothing to do with it. I think she is probably a very good photographer and think you will like the pictures. I told her I did not know if you paid for the originals or how much—and that if you did pay for them you would pay her at the usual rate—but that in any event you would have them credited to her.

Thank God to be off the subject of photography.

I asked a (Mrs.) Emily Holmes Coleman to send you her novel about an insane asylum. (She was in one for a while as a patient and, I think, can write) I have never read it, but she was going to send it to Boni and Liveright (who published a book on psychology by her husband) and I prefferred if it should chance to be good that you see it.[3]

I would like to have finished the novel—but (1) I have been laid up and out a good deal.

(2) It took me 5 years to write all the stories in In Our Time.

(3) It took 5 years to write the ones in Men Without Women.

(4) I wrote Sun Also Rises in 6 weeks but then did not look at it for 3 months—and then rewrote it for another three months. How much time I wasted in drinking around before I wrote it and how badly I busted up my life in one way or another I cant fit exactly in time.

(5) I work <u>all</u> the time. But I dont think I can make even an irregular schedule and keep up the quality. I know very well I could turn books out when they should come out. (And you have been very damned decent about not even asking me too or putting any pressure on me) but we only want good ones—Both of us. You see my whole life and head and everything had a hell of a time for a while and you come back slowly (and must never let anyone know even that you were away or let the pack know you were wounded). But I would like to write a really damned good novel—and if the one I have 22 chaps and 45,000 words of done doesnt go I will after I get to

America I will drop it and put it away and go on with the other one I am writing since two weeks that I thought was only a story but that goes on and goes <u>wonderfully</u>.[4]

The first one was supposed to be a sort of modern Tom Jones. (Never mention that because I do not invite comparison) but only to name the sort of book) But there is a <u>very very</u> good chance that I dont know enough to write that yet and whatever success I have had has been through writing what I know about—

I know very well that Scott for his own good should have had his novel out a year or two years ago[.] I dont want you to think that I am falling into that thing or alibi-ing to myself. But this next book <u>has</u> to be good. The thing for me to do is write but it may be better not to publish until I get the right one.

I should have gone to America two years ago when I planned— I was through with Europe and needed to go to America before I could write the book that happened there. But I didnt go—but now have, suddenly, a great kick out of the war and all the things and places and it has been going very well.

My wife says that she will see that I'm bled just as often as I cant write— judging by the way it's been going this last week. Hope to be able to work on the boat. If I find I've any readers in America will change my name.

This letter is long enough to be a bitter test of your friendship to have to read—

Also I would appreciate a copy of Men Without Women

being sent and charged to my account to W.W. Stigler

    Hotel Noble

    Jonesboro—Arkansas.

I will pay the account anytime it reaches $5.00 (five dollars Thanks very much for the offer of money. I will wire when I need it.

I am glad you are publishing Morley. I was never off of him but only a poor correspondent—[5]

Yours always,
Ernest Hemingway.

I will write you next from Florida.

Helen Breaker would like to get her pictures published in the magazines. The more expensive (I imagine) the better.

What about Foreign Translations? For when I'm back here. I am sure I could have gotten you Lückners book if I had known you wanted it and that you did not have someone after that sort of thing. Or wouldnt you have wanted it? I thought it a grand Book. The Last Privateer it was in the French edition. His early life and the Sea Adler part were wonderful.[6]

PUL, ALS

1 As reported in the "Around the Town" section of the *New York Herald* Paris edition on 6 March, EH "was wounded about the head when a skylight crashed on him, at his home Sunday [March 4] morning" (quoted in Reynolds *AH*, 166).

2 Helen Pierce Breaker (1890–1936), a photographer and one of Hadley's close friends from St. Louis. In his response of 10 April 1928, Perkins would report that these were "by far the best pictures we have seen of you." The scar on the forehead, however, would require explanation, he wrote (PUL).

3 Emily Holmes Coleman (1899–1974), American expatriate poet, novelist, and society editor for the Paris *Tribune*. Her novel, published as *The Shutter of Snow* (New York: Viking, 1930), drew upon her experiences as a patient in a mental hospital. Her husband, Loyd Ring Coleman (1896–1970), and Saxe Commins (1892–1958) had published *Psychology: A Simplification* with Boni & Liveright in 1927.

4 EH refers to the start of his novel *A Farewell to Arms*, which Scribner's would publish in 1929. The manuscript containing twenty chapters of the unfinished novel he set aside is housed at JFK (Hemingway manuscripts, item 529b). For a discussion of those chapters, see Reynolds *AH*, 145–47, 247.

5 In his letter of 1 March 1928, Perkins wrote that Scribner's planned to publish a book of stories by Morley Callaghan titled "American Made"; it would be retitled *A Native Argosy* when published in 1929.

6 *Le Dernier Corsaire* (Paris: Payot, 1927), the title of which EH translates as "The Last Privateer." The French translation of a book originally published in Germany as *Seeteufel: Abenteuer aus meinem Leben* (1921), it is an account by German officer Count Felix von Luckner (1881–1966) of his adventures as a privateer in the service of the German government. Luckner's seafaring exploits were first related in English by Lowell Thomas in *Count Luckner, the Sea Devil* (Garden City, New York: Doubleday Page, 1927). The "Seeadler" ("Sea Eagle") was a three-masted sailing ship von Luckner commanded during WWI to raid, capture, and sink Allied merchant ships.

To Pauline Pfeiffer Hemingway, [c. 28 March 1928]

Dear Miss Pfeiffer or ~~should~~ may I call you "Mrs. Hemingway?"——

We are five or ten days out on our trip or tripe to Cuba which promises to extend indefinitely into the future.[1] I have often wondered what I should do with the rest of my life and now I know— I shall try and reach Cuba

It is certainly hell to try and write. You are so handsome and talented and your throat never gets sore and you never say "Perhaps my husband Mr. Hemingway cant play well enough to interest you."

But you cant stop this bloody ship going up and down. Only Mothersills can do that and she not for long.[2]

I have been reading about the accomodations on the other liners—the Orcoma, Orita, Oroya, etc. and they all have gymnasiums and beds and double beds and nurseries for the resultant infants but our boat has little cells at $250 a cell and a man might as well have paid 250 to some good monastic order (if they would take that little)[3]

I have discovered what makes our Indian friend look furtive—his neck is so short that he has to turn his shoulders when he looks around. You on the other hand have no defects but this boat is The Royal Mail S Packet and I have no [inspiration?] except the something that was caught in this pen (one of your eyelashes maybe) and now it's gone and what's a guy to do.

Anyway I love you and if you forgive this bad letter I will write a good one sometime. Only lets hurry and get to Havana and to Key West and then settle down and not get on Royal Male Steam Packets any more.

The end is weak but so is Papa.

Love from Papa.

JFK, ALS; letterhead: R.M.S. "ORITA."

1 EH and Pauline were aboard the Royal Mail Steamer *Orita*, which left La Rochelle, France, on 17 March 1928 and arrived in Havana on 1 April.
2 Mothersill's Seasick Remedy, a patent medicine containing chlorbutanol, manufactured by the Mothersill Remedy Company, Detroit.
3 The *Orcoma* and *Oroya* of the United Kingdom's Pacific Steam Navigation Company, sister ships to the *Orita*, were among six "'O' Steamers" of the Pacific Line Mail Service that operated between Liverpool and Valparaiso, with stops in La Rochelle and Havana.

To Maxwell Perkins, 7 April 1928

MZ A59 12 NM = KEYWEST FLO 7
MAXWELL PERKINS=
CHARLES SCRIBNERS NEWYORK NY=

ADDRESS GENERAL DELIVERY KEYWEST FLORIDA FOR A WHILE
WORKING HARD BEST REGARDS=
HEMINGWAY.

PUL, Cable; Western Union destination receipt stamp: 1928 APR 7 PM 2 39

To Clarence Hemingway, 10 April 1928

MPB65 24
KEYWEST FLO 10 1049A
DR C E HEMINGWAY
HOTEL IDLEWILD STPETERSBURGH FLO
LEARNED YOU FLORIDA FROM LETTER FORWARDED PAIRS STOP
HOW ABOUT COMING HERE FEW DAYS FISHING HAVE CAR AND
TACKLE ADDRESS KEYWEST LOVE TO MOTHER[1]
ERNIE.

UT, Cable; Western Union destination receipt stamp: 1928 APR 10 AM 11 23

1 Clarence, Grace, and Clarence's brother Willoughby Hemingway visited with EH and
Pauline in Key West on 10 April 1928, the day EH sent this cable to their hotel in
St. Petersburg, Florida, but the meeting was apparently by chance. Marcelline recalls that
their parents and uncle encountered EH fishing on the dock in Key West when their tour
group arrived on its return from Havana, where they had spent Easter, 8 April 1928
(Sanford, 227). This cable establishes that EH knew of his parents' planned trip to Florida
but had no advance knowledge, apparently, of their visit to Cuba and Key West. In her letter
of 5 March 1928, sent to EH in Paris, Sunny wrote that Grace and Clarence would leave Oak
Park on 19 March for a one-month stay in Florida, and that may have been the letter EH
received in Key West on 10 April (JFK). Grace's letter of 11 March [1928], mentioning the
upcoming trip to Florida and Cuba, was forwarded from Paris to Key West but did not
arrive until 18 April (JFK). In a letter to EH dated 11 April 1928, Clarence wrote, "Like a
dream to think of our joyous greeting & visit with you at Key West last evening" (JFK).

To Waldo Peirce, [13 April 1928]

Muy Amigo Mio—

You and Eddy were damned nice to send that wire. It came just as we
were shoving off.[1] I suppose Ivy told you how the skylight fell—but I don't

insist on any version and anybody can believe anything they bloody well please. I would have wired you but didn't know where to get you.

Today a letter came from a Big Creative Artsman named Rockwell Kent saying that you suggest that I would be willing to write an article on yr. paintings for creative Art its-self. Makeing it 1200 1500 words long copy in a month from date. date being March 15—a month from then is April 15 or day after tomorrow. I can't do it in that time Rockwell.[2]

Listen Chico—I know how these things happen— Mr. Kent says we ought to have an article on yr. stuff Waldo. Uhuh you say. Who could we get to do it he says. Jeesus christ man how should I know? you say. Tell me somebody that's seen it, he says. Jesus Christ everybodyy's seen it. You've seen it. Kent—Has Hemingway seen it? You— Sure I supose he's seen it. Kent—Would he wrie about it? You—Jesus Christ man how should I know if he'd write about it. Write and ask him etc. etc.

Well I will be happy to wr[i]te ab[o]ut it. But in order that I not make a horsesass of both of us (this Creative Art being written evidently for and by painters) you write it and send it to me and I will knock out some of the better punctuation marks and sign it. I'll write some more too. But you write the body of it and send it to me right away. All I could write now is that I think you are a hell of a fine painter and could have been Goya or Greco if you would have been born at the right time but that aint 1500 words. You give me the dope. All articles about people or their work are shit and the only way to do it is to do it good and strong and have it full of dope. Write me 1200 words on how good you are and then I will add how you make a bum out of Elliott, MacLeish Shakespeare and Giotto[3] and my personal remeniscenses of you drunk and we will send it to this damned Creative Artsman. I will write him now that I am doing it. But send me the copy right away.

Pauline and I both felt terribly about your mother dying when you were on the way over to see her.[4] We wanted to cable and to write and then like bastards did neither. But we are always with you.

Ivy looked grand when we saw her.

Pauline is in fine shape. We are going to have a baby in June or July. This is a grand place—all talk Spanish— I work and we go out on the keys and catch Red snappers, amber jacks and lose barracudas every day. They are like muskies only run up to a hundred pounds and I can't hold them on my flyrod. Landed a four foot shark on the damned fly rod this morning though Pauline 2 snappers and me four. They are built like bass and fight like hell. The flyrod is getting to look like it had been used for lifting garbage cans up to the fourth floor. We sell the sharks to the OceanvLeather Company.[5] But you can't make a living at it with flyrods at 40 bucks.

I wish the h[e]ll you would write a novel. I'll write the preface and three introductions to every chapter. Know the words for that but want you to help me out on the painting.

[*The bottom inch of the page is torn away and missing. The remainder of the letter appears on the verso:*]
brings Bacardi, Fundador, Rioja Alta every day.[6]

This is a grand place. Population dropped from 26,000 to 10,000 in last ten years. Nothing can stimulate it.

Pauline sends her love.

Always,
Ernest

You tell Kent I'm writing that piece and Christ we'll save a letter.
No mosquitos
Fine breeze—hot as Spain and cool at night.

Colby, TLS with autograph postscript

1 Although the cable remains unlocated, Peirce mentioned it in his letter to EH of 10 March 1928, saying that Eddy Tilyou had seen a report in the "Brooklyn Beagle" of EH's having been "knocked out by a god dam sky-light" and expressing concern (JFK). The *Brooklyn Eagle* published an article on 7 March 1928 headlined "Novelist Hurt in Paris," reporting that EH had "spent an hour and a half on the operating table while surgeons tied the ends of four arteries" (12). The report was sent on 5 March 1928 by "Special Cable to the Eagle" from its Paris bureau, which was headed by Guy Hickok.
2 As editor of *Creative Art: A Magazine of Fine and Applied Art*, Rockwell Kent (1882–1971) had written to EH on 15 March 1928 asking if he would contribute an article on Peirce's paintings, as EH describes here. Delivery of Kent's letter was delayed, as it was sent first to Paris and then forwarded to Piggott before reaching EH in Key West (JFK).
3 Giotto di Bondone (c. 1266–1337), Italian painter.
4 In his letter, Peirce reported he "had a bitch of a crossing—but was glad to avoid the horror of urban burial—out at sea." Anna Hayford Peirce (1856–1928), an accomplished photographer, died on 8 February and was buried two days later at Mount Hope Cemetery in

Bangor, Maine. Peirce sailed from Le Havre aboard the *De Grasse* on 8 February and arrived in New York City on 17 February.
5 Patents issued in 1919 and 1920 for removing the scales from shark skin were assigned to the Ocean Leather Corporation of Newark, New Jersey, the principal U.S. processor and producer of shark leather used for manufacturing shoes, luggage, and other products.
6 Brands of Cuban rum and Spanish brandy, and red wine from the Rioja Alta region of northern Spain.

To Maxwell Perkins, 21 April 1928

April 21–1928
Key West Fla.

Dear Mr. Perkins,

I'm terribly sorry to hear about Scott. Could you tell me the name of his ship and I will send him a cable.[1] Perhaps it would be better to wire it [*EH insertion*: the name of hi[s] boat or where he is] in a night letter as this place seems to be a long way from New York by mail. I wish he would finish his novel or throw it away and write a new one. I think he has just gotten stuck and does not believe in it any more himself from having foole[d] with it so long and yet dreads giving it up. So he writes stories and uses any excuse to keep from having to bite on the nail and finish it. But I believe that everybody has had to give them up (novels) at some time and start others. I wish I could talk to him. He believes that this novel is so important because people came out and said such fine things about him after the Gatsby and then he had a rotten book of stories (I mean there were cheap stories in it)[2] and he feels that he must have a GREAT novel to live up to the critics. All that is such (   ) because the thing for Scott to do is WRITE novels and the good will come out with the bad and in the end the whole thing will be fine. But critics like Seldes etc. are poison for him.[3] He is scared and builds up all sorts of defences like the need for making money with stories etc. all to avoid facing the thing through. He could have written three novels in this length of time—and what if two of them were bad if one of them was a Gatsby. Let him throw away the bad ones. He is prolific as a Gueinea pig (mis-spelled) and instead he has been bamboozled by the critics (who have ruined every writer that reads them) into thinking he lays eggs like the Ostrich or the elephant.

Glad you saw Waldo Pierce. He wires he is coming down here. I don't just know when but hope it will be soon. Dos Passos is on his way too. I don't know for how long.

Have been going very well. Worked every day and have 10,000 to 15,000 words done on the new book [*FTA*]. It won't be awfully long and has been going finely. I wish I could have it for Fall because that seems like the only decent time to bring out a book but suppose, with the time necessary to leave it alone before re-writing, that is impossible. I forget when I got the mss. for the Sun to you but think it was sometime pretty early in the Spring. Please tell me if I am wrong. Would like to finish this down here—if possible— put it away for a couple or three months and then re-write it. The re-writing doesn't take more than six weeks or two months once it is done. But it is pretty important for me to let it cool off well before re-writing. I would like to stay right here until it is done as I have been going so very well here and it is such a fine healthy life and the fishing keeps my head from worrying in the afternoons when I don't work. But imagine we will have to go someplace for the baby to be born around the end of June. Ought to leave a month before. Still if I keep on going there will be a lot done by then.

It is hot here but there is always a cool breeze and it isn't hot in the shade and you can sleep at night.

After I get the novel done—if it is too late for this fall—I could do quite a lot of stories and that would keep the stuff going until the next fall and then the novel would come out and we would have stories enough for a book of them to follow it.

Have been ctahcing tarpon, barracuda, jack, red snappers, etc. Caught the biggest tarpon they've had down here so far this season. Sixty three pounds. The really big ones are just starting to come in. They get them up to 125–140 lbs. Also a barracuda on a fly rod. Great quantities of sharks, whip rays and other vermin. We sell the fish we get in the market (the edible ones) and get enough to buy gas and bait. Have been living on fish too. Tonight is a big night (Saturday) although not so cheerful because another cigar factory has closed down.[4] This is a splendid place. Population formerly 26,000—now around ten thousand[.] There was a pencilled insription derogotory to our fair city in the toilet at the station and somebody had written under it—'if you don't like this town get out and stay out.' Somebody else had written under that 'Everybody has.'[5]

Would appreciate your asking them to send and charge to me 3 Sun Alsos and 3 Men Without Womens. (As soon as possible) Nobody believes me when I say I'm a writer. They think I represent Big Northern Bootleggers or Dope Peddlers—especially with this scar. They havent even heard of Scott. Several of the boys I know have just been moved by first reading of Kipling. A man introducing Robert Service's works would coin money if there was any money to coin—but there isn't—[6]

Yrs. always,

Hemingway.

Hope I get nothing incriminating as they open my mail.

What about the Books— I havent seen Men Without advertized for a long time.[7]

PUL, TL/ALS

1 In a letter to EH of 10 April 1928, Perkins reported that he had seen Fitzgerald at a luncheon attended by *Dial* editor and critic Gilbert Seldes. Fitzgerald took Perkins aside to tell him that he was depressed and had "made no progress with his novel for a long time, always having to stop to write stories." Perkins also mentioned that the Fitzgeralds expected to leave for Europe on 21 April (PUL; *TOTTC*, 70).

2 *All the Sad Young Men*, Fitzgerald's story collection published by Scribner's in February 1926.

3 The empty parentheses are EH's. In a glowing review of *The Great Gatsby* in the August 1925 *Dial*, Seldes called the novel a major achievement and a masterpiece of rare "technical virtuosity" and aesthetic integrity ("Spring Flight," 162).

4 The cigar industry in Key West began in 1831 and peaked in the 1880s with dozens of factories operating. Union worker strikes, fires, hurricanes, and the lure of lower taxes elsewhere contributed to its decline in the early twentieth century as the center of production shifted to Tampa and Ybor City, Florida.

5 The remainder of this letter is handwritten.

6 Robert W. Service (1874–1958), popular and prolific English-born Canadian poet and fiction writer known for his writings about the Yukon Gold Rush, including more than forty-five poetry collections.

7 In a letter to EH of 19 April 1928, Perkins wrote that the sales of *MWW* were at 19,000 copies but did not mention sales figures for either *TOS* or *SAR* (PUL). In a letter of 27 April, he would explain that Scribner's had "eased off" advertising *MWW* due to other book publications, slow business, and its being a "presidential [election] year" (PUL).

To Clarence Hemingway, [23 April 1928]

Dear Dad—

It was certainly grand to see you and mother and uncle Bill and we enjoyed it tremendously.[1] You were very good to send me the maps and information and the pictures. I did not know whether a letter would reach you at Bryson City as Sunny had said you would be back in Oak Park the 18th. Am sending this to Oak Park anyway and if you should have stayed on perhaps they will forward it.[2]

Have been working hard and hope to stay here until my book [*FTA*] is finished. Also had some fine fishing. Landed a 63 pound tarpon (weighed) and a five foot barracuda. Caught a small barracduda on the fly rod and some jack and many snappers. We have been living on snappers and grunts. Going out after tarpon again to night. Last night went out about six o'clock but didn't land any. Got a ten pound jack though that fought very well.

This is just a note as must get to work. Love to all the family

Ernie

JFK, TLS; postmark: KEY WEST / FLA., APR 23 / [10 AM] / 1928

1 EH's uncle Willoughby Hemingway was a physician and missionary who in 1904 settled with his wife, Mary, in China, where they founded a hospital and a school of nursing in Taiku (P. Hemingway, 294). Willoughby was home on a break "from his medical missionary duties in strife-torn China" (Reynolds *AH*, 171).
2 With a letter of 13 April 1928, Clarence sent maps and information for EH's planned trip to the north. He and Grace had traveled by train to Bryson City, North Carolina, where Grace stayed to paint the scenery while Clarence left for Freeman House, "the Highest Cabin in the whole Appalachian Mountains," where he went trout fishing. Apparently EH had not yet received his father's postcard of 18 April 1928 saying that he and Grace planned to leave Bryson City on 20 April and expected to arrive in Oak Park the next day (JFK).

To Barklie McKee Henry, [13 May 1928]

Box 53

Key West

Florida

Dear Buz— What a fretting shame to miss you. I would have loved to go to Spain or Norway or anywhere but especially Spain or Norway. But came to

Key West instead.[1] Have been bumming around the Keys having a grand time[.] Hope I'll see you in New York in the fall.

I'll send this to the Guaranty and feel terribly bad not to see you—we could have had a good time. Maybe you will see Hadley— She banks at the Guaranty and lives at 98 B^d Auguste Blanqui— Bumby's worth a trip to the XIIIth arrandisment to see.

Am working like hell on a novel [*FTA*]—done 167 pages[.] Am in the worst part and cant write letters but do wish I could have seen you and Barbara and it would have been grand to visit Spain—a country I have always hoped to visit.

You are a good guy but write oftener.

yrs. always.

Ernie

PUL, ALS

1 In a letter of 16 March [1928] sent to EH in Paris, Henry wrote that he and his wife, Barbara, planned to come to Europe around 17 May and wondered if EH wanted to join them for a trip to Norway or Spain. The letter was forwarded from Paris to Key West, where the postmark indicates it arrived 23 April 1928. The envelope bears EH's note, "Answered May 13" (JFK).

To Henry Strater, 13 May [1928]

May 13

Dear McTigue:[1]

How the hell are you and yr. wife Maggie and yr. numerous children?[2] I and wives am very well and happily situated here in this decreasing metropolis of 10,000 souls (50% Cubans) formerly a population of 26,000.

Dos was down and we have had swell fishing and drinking and I have written 167 pages on my newest (and let us hope best gentlemen) novel (Christnose what it is all about) but this is a fine place to write it. But working like a bastard at 7 till 1 a.m and then going fishing every day have been too pooped to write letters.

All the news down here is that "Young" Stribling can now hit.[3] Take it or leave it. We will get together in the fall.

Berg is just another jewish boy.[4]

The good ones in Yarrup are Tassin and Humery— Scillie, Routis, Kid Francis, Laffineur and Len Harvey. Details on request.[5]

May not come to N.Y. at all but we could arrange to meet somewhere outside of the shitty limits.[6]

My god I will be glad to see you.

Write me care Paul Pfeiffer—Piggott, Arkansas— Will be here another week or ten days—address Box 53 Key West Florida. Caught hundreds of lbs. of barracudas—Tarpon up to 70 lbs.—one sailfish etc. Christ this is fine country. Viva D'America. Must strike some large center of population to have a baby some time in June. Kansas City perhaps[.] Want to finish my book. Love to Maggie and David and your hundreds of other children

Keep some Bourbon. Also some Rye.[7]

Yrs. always, Hem.

PUL, ALS

1 In his letter to EH of 25 April [1928], Strater mentioned several professional boxers (JFK). EH alludes to Irish-born American heavyweight boxer Mike McTigue (1892–1966).
2 At this time the Straters had two children, David and Martha, aged 7 and 2½ years. EH may be making a joking reference to Strater's known infidelities.
3 William Lawrence "Young" Stribling, Jr. (1904–1933), American heavyweight boxer who earned his nickname during his first professional fight at age sixteen. Of 286 total career fights, he lost only 12.
4 Jackie "Kid" Berg (né Judah Bergman, 1909–1991), English welterweight and lightweight boxer whose style in the ring earned him the nickname "the Whitechapel Windmill." In his letter of 25 April, Strater wrote, "They are touting an English lightweight named Berg here."
5 French featherweight boxer Robert Tassin (1908–1972); French lightweight Gustave "Tiger" Humery (1908–1976); Belgian bantamweight Henry Scillie (1904–1953); French featherweight André Routis (1900–1969); Italian-born French bantamweight Kid Francis (né Francesco Buonaugurio, 1907–1943); French middleweight Yvan Laffineur (b. 1904); and British heavyweight Leonard Harvey (1907–1976).
6 EH's pun on "city limits" may have been provoked by Strater's comment, "New York is a terrible place."
7 Strater invited EH to visit him at 1 Lexington Avenue in New York City, and wrote, "there is excellent Bourbon & Rye at the above address."

To Dorothy Connable, [14 May 1928]

Box 53
Key West
Florida

Dear Dorothy

It was grand to hear from you and I wish we could have come through New York. But took an 18 day boat via La Rochelle, Santander, Coruña and Vigo to Cuba and Key West finally. This is a fine place a little like Petoskey but deader and very fine fishing. Ive been working very hard on a novel and have 167 pages done and am so tired after writing always that this is a bum letter. But I do hope I'll see you—not alone hope but will see you. Where will you be in the Fall and Summer? I dont see any chance of getting to N.Y. until fall. May go to Walloon or Petoskey for a week or so this summer.[1] Havent any plans except to finish this book and move north by way of Arkansas. Might go to Republican Convention in Kansas City.

How are your Mother and Father? I had Ralph's announcement and meant to cable.[2] Please forgive a rotten letter. I haven't even written Greg [Clark] I've landed. I am afraid I will lose all my friends.

Yours always affectionately,
Ernest Hemingway.

phPUL, ALS

The date "May 14 1928" is written in another hand at the top of this letter.

1 EH would not visit Michigan that summer.
2 Dorothy's parents, Harriet Gridley (b. c. 1870) and Ralph Connable (1865–1939), and her brother, Ralph, Jr. (b. c. 1900). EH met Harriet Connable in Petoskey in December 1919 and worked in their Toronto home as a live-in companion for their disabled son in early 1920. EH probably refers to an announcement of the wedding of Ralph, Jr., and Edna Emma Bush (b. 1903) on 27 September 1927.

To Maxwell Perkins, 31 May [1928]

Piggot—ARKANSAS
May 31

Mr. Perkins—

There was no Lady Ashley in Burke's or Debrett's Peerage when I sent you the Sun Mss and none in either of those stud books when I corrected the proof. A young Ashley married a girl out of musical comedy the summer after the book came out. She might as well try and sue Robinson Crusoe.[1]

You've probably seen Waldo. We had a grand time— I worked every morning too and did 200 pages—200 words or so to a page—in Key West. Am now at the above address—a christ offal place. Hope to get up to Michigan soon. Am delayed by impending child birth probably to take place at Kansas City or some such great obstetrical center.

Last winter (IE) the winter before last—I tried to argue Thornton Wilder out of Boni and Boni (He was commissioned to argue me into [*ditto mark*: Boni and Boni]) but am afraid he would now have more arguments. I thought Bridge of S.L.R. was a fine book of short stories— 2 splendid ones—The Esteban and I think the other was about a little girl who worked for the Mother Superior. He can write very very well. Also a nice boy.[2]

I think I will have to get a large advance on my next book to insure to assure it being advertized in Florid and gigantic manner in order that Scribners must sell a large number of copies to get the advance back. Glenway Wescott, Thornton Wilder, and Julian Green have all gotten rich in a year in which I have made less than I made as a newspaper correspondent— And I'm the only one with wives and children to support.[3]

Somethings going to have to be done.

I dont want the present royalties until they are due. But I would like to make a chunk of money at one time so I could invest it.[4] This bull market in beautiful letters isnt going to last forever and I do not want to always be one who is supposed to have made large sums and hasnt and doesn't. If I have as many accidents right along as I've had this last year they will be having to give a benefit for me in a couple of years. It did seem as though they laid off advertising Men Without Women when it was still going well just as much as they jumped out with enormous ads for Thorntons book the minute it started going. Of course I know nothing about it but after the first of the year—when Men Without was still selling well—it seemed as though they were satisfied with the sale and pretty well laid off.

Anyway am working steadily on the present novel and it seems to go well—and finally—I hope—toward an end. When I get it done I think I will go back to the one I dropped after 60,000 and finish it— It seems now as though it had never been difficult to work but I suppose that time will come again.

I dont think Mrs. Breaker will mind your having removed the scar. It seemed to bother her—the scar and she wanted to remove it. But I thought that if you give a photographer an inch they will remove an ell.[5]

Yours always,

Ernest Hemingway.

Address Piggott Arkansas for a while. They will forward.

PUL, ALS

1 In a letter to EH of 24 May 1928, Perkins reported that Scribner's had recently been threatened with a lawsuit by a woman named Lady Ashley, who "considered the use of the name Lady Ashley for the heroine of 'The Sun Also' libelous." After discovering that "the lady was not Lady Ashley at the time the book was published," Scribner's nevertheless offered "to publish a statement that the Lady Ashley of the book was not the Lady Ashley of fact" which, according to Perkins, would have been "excellent advertisement anyhow." However, Perkins wrote, "It rather looks at the moment as if the matter has been dropped" (PUL). *Debrett's Peerage and Baronetage*, reference publication founded in 1769 providing genealogical details of Britain's royal and titled familes. Robinson Crusoe, the protagonist of the novel *Robinson Crusoe* (1719) by Daniel Defoe (c. 1660–1731).
2 *The Bridge of San Luis Rey*, by American author and playwright Thornton Wilder (1897–1975), was published in 1927 by the firm Albert & Charles Boni, Inc. In 1926 Albert Boni (1892–1981), co-founder of Boni & Liveright, and his brother Charles Boni (1894–1969) had purchased the publishing house of their uncle Thomas Seltzer and renamed it. Set in eighteenth-century Peru, Wilder's novel centers on five persons who fall to their deaths when a bridge collapses. The two "splendid" stories are Part Two, "The Marquesa de Montemayor," and Part Three, "Esteban." The book was awarded a Pulitzer Prize in 1928.
3 EH refers to the success of Wescott's *The Grandmothers: A Family Portrait* (1927), Wilder's *The Bridge of San Luis Rey* (1927), and a novel by French-born American writer Julien Green (1900–1998) published in French as *Adrienne Mesurat* (Paris: Plon, 1927) and translated into English as *The Closed Garden* (New York: Harper, 1928). EH is probably alluding to the homosexuality of all three writers, without "wives and children to support." In his reply of 4 June 1928, Perkins remarked that Green's financial success "was chiefly due

to a new element in publishing . . . The Book of the Month Club. That now represents a very large sale though at a very low royalty. It gives a book a splendid advertisement." While speculating that a book by EH would stand a good chance for selection, Perkins wrote that a book such as *SAR* might be "too <u>strong</u>" for the club's audience and for those judges with conservative tastes (PUL).

4 The contract for *MWW*, dated 27 May 1927, calls for the first royalty statement to be provided six months after the date of publication and "settlements to be made in cash, four months after date of statement" (PUL). In his letter of 19 April 1928, Perkins reported that nearly 19,000 copies of *MWW* had sold in the six months since its publication on 14 October 1927, adding "you can have any or all of the $3,718 due, whenever you want it" (PUL).

5 In his letter of 25 May 1928, Perkins reported that Scribner's had removed the scar on EH's forehead from Helen Breaker's photographs of him (PUL). One of the portraits would be used on the dust jacket and in the advertisements for *FTA*.

To Clarence Hemingway, 1 June [1928]

Piggott

Arkansas

June 1

Dear Dad—

Got safely up North thanks to your good map. Drove from Key West here in six days—needless to say at that rate of going didnt see anyone along the route. I was anxious to get the trip over and back to work on my book [*FTA*]. Have 238 pages done now— Did nearly 200 at Key West.

Caught 5 Tarpon altogether— Largest 75 lbs.—smallest 40 lb. Caught 3 amberjacks, 1 very big King fish—60 or so barracudas—many jack crevalles— groupers, snappers, Whip rays, sharks, (all kinds of hammerheads, man eaters, nurse sharks etc.)

We went out to Marquesas Islands—way out in the Gulf—beyond the last keys and there had the best tarpon fishing and shooting—plover, cranes, curlew etc.

You will have to come down next time and go on a trip to Marquesas— Waldo Pierce landed a 150 lb. Tarpon—6 feet five inches long. Took 1 hr. and 20 minutes—in the channel inside the atoll of the Key— I landed one weighing over 60 lbs. on bass tackle—no brake nor drag on the reel not even a click—took a full hour. He jumped 12 times.

Harpooned many big sharks and whip rays.

When do you plan to go North? I would like to come up to O.P. maybe for a few days in the next 2 weeks—may not be possible. It is too late for Pauline to travel except toward a hospital. The baby is due the 27th of June according to Dr at Key West's calculations.

I wish we could come to Walloon— If the baby is born at K.C. I dont know how soon we could travel.

Who has the Loomis cottage?

If we came to Walloon could we get a cook and a nurse?

When will you be at Windermere and for how long?

I find I am very homesick for The North.

Is there a good hospital at Petoskey? Could Pauline have a baby there as comfortably as at K.C?

I wish you would write me about this right away if you have time.[1] I think it would be better if she could get out of the heat. At least for the hottest months after the baby is born.

Please give my love to Mother and the kids. What is Aunt Arabelle's address in KC. and new name?[2] I have it in Paris but didnt bring it. If we go to Kansas City we will leave about ten days or two weeks from today. If you or Mother will send me Aunt Arabelle's address I could write her. Perhaps Mother would write her and tell her Pauline and I are coming to K.C.

I am sorry not to have written more and oftener but it is almost impossible to write a letter when you are writing as hard as I am on this book. I am apalled at the urgent letters I should write. So far the book is going well.

Best luck to you.

With love from
Ernie

JFK, ALS; postmark: PIGGOTT, ARK, JUN / 1 / 6 pm / 1928

1 In a letter of 4 June 1928, Clarence would reply that Marcelline and Sterling Sanford had bought the Wayburn-Loomis Cottage on Walloon Lake in northern Michigan two years earlier. Clarence welcomed EH's visit "any time" but predicted that the family would probably not go up to Windemere until after July Fourth. He advised that the baby be born in Kansas City or St. Louis, "as the Petoskey Hospitals are really only best for local

emergencies" and there was a shortage of local nurses and maids. He also offered his services as obstetrician if they wished to have the baby at the Oak Park Hospital (JFK). In a separate letter, also dated 4 June 1928, EH's mother wrote, "I hope Pauline, that you are as comfortable as possible. Its a hard few weeks ahead of you—but . . . it is bound to be over with soon—and then you will feel it has been all so worth while. Keep up your courage, dear girl" (JFK).

2 Fanny Arabell Hemingway, the widow of Clarence's brother Alfred Tyler Hemingway, had married Clarence Erasmus Shepard (1869–1949) on 31 December 1927. In his reply, Clarence would give her new name and address as "Mrs. Clarence E. Shepard, 1300 West Santa Fe Road, Kansas City, Mo."

To Grace Hall Hemingway, 1 June [1928]

Piggott
ARKANSAS.
June 1

Dear Mother—

Would you be very good to me and forward the enclosed letter to Aunt Arabelle in Kansas City— I havent her address and am afraid I would misspell her name.[1]

It is pretty hot here but Key West was a fine place.

Coming north Tennessee was beautiful. This is a punk note only because I've written 2500 words on my bloody book—& a letter to Dad and the enclosed to Aunt Arrabelle— I'd appreciate it greatly if you would address it and send it off right away. She wrote me when she was to be married and like the lousy correspondant that I am I never answered—now I want very much to see her and want to set our correspondance straight.

How is ART?

Literature is very hot and sweaty today.

Love from
Ernie.

Pauline thought you and Dad were fine.

PSU, ALS; postmark: PIGGOTT / ARK, JUN / [*illegible*] / 1928

1 The enclosed letter to Aunt Arabell remains unlocated.

To Maxwell Perkins, 7 June [1928]

June 7
Piggot
Arkansas

Dear Mr. Perkins—

You are certainly right that the thing to do is to complete the mss. first— and it looks now as though I would get through the first draft by July perhaps. Have 279 pages done—maybe it will be very good. I hated terribly to leave Key West but got going well again after a week— The next jump is to Kansas City— Then after the baby is born and the book done I will take a couple of fly rods and go out to Idaho for 2 or 3 weeks— Then pick up my family, here or in KC. and go north somewhere until Fall— Will come through N.Y. in the fall sometime on the way back to Paris— I'll rewrite this novel [*FTA*]—then finish the other one—then do some stories.

Wasnt Waldo's tarpon a wonderful fish? He had lost seven before that and after he had this one on 40 minutes I bet 5.$\underline{^{00}}$ to 3.$\underline{^{00}}$ he would lose it. When it jumped it made a noise like Wm. Howard Taft diving. But he landed it.[1] I wish you could have seen him. I wish you would come with us next time. It is a wonderful life at the Marquesas. Dos Passos said he had the best time he'd ever had in his life. I can write a fine story about that country—wish this bloody book was finished so I could do it.

Is Meyers coming back? I was very much impressed with him in Paris. Took him around to Waldos but Waldo wasnt home or was drunk or painting in red flannel pants or something.

Does Mr. Struthers Burt the Foe of the Vicious City etc live out in Idaho? I would go and see him. Any man so opposed to VICE must have liquor.[2] I have been consistantly taken for a Govt. Rev. Agent or a bootlegger all over America so far—neither way gets you any liquor in the country. In the cities you talk Italian to get wine and ask a cop where to get beer. Gents that you give a lift to when they have fallen overboard from Buicks, Lincoln's, Chrystlers etc give you whiskey. I only drink the whiskey of Living drunks.

None of this finishes a novel—

Yours always
Ernest Hemingway.

I didn't know Thornton was leaving the Bonis.[3] He is very honorable and conscientious so he must have some reason or have fallen among peculiarly plausable thieves. I have heard several of them talk and they are all plausable (I'll try it with an i)— Thornton has no experience of the wicked world and he probably believed some of them. Anyway the Bonis—no matter how brilliant—I dont believe are altogether honest—and the small irritations of dealing with clever and not completely honest people may have gotten on his nerves. But he should have held a public auction of himself to the highest bidder rather than let some particularly smooth one tell him what <u>he</u> (the smooth one) could do for him (Thorton).

I think it's fine though that Thornton—without any business sense— writing the best he can and not cheapening should make more than Scott trying to play the market and watering his talent in the Post. Makes you believe in something. I don't know what.

PUL, ALS

1 In a letter of 4 June 1928, Perkins had written that "Waldo has been here and told me all about Key West and Dos Passos, and how he, Waldo, caught the biggest fish, and he showed me many splendid pictures of the three of you and of the fishes" (PUL). William Howard Taft (1857–1930), twenty-seventh president of the United States (1909–1913) and Chief Justice of the Supreme Court (1921–1930). Taft's weight at times exceeded three hundred pounds.

2 Maxwell Struthers Burt (1882–1954), a Scribner's author whose recent books included *Diary of a Dude Wrangler* (1924) and *The Delectable Mountains* (1927), was an advocate for the unspoiled American West. Since 1912 he had owned and operated the Bar B C Ranch near Jackson Hole, Wyoming, and popularized dude ranch vacations for Eastern city-dwellers. In his response to EH of 18 June 1928, Perkins would give Burt's address and write, "I can tell you there are few people he would be more delighted to see than yourself whom he immensely admires. He is a most furious foe of prohibition (he is always furiously for or against) and can certainly produce the best that is available in the U.S., or pretty near it" (PUL). Burt's anti-Prohibition essay "The Dry West" appeared in the February 1928 issue of *Scribner's Magazine*.

3 Perkins had written to EH that "Boni & Boni did beautifully by" Thornton Wilder and that it seemed to him "a little rough that he should be leaving them now after his contract, which includes one more novel, runs out" (4 June 1928, PUL). Wilder's next book, *The Angel That Troubled the Waters and Other Plays* (1928), was published by Coward-McCann of New York City. He would return to Boni & Boni for the publication of his novel *The Woman of Andros* (1930).

To Marcelline Hemingway Sanford, [8 June 1928]

Dear Ivory—

I lost your fine letter on a fishing trip— It dissolved in the pocket the 4th time I went in the water—so I didnt realize how soon you were going— Wrote the family and am writing now—will send you a wire to the boat.[1]

Hadley's address is 98 B^d Auguste Blanqui, Paris XIII. She can tell you tousands of places to eat, buy clothes, etc.

If you want a tailored suit go to O'Rossen in the Place Vendome.[2]

Millions of citizens will recommend places to you— It is some peoples main life to get people to go to the wonderful attractive little places they found themselves. So I wont bother you with many. However—

Eat outside at the Pavillon du Lac, the restaurant of the Parc Montsour[is], get fresh trout—tournedos and asperagus—and drink Pouilly (white) and St. Estephe (red) with the tournedos. It's grand there on a warm evening.[3]

Eat at the 4 Sergents du La Rochelle 4 B^d Beaumarchais (on the Place du Bastille). Eat anything but drink Richebourg, the best burgandy in town— They have it in magnums if youve any friends with you. But for Christ sake dont tell people to go there because there are only five magnums left. All their wines are lovely. Try the Margaux (red bordeaux) Tell the wine waiter your my sister.[4]

Go to Brasserie Lipp on B^d Saint Germain opposite Cafe des Deux Magots for Beer—potatoe salad and choucroute garnie. Best beer in Paris.[5]

Eat to spend money at Foyots, Tour D'Argent etc. But still spending money you can eat better at Laperouse and if you want to get your hair cut or a permanent go to Antoine's in Rue Cambon, only decent coiffure in Paris.[6]

If you want the best perfume there is, get Chanel's Gardenia at Chanel[7]— also on rue Cambon.

Go to the Ritz for a cocktail and see the fraternity pins. I wish to God I was there to take you to the real places but we're not. Mrs. Moody will know all the places but they arent my places.[8] Best love and good luck.

I've no friends in Paris in the summer time so am not giving you any letters. Everybody is out of town. If you want a fine place to go, go to Saint Jean de Luz on the Basque coast. Swimming and everything else.

If you want to go to Pamplona, it is the 7th 8th 9th 10th 11th and 12th of July— Go to Don Juan Quintana at Hotel Quintana and tell him you are my sister and he must get you tickets. Give everybody my love.[9]

So long kid and I hope you get this.

Love always—

Ernie

JFK, ALS

1 As EH told Marcelline in the following cable, dated 8 June, he had sent this letter to the *Olympic* of the White Star Line, on which Marcelline sailed from New York for France that day. In a postcard to EH dated 14 June 1928, "20 hours out from Cherbourg," Marcelline would report that his letter and telegram had reached her ship in time and that she was thrilled to get them.

2 O'Rossen, fashionable Paris-based tailoring firm located at 12, Place Vendôme.

3 The restaurant Pavillon du Lac in the Parc Montsouris on the Left Bank. In Chapter 4 of *SAR*, Jake Barnes and Brett Ashley arrive by cab at the Parc Montsouris, but "the restaurant where they have the pool of live trout" is closed. Tournedos, filets of beef tenderloin. Likely Pouilly Fumé (a Sauvignon Blanc with smoky flavor from the Loire Valley) or Pouilly Fuissé (a Chardonnay from the Mâconnais region). Saint Estèphe, a robust, earthy red wine from the Médoc region north of Bordeaux.

4 The 1924 Baedeker guide to Paris recommends Restaurant des Quatre Sergents de la Rochelle at 3, boulevard Beaumarchais, in the Place de la Bastille (Baedeker's *Paris*, 19). Richebourg, a distinctive red wine from a Grand Cru vineyard in the Côte de Nuits region of Burgundy. A magnum wine bottle holds about 1.5 liters, twice the usual volume. Château Margaux, a fine red Bordeaux wine from the Médoc region. In Chapter 19 of *SAR*, Jake Barnes drinks a bottle of Château Margaux "for company."

5 The Brasserie Lipp, at 151, boulevard Saint-Germain, opposite the Café les Deux Magots at 6, Place Saint-Germain des Prés. In the "Hunger Was Good Discipline" chapter of *MF*, EH describes a meal at Lipp's that includes a large mug of "very cold and wonderful" beer, two orders of *pommes à l'huile*, and "a *cervelas* . . . a sausage like a heavy, wide frankfurter split in two and covered with a special mustard sauce." Jules Pascin, in "With Pascin at the Dôme," tells EH, "if you really liked beer you'd be at Lipp's" (*MF*). EH and James Joyce share a drink of sherry at the Deux Magots in "The Man Who Was Marked for Death" (*MF*). *Choucroute garnie*, an Alsatian dish of meats and sauerkraut.

6 Identified by the 1924 Baedeker guide to Paris as the only two "Restaurants of the Highest Class" on the Left Bank, Foyot (22bis, rue de Vaugirard and 33, rue de Tournon) opened in 1848, while the Restaurant de La Tour d'Argent (15, Quai de la Tournelle and boulevard Saint-Germain) is described as "the oldest restaurant in Paris, founded as a hostelry in 1582" (Baedeker's *Paris*, 15). In Chapter 3 of *SAR*, when the prostitute Georgette questions Jake Barnes's choice of restaurant, he wonders if she might prefer Foyot's. Lapérouse (51, Quai des Grands Augustins), also on the Left Bank, in a seventeenth-century townhouse

beside the Seine, was frequented by Émile Zola, George Sand, and Victor Hugo. Known as "Monsieur Antoine," Polish-born Antoni Cierplikowski (1884–1976) opened his hair salon at 5, rue Cambon in 1912 and became known for popularizing the "bob."

7 Gardénia, a scent created by perfumer Ernest Beaux and launched in 1925 for Chanel, the company headed by designer Gabrielle "Coco" Chanel, whose shop was at 31, rue Cambon.

8 Anna Addison Moody (1877–1965), Marcelline's travel companion, was married to John Edward Moody (1868–1958), entrepeneur and financial analyist who founded the firm John Moody & Company in New York City in 1900.

9 On 2 July 1928, Marcelline would send EH an enthusiastic letter from Saint Jean de Luz, where she planned to stay for about ten days. She wanted to travel to Pamplona, but her travel companion was unwilling (JFK; Sanford, 335).

To Marcelline Hemingway Sanford, 8 June 1928

LRA 71 26=PIGGOTT ARK 8 1031A
MRS S S SANFORD=
STEAMSHIP OLYMPIC SAILING MIDNIGHT JUNE 8 NEWYORK NY=
SENT LETTER TO BE FORWARDED TO GUARANTY TRUST PARIS IF
MISSED BOAT STOP HADLEYS ADDRESS NINE EIGHT BOULEVARD
AUGUSTE BLANQUI PARIS THIRTEEN STOP LOVE AND LUCK=
ERNIE.

JFK, Cable; Western Union destination receipt stamp: 1928 JUN 8 PM 1 02

To Maxwell Perkins, 12 June 1928

KA559 18 NM=KANSAS CITY MO 12
MAXWELL E PERKINS=
CHARLES SCRIBNERS SONS NEWYORK NY=
PLEASE ADDRESS MAIL CARE MRS MALCOLM LOWRY 6435
INDIAN LANE[1] STOP LOOKS LIKE AL SMITH=[2]
    HEMINGWAY.

PUL, Cable; Western Union destination receipt stamp: 1928 JUN 12 PM 7 37

1 Having come to Kansas City for the birth of their child at the Research Hospital, EH and Pauline stayed at the home of William Malcolm Lowry (1884–1953) and Ruth White Lowry (1884–1974). Ruth was the half-sister of EH's Aunt Arabell.

2 As EH predicts, Al Smith would be nominated as the Democratic candidate for president at the party's national convention, held 26–29 June 1928 in Houston, Texas.

To Waldo Peirce, 17 and [c. 19] June [1928]

June 17

Muy Waldo mio—

The address on the back of this is where we are for a while until little Pilar arrives and then for a couple of weeks afterwards while Pauline is in the hospital.[1] She is in fine health and the doctor says everything should marche.[2] The trip to Piggott wasn't bad. [T]hen worked like a bastard in Piggott and finally came on here. That Berenson story was a wonder. What an empty arse hole a kike patron of the arts can be. Using the old envelope gag on you.[3] As I pound this mill I see in the book case a vol called Understanding Our Children

Pierce

Frederick, I see by the title page, not Waldo.[4] The convention was too shitty to write about. I am now on page 311 in the book [*FTA*]. Hope to finish it in a month. You write the best letter of anybody in the cockeyed world and what a lousy letter this is. I'm all written to hell out and pooped. Plenty of liquor out here. Also some good polo. There is a swimming pool in the yard and nice trees and I work in the morning then have lunch then go over and watch the polo have a few drinks in the locker room while guys sit around getting dressed and smell a little sweat and bull a little then come home go swimming have supper read Zane Grey on his battles with the monsters and then go to sleep.[5] Bought the Zane to send to Charles and am reading it first so as to be able to discuss it intelligently with Charles when we talk Literature.[6] It is a pretty good one too. Broadbill Swordfish and Tuna. Off Nova Scotia—biggest Tuna weighed 758 lbs. Biggest Swordfish 582. Wish the hell we could do some more fishing. After the baby is born I may go out to Idaho. They say there is swell fishing there and I could work on the bloody book and fish when I get through. Piggott is a grand place to shoot but the law is on. I would come to Maine but it is a hell of a way with me only a day or so away from Wyoming here. This is a nice town with some good guys. Simple as hell everybody with lots of money doing all the things the English do without english accents and no bloody snobbery.

Once I get this book done will leave it alone a couple of months and maybe do some stories—then go back and re-write it. I believe a writer deserves all the dough he makes even it if is a million. Writing a novel if you write hard instead of easy is a hell of a job. Am on the last leg now. Know how it comes out anyway.

There is a big black police dog from Germany here with police training who is trained to sieze and hold anybody he doesn't know. He knows me finally. Also to disarm you if you have a pistol. Mine is in my trunk under the bed.

Maybe Al Smith will get elected if enough people get to believe the story that Hoover once voted in England. Who for I wonder? Queen Victoria?[7]

I will let you know when Pilar or Patrick is born. If you will turn Papist you can be a Godfather.

Anyway love from Pauline— Hope Ivy's there by now. Give her my best.

su amigo Ernesto

I miss not going to Pamplona—first time I've defaulted in a hell of a long time. Hope it rains or that the bulls have no balls.[8]

[*On verso:*] a couple of days later—

Your letter came and one from Charles. George Brooks won the primaries and it seems there actually was a man there with a beard who was trying to buy the ice plant. Mimi caught one that was six feet one inch long and weighed 102 pounds.[9] In the old days before yours put a stop to the estimating and started weighing it would probably have been a 140 pounder. You don't owe me any money at all of any sort. As a matter of fact I owe you money so keep the 25 and tell them put the picture up in every Water in America Hemingway's Pile Remedy. It looks fine.[10] Wish the hell I was up in Maine with you. Maybe the guy's grouper got caught in the rocks like that one of mine where I had to tow the whole boat on my line back to the rocks and he thought that the grouper ounce for ounce and pound for pound the strongest fish that swims.[11] I can't wait to get out on the reef and

Mascot Shoals again. Next time we'll hit it when the Kingfish are running. The scotch here is only caromel, rainwater and alcohol—damn little of the last even. I drank all one night until sunrise and couldn't even get a breath. Holder certainly has it all over Zane [Grey]. But give me Zane over VanCampen.[12] Maybe we should do a fish book for all time. It would be fine for Scribners. I'll write the book and you do color plates and photographs. We&d get a graphlex or a good automatic movie camera and then enlarge from the movies. You could do some wonderful pictures and we'd have them sell the book for $22.50 and it would be a classic. That is the kind of book I'd like to do. We would get a big advance on

[*On recto of page, typewritten upside down in the space below EH's typewritten signature and postscript*:]

    continued from back side

the book, enough to buy all our tackle, pay for the boat and all expenses. I could make the book just a straight running story and make it funny as hell. We would get Dos to go along and Charles. Go down in the winter and fish Shark River and around the Cape and all through there—all along the Keys—stop and kid the milliardaires at Llong Key—go out to Marquesas, Dry Tortugas, and the Bahamas—anhcoring at Havana for a while—with chapters on the fishing, yencing, pelota etc. there. Catch Sword Fish and everything. Wouldn't that be a trip?[13] Scribners could serialize it and I could make it funny as hell. We could have funny pictures and serious ones. It would be a saga of fishing and drinking. I think would make a swell book. What do you say?

Colby, TL with typewritten signature

The first part of this letter, dated "June 17," responds to Peirce's letter of 9 June 1928, addressed to EH at the Pfeiffer home in Piggott and forwarded to Kansas City (JFK). The second part, written "a couple of days later," responds to Peirce's letter of 12 June 1928, also mailed to Piggott (JFK).

1 The letter is written on the verso of stationery embossed with the address of the Lowrys' home, where EH and Pauline were staying: 6435 INDIAN LANE / KANSAS CITY, MISSOURI.

2 *Marcher*: to work, function, go (French).

3 Bernard Berenson (né Bernhard Valvrojenski, 1865–1959), Lithuanian-born art critic and a connoisseur of Italian Renaissance art. In his 9 June letter, Peirce wrote that a cousin of Berenson had owed him $250 "for a little picture" purchased two years earlier, but when

the man finally handed him an envelope, it contained only $100, along with a note promising future payment of the remainder (JFK).

4 *Understanding Our Children* (New York: E. P. Dutton, 1926), a book on child psychology by Frederick Pierce (1878–1963).

5 Polo had been a popular sport in Kansas City since 1898, when the Kansas City Country Club bought land for polo fields and regular matches were first held. The Lowry home was less than two blocks from the southern edge of the Country Club. Zane Grey (1872–1939), best known for his popular adventure novels, especially of the American West. EH refers to *Tales of Swordfish and Tuna* (New York: Harper, 1927), a nonfiction account of Grey's fishing ventures. EH and Peirce often referred to large fish as "monsters."

6 Charles P. Thompson (1898–1978) managed his family's fishing business and marine hardware store in Key West and introduced EH to big game fishing. Charles and his wife, Lorine C. Thompson (1898–1985), a public school teacher from Richmond, Georgia, became close friends of EH and Pauline. Charles would join EH and Pauline on their African safari (December 1933–February 1934) and serve as the model for Karl in *GHOA*.

7 Herbert Hoover would defeat Al Smith in the 1928 presidential race and serve as thirty-first President of the United States from 1929 to 1933. Hoover had lived abroad for extended periods between 1897 and 1919. EH refers to charges that Hoover had voted in England while he was living there; although his name appeared on London voting rolls, it was never proven that he actually had voted in a British election. Queen Victoria (1819–1901) was monarch of the United Kingdom from 1837 until her death.

8 In Chapter 16 of the *SAR* typescript, Mike tells Jake to tell Romero that "bulls have no balls." Because of Scribner's concerns about suppression, the wording was changed in early editions of *SAR* to "bulls have no horns." In 1953 Scribner's quietly restored EH's original wording to subsequent editions.

9 George "Georgie" Brooks (b. 1876), assistant district attorney in Key West, had introduced EH and Charles Thompson. In his letter to EH of 12 June 1928, Thompson reported "Memie's" feat, but she remains unidentified (JFK).

10 Scribner's had sent Peirce $25 for a portrait drawing of EH that he had delivered to Perkins. Describing it as "very definite and simple," Perkins told EH the sketch would be used for publicity "right away" (4 June 1928, PUL) and, with a letter of 18 June 1928, sent him a copy of it (PUL). In his letter of 12 June, Peirce referred to the drawing as "that black and white bean of you suggesting the act of thinking." Feeling indebted over expenses incurred during his stay in Key West, he offered to send EH the $25, saying it was "much less than I owe you even if its more than your mug is worth" (JFK). Peirce's 1928 portrait of EH is included in the plate section of this volume.

11 In his 12 June letter Peirce wrote, "What do you think of a guy that sends a small grouper all the way to Bangor Maine to be stuffed."

12 American naturalist and sportsman Charles Frederick Holder (1851–1915), author of *The Big Game Fishes of the United States* (New York: Macmillan, 1903), a copy of which EH owned (Reynolds *Reading*, 137). Van Campen Heilner (1899–1970), American naturalist and sportsman known for his books on fishing and duck hunting.

13 In a letter of 22 June 1928 Peirce would reply, "You can count me in on your trip anytime . . . Ill get a movie etc—& well really produce a saga—as you say" (Colby).

To Don Carlos Guffey, [c. after June 1928]

To Dr. Guffey
this copy emasculated and anglicized by Jonathan Cape for British
consumption

Ernest Hemingway.

Christie's catalog, New York, Masterpieces of Modern Literature: the Library of
Roger Rechler, Lot 149 (illustrated), Inscription

EH inscribed a copy of the first English edition of *In Our Time*, published by Jonathan Cape on
23 September 1926. The date of EH's inscription is uncertain, although it was most likely
sometime after Dr. Guffey delivered EH and Pauline's son, Patrick, on 28 June 1928. EH would
give Guffey other inscribed books during the early 1930s.

To Mary Pfeiffer, [2 and 3 July 1928]

Monday Five PM

Dear Mother—

Pauline was a lot better this afternoon. The gas had gone down and
Patrick was getting a good supply of milk. It seems to be cooling off a little
and I hope tomorrow, if the gas stays down, she will be much more
comfortable. I think that is all the news.[1]

I would write more but have been at the hospital most of the time. Am
going to try and do something on my book tomorrow morning. I think I
had better get out of the writing business and into something else.

Best to all the family. I am sorry to have missed Karl.[2] Hope he found
enough arrows for the cross bow. You ask in your letter what effect the
operation will have on Pauline. The doctor said the wound will take ten days
to heal normally. Then she should stay in the hospital another week or ten
days and then she can come to Piggott but must stay upstairs and not do any
walking up or down stairs or lifting. The doctor said she shouldn't have
another baby for three years if she did not want to become a cripple or a
corpse.

Tuesday A.M.

I just called the hospital and they said Pauline had the best night yet, that the distention was gone down and that she felt hungry for the first time. She is much better. Will mail this now on my way to the hospital. With the good news got a morning's work done.

Love to all,

Ernest

Tell Mr. Pfeiffer I certainly admire his levee. Hope this hot weather will prevent any more floods.[3] Please tell Jinny to hang onto the present she has for me and not to mail it. I will write her.

PUL, TLS

1 Pauline had delivered Patrick by Caesarean section at the Research Hospital, Kansas City on 28 June at 7:30 p.m. after eighteen hours of labor, and she was experiencing the aftereffects of abdominal surgery.
2 Karl Gustavus Pfeiffer (1900–1981), Pauline's brother.
3 Heavy rains had caused flooding in Missouri and Arkansas in late June. In a letter to Pauline and Ernest of 1 July 1928, Paul Pfeiffer reported that the fields were so wet that farmers could not enter them to harvest the crops. The St. Francis River had risen to record high water levels. Pfeiffer, who was on the board of directors of the St. Francis Drainage District, wrote, "With much emergency work we saved all the Ark side levees but 3 bad breaks on Mo side with much loss to the poor farmers" (JFK).

To Clarence and Grace Hall Hemingway, 4 July 1928

July 4 1928

Dear Dad and Mother—

Thank you both for your very good letters. We have named the boy Patrick. He is very big strong and healthy. He is too big in fact as he nearly killed his mother.[1] They had to do a cesaerian finally and I have been very worried about Pauline since but today her temperature is down to 99 8/10 and the gas distention is subsiding. She has suffered terribly.

It has been over 90 in the shade here ever since the day the baby was born. Conditions have not been ideal for finishing my novel.

You speak about coming to Windermere but Mother says you will be gone August 19th so I do not see, at this date, how we are to make it.[2] I saw my time clear to run up to Oak Park to pay a visit a while back before the baby was born but when I wrote you advised against it. We can do no jumping around with a baby that age in the summer time and wherever we go must stay for a while. I wrote Dad from Piggott asking about getting a cottage at Walloon but was discouraged.

I will try and write Uncle Will and family as you suggest but have been spending a great deal of time at the hospital and have not been able even to do my urgent work.[3]

Please give my love to Sunny and tell her the reason I have not written her is because I have been swamped with work.

Love to all

ERNIE.

Pauline said to thank you very much for your letter, Mother. She would like to have answered it but has been very very sick.

JFK, TL with typewritten signature

This letter was enclosed with EH's letter to his parents dated 15 July [1928]. Clarence would acknowledge their receipt in a letter to EH of 18 July 1928 (JFK).

1 EH would echo this statement in the final chapter of *FTA*. Asked if he is proud of his newborn son, delivered by Caesarean, Frederic Henry responds, "No, . . . He nearly killed his mother." In a letter to EH of 29 June 1928, Clarence reported that EH's telegram had come that morning "announcing the arrival of nine pound boy" (JFK). Grace's letter to EH has not been located.
2 In his letter to EH of 24 June 1928, Clarence wrote, "Keep us posted as to 'Events.'— Think you were wise 'Storking in K.C.'— Hope you can get up to Windemere later" (JFK).
3 Clarence's brother Willoughby had been visiting Oak Park with his wife, Mary, and their daughters, Winifred and Adelaide. In his 29 June letter, noting that they would leave from San Francisco for Hawaii aboard the *Malolo* on 14 July for a visit with EH's Aunt Grace en route to Japan and China, Clarence urged EH to "Write them a steamer letter."

To Waldo Peirce, [c. 6 July 1928]

Capitalista Enorme:[1]

Glad to hear and the longer the letters the better. Hope by this time the trout have advanced in size from the prick passive to the prick rampant.[2] I am waiting to hear how you catch the largest bloody trout ever caught in the state. Your style adapts its-self better to the more monstrous. Let you hook one big enough and you'll land him. I wish the hell I was fishing instead of being here with the bloody thermometer over ninetey every day since Don Patricio entered this world by the same process as J.C. (not as you think our Lord but Julius Cesear) It was a very near business for Pauline. Eighteen hours of labor with the thermometer at 97 then no results at all— Patrick built like a brick shit house across the shoulders—finally the old cesaerian. Nothing for a guy to watch when his affections are involved. Nor in any sense the ideal way to kill time while woiking on a novel. Pauline was pretty dam [*diamond-shaped hole cut out of MS, missing text*] afterwards. Suffered like we know nothing about. Anyway she is getting [*hole in MS*] take her and the heir of all the penniless Hems of History down [*hole in MS*]en shove off for Wyoming. Bill Horne is going to ride out with me from he[*hole in MS*]y I used to know in the autoambulanzia.[3] Will prospect—locate the fishing and then wire you to come on. Have never seen the coekeyed west and if you've never you'd better see it. The flies, mosquitoes etc. re all killed off by the first frosts in August and then they say the fishing just starts to be good. T[h]ousands of trout and big ones. Rainbows, cut-throats, brooks, dolly vardens, grayling, golden trout etc. We will butcher them all. I have 4 qts. Scotch. We'll get some more. Should be fine fishing trout on good cold wadeable streams in the mountains wit Elks, bears, dude ranchers etc. to shoot at. Have got a 22 cal automatic colt—shooting long rifles, and a 410 ga. shot gun. Sage hen season opens in Wyo,ing Aug. 1st. Rattle snake season open all the time. They say it is fine country. I will write you all the dope. Horny bill can only stay two weeks from office to office— I plan to stay four. You could drive back wit me as far as Piggott—or St. Louis if Arkansas means nothing to you and you want to get back to Maine.

I am glad as hell you have all that timber. Be careful with it and watch where you lay your buts down.[4] I think we will all need it before so damn long. I think it might be a good idea if we could get Dos and you and I and give up all forms of Art including the little theater movements thus leaving art completely constipated while we fish—[5] Fishing is certainly thr best thing there is. We might as well find out about this western fishing because maybe it is fine. I would like to fish where I could catch a christ awful amount of trout with out working too hard for them. It was like that when I

was a kid and maybe it is somehwre still. They say the middle fork of the
Salmon River in Idaho (no roads within fifty miles) is the best fishing in the
world. You have to pack in on hoss back. We'll get a guide and the horses
and bloody well pack in and catch some of those big bastards and shoot
some stuff and have a real trip. To hell with sitting around the dude ranches
with a trip like that to take. They say it is the wildest country left in the
D'america and after I fisnish this bloody book and get i[*hole in MS*] a little
while out there we'll need a trip like that. The flies and mosquitoes sh[*hole
in MS*] We could camp on the river and have a swell life. Get some [*hole in
MS*]ok and all and caress the pack animals. What do you think?

That is tough about Pat. I will write but what can you write? Best to
cable.[6]

So long you feudal landowner. We'll take a swell trip. We ought to be able
to buggar civilization completely pn the middle fork of the Salmon. Look at
it on the map. They say it is almost untouched. Lots of them run up to six
and eight pounds. Jump like tarpoons. Would be a swell trip.

Write,

ssqbsm (in theory)[7]

Ernesto

Colby, TL with typewritten signature

Some text is missing where the letter was folded and scissor-cut at the fold marks, creating two
diamond-shaped holes in the paper.

1 *Capitalista Enorme*: Enormous Capitalist (Spanish). In his letter of 28 June 1928, Peirce
reported that he was to receive "two ninths" of an inheritance "valued at some two million
and a half." It was enough, Peirce wrote, "to keep us in rods reels flies licker worms wenches
etc." (JFK).

2 Peirce's 28 June letter to EH was typed single-spaced on two legal-sized pages with a lengthy
handwritten postscript. Fishing a stream "lousy with trout" near his home in Maine, he
reported, "I caught one trout about the size of my prick which was some fish—for
diminuativeness."

3 William D. Horne, Jr. (1892–1985) and EH met while serving in the American Red Cross
Ambulance Service during WWI. The two briefly roomed together in Chicago in 1920, and
Horne was in Hadley and EH's wedding party. In a letter of 12 January 1928, shortly before
EH began drafting *FTA*, Horne had encouraged him to "write the war," saying, "It hasn't
been done yet—not even almost nearly close, and oh Jesus how you could do it" (JFK). The
pair would join up for a road trip to Wyoming in late July 1928.

4 Peirce's family fortune came from timberlands. In his 28 June letter, Peirce wrote that while
he was out fishing, the fire warden "took me name as if I wanted to burn down my

inheritance which in the paper that same morning had been announced." The value would depend on "cutting, forest fires etc.," Peirce said, adding "I shall piss copiously on all my trees as fire protection first & to make em grow greener bigger and pulpier."

5 In his letter, Peirce expressed contempt for art colonies, such as Provincetown and Woodstock, and wrote that he much preferred the wilderness of Maine and fishing. Dos Passos was then on the board of directors for the New Playwrights Theatre, but would resign after the closing of his play *Airways, Inc.*, in 1929 (Townsend Ludington, ed., *The Fourteenth Chronicle: Letters and Diaries of John Dos Passos* [Boston: Gambit, 1973], 369, 390–91).

6 Peirce wrote he had just learned that Patrick Morgan's mother had died suddenly and said he and EH should write to him, although he did not know Morgan's Paris address.

7 Abbreviation for *Su servidor que besa su mano*: Your servant who kisses your hand (Spanish).

To Henry Strater, [c. 6 July 1928]

6435 Indian Lane
Kansas City Mo.

Dear Mike—

Where did that horses ass Hartmann get any such shit as that your letters made me sore? He and his lady wife delight to make trouble if possible. Still I like him but she is just another nut.[1] Drove here from Key West.

I would have written you sooner but yr. letter came the day I left Key West and was so pooped from driving and anxious to get back on the novel that I put off writing and never wrote.[2] Have another son Patrick nine pounds—18 hrs. labor and a cesaerian. Pauline is about out of the woods now. Poor kid.

Have 388 pages foolscap done on novel—will boil down to 250 type—am about three quarters through maybe. Thermometer 92, wife that your crazy about in the hospital dangerously sick—all the ideal conditions for working.

Well kid this seems to be all of this letter which is no letter but just a communication to show you how fond Mr. Hemingway is of youse.

Have six bottles Scotch two of bourbon one of rye and no appetite for it. Too hot. My neck's too thick to drink this weather. Humidity of 96. Drink a little just the same. Do you know Waldo Pierce? He is a hell of a good guy and my Tarpon Fishing partner at present at Bangor Me. If you are near there get ahold of him. We will be in N.Y. in the fall. When will youse be back? I plan to go to Idaho from here to fish some trout. Would come to Maine but am a hell of a long way while not far from Idaho. Probably wont get anywhere.

My love to Maggie and salutations to your numerous and talented progeny.

Hem.

PUL, TL with typewritten signature

1 Hartman had married German-born Gusta Frank (b. c. 1885) in 1913.
2 EH may refer to a letter Strater had sent to Key West in an envelope postmarked "19 May 1928, N.Y." that survives at JFK; the letter itself remains unlocated. EH left Key West on the long road trip to Piggott around 25 May.

To Evan Shipman, [c. 6 July 1928]

Dear Evan—

Just got your letter.[1] Pauline had the baby after 18 hrs. labor and a cesaerian. She is going to come out all right but was awfully sick. The baby is named Patrick and is big, too big, brown and healthy.

My address here is 6435 Indian Lane K.C. Mo. For two weeks more anyway. We had a wonderful time down on the keys. Have done 388 pages on my book and ought to finish in another month.

Where are you and what are you doing? I hope to go out to Idaho on a fishing trip once Pauline is better and out of the hospital.

Pierre can stick 1000 dollars up his ass. Glad Miro has had a success.[2] When you write him give him my bewt. Andre too.[3] I am trying to work and it is hard with thermometer 92—Pauline sick etc.

Write me the dope. I want very much to see you.

Yrs. always,
HEM

Channick, TL; postmark: KANSAS C[ITY; *rest torn away*]

EH addressed the letter to "Evan Shipman Esq. / 21 Beekman Place / New York City / N.Y." The conjectured letter date is based on the postmark on the envelope verso, which indicates that the letter reached New York City on 7 July 1928.

1 EH is responding to Shipman's letter of 6 June 1928, sent from Boury en Vexin, just before Shipman's departure for New York City (JFK).

2 French art dealer and gallery owner Pierre Loeb (1897–1964) organized an exhibition of works by Spanish painter Joan Miró (1893–1983), held 1–15 May 1928 at the Galerie Georges Bernheim in Paris. Shipman wrote, "Pierre says he will give you $1000 (dollars) for the picture if you want to sell—I told him you'd tell him next year" (JFK). Loeb may have wanted to buy Miró's painting *The Farm* (1921–1922), which EH had purchased in 1925 for 3,500 francs, equivalent to about $166 at the time.

3 André Masson (1896–1987), French painter whose Paris studio at 45, rue Blomet EH likely first visited in 1922 or 1923 with Gertrude Stein. Masson's triptych of oil paintings, *The Forest* (1922–1923), along with another of his paintings that EH purchased in Paris, *The Throw of the Dice* (1922), are now part of the Hemingway Collection at JFK (Colette Hemingway, *in his time: Ernest Hemingway's Collection of Paintings and the Artists He Knew* [Naples, Florida: Kilimanjaro Books, 2009], 11–18). Masson had sent EH "his best" via Shipman's letter of 6 June.

To Leonore Ovitt, [c. 15 July 1928]

Dear Miss Leone Ovitt

The Oak Parker

You are certainly an unattractive little nest egg of other peoples ideas and phrases[1]

Ernest Hemingway

JFK, ACDS

EH drafted this cable on the verso of a letter of 28 June 1928 from Waldo Peirce (JFK). In the following letter to his parents, dated 15 July 1928, EH writes that he "was going to send" a wire to Ovitt with this wording but apparently decided against it.

1 EH was incensed by Ovitt's review essay, "Ernest Hemingway, One of Ours," that had appeared in the *Oak Parker* on 29 June 1928, which his father had enclosed in his letter to EH of 2 July. "There is no other Oak Park writer who has made so definite and overwhelming a contribution to literature," Ovitt conceded, but she attacked EH's work, particularly *SAR*, declaring "Mr Hemingway apparently hasn't an ideal to his name" (32).

To Clarence and Grace Hall Hemingway, 15 July [1928]

July 15

Dear Dad and Mother—

Am sending you the enclosed letter which I thought had been mailed long ago.[1] Pauline will write as soon as she is able to thank you for the lovely presents to Patrick. He is gsining well and seems very strong—weighs 9 lb. 10 oz.

Thanks very much Dad for sending me the clippings—the one by the local village critic was charming.[2] I never read a collection of such drool—was going to send her a wire saying "You are an unattractive little nest egg of other peoples ideas" but didn't want to notice the young lady. Have been working very hard all the time plus the strain of Pauline's danger (now all past) plus the heat—consistently over 90 and now have 456 pages done—and a third more to go. Am taking Pauline and Patrick to Piggott then going out somewhere where I know no one and try and finish the book. I'd love to come to Windermere but can't work and see anyone and would be as pleasant for you to have around as a bear with carbuncles until this book is finished. Must get back at it now.

Please give Ura my love and tell her how much we appreciated her grand present.[3] I will write her but am so shot from working day and night and being at the hospital all the time that I can't write a decent letter.

Best love,

Ernie.

Hadley's address is 98 Boulevard Auguste Blanqui

Paris XIII

France

She and Bumby are both very well and are going to the mountains the first of August.

JFK, TL with typewritten signature

1 EH enclosed his letter to his parents of 4 July 1928, as confirmed by his father's reply of 18 July 1928 (JFK).
2 In addition to Leonore Ovitt's review in the *Oak Parker*, "Ernest Hemingway, One of Ours," his father had sent Harry Hansen's "First Reader" column from the 2 July 1928 *Chicago Daily Journal*. Hansen wrote about Scribner's "latest find," Morley Callaghan, whose stories "A Regret for Youth" and "A Predicament" appeared in the July 1928 issue of *Scribner's Magazine*. Hansen aligned Callaghan with EH as one of "the younger writers [who] are breaking into the established magazines without compromising their work" (6). In his letter of 2 July 1928, Clarence remarked, "Enclosed clippings you may read with interest—. All good advertising me thinks!" (JFK).
3 In a letter to EH and Pauline postmarked 11 July 1928, Ursula wrote that she had sent "a little sweater for the new relative in K.C." (JFK).

To Archibald MacLeish, 15 July [1928]

Write to Indian Lane address
July 15
(All France wit a headache)[1]

Dear Mac—

Well whom should it have been but little Patrick. Now ready to leave the hospital and weighing nine pounds and seven ounces. Eight pounds twelve ounces when born. I myself weigh 186 pounds. What do you weigh? What does Mrs. Mac Leish weigh? Everyone should know their weight. I have no idea what my grandfather weighed and now he is dead. Poor unfortunate grandfather.

My God I would like to see youse guys but what are the chances? I am now on page 455 (one of the shittiest yet and I hoped it wd. be one of the best)—as near as I can figure out I will go on writing this book forever. I am next going to try writing in Wyoming. I have had some success writing in Key West—writing in Piggott was equally difficult—writing in Kansas City has charms of its own but have we given the great west a chance? No. Therefore I will hope to conclude the volumne in Wyoming. If it doesn't go well I will move on to Idaho. Will probably finish neck deep in the Pacific oceon. Does this take me toward Conway? Would that it did. However I can't stay in Wyoming indefinitely. We got to go east sometime. Whan do the fussballspielen start?[2] How are your trout coming on? Don't shoot that woodchuck he may be Harold Stearns.

I wish to hell I had some plans—but have only de hopes—and only the one hopes—to finish this bloody book. The night Patrick was born I wrote out a long telegram to you. Carried it around in my pocket several days. Found I had not sent it. Decided it was better to write—am now writing and you can see what a pitiful performance that is.

Pauline is fine now. Patrick also. He looks like a cross between Jinny and an ape and has the widest shoulders and thickest forearms and wrists in the world—I mean the hospital. Pauline sends her love and luck to Ada. Papa too. Hope youse are all well. If you aren't writing litrachur (Influence of Pound on Hem's style) or doing obstetrics write me another letter. Once

I get this fooking book done (it rides me and poops me all day and all night)
I will write you out of house and home wit letters.

I never gave up anything especially not youse nor drink[.] How about a
bottle of Saint Estephe and a sight of old mac?

Pappy

LOC, TLS with autograph postscript

1 EH penciled these three lines in the top and right margins of the first page after he finished
typing the letter. He refers to hangovers resulting from the previous day's Bastille Day
celebrations, the Fête Nationale, commemorating the storming of the Bastille on 14 July
1789 at the beginning of the French Revolution.
2 *Fussballspiele*: football games (German).

To Benjamin Tyley Hancock, 21 July 1928

July 21 1928

Piggott Arkansas

Dear Uncle Tyley:

I have wanted very often to write but have been working so hard on a
novel that when I get through work there is nothing much left to go on
paper. We did have some fine fishing though in the Florida keys tarpon,
barracuda ... jack, snappers, and kingfish, and Spanish mackerel. I got
seven tarpon altogether but none weighed over 75 pounds. Waldo Pierce
who was fishing with me caught one that weighed 150 lbs. 6 feet 8 inches
long. He fought over three hours ... Waldo is sending me some pictures
and I will send them, to you ...

Have been in Kansas City lately. We had a son born there June 28.
Pauline had a very bad time but she and the boy are both well. Today is my
birthday and I remember the fine times we had at the lake together. I don't
know anything about the Tunney-Heaney fight. Tunney (if he has kept his
accuracy) should win. But Heaney has been fighting hard and often while
Tunney has been studying literature and he may upset things ...[1]

Your always affectionate nephew ...

Ernest

Sotheby's catalog, New York, 21 June 2007, Lot 111 (partially illustrated), ALS

This transcription derives from the auction catalog description and partial illustration of the letter.

1 Gene Tunney, reigning world heavyweight boxing champion, would defeat New Zealand-born heavyweight Tom Heeney (1898–1984) in New York City on 26 July 1928 and retire after the fight. Known for his love of literature, Tunney had recently made news by lecturing on Shakespeare's *Troilus and Cressida* for a class taught by William Lyon Phelps (1865–1943) at Yale University ("Tunney Tells Yale About Shakespeare," *New York Times*, 24 April 1928, 1, 5).

To Waldo Peirce, 23 July 1928

July 23 1928

Piggott.

Well it looks like no trip to Salmon river. Probably was pretty bloody impractical anyway— Christnose Wyoming and Idaho a long way from Maine.

I am no nearer finished on my fooking book than ever—now on page 478 or something like that and six weeks more work. The bloody heat ruins my head. Also the cries of Patrick. We came down here from K.C. leaving at 6 pm—train at Jonesboro 4 hours late— Supposed to arrive at Piggot at 9 something a.m arrived at 2.45 pm— 94° in K.C-—93° here—over 90 all the time.

Pauline is well now and getting strong. Patrick is like a bull—bellows like a bull too. Why you ever wanted to be a Father I dont appreciate.

I leave here night after tomorrow for K.C. then leave Sat. morning for Wyoming—no idea where. But someplace where there is a good stream and I can fish ½ day and work the other half. Will finish book. Patrick is on a bottle so Pauline can come out in Sept. and we will have a short time together without muchachos yelling all the time.[1] Then come back. Go east. Get boat to Paris.

Am about broke. Made no money this year—haven't written or sold a story—done nothing but work on this book. Book probably shit—but will hit Scribner's for an advance on it to carry us back to Francia. It is not enough to just jam ahead writing all the time—needs more than that— I need tranquility in the head and not too much heat—also need fishing or bike riding— To hell with motor car riding. I miss the bull fights like hell.

How are Ivy and Pfifi?[2] Never curse Ivy for not giving you kids— It is 100 to 1 they bellow and if they do they drive you bughouse. Then when they grow up whats to say but what they will be shits.[3] I must write this book and not just write it—which alone is hard enough to do—but make it good— To hell with novels—

Last letters I had from you were a note from Boston and letter from Bangor when you were going up to get Ivy.[4]

Provincetown sounds like like the cul of Cape Cod. I think of it as full of Bodenheims.[5] Wish we were out on the Gulf Stream or on some good stream— Christ I will be happy if I get this book done and any good. I have been cogida so much while doing it that my faena (performed daily) is that of a very groggy bastard—[6] There are no fooking alibis in life—the stuff is good or not— Your reasons for it not being so good arent worth a turd— Have to make it good— Temptation is just to make it—

Well let me hear from you— Write to Piggott—they'll forward it as soon as I get an address—

Love to Ivy—

Don Ernesto Mierde[7]

Colby, ALS; postmark: ST. LO[UIS AND JON]ESBORO / R.P.O. / 1906, 23 / JUL / 1928

1 *Muchachos*: children (or boys) (Spanish). In his response of 26 July 1928, Peirce would write, "Must be hell trying to finish book & lock step with propogation etc. Youre right there are no alibis . . . . . Children should be had if at all when you and the girl are young, park em with the grandparent afterwards, who are of the age to care and enjoy them, then look em over on return from Mesopotamia" (JFK).
2 "Pfifi" is the little dog that belonged to Waldo's wife, Ivy. In his letters to EH, Peirce refers to the dog variously as "Peepee," "Pheephie," or "Fifi" (JFK).
3 In a letter of 20 July 1928, congratulating EH on Patrick's birth, Peirce observed, "Having no offspring I have only the machinery of life, that is of holy bedlock to contend with, without the major consolation, penalty or reward as you like" (JFK).
4 In a letter of 11 July from Boston, Peirce reported he had just spent three days in Provincetown and was en route to Montreal to meet his wife, who was arriving on the *Emperor of Sutherland*. The next day he sent EH a letter from Bangor, Maine (JFK).

5 *Cul*: ass (French). Peirce made derogatory comments about Provincetown in his 11 July letter, calling it a "squirrel caged art colony."

6 *Cogido*: injured, wounded by a bull's horn; *faena*: matador's work with the bull (Spanish).

7 *Don*: an honorific, comparable to "Sir"; *mierda*: shit (Spanish).

To Maxwell Perkins, 23 July [1928]

July 23

Dear Mr. Perkins:

I've written you a couple of times but not sent the letters. The child is a boy, Patrick, very big dark and strong seeming. Pauline had a very bad time— Cesaerian (can't spell it) and a rocky time afterwards— I was worried enough. Am now on page 486—it must average 180 words to a page—am going out to Wyoming starting the end of this week. Will finish the book there. There will be a lot to cut and I will leave it alone and re-write it when we get back to Paris in Nov. It should be ready to serialize in Feb. anyway. How much $\left\{ \begin{array}{c} \text{would} \\ \text{will} \end{array} \right\}$ the magazine pay for it?[1]

Am damned sick of the heat. Been over 90° almost everyday for nearly a month. Patrick being on a bottle Pauline will be able to leave him here with her family and come out to Wyoming in September for a month if everything goes well.

I hope you are having a good vacation. I have heard nothing from anyone except the Maine fishing news from Waldo. Made some money playing the races.

There seems to be no news.

Yours always,
Hemingway.

I wish the boy had been one of your girls.[2]

Address

Piggott

ARK.

They will forward as soon as I get a Wyoming address.

PUL, ALS

1 Perkins, who spent July vacationing in Vermont, replied to EH on 1 August that he would check with *Scribner's Magazine* editor Robert Bridges "and others" (PUL). On 8 August, he would write that Scribner's was ready to pay its highest possible rate for a long serialization, with its top rate for Galsworthy and Wharton running around $10,000. Perkins conceded that the amount did not "compare well with the twenty-five to forty thousand dollar payments sometimes made by the popular magazines" (PUL; *TOTTC*, 74–75).

2 Perkins and his wife, Louise Saunders Perkins (1887–1965), had five daughters. Bertha (1911–2005), Elizabeth (1914–1974), Louise (Peggy; 1915–2013), Jane (1918–1979), and Nancy (1925–1984).

To Evan Shipman, 23 July 1928

24N B 14

PIGGOTT ARK 1030A JUL 23 1928

EVAN SHIPMAN

23 BEEKMAN PLACE

LEAVING WYOMING PAULINE PATRICK AT PIGGOTT COMING EAST IN OCTOBER WISH COULD SEE YOU

    HEM

    1216 P

Channick, Cable

EH was about to travel to Wyoming from Piggott.

To Guy Hickok, [c. 27 July 1928]

Dear Copernicus—[1]

Whenever I begin to mis Paris there is always some little item in the paper about how Professor Ritchey will be able to see men on Mars (if there aremen) with his new telescope. Of course, he doesn't think there are men but if it will please the A.P. he will look for them and if they are there he will see them.[2]

Patrick, weighing nine pounds was born in Kansas City. He looks like Count Salm and we hope will show talent along that line as if he keeps on yelling it is a cinch I won't be able to write and support him.[3] They finally had to open Pauline up like a picador's horse to lift out Patrick. It is a different feeling seeing the tripas of a friend rather than those of a horse to whom you have never been introduced. Anyway the thermometer went to

90 the day Patrick was born and zstayed there or above for three weeks—
Nearly killed Pauline who (to continue the horse motif) blew up with gas
like the same rosinante after the tripas removed if left in hot place.[4] But
everything all right finally and no one dead and Patrick back to Piggott on a
bottle—on several bottles— His father on page 482 of his monumental
opus—leaving tomorrow for wyoming in the ford—seeing damerica first.[5]
Will find a place where can fish and work and finish the bloody book.
Thanks like hel for going around and paying the merchants. You did write
to hang ont[o] the receipt. I know how christawful busy you are with the
bastardly tourists who would be bad enough in any event but all coming
from Brooklyn are therefore the cream and you were damned fine to pay the
govt. Also to send the auto and echo.[6] Write to Piggott.

Pauline is coming out to Wyoming in Sept. if all goes wel—this typer is
not mine and I don't know where the margin release is—am not trying to
pull and ezra on you with fancy spellings.

Pauline is o.k. after the cesaerian—scar tight—looks fine and feeling good
now but had a near thing— I'm going to find someplace in wyoming where
it will be comfortable and good fishing in th[e] front yard and then we will
come east in oct. stay three weeks maybe and then back to Professor
Richeyville where I trust you will have a lot more fascinating dope on
telescopes. You certainly had a grand idea that you were not Richey's press
agent just because you weren being paid for it. I wish the Swedes would
arrest Zappi and try him for murder. I should think they would. That would
be a good thing rather than wait for them to get home and let a wop court
whitewash the dirty swine.[7] Write. Pauline says your letters were all that
made her want to live in the hospital.

I may have written you giving you the dope on the operation before. If so
pardon repetition. I a have been too groggy to recognize my own corner.
Happy touristing to you—

Ernest

phPUL, TLS

1 Polish astronomer Nicolaus Copernicus (1473–1543), known as the founder of astronomy,
is credited with proving that the earth revolves around the sun.

2 American optician and astronomer George Willis Ritchey (1864–1945). Hickok's article on Ritchey, "Builds World's Biggest Telescope," which appeared in the 27 May 1928 *Sunday Eagle Magazine*, mentioned that Ritchey had been "decorated in Paris with the ribbon of the Legion of Honor" (7). A.P.: Associated Press.

3 Austrian tennis player and nobleman Count Ludwig von Salm-Hoogstraeten (1885–1944). His 1924 marriage to an American heiress (against her parents' wishes), their subsequent separation and child custody fight, and their Paris divorce on 13 April 1927 (one day before EH and Hadley's divorce became final) received extensive newspaper coverage at the time.

4 *Tripas*: guts, entrails (Spanish). In the first act of the bullfight, a *picador*, mounted on horseback, thrusts a lance into the neck muscle of the charging bull. Before protective padding for picadors' horses was required by Spanish law in June 1928, horses were frequently gored and often killed, as EH describes in *IOT* (Chapter 10) and in defining the terms *peto* and *pica* in *DIA* (Glossary). Rocinante is the name of Don Quixote's bony old horse, derived from *rocín*, Spanish for a hack or nag.

5 Allusion to the "See America First" advertising campaign promoting national tourism.

6 *L'Auto*, founded in 1900 as *L'Auto-Vélo*, a French daily sporting newspaper best known for sponsoring and promoting the Tour de France starting in 1903. *L'Echo des Sports*, a competing French sporting newspaper.

7 Italian explorer Captain Filippo Zappi (1896–1961) had been aboard the dirigible *Italia* when it crashed in the Arctic on 25 May 1928. Zappi and Italian navigator Adalberto Mariano (1898–1972) were rescued, but they reported that Swedish meteorologist and scientist Dr. Finn Malmgren (1895–1928) had died. The accident report was mired in controversy, as some suspected them of murder and cannibalism.

To Josephine Herbst, 27 July [1928]

Kansas City, Mo.

July 27

Dear Jo—

I am on my way to Wyoming and dont know address there—but if you know send some galleys of your book to me

c/o Ernest Hemingway

Piggott

ARKansas

they will forward them as soon as I have an address— Will wire my address to Piggott as soon as I have one. Will be very glad to say something about your book. Anything you want. I hope you have good luck with it.[1]

John [Herrmann] says it is a fine book—

Best luck to you both— I am trying to finish one. That's why am going to Wyoming find some place quiet

Yours always

Ernest Hemingway

Yale, ALS; postmark: KANSAS CITY / MO., JUL 27 / 6 PM / 1928.

1 Herbst had asked EH to write a blurb for her first book, *Nothing Is Sacred* (New York: Coward-McCann, 1928).

To Barklie McKee Henry, 27 July [1928]

July 27

Dear Rock Climber—[1]

The pen is too bloody scratchy— By gawd yes we will see you—in the fall—[2] We'll land in N.Y. and get a trained nurse for Patrick (who weighed 9 lbs—most of it shoulders and had to have a cesaerian) but Pauline's all right now—) and stay at the Brevoort and see you and the fights and the football games—and go up to Conway Mass. and see Archie MacLeish and shoot all the grouse he's been raising so humanely—

Am on Page 486 in spite of cesaerians, no wine, no fishing since Key West—and am enroute to Wyoming to sprint on the finish—need a trout stream and some cool weather. Patrick's on a bottle so Pauline can leave him with her people and come out in September and we will fish and shoot for a month and then pick up Pat and move east.

I wish to hell I was in the Guaranty Trust instead of trying to write— work 24 hrs. a day—never sleep—don't give a damn about anything— exept getting it done—then find that it's not enough to drive it doggedly on—have to make it good at the same time—always cockeyed discouraged—stuff they praise seems like merde to him that writes it because it isnt what you worked for—feel fine just a while each day after you've finished work—then worried about the next. If it wasnt that I am so utterly unhappy if I dont write would go in the bank with you if they'd take me. or I'd sail a boat for somebody or teach skiing—may yet.[3] But when this book is finished then comes the fine time—and that will be about when we'll hit N.Y.

I am cockeyed crazy about shooting again so if you can feed up any sparrows around Westbury start fattening them. [*Heavy EH cancellation of what appears to be an entire sentence*] That that's crossed and was an idea I had that I'm too bloody worn out with the train etc to go into. Had a fine career for you if you were through writing. Anyway Key West was wonderful. Old Dos Passos and Waldo Pierce were there. We had grand fishing and I worked well. My very best to Barbara

Yours always
Ernie.

You must come down to Key West sometime. It's lively—but you have to have your own gang. Will be there in two years again. Ill tell you about it when we see you.

[*At the top of the first page of the letter, EH drew an arrow pointing to the letterhead and wrote*:] From this address they will always forward

JFK, ALS; letterhead: 6435 INDIAN LANE / KANSAS CITY, MISSOURI

1 In his letter to EH of 20 June 1928, Henry confessed that he had been frightened while rock climbing in Germany (JFK).
2 Henry invited EH and Pauline to visit him and his wife, Barbara, at their home in Old Westbury, New York, on Long Island.
3 Henry wrote that he had accepted a position with the Guaranty Trust Company and hoped EH would not snub him if they met on the street.

To Waldo Peirce, 9 August [1928]

Aug 9
Big Horn—Wyoming

Dear Mr. Purse—

In yr. last letters you sound slightly peacock-pecked. By gawd you write a noble letter though.[1] I wish I'd come to Maine instead of out here. It's damned lovely country though— Looks like Spain— Big Horn Mts ringers for the guadaramas only on a bigger scale— Same color—Same shape.[2] Drove here in 3 days from K.C. 340 — 380 — 320— Jack rabbits with ears as big as mules— Came to a ranch (sic) of a friend where there were 15 girls! Shit. Worked and fished as follows—

1st day	2nd Day	3rd Day
Worked 4 pages	worked 4½ pages.	Worked
Fished with Bill	Fished with 2 girls	0
Horne caught 12	caught ②= two	Zero
		Fished by self
		alone caught
		30 = limit

Got up at 6 A.M on morning of 4th day and left witout saying goodbye.

Went into Sheridan where stayed at Old Hotel and worked 9 — 6½ — 9 — 11—then came out to empty ranch without Dudes and Did 17½ yesterday—bloody near 2550 words—[3]

Probably shite too— I wish to God Pauline would come out and that I would get this book finished before she comes. Am lonely as a bastard— Drank too much last night and feel like anything but work now— Eat too much too at the ranch house. Splendid guys.

I'm glad you are getting such a splendid lot of dough— It will take money to keep us in muttonfish— Pauline wrote Mr. Pfeiffer was delighted with the pictures— It was bloody nice of you to send them— Piggott is the best permanent address altho I'll be here at Big Horn for two weeks more anyway—[4] Address—Big Horn—Sheridan County—Wyo.— Big Horn is 4 houses and Gen Store Post office. Patrick now weighs 12 pounds— Looks like Chinese woodchuck.

This country around here has been settled too long. When Pauline comes we will go over across the mountains and up around Cody—then through the Park maybe after the hotels are closed and out the southern end through Jackson's Hole.[5] They charge you $50 for a licence to shoot an Elk. If they paid me $50 to shoot and dress one I would do it but not a cent less.

So far have shot 2 marmots—(rock dogs) almost as big as Badgers—with the pistol and the head off a water snake. Of the 30 trout I caught 26 were eastern brook and 4 rainbows— I was within 5 of the limit at 3.30 pm— (7 inches keep) and then slipped back a lot to only keep good ones. I bought a 12 ga Winchester Pump which will come in handy around Key West— I'd like to have seen the hurricane there— By God that's a fine place—[6]

We will come to Maine sometime. We got to go back to Paris this fall sometime— Go to Spain next Spring maybe then come over to Key West early enough for good monstering the next winter— I've got to see some more toros— By gawd every Sunday this summer at 5 oclock in the afternoon my whole life seems pointless— I wonder how they were at Pamplona—my bull fight papers havent come. Valencia is the best— 7 bull fights on 7 successive days starting July 25— Swim in between in the Mediterranean at Grao— Ride out on the train—dodge turds in the water— Damned good though—eat out there on the beach—or back at Valencia with an ice cold pitcher of beer—arroz valenciano—good meat—melon— That's where I'd be now instead of here trying to write—[7] To hell with novels— I've written 548 pages— I could write a short story of 12 pages and feel fine and probably it would be better stuff—as it is have been in a state of suspended something or other for 3 or 4 months now— Glad to see the pictures of old Kate— Norm Matson has fattened like a calf. Susan I never cared for. Too worthy and noble. Nice enough—[8]

Always send any writings.

> Que le bon dieu vous allways—
> Su amigo Hemingstein.[9]

Colby, ALS

1 The salutation "Mr. Purse" may be wordplay on Peirce's name, alluding to his recent inheritance. In letters to EH of 20, 26, and 28 July, Peirce detailed problems in his marriage, including Ivy's unhappiness with his lifestyle and his resistance to her demands. In his 26 July letter, he complained that it took Ivy "three days, one medico, one osteopath, one vet for Peepee, and all the servidors in masse formation to pull through after voyaging one day with native Maine State helpmeet. Wo-man thy name is asperine" (JFK).

2 EH compares the Big Horn Mountains of northern Wyoming and south central Montana to the Sierra de Guadarrama, a mountain range north of Madrid that forms the frontier between the provinces of Madrid, Segovia, and Ávila.

3 When EH and Bill Horne arrived on 30 July at the crowded Folly Ranch outside Sheridan, Horne's fiancée, Frances Thorne (1904–1991), joined them. A "Log of Folly Ranch" for 1928 shows that EH was officially in residence from 30 July to 18 August (Baker *Life*, 597), but biographies report that EH left for the Sheridan Inn on the fourth day and stayed there until he moved to Eleanor Donnelley's Lower Ranch on 8 August (Baker *Life*, 195; Reynolds

AH, 187). In the left margin of the letter EH wrote his calculations showing how he arrived at the figure of 2,550 words:

$$[17^1/_2]$$
$$\underline{150}$$
$$\overline{850}$$
$$\underline{17}$$
$$\overline{2550}$$

4 Peirce wrote in his 20 July letter that he had "a lot of enlargements" of photos of their Key West fishing expedition for EH and, not knowing where EH was, had sent them to "Mr. Pfeiffer" in Piggott, referring to Pauline's father, Paul.

5 The town of Cody in northwestern Wyoming is located near the East Gate of Yellowstone National Park, established in 1872 as America's first national park, spanning parts of Idaho, Montana, and Wyoming. Jackson Hole is a valley about 15 miles wide by 80 miles long bounded by the Gros Ventre and the Teton mountain ranges in western Wyoming near the Idaho border.

6 The first of several hurricanes hit the Florida coastline on 7 August 1928, with winds reaching 105 miles per hour.

7 El Grao, the port area of Valencia, on the Mediterranean, about 3 miles east of the city's center. *Arroz a la valenciana* or *paella*, a rice dish that in Valencia traditionally would include seafood.

8 Among EH's papers at JFK is a photo of Kate Smith and American writers Norman Matson (1893–1966) and Susan Glaspell (1876–1948) that Peirce took during his three-day stay in "stinking" Provincetown, made tolerable by "bright-eyed Kate," as he reported in his 11 July letter to EH (JFK). Glaspell's feminist play *Trifles* (1915) was one of the first offerings by the Provincetown Players. She and Matson were romantically involved from 1924 to 1932.

9 *Que le bon Dieu vous garde*: May the good Lord always watch over you (French). *Su amigo*: your friend (Spanish).

To Evan Shipman, [c. 10 August 1928]

Big Horn
Sheridan County
Wyoming

Sheridan, Wyoming

OLLY RANCH
Big Horn, Wyoming

Sheridan
Wyoming

Dear Evan— Damned glad to hear from you and that you are out for AL.[1] I am out here all alone and working like a bastard[.] 574 pages now done— It's what I showed you the start of— Hope it's good—

Patrick weighs 12 pounds now— Pauline's going to leave him in Piggott with Jinny and her folks and come out here in a week— This country is like Spain

I get good beer from the brewery—good wine from a wop—$4 a gallon—too bloody much but good— Beer 1\underline{00}$ a gallon—good as Lipps—[2] Hot as hell—hot wind blows but cool in the mountains—

I'm lonely as a bastard—hope this book gets done soon—know no other way of getting it done than writing it— Write to me again— I dont like to shoot deer but love to shoot partridges— Have you any of those?

I hope things go all right— Anything you can write about Kid I'll be glad to answer but cant guarantee value of my advice.[3]

Morley Callaghan's stuff in Scribners seemed like TRIPE to me— Especially his fight story—[4]

Sun Herald could write darned well—[5]

I went to the races at Kansas City and won 158 dollars in 2 days on $15 capital— Lost all but 18 of the profit on last day of meeting— Didnt cash a ticket— Punk races but damned exciting on a little track—[6]

Pauline had a tough time—heat cesaerian etc but was brave as hell and god knows Ill be glad to see her out here—we will fish up in the mts—then cross the Big Horn mts to Cody—go through the Yellowstone Park after the season is closed—then to Jackson Hole country to shoot ducks and geese maybe. I hope I get the book done by Sep. 1st— Write me again— Piggott will always have my address. Good luck old kid HEM.

I hope we can come in the fall.

Channick, ALS; letterhead: Sheridan, Wyoming / [*EH cancellation*: FOLLY RANCH; *insertion above cancellation*: General Delivery] / Big Horn, Wyoming

1 In his letter to EH of 5 August [1928], Shipman declared his support for the Democratic Party's presidential candidate: "I'm on the wagon (band-wagon) for Al Smith. Communist or no Communist" (JFK).
2 Brasserie Lipp in Paris.
3 Shipman wrote that there was "a lot" he wanted to tell EH but did not include in his letter, saying, "On the whole, things are not hitting just on all eight and I miss you as the Adviser." Responding to this letter on 29 August, Shipman would recount his troubles with his work and his failed relationship with Harriet Mann (JFK).
4 Callaghan's "A Regret for Youth" and "A Predicament" appeared in the July 1928 issue of *Scribner's Magazine*. His fight story, "Soldier Harmon," was published in the August 1928 issue.
5 In his 5 August letter, Shipman mentioned that he had received a letter from Harold Stearns saying he was back at work at the *Baltimore Sun*. Shipman also reported that he was reading

a book by Stearns and "was surprised by how good it was." Stearns had also written a racing column for the Paris edition of the *New York Herald*, likely prompting EH to pun on the name Harold/Herald.

6 EH probably attended races at the Riverside Jockey Club, opened in 1928 in Riverside, Missouri, north of Kansas City.

To Isabelle Simmons Godolphin, [c. 12 August 1928]

Dearest Izz—

Well that was a <u>grand</u> letter—I dont know what an introvert is either but if that is what you are may all my children be them.[1]

Patrick weighs 12 pounds and is old enough to stay with his grand parents— Pauline is going to come out here in a week now. Thank God. I was beginning to get sheepherder's madness— Am on Page 574— I hope to get it done soon— It has certainly gone on and on and on but yesterday I read over the Mss.— It just arrived from Piggott— I was afraid to carry it around—you may recall my losing some Mss. once—[2] Anyway read it and it seemed swell—cockeyed wonderful—so much so that I (afterwards) drank nearly a gallon of wine and ½ gallon of beer and now have gastric remorse today and cant work at all—but will in a little while anyway. All I do is work and work— Never write letters—but love to get them— You certainly presented the town in a masterly way— Those rag rug weavers—[3]

Got to stop— All the juice has to go in the book— Isnt much juice today. Have to get going again— I am <u>certain</u> I wrote from Key West— Please write again— Give my heartiest to Sim—[4]

Yours always—

Ernie

PUL, ALS; letterhead: Sheridan, Wyoming / [*EH cancellation*: ~~FOLLY RANCH~~; *insertion above cancellation*: General Delivery] / Big Horn, Wyoming

1 EH is responding to a letter Godolphin sent from Oak Park to Piggott which was forwarded on 9 August 1928 to Wyoming ([5 August 1928], JFK).
2 EH alludes to the loss of the suitcase containing nearly all of his early writing, stolen from Hadley at the Gare de Lyon in Paris on 2 December 1922.

3 Isabelle's letter contained a numbered list of fifteen items of Oak Park news and gossip, including a report that their friend Dick Hill (1901–1961) "married the girl" (Juliana Armour Lincoln, 1899–1961), and the couple "wove rag rugs all winter." Envious of EH's freedom to roam, Godolphin wrote, "Good God this is a hell of a town & I wouldnt go into detail about it to anyone except Your honor—and that after repeated requests."

4 Howard L. Simmons, Jr., one of Isabelle's younger brothers.

To Maxwell Perkins, [c. 12 August 1928]

Dear Mr. Perkins—

I was glad to hear from you and hope you are in good shape— Meyer wrote you had gotten run down before you left and I do hope you are all right now.[1] You represent Scribners and my entire publishing future to me so for Gods sake take care of yourself if for no other reason.

The book is now 575 pages along— I had my wife send me out the entire mss here to General Delivery—Big Horn—Sheridan Co. Wyoming— I had been afraid to carry it around. And yesterday I read most of it and it seemed so good that I drank a gallon of wine and forgot to eat supper and so cant work worth a damn today—but when the gastric remorse is gone will start up again tomorrow morning.

I've only fished 3 times—caught 30—the limit the last day—been driven by the writing—don't want to see anyone—only to get the bloody book done and have it be some good. As soon as Ive finished work for the day am frightfully lonely— But my wife is coming out in a week now. I had hoped to finish the thing before she came but it seems to go on and on— Should be done by the first of September now anyway— Am all alone at an empty Ranch house lot with a Rancher and his family about ½ mile away.

I bring them beer and we all tell each other great damn lies about hunting, fishing, fighting, bull fighting etc. Thank God there are no bulls to prove me a liar.

We can talk about the book serial etc. when its done and I'm in N.Y. It's a terrible mistake to talk about a book.[2] This country is a lot like Spain— I have found a fellow who was in the Foreign Legion who gets me beer and a good wop for wine— Splendid beer—

The Sage Hen season opens Wednesday—one of the Ranch hands and I are going to get up before day light and go North of Ranchester to try and get some— I stayed at a more or less Dude ranch 3 days and nearly went crazy[.] Came down into Sheridan and stayed at a Hotel there then a friend offered me this vacant place to live at. I will be awfully happy to get this book done and drink and fish and have some family life— Patrick now weighs 12 pounds and is old enough to stay with his grandparents. Thank Meyer for a good letter and tell him I'll write him.

How many more copies has Men Without Women sold?[3]

Will you have them send a copy of Men Without and The Sun to Howard L. Vickery [Editor] The Sheridan Post Enterprise—Sheridan Wyo.— He introduced me at the Brewery and also writes book reviews.

Some woman bawled me out for being an ex patriate and I said good God you can't call a man an ex patriate in Kansas City.

PUL, AL; letterhead: Sheridan, Wyoming / [*EH cancellation*: FOLLY RANCH; *insertion above cancellation*: General Delivery] / Big Horn, Wyoming

1 EH is responding to Perkins's letters of 1 August and 7 August 1928. Wallace Meyer, who filled in for Perkins at Scribner's during Perkins's July vacation, had written to EH that when he saw Perkins in June he was disturbed to see "how completely gone he was—one of the tiredest men I've ever seen in my life" ([July 1928], JFK).
2 In his letter to EH of 14 August, which Perkins apparently wrote before receiving this one, he would again express Scribner's interest in serialization (PUL).
3 Perkins would report in a letter of 30 August that "between 250 and 300 copies" of *MWW* had sold since 1 August, bringing the total "above 20,000" (PUL).

To Guy Hickok, 18 August 1928

Aug 18 *[192]*8

5 pm

~~Dear Smith—~~

~~Often wonder what happened to you or where you are.~~

⟨Shit to Smith⟩ Hickock Noble Hickock— See the Steffenses have been wedding each other publicly in Am. Magazine. Wait till Pauline and I tell the inside story of our lives.[1]

Patrick now weights 12 1/2 lbs and is sojourning chez son granmere at
Piggott— Pauline was due here at 3.20 p.m. Its now past 5 train not in yet.
I'm on page 600 and only about 2 days from the end—The bloody end—
Have been here 1 mo or more—good beer from the brewry—good wine
from a wop— A nice French family (bootlegger) where we sit on the vine
shaded porch and drink as at the Double Maggots— Youth will be served.[2]

Have done nothing but work— Book either wonderful or the old shite.
Love to Mary—[3]

Address always Piggott— Write to us you loafer—nothing to do but
entertain a few pleasant folk from Brooklyn— And then you complain.

Never mind[.] We'll be back in Nov. We're going up in Big Horn
mountains to fish[4]—then over to the Park after the season and down in
Jackson Hole to shoot ducks and geese— Never travel with less than 3
shotguns now—

Love from me and Pauline who I hope is now only about 15 minutes
away—

Ernest

Neville, ALS; letterhead: The Sheridan INN / Sheridan, Wyo.

Although EH dated and signed this handwritten letter, he repeats himself in a letter written to
Hickok on [c. 5 September 1928]. This may be an unsent draft.

1 Lincoln Steffens (1866–1936) and Lenore (Ella) Sophie Winter (1898–1980), Australian-
 born journalist, married in 1924 and had a son the same year. The August 1928 *American
 Magazine* included an article by Lincoln titled "Becoming a Father at 60 Is a Liberal
 Education." The next month's issue featured an article by Ella, "The Advantages of
 Marrying an Older Man." An accompanying photograph of the couple and their infant
 son was captioned: "'There is a big element of doubt in marrying a young man,' says Mrs.
 Steffens, 'but when a girl picks out a man whose character, reputation and income are
 established, she knows what she is getting!'" (29).
2 French-born Charles Moncini (1884–1955), a truck driver, and his wife Alice (b. c. 1895),
 who cooked and served meals. The couple produced and sold wine and home-brewed beer
 at their home on Val Vista Street in Sheridan (Baker *Life*, 196; 597). "Double Maggots" is a
 reference to the Paris café Les Deux Magots.
3 Guy's wife, Mary E. Hickok (née Heinline, 1892–1983).
4 EH planned to take Pauline to the rustic Spear-O-Wigwam dude ranch, about 30 miles
 south-southwest of Sheridan in the Big Horn Mountains, at an elevation of 8,300 feet.

To Josephine Herbst, 25 [August 1928]

[*Received at*] Frenchtown N J 11.45 PM 2 QU 54 N L Sheridan Wis 25

Josephine Herbst

Frenchtown N J

Sorry delayed was on a trip in the mountains and didnt get book nor wire Stop Quote nothing is sacred ~~or~~ [*Insertion*: is] a ~~good~~ [*Insertion*: ~~very~~ fine] book it does not need blurbs it needs readers stop Josephine her best is [*Insertion*: an] honest writer and it is the honest writers who are great writers when all the [*Insertion*: so called] "great" writers are dead,

Ernest Hemingway.

Yale, Cable

This night letter (as indicated by the symbol "N L" in the first line) is typewritten on a Western Union cable form, with autograph cancellations and insertions in black ink in an unknown hand.

EH is sending his endorsement of Josephine Herbst's first book, *Nothing Is Sacred*. The published blurb on the dust jacket would read: "ERNEST HEMINGWAY—A fine book by an honest writer" (Bruccoli and Baughman, 12).

To Waldo Peirce, [c. early September 1928]

August [*192*]8

Muy Waldo Mio—

Nothing from you in a hell of a while. Hope you're not laid up. Pauline came out and I finished the damn book—first draft—finally— Then we fished— Caught 30 apiece every day— None over 15 inches but damn nice trout— This is a cockeyed wonderful county—looks like Spain—swell people— Every time I go out and see it I wish you were here to paint it.

Saw old Wister—sweet old guy writes damned well too—[1]

Went on a trip—shooting prairie dogs with the pistol from the car[.] Shot and recovered 8— They are like getting planes in wartime— For Every one that is confirmed you lose a bunch down the holes—only unlike the war you go home at night— We go shooting (chickens) on the Crow Indian

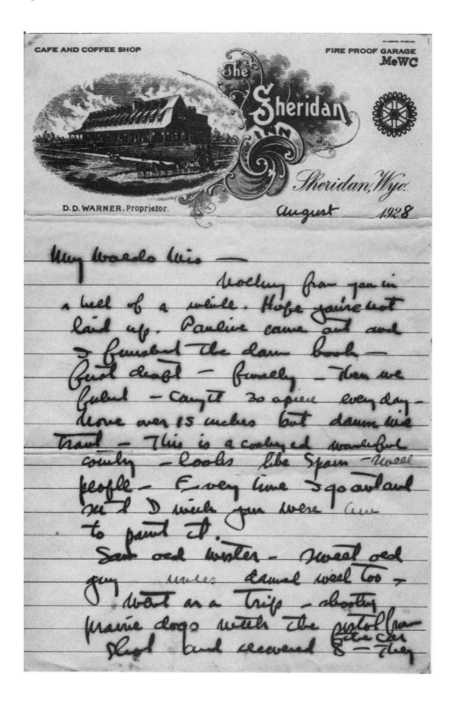

reservation next week then home to Piggott—then east at end of Oct.[2] Then to Key West for all winter—

Better than trying to keep warm on grogs Americaines—just decided to go down. You come too and we will butcher the bloody monsters and swim all winter.

Write to Piggott

Pauline sends her love—she is strong as a goat again[.] Pat weighs 18 lbs now parked with his grandparent [*Ditto marks*: now]

Love to Ivy.

Write[.] Yours in haste HEM.

Colby, ALS; letterhead: The Sheridan INN / Sheridan, Wyo.

Although EH wrote "August [192]8" in the letterhead's designated spot for the date, his reference to hunting on the Crow Indian reservation "next week" suggests he either misdated the letter or continued writing it into early September. The prairie chicken hunting season on the reservation opened 15 September 1928. Reynolds points out that Baker misdated the letter as "c. 23 August 1928" (*SL*, 284), and that "it was probably written at least two weeks later" (*AH*, 255).

1 EH and Pauline had visited novelist Owen Wister in Shell, Wyoming, where he was vacationing at the Trapper Creek Lodge, built in 1927 by the Wyeth family (of the Wyeth Pharmaceuticals company) on the well-established dude ranch they had purchased the year before.
2 The Crow Indian Reservation in south-central Montana, bordered by Wyoming to the south.

To Guy Hickok, [c. early September 1928]

Dear 'Cock—

The old spedometer now is 7609 miles—first draft of book finished 600 some pages—Pauline all well and husky—been out here two weeks—Pat chez his grandparents—weighs 15 lbs. Looking very Chinese—we've caught tousands of trout—almost literally— How are the bloody sweat of brooklyns balls?

Dont ever get the idea you could quit your job and make a living over here just because you could once upon a time— Nobody can now-— I'd be starving to death if I hadnt spent all that time stewed in the quarter and ruined my digestion so as to write The Sun Also Rises. Honest toil only gets a man into jail as a vagrant—

We go from here to Piggott via K.C. then I'm going to Chicago then we go to N.Y. Then maybe back to Key West again. I see where Steff and Ella writes True Confessions for the American mag. Why don't you write the dirt on your married or unmarried life—or me write the inside story of my marriage with a girl two days my junior. When do you suppose young Peter Steffens will begin to write his version? Will he have any prewombal memories? Will he name any one?[1]

How are you? Have you seen Hadley or Bumby lately? We have driven daily over bloody mountains that make the Appenines look like the back steps to the urinoir—but no vines on their slopes—many a still though— But the beer from the brewry is good here— This is a punk letter but write Kid— The tourists must be slackening now[2]—[a]fter the 10,000 times I've defended Ezra to get a letter like that[3]

> Pauline sends her love—
> Best to Mary—
> Yours always
> Ernest

phPUL, ALS; letterhead: The Sheridan INN / Sheridan, Wyo.

1 Peter Stanley Steffens (1924–2012), son of Lincoln and Ella Steffens.
2 In his letter from Paris of 20 August 1928, Hickok wrote, "Smany tourists these days ca't astronomise at all. May be no moon nor mars any more sfar as I know, may have all been eaten by caterpillars" (JFK).
3 Hickok wrote part of his letter to EH on the verso of an undated letter he had received from Ezra Pound. In it Pound complained that he had not heard from EH, referring to him as "our bloodyminded friend (at least he was)" and as "the august Mr Hem. (who was last heard of in connection or at least conjunction if you are literal minded with that loose liver Mr Sink lair Lewis, and lougdly mouthedly denouncing all highbrows (sech as yew an me)."

To Maxwell Perkins, [c. early September 1928]

Dear Mr. Perkins—

Thanks for the letter with the check.[1]

I've not received Strange Fugitive yet and would like to see it. From the advertizements in the magazine I got the impression you were booming him as a newer and better Hemingway of some sort—grooming him in case the present Hem should be slipping. I read the two stories that were in the magazine in the station at K.C. worried to see whether the new H. was better than the old—then read there was to be a prize fight story next month bought it—read it and haven't worried since.[2] I feel like a boxer when his opponent hits him flush in the jaw with a right hand and he say's "Is that all you got" and knows the other guy cant hurt him.

The first draft of the book [*FTA*] is finished—we've had a fine time ever since—bummed all over—caught our limit of trout nearly every day—saw Struthers Burt one evening— Have driven 7600 miles in America this Summer— We come to N.Y. the middle of Oct—first of November— Hope to see Scott then—[3] Dont tell anyone but we wont be going back this fall— will stay in Key West—to rewrite the book— That was where I went best writing it and it should be a grand life— Will get Waldo down— Couldnt you come down in the winter? If we could work up some good excuse?

I havent thought about serialization much—need the money but am afraid the magazine wont take a chance under Dr. Bridges— I am sure he would not have run The Sun—[4] He wanted me to cut 50 Grand— Owen Wister—who seems a fine man—told me he was once going over some letters of Roosevelt's for his sister and all the good ones were one's B. had refused for the magazine.[5]

So I dont know how much hope to give myself— But now my earnings are down to $90 a month again must look forward to something as life is expensive.

The fate of my stuff has been to always be turned down as too something or other and then after publication everybody say that of course they could have published it and it would have been fine— I think you'll like the book— The Mss. is in the safe in the bank at Piggott—

I did not mean to be catty about Morley [Callaghan]— I have read <u>much much</u> better stories by him than those in the magazine— I think he will be a very fine writer and I'm awfully glad you have him— I want to see his book—

Writing whether you want it or not is competitive— Most of the time you compete against time and dead men—sometimes you get something from a living $\left(\begin{array}{c}\text{contemporary}\\\text{competitor}\end{array}\right)$ that is so good it jars you—as the story of Esteban in Thornton's last book.[6]

But as you read them dead or living you unconsciously compete— I would give 6 mos. of life to have written it.

You know the ones you have no chance against and the others that, with luck, you can beat. Living and dead. Only never tell this to anyone because they might call it the megalomania or simply swollen head.

We hunt (shoot) next week on the Crow reservation then back to Piggott via K.C. I'm going to Chicago for a few days then we'll come to N.Y. May drive.

Pauline is well and strong again and we are both in very good shape. This part of the country is very like Spain— I can see how happy the Spaniards must have been when they found it— The only draw back is Dude Ranches— I could write a piece Dude Ranches vs. The West— They are frightful places [*EH insertion*: Like either the Social Register or War time Y.M.C.A.]—but the cabins and tents where the tin can tourists and sagebrushers stop are grand.[7]

Yours always

Hemingway.

PUL, ALS; letterhead: The Sheridan INN / Sheridan, Wyo.

1 With his letter of 14 August 1928, Perkins sent EH a check for $3,718.66 in payment of royalties for *MWW* (PUL).
2 In the same letter, Perkins told EH he would send a copy of Callaghan's novel, *Strange Fugitive*. The July 1928 *Scribner's Magazine* featured two stories by Callaghan, with an introductory note placing him "in the front rank of the younger writers" and noting that "on the other occasion when we presented two stories in the same number the writer was Ernest Hemingway" (37). Callaghan's story "Soldier Harmon" appeared in the August 1928 issue.
3 In his letter of 30 August, Perkins asked when EH was going to come to New York as Perkins hoped to see Fitzgerald around mid-September and thought EH "would enjoy seeing him established at Ellerslie Mansion on the Delaware" (JFK).
4 In his reply of 17 September 1928 to EH's concern that *Scribner's Magazine* editor Bridges might be unwilling to serialize *FTA*, Perkins acknowledged "the one danger" would be if there were "some element that would unfit it for magazine use,—as there was in The Sun Also." However, Perkins also wrote, "There is nothing that Scribner's wants as much as a serial by you" and said that Scribner's was ready to let EH determine the size of the advance and to pay it "any time from now on" (JFK; *TOTTC*, 77–78).

5 *Scribner's Magazine* published a nine-part series from September 1919 to June 1920 titled "Theodore Roosevelt and His Time—Shown in His Letters," edited by Joseph Bucklin Bishop. The final installment, "Roosevelt to Authors and Artists," includes four letters Roosevelt wrote to Wister. In 1930 Wister would publish his *Roosevelt: The Story of a Friendship, 1880–1919* (New York: Macmillan).

6 A character in Thornton Wilder's 1927 novel *The Bridge of San Luis Rey*.

7 The term "dude" originated in North Dakota and Wyoming to refer to a city-dweller or non-Westerner vacationing in the West, especially those able to afford train travel. The Social Register, a directory of socially prominent American families, originated in the 1880s when the "visiting lists" of the New York City elite were compiled into a single volume. "Sagebrushers" originally referred to those who traveled by covered wagons and later by automobile. As a result of the growing popularity of automobile vacation travel, the Tin Can Tourists of the World was organized in 1919 and held biannual meetings for caravanners.

To Madelaine Hemingway, [c. 7–10 September 1928]

Dear Nunbones—

Glad to hear from you kid and at once figured on you going with us— then all off and you arent going till Spring. Well anytime you want to go or come with us you are bloody welcome.

It looks now as though we would not go over until Spring ourselves—may spend winter at Key West—you could come down there and stay with us if we get a house—wonderful fishing—swim all winter and then shove off with us or what have you— Are you committed to the Pickard wench? or not?[1]

Anyhow there is plenty of time to arrange now. Save cash. Dont buy clothes. Pauline will help you get some clothes— She knows all about covering for the human frame as she ran Vogue and knows where to get body covering all over the world and what type of same to purchase for maximum results at minimum expense.

So dont buy any clothes till you see the whites of our eyes.[2]

We are having a fine time—caught 100s of trout—shooting prairie chickens next week— Have finished first draft of my book— Write to Piggott—Arkansas—

Best love to you and all the family—

Your always
Bro
Ernie

PSU, ALS; letterhead: The Sheridan INN / Sheridan, Wyo.; postmark: SHERIDAN / WYO. / SEP 10 / 9 PM / 1928

Although this letter date is postmarked Monday, 10 September 1928, EH's comment about shooting prairie chickens "next week" suggests he may have written it a few days earlier. The prairie chicken season on the Crow Reservation opened on Saturday, 15 September 1928.

1 EH is responding to his sister's letter of 4 August, sent from Petoskey, Michigan, and forwarded from Piggott to Big Horn, Wyoming, on 10 August 1928. Sunny hoped to join the Hemingways on their return trip to Europe, assuming they would be going back that fall. Alternatively, she suggested that she and her friend Miriam Rickards (b. 1906) could visit the Hemingways in Europe in spring 1929, but her preference was to travel with EH (JFK). In her response of 26 September [1928], Sunny would enthusiastically accept EH's invitation to spend the winter with them in Key West, but she insisted that the twenty-two-year-old Miriam, who had stayed home from college to work and save for the trip to Europe, should be allowed to join them for the trip in the spring. When Sunny sailed to Europe with EH and Pauline in April 1929, Miriam made the transatlantic crossing separately, meeting Sunny in Europe (JFK).
2 Pauline was working for Paris *Vogue* when she and EH met in 1925. EH plays on the saying "Don't fire until you see the whites of their eyes," typically attributed to Colonel William Prescott, American Revolutionary War leader, who commanded the troops at the Battle of Bunker Hill on 17 June 1775.

To Archibald MacLeish, [c. 9–13 September 1928]

Dear Mac— Well the book is finished— Pauline came out. We've been having a grand time. Been all over Wyoming— It's like Spain and this time of year is lovely—

We caught 30 trout a day apiece for damn near a week— Met grand people— Bums of every sort— Going up with old Willie Spears[1] Round up Wagon on the Crow Indian Reservation this week to shoot prairie chickens, sage hens and grouse when the season opens the 15th— Then back to K.C. and Piggott— Patrick weighs 16 lb. We're coming in Oct—last part—maybe be drive— I've driven 7400 miles through Lamerica—maybe we'll stay down in Florida at Key West this winter if you'll come down— It is lovely there and I can re-write my book[.] That was where I went best when I was writing it— Swim all winter— Everybody talks Spanish— The old Gulf stream just seven miles out and all the uninhabited keys to sail to. Good Spanish wine from Cuba on every boat— Whiskey 5\underline{^{00}}$ a quart—Bacardi 4$\underline{^{00}}$ Fundador 4$\underline{^{:50}}$— We'll get a house and two niggers—one for Patrick; one to cook and stay till April then go to Paris. Will you and Ada come down? The fishing is as exciting as war only you can go home nights. Grand people.

How are you going yourself Mac? The west is a damn fine place.

Write to Piggott.

Do you really want us to come to Conway? What are some dates on football games? Love to you and Ada and Mimi and Kenny and Pedro—[2]

Pappy

LOC, ALS

1 Willis Moses Spear (1862–1936), owner of the Spear-O-Wigwam Ranch and state senator of Wyoming (1918–1932).
2 In his letter of 12 August [1928], MacLeish encouraged EH and Pauline to visit him and Ada in Conway, Massachusetts, in late October or early November "because there will be football & deer shooting" (JFK). MacLeish also commented on the recent birth on 7 August of their third child, Peter, whose name ("Pedro" in Spanish) would later be changed to William Hitchcock MacLeish.

To Sylvia Beach, 14 September [1928]

Sheridan
WYO
Sept. 14.

Dearest Sylvia—

We have a son named Patrick— Also the new book done— Wonderful fishing out here. Did my book ever come out in French—have never seen or heard of it.[1] Have driven 7600 miles

Love to you and to Adrienne
from Pauline and Hemingway

PUL, A Postcard S; verso: color painting image of a man wearing a broad-brimmed hat and gripping a rifle, with a dog at his side and a horse grazing in the background, captioned "A Sheep Herder"; postmark: SHERIDAN / WYO., SEP 15 / 11^{30} AM / 1928

1 *Cinquante mille dollars* (Paris: Éditions de la Nouvelle Revue Française, 1928), a book of six of EH's stories in French translation. In addition to the title story, "Fifty Grand," the

collection included "My Old Man" ("Mon Vieux"), "The Undefeated" ("L'Invincible"), "The Battler" ("Le Champion"), "Indian Camp" ("Le Village Indien"), and "The Killers" ("Les Tueurs").

To Clarence and Grace Hall Hemingway, 17 September 1928

C159 50 NL=SHERIDAN WYO 17

DR AND MRS C E HEMINGWAY =

600 NORTH KENILWORTH AVE OAKPARK ILL

DONT KNOW IF SMOKY TRIP POSSIBLY WILL WRITE FROM KANSASCITY WRITE ME CARE RUTH WHITE LOWRY WHEN EXACTLY YOU PLAN TO LEAVE AND WHO[1] GOING TO START KANSASCITY TOMORROW BEST LUCK TO YOUR SHOW MOTHER[2] ID PLANNED STOP OAKPARK EARLY PART OCTOBER ENROUTE EAST BUT PLANS NOT DEFINITE YET LOVE =

    ERNIE.

PSU, Cable; Western Union destination receipt stamp: 1928 SEP 17 PM 9 26

On the back of this telegram, Clarence wrote, "Sept 20. 1928 Wrote Ernest at 6435 Indian Lane c/o Mrs Lowry K.C. MO—Impossible to set any date for Smoky Mt trip.— Ask him if he can come up here in Oct.— Let me know at once or Could he go."

1 On 20 September 1928 Clarence would reply that definite plans for the Smoky Mountain trip were "not yet possible," but he wanted to know if EH would be able to make the trip with him. "I did so want to go," Clarence wrote, but there were new obstacles, including an increase in his work (JFK). Apparently EH responded, but that letter remains unlocated. In a letter of 26 September 1928, Clarence would thank EH for "yours of yesterday from Kansas City" and write that he was "now entirely willing to give up the Smoky Mts. trip this Fall" (JFK).
2 Grace's art exhibit, "Studio Tea and Exhibition of Western Landscapes," was held 21–23 September 1928 at the Hemingway home at 600 N. Kenilworth Avenue in Oak Park.

To Henry Strater, 23 September [1928]

Sep. 23

Dear Mike—

    When we were in Cody some mail was forwarded out to Sunlight— I called up and asked them what it was and they said it was two letters from

Piggott and one from Agunquit* so I fugured that was you—asked them to forward the mail to Jackson Wyo—where we were going and so far have never gotten it. So if you wrote me a letter and I didn't answer this is why. Maybe it will be at Piggott. If you didn't write you sonof a bitch read no further. How the hell are you anyway? I've finished the first draft of my book 600 something pages and had a grand summer. Patrick weighs sixteen pounds— Pauline is in grand shape. Bumby has been mountain climbing in Savoy. We are going to Key West for the winter and not back until Spring. Don't know when I get to N.Y. Want to see some fights. Planned on coming in Oct. or Nov. but don't know now. Got to re-write this book. Where are you going to be and how? Why don't you come down to Fla for some of the winter with swell fishing sailing and swim all the time. I will keep the barracudas off of you with a baseball bat or if you feel low you can let one have the works and solve all your sexual problems. address Piggott— Arkansas. Do you know the dates of any fights? Could you find out at the Garden by calling up maybe? or at any of the other clubs. I would like to see this new nigger Jack Thompson or any of the filipinos or mecs or Jimmy MacLarnin—wd like to see some sockers.[1] I think Paolino [Uzcudun] can whip most of the heavies. Stribling if he can hit now and will take chance might be pretty good. Love to Maggie.

Hem.

PUL, TL with typewritten signature; letterhead: 6435 INDIAN LANE / KANSAS CITY, MISSOURI

1 EH refers to Madison Square Garden in New York City. Cecil Lewis "Jack" Thompson (1904–1946), African American boxer and two-time welterweight champion known as "The Frisco Flash." James McLarnin (1907–2004), Irish-born welterweight boxing champion, considered one of the great welterweights in history.

To Waldo Peirce, [23 September 1928]

Waldo enorme—

My god that was a brilliant bit of testimony by Mr. Pierce the old tree expert and root puller.[1] I was certainly glad to hear from you—we didn't see a damned warden the whole time. Caught maybe 600 trout altogether—for while were taking the limit apiece—30 over seven inches. Only got three big ones—cut throats—2 2½ and 3½ lbs—those three in the Snake river. It would have been wonderful fishing there but the water was too high andwe couldn't wade. When they shut off the big irrigation dam the water goes down the end of Sept. and the fishing in grand. We went Prairie chicken shooting and got nine. Bloody fine birds. Now damn glad to get back to work—lips all burned off by the sun and alkali—worse sunburned than they were at Key west. Drove 394 miles one day coming back—drank whiskey and ate apples—fine cold day with the wind blowing a gale—smooth gravel roads across Nebraska. We'll go out to wyoming together next time. It is a cockeyed swell country—like Spain only full of fish and game and bloody few wardens. They let you fish until November 15— I hate the bloody wardens—it would be all right and you would respect them if they did not break the law at all times themselves— Met a guy in Wyo who was employed last year by Game commission to kill of predatory animals to protect the antelope but he said he just couldn't resit taking shots at those damn antelope—first he would just shoot near them to make them run faster then he commenced to bag them and ended up by eating antelope all fall and winter. Game protection in the U.S.A. Nearly all the wrdens I have known have been skunks. Maybe got prejudiced on acct. of being chased and having to leave home at age of 13 by two wardens. If they get bumped off tant mieux. I am bloody glad they didn't find your short trout.[2]

Mike Stratervis a good guy. I haven't seen any of his painting for a long time but I thought some was pretty good. He made some swell drawings for that book of Cantos of Ezras.[3] I think this part of the country—Nebraska, Okla, Wyo Col has a good chance to go for Al [Smith].

This is Sunday morning been to messe gotta eat sunday dinner with relatives so must stop. We leave tomorrow for Piggott—then do some work—maybe go up to Chicago. Not decided about N.Y. Maybe go direct down to Key West. When will you be down? Best to Ivy. We could go up in the everglades and shoot wild turkeys and wild hogs. Let's make a bum out of that lying VanCampen Heileman / We wrote Charles to get us a house.[4] Maine will get bloody cold—fall is the best time but then when the fall is over come on down and we will start scientific butchery of the monsters. Vino rioja and Fundador ole espana! a los toros del mar!⁵ We can ride some of those nurse sharks for the movies. The talking movies. Benchley is a success in the talking movies—how would a talking movie of a good struggle with the monsters be?⁶

SSQB.M.

Ernesto.

Colby, TL with typewritten signature; letterhead: 6435 INDIAN LANE / KANSAS CITY, MISSOURI

1 *Enorme*: enormous (Spanish). In his letter of 12 September 1928 (JFK), Peirce enclosed a clipping of an article in the *Bangor Daily Commercial* (20 August 1928) covering a municipal court trial in which James A. Gallagher (1892–1961) was charged with showing prohibited film reproductions of the Tunney–Dempsey and the Tunney–Heeney fights at a theater in Bangor. Peirce had been called as a witness to testify as to the identities of the boxers. As in other letters of September 1928, Peirce also mentioned his work of clearing land for planting and pulling up unwanted trees at his family's place in Bangor.

2 In his letter, Peirce described having been stopped after a fishing trip by two armed game wardens looking for "shorts," fish under the six-inch limit; they did not discover the twenty "minnows" Peirce had kept for a "fry" and hidden in the fold of the car's lowered top. In July 1915 EH had fled from a local game warden who pursued him for having shot a blue heron at Walloon Lake, later turning himself in to the judge at Boyne City and paying a fifteen-dollar fine (*Letters* vol. 1, 21–22). That incident was the basis for EH's final Nick Adams story, "The Last Good Country" (*NAS*), which he left unfinished. *Tant mieux*: so much the better (French).

3 Peirce reported meeting Strater—who "seems too nice a feller to paint well"—in Ogunquit, Maine. Strater had illustrated Ezra Pound's limited edition *A Draft of XVI. Cantos* (Paris: Three Mountains Press, 1925).

4 EH and Pauline were in communication with Charles and Lorine Thompson regarding a rental house in Key West.

5 Vino rioja, red wine from the Rioja region in north-central Spain. The Fundador brand of Spanish brandy, made in Jerez, was first marketed in 1874 by the firm of Pedro Domecq. *A los toros del mar*: to the bulls of the sea (Spanish).

6 Peirce had prepared an illustrated manuscript titled "Hemingway Among the Sharks," set in the "Marquesas Keys—Gulf of Mexico" and dated "May 10 1928" (Sotheby's catalog, New York, 5 December 2013, Lot 114). The manuscript consists of a handwritten dialogue and watercolor illustrations depicting Bill Smith, Waldo Peirce, and EH in action in a boat surrounded by sharks. At the time EH wrote this letter, Robert Benchley had been featured in two 1928 talking movies, *The Treasurer's Report* and *The Sex Life of the Polyp*. In December 1928 he would appear in *The Spellbinder*.

To Sylvia Beach, 24 September [1928]

Piggott.

Sep. 24

Dear Sylvia:

I have finally gotten a letter from Duplaix after various voyages and have sent him a list of thirty friends and citizens (influential citizens) to send $^{\$}$50,000—to. (The book not the money)[1]

I told him you would have their addresses and as I cant write <u>dedicases</u> due to ① not being there ② not being able to spell my sentiments I enclosed 30 of my cards.[2] Is there not some card the publishers have to insert saying the author is out of town or pregnant or something so that he cannot sign the book himself? It would be a good idea to insert a liberal supply of these cards.

As Herr Duplaix de Weymar is not overly strong maybe you could plunge your elaborate and efficient office force into sending out these volumnes. There are 30 to go out. I enclose a cheque to apply on postage, paper and the better sorts of glue. I told the Rev. Duplaix to take the list around to you— Some of these estimable people he may have sent copies to already. I told him I would pay for all copies over what I was entitled to but imagine I should get some as all these except about 4 or 5 to gents such as yourself and Adrienne, Joyce and MacLeish are for furthering the progress of the book. I would clearly appreciate it if you will help me out on this—

Also I would like to send a copy to Monsieur Rene Pottier my landlord hoping that he would thus think of me kindly and perhaps renew my lease which runs out next Jan—not this Jan. but December 1929—[3]

What should I say in a dedicase to my landlord— Consult with the highest authorities y compris Monnier or surtout Adrienne and send me a dedication to Monsieur Pottier to copy into one of the six volumnes I am asking Old De Weiner to send me direct. I will sign yours and Adriennes and people I really know when I come back. Send me something to write that will make M. Pottier not congé me when my bail is up. Then when I send him the next rent check will send the book too.[4]

I would also like to send one

au redaction

Le Toril

38, rue Roquelaine

Toulouse.

thus maybe obtaining the suffrance of los aficionados[5]

Anyway how are you? Did you have a good vacation? I hope you are husky and having a fine time. My book, (first draft) is finally done (or dung)[.] Pauline is strong and well again. Pat is like a dark Bumby—weighs 16 ½ at 3 months and is strong and laughs all the time. Pauline nearly died with him— He was too big and she had to have a Caeserian and the weather never got below 90° for 3 weeks. But we had a fine time afterwards out on the Crow Indian Reservation shooting and fishing. Now back to work again.

Best love to you and to Adrienne from us both

Yours always,
Hemingway.

P.S.

I forgot that my cousin

Ruth White Lowry

6435 Indian Lane

K.C.

MO.

wants some French childrens books for her daughter Rutherford who is 3—and has a French governess. She asked me to write you to ask if you could send some— Bumby has a good book of songs with Sur Le Pont D'Avignon—Le Bon Roi Dagobert—Frere-a Jacque-ah etc that might do for one and any others you have— I enclose 150 francs on the check for that and postage— Let me know if there is any more charge. If any of this runs over apply it on my subscription[.] You could send them direct to her.[6]

PUL, ALS; postmark: PIGGOTT / ARK, SEP / 27 / 5 PM / 1928

1 *Cinquante mille dollars* (*Fifty Grand*) was translated into French by Georges Duplaix under the pseudonym Ott de Weymer.
2 *Dédicaces*: inscriptions, dedications (French).
3 In her letter of 30 January 1929, Beach would return EH's check with apologies for having been unable to carry out EH's request because she, her office staff, and her partner Adrienne

Monnier had all been sick and overloaded and because Duplaix, who had disappeared without leaving a forwarding address, reportedly had already sent out all the copies of *Cinquante mille dollars* (JFK).

4 *Y compris Monnier* or *sourtout Adrienne*: including Monnier or above all Adrienne; *donner son congé à*: to give notice; *bail de loyer*: rental contract (French). In her 30 January response, Beach would advise EH to simply give his landlord a copy of the book after returning to Paris. She had met with the landlord's son, Philippe Pottier, and learned that there was much enthusiasm for EH's book.

5 *À la rédaction*: To the editorial staff or office (French); *suffrage*: approval (French); *los aficionados*: the enthusiasts or fans (Spanish). *Le Toril: Revue Tauromachique Indépendante Illustrée*, taurine newspaper established in Toulouse in 1922. EH subscribed to it from 1925 to 1927 (Mandel *HDIA*, 104). Jake Barnes reads *Le Toril* in Chapter 4 of *SAR*, and it is among the bullfight periodicals (*revistas*) EH describes in the *DIA* glossary. He describes the *toril* as "the enclosure from which bulls come into the ring to be fought."

6 Rutherford Lowry (b. 1926), daughter of W. Malcolm and Ruth White Lowry. Beach would reply that Jinny Pfeiffer had located and dropped off the children's books, and that Beach would mail them as EH requested.

To John Herrmann, 26 September [1928]

Sept 26

Piggott

Arkansas—

Dear John—

I hope Jo got the wire about her book—[1] I had a hell of a time to get it to her in time as I was up in the mts in Wyo working like a bastard and my mail was sent somewhere else by mistake—some I just got here yest— Had been forwarded 5 times— I finally got the galleys and wrote some bloody wire and sent it to Erwinna Pa. and also to a N.J. address she sent me hoping she would get one or the other. But sent to Josephine Herbst instead of Josephine Herbst Herrmann— Hope it came anyway and made some sense—dont know how much. Have the 1st draft of new book done now—also a new son named Pat—weighs 16½ lbs. at 3 mos. Were you really in K.C. during the Rep. Convention? I wish the hell I had known it.

How are you going? I hope Jo's book will go big—but no book goes big when you need it—only afterwards when you dont need it and it doesnt mean a damn thing—

You are a hell of a good writer ~~and~~ Every once in a while I read your stuff again and it has only one fault—kick my ass if you want at this point— What Happens (with or without capitals) is always damned fine but you let it happen in a vacuum sometimes—you could just as easily make it happen somewhere[.][2] Make the <u>place</u> as well as the people and and action— Then you would knock them all for a row of cesspools. Maybe I wrote you this before. I thought about it and meant to and if I did kick me again in the same place. You see what I mean—that action does not want to take place without taking place somewhere— You must make the place too— I dont mean just description— <u>Make</u> it. You are a good writer and can make bums out of all of them if you will do that.

Write me to Piggott if I wrote you this before and I'll stop. Will stop anyway—but I think about your stuff a lot and that is what I think. You are a better writer than Jo because you have more talent— (<u>Don't for God's sake tell her this. She has talent enough God knows</u>) (But you could butcher them all.) You both are honest as hell and when I see you doing this— (leaving out the place where it happens) I tell you as though you were a boxer who did not keep his jaw covered against a hook— But as I say kick me—nobody has any business telling anybody else anything— Maybe I wrote you this <u>three</u> times— Anyway good luck and so long and my best to Jo and every sort of luck to her— She knows how I liked her book from the wire I hope.

Yours always

Hem

We just got in last night— Have driven 9200 miles—not so bad for an old ex patriate— Montana and Wyo are damned fine.

Cohen, ALS; postmark: PIGGOTT ARKANSAS, SEP 26

1 EH refers to the cable he sent Josephine Herbst on 25 [August 1928] with his endorsement of her novel *Nothing Is Sacred*.
2 *What Happens* (Paris: Contact Editions, 1926), Herrmann's novel about a young man's high school and college experiences. In 1927 a U.S. district court ruled the work obscene, and 300 copies of the book were destroyed.

To Archibald MacLeish, 26 September [1928]

Piggott

Sept 26

Grüss Gott Herr MacLeish!—[1]

I wish to god we had some dates kid but anyway will let you know as soon as we have.[2] We butchered the Prairie Chickens—lovely birds—and then drove back here via K.C. The cotton is as white as a Mammy Song— However Mr. P. [Pfeiffer] stands to lose $25,000—floods and one thing and another. By all the laws of civilization we aught to look after Pat for a while otherwise you'd see us this week end— Pat weighs 16½ lbs and seems as solid as the proverbial great Yale team— He laughs all the time and seems to have Bumby's legs and disposition. When is the Yell-Harvard game? I cant figure until I hear from Key West whether it is better to go right down there and install then come up to youse or go east and then down— Patrick complicates things. Coming back across Wyoming and Montana looked like the trip we took to Saragossa. But there was no jota dancing and the bulls cared more for fucking than fighting.[3]

I would as soon see any football games as classic games— I just wondered what date the Harvards played them in order to know the terminus of the season. Pauline is strong as ever—stronger— The month in Wyo. fixed her up grandly but she has a scar that makes my forehead look like nose picking (a pretty simile) We had a swell time and I am anxious to start rewriting the book— Do you know anyone coming over from Europe that could bring Bumby— He is easy to travel with and a good companion— I want to get him to go fishing with this winter in Key West any time Hadley can spare him. I would pay his expenses and meet him in N.Y. Then he and I could drive down to Florida together— Love to Ada— I'll write you the minute we have any dope on coming east.

Fall is a hell of a fine time of year—give it to me over Spring any bloody time—

Yrs.

Pappy (pride of the Papacy.)

After this book when they see I am no great catholic writer they will kick me out on my shall we say ass.

LOC, ALS

1 *Grüss Gott*: God be with you (literally "Greet God"), German greeting popular in Austria and southern Bavaria.
2 In his letter of 20 September [1928], MacLeish again invited the Hemingways to visit his family in Conway, Massachusetts and asked for possible dates (JFK).
3 *Jota*: a Spanish folk dance originating in Aragon in northern Spain.

To Guy Hickok, 27 September [1928]

September 27

Dear Guy—

I'd write oftener but there is no typewriter— Today have been paying bills— Bill's all paid. Speaking of Bill's I don't see any reason why Sally shouldn't have been born in Brooklyn. Have you ever seen anything of that sort? Anything to make it seem improbable?[1] Patrick looks like Bumby only dark—laughs all the time—sleeps all right. (So far) He's about the same size as Pauline right now—how the Lord expected him to be born I can't figure— He certainly would have killed her except for a hell of a lot of surgery. As for Scott and it being called A Lack of Passion that is shit— So far it isnt called anything— I wrote a long story once about a bull fighter— never published it—called A Lack of Passion and suppose Scott—not to be at a loss—~~called~~ took that for a title.

I hope to vote for Al in Illinois—will return to birthplace for that alone.[2]

We had a hell of a good time on the Indian reservation shooting the Indian's Prairie chickens. I go everywhere in America under the name of G. Hickock in case I should get into any serious trouble. I suppose Malgrem preferred to die rather than eat an Italian—I can see his view point—[3] Poor Bretonnel what did he have?[4] Somebody should have told him it was no worse than a bad cold. All the boxers I knew are blind or dead or walking on their heels—all the newspaper men I started with are dead from drink or syph or alimony, or in monasteries (Steve O'Grady)[5] I am getting to be an old man. You are old Father Steffens the young man said and your child looks like Guy— So Steff said I will prove my fatherhood in the magazines.[6]

My cousin Ruth White Lowry (there's a Ruth Lowry who is a friend of Mabel Walker Wellabrandt)[7] was in Tulsa and a news vendor tried to sell her The Sun Also Rises which she claimed was an <u>absolutely</u> <u>true</u> book— A friend of Mr. Hemingway's told her—he was very badly wounded in the war you know—the vendor gave her the names of all the people— And who do you think the Jew was? Two guesses.

Ford Maddox Ford!

Our Ford. Ford it seems is the Jew in Papa's book. Well that makes writing worthwhile.

I see by the advertizing pages of the August N.R.F. that I've a book out and that the other old shark and mutton fish man Jack Passos has too.[8] Well we local boys certainly make good. I don't know good what. Good merde maybe.

Pauline said she had a fine letter from Mary and is going to answer it as soon as she get's Pat organized— She has just taken him over from Jinny and is not yet in form.

How are your children Hickok? How many have you now?[9] I have only two but they are both boys and are by different mothers—old Hem the boy getter— Boys guaranteed—the fee is within everyone's reach. Reach for it and see— I must be careful to avoid anything which would corrupt the young in case you have any of the young around your office. That bloody Tunney— You make him sound the best of anybody yet but if he writes his own stuff—and it reads like he does—I'd like to shoot him.

So long Guy—we wont be back till March so I will write often to stand in with you— If we were coming back in the fall I wouldnt write at all— I am cockeyed nostalgique for Paris—for Buffalo and the Parc du Prince and the rue de la Gaitre and the bloody Luxembourg with the leaves fallen and riding down the Champs Elysees on the bike from the Etoile to the Concorde[10]—and for everything to drink—Cinzano and Lipp's Beer and I could drink 200 bottles of St. Estephe—that's what I miss—not the

burgundys or Chateau Yquems[11] of literature but good 6 to 11 franc
Bordeaux—but I got to rewrite this book and get a belly full of D'america so
I'll have some stories to write when I come back—then we'll be back the end
of March for Spring—going to Key West—can speak Spanish there fish and
drink when through work.

Yours always— Ernest

phPUL, ALS

1 Bill Bird's wife, Sally (née Sarah Costello, 1892–1963), was born in Brooklyn, New York, on 5 July 1892.
2 Democratic presidential candidate Al Smith. EH would return to Oak Park in October but did not stay in Illinois long enough to vote there on election day, 6 November.
3 In his letter to EH of 7 and 20 August 1928, Hickok had commented, "They should try Malmgren's ghost for not eating Sappi" (JFK), a reference to rumors that Swedish scientist and explorer Finn Malmgren had been killed and cannibalized by Captain Filippo Zappi, who survived after the dirigible *Italia* crashed in the Arctic on 25 May 1928. (See EH to Hickock, [c. 27 July 1928].)
4 Fred Bretonnel (1905–1928), French lightweight boxer, had hanged himself at the age of twenty-three on 4 September 1928 in Paris.
5 Steve O'Grady (1877–1923), theatrical promoter and journalist who had worked for newspapers across the United States, including every paper in Kansas City. He was famed both for his heavy drinking and his strong Catholic faith, which led him to spend six months in a Franciscan monastery.
6 EH refers to Lincoln Steffens's article "Becoming a Father at 60 Is a Liberal Education" (*American Magazine*, August 1928).
7 Mabel Elizabeth Walker Willebrandt (1889–1963), U.S. Assistant Attorney General (1921–1929) known for her strict enforcement of Prohibition. She served as chair of the credentials committee at the 1928 Republican National Convention, the first woman to hold such a position for either of the major parties. Her active campaigning for Herbert Hoover during and after the convention was depicted in some newspaper accounts as a conflict of interest with her position in the Department of Justice.
8 The August number of *La Nouvelle Revue Française* included advertisements for EH's *Cinquante mille dollars* (*Fifty Grand*) and for the French publication of John Dos Passos's *Manhattan Transfer* (Paris: Gallimard, 1928).
9 Guy and Mary Hickok had two children, son Robert C. (1915–1995) and daughter Andrée (1920–2012).
10 Stade Buffalo and the Vélodrome du Parc des Princes are both bicycle racing tracks, the former in the southern suburb of Montrouge and the latter in southwest Paris. The rue de la Gaîté is a street famous for its entertainment, including the Théâtre Montparnasse and the music hall Théâtre de la Gaîté-Montparnasse.
11 Château d'Yquem ranks in a class by itself (*Premier Cru Supérieur*) as the finest of Sauternes in the 1855 Official Classification of Bordeaux wines.

To Owen Wister, 27 September [1928]

Piggott—Ark. Sept 27

Dear Mr. Wister—

While we were up in the Clark's Fork country we decided not to go back
to Paris this fall but down to Key West instead. So I feel very badly not to be
going to see you there in November. Back here in this dull, overfoliaged,
shut in country I'm very homesick for both Wyoming and France— I wish
we were taking the boat and that we would see you— But Florida is a fine
place (periodically scoured clean by storms and financial disaster) and if
you go to Palm Beach perhaps you will come to Key West and see us. It's not
a long trip on the train—or I could come up and get you in the car. It is a
lovely drive and in Key West they all speak Spanish and there are several
fine saloons where they have Fundador, Tres Cepas, Vino riojo, (and all the
products of the Domecq's) and, if you are not drinking and want any vile
waters; if you let me know in advance which waters they are I will try and
have them stocked both in the house and in the saloons—[1] So that we may
sit and drink something and talk a great deal.

It did me much good to see you and we hope you will come and do us
much good again—but you would be very welcome even if it was certain
that you would do great and elaborate harm.[2]

We had good fishing in the Sunlight river and the Clark's Fork up toward
the Montana line—between the Asaroka and Beartooth Mts. Went Prairie
chicken shooting with Uncle Willie (Senator) Spear on the Crow
reservation and had a wonderful time— Will stay here a week or so then go
East until the middle of November—then down to Key West where we are
trying to get a house. It was there that I had the best time and worked best so
I thought it would be better to re-write the book there and by staying that
long I would know something about the place and could write some stories.
So it's better to to be homesick for Fall in Paris now and go there in the
Spring than to go back and be really homesick for Key West and not able to
go there—and then come back, perhaps to find they had spoiled it.

I hope you have a good trip and good luck with Aix-les-bains—(have had
a son there all summer and have an elaborate post card acquaintance with it
and environs)— We both loved meeting you and I hope we can meet

somewhere this winter. I might be coming up to N.Y around Christmas to meet my boy who comes from France—but Key West would be very fine— I cant tell you how disappointed we are not to see you in Paris—

Yours always,

Ernest Hemingway.

LOC, ALS; postmark: PIGGOTT, ARK, SEP / 29 / 5 PM / 1928

1 Fundador and Tres Cepas, brandies produced by the firm of Pedro Domecq, founded in 1730 in Jerez, Spain. Vino rioja, wine from the Rioja region of north-central Spain.
2 After EH visited him in Wyoming, Wister wrote from Bryn Mawr, Pennsylvania, shortly before he was to sail for France, "I loved seeing you. Not since I talked with Henry James at Rye in 1914 have I opened up at such a rate" (13 September 1928, JFK). Wister asked when EH planned to return to Paris, where he hoped they could meet again.

To Evan Shipman, 27 September [1928]

Sept 27

Piggott

Ark.

Dear Evan—

I know this will be bad news for you as it was for me. Dont know yet when we get East or for how many days— Fall is lovely all the way here— We had swell prairie chicken shooting in Montana— Think the West may go for Al[.] Hope so.[1] Your letter was damned good and bloody welcome. I do wish like hell you would write some stories or a novel— You are the only guy whose stuff it would be exciting for me to read or who could write something great and I wish to hell you would do it.

Callaghans story about Soldier Jones was peurile affected faking merde.[2]

I did not think he would turn out a faker. You are right about Dos too. He is bloody good. He wrote from the Volga—was having a grand time.[3] Maybe you will come down to Key West this winter when Dos is down—we can have a fine time there— We are just back in Piggott and cant leave yet as Pauline is just taking over Pat— He looks like Bumby (only dark) and weighs 16 1/2 lbs.

I had a card from Miro from Spain and wrote him one—[4]

Write me to Piggott

Pauline sends her love too.

> Yours alway
>
> Hem

Channick, ALS; postmark: [PIGG]OTT / ARK., SEP / 28 / 9.30AM / 1928

1 Al Smith would lose in every Western state, with Herbert Hoover winning the 1928 presidential election in a landslide.
2 Morley Callaghan's story "Soldier Harmon" is based on Canadian heavyweight John Horace Beaudin (1897–1942), who fought under the name of "Soldier Jones," and his bout with Harry Greb on 5 November 1923 in Pittsburgh.
3 During his 1928 visit to the Soviet Union, Dos Passos traveled down the Volga River; he left the United States for Europe in May and would return in December 1928.
4 This correspondence between EH and Joan Miró has not been located.

To F. Scott Fitzgerald, [c. 28 September 1928]

Dear Mr. Fizzgeral—

A letter some time ago from MaxwellEEPerkins let me in on the little secret that you work eight hours every day—Joyce I believe worked twelve. There was some comparison between how long it took you two great authors to finish your work.[1]

Well Fitz you are certainly a worker. I have never been able to write longer than two hours myself without getting utterly pooped—any longer than that and the stuff begins to become tripe but here is old Fitz whom I once knew working eight hours every day. How does it feel old fellow? What is the secret of your ability to write for eight hours every day. I look forward with some eagerness to seeing the product. Will it be like that other great worker and fellow Celt? Have you gone in for not making sense? If I could only take the slight plunge to going in for not making sense I could work ten and twelve hours a day every day and always be perfectly happy like Gertrude Stein who since she has taken up not making sense some eighteen years ago has never known a moments unhappiness with her work.

You dirty lousy liar to say you work (write) eight hours a day.

Send Lorimer a story hell. I'm letting you send Lorimer stories for both of us.[2]

Finished my first draft of the bloody book a month ago—going east now in a couple of weeks. Wanted to write some stories here but laying off writing for a month lost all impetus and now feel too healthy and at the same time mentally pooped. God I worked hard on that book. Want like hell to start re-writing but know I ought to wait a while still.

Just got back from Montana went there from Wyo.—had a grand time. Pat has doubled his weight in three months—weighed 9 something to begin with. He looks like Bumby only dark—never cries laughs all the time— sleeps all night built like a brick shithouse. I am thinking of advertising in the Nation or some such suitable medium.[3] Are your children Rickety, deformed, in any way unsatisfactory. See E. Hemingway (then pictures of the product—all by different Mothers) Perhaps He can help You. Mr. Hemingway understands your problem. He is the author of Mr. and Mrs. Elliott. He knows what you are up against. His own problem is different. Mr. Hemingway has to avoid children. Since the age of fourteen he has been embarrassed by a succession of perfect Little Ones. Now he has decided to make this great gift available to All. Tear off the enclosed coupon and mail it in a plain stamped envelope and you will receive his booklet Perfect Children for You All.

Just send the coupon and your photo and you will receive a personal answer from Mr. Hemingway himself.

Do not confuse Mr. Hemingway with Mr. FitzGerald. Mr. FitzGerald it is true is the fother of a very perfect child with, we must admit, a delightful English accent (a thing Mr. Hemingway cannot guarantee his clients) But Mr. FitzGerald is what is known in the profession as a 'one time performer'. You may take Mr. Fizzgerow if you wish but, in the end, you will be sorry. Mr. Dos Passos, however, we must strongly counsell against. For your best interests do not take Mr. Dos Passos. Mr. Dos Passos is practically 'sterile'. You all know what that means. Mr. D.P. cannot have children. Poor Mr. D.P. It is true Mr. Hemingway sometimes envies Mr. Dos Passos but that is just another proof of Mr. Hemingway's real worth to You.

There has lately been a movement on foot to take mr. [*burn hole*] Delicacy forbids us to give Mr. [*burn hole*] first name (or last name). We cannot counsel too strongly against this. Do not press us for our reasons.

Mr. Donald Ogden Stewart has had a certain amount of publicity lately in this connection but after mature consideration we feel that we cannot conscientiously recommend Mr. Stewart. Mr. Stewart may be a 'one timer'. There is no greater waste of money in modern social hygiene than the employment of a one timer.[4]

Then there is the religious issue. Mr. Hemingway has enjoyed success under all religions. Even with no religion at all Mr. Hemingway has not been found wanting. In the matter of Creeds, as in Colours, he is not a Bigot.

You understand, my dear Fitz, that none of this is personal. When I say Hemingway I may mean Perkins or Bridges. When I say FitzGerald I may mean Compton MacKenzie or Stephen St. Vincent Benet the wife of the poet Eleanor Wylie.[5] When I say [*EH heavy ink cancellation: illegible word*] I may mean Horseshit. None of this is even the slightest bit personal or 'mean'. Just good old big hearted Hem speaking ~~this is being~~. We are on the air tonight through the courtesy of the Kansas City Star and associated newspapers. Oh my this really is a fight. I wish you all could see Tommy Heeney's left eye. Now they are at it again.

Where are you going to be the end of Oct. How's to get stewed together Fitz? How about a little mixed vomiting or shold it be a "stag" party.

Write me to Piggott (Arkansas)

Ernest[6]

Glad you are friends with Murphy's[7] [*EH heavy ink cancellation: illegible line of text*]

[*EH cross-hatch cancellation of autograph postscript*: I would rather stay friends with, say, Mike Ward than be in and out of being friends with, say, Saint Paul or other rich and noble characters. But then the [*EH heavy ink cancellation: illegible word*] aren't Saint Paul nor are they Minneapolis. They are figures in a ballet. A very attractive Ballet. Use that sometime in the Post, Kid.]

[*EH marginal insertion to the left of cancelled autograph postscript*: This is crossed out—Old Hem never speaks nor writes in criticism of his friends and they are my friends.]

I see Glenway or Nuway (the back way) Wescott used your sailors in Villefranche scene in Goodbye to Wisconsin—in a story called the The Sailor (so you wont have to read through it all.)[8]

PUL, TLS with autograph postscript

Although Baker dates this letter "c. 9 October 1928" (*SL*, 287), similarities in content and phrasing between this and the following letter to Perkins dated 28 September 1928 suggest they were written close together. The conjectured letter date is based on EH's mention of having "just" returned from Montana (he arrived in Piggott on 25 September), his description of three-month-old Patrick, and his comment that he finished writing *FTA* "a month ago." The letter is in poor condition, with a tear along the horizontal fold, two burn holes, and heavy cancellations in ink that has bled through the paper and obliterated text on both sides.

1 In his letter to EH of 8 August 1928, Perkins quoted a letter he had received from Fitzgerald, who wrote from Paris: "I was encouraged the other day when James Joyce came to dinner, when he said, 'Yes, I expect to finish my novel [*Finnegans Wake*, 1939] in three or four years more at the latest', and he works eleven hours a day to my intermittent eight. Mine will be done <u>sure</u> in September" (PUL; *TOTTC*, 75). Fitzgerald's letter to Perkins [c. 21 July 1928] appears in full in John Kuehl and Jackson Bryer, eds., *Dear Scott/Dear Max: The Fitzgerald–Perkins Correspondence* (New York: Scribner's, 1971), 152.

2 In a letter to EH of [c. July 1928], Fitzgerald had advised him to send a story to George Horace Lorimer, editor of the *Saturday Evening Post*. The *Post* paid Fitzgerald extravagant sums for his stories but had rejected EH's submissions (JFK; Bruccoli *Fitz–Hem*, 97–98).

3 An American weekly magazine founded in 1865, *The Nation* focused on politics and culture.

4 Stewart's first child, Ames Ogden Stewart, had been born in May 1928. He and his wife, Beatrice, would have a second son, Donald Ogden Stewart, Jr., in 1932.

5 Compton Mackenzie (1883–1972), prolific Scottish novelist whose *Sinister Street* (published in two volumes in 1913–1914) is named in Fitzgerald's *This Side of Paradise* (1920) as one of the "quest" books that inspired protagonist Amory Blaine to openly question the institutions at Princeton (Chapter 4). Wylie's third husband, William Rose Benét, was the brother of Stephen Vincent Benét (1889–1943), whose name EH conflates with that of another American poet, Edna St. Vincent Millay (1892–1950).

6 The letter is typewritten up to this point; the remainder is handwritten.

7 In his [c. July 1928] letter from France, Fitzgerald reported that he and Zelda were once again friends with the Murphys.

8 Glenway Wescott's story "The Sailor" in *Good-Bye, Wisconsin* (New York: Harper, 1928) treats American sailors at Villefranche; Fitzgerald's *Tender Is the Night* (1934) includes a similar incident (Book 3, Chapter 8). After his novel was published, Fitzgerald would write to EH, "By the way, I didn't read the Wescott story of Villefranche sailors till I'd done my own version, and got a pleasant letter from him in regard to the matter" (1 June 1934, JFK;

Bruccoli *Fitz–Hem*, 174). In a letter of 20 February 1934, Wescott thanked Fitzgerald "for the friendliness with which you refer to our overlapping inspiration" and called his own use of the incident "accidental precedence" (Matthew J. Bruccoli and Margaret M. Duggan, eds., *Correspondence of F. Scott Fitzgerald* [New York: Random House, 1980], 330).

To Maxwell Perkins, 28 September [1928]

Piggott

Sept. 28

Dear Mr. Perkins—

I hope the hay fever is over. There's nothing worse and I do hope it is finished now. Arriving at Piggott I found two letters from you and one from Guy Hickock who said ~~he~~ sat, "next to me Scott Fitzgerald very white and equally sober—"[1] So you can add that to your reports though by now Scott may be back. I hope he is and that he is in good shape—though I dont know why I should wish him in US. for his own good— He wrote the Gatsby in Europe— He drinks no more there and what he does drink is not poisonous. Im awfully anxious to see him.

Coming back here I am anxious to start re-writing the book— But it is only a month since I finished it and it probably is best to let it lie until we get settled in Florida. I finished the Sun in Sept. and did not start re-writing it until December— This will not take as much re-writing as each day to start with (while I was working on it) I wrote over what I had done the day before. But I want to make sure that I leave it alone long enough so I can find the places where I get the kick when writing it and neglect to convey it to the reader.

I appreciate the offer of the check for $5000 and nothing would please me more.[2] I want to get together about 15000 to buy bonds with when I get to N.Y. in the attempt to add $75.$\underline{^{00}}$ a month to our income—$100.$\underline{^{00}}$ if possible if I can raise 20,000. Money in the bank does me no good at all—it simply vanishes. That is why I haven't cashed the $3700 royalty check—but if I can save in chunks and invest we can live very well on the income. Pat was very expensive and liveing in U.S. with nurse cook etc plus travelling is expensive too. So I want to make an investment before I dribble my capital away. With the 3700 and some other I have picked up have about 5000 to invest now and want to get enough more to do some good.

The only draw back to accepting the 5000 advance is that I quite gratuitously promised Ray Long I would let him have the first look at my next book if I decided to serialize it.[3] I did this to shut them up when they were worrying me with propositions while I was working.

To be completely frank I would greatly prefer to serialize in the Magazine—I do not care for serializing in Cosmopolitan and the difference of a few thousand—2 or 3—would not make me switch from Scribners to the International Magazine Co. I think it would be a good thing for me to serialize because it is not a good plan to wait <u>too</u> long between appearances and as will not have a book out this fall—nor until next fall—due to working so long on this one—it is good to keep something going.

As I said the money would be very welcome. I would write Ray Long and tell him but am afraid he would think I was trying to bid him up which is the last thing I want. If you can see anyway out of this I would be very happy. In the meantime I feel like a damned fool not to take the check— I worry about the whole business and am prevented from writing the stories I wanted to do now in between by worrying about these bloody money matters.

Yet I know, and that is what worries me—that so far I have made no money—nor been able to get any ahead—and I have attended enough benefits for people who did make money and did not hang on to it so that I have no idea but that it is an absolute necessity to get some ahead.

Also on the other hand it would be no fun if the book was adjudged un-serializable to send the money back.

So that is the situation—if this letter is muddled perhaps it is because the situation seems muddled— Perhaps you can clarify it. If the hay fever season is not over don't try!

Anyway the encouraging thing is that I believe maybe the book is pretty bloody good—and I've 40,000 words on another one to follow it—have never felt better or stronger or healthier in the head or body—nor had better confidence or morale—haven't been sick since I've been in America—knocking on wood—nor had an accident—more knocking. The last few days my good eye—that I cut last winter has been bothering me and that and worrying about the money has slowed me up—but today it is all right—

This letter has dragged on long enough— Perhaps on re-reading your letter I would not be breaking my promise to Long by taking the check— Anyway you will know—[4] I dont think I would accept his offer no matter how much it was— There's also a good chance he wouldnt want it. No one may want it. I suppose that's really why I want the cash in hand! Anyway you will know where I stand and what I can and cant do. Your conscience is as $\left\{ \begin{array}{l} \text{good} \\ \text{bad} \end{array} \right\}$ as mine.

So good luck anyway and I certainly appreciate the offer.

Yours always

[signature has been cut out]

PUL, ALS

1 EH is responding to Perkins's letters of 17 and 21 September 1928; in the earlier letter, Perkins had reported that he was "in one of those desperate states that come toward the end of the Hay Fever Season!!" (JFK; *TOTTC*, 77–78). The letter from Hickok that EH quotes remains unlocated.

2 In an "unprecedented" move, Perkins had offered to send EH a $5,000 check as a nonbinding advance on serial rights to *FTA*, sight unseen, to run in *Scribner's Magazine* (21 September 1928, PUL; *TOTTC*, 78).

3 In his letter of 24 June 1927 to Mildred Temple, EH had rejected a generous offer from Hearst's International Magazine Company, for which Long served as editor in chief.

4 With his letter of 2 October 1928, Perkins would send EH the check for $5,000, to serve as an advance on the book if EH decided to let Long serialize it in *Cosmopolitan*. Meanwhile, Perkins advised "forgetting the question, wholly, until the manuscript is finished" (PUL; *TOTTC*, 80–81).

To Waldo Peirce, [c. 29 September 1928]

Dear Mr. Purse;

What the hell? Was there only one pair of moccasins? Didn't Ivy get a pair too?[1] I thought I might I might take refuge in the fact that the paper was torn to claim there had been two pair when they started by by gawd there was only one—if I had not been a bloody fool I would have got a pair for Ivy but like a bloody fool never thought they would be any good to her. Women claim they break the arch flatten the foot etc. Tell her for me I regret like hell not moccasinning her and will at the first opportunity.

We are back in Piggott and I am homesick as hell for Wyoming, Paris, Zaragoza, Key West—anywhere a man can get good wine and have the fall to sit out in in front of a cafe or on a boat or ver los toros.[2] Have to stay here for two or three weeks while Pauline's Mother goes on a trip with her sister. They have been bloody good about Pat all July and August and most of September. Then we'll park him again and come on east and then I'll go down to Key Westb in the car maybe from N.Y. and Pauline come back and pick up Pat and go down.

Pat is a good baby, sleeps all night, doesn't cry much—laughs a lot—lies and plays with my gun by the hour. Seems husky as hell so far—doubled his weight in two and a half months. Thats all the obstetrical news.

I wish the hell I was in Paris now but there is no use to go over have the autumn last three days—then rain and sit in front of the Deux Magots and look at the fairies and lesbians and wish the hell I was at Key West with the bloody monsters. Better to get a bellyful of the monsters and get back when the Spring starts then can go to Spain in the summer;. Spain is such a bloody fine country— Wyoming looks like it but there is a hell of a differenve between looking like it and being it. I wish the hell I'd been born there and could write Spanish—by Gad wouldn(t a man be a writer then. Instead when you write about it you always feel you are shooting on posted land or fishing after the season. It's 84 now on the front porch where the shade is and this is not the front porch but upstairs at the back of the house and it must be about 108— Hot as hell.

Freddy Betonnel hanged himself in the dining room. Let Charlie Sweeney explain that one.[3] When they cut him down he was dead. 23 years old.

Would you like the autos? I can send them to you a week's collection at a time. Frantz won the Tour. Leducq was second.[4] The boxin season has just opened at Wagram.[5] Molina was hit by a train while driving an auto and all smashed completely to hell. WOn't be able to box again. Humery knocked out Johnny Cuthbert last summer.[6]

What do you hear from Sweeney? The N.R.F. published one of those photos you sent Sylvia in an ad and said Hemingway had given himself since youth to la peche aux grandes tortues![7] Have a box with two praying mantis in it. They look like Al Brown and catch flies like barracudas taking a live grunt—if you take the partition out they fight like hell—like the British school of boxing—jabbing and footwork. Will see if I can get you a couple. You feed them live flies and they catch them and eat them.

If I can't go to the queensborough A.C. or Wagram by gad I can always remove the partition from between my mantises.[8]

So long.

Ernest

Colby, TLS

1 "I wear the royal Big Chief Shiting Bull Bison Beaded Buskins with great comfort & delight," Peirce told EH in his letter of 25 September 1928 (Colby).
2 *Ver los toros*: to see the bulls (Spanish).
3 Charles Sweeny (1882–1963), an American-born soldier of fortune whom EH met in Constantinople while covering the Greco-Turkish War for the *Toronto Star* in 1922. He is the likely prototype for Colonel Boyle in *GOE* and would serve as an honorary pallbearer at EH's funeral in 1961.
4 The French sporting newspaper *L'Auto* sponsored the Tour de France. Nicolas Frantz (1899–1985), Luxembourgian professional cyclist and winner of the 1927 and 1928 Tour de France. He won the 3,360 mile race on 15 July 1928 after riding for twenty-nine days. French cyclist André Leducq (1904–1980) would take first place in 1930 and 1932.
5 Salle Wagram, a nineteenth-century hall on the Avenue de Wagram in Paris, was a frequent venue for boxing matches.
6 French middleweight boxer Barthelemy Molinero (b. 1904), better known as Bart (or Bert) Molina, retired from boxing in 1928. In a bout in Paris on 8 May 1928, French lightweight boxer Gustave Humery knocked out English lightweight Johnny Cuthbert (1904–1987), avenging his knockout by Cuthbert in their previous fight on 27 September 1927.
7 N.R.F. refers to *La Nouvelle Revue Française*. *La pêche aux grandes tortues*: Fishing for large turtles (French). Among Beach's papers at PUL are photographs Peirce took of the 1928 fishing expedition in Key West, including photos of turtles the group had caught.
8 Al Brown (né Alfonso Teofilo Brown, 1902–1951), Panamanian-born bantamweight boxer notable for his tall, gangly build and exceptionally long reach. The Queensboro Athletic Club in Long Island City, New York, held boxing matches.

To Waldo Peirce, [c. 1 October 1928]

Why the hell don't you write some pieces? (Don't start as a novel if that is too bloody long and keeps your nose on the grindstone too long but start as anything—a story or any damn thing BUT THEN FINISH IT You could write a damned fine story about the gt. fight film trial. The stuff you wrote me was bloody fine. What the hell business have you to worry about the commercial end of it anyway?[1] The only thing to do is to write it—I never think about anything else. Why the hell should you. Write it—if you want to write about anything Mother, father brother wife bootlegger bastard son or anything else for god's sake put it in. There are no punches pulled in literachur—if you pull them they walk out on you. What you ought to do is write you big lazy bastard— My god it is hard for anybody to write. I never start a damn thing without knowing 200 times I can't write—never will be able to write a line—can't go on—can't get started—stuff is rotten—can't say what I mean—know there is a whole fine complete thing and all I get of it is the bacon rinds— You would write better than anybody but the minute it becomes impossible you stop. That is the time you have to go on through and then it gets easier. It always gets utterly and completely impossible. Thank God it does—otherwise everybody would write and I would starve to death—but the thing is the bastards do not know that it is just when it is all foutu that you continue on and make someth[ing] out of it. And because you got tired don't think that you have [t]o then let it go all to slop— demarre again—or lay off until the next day.[2] Only other thing I know is don't write too much at a time—you start that way and at every performance fook yourself completely dry and then are empty—with consequent interstitial remorse—a novel—a long one—is 100,000 words long— If a guy does only 500 words a day—which seems like nothing when you do it and you feel you have been loafing you would have the bloody thing done in 200 days—1000 words a day means only about three months. A hell of a good novel can be only 40,000— There is nothing to it once you get going and take it through the point where you first stall completely. Most guys write on as long as they have any juice—that is bloody good for the sht. story but on a novel you can't do the same thing any more than you can run the mile at the same pace as the 100.

This is all shit of course and you are probably the guy who told it to me— only when anybody can write as bloody well as you can it would be a hell of a pleasure to have them write more. There isn't any commercial end to good writing. Throw that out. Whatever you get for it is luck. You can write anything you want and there is always some place you can get it published if it is good.

The noted Philadelphia Bill is half kike anyway and so it is reallyna boon to humanity— Let's hope nob[o]dy ever gives him a box of dragee d'Hercule— I wonder what part the little turk plays in the great Restoration Comedy. But what proof have we that there was ever anything to restore. Are there any proofs of original potency.[3] He is the guy you know who went around telling people when I hadn't a sou to my back and was bloody well walking around the block instead of eating lunch to hold down the family expenses in Paris at one time in the old days— We lived almost entirely on poireaux which I purchsed to the greatest advantage—became one of the greatest judges of poireaux in the world—and old Jack Passos the Muttonfish kid—had pawned his typewriter—or rather tried to but they wouldn't give him any thing on it after he stood in line an hour and a half because he had no papiers— I was purchasing high grade milk from the champs des courses d'auteuil for Bumby and poireaux for Hadley, myself and occasionally Passos—[4] We were having a bloody fine time but not a bloody sou—had laid off newspaper job to "write" and had every story in Men without and In Our Time come back at least four times from every magazine in America (all of them now having discovered great stuff in them and eager for stories damn them to hell) Me boxing at Lerda's in order to get billet de faveur as a poxer to go to the Cirque and see Mascart and Ledoux and Routis and Ledoux—Criqui and Billy Mathews etc.[5] This son of a bitch William Rothenstein B——— [William Christian Bullitt] went around telling everyone that I was feigning poverty and was in reality rich as hell— in fact just like he was—but was feigning poverty in order to getin with artists and writers instead of going around with my fellow big bondholders. He told Archie MacLeish that I had an income at that poireaux period (like Picasso's blue period) of $12,000 the while I was teaching boxing, instructing in ski-ing and my only source of jack the money paid by the noble citizen and prominent jewish buggar and great art dealer Alfie Flechtheim who was featuring my obscene poems throughout the fatherland.[6] So anything I hear about the great Bill is not calculated to plunge me into a sea of lachrimosity— Of course the late clipping queen is no aphrodisiac—perhaps she has been a sedative—perhaps the clippings are so well read that they no longer arouse William. We should get some new clippings.[7]

I thought I would be able to write some stories during this two weeks—may still—but seem unable to do anything but letters. Want to start re-writing the novel but know it's too soon. Finished it only a mo. ago. So am training. Put on a sweat shirt, long und[e]rwear and shoes and run over the countryside—then exercise and shadow box, lost six pounds yesterday—came down to 184 from 190 in a forenoon! Will come down to 178 and then lay off. Stiff as a board. Torture to run. I run pretty fast for three minutes—then jog slowly—then fast again—natibes all think old man Pfeiffer has a crazy son in law. Am regarded with great suspicion by those hereabouts in the countryside anyway—popular belief is that Pauline ma[r]ried a man who couldn't support her and came home and camped on the family. One of the worst aspects is that we shoot up about 100 shot gun shells at clay pigeons every day—they all thank God they haven't a son in law that not only won't work but shoots off about 4 dollars wortof Money like that You get damn few good guys in the middle west. North they are good and south too—also east and the west starts visibly at the boundary (west) of Nebraska—out in the middle west you get the suspicious, bigoted, mean and especially conceited Yokel— I enjoy insulting them whenever they are snotty knowing I can knock the shit out of them and trusting they [w]on't draw a knife— But having lived wit[h] and among the eytalians I would rather fight a guy who had a knife and no talent with same than a guy with a good left hook and I don't think there is a guy who can fight between SaintLouis on the north and Little Rock on the south. Training makes me feel both mean and snotty so should cut it out before some guy knocks the can off me. Got started by boxing in K.C. with Hall Smith another expupil of Sam Langford (they are in number like Mayflower or Leviathan cabin passengers) and John Fennelly who was a welter weight champion in the navy on the coast also college intercollegiate champion. He is now in N.Y. and claims to box a lot with Jeff Smith. He had a fancy left hand but was not unhittable. Hall a big hulk as easy to hit as say Bouquillon but muscle bound

[t]o something on acct. being a swimmer—once beat Duke Kahonomoku but soon took up yencing which did not have the same effect on the Duke.[8]

Well this seems to be all— Hall is now in N.Y. A good guy out of the wreckage of a spoiled guy—was an ivory killer in the Belgian congo for a while—hates the Belgiums—was at one time a dreadful turd but now is a good guy. We went to the races and I ran 17 bucks up to 186 in two days to drop all but 30 on the last day of the meeting. I would be worried as hell about Pauline in the orspital and take it out working with Hall with the gloves— [H]e weighed 193 and I dropped him a couple of times with the 14 oz. gloves— I say 14 they may have been less or more—biggest he could buy— He wanted to learn to fight—not to box—said he had taken boxing lessons all his life and knew nothing about fighting— Gave him such an appetite for gore that he went out and beat up a guy at the country club— just across the road—practically gratuitously—knocked him down 14 times—thought it very courteous of the guy to keep on getting up himself— I would have tried to grab his feet or bite his ankle— Time to go down and buy more shotgun shells— Love to Ivy et Evviva la Orticultura[9] Pauline sends her best.

Ernest

PUL, TLS

1 In his letter to EH of 27 September [1928], Peirce wrote, "I'm a damn fool not to sit down & write something serious," saying, "I could sit down & write you a novel—just for the fun of it—but I am chilled by the business end—arnt you—especially if there aint any contract" (JFK).

2 *Foutu*: over, done for; *démarrer*: to start up (French).

3 William Bullitt, son of William Christian and Louisa Horwitz Bullitt, was a native of Philadelphia. "Bull Billet," Peirce wrote in a 26 September [1928] letter to EH, "had lost or bantered away or duly frozen to death the erectile in his tissue in Shittenhouse Sq. [Rittenhouse Square] Philadelphia, last in the National League. and not all the King's hosses, whores or Mustapha Kemal's White Pearls or loose jyants of louise bryants can put it together again" (JFK). EH alludes to the 1904 French farce *Les Dragées d'Hercule* (*Hercules' Sugar-Coated Pills*) by Paul Bilhaud (1854–1933) and Maurice Hennequin (1863–1926), in which a lecherous man is empowered by the sexual stimulant "Spanish fly."

4 *Poireaux*: leeks (French). EH had recounted Dos Passos's failed efforts in 1924 to pawn his typewriter in Paris in a letter to Stein and Toklas [c. 28–31 August 1924] (*Letters* vol. 2, 151–53). *Champ de courses*: racetrack (French). EH refers to the Hippodrome d'Auteuil, the horse racecourse built in 1873 at the edge of the Bois de Boulogne in Paris.

5 Complimentary ticket (French). Louis Lerda, a Frenchman who boxed in America as "Kid Adler" during the late 1800s, became a boxing manager and ran a boxing club in the Latin Quarter of Paris where EH frequently sparred. Charles Ledoux (1892–1967) and André Routis, French featherweight boxers. Routis had defeated Ledoux on 22 January 1924 at the Cirque de Paris for the French bantamweight title. Eugéne Criqui (1893–1977), French featherweight boxer. Billy Matthews (1901–1967), English featherweight boxer.

6 Alfred Flechtheim published several of EH's poems in his German magazine *Der Querschnitt* in late 1924 and early 1925, including "The Soul of Spain with McAlmon and Bird the Publishers," "The Earnest Liberal's Lament," "The Lady Poets with Foot Notes," and "The Age Demanded." In a letter of 22 April 1925 to Dos Passos, EH reported that Flechtheim was going to publish a book of his "dirty poems" to be illustrated by Pascin, claiming that such poems were his "only source of income" (*Letters* vol. 2, 323). The poetry volume never materialized.

7 Although the context is unclear, EH is responding to Peirce's comment in his 26 September letter that "This time Louise [Bryant, Bullitt's wife] must have gotten away with more than the clippings."

8 Walton Hall Smith (1898–1955), longtime boxing and hunting acquaintance of EH's. Sam Langford (1883–1956), black professional boxer from Nova Scotia whose twenty-four-year career involved more than 300 bouts against boxers ranging from welterweight to heavyweight. John Fauntleroy Fennelly (1899–1974), briefly a news reporter for the *Kansas City Star*, had been a welterweight boxing champion at Princeton and served in the U.S. Army during World War I. Jeff Smith (né Jerome Jeffords, 1891–1962), also known as the "Bayonne Globetrotter," middleweight boxer from New Jersey. Moise Bouquillon (b. 1903), light heavyweight boxer also known as the Iron Man of France. Duke Kahanamoku (1890–1968), Hawaiian-born Olympic medalist in swimming in 1912, 1920, and 1924.

9 *Evviva la Orticoltura*: Long live Horticulture (Italian), a reference to Peirce's labors on his land in Maine.

To Madelaine Hemingway, 1 October [1928]

October One

Dear Nunbones—

Glad to hear from you again.[1] I'll be seeing you inside of two weeks when I plan to darken the door of the parental mansion and then we can discuss one thing and another. Stuck here for the moment due to Patrick— Pauline's sister Jinny and her Mother left this morning on a trip for two weeks—they have been taking care of him while we were off in Wyoming.

(have b ecome a demon Ford driver—we did 394 miles in one day starting after nine o clock in the morning.[2] Have driven over 9000 miles in the insect and only been passed twice on the road in that time! It will make 65 m.p.h. and will stay over 50 all day if the roads permit. I am thinking of attempting to drive to O.P. in a day from Piggott. That is only a little over 550. The only trouble is that after a trip I do not know whether to put the car in a garage or simply touch a match to it.

Patrick is a fine kid—has doubled his weight in three months—never cries—is very good looking—like Bumby only dark—laughs at any joke— plays with my gun by the hour. I am thinking of advertising as a male parent-— Exceptional children for All Mothers—are your children deformed, underweight, rickety? E. Hemingway son of Grace Hall Hemingway the Paintress— Perhaps He can help You.

Tell Car[o]l I have a large photo for her in answer to her request for something to make a bum out of the other girl's pictures of Ruchard Halliburton the daylight Canal swimmer. Will bring it. Is Carol still in High School? Or if she has graduated what is she going to do?[3] Give me a little dope. How is my noted brother the sensati[o]nal violinist? I hope you are going to vote for Al Smith.

I'm sorry Izzy's kid doesn't look so good but it will have one advantage of having as mother about the best and most sporting character I've ever known.[4]

Glad to her Meriam is such a fine girl. Tear a little time from your tooth extracting and write me again.[5] A letter in Arkansas is worth nine any place else.

Regards to all the members,

yr. affct bro.

STEEN

PSU, TL with typewritten signature

1 In her letter to EH of 26 September [1928], Sunny expressed excitement at the prospect of spending the winter with EH and Pauline at Key West and traveling with them to Europe the following spring (JFK).
2 The Model A Ford coupe was a gift from Gus Pfeiffer, intended to await EH and Pauline upon their arrival in Key West in early April 1928. Although its delivery was delayed, it appears in the family photos taken in Key West on 10 April 1928 during the brief visit by EH's parents and Uncle Willoughby (included in the plate section of this volume).
3 EH's sister Carol was then a junior in high school, in the OPRFHS class of 1930. Richard Halliburton (1900–1939), American adventure travel writer, had just swum the length of the Panama Canal in August 1928.

4 Sunny reported in her 26 September letter that Isabelle Simmons Godolphin's baby was "awfully scrawny and has an ugly birthmark on its face— Not what I would call a good specimen, but I suppose she loves it."
5 EH refers to Sunny's friend Miriam Rickards and to Sunny's work as a dental assistant.

To Maxwell Perkins, 11 October 1928

Oct 11, 1928

Dear Mr. Perkins—

Thanks very much for sending the check. I will hang on to it and we or rather you can decide what it is for later. I imagine when I see Ray Long or some of his under Rays I can fix it up with them as you suggest. We will see anyway. I don't see why they shouldn't.[1]

Have a story about ¾ done.[2] Will be leaving here as soon as it is finished to see Chicago and Toronto en route to N.Y. What about Scott? I am awfully anxious to hear.[3]

Is Morley Callaghan in Toronto? Would like to see him.

Nigger to Nigger is very very good. I enjoyed it greatly. Thanks very much for sending it and also for the Aiken book. His story about the fellow rapping on the wall very funny and the old whore lady quite sad. Haven't read any others yet.[4]

Anyone that would say hay fever was imagination could probably prove that child birth was too. My father had it and I was always grateful to it because it kept us increasingly further north when I was a kid—but I know how hellish it is. I get the same feeling from dust. But it goes away after a couple of days.

Instead of thinking Zelda a possible good influence (what a phrase) for Scott—I think 90% of all the trouble he has comes from her. Almost Every bloody fool thing I have ever seen or known him to do has been been directly or indirectly Zelda inspired.[5] I'm probably wrong in this.[6] But I often wonder if he would not have been the best writer we've ever had or likely to have if he hadnt been married to some one that would make him waste <u>Everything</u>. I know no one that has ever had more talent—or wasted it more. I wish to god he'd write a good book and finish it and not poop himself away on those lousy Post stories. I dont blame <u>Lorimer</u>. I blame Zelda.

[*EH bracketed the previous paragraph and wrote in the margin*: I would not have Scott imagine I believed <u>this for the world</u>.]

Yours always,

Ernest Hemingway.

Will leave here in about three days. I'll give you an address in Toronto.

PUL, TL/ALS

1 The check for $5,000 that Perkins sent EH with his letter of 2 October 1928 was an advance to be applied toward either the serialization or the book publication of *FTA*, depending on EH's arrangements with Ray Long. Perkins had advised EH to tell Long that it seemed "only fair" to let *Scribner's Magazine* serialize the novel since it was "the first general magazine" to publish his stories and Scribner's was publishing his books (PUL; *TOTTC*, 80–81).
2 "Wine of Wyoming," based on EH and Pauline's conversations with the Moncini family during their stay in Wyoming, would not be completed until 1930, when Perkins asked for a submission to *Scribner's Magazine*. The story would appear in the August 1930 issue and would be collected in *WTN* (1933).
3 "I don't know what the devil Scott's up to," Perkins had written in his letter of 17 September 1928: "I hear bad reports of him, but probably untrue" (JFK). In his letter of 2 October 1928, Perkins reported that Fitzgerald had sailed for the United States on 29 September (PUL).
4 Perkins had sent EH two 1928 Scribner's publications: *Nigger to Nigger* by Edward Clarkson Leverett Adams (1876–1946), a collection of stories, sketches, and poems set in South Carolina; and Conrad Aiken's short-story collection *Costumes by Eros*.
5 In his 2 October letter, Perkins wrote that he was surprised Zelda did not "show some sense about spending money. Most of their trouble, which may kill Scott in the end, comes from extravagance."
6 The letter is typewritten to this point; the remainder is handwritten.

To Henry Goodman, 12 October 1928

Piggott

Arkansas.

Oct 12—1928

Dear Mr. Goodman:

I do not believe I can give my consent to your reprinting in a book the letter I wrote you in reply to your request for information for your pupils.[1] If you had written me at the time that you were contemplating a book made up of letters from writers and their stories it would have been different. But as it looks to me you are publishing a book which has been in part written by proffessional writers—without renumeration—and without the understanding that their work was to be published.

A man who writes for his living, Mr. Goodman, is very often glad to contribute his work to any charitable cause. He should not be asked for a statement or a piece of writing for one purpose if it is really intended for another—and if he gives his permission he is injuring rather than aiding other writers. Personally I doubt greatly whether the teaching of short story writing is anything but harmful to the ends of literature— It has been going on for a number of years and I have encountered no stories by Short Story Taught writers which seem worth a damn. Perhaps you have.

However because I disapprove of your project I have no desire to cause you any personal loss or inconvenience; I will therefore give permission for you to use my letter and republish The Killers (provided Scribner's also give their written consent) if you will (1), send me care Charles Scribner's N.Y. a proof of my statement to insure accuracy of quotation and (2) give to the member of your class whom you consider the <u>worst</u> and most <u>unpromising</u> writer of the short story a sum equal to the fractional part of the advance and royalties which I would receive if I were to be paid for my work on a royalty basis. I.e. if you are publishing the work of ten writers and receive an advance of two hundred dollars the pupil designated should receive 20 dollars. (3) That you include this letter in the forthcoming book. This last condition to be conditional on the judgement of Mr. Alfred Harcourt for whom I have the greatest respect. If Mr. Harcourt thinks it inadvisable to include this letter I would respect his judgement.

The other conditions, however, are quite arbitrary.

Wishing you personally the greatest success,

Yours very truly,

Ernest Hemingway

JFK, ALS

1 In a letter to EH of 17 September 1928, Goodman requested permission to reprint EH's letter to him of 16 January 1928 to accompany "The Killers" in a volume of views and works of contemporary short-story writers that was scheduled for publication by Harcourt, Brace, & Company (JFK).

To Henry Goodman, [21 October 1928]

[Excerpt as published in Christie's catalog:]

. . . I am sure that the book came about as you say and I am very glad for you to print my letter and also "The Killers" if Scribners give their permission—if there is a fee that is customary that will be a matter for them to arrange with you.[1] I hope you will have great success with the book—it never occurred to me that you would plan to take advantage of writers—nor plot to defraud them— I believe you can see my standpoint—at least I wrote it in the last letter. However, having read your letter it is quite changed . . .

Christie's catalog, New York, 16 December 1983, Lot 418, TLS

1 EH is replying to Goodman's letter of 15 October 1928 (JFK), in which Goodman defended his motives against the implied charge of deception that EH had expressed in his letter of 12 October 1928. In his book *Creating the Short Story* (New York: Harcourt, Brace, 1929), Goodman would include verbatim EH's letter of 16 January 1928 with only minor punctuation refinements, together with "The Killers," acknowledging permissions by the author and by Scribner's and noting the story's prior publication in *MWW*.

To Maxwell Perkins, 23 October 1928

ND184 35 DL= CHICAGO ILL 23 153P
MAXWELL PERKINS=
CHARLES SCRIBNERS SONS=
WILL BE CARE WILLIAM D HORNE THE WHITEHALL 105 EAST DELAWARE PLACE CHICAGO[1] UNTIL NEXT TUESDAY OCT 30 WIRED SCOTT ELLERSHEY MANSIONS WILMINGTON DELAWARE WOULD THAT REACH HIM THANKS FOR CALLAGHANS ADDRESS=[2]
=HEMINGWAY.

PUL, Cable; Western Union destination receipt stamp: 1928 OCT 23 PM 3 27

1 In a letter of 17 October [1928], Bill Horne had invited EH to stay with him and his roommate at the Whitehall, a luxurious new apartment house built in 1928 near Michigan Avenue in Chicago (JFK).
2 In his 16 October letter to EH, Perkins had sent Callaghan's address: 35 Woolfrey Avenue, Toronto (PUL).

To Waldo Peirce, [31 October 1928]

Wednesday

Dear Waldo—

Pauline reports the fish are bloody fine and we will look at them until we can get a fly out on the stream in Galicia again next summer— Damn glad to hear from you, Pat and Unser Max at lunch[1]—we leave here Thursday night arrive at MacLeish's direct in Mass. (Conway) leaving train at Greenfield— Spend 2-3 days and go to New Haven to see the Dartmouth vs Yale—[2] Then to N.Y. Wont tell anybody we're there and see some fights etc.[3] (The Aquariums)[4] Will be in N.Y until Nov 17— See you there Eh?

Did you shoot the grouse with that all purpose gun? I am going to try and shoot some of Archie's with the 20 ga.[5]

Will write you from Conway—you're picture of you, me, the Telephone and Sherry King, and El Desencajconamento de los Toros en los corrales de gas is on display here at AM. Shit Show in Fart Institute— Only picture in show except your Regina Cucina—[6] But by Christ they have some Winslow Homers that give me the same feeling I get from the Monsters or a Faena de Belmonte—[7] You've got to <u>Paint</u> more Chico— Time is short and art longer than the whang of John Arthur Johnson—[8] That guy Winslow Homer was a swell painter and you are a swell painter and for christ's sake work hard— I've got to work hard too—

Going to 6 Day with Wegg tonight—just learned he was in town—[9] I'll be damned glad to see you—

Nick the Greek is broke here now—[10]

This town full of [class ?] whiskeys etc. All bootleggers working for the Republicans Fat chance—

Ernesto

Colby, ALS; letterhead: THE WHITEHALL / 105 EAST DELAWARE PLACE / CHICAGO

1 *Unser*: our (German). In a letter of 24 October 1928, Peirce reported that he, Pat Morgan, and Perkins had met for lunch and that everyone wanted to know when EH would be in New York (PUL).
2 In a home football game on 3 November 1928 in New Haven, Connecticut, Yale would beat Dartmouth by a score of 18–0.

3 On 16 November 1928, EH, Pauline, and Mike Strater would attend an evening of six boxing matches at Madison Square Garden. They planned to meet Evan Shipman at the event but never found him among the crowd of 19,000 spectators.

4 Probably the New York City Aquarium, founded in 1896 and located in Clinton Castle in Battery Park at the southern tip of Manhattan until 1941. EH had visited the Aquarium in 1918 while in New York for training before sailing for Italy to serve with the ARC Ambulance Service in WWI (*Letters* vol. 1, 98–99).

5 Peirce had written of his plan to "rustle up the ruffled grouse" with a "'handy gun'–28 sawed off single shot shot gun in pistol form." He illustrated the letter with a color sketch of himself with the gun, two small dogs, and a sage chicken, with the caption "What chance has a poor bird against this gang? Answer—Every—" (9 October 1928, JFK).

6 Peirce's paintings *Bulls at Pamplona* and *Our French Cook* (which EH dubs "Regina Cucina," or "Kitchen Queen" in Italian) were on display at the Forty-First Annual Exhibition of American Paintings and Sculpture held at the Art Institute of Chicago, 25 October–16 December 1928. "El Desencajonamento de los Toros en los corrales de gas" translates as "The Unloading of the Bulls in the gas corrals," a Pamplona place name reflecting the site's former use as a gas factory. In that painting, reproduced in the exhibition catalog, EH and Peirce are depicted among the crowd of onlookers at the event. "The Telephone and Sherry King" remains unidentified.

7 Winslow Homer (1836–1910), American painter best known for his marine paintings. Twenty-two Homer watercolors were on long-term loan to the Art Institute of Chicago from Martin A. Ryerson (1856–1932) before becoming part of the permanent collection in 1933. The 1928 exhibit included several moody seascapes such as *Stowing Sail, Bahamas* and *Gulf Stream*, depicting human effort outsized by the raw force of a threatening sea. EH and Peirce used the term "monsters" to refer to the big game fish they encountered during their expeditions from Key West. *Faena* means "work" in Spanish; EH employs it here in reference to the bullfighter Belmonte as "the sum of the work done by the matador with the muleta in the final third of the bullfight" (*DIA*, Glossary).

8 "Life is short and the art long," aphorism credited to the Greek physician Hippocrates (460–377 B.C.). Arthur John Johnson was the birth name of African American heavyweight boxing champion Jack Johnson.

9 The Chicago Six-Day Bicycle Race was held from 29 October to 4 November 1928. Wegg remains unidentified.

10 Nick the Greek, nickname of professional gambler Nicholas Andreas Dandolos (1883–1966), who moved to the United States from Crete at the age of eighteen and lived on and off in Chicago. He once lost all his horse race winnings (about $500,000) in a card game and claimed to have gone from rags to riches seventy-three times during his career.

To Madelaine Hemingway, 13 November [1928]

November 13

Dear Nunbones—

The dope now is that we leave Nov 18 from Philadelphia after the Yale-Princeton game.[1] Pauline will go direct to St. Louis and Piggott probably and you and I will drive down— We ought to start at least by the morning of the

21st (Early in the morning) Have to be in Key West by Nov. 27th You and I will probably drive as far as Jacksonville Fla and you can go on then on the train with Pauline and Pat— She has to lay over a day there between trains—

It ought to be a fine trip down— We ought to have the car in shape all ready to go when I get there—

[*EH bracketed the following three paragraphs:*]

It ought to go to the local <u>Ford</u> garage and have the oil drained and changed— (Re-Filled with 5 quarts of <u>Mobiloil A</u>.)

Be <u>greased</u> and <u>oiled</u>— Especially the <u>CLUTCH-COLLAR</u> greased— Water put in the batteries—the DIFFERENTIAL checked (To see if it needs grease) and if possible the <u>Speedometer fixed</u>— It sticks now at 35 Miles— Also there is a squeak in the motor which is caused, I believe, by the <u>Timer</u> or rather the <u>Distributor</u>—which needs to be oiled— It is a little rusty or dry probably. If you will drive the car to <u>Snows</u> or whatever the official Ford place is and take this letter and ask them to do the things I've mentioned above and have it all ready to Roll by the afternoon of November 20th.[2] If Dad has drained the radiator be sure and put water in before you start out to Snows.

I hope you wont mind doing this as it will help us like the deuce to be all ready to go. You pack the things you need on the trip going down in one suit case and we can Express the other suit case or whatever you have down to Florida if there is not room for it in the car. There will be plenty of room for your racket etc.

We have heard from Key West and have a fine place which will be vacant November 20th— Have wired taking it.[3]

You wont need many clothes on an automobile trip— Is there anything you need or want here in N.Y? If so wire us here at the Brevoort and will get it for you.

Pauline sends her love. Best to all the merchants. Better take the car around when you get this so they will have time to fix the speedometer— If they cant have it fixed by the 20th dont let them fool with it. I dont want it sent away and not back. What is the matter is that it sticks at between 35 and 40 and does not register until it jumps up above 50 again—very annoying.

Best love—

Ernie.

PSU, ALS; letterhead: Hotel Brevoort, New York; postmark: NEW YORK, N.Y. STA. D, NOV 13 / 1³⁰ PM / 1928

1 The Hemingways and the Fitzgeralds would be among the crowd of 56,000 at the 17 November 1928 football game at Palmer Stadium in Princeton, New Jersey, where Princeton beat Yale by a score of 12–2.
2 Snow Brothers Inc., an authorized Ford and Lincoln automobile dealership and service shop established in 1914 by Lynn S. Snow and Earl C. Snow at 1011 South Boulevard in Oak Park.
3 In a special delivery letter to Pauline forwarded from Piggott to the Brevoort Hotel in New York City, Lorine Thompson wrote that she had found a "nice cottage" being vacated by the tenant on 20 November ($60 per month for the two-bedroom house and garage) and asked that they write or wire her at once ([c. 6 November 1928], JFK). EH's wired response has not been located.

To F. Scott and Zelda Fitzgerald, [18 November 1928]

Sunday Night

Dear Scott and Zelda—

The train is bucking and pitching or bitching (but not listing anyway)

We had a wonderful time— You were both grand— I am sorry I made a shall we say nuisance of myself about getting to the train on time— We were there far to too early— When you were in the hands of the cop I called on the phone from our platform and explained you were a great writer— The cop was very nice— He said you said I was a great writer too but he had never heard of either of us. I told him rapidly the plots of some of your better known stories— He said—this is absolutely literal—"He seems like a Dandy Fellow"—thats the way cops talk—not as they talk in Callaghan's works.

Anyway we had a grand time, and Ellersley Mansion is the most cock eyed beautiful place I've ever seen—¹ Pauline sends her love—

Ernest.

I'll write our address in Key West when I know it—
Piggott Ark will always reach us.

PUL, ALS; letterhead: Pennsylvania Railroad / "Spirit of St. Louis"

1 EH was en route to Chicago after an overnight stay at Ellerslie, the stately mansion in Edgemoor, Delaware, that the Fitzgeralds had leased for two years beginning in the spring of 1927.

To Archibald MacLeish, [c. 3 December 1928]

Our address

Box 323 Key West

Dear Archie—

This is not Pappy's own choice in paper— But anyway Kid—read your poem The Shapespeare of William MacLeish on the train that day for Boston and it was really grand—[1] I'm not a critic so I dont know what to say but it gave me a thrill that I usually get only from paintings by great guys or sometimes writers very rarely and then usually dead. I am afraid you are a great poet and I may have to sock you a few times to keep from being awed— It was so good I thought maybe I was crazy so I gave it to Pauline and she felt the same way— Then I got Evan [Shipman] and had him read it all the way through and he said it was a Fine Poem and that Baby is hard to please. So if that is any good to you— Also told what I thought to Galantiere, Scribners etc. Not what I think matters any where near as much as what Evan thinks— He knows! We drove from Piggott to Miami in 3 days—385 first day—447 the 2nd and 528 the 3rd day— I went to sleep 3 times about midnight on 3rd day— got out and walked around—(was alone) slapped my face hard then drove on—went to sleep again and drove off the road at 55 M.p.H! Nothing smashed but blew a tire— Stayed awake then until reached Miami at 1.30. A.M. Have the book going well— So far like it fine— Bumby arrives day after tomorrow on the Isle De France and I bring him down the next day—[2] My sister Sunny—Pauline and Pat are well— Key West is fine— We fished out in the Gulf stream Sunday and caught 3 Kingfish (lost a sail fish (I was going to send you his outer boards) caught ½ doz barracudas—a Bonita—1 grouper—1 Spanish Mackerel— Day was lovely— Wish you'd come down later on—

Jinny sails from N.Y about Jan 5th to go to Suisse and ski— She wants to see you and would come up for a day—if you want her to come write her to Piggott— She is very fond of youse— She and Pauline and I went duck shooting and got 8— We got 6—they got 2 alone the day before[.][3] It was too early— Sometimes they come in flocks to the blind so that the water is covered— There are 100s of thousands of quail and the country is lovely in the fall— Some fall—the one after next youse come down for 10 days and we will have the finest shooting in America plus all the St. Estephe and Margaux I can carry from Chicago— Have it stored there— Love to Ada and Mimi who was so lovely and solid too and [*EH insertion*: (Kenny and)] old Mac

Pappy.

I think maybe we are both going good— When you were afraid to show it to me, I knew that was a good sign— That's the way it is with the best stuff— It's a wonderful poem—

LOC, ALS; letterhead: HAVANA SPECIAL / NEW YORK–KEY WEST–HAVANA / PENNSYLVANIA RAILROAD / RICHMOND FREDERICKSBURG & POTOMAC R.R. / ATLANTIC COAST LINE RAILROAD / FLORIDA EAST COAST RAILWAY

1 *The Hamlet of A. MacLeish*, a long poem published by Houghton Mifflin in October 1928. In his reply of 14 December [1928], MacLeish would write that EH's praise meant much to him, especially since the book had received "perfunctory notices and tepid hostility" (JFK).
2 Although EH himself would arrive in New York aboard the Havana Special train the "day after tomorrow" (5 December), Hadley and Bumby would arrive in New York on the *Ile de France* on 4 December 1928.
3 Sunny recalled in her memoirs that on their long drive from Oak Park to Florida in November, she and EH stopped at Piggott "long enough to go sunrise duck hunting" (M. Miller, 117–18).

To Maxwell Perkins, 6 December 1928

NA610 19=PRR DEPOT TRENTON NJ 6 453P
MAXWELL E PERKINS=
CHARLES SCRIBNERS SONS 5 AVE AND 48 ST=
PLEASE WIRE $100 IMMEDIATELY WESTERNUNION NORTH
PHILADELPHIA STATION MY FATHER DEAD MUST GET FIRST
TRAIN CHICAGO:[1]
=ERNEST HEMINGWAY.

PUL, Cable; Western Union destination receipt stamp: 1928 Dec 6 PM 5 19

A sticker affixed to the top left corner of this telegram reads: "an Answer is expected *by* the sender of this message. Please give it to the messenger or telephone it to . . .. WESTERN UNION."

1 EH and Bumby boarded the Havana Special on 6 December at 3:20 p.m. in New York City, bound for Key West. When the train stopped at Trenton, New Jersey, EH received a relayed cable that his sister Carol had sent from Oak Park saying "FATHER DIED THIS MORNING ARRANGE TO STOP HERE IF POSSIBLE" (JFK). She did not mention that Clarence Hemingway had shot himself. EH left Bumby in the care of a Pullman porter to complete the journey to Key West while he himself switched trains in Philadelphia and hastened to Chicago.

To Maxwell Perkins, 6 December 1928

NB64 6=GO PHILADELPHIA PENN 6 808P

PERKINS, CHAS SCRIBNERS=

5 AVE AND 48 ST=

DISREGARD WIRE GOT MONEY FROM SCOTT=[1]

HEMINGWAY.

PUL, Cable; Western Union destination receipt stamp: 1928 DEC 6 PM 8 32

1 Realizing his cabled request for $100 might miss Perkins, at the North Philadelphia station EH tried unsuccessfully to reach Henry Strater by phone. He then contacted Fitzgerald, who personally delivered the money to him when his train arrived at the station in Philadelphia.

To Madelaine Hemingway, [7 December 1928]

MADELEINE HEMINGWAY

1100 South Street

Key West

Florida

Mother Says Disregard First letter CHEERFUL ONE SENT TONIGHT EVERYONE FINE REALLY ALL SEND LOVE Duke too[1] FUNERAL TOMMORROW[2] planning LEAVE Saturday night LOVE ERNIE

JFK, ACDS; letterhead: 600 NORTH KENILWORTH AVENUE / OAK PARK, ILLINOIS

1 Duke T. Hill, Jr. was an Oak Park beau of Sunny's. In a letter to EH of 11 August 1929, Grace would express regret that Sunny had broken off their engagement (JFK).

2 On 8 December 1928 an article in the *Oak Leaves* announced that funeral services for Clarence Hemingway would be conducted at the First Congregational Church "at 2 o'clock on Sunday afternoon by Dr. Alber" (82). However, as EH mentions in several of his letters, the funeral took place on the afternoon of Saturday, 8 December.

To McIntyre (Pullman porter), [c. 7] December 1928

McIntyre
Pullman Porter
Car E72
Havana Special for Key West
Daytona Beach

Please wire me collect IF Bumby allright
Ernest Hemingway
600 N. Kenilworth Ave.
Oak Park
    Illinois—

JFK, ACDS

Marcelline recalled that on the day of their father's funeral, EH, "almost frantic with worry," kept calling the telegraph company to see why he had received no response to his cable about Bumby. Finally the wire arrived with the Pullman porter's report, "The boy had a good night's sleep" (Sanford, 233).

To Pauline Hemingway, [7 December 1928]

Pauline Hemingway
1100 South Street
  Key West
    Florida
~~All My Love~~ Bumbys Regime IN Letter IN HIS BAG Leaving SATURDAY UNLESS WIRE ~~Best~~ ALL MY LOVE ERNEST

JFK, ACDS, letterhead: 600 North Kenilworth Avenue / Oak Park, Illinois

To Eleanor Chase, [c. 8 December 1928]

[*To*] ELEANOR CHASE
[*Street and No.*] ON BOARD THE CHIEF
[*Place*] SANTA FE TRAIN LEFT CHICAGO FOR LOS ANGELES
FRIDAY 8.15 P.M.

LEARNED AT TRAIN MY FATHER DIED THURSDAY SO DIDNT
GET BOOK BUT APPRECIATE YOU SENDING IT BEST LUCK AND
LOVE TO DOTTY[1] ERNEST HEMINGWAY
[*Sender's Permanent Address*] Ernest Hemingway 1100 South Street Key
West Fla.

JFK, ACDS; letterhead: WESTERN UNION

1 In a cable of 6 [December] 1928 addressed to EH aboard the Havana Special bound that day
for Florida, Chase wrote that she had sent a copy of her novel *Pennagan Place* (New York:
J. H. Sears, 1928) to reach him on the train. She invited him and Pauline to visit her in Palm
Beach and asked him to wire her aboard the Santa Fe Railroad Chief train leaving the next
night from Chicago (JFK). "Dotty" is Dorothy Parker, whom Chase knew through her
publishing connections.

To Maxwell Perkins, [9 December 1928]

Corinth Miss
Sunday

Dear Mr. Perkins—

Hope to be back at Key West Tuesday morning and at work on the book
again. My Father shot himself— Dont know whether it was in N.Y. papers.

I didnt see any of the papers. I was very fond of him and feel like hell
about ~~naturally~~ it. Got to Oak Park in plenty of time to handle things—
Funeral was Sat. aft—

Have everthing fixed up except they will have damned little money—
went over all that too. Realize of course that thing for me to do is not worry
but get to work—finish my book properly so I can help them out with the
proceeds. What makes me feel the worst is my father is the one I cared
about—

You dont have to write any letter of condolence to me— Thanks very much for the wire—[1] There was no immediate need for money— When I get the serial money I will try and fix them up—

For your own information (Not Scott) there are my Mother and two kids Boy 12, girl 16 still at home—$25,000 insurance—a $15,000 mortgage on the house— (House should bring 10 to 15 thousand over the mortgage but sale difficult) Various worthless land in Michigan, Florida etc. with taxes to pay on all of it. No other capital—all gone— My father carried 20–30 yr. Endowent insurance which was paid and lost in Florida. He had Angina Pectoris and Diabetes preventing him from getting any more insurance—

Sunk all his savings, my grandfather's estate etc in Florida.

Hadnt been able to sleep with pain etc—knocked him temporarily out of his head.

I have what I hope wont prove to be the grippe—so excuse such a louzy letter— Thought you might be worrying so wanted to give you the dope—

Yours always,

[*signature has been cut out*]

PUL, AL; letterhead: Illinois Central System

1 In response to EH's cable of 6 December, Perkins sent a cable to him in Oak Park with the message "Terribly sorry. Will gladly wire any money you want" (6 December 1928, PUL).

To F. Scott Fitzgerald, [c. 9 December 1928]

Dear Scott— You were damned good and also bloody effective to get me that money—

I had like a fool only 35–40 bucks with me after Xmas shopping—plenty for food and tips enroute to Key West—

My Father shot himself as I suppose you may have read in the papers.[1]

Will send you the $100 as soon as I reach Key West—or have Max Perkins send it—

Thanks again like hell for your werry admirable <u>performance</u> as we say in the automotive game.

I was fond as hell of my father and feel too punk—also sick etc.—to write a letter but wanted to thank you—

Best to Zelda and Scotty—

yrs always

Ernest.

PUL, ALS; letterhead: Illinois Central System

1 The *Chicago Tribune* reported Clarence Hemingway's suicide the following day, noting, "The weapon he used was a .32 caliber pistol that his father, Anson T. Hemingway, had carried while commanding troops in the civil war" ("Dr. Hemingway, Writer's Father, Ends Own Life," 4). His photograph was featured in the back page photo section with the caption "Physician Suicide" and a page reference to the story. A short report, "Author's Father A Suicide," also appeared on the front page of the *New York Evening Post* (7 December 1928).

To Mary Pfeiffer, 13 December [1928]

Thursday Dec 13

Dear Mother Pfeiffer—

What you want to hear about no doubt is Pat—who is very fine and happy and seems to have a lot of color this morning. I think he is starting some teeth because—he seems a little like it. The truth is that I can't write a letter— I was planning to write you and Mr. Pfeiffer on the way back from N.Y. but instead had the trip to Chicago etc/. I was awfully fond of my father —and still feel very badly about it all and not able to get it out of my mind and my book into my mind) also got the grippe and you know how clearly that makes you think—a certain amount of headwork must be done with the nose because when mine is stopped up the head doesn't work at all. Pauline probably wrote you all about everything but I wanted to send just a line to tell you that I want to write and I will write—but just now I feel so very bad that I can't write a letter. As soon as things get going, tell Mr/ Pfeiffer, I'll be writing him. Hope everything is fine and the cotton o/k/.

Much love to you and to Jinny, Tell her Bumby is fine and sends her his love.

Ernest

PS.

I fixed the practical side of things up in Chicago as well as I could—got it organized. And as soon as I get this book done and some more from Scribners will be able to do something more. Also got them pretty well cheered up but couldn't cheer my self up after I went away. My father had been having much pain and hadN't been able to sleep and the poison of all that knocked him out of his head. I wrote him a long letter on the train Monday night enroute to N.Y. and mailed it from Jacksonville—telling him not to worry but to keep his courage up and especially not to worry about finances because I could always raise cash from Scribners and would see that he had nothing to worry about etc/ and it came to the house on Thursday 20 minutes after he had gone upstairs and shot himself.

It was from that letter that they found what train I was leaving on and wired me on board the train. He was going through that time of a man's life when things are liable to seem the very blackest and most out of proportion too. Anyway I must stop now and get to work. Bumby goes to kindergarten in the mornings— We have a nigger that does the housework and one that comes at 3 o'clock to take out Pat in his carriage and Bumby—but at that Sunny and Pauline are busy all the time.

The P.S. seems longer than the letter—

Please give my best to Mr. Pfeiffer and greetings from Pat— Tell him I drove from Piggott to Miami in three days—going via Memphis—Corinth, Bermingham—Montgomery, Tallahassee, Jacksonville—Miami— Drove 527 miles the last day from Tallahassee to Miami 440 the day before. Wonderful road all that last day— St. Augustine was about the prettiest place along that coast— West Palm Beach looked like the devastated regions in France right after the war—[1] Miami very nice—but a poor copy of Havana. You might like to winter there [*EH drew arrow pointing to* "Havana"].

PUL, TLS with autograph postscript; postmark: KEY WEST / FLA., DEC 13 / 4 PM / 1928

1 On 16 September 1928 the Okeechobee hurricane hit the Florida coast near West Palm Beach, devastating the area and killing an estimated 1,770–2,300 people.

To Grace Hall Hemingway, Leicester Hemingway, and Carol Hemingway, 19 December [1928]

December 19

Dear Mother Les and Deef)—[1]

Merry Christmas from the old Steen and all his family. We are thinking of you and hope you are all in splendid shape and going well.

If Marce and Sterling [Sanford] are there wish them Merry Christmas from us too. I haven't sent them any presents because there is nothing here to send and I don't want to insult them with a check but know you won't mind because I never was a shopper anyway. Have had the grippe and a filthy throat since leaving Chicago but worked every day and by the time you get this will doubtless be healthy. Sun [Sunny] is O.K. now too. Pat, Bumby and Pauline flourishing.

Best love and again wish you as merry a Christmas as I know Dad would have wanted you and us all to have.

Best love to everybody,

Ernie.

UT, TLS; postmark: KEYWEST / FLA., DEC19: / 1928

1 One of Carol's nicknames; as Sunny recalled, "Carol called herself Dee, then it got to be Deefish, then Beefish, until finally Beefy seemed like her real name" (M. Miller, 57).

To Henry Strater, 22 December [1928]

Dear Mike— Thanks for the letter. I was sorry to bother you that night but was on the train when I got the wire and had to get off at North Philadelphia and didn't have enough jack for a ticket to Chicago. They wouldn't cash me a check but would let somebody deposit the dough at any Penn. Station.[1] Finally got it from Scott who came into the Central Station at Philly with the dough six minutes before the train left. No use writing about my father that is for me to—but appreciate your letter like hell. Old Hem the writer at present engaged in writing—this book [*FTA*] has taken more on the button that Battling Nelson and Stanley Yokum combined[2] so I would esteem it a favor from you, Mr. Strater—(being a gent of whom I am very fond) not to shoot yourself—nor have any cesearian operations nor anything of that sort until old Hem the writer has finished this book/. Also don't lose all your money. I warn you until this book is finished I cannot positivcly take on any more people to support.

Also don't forget you are coming down here and bring your out board motor with you—you is collective and means your wife Maggie or Magi (Three Wisemen) Strater. The Casa Marina opens the first. It's only two blocks from us.[3] Swimming swell now.

I have only been out twice but we butchered them. The Gulf Stream is as fine as ever. The temperature is 78 today—Saturday Dec. 22. Out where we can go on trips there are big flocks of curlew and eskimo plover and all sorts of shore birds. I bought a harpoon gun—to fire from the shoulder—at Abercrimbie and Fitch's.[4] Saw four big sailfish last time out and hooked one and got him to the boat. Also have purchsed some genuine made in Swiss Absinthe on which I can get COCKEYED in two drinks. Have two barrels of blue rocks.[5] Ought to be through the book by the first week in Feb. Don't bring anybody but your wife and members of your family with you. Love to Maggie from us all. Bumby in splendid shape. He caught three barracudas trolling with a hand line.

Yrs/ always

HEM

PUL, TL with typewritten signature

1 In a letter to EH of 8 December [1928], Strater wrote, "Sorry I was out when you needed me worst" (JFK).

2 Battling Nelson (né Oscar Mattheus Nielson, 1882–1954), Danish-born American boxer who twice held world lightweight championships; he retired from the ring in 1920. Stanley "Kid" Yoakum (b. 1890), lightweight from Hartford, Connecticut, who fought between 1910 and 1925.

3 The Casa Marina, a luxurious beachfront hotel that opened in 1920 on the south shore of Key West. It was conceived as a destination resort by Henry Flagler (1830–1913), owner of the Florida East Coast Railway and its Over Sea Railroad extension that connected Key West and the Florida mainland north to Jacksonville.

4 EH's harpoon gun was an adapted Springfield rifle he purchased earlier that month in New York City at Abercrombie and Fitch, an upscale outdoor sporting goods store founded in 1892 by David T. Abercrombie (1867–1931) and Ezra Fitch (1865–1930).

5 Blue rocks, clay pigeons used in trap shooting. The name derives from the blue rock pigeons used as targets before live bird shoots were prohibited in most states around 1900.

To Archibald MacLeish, [c. 23 December 1928]

Dear Archie—

The Bitch and Bugle review was ridiculous— I know such tripe is irritating but in this particular case remember that the Hound etc. reviewed Hills Like White Elephants as follows—another of these stories by Ernest Hemingway in which there is endless meaningless conversation interrupted only by one character asking the other to have a drink.[1]

They dont know anything kid. If you gave them pure never before published Shakespeare which no one had told them was Shakespeare they would sneer it off the boards and prove how it derived from Benet, Robinson and The Embattled Humanists.[2]

Your poem is a damned wonderful poem and completely yours— It needs no Hamlet—no more than Ulysses needed that horse shit Odyssey frame work— But the frame work doesnt hurt it and if it pleases you fine— Just as the Odyssey pleases Joyce[3]—and considering and realizing and seeing what is supposed to be criticism—I think there could be no better sign than the way the poem is being received.

You know what I think of Kirstein— I told you and Hester Pickman that night in Boston— It isnt just that his magazine disliked a piece of mine— It was that they failed utterly to grasp or understand or appreciate a good piece—[4] They do not know anything— When people know nothing and cannot learn— Education is only a handicap— It only makes them suspicious—

Kirstein has youth, the freshness of Youth and money— He has no intelligence. He is a dull boy—a very very very dull boy— The more educated a dull person becomes the worse they are— The only thing is we should be snotty to them rather than friendly to keep them in their place. Valery is 75% poetry and intelligence and 25% snot.[5] You have to snot them probably. I havent tried it but may take it up.

Now I got to get to work— You wrote a swell letter—you were right about what I shouldnt do—[6] Am keeping my mind on my work but what socks on the jaw this book has taken! All this talk about how different the Elizabethan age was gives me the shits— I see very little difference— V. Woolf etc.

see more because they do not see what goes on now— I see one age going on all the time— But it doesnt go on in Bloomsbury— I may be wrong of course—[7]

Ernest.

LOC, ALS

1 "Am Not Prince Hamlet Nor Was Meant To Be," a negative review by R. P. Blackmur (1904–1965) of *The Hamlet of A. MacLeish*, appeared in the January–March 1929 issue of *Hound & Horn: A Harvard Miscellany* (167–69). MacLeish had sent EH a copy of the review with his letter of [17 December 1928] (JFK). EH paraphrases the unsigned critique of "Hills Like White Elephants" that had appeared in the first number of *Hound & Horn* (1927): "In the August number [of *transition*] there is one of those stories by Hemingway in which the male character asks the female character several times if she won't have another drink. The latter usually accepts" (72).

2 EH may be referring to either William Rose Benét or Stephen Vincent Benét and to American poet Edwin Arlington Robinson (1869–1935), who had received Pulitzer Prizes in 1921, 1924, and 1927. *Hound & Horn* was sympathetic to New Humanism, a conservative school of criticism developed in the early twentieth century by Irving Babbitt (1865–1933) and Paul Elmer More (1864–1937) that emphasized the moral significance of literature. EH would parody the movement in "A Natural History of the Dead" (*DIA* and *WTN*).

3 Joyce's *Ulysses* takes its structure from Homer's *Odyssey*.

4 Lincoln Kirstein (1907–1996) founded the literary magazine *Hound & Horn* in 1927 with Varian Fry (1907–1967) while both were attending Harvard University. Hester Marion Pickman (née Chanler, 1893–1989) and her husband, Edward Motley Pickman (c. 1887–1959), were members of the Boston elite and good friends of the MacLeishes.

5 Paul Valéry (1871–1945), French Symbolist poet and essayist whom EH had met at Beach's Shakespeare and Company. Valéry had been elected to the Académie française in 1925 and had recently published *Poésie: Essais sur la poétique et le poète* (1928).

6 After learning of Clarence Hemingway's suicide, MacLeish wrote, "You must not let your mind work over and over the way it happened. I know how your mind works round and round your pain like a dog in cover going over and over the same track and what a torment it is to you. But now you must not" (14 December [1928], JFK).

7 EH may be referring to Virginia Woolf's "The Elizabethan Lumber Room" (*Common Reader*, 1st series, London: Hogarth Press, 1925).

To Grace Hall Hemingway and Family, 24 December 1928

C88 5 =KEYWEST FLO 24 1153A

MRS C E HEMINGWAY AND FAMILY=

600 NORTH KENILWORTH AVE OAKPARK ILL=

MERRY CHRISTMAS AND MUCH LOVE=
ERNIE SUNNY PAULINE PAT AND BUMBY.

UT, Cable; Western Union destination receipt stamp: 1928 DEC 24 AM 11 19

To Marcelline Hemingway and Sterling Sanford, 24 December 1928

MZA106 6 NM GTG=KEYWEST FLO 24
MR AND MRS STERLING SANFORD=
600 NORTH KENILWORTH AVE OAKPARK ILL=
VERY MERRY CHRISTMAS TO YOU ALL=
ERNEST PAULINE SUNNY BUMBY AND PAT.

James Sanford, Cable; Western Union destination receipt stamp: 1928 DEC 24 PM 5 15

To Mary and Paul Pfeiffer, 4 January 1929

January 4, 1929.

Dear Mother Pfeiffer and Patrick's Grandfather:

You ought to have a lot of letters now that Jinny is gone and all your children and grand children away. It is not so easy to write when we do not know where you are going to be but I must write now to thank you for the fine Christmas present. It was a grand present and I certainly appreciate it.

Everything goes finely here. Pat has gotten his second tooth through today. They are both on the lower jaw in the middle. He is very happy and reasonable and good and inherits from his mother the ability to let it be known if he is mistreated. Treated well he is splendid. So I will try and treat them both well.

I've tried to get some pictures of him but the trouble is to get him in the light and not have his face squint up—and the other trouble is to get him when his face has no mosquito bites of any sort. If he has a mosquito bite it is as prominent as a mountain would be on a relief map of Florida. But I can promise you he looks exactly the same excapt that he has the beginning of the teeth that will eventually complete his smile.

I have gone over my book entirely in pencil and have twelve chapters of it all finished and typed. That is a little over a third. It ought to be done by the end of the month. As I've read over some of the chapters twelve or more times am at the state when I wish it was much much better and yet can't get it any better.

We wrote Jinny letters to the boat and sent her and Catherine a wire yesterday.[1] Had a letter from her from Pittsburg on her way east.

I can't thank Patrick's Grandfather enough for all the forwarding and expressing of things down here. You certainly have done many things for us and looked after us wonderfully.

You, Mother Pfeiffer, haven't sounded very cheerful in some letters lately but you musn't be that way because of everyone going away because you will have a hard time to keep us away from Piggott and your grandson Pat ought to be even better when he come again. When we leave here I am am going to grease up all our guns and box them and ship them to Piggott to store as hostages until we come back. We won't be there next fall but we will the fall after in time for the quail and duck hunting. So because I didn't shoot any out of season don't let any body else but Karl [Pfeiffer] shoot them until we come back and we can shoot without breaking any laws.

Bumby was crazy about his accordion and can play what we hope some day will be pieces on it.

This letter had better stop because everyone is going to bed and the typewriter is noisy.

Best love to you all and we hope you find the desert you are looking for for the winter. Waldo says North Africa is a fine place. He lived there, near Tunis, for a couple of years I think. There are fine trips you can take back in the country. Morrocco is a fine country. Waldo and Dos Passos both thought it was wonderful. It's not hard to get to. The Compagnie Generale Transatlantique (French Line) have all the dope on it.[2]

Let us know what you are going to do. I wish we were going to see you. If you go to N. Africa may be we will in the Spring. Thank you again for the wonderful Christmas—we still eat the cake.

Yours always,

Ernest.

PUL, TL/ALS; postmark: KEY WEST / FLA., JAN 4 / 6 PM / 1929

1 Jinny Pfeiffer returned to Europe in early January. Katherine Coffin (1903–1977) was Pauline and Virginia's cousin and a high school teacher in Carroll, Iowa. The *Waterloo Evening Courier* reported on 17 December 1928 that "Miss Catherine Coffin, daughter of Mr. and Mrs. Charles A. Coffin, Cedar Falls, will sail on Jan. 7 from New York for a six months' tour of Europe," the school board having granted her a leave of absence for the remainder of the year. It reported, too, that in France she would meet her cousin, Miss Virginia Pfeiffer ("Will Tour Europe," 16).
2 The Compagnie Générale Transatlantique, whose passenger liners served in Europe, the Americas, the Middle East and North Africa.

To Waldo Peirce, 4 January 1929

Jan 4 1929—

Where the hell are you kid? I've waited to hear before shooting a letter but might as well write to Bangor. Everything is bloody fine here. My book one third entirely finished—been over it all in pencil—have twelve chapters typed. Should be done by the end of Jan.

My old man shot himself as you may have read in the paper[.] Hell of a lonely way to die. Combination of losing all his money, not being able to sleep, finding he had diabetes and the good old pain of Angina pectoris. Poor old boy.

On the other hand we shoot lots of snipe here. They are bloody fine to eat. Got 12 yesterday—twenty a couple of days before—fifteen a couple of days before that.

Everything is the same here and damned lovely place too. I have been bait casting with those spoons you gave me and the light steel rod and good old bait casting reel. Got sixteen jacks casting from the breakwater by the old fort.[1] They are damned exciting that way. Also used the light rods out on the reef and have caught spanish mackerel, and barracudas.

Went out Sunday and Charles caught a 8 and half foot sailfish. A good deal heavier than mine of last year. Crawfish and stone crab season open—also fresh shrimps. We live high. Bumby caught five jacks. I cast out and let him reel in and hook them. There have been big schools in shore. Out on the reef it is alive with fish) big amberjacks, Kingfish, barracudas. Kingfish are the classiest to catch. Fast as trout and great jumpers and runners in on you.

Am getting a sewed in ground cloth, bobbinet window, insect proof explorer model tent to camp at Marquesas with. It out to be the works. We could get a couple maybe and it would be classy. They are the sort used in the tropics and are guaranteed sandfly proof. There are lots of Kingfish and mackerel in that channel between Marqueasa and Boca Grande.[2]

Charles [Thompson] and Bra send you there best.[3] Also Pauline and Bumby. We have your trout and landlocked salmon picture on the wall in the dining room. It is a lovely picture and a really swell one. I like it better every day and liked it like hell to start with.

Write me the dope and when we will see you. Have gotten some of the old swiss pre-war export Pernod that makes me cockeyed in two drinks.[4]

Have a harpoon gun too—old springfield carbine 45–70—shooting a toggle dart—

Weather fine and water good for swimming.

Su amigo

Ernesto.

Colby, TLS

1 Fort Zachary Taylor, located at the end of Southard Street in Key West. Named after Zachary Taylor (1784–1850), a former U.S. Army general who served as twelfth president of the United States from March 1849 until his death in July 1850, the fort was strategically important during the U.S. Civil War.
2 The Boca Grande channel runs from the Gulf of Mexico to the Florida Straits, separating Boca Grande Key (approximately 12 miles west of Key West), and the Marquesas Keys, about 7 miles farther west.
3 Edward "Bra" Saunders (1876–1949), a charter boat captain and fishing guide in Key West who befriended EH in the spring of 1928.
4 Pernod absinthe was produced by distilleries founded by Henry-Louis Pernod in Couvet, Switzerland, and Pontarlier, France, around the turn of the nineteenth century. Its potency and reputedly dangerous mind-altering properties attributed to the wormwood it contained led Switzerland to outlaw production of absinthe in 1910, followed by bans in the United States in 1912 and in France in 1915. In the 1920s the firm of Pernod Fils created a wormwood-free anise spirit, also known as "Pernod."

To John Dos Passos, [4 January 1929]

Drama Heil you poor bastard!

Well kid how does it feel to be back? Back to the drama? Drama my ass. The last letter we had from you was from Warsaw—home of the Pans. Dostoevsky had the dope on those babies. By now you ought to be back. As soon as the drama has you on your ass or as you get the drama visa versa come down here.[1]

We are much poorer than when you were here before [b]ut have an entire house and are living exclusively on fish and game. It is the crawfish, stone crab and fresh shrimp season also snipe. Shot 12 yesterday! 20 day before yesterday and fifteen two days before that. Every other day we shoot snipe for the day after. My old man shot himself on the other hand (not in the other hand. In the head) as you may have read in the paper. I have my bloody book all gone over in pencil and one third typed. Should be finished by the end of Jan. But any time you want to come down is a good time. Am getting a tent with a sewed in ground cloth against the mosquitoes etc. and we will camp at Marquesas. There is good shooting there (Bra holds out as a great advantage that you can shoot them off the nests there and they can't stir) and swell mixed Harpooning and fine fishing in the gulf. Have got 2 bottles of the real old Swiss Pernod that will make you think you are Philip Barry or Kosciusko.[2] The Marquesas are in the form of an Atoll or atol with channels inside and a fine sand beach. That's where we got the big tarpon.

There's nobody down here. I got three of those telescoping steel rods and bait casting reels and have only broke one. The fish are 90 times as plentiful as last spring. When the last Norther blew a school of jacks damn near a mile long came into the harbor and sub-base and fishing off the breakwater by the old fort—casting out spoons with the steel rods we caught 75 one morning. Bumby got five. They broke my line I don't know how many times milling around when one would be hooked—twenty or thirty of them would fight for the spoon when you cast out.

Have been working so hard that have only been fishing out in the boat on Sundays— Last Sunday Charles Thompson caught an 8ft/ 6inch sailfish—a bastard. We cut him up and eat him tonight. We got some big amberjacks and groupers and lots of spanish mackerel. The Gulfstream is wonderful now it's as full of fish as the old passenger pigeon or buffalo days.[3]

We live cheap as hell except for buying liquor which hasn't increased in price any. Fundador, bacardi, rioja alto, cinco perlas, Hay todo senores.[4]

What do you think of Horschitz. By god I couldn't have gotten a better translator She may be wrong but she's always Horschitz.[5]

If you want to work come on down and work at the overseas. We have a jig cook and fine meals. Pauline sends her love and says to come as soon as you can. I want like hell to see you. Stay a long while. You can work as well at the Overseas as any place.[6] It's cheaper here than anywhere and as long as the snipe hold out we will have meat twice a week anyway. I am due to take a rest anyway. Have been working like a sourd.[7] Never miss a snipe. Cant afford to. I figure that at 4 cents apiece (the price of shells) they are a good buy. We are here until the end of March then go to Paris. Kids are healthy.

Write me the dope.

Yours always,

Hem

Address

Box 323

Keywest.

UVA, TLS

1 *Heil*: hail, a German salute. Dos Passos, recently returned from his travels in Europe and the Soviet Union, was working on his play *Airways, Inc.*, which would be staged 19 February–17 March 1929 by the New Playwrights of New York during the theater's final season. Dos Passos had written to EH from Warsaw that he was returning to New York, "to take my annual licking at the hands of the American Drama." Warsaw seemed to him "a horrible dump" that made him realize "how swell things are in Russia" by comparison ([24 December 1928], JFK). *Pan*: term for a Polish nobleman. Dostoevsky's *The Brothers Karamazov* features two Polish noblemen who are card sharks and con men.

2 Thaddeus Kosciuszko (né Andrzej Tadeusz Bonawentura Kościuszko, 1746–1817), a Polish-born engineer and military hero in Poland, Belarus, and Lithuania. He left Poland for America in 1776 and established an honorable reputation for himself as an engineer in the Continental Army during the American Revolution.

3 Both the passenger pigeon and the American buffalo once existed in abundance in North America. Passenger pigeons became extinct by the early 1900s. Of an estimated 30 to 60 million buffalo in the early nineteenth century, fewer than 1,000 remained by 1899, and only strong conservation efforts saved the species.

4 Brands of Spanish brandy and Cuban rum, a variety of Spanish wine (Rioja Alta), and Cinco Perlas, a brand of sherry from southern Spain. EH likely means to say in Spanish, "Hay de todo, señores": "There is everything, gentlemen."

5 Annemarie Horschitz, later Horschitz-Holt (née Rosenthal, 1899–1970), translated more than twenty of EH's books into German, starting with *Fiesta* (*SAR*) in 1928.

6 The Over Sea Hotel at 917 Fleming Street in Key West.
7 *Comme un sourd*: like one possessed (idiomatic French).

To Henry Strater, [4 January 1929]

Dear Mike—

Didn't you say you had an outboard motor and could or would have it shipped down here? There is a distinction between them two words and if it isn't practical to—don't. But it would be fine as hell to have for all sorts of trips around the keys and up in the channels and trolling in the harbor and sub-base.[1]

A school of jacks (Horse Crevalle) damned fine eating and fighting fish—the school nearly a mile long came in with the last norther. I bait casted with light rod and spoon hook and the first five I hooked the others broke the line by milling around and raising such hell. With a longer copper leader and a spoon and same light rig landed sixteen in a couple of hours fishing off the breakwater. Four of us caught 75. They weighed up to twenty pounds. They've been fooling around just outside for wekks and with an outboard would be cinch to get into.

I Have a square sterned skiff it would go on and could get a bigger one. When are you men coming down? The book is a little over a third done. Have been all over it once in pencil and have twelve chapters all complete-ed on the machine. Should be finished by the end of this month. Haven't been fishing out in the gulf stream except on Sundays but last Sunday the gulf was as full of fish as America in the old passenger pigeon or buffalo days. We got a 8and a half foot sailfish—big amberjacks, yellow jacks, black groupers, barracudas, and a bunch of spanish mackerel. I got one ten pound mackerel which is a bloody big mackerel on a fly rod.

Have a harpoon gun for you to use—to fire from the shoulder—a springfield 45–70——accurate range of the toggle dart 35 feet. Lots of porpoises come right in the sub base.

I don't know whether it would be practical for you to send down the outboard but it would be swell to have. I will pay Express Collect—Address 1100 South Street—

Also have had fine shooting. Got 12 snipe yesterday——twenty a couple of days beforev—fifteen two days before that. Go out in the afternoon in the car when I'm through work.

Swimming is swell. There are still some mosquitoes but hope this present Norther will take them out. The Casa Marina is open. I'm getting a sewed in ground floor 9 by 9 7 feet high in front tapering to 2 high in back insect proof tent to camp out at Marquesas in. We could go out in a big boat with all our outfit—fix up a camp on the beach (there is a swell sand beach) then let the big boat go back and use the outboard for harpooning and to run out to the reef with. Wonderful shooting there too. All kinds of snipe, plover, curlews, willets, etc/ The snipeare cockeyed fine eating.

Best to Maggie,
So long, Hem

PUL, TL with typewritten signature

1 Strater would reply that he certainly could send the motor, but warned, "I neglected to say that it was a racing motor. Fast as hell, & temperamental as Ezra" and not really suitable for a fishing boat (9 January 1929, JFK).

To Maxwell Perkins, 8 January [1929]

January 8—

Dear Mr. Perkins—

Have 20 chapters done and typed [*EH insertion*: must be around 30,000 words]—have been over the whole thing once in pencil and re-read it all. Going good but have been working 6–10 hours every day and will be glad to lay off and take a trip when you come down—

All you need is some old clothes and tennis shoes—better bring tennis things and racket—any sweaters you have—but we have plenty if you havent any—I must have 15—all sizes—

The Gulf stream is alive with fish now—really— It's like the old wild pigeon and Buffalo days— I've fished every Sunday— We got a 8 ft 6 inch sailfish a week ago. Last Sunday day before yesterday—were out salvaging liquor from a boat that went on the reef coming from the Bahamas— Got 14 bottles of Chateau Margaux among other things— Boat had about $60,000 worth of liquor on her but everybody else was salvaging too[.] We got caught in a storm and I was afraid I might Shelley-out on you for a while.[1]

Dont let anyone bluff you out of coming down— It's the only way you can get this Mss. Anytime after next week that you want to come will be fine — I'm getting a carbon made of the Mss. Have about 15 or 20 chapters more to do. But will be glad of some company. I expected Archie MacLeish down this week but he wired he was in some sort of a jam and couldnt come.

Would you send Scott $100.[00] I borrowed from him in North Philadelphia— I didnt want to draw it till after the first of the year to hold down my last years income figure.

Have bought a fine 9 x 9 ft insect proof tent with a sewed in ground cloth so we can camp out at the Marquesas where Waldo caught the big tarpon if you want. There's lots of shooting if you like to shoot— Got 9 snipe yesterday after I knocked off work—20 a couple of days before—15 before that— They are very good with the Bordeaux— Have some pre-war absinthe too but it makes too crazy dreams so am saving it for you and Waldo.

Best wishes for the New Year—

Ernest Hemingway

PUL, ALS

1 English poet Percy Bysshe Shelley drowned when his new sailing boat, the *Don Juan*, was engulfed during a violent storm in the Gulf of Spezia off the Ligurian coast of Italy.

To Guy Hickok, 9 January 1929

January 9—1929

Dear Guy

Well Hickock I must dig out that 5 cents in stamps and send off this letter. I hear there are some pretty low temperatures in the old country and you can never tell whwn you may need an good pipe drainer.[1]

See somebody has bought the Eagle so perhaps this will find you out on what we may learn to call yourass but let us hope not.[2] I hope not because I could not take you and all your family on just at present. Maybe next year. Undoubtedly next year. Count on me for next year kid but this year my father shot himself and left me with all the rest of his family so I am very busy. But next year kid I will fix you and Mrs. Hickock and little Bobby and Andree up fine. Am now re-writing my book on the typer. Final and last stage beforevtype setting. Have gotten to chapter twentysome and am going all right. This monumental opus has covered some 6 or seven hundred pages in the longest longhand in the world. It has been in process since last February. Placed end to end it would guarantee coitus at least interruptus between practically anything you can mention.

Pauline is fine also Patrick. Also Bumby. Have a sister down here too. She is not such a success but you with your taste for circus performers and eagle visitors would like her.[3]

God be with us Hicjkock but I am pooped tonight and can't write much more. But would have written sooner kid but for my father shooting himself and one thing another) including 10,000 miles in two weeks travelling around straighteneing one bit of horseshit and another up and ever since been working like an old Eagle Correspomdent just befoe the boat leaves. So hope you will enjoy my long tale of transalpine fornication encluding the entire war in Italy and so to BED. Write me again when you get this and once I get this book done—only twelve chapters more to do—will write anyway without hearing from you

Saw Steff [Steffens] in N.Y. Waldo is coming down here in February. I am dead broke but will get passage etc/ from Scribners and arrive early in April. They are going to serialize. Ray Longs offered me twice or three times what they would pay but didn't know then how badly and how much money I needed. But anyway will tell all these people they can starve anywaysoon. Should get 15,000 from Scribners will turn a portion of it over to my relatives on the promise that they shall have a little more if they never write me. Nothing if they do.

Love from Pauline and to Mary—

Ernest

phPUL, TLS

1 In February 1928 EH returned to Paris from a skiing vacation in Gstaad to find that frozen water pipes had burst in his apartment, as noted in his letter to Hickok of [c. 5 February 1928].
2 Newspaper magnate Frank E. Gannett (1876–1957) purchased the *Brooklyn Daily Eagle* on 7 January 1929. Hickok would write to EH in a letter of 29 January [1929] that the *Eagle* had become "a link in a chain owned by a Dry named Frank Gannett, who also owns fifteen other links. I don't know yet whether it is a chain of wursts or betters" (JFK).
3 EH's sister Sunny was helping to care for Patrick and Bumby and with typing the manuscript of *FTA*. EH may be alluding to tensions between Pauline and Sunny, who recalled feeling that Pauline put her "on a servant level," and to Sunny's active social life in Key West. According to Sunny's memoirs, Pauline wrote to Grace that Sunny was "being much feted and has the town by the ears." (For Sunny's account of her stay in Key West, see M. Miller, 109–17.)

To Maxwell Perkins, 10 January [1929]

January 10—

Dear Mr. Perkins:—

After you come down here you will be able to go back and make hash out of all the 15 yr. old boys and 60 yr. old fat men the handball king can find. But seriously handball is a knack too and probably the fat man was a specialist at it as the kid was.[1] It's one of those things like punching the bag that are no criterion of Honest Worth. Anyway you come down anytime now and we will have a fine time—

My sister and Pauline are both typing on the book today and I will have 29 chapters in type by night. Have finished 413 pages of the hand written mss. I will pretty surely have it all ready for you to take back—that is if you come down. If you don't come down you wont ever get it.

I'll try and get a New Republic for the Sonnets. She always seemed to me personally like a lecherous cat but I'd hoped she would confine herself to staying in love with Shelley and thus give Bill Benet a break.[2] It is awfully tough on him— I'm glad the sonnets are good. I did not know she was dead until I saw some reference to it in the paper last week. What did she die of?

Thanks about the money.[3] I dont need any until I get the book done

Let me know when to look for you. You can get in a lot of tennis down here— There are good courts and my sister is not much good but plays a strong game and you can get a work out with her anyway. I wrote Waldo and suggested he come too— But [i]t may be too soon for him to leave Bangor—

15 naval planes came down and have scared away all the snipe— But the planes will go and we may get ~~not~~ some new snipe who will not be so highly educated as to shotgun ranges— Had 14 for dinner again last night— But they were hard to get—

The boatman we fish with thinks it is a great waste of ammunition to shoot snipe when he says he can take us to a rookery where we can shoot white herons. Right on the nests! The local ideal of the sporting life.

Yours always

Ernest Hemingway.

PUL, ALS

1 EH is responding to Perkins's letter of 9 January 1929 and his amusing account of being beaten at handball first by the instructor, then by a fifteen-year-old boy, and then by a fat man "not far from sixty" (JFK).

2 Perkins referred to the recent death of Elinor Wylie (on 16 December 1928) and recommended her "magnificent sonnets" in the *New Republic*. Wylie dedicated her poetry collection *Trivial Breath* (1928) to Percy Bysshe Shelley, and her novels *The Orphan Angel* (1926) and *Mr. Hodge and Mr. Hazard* (1928) also reflect her passion for Shelley. Wylie was known for her tumultuous love life, and Perkins confided to EH that she had planned to leave her husband, "poor Bill Benet who worshipped her" (JFK; *TOTTC*, 84–85).

3 Perkins had asked EH if he needed money "in view of all that's happened" (*TOTTC*, 85).

To Henry Strater, 11 January [1929]

Jan. 11

Dear Mr. Angelo)

I am no outboard Lindboig and if the motor is anything like EZRA you had better let Reggie keep it. I did not know it was moteur de course. I thought it was maybe a plain put-put that would throttle down to troll and shoot snipe with.[1] We had 15 again yesterday) That puts us into the second hundred but have bloody near exterminated the local product and must lay off a few days for more to come down from the north. Fine swim today. Also on Chapter 30—don't think there are more than 42 chapters all told so I'll be finished by the first. Have been working like a bastard. You can read the carbon if you want[.] The boats from the Casa Marina have been getting lots of sailfish—one has ten so far. They are the classiest fish I know. But to eat give me the snipe. A rum boat ran aground on the reef and we got 14 bottles of chateau Laffite off her—also have 12 bottles amontillado fino of the old Cinco Perlas.[2] The absinthe is half gone so you and maggie better hurry.

You can get all your fish tackle here. Charles Thompson has everything at his marine hardware store. Shells are better borught maybe. Bring a couple of boxes of No. 9 or 10 to fit your gun for snipe. The season closes Jan 31 but on the Marquesas where we will take a trip there isn't any season and we will butcher a lot to bring home and have with some of the chateau Lafitte. Bring plenty of Merry Widows)[3] You can bring a doz or so for old hem too if you wish. A regular jockstrap will keep off the barracudas. It takes the smell of blood to really arouse them.

The reason I wrote about the outboard instead of getting one was because am in very economical streak due to my old man having bumped himself off without a seed and have his large family to support thus having taken all my cash etc. and are broke but in no need of charity except in the case of motors if they were on hand.

It will be bludy fine to see you and your beautiful and sterling wife MAGGIE

Love

Hem.

PUL, TLS

This one-page letter is typewritten on the verso of what appears to be a discarded draft page from *FTA*, bearing the single typewritten sentence: "'How many have you got Etorre?' I asked."

1 In his letter to EH of 9 January 1929, Strater reported that his outboard motor, as "temperamental as Ezra," was in Ogunquit, Maine, at the garage of Mr. Jacob, known to his friends as Reggie (JFK). The Ogunquit garage was owned by Reginald F. Jacobs. *Moteur de course*: racing engine (French).
2 Château Lafite, a wine from vineyards of the Médoc region of Bordeaux dating back to the seventeenth century and acquired by Baron James Mayer de Rothschild in 1868; in the 1855

vintage rankings of the Universal Paris Exposition, it was rated a "leader among fine wines."
Amontillado fino, a fine aged Spanish sherry. Cinco Perlas (Five Pearls), a brand of sherry
produced in Southern Spain.

3 "Merry Widows" are wooden, jointed fishing lures with triple hooks.

To Waldo Peirce, [c. 11 January 1929]

Muy Illustrissimo Senor y Amigo Mio—[1]

Got your letter from Bangor the day after I wrote.[2] Come on down chico
anytime. I'm on chapter 30 of my book and have only about ten more to do.
Bra [Saunders] salvaged 45 bottles of gin off a rumboat from Bahamas that
ran aground on the Eastern Dry Rocks and has 4 saved for you.[3] He told me
to write you to come on down or he couldnt guarantee to keep it. I have 14
bottles of Chateau Laffitte and 12 of Cinco Perlas Amontillado Fino and a
bottle of real old Swiss Pernod.

Will be bloody glad to see you. The Gulf is <u>alive</u> with fish—Kingfish—
Spanish mackerel etc. Were out on Sunday looking for liquor where the
boat grounded and got in a hell of a storm. Waves went clean over Bra's
boat— Blew like a bastard. Have shot all the local snipe and want to go out
to Marquesas for some.

Archie MacLeish was due here this week but wired he couldnt come.

I am lonesome to see some of youse guys. Max Perkins is due to come
down here the last of Jan to get my Mss and stay a week. Why dont you
come down then and then stay on. We could show old Max life among the
monsters.

I dont want to drag you away from staying with your old man but am in
need of society and want you down whenever you can come.[4]—but if you
shouldnt leave until say the middle or so of Feb why dont— Dont let me kid
you out of staying if you ought to stay. But miss you like hell down here. We
leave the 27th or so of March. Old Dos will come down after his play blows
up. I want to go to Tortugas. We can have some swell trips and good sun
and swimming and, as I say, there is this vin and always Fundador.

Pauline send her love— Pat is well and husky and Bumby sure death on Jacks and Barracudas— He said I know what a son of a bitch is. It's a great big fish.

Charles and Lorine [Thompson] send their best. Also Bra

Yours always
Ernest.

Colby, ALS

1 *Muy ilustrísimo señor y amigo mío*: Most illustrious sir and friend of mine (Spanish).
2 Peirce's letter of 1 January 1929, postmarked on 2 January from Bangor, Maine (JFK), apparently had reached EH on 5 January.
3 Eastern Dry Rocks refers to a coral reef surrounded and covered by shallow water located approximately 5 miles southwest of Key West.
4 Peirce had written, "I'll have to hang around here a little—just for the old man." His father, Mellen Chamberlain Peirce (1846–1936), was a timberlands businessman and director of the Dirigo Ice Company of Bangor. Waldo expected to go to Key West in March or April.

To Guy Hickok, 14 January [1929]

Jan 14

Dear guy:—

No. (1) of these was received first. No (2) the one about 8 days delay was received <u>today</u> Jan 14. It was forwarded by the concierge.

I knew you had paid the bloody taxes so I didnt pay any attention to No. (1)—

Any way if this should be paid will you pay it with the enclosed which is designed to translate into Francs and I hope cover the taxi ou will need to go to the damned recette and perception of the XI$^{\underline{\text{lin}}}$ 80, rue Bonaparte, 80.[1]

I am on Chapter 34 and working like a bastard to get it (The book) done by the end of January.

If there are any francs left over buy yourself a drink of Golden Horse and think of old Hem.[2]

I hope this will not be as hard or difficult as pipe unfreezing— Remember I tried to save you all the trouble possible by draining the heating system. I certainly appreciate like hell you paying this.

Best to Mary.

Pauline sends her love.

Ernest

phPUL, ALS

1 *Perception de recettes fiscales*: office of revenue collection (French). EH enclosed two tax
notices along with 65 dollars, which Hickok would exchange for 1,651 French francs and
use to pay the 1,589.13 French francs in taxes that EH owed in Paris (Hickok to EH, 29
January 1929, JFK).
2 Golden Horse, a brand of cognac produced by the Seguinot firm, founded in 1890 in the
Vendée department of France.

To Waldo Peirce, [c. 14 January 1929]

Waldo Nievoso—

You ought to have the bludy snow by now if the Cuban papers dont lie. El
Mundo reported 24 below zero in Chicago last night.[1]

Rec'd yours and Renee's letters last night— Present my compliments to
Renee and tell her I'll write her when I get back from this trip.[2]

I understand how you'd better stay up there for quite a while.[3] When I
wrote before urging you to come down pronto thought you might be fed up
with the Banging of Bangor. But now will look for you any old time you
show— But get here by the first of March Kid if you can.

Mike Strater's coming down for 2 weeks the 1st of Feb. Havent heard
from Max. I'm on chap 34 with only about 10 more to do into type. Have
been going over the typescript up to where it leaves off. I've got a carbon and
you can read the damn thing when you come if you want.

Am going off this aft with Bra on a two day trip he's making Kingfishing
toward Tortugas—about 30 miles beyond Marquesas. Hope he strikes
them.

Shot 7 Snipe yesterday. 10 the day before. Hit 21 out of 25 clay pigeons
with the 410. Have a barrell and a half left and we will shoot them when you
come down—

Archie couldnt come because they were frozen out of their house at Conway— Heating problem didnt solve.

My best to Reneé—

Yours always

Ernest.

There are 10s of 1000s of Snipe in big flocks on the flats but they fly up out of range— Need decoys and a blind. You could lie flat and decoy behind your barbe—[4]

Wish I'd let mine grow—too late now to fool them.

Colby, ALS

1 *Nevoso*: snowy (Spanish). The Havana newspaper *El Mundo*, affiliated with the Associated Press, apparently carried reports of the record cold then sweeping the Midwest and New England.

2 In his letter to EH of 26 September 1928, Peirce described a servant who worked for his father and to whom he had taken a liking: a "little girl in old house named Rainey . . . I call her Renée and tell she is mine" (JFK). At Peirce's urging, the young woman, Ada Rainey (1909–1969), wrote EH a letter saying, "Here's hoping we see you here in Bangor this summer," signing it, "Fondly Yours, Renee." Peirce enclosed her letter with his own of 11 January [1929] (JFK).

3 Peirce wrote that he wanted to stay in Bangor "til Feb anyway—& I want to paint the old man etc—while still here—he's 81." On the night of 13 January 1929, Chicago experienced record cold temperatures, dipping from –11° to –15° Fahrenheit, the equivalent of –24° to –26° Celsius (*Chicago Tribune*, 14 January 1929, p. 1).

4 *Barbe*: beard (French).

To Archibald MacLeish, [c. 14 January 1929]

Dear Archy—

I feel like bloody hell naturally that you couldnt come. Had it all settled too—wanted to go exploring in the boat and snipe shooting and fishing and get cockeyed and have you read my book. But shit Kid we will go another time— You had a terrible break on the damned weather— I dont know about Bank accounts except that ours is bloody low.[1]

About people in Chicago[.] I have one friend Bill Horne who lives at the Whitehall—105 East Delaware Place—and he has 6 or 8 bottles—maybe it's only 3 or 4 –of Margaux and Chateaux of mine which I now see were destined by God to help one or two evenings in Glencoe.[2] So I will ask him to bring them out or you might call for them sometime when he's at home. His rooms are a good place to get a drink anyway. He can get you good Scotch if you want to have some.

The name is—William D. Horne Jr.

Whitehall Apts.

East Delaware Place

Cuban paper says its 24 below in Chicago! Get some Scotch from Horney! He has some of that Napoleon Fine in the house too I think.[3]

Horney works for Green Fulton Cunningham— They are in the telephone book.[4] The Whitehall is too. I'll write him and tell him you'll pick up the wine[.] You could go by some evening after 5 and he would put it in a suitcase for you and you drink it to us.

Must stop writing now—going on a 2 day and night trip with a boat that is going after King fish down toward Dry Tortugas— Professional King fishers. They carry Pappy as a Puller. Hope to catch 8,000 pounds. I hope not. That's too many to Pull.

The clay pigeons and trap went to Conway from Chicago by freight. They'll be there for Spring anyhow.

It's suddenly occurred to me that you might still if money or something or anything broke better come down here from Chicago. If there is any chance come just like that— You could just come in a minute— Bring Ada and leave Mimi with your mother— Come like bums and live with us like Kinks—we have such good food and wine and fine swimming you wont mind no Luxe— Ada would certainly be a fine gift to Pauline and we would go on trips. Pauline says to come like Bums dont spend any money but car fare and bring only enough for your hotel rooms and we will live like Kings—

Yours always with love to Mimi and Ada—

Pappy—

There are thousands of snipe in flocks on the flats— But hell to get in range—worked hard for 7 yesterday—

Am on chapter 34—only about ten more to do.

Or abandon all hope of money and come down here Bodily with all your establishment and live at the Casa Marina— That's what we all should have done to start with and when the bills come due say "Sir show me the door!"

LOC, ALS

1 In a letter to EH of 11 January [1929], MacLeish lamented that his finances would not permit him to travel to Key West, and he would be spending the rest of the winter in Chicago ("this ash can!"). He asked EH, "Do you know any human beings in Chicago?" (JFK; Winnick, 220–21).
2 MacLeish was a native of Glencoe, Illinois, a suburb about 18 miles north of Chicago, where he was staying at the family home, Craigie Lea, on a bluff overlooking Lake Michigan.
3 Napoleon, a premium grade of fine, well-aged cognac.
4 The Chicago office of the Green, Fulton, Cunningham Company, an advertising firm, was located at 300 North Michigan Avenue.

To Maxwell Perkins, [c. 18 January 1929]

Dear Max—

I'm sorry to have mistered you so long— Early got the habit of mistering anyone from whom I received money—on the theory of never make a friend of either a servant or an employer— But we have been friends for a long time and it is cockeyed splendid that you are coming down.[1] Anytime now is fine— Waldo cant come I'm afraid. He doesnt want to leave Bangor until the end of February— Hes really just gotten there—

Got 1500 gold marks from Rowohlt my German publishers— They published The Sun in Nov and it has had very much comment and whoopee reviews— They are bringing out Men Without in February and want to publish In Our Time in the late Spring or summer—following with the new book as soon as they can get it translated next Fall.[2] They are an industrious people and always overdo everything. They have come up from 500 to 1500 marks advance so the book must be doing something.

Laid off work yesterday and the day before and went down toward Tortugas Kingfishing for the market— We did not hit them the first day nor yesterday until on our way in at 3 o'clock—then struck them and they were absolutely wild—using two hand lines and a rod we caught over

2,000 pounds of them between 3 and 6— Filled up the cockpit of the boat— Early in the afternoon we had harpooned a big loggerhead turtle weighing about 400 pounds and later on needed his room for Kingfish and we could not lift him to get him overboard. The Kingfish sell for 6 cents a pound at the dock.

They jump high up in the air—sometimes 6 feet clear of the water and turn and come down on the spoon— I trolled only about 30 or 40 feet behind the boat—used a heavy rod and they fought clear of the water most of the time— When we were in the middle of the school you could not let the spoon go clear of the boat before they grabbed it— It took about 300 fish to make 2000 pounds—gutted—

We got in last night at ten oclock— They typed up through Chapter 34 while I was gone— Must get to work now and read the typing— Book will be finished by middle of next week. When will you be down?

Best always,
Ernest Hemingway.

PUL, ALS

1 This is the first letter in which EH addresses his editor by his first name instead of "Mr. Perkins." In a letter of 15 January 1929, Perkins wrote that he was trying to arrange to visit EH in Key West and in an autograph postscript added, "For Gods Sake un-Mister me anyhow" (Hemingway Collection of the Museum Ernest Hemingway of the Republic of Cuba in the Hemingway Collection of the John F. Kennedy Presidential Library and Museum). Perkins's postscript is not present on the carbon copy of his letter in the Scribner's archives at PUL.
2 Rowohlt had published *SAR* as *Fiesta* in 1928 and would publish *MWW* as *Männer* in October 1929 and *FTA* as *In Einem Andern Land* in 1930. Rowohlt would publish *IOT* as *In Unserer Zeit*, but not until 1932. All were translated by Annemarie Horschitz.

To Waldo Peirce, [c. 18 January 1929]

Muy borracho y bangoristo mio—[1]

Got back from the no man's land trip with Bra and founf your letter of the 16th. It will be bloody grand to have you down chico.[2] I wrote last saying come any old time later on because I thought you might think I was trying to pull you away from your duties toward the old man and Renee. Any time you come will be damned fine and the sooner the better. Had a letter from Max that he was coming but didn't say when. Mike Strater claims to be coming the first of Feb.

Weather is wonderful today—like the best of the days we had. Bring a tennis racket with you. They have good courts at the Navy Yard and we have passes and it's a good way to get up a sweat. Swimming is swell. Lots of sailfish in the gulf. Have 2 bbls. of clay pigeons. You might bring some 410 ga. shells— NO. 7and a half or 8 or 10 shot. Have 2 410 ga / guns a winchester 12 pump and a twenty ga. double bbl/ The 410 is a swell gun to shoot clay pigeons with with the hand trap as you can't throw them out of range and the shells only cost about 2.75 or 3.00 a 100. I have a 22 colt automatic with 3 magazines.

We fished at No man's land— 2hrs/ and 45 minutes run beyond Marquesas for two days—anchored at the beach where we struck all the nurse sharks for the nights. Never hit the kingfish at all. Then on our way home down the gulf we struck a big turtle) 400 pounds—hell to get in—and afterwards I was trolling with the rod and suddenly we hit the kingfish at 3 o'clock. They jump high up in the air and turn and come down on the spoon. I lost four spoons and three squids—trolled only about fifty feet behind the boat and rough-housed them in. Saw every strike. The school would swim along under the boat and you could not get a spoon out before they hit it.

They used two hand lines and I used the rod and we got 1800 pounds of them between 3 O'clock in the afternoon and six. I caught 60 some on the rod. Never was more pooped in my life. Big smashing hard fighting jumping sons of bitches. Bra sold the catch for 7 cents a pound. We wanted to throw the loggerhead overboard to make room for more kings but were too pooped and the deck too slippery to lift him.

Bra wants to sell his boat and buy one with a cabin you can stand up in and ventilation forward and bunks for four. He claims he can get 900 for his boat from a man who wants her for sponge-ing and buy this new one that is on the ways now for that—she was ordered by a rich guy who wanted her for crusing along the keys with his family and then cancelled when he found a boat at long key. Then he only needs 300 for a motor— He said if we could loan him the money for the motor I.E. $300 he'd carry us crusing for nothing whenever we wanted to go all the time we are down this spring and guarantee to repay the money next year. Put the papers of the boat in our names if we wanted. I said I could loan him 100 and didn't know about you. You might be broke. Told him if I got enough dough from Scribners for serializing [*FTA*] might be able to let him take the whole three. He is good pay all right Charles [Thompson] says but hasn't been making any money on parties this year because his boat is too old, slow, hasn't enough cabin room and isn't chic. I would as soon loan Bra 100 as a lot of the shites that I've loaned that to around the quarter. He has good weather today and ought to clean up on the Kingfish again. By god they are exciting to catch. You remember the one we got that day out at mascot shoals? All like that and some that would weigh 40 to 60 pounds. Marqueas looked lovely. Didn't have any mosquitoes or sandflies sleeping on the boat. I didn't see any on shore either. Anyway have that new fine tent with floor cloth. Don't think I am letting you in for any money bleeding or attacks on the Purse capital Chico. I told Bra there was a good chance that you might be dead broke.

I think though that between us and the Scribners we ought to be able to raise the trois cent[3]—will simply add it to the price of serilization. Hope the hell they take this great pistermass for serialization. Otherwise we will swim the atlantic and make a bum our of Ederle and Lindboig combined.[4] Max said in N.Y. he was sure they would. But you never can tell how they feel about a new one with all the words and one thing and another. Am bloody anxious for you to read it to tell me what the hell you think. Will have a carbon for you. You can spot shite as far as the average buzzard and can tell me if you detect it and will remove same.

Anyway Chico come as soon as you can with your conscience— I don't want you to get remorse that you didn't stay. But you'll be more welcome than I can say. (one sentence on top of anothr[5] Why don't you start painting your father right away and then come down when you get him well done. Certainly he can be no worse to paint than the great Sweeney who poses with a brush in his hand ready to aid the artist at any time by helpful criticisms.[6]

Charles sends his best. Also his wife and Bra. Bra has 4 bottles of gin for you. I am holding some of the absinthe and have 8 bottles of bordeaux—and 8 of Xeres seco still[7]—started with 14 of one and 12 of the other.

Must lay off now and get to work.

Give my very very best to Renee. She wrote me a fine letter and I will write her as soon as I get going.[8] Am driving on the book to have it done by the middle of next week. Must go over the typing they did while I was gone. Love from Pauline. Best always.

Ernesto

Colby, TLS

1 *Muy borracho*: very drunk (Spanish). EH's invented word "bangoristo" is a play on Peirce's residence in Bangor.
2 After returning from a two-day fishing trip with Bra Saunders beyond the Marquesas Islands, EH read the letter of 16 January that Peirce wrote saying he expected to visit EH in Key West "the first part of Feb" (JFK).
3 Three hundred (French).
4 American swimmer Gertrude Ederle (1905–2003) who, in 1926, became the first woman to swim the English Channel.
5 As EH notes, he had typed the preceding sentence over the first portion of the following one, although both are legible.
6 Referring to Charles Sweeny in a letter to Maxwell Perkins years later, EH would write, "Ask Waldo about the time he was painting Charley's portrait and Charley finally started painting it himself. Boy I'd like to have that confidence" ([c. 4 or 11 February 1940]; *SL*, 502).
7 *Xeres seco* (or *jerez seco*): dry sherry (Spanish).
8 A reference to Renée's letter of 11 January 1929, enclosed with Peirce's of the same date. Renée had asked about the weather and fishing, and noted the recent loss of Peirce's "boyish form since he has been eating my pies . . . his trousers all come within an inch or two from meeting" (JFK).

To Maxwell Perkins, [22 January 1929]

Tuesday.

Dear Max—

Finished the book [*FTA*] today— The weather is fine—76°— So come on down— Maybe I'll get a letter today or tomorrow from you— Too pooped to write more— But the sooner you come down the better—

yours always,
Hemingway

The Casa Marina would be a good place to stay maybe— There are very few people there— The Concha is comfortable but in center of town and the Overseas primitive cuban and old fashioned.[1] You dont need to decide where you stay till you look them all over— You can send your mail care of me. It will be fine to see you. Best regards to Wallace Meyer.

PUL, ALS

1 La Concha, a seven-story hotel that opened in 1926 at 430 Duval Street, the highest building on the island. The Over Sea, a three-story wood-frame hotel with a hundred rooms, charged a dollar a day and was located at 917 Fleming Street, a mile from where EH was living. On 25 January Perkins would respond, "I'll take your decision on hotels. I think it would be much like mine. I would prefer one where there aren't many people" (PUL).

To Maxwell Perkins, 23 January 1929

ND46 11=KEYWEST FLO 23 404P
MAXWELL E PERKINS, CHARLES CRIBENS SONS=
                    5 AVE AT 48 ST=
TAKE WHATEVER CAN GET FINISHED BOOK YESTERDAY
SPLENDID TO SEE YOU=
        HEMINGWAY.

PUL, Cable; Western Union destination receipt stamp: *Received at 41 East 46th Street, New York* / 1929 JAN 23 PM 4 41

Earlier that day, Perkins had sent EH a cable stating: "Fox Film considering KILLERS for two reel movietone. Might get twenty-five hundred more likely two thousand. Wire decision" (23 January 1929, PUL). Nothing would come of this offer.

To Charles Scott, 23 January 1929

Key West Florida
Jan 23, 1929

Dear Mr. Scott—

I remember receiving the other photograph you sent and autographing it and sending it back. I believed I recalled having a note of acknowlegement from you— But my memory may have betrayed me.

In any event I am very honored to sign this.[1] I have just finished a long novel that I have been working on since last February— It should be out next fall— Perhaps appearing as a serial in Scribners in the meantime.

Thank you for sending me the picture—

With best regards
Yours very truly
Ernest Hemingway.

UVA, ALS

1 The portrait photograph of himself in a fedora and overcoat. Scribner's used the photo on the rear jacket of *SAR* beginning with the seventh printing in March 1927.

To Russell Spencer, 23 January 1929

[*Excerpt as published in Parke-Bernet Galleries catalog:*]
"... Maxwell Perkins who pretty well runs the editorial end of Scribners, is coming down here next week to get the MSS. of my book I've just finished ..."

Parke-Bernet Galleries catalog, sale of Frank J. Hogan Library, New York, 23–24 January 1945, lot 248, ALS

According to the catalog description, this letter, with the addressed envelope, was laid in a copy of *A Farewell to Arms* ("FIRST EDITION. ONE OF 510 COPIES, SIGNED BY THE AUTHOR. FIRST ISSUE, without the notice regarding the characters in the book"). The 1¼-page letter to Russell Spencer, sent from Key West, Florida, "apparently refers to the present work." The catalog listing is reproduced in facsimile in *Hemingway at Auction*, compiled by Matthew J. Bruccoli and C. E. Frazer Clark Jr. (Detroit: Gale Research Company, 1973), 23. The facsimile includes a handwritten marginal notation indicating that the book and letter together sold for $27.50.

To Henry Strater, [23 January 1929]

Dear Mike—

Forgot to say to bring your tennis rackets! Bring your bathing suits too. Swell weather and fishing wonderful now— Finished my book yesterday.

The Casa Marina is probably the place for you men. I will go over and ask them about rates if you want or you can look at all the hostilleries when you come down— Think the Casa Marina is around 8 seeds a day American plan with weekly rates.

Look forward to seeing you. Write when you will be down—

Best always—

Hem

Sharkey must K.O. Christner if he is to draw at Miami. Hope he wades in and K.O. Christner hangs one on him for a row of open cess pools. Such things have been done. Sharkey may fight a cautious slop match. They all are doing everything for dear old Tex. You hurry and come down here for Dear old Tex.[1]

Hem

PUL, ALS; postmark: KEY WEST / FLA, JAN 24 / 12 [*illegible*] M / 1929

1 Famed boxing promoter Tex Rickard had died 6 January 1929 from complications following surgery for appendicitis. Jack Sharkey would defeat Meyer Wilson "K.O." Christner
(1896–1979) in a heavyweight fight by decision on 25 January in New York City. Sharkey
would go on to win by decision against Young Stribling on 27 February 1929 before a crowd
of 35,000 at Flamingo Park in Miami Beach.

To Josephine Ketcham Piercy, [c. after 23 January 1929]

Dear Miss Piercy:

I do not know any valuable advice to give your pupils about writing
except to continue.[1] I do not know of anyone who wrote prose well to start
with; although there is a sort of completely articulate writing that is done by,
usually, very young English writers. I should think that the danger of this
would be that the young writer puts everything he or she knows into the
first book and because he or she is able to express ~~themselves~~ it all the book,
with the freshness of youth, is a success—. The young writer then becomes a
professional writer and continues to write books although he or she never
sees or learns anything moe; being too busy writing to have anything
happen to himself or herself. So perhaps it is good that it is usually very hard
to learn to write.

About practical advice; the only practical advice that I know is to
write with pen or pencil and try to have each sentence make sense, to
yourself at least. If it makes sense to you, and you are honest, it will
eventually make sense to some one else. If you write by hand you will
write slower.

Some things are written at great speed but they need to be gone over
slowly.

I wrote a book called The Sun Also Rises in six weeks—starting it on
my birthday the 21st of July in Madrid and continuing on the train to
Valencia, in Valencia each day during a week of bull fights, on the
train again to Madrid, on the train to Hendaye, in a hotel there and
finishing it the 6th of September in Paris. I did not look at it again
until I re-wrote the first half of it in Austria in December. Took a trip

to N.Y. and re-wrote the last half when I came back. The re-writing took six weeks. I was never satisfied with the book but could do nothing more about it.

Two short stories The Killers and Today Is Friday I wrote on two successive days in Madrid starting the 15th of May of one year when there was a snow storm and the bull fights were called off

Cohen, AL

1 Josephine Piercy, then an instructor in the Department of English at Indiana University, had written to EH requesting his advice for her students about the principles of good writing and asking for a sample illustrating the writing process. This appears to be a draft of the letter that follows in this volume. EH's cancelled remark in the following letter that he was "finishing the rewriting of a book" and his reference to his "new book" suggest that he responded to Piercy after completing *FTA*. As he reported to others in preceding letters, he finished the revisions on 22 January 1929.

To Josephine Ketcham Piercy, [c. after 23 January 1929]

Box 323

Key West

Florida

Dear Miss Piercy—

I would have written you sooner but have been ~~finishing the rewriting of a book~~ working—besides I do not know anything to tell you of any use to your pupils except, possibly, to continue. ~~Almost~~ Everyone writes prose badly to start but by continueing some get to write it well.[1] Stop or go on is the only advice I know. As for the practical side; I believe the typewriter is ~~the~~ A curse of modern writing. It makes it too easy and the writing is solidified in type and is hard to change when it might still be kept plastic and be worked over and brought nearer to what it should be before it is cast in type. This all sounds very high flown but you must remember that you are asking some one engaged in a craft which they are constantly studying, practicing and trying to learn more about to concentrate what they have learned, or think they have learned, into a letter. All this can bring is generalities, which are useless.

I should think it might take a lifetime to learn to write prose well; your own prose that is; for if it is not your own it is of no value. Then if you had spent your life doing it perhaps you would have nothing to write about.

The ideal way would be to live and then write or live and write at the same time. But it is very hard to serve two masters and a writer is very lucky if he has only two.

At any rate what we should avoid is developing a lot of completely articulate young professional novelists just out of the University who write one interesting novel; well written in anyone else's way of writing; interesting fresh because it has youth; and successful for any of the above reasons—then to be followed by other novels, demanded by the success of the first and because the author is a professional writer, and all the time the author never living any life or learning anything or seeing anything because he, or even more possibly she, is so busy writing novels.

You can study how this works out in England.

You can use any story of mine you want. Liveright published In Our Time—Scribner's all the other books. You can write them for permission.

I do not know if the enclosed page of Mss. is what you want. It is an attempt to get a sentence right— I've taken it out of the Mss. of the new book. As far as I know the sentence never was gotten right. So it does not prove anything! I work like hell to get them right. Sometimes you have luck and it is much easier.

I wish you much luck with the book.

Yours very truly
Ernest Hemingway.

[*Enclosed manuscript page:*]

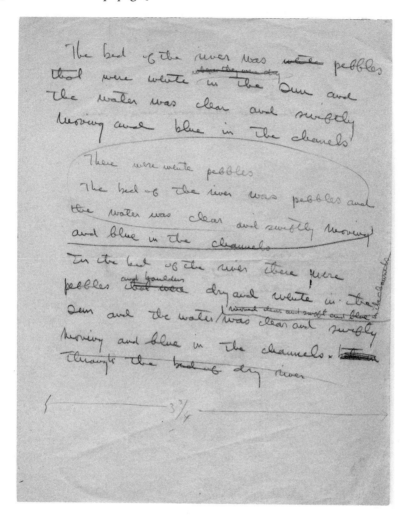

IndU, ALS

1 Piercy included much of this letter, almost verbatim, in her book *Modern Writers at Work* (New York: Macmillan, 1930), along with EH's story "Cat in the Rain" (*IOT*). On the page facing the letter in Piercy's volume is a reproduction of the draft manuscript page of the opening of *FTA* that EH enclosed with this letter. The caption reads: "*Facsimile of a page of manuscript by Ernest Hemingway showing how he revises a sentence*" (489).

To Luise Sillcox, 27 January 1929

January 27, 1929

Dear Miss Sillcox:—

Thank you very much for your letter of January 24 informing me of election to the Literary Council of the Authors' League.[1]

I did not receive your earlier letter of January 4 but, as I have been travelling, perhaps it will turn up.

I appreciate the honor of being elected to the council very much. On the other hand I travel around quite a lot and my mail is sometimes delayed or lost so that, practically, it might be better to have some one else in my place who could be of more use. Still if, knowing my drawbacks as an active member, the members of the council should still wish me as a member I will be very glad to do whatever I can and certainly appreciate the distinction.

With all best wishes,

Yours very truly,

Ernest Hemingway.

Key West, Florida

Box 323

P.S. Would it be too much to ask you to send me a copy of your first letter, if it contains additional information I should have, and a list of the other members of the council.

E.H.

My address is Box 323 Key West—Florida for the next two months. After that it will be

$^c/_o$ The Guaranty Trust Co. of N.Y.

1, rue des Italiens

Paris France.

They or Scribner's will always forward my mail wherever I may be.

Private Collection, ALS

1 The Authors' League of America was founded in New York City in 1912 by Arthur Cheney Train (1875–1945), a Harvard-educated lawyer and an author of legal fiction, to represent the interests of writers and to advocate copyright protection, fair contracts, and free expression.

To Guy Hickok, [late January 1929]

HICKOCK

EAGLE

PARIS

HAVE SOMMATION AVEC FRAIS[1] From Tax Bureau 80 Rue Bonaparte
For ~~Fifteen hundred~~ 1589 Francs 13 centimes dated January 18 Has this
been paid If not wire and I will cable you the money ~~Book finished~~ Hate To
Bother you but dont want To Be Sold Out

ERNEST

JFK, ACDS

1 *Sommation des frais*: notice of charges (French). In his letter to EH of 29 January [1929],
  Hickok would reply with an account of his payment of EH's taxes and enclose a receipt (JFK).

To Waldo Peirce, 7 February [1929]

Feb. 7 (?)

Thursday—

Bloody fine letters from you. Four in one day—and 5oo shells—yhen a
fine one today with illustratiyuns.[1] It will be wonderful to see you. Max P.
has been here for a week. That's why I haven't written— Up every morning
at five thirty to start on trips—home after dark pooped and just able to make
the bed (not arrange the [c]overs but enter them) to start again the next
morning. Trying to give yhe guy a month's fishing in a week. He got a
tarpon last night—big bastard in the jack channel—in a hell of a storm—
came up just as we hooked him and blew so they gave us up for lost as d
were out till ten last night looking for us. Hooked the tarpon way up in the
little river of the jack channel and didn't land him until way toward key west
from the old schooner. Water going over the boat all the time rough as blue
hell—bwe were on our way home from Jewfish channel with Max, Waldo
and Burge in the little boat—[2] Pauline hooked one and played him
beautifully on six oz. rod and got him to the boat— burge gaffed him and
had him inside the boat over the rail when he gave a terrific flop and went
over the side. I dove after him and followed him down in the water—got my

hands on him but too slippery to hold. If I'd had the gaff could have got him MAYBE. When yhe big blow started Bra and Charles went out to find us— they went toward Jewfish and missed seeing us tied to the big tarpon of Max' out by the old Marie. So far have caught three tarpon and a sailfish— Pauline one—me one and Max one— Counting the one in the boat as coaught which you don't need to. I landed a sailfish on the 6 oz/ rod last Saturday. Also some cockeyed wonderful dolphins.

Fine to bring Kate [Smith] if you want and can get her along. Extend her heartiest welcome.

Max leaving tonight. Mike Strater got here Monday leaves the end of next week.

They probably won't be able to serialize my book after all it seems—said they would and now of course it is too much like the old process for them to take it. It is what always happens. Then afterwards they say why of course they could have puplished it. We are up shite creek financially but in no need of borrowing money so don't worry Chico.[3] I know how when people think you have some dough they gather like buzzards. We are perfectly all right and I can borrow all I need from Scribners. Will start a story tomorrow—except that it of course too will prove what is called Unavailable—but we will give it to one of those highbrow merchants you know and cash that way. I hate the damn magazines anyway. They all have turned down everything I write except old Sedgwick. Max read the book and first day said Magnificent— second day magnificent—thrid day magnificent—a great book ernest relly a great book—fourth day he was so under spell couldn't eat or shite like doctor tanner but grave doubts about it being able to be serilized.[4] Of course they had told me and assured me absolutely that they would serilize it. But that never cuts any ice. To hell with them all.

Come on down and we will work and fish and eat and drink and swim and shoot and go to the Tortugas. Dos [Passos] ought to be down. Marquesas is a swell place. I have the dope on tortugas and a harpoon gun and we will get swell pictures/ Pauline sends her love.

Best to you kid— Thanks like hell for sending the shells.

Ernest

Colby, TLS

1 EH likely is responding to three letters that Peirce wrote on 29 January and to another letter of 2 February 1929 (JFK). Two were illustrated with Peirce's drawings. In response to EH's letter of 11 January, Peirce had arranged for the local hardware store in Maine to send EH 500 shells, "so you can pump away till I get there" (29 January 1929, JFK).

2 Jack Channel and Jewfish Channel are on the Gulf of Mexico side of the Florida Keys, approximately 4 and 8 miles, respectively, from Key West. EH's mention of "Waldo" in the little boat is a slip; his companions on that trip were Perkins and perhaps Strater. Birchland "Berge" (or "Burge") Saunders (1897–1970), like his half-brother Bra Saunders, worked as a fishing guide.

3 Peirce wrote in one of his three letters of 29 January that his father had lots of money but was tight and that he himself was "spending nothing here living on soup and beans."

4 Henry S. Tanner (1831–1919), American physician who completed an experimental forty-day fast in 1880 to prove the health benefits of fasting.

To Waldo Peirce, [8] February [1929]

Friday Feb. (?)

Wrote you yesterday in a hell of a bloody hurry—worse hurry today because trying to write a story— But find on reading your letters that I didnt mention—

(1) Tackle—you can get it all here. Charles has some swell rods and a good reel

(2) To thank Reneé for the Valentine—Lovely valentine. Give her my best—

(3) The Fight or maybe fight— Although you would think they had got to fight what with Max Schmelling Paolino etc. to take over if they were a flop— It might be a grand fight and fun to go up to Miami.[1] It would be swell to go to but we are broke— And dont want you throwing away jack to stake us. We hope to be your only friends that dont cost you any dough.

Bra is making some money now and has put off getting the boat until next year. So you wont have that to worry about anyway.[2] But the old boy is a damn sight more worth staking than the staking I've done of guys like Pat Guthrie, Stearns and Co.[3]

Reading your No. 3 think you have right dope on Kate being complicated to travel with— However we'd be glad as hell to see her.[4] The best part of what you get down here you dont need any virgins on.

You might bring 500 Lesmok Kleanbore 22 Cal. L. R. as if we get to shooting hand illuminated targets they will go fast.[5] That's all I think of. I have $60.$\underline{^{00}}$ hand illuminated Abercrombie and Fitch Harpoon gun that I bought when a little tight— It shoots a fine harpoon though.

Snipe season over except at Marquesas. We can get plenty there. Hurry
on down. It will be wonderful to have you. We'll take some swell trips to
Marquesas and Tortugas— Bra wants us to go over to the Cape and
Everglades— Claims mosquitoes all dead.

Yours always—
Ernesto.

I have (1) Mother (2) Sisters (1) Brother (1) Wife (1) (Ex-wife)—(2)
children to contribute to support of— Also two house niggers— So must get
to work—and when I finish a story no magazine will touch it— (I suppose as
Max says Scribner's is a Family magazine tho) They will probably run a
serial by Morley Callaghan instead. Anyway I got these envelopes off of
them! Max had a wonderful time I think— He pulled out last night.—

Colby, ALS

1 EH refers to the heavyweight title elimination bout between Jack Sharkey and Young
  Stribling on 27 February 1929 in Miami Beach. In two of his 29 January letters, Peirce
  expressed interest in attending that fight. German boxer Max Schmeling (1905–2005)
  would defeat Paulino Uzcudun of Spain in a heavyweight bout on 27 June 1929 in New
  York in Yankee Stadium.
2 In the letter of 29 January 1929 wherein Peirce mentioned he was short of money, he
  nevertheless offered to buy a new engine for Bra's boat with or without EH's support and
  enclosed money for that purpose (JFK).
3 Both Pat Guthrie and Harold Stearns, like the *SAR* characters for whom they served as
  prototypes, lived beyond their means and at times on borrowed money.
4 "Kate Smith seems too dam complicated to travel with and I like to move when I start, he who
  travels fastest travels alone," Peirce wrote in the 29 January letter he marked "letter no.#3" (JFK).
5 "Lesmok" gunpowder was developed in 1911 by the E. I. du Pont Company of Wilmington,
  Delaware, to produce "less smoke" than other powders used in .22-caliber cartridges; it was
  adopted by several ammunition manufacturers and was in use into the 1930s. The Remington
  Kleanbore .22 Long Rifle cartridges were produced by the Remington Arms Company of
  Ilion, New York, which in 1926 introduced Kleanbore technology, a noncorrosive primer that
  made it unnecessary to wipe corrosive residue from the bore of the gun.

To John Dos Passos, 9 February [1929]

Feb 9.

Dear Dos—

Enclosed came today[.] For god's sake come down.[1] The road isnt
finished—45 mile water gap still and the County Treasurer absconded with
all funds and they've closed the schools—let alone build the road.[2]

Tarpon are in and have caught two—lost a big one last night at the boat—we're here until middle of March—absolutely broke may not be able to ever leave but lots of liquor off a wrecked booze boat.

Waldo comes down next week. Come on down. Saw at least 100 tarpon last night out by the Jack channel.

Pauline sends her love.

Come on down and we will go to Tortugas— Waldo has some Jack. His mother died.[3] My old man shot himself but it was no help financially—On The Contrary!

Come on down kid— You must have thought me a shite not to write

Hem

No eyes dropped out yet.

UVA, ALS

1 In a postcard to EH of 20 December [1928] sent from aboard the *Columbus* as he was returning from Europe to New York, Dos Passos wrote, "Drop me a line as to the life and habits of Key West, or thereabouts," adding, "I dont know where I'm going to live, if at all" (JFK). EH's enclosure remains unidentified. Dos Passos would visit EH in Key West that March.

2 By 1928 the Dixie Highway connecting Florida City to Key West was complete except for a 40-mile gap between Lower Matecumbe Key and No Name Key, which were connected only by ferry service. EH refers to the arrest on 17 December 1928 of Monroe county clerk D. Z. (Davoult Zair) Filer (c. 1898–1930), who had embezzled $19,000 of the funds needed to complete the Dixie Highway. The end of the Florida Land boom in 1927 and later the Great Depression also played a major part in stalling the road project, which would not be completed until 1938. Hundreds of U.S. war veterans sent in to complete the highway were killed by the 1935 Hurricane, as EH would later describe in his 1935 *New Masses* article "Who Murdered the Vets" and 1937 novel *To Have and Have Not*.

3 Jack, slang for money. Anna Peirce had died in February 1928, but Waldo's financial situation was complicated by his father's protective attitude toward her estate, as Peirce would write in his letter to EH of 15 February [1929] (JFK).

To Frances Thorne, 12 February 1929

NOTES AND TRANSCRIPTS FROM LETTER OF ERNEST HEMINGWAY TO MISS FRANCES THORNE (later Mrs. William Horne), c/o Mrs. Robb Sagendorph, 1060 Park Avenue, NYC, as she was on point of leaving for Europe.[1]

dated Key West, Fla.

Feb. 12, 1929

Dear Bunny:

Hopes weather will be good in Spain during her trip. "I've had it snow in Madrid in the middle of May."

Commiserates with her on death of her fiance, Ernie Wadd. "My own father had shot himself and I felt too bad to write" at the time. "We all have to die and if you have a fine religion that takes any of the curse off . . . The only thing I learned from the war was never discuss casualties and it works pretty well for peace, too."

"If you go to Spain in a motor from the Riviera you'll go through Provence which is a lovely country and you ought to see Nimes and a place called Les Baux and San Remy and the finest walled town left (and not just a show place like Carcassonne) in Aigues Mortes—straight down on the Mediterranean from Nimes and almost on your main motor road which goes through Nimes— Semel to probably Montpellier and on to Perpignan and the Spanish frontier. Aigues Mortes is a wonderful sight looking back at it from the sea. The road goes from it about 5 miles to the sea where there is a little port called Le Grau du Roi along the canal St. Louis built to go to the Crusades from. . .² Provence is cockeyed beautiful."

Nota bene: Much later Hemingway began a novel with locale at Aigues Mortes. See letter of Mary Hemingway on his still unpub. work filed under 1958–1959.³ He had also been there with Pauline in May 1927

"Barcelona. . . big and dusty and strange. . . some of the most unbelievably ugly bldgs in the world but there is a high hill above the town with a restaurant you can reach by a funiculaire with a great view out all over everything."⁴

He recommends a white wine called Diamante and a red one called Rioja alta or Rioja claret. Recommends Valencia, Malaga, Alicante, and esp. Ronda—"a wonderful place. . . lovely hotel. . . on the edge of a gorge. . . and is marked **** in old Hem's Hand Prepared Baedeker."

Advice on bullfight: sit in box (pahcos).⁵ "Remember it is all wrong and immoral and indefensible but you can't do anything about it and sometimes it is beautiful and wonderful."

Says his book is all done (FTA). Says Bumby, Pat, and Pauline all fine. Says will be leaving for Paris latter part of March, and address will be 6 rue Ferou, Paris VI.

Says Jinny Pfeiffer is now skiing at Gstaad.

PUL, Typewritten notes and partial transcription of EH letter

1 These notes and the partial transcription of EH's letter by Carlos Baker are reproduced here verbatim from his files (Carlos Baker Papers, CO365, Box 5, folder 6, PUL). Beatrix Thorne Sagendorph (1900–1985), Frances Thorne's sister, was an artist married to journalist Robb Sagendorph, who later founded *Yankee* magazine.
2 King Louis IX of France (1215–1270), leader of the seventh (1249–52) and eighth (1270) Crusades. He was canonized in 1297.
3 The novel was posthumously published as *The Garden of Eden* (1986), edited by Scribner's from EH's unfinished manuscript of some 2,400 pages (items 422–422.9, JFK). Mary Welsh Hemingway (1908–1986), EH's widow, whom he met in London in 1944 and married in Cuba in 1946 in his fourth and final marriage.
4 EH likely refers to Tibidabo (elevation 1745 feet), the highest hill in the range to the northwest of Barcelona, scaled by a funicular railway that began service in 1901. A hotel-restaurant at the top afforded panoramic views over the city and the Mediterranean Sea. Montjuïc, overlooking Barcelona from the south, was developed as the site of the 1929 World Exposition. The funicular went into operation on 24 October 1928, ahead of the exposition, which would be officially opened by King Alfonso XIII of Spain on 19 May 1929.
5 *Palcos*: boxes for prime seating at a bullring (Spanish).

To Sylvia Beach, 12 February [1929]

February 12
Birthday of Lincoln the Lover
See Atlantic Monthly[1]

Dearest Sylvia:

I was so so glad to hear from you and so <u>awfully awfully</u> sorry to get the bad news of Mrs Joyce, of you being sick, and of Adrienne with the grippe.[2] I was a swine to bother you about the books in the first place and I only hope that now you and Adrienne are both well and and that poor Mrs. Joyce will be all right. I hope the operation is over and everything all right or that the doctors were wrong and perhaps didnt have to operate.

Duplaix and his troubles do not touch me as anything happening to you or Adrienne or anyone dear to you— But I am awfully sorry he and his wife are in trouble.[3]

I do hope things are all right with you again. About the book— To hell with the book— If it doesnt go that is the publisher's hard luck not mine. I saw a stinking review by that big monument of business acumen Victor LLona—and to hell with him too.[4]

My new book is finished— I think you will like it better than any I have ever done— I hope so— Scribner's promised to serialize it— But now are afraid of it— They say after all theirs is a <u>Family Magazine</u>! So it will be out in the fall in the regular way—

My father shot himself in December so now—after having left my family when I was 14 and never taking anything from them—I now finally have the responsibility of them—[5] He left practically nothing except my mother and two children still in school. Poor old boy he had tough luck investing money and speculating and then got sick.[6]

But my book is fine and Pauline is well and I am crazy about her— Pat and Bumby are well and fine kids—and I have been healthy and working very well—better than I ever did— So I have no kick— We plan to sail about the 20th of March from Havana via Vigo, Coruña and Gijon for France. It will be wonderful to see you again. We should be in Paris by the middle of April at the latest.

I am so sorry to have bothered you about the books at all and I wish you would keep the check and apply it on my subscription which is always overdue—

Best love always
Hemingway.

Do you see how our old friend Routis is Champion du Monde. Pladner too will be.[7]

I know what hell facial neuralgia is.

PUL, ALS; postmark: KEY WEST / FLA., FEB 12 / 6 PM / 1929

On the envelope verso, EH wrote: "Caught 8 ft. Sailfish and some big tarpon. / Bumby is having a wonderful time."

1 U.S. President Abraham Lincoln was born on 12 February 1809. Three articles by Wilma Frances Minor (pen name of Wilma Willows, 1898–1965) purporting to contain newly discovered love letters between Lincoln and Ann Rutledge (1813–1835), daughter of a New Salem, Illinois, businessman and tavern owner, ran in the December 1928, January 1929, and February 1929 issues of the *Atlantic Monthly* under the title "Lincoln the Lover." It was later determined that Minor had forged the letters.

2 Nora Barnacle Joyce (1884–1951) was James Joyce's companion beginning in 1904; they wed in 1931. After exploratory surgery in November 1928 revealed a tumor, Nora received radium treatments, Beach reported in her letter to EH of 30 January 1929 (JFK), and in February underwent a hysterectomy. Beach wrote that she herself had suffered from facial neuralgia and that Adrienne Monnier had two relapses of the grippe while correcting the proofs of the French edition of Joyce's *Ulysses*, published by Monnier in February 1929 (JFK).

3 According to Beach, EH's French translator Georges Duplaix and his wife, American translator Lily Duplaix (née Wheeler, 1905–1997), had rushed to the South of France in the fall of 1928 after Lily fell seriously ill with tuberculosis.

4 EH is responding to Beach's report that the distribution of *Cinquante mille dollars* (*Fifty Grand*) was not properly handled because EH was away from Paris at the time of its publication in 1928 and because Duplaix, who translated it, was distracted by his wife's illness. Victor Llona had written a review of *Cinquante mille dollars* that appeared in the January 1929 issue of *Nouvelle Revue Française*. EH likely is alluding to the poor reception and sales of Llona's translation of *The Great Gatsby* (*Gatsby le Magnifique*), for which Fitzgerald had paid the translator's fee.

5 EH did not move away from his family in Oak Park until he was eighteen (not fourteen), when he took a job as a cub reporter at the *Kansas City Star* in October 1917, a position his uncle, Alfred Hemingway, helped to arrange.

6 Starting in 1924, Clarence Hemingway had bought several real estate lots in Clearwater, Gulfport, and St. Petersburg, Florida, which he financed in part with a $15,000 mortgage against the Oak Park house. By the end of 1926 the real estate bubble had burst, creating financial stress and casting doubt on the investments' prospects and on Clarence's ability to make mortgage payments. For a detailed study of the Florida investments, see John Sanford, "A Garden of Eden, or, Hemingway's Last Lot," *North Dakota Quarterly* 66, no. 2 (Spring 1999): 159–63.

7 French featherweight boxer André Routis had won the world featherweight title against American Tony Canzoneri (1908–1959) on 28 September 1928 at Madison Square Garden in New York. Émile "Spider" Pladner (1906–1980), a French boxer, would become the world flyweight champion in March 1929.

To Maxwell Perkins, 14 February 1929

ND322 4=CA KAYWEST FLO 14 330P

MAXWELL E PERKINS=

SCRIBNERS 597 FIFTH AVE=

AWFULLY PLEASED PRICE OK=

=ERNEST HEMNYWAY.

PUL, Cable; Western Union destination receipt stamp: 1929 FEB 14 PM 3 56

EH is responding to a telegram of 13 February 1929 from Perkins offering $16,000 from *Scribner's Magazine* for serial rights to *FTA* (PUL; *TOTTC*, 86).

To Maxwell Perkins, 16 February [1929]

Feb 16—

Dear Max—

Here are the pictures of your fish. It was wonderful to have you here. We all enjoyed it very greatly. I would have written before but caught my old bad throat clearing fish out of the ice house and was in bed with the throat pretty bad. Before it happened—the Sunday after you left—had a wonderful day in the gulf stream— It was calm, almost oily— Hooked a sailfish that ran out 250 yards of line on the Vom Hofe reel and light rod and had 40 minute fight. He was just over 8 feet long— Record here for this year— Completely pooped me with the light tackle— He seemed strong as a tarpon— 1/2 hour later Charles [Thompson] hooked a Mako shark out in the Gulf and fought him 3 hrs and 20 minutes— The shark jumped like a tarpon—straight up high clear of the water— He lost him—after finally bringing him to gaff (and having the heaviest tarpon rod break) when the hook straightened— All the other boats came around to see the fight— We were way out where the big tankers were passing— Mike [Strater] gaffed him 3 or 4 times but he couldnt hold him. I never saw a fish jump more beautifully— We hoped of course he was a Marlin—he was bigger than the one at Casa Marina— but he was a shark of a sort nobody had ever seen around here— So we called him a <u>Mako</u>—the kind they have in New Zealand that jumps so wonderfully—

I'm awfully glad they are going to serialize and the Price is fine.[1]

About omissions—they can only be discussed in the concrete examples—[2] I told you I would not be unreasonable—I dont mind the leaving out of a word if a blank is left if the omission is unavoidable and as for passages—almost every part in the book depends on almost every other part—you know that—so if a passage is dropped—there should be something to show it— That will not hurt the serial and will help the book. People might be curious to see the book and see what that passage contained. It's not a regular serial anyway.

My point is that the operation of emasculation is a tiny one— It is very simple and easy to perform on men—animals and books— It is not a major operation but it's effects are great— It is <u>never</u> performed <u>intentionally</u> on books— What we must both watch is that it should not be performed unintentionally—

I know, on the other hand, that you will not want to print in a magazine certain words and, as you say, certain passages. In that event what I ask is that when omissions are made a blank or some sign of omission be made that isnt to be confused with the dots . . . that writers employ when they wish to avoid biting on the nail and writing a hard part of a book to do.

Still the dots may be that sign— I'm not unreasonable— I know we both have to be careful because we have the same interest i.e. (literature or whatever you call it) and I know that you yourself are shooting for the same thing that I am. And I tell you that emasculation is a small operation and we dont want to perform it without realizing it—

Anyway enough of talking—I am not satisfied with the last page and will change it—but the change will in no way affect the serializability (what a word.)

I think you are very fine about the price—if I havent said more about it it is because while we are friends I am no blanket friend of the entire organization and have the feeling, from experience, that the bull fighter is worth whatever he gets paid. However I think you are fine about the price. You are very generous and I appreciate it. I may want some of the money quite <u>soon</u> will write. This letter in great haste

Best to you always,

Ernest Hemingway.

Thanks ever so much for the books. So far have received the Russian one —one story—The horse thieves—only one I've read is <u>splendid</u> almost all the way.[3] I'll read the one you recommend tonight.

Now will look forward to when you come to Piggott for the shooting. Ideal wing shooting the ducks so thick you can shoot at one and hit another!

PUL, ALS

1 Perkins told EH in his letter of 13 February 1929 that the offer of $16,000 to serialize *FTA* was "more than we ever paid anybody else" (PUL).

2 In his 13 February telegram offering serialization, Perkins noted that the first installment would be printed with some "blanks" and that additional omissions might be made in later installments, but only with EH's approval (PUL; *TOTTC*, 86); in his letter of the same day, Perkins elaborated on that possibility (PUL).

3 Probably Anton Pavlovich Chekhov (1860–1904), *The Horse-Stealers and Other Stories: From the Russian by Constance Garnett* (New York: Macmillan, 1921).

To Maxwell Perkins, [c. 18 February 1929]

Dear Max—

The books are grand—Homer—Vishnu Land—Philadelphia Jack O'Brien and the grand wonderful Waterfowl and Waders— I had no idea that was a thousand dollar book when I asked for it. It's a good book. Thats Pauline's and my idea of a book. Thanks ever so much for them.[1] They are all wonderfully welcome.

We are sending your T-shirt and Shark jaw—

I've fished ever since you left— No more tarpon— at Jewfish Channel yesterday we saw literaly hundreds of them rolling but not one strike. Am trying them tonight in the little boat in the Jack Channel. Mike Strater goes Friday— It's been fine to have him but will be glad to work again. I have 10 pages done on a story—14 I guess—[2]

Pauline hooked and landed a 53 lb Amberjack on the light 6 oz. rod— We got in a school and hooked 3 at once— No one paid much attention to Pauline who fought hers from the [*EH insertion*: up on the] bow— We took it for granted her fish was smaller and Mike and I were both fought out with our own—when we landed them[.] Mine was 51—Mike's in the 40s and Paulines 53! The lines had to be crossed and uncrossed like Maypole dancing— Pauline's ran out all but about 10 ft. of the line in the Vom Hofe reel.[3] We caught 6—all over 40 lbs and the biggest 56 lbs. Put back all but 4— They pull hardest of all fish I think but dont jump. They'd be wonderful if they jumped. Tarpon fishing yesterday and not a strike— I harpooned a porpoise with the harpoon gun and he broke the line— We were in a great school of them—6 right under the bow— We wish you were down here— The weather has been hot and fine— Thanks <u>ever</u> so much for the books—

Yours always,

Ernest Hemingway.

PUL, ALS

1 *The Iliad of Homer*, translated by Andrew Lang, Walter Leaf, and Ernest Myers (New York: Modern Library, 1929); Stanley Warburton, *An Avatar in Vishnu Land* (New York: Scribner's, 1928); Philadelphia Jack O'Brien and S. E. Bilik, *Boxing* (New York: Scribner's, 1928); and Hugh B. C. Pollard, *Wildfowl & Waders*, illustrated by Frank Southgate (London: Country Life, 1928), which was issued in a limited edition of 950 copies and featured colored plates with letterpressed guardsheets.
2 Possibly an early start of a story that would later become "A Natural History of the Dead," published in *DIA* (1932) and in *WTN* (1933) (see Smith, 231–33).
3 Edward vom Hofe & Company of New York was renowned for its top-of-the-line fishing tackle; the company received the first of several patents for its reel mechanisms in 1879.

To Evan Shipman, [c. 20 February 1929]

Dear Evan—

I'm worse than a skunk not to have written but have been working and every other thing. Book done finally. On the train after I left you got a wire my father was dead. Had to leave it at Phil. and go to Chicago. He shot himself poor old boy. So there was all of that and in the middle of re-writing the book. Hell to pay. (Got the flu in Chicago) Finally finished it—the book. I wish to hell you could read it. Think you'd like it. It's the best I've ever done I think really.

You are swell to write us to stay with you but we'll be sailing from Havana— about the 20th of March. Keep at the novel.[1] They go slow as hell— Just do some every day and stop always while it's going good—that's the mechanics of it— Never write on until you're all pooped[.] that makes it too hard to pick up — You dont want to have to demarre new every time[.] Continue on your lanceé— Ask Old Hem he knows— They are hell to write—[2]

Scribner's are going to serialize it although they are scared to—

Pauline sends her love— I caught a hell of a big sailfish—8 feet—also a smaller one and some tarpon— Pauline landed a 53 lb. amberjack by herself on 6 oz. rod— They are the hardest fighters of all— But dont jump.

Write me. I'll try and write from now on.

Bumby is fine and husky like the old days he's gained 9 lbs. Pat in fine shape too—

Best to you always,

Hem

Channick, ALS

The letter date is conjectured relative to the letter from Shipman dated 15 February [1929] to which EH is responding.

1 In his letter Shipman invited EH and Pauline to stay with him in New York City. He also reported that his novel was progressing more slowly than he had expected (JFK).
2 *Démarrer*: to start up; *continuer sur sa lancée*: to continue to forge ahead (French).

To Owen Wister, 20 February 1929

February Twentieth.

1929.

Dear Owen Wister:—

Thank you for your letter of February fifteenth.[1] I did not deserve another letter and you were very good to write it. We would have loved to come to Long House—and would have—but everything went to pot very suddenly.[2] When I was to go east to get the boy my father shot himself—a very lonely way to die—and since I've had his family—whom I left when a kid because we did not get along—to more or less look after—being at the time in the middle of the worst part of all—the re-writing—of this book. So I had no other life but the re-writing—but all the rest of it going on too— Now the book is finished. Scribner's—Max Perkins that is—was afraid they couldnt serialize it. But took the Mss. back to N.Y and last week wired that they would serialize— Setting up the first installment with some blanks in place of certain words. It seemed Mr. Bridges—the Editor Laureate—liked it very much— The only explanation is that he didn't know what it was about—that seems reasonable. I wish there was some way you could read it and tell me what you think—I've had hell's own time writing it and worse re-writing it—

Max Perkins raised the question of omitting certain passages—"never more than a few lines" and I wrote back that it is a very simple operation to emasculate anything—a boar or a man or a book. The operation is not a Major one but the effect is Major. No one ever does it to a book on purpose—but it is so simple and easy to do that it is liable to be performed unwittingly—and then it's done.

So I dont know about the omission business—[3] When you write you omit everything you can— on the other hand if they left a blank where the[y] made deletions in the magazine and gave the text in full in the book it might be all right. What do you think? It all depends on the specific example of course.

You wrote a fine letter from France and this letter is only stable gossip— I wanted to ask you about this very silly seeming committee of something or other of the Author's League that I see by a letter from them, that we are both members of. What about it? The business of classes etc seems idiotic— I thought—if you said the word—we might resign. Both of us resign in a body. Or if it is a good thing tell me— I did not know—until I got this letter—who were members—and then there was an appalling list of projected new members and it all made me feel as though somehow we were in with a bad lot— But if it's all right tell me.[4]

Are you coming South? We would like very much to see you. We are here until the middle or end of March. Then sail from Havana[.] Please tell me if you are coming south. We are in more or less of a cottage but could put you up at a very imposing looking hotel on the sea very close to the house. Waldo Pierce is coming down and we could go fishing.

We'll be in Europe for a year perhaps and then we could see you at Long House if you would stil have us when we come through. My wife sends you her best greetings. She, and both the boys are well. We've caught some big sailfish and some medium sized tarpon. Had good snipe shooting until the season closed. The tarpon are beginning to bite now.

I called up Buzz Henry in N.Y. but could not reach him. Have you his address? I tried to get him through the bank but failed.[5]

With best wishes to you always,

Ernest Hemingway

LOC, ALS; postmark: KEY WEST / FLA, FEB 2[1] / 930 AM / 1929

1 With a letter to Perkins of 15 February 1929, Wister had enclosed a letter to EH, asking Perkins to forward it "to the young phoenix" (PUL). In his own letter to EH dated 19 February 1929, Perkins wrote that Wister considered it "the best possible news" that Scribner's was going to serialize *FTA* (PUL). Wister had written to Perkins, in a letter of 18 February, that he had "begged" Charles Scribner to serialize the novel and declared his readiness to be of use to Scribner's "in E. H.'s cause" (PUL).

2 In a letter to EH of 17 October 1928, Wister wrote, "if you come to meet your boy at Christmas, come a day or two in advance, and stop off at Philadelphia, you and your wife,

and stay with me . . . and make us all very happy" (JFK). Long House: Wister's residence in
Bryn Mawr, Pennsylvania.

3 Wister would respond that omissions in the serialization did not matter and could be
restored in the book. "Magazines have a special responsibility. They're subscribed for. But
nobody's obliged to buy a book. So put it in the book and never mind the magazine" (27
February 1929, JFK).

4 "Give the Authors' League Committee the benefit of the doubt. I think those things are
always silly," Wister would advise. The Authors League of America was founded in 1912
with almost 350 members, including book authors, magazine writers, and playwrights, to
protect copyright matters. The list of committee members that Luise Sillcox sent EH has not
been located.

5 Wister would reply that there was "no better address" for Barklie "Buzz" Henry than
Guaranty Trust Company, New York, where Henry worked from 1928 to 1930.

To Grace Hall Hemingway, [20 February 1929]

Dear Mother—

Thank you very much for your letters and the enclosures.[1] I appreciated
very much your sending Dad's watch and am very sorry you were unable to
locate his account books so that the collections could be made.

I would be very glad if you would send me a list of the taxes to be paid
together with the amounts and to whom they are to be paid—all details
necessary—and I will pay them promptly as soon as I receive the list.[2]

The latest news is that Scribners—after first thinking they would be
unable—are now planning to serialize the book. I have not yet received the
money but should soon. When I get it will either arrange to have a check for
$100.^{00} sent you each month—or what will be better and save mailing—will
write 12 checks for 100 each dated the first of each month for the next 12
months and send them all together.[3]

That way you can cash each check as it comes due. Cash the first one at
once and the others the first of each month.

Please tell me if you need any ready cash— I could send whatever ready
cash you need now as well as the monthly checks.

Until I heard about the serialization was pretty badly worried— I knew I
could pay the taxes but we were low in funds ourselves and I wanted to get
the monthly check business organized.

So now please send me a list of the taxes and to whom they are to be paid and I will see they are paid at once. Now is an awfully bad time to sell Florida real Estate but I will pay the taxes until a good time comes for disposing of it.

Best love to Carol and Less and dear Uncle Tyley— I hope things are going well with you— We will be leaving toward the end of March—

Your affect. son
Ernie.

Will be down in Florida in a year or two again and like Dad the taxes will give me a good excuse to go to St. Peteresburg. I have been making enquiries and now is the worst possible time to sell. Land that sold for $2,000 an acre during the boom is selling now for $50^{00}[.] But Dad's stuff—being city lots will always have a certain value.[4] I will continue to pay the taxes and we can sell it when the market is better— In the meantime $100 a month is more or as much as you would get as safe interest on the principal invested in Florida—if you had the principal. I trust you are getting the insurance money and having the bank invest it. I count <u>absolutely</u> on you to do that.

Ernie.

I hope that you can assure me that Carols and Leicester's allowances can be kept up with this sum coming in.[5]

IndU, ALS; postmark: KEY WEST / FLA., FEB [20] / 6 PM / 1929

On the flap of the envelope EH wrote: The cookies were <u>delicious</u>. Thank you so much.

1 In a letter of 2 February 1929, signed "Your loving Mother Gracie," Grace wrote that she had sent a parcel with cookies (JFK). She also enclosed a letter that she had found among his father's belongings and thought EH would enjoy (JFK). In another letter of the same date, Grace wrote to Pauline, "How I wish we were nearer so we might do things together" and asked her to give Bumby and Patrick "a good squeeze for their grand mother" (JFK).
2 Although Grace had not yet received the tax bill for the Florida properties when she responded on 24 February 1929, she expected that $400 would cover it and asked EH to send her that amount. In the rest of the letter, she detailed her financial situation. She planned to use her savings from the sale of her paintings for the property tax of $400 on the house, and Sterling Sanford, Marcelline's husband, was going to cover the semi-annual mortgage payments of $450 in May and November. With advice from Sanford and her bank, she had invested Clarence's life insurance of $21,000 and the $1,000 in his checkbook in a mixture of bonds and real estate mortgages, with the total $22,000 averaging her 6% or "$110.^{00} a month when it gets going" (JFK).
3 "Surely God will bless you when you have such a generous heart," Grace would respond in her 24 February letter, "its like being reprieved when you expected to hang. An income of $200.^{00} a month instead of $100.00 is all the difference between comfort and poverty."

4 Clarence owned six properties in St. Petersburg, four in Clearwater, and four in Gulf Port, according to Grace's letter to EH of 7 April 1929 (JFK).

5 Grace would respond in her 24 February letter that she could now resume giving Carol her former allowance of ten dollars a month and lunches amounting to six dollars a month. Uncle George had offered to supply clothes for Leicester, who needed only two dollars a month for spending money.

To Maxwell Perkins, 23 February [1929]

Feb 23

Max—

Have gone over the galleys and returned them to Mr. Bridges. The blanks are all right <u>so far</u>. I'll consent to the omision of the lead pencil encircled passage in galley 12—It is bad for the story to omit it but does not cripple it. I would never consent to its omission in a book.[1]

In the foreward at the start of galley (1) I eliminated the words <u>of the sordidness</u>—they add nothing, give people a word to attack with and weaken the statement.[2] Remember more people review the blurb than ever do the book.

I'm not trying to give sordidness—have avoided it as much as possible—

———

Do you still care for the title?

I think the book so far looks fine in type— That is very good type too. I had a fine time reading it for the first time in type.

Could you send me a list of how much money I received from Scribners in 1928— So that I may make out an income tax.[3]

Also would you send me a check for 6,000 of the 11,000 due on the serial?[4] I want to send some money to my family.

A norther today. It's Saturday night and Charles and I were going tarpon fishing tonight with the full moon but maybe not with the norther blowing[.] Everyone sends you their best wishes.

I wrote Owen Wister.

Best always—
Ernest Hemingway.

Evan Shipman's address is 19 Beekman Place if you want to communicate with him about that poem.[5]

PUL, ALS

1 Bridges had objected to Frederic Henry's fantasy of going to a hotel in Milan with Catherine Barkley. When he mailed EH the marked galley proofs for the first installment of *FTA*, he remarked, "In these things we have to consider a constituency that has followed the Magazine for a great many years" (19 February 1929, PUL). Although it did not appear in *Scribner's Magazine*, the passage beginning "Because we would not wear any clothes" was restored in Chapter 6 of the book version.
2 The editorial statement in the first galleys included the sentence "It is a love-story woven with such a picture of the sordidness of War as would discourage either victors or the conquered from that terrible solution of international troubles." In the published version, "of the sordidness" was omitted, as EH wished.
3 With his letter of 1 March 1929, Perkins would enclose royalty reports of the past six months' sales of EH's books, not counting 949 copies of *SAR* (JFK).
4 Perkins would send EH a check for $6,000 on 27 February 1929. In fall 1928 EH had already received a $5,000 advance on the $16,000 Scribner payment for the *FTA* serialization.
5 The address printed on Shipman's personalized letterhead envelopes is "21 Beekman Place / New York."

To Guy Hickok, 26 February [1929]

Feb 26

You're certainly a fine guy and I hope it wasnt too bloody much trouble—[1] The book is finally finished and will be serialized starting in the <u>May</u> number of Scribners—to run through <u>Oct</u>. They don't know what the hell it's about or they wouldnt touch it. But it's a sweet book—I'm damned if it's not. I'm using the dough to support all members of the Hemingway family— If you can prove your name is HEM and not Hickock you will automatically be supported— Just like the [Gundersons?] in the Great War—

Hope your tendon is O.K. Sometimes they <u>never</u> get well. Pat has 4 teeth—Bumby weights 52 lbs—46 when he hit here—

I caught 8 ft. sailfish—also smaller one—also big tarpon- - Pauline caught a small tarpon and a 52 lb. amberjack on a 6 oz. rod. You ought to have seen her. We all had fish on—3 at same time— Nobody paid any attention to Pauline's fish— Thought she naturally had on a girl's size fish— Mike Strater and I each got completely pooped landing ours—Mine 51—his 46—

then Pauline shipped hers and he was a 53 pounder—hardest pulling fish there is—

Waldo comes down tomorrow—Dos Passos soon— Then we shove via Havana and come over to see youse guys—

Hold your Golden Horses—

Will write soon—

Ernest

Pauline send her love to you both.

phPUL, ALS

1 In his letter to EH of 29 January [1929], Hickok related the challenges he encountered while paying EH's taxes for him in Paris (JFK).

To Owen Wister, 1 March [1929]

March 1

Dear Owen Wister:—

It was damned sweet of you to send the check. I would keep it if I could because it was so fine of you to send it; a good wine needs no bush and a good letter no check; but a check is always fine in a letter and I know nothing more exciting than to open a letter from a man who's approval is completely satisfactory and enough to make me happy and also find a check for 500.$\frac{00}{}$.[1] You see I'm treating it from its most casual aspect. More Seriously, you were very fine to send it and I know that the bitterest tragedies are money tragedies and I would keep the check absolutely if it were that bad. This present show, though, I can swing all right so far. It would be fine if you would let me send this back now and know I could ask you to let me have it if things were ever bad enough. I cannot tell you how much I appreciate your sending it and the way you sent it. Max Perkins getting them to serialize pulled me out of the hole.

(1) If you're damaged goods [*EH insertion*: about taking care of the human machine.] let me be damaged like [*EH insertion*: (as)] you [*EH insertion*: (are)] at 68 and I'll be happy. In 1919 I had, still have, an aluminum kneecap, bad heart (fine now) hole in the throat about 2 inches

deep (all right now) but have to watch it—also after effects of concussion of brain couldnt sleep, etc. (all right now) various other minor infirmities. Now I'm in good shape but dont ~~look forward to~~ expect a long life—burned too much too early. But will certainly avoid knife throwers. I dont recall anything of that report except something about a knife thrower. My impression though is that I threw the knife in what seemed to be a final exhibition of knife throwing and that the first knife was somewhat successful but either the 2nd or 3rd knife struck Capt. E.E. Dorman-Smith of His Majesty's Fifth Fusiliers on the top of the head and he behaved very nobly about it but that my wife made me give up knife throwing permanently. At any rate have not cast a knife since that date—sometime in 1925—but always have a fellow feeling for any still practicing knife thrower and may have lent a hand as a target.[2]

I wish so that you were coming down and we could talk—but tell me what Kipling said. Something might happen to him or to yourself and then I'd never know![3] Doesn't the train go through Tours? I'd have sworn it did. It goes through Angouleme anyway. I'd have sworn it stopped just outside of Tours— Let me see Paris— Orleans—Blois—Tours Chatellerault Poitiers—Angouleme—Bordeaux—Dax—Bayonne— But maybe it isnt true—[4] I hate to have tried to deceive Justice Holmes—[5] If people should ever read the book in a year or two maybe they will think "back in those days" it did go through Tours. I'll take your word on the [Authors' League] committee—or Tours too for that matter and certainly for Saint Pierre de Corps.

I'm glad your boy is all right again from the flu. If you tell the other boy that we live at 6 rue Férou in Paris and will be most happy to see him when he comes to Paris both Pauline and I will be very pleased. Please tell him to come and see us.[6]

Benet's book I haven't read. His other books, the fiction, not the poetry which I havent read—I thought were tripe. I'm glad if it's so good. In principle I suspect an epic by a man who can't do a small thing well. The Civil War its-self is so fine that there is always the danger that it is the Civil War which receives the homage and not the book. (Of course it should anyway—but that's History.)[7] You, too, knowing about the war of the Secession and having written and studied history bring more to it than a writer should expect from a reader.[8] This talking of a book I havent read is most certainly tripe— But when you've seen a man practicing your own craft in sloppy dishonest way (This from an old railway inaccurist!) it prejudices you against his craft—though one is liable to be very silly and wrong and find him very good. And of course the real reason I could not read Benet's book was because the print was too fine!

I hope so that you'll like the book— They start it in May and finish it in October in the magazine— In the proofs of the first installment they removed the name of Our Lord and left it in blank and did several harmless things like that but held out for the removal of a passage not at all obscene but which conveys the effect of lewdness if left out. That's their lookout. The book starts at Gorizia goes to the front, hospital, back to Milan back for Caporetto—the whole of that—(or I wish it were—or hoped it would be) back to Milan—Stresa—Switzerland and the end. You see I wrote The Sun Also in 6 weeks—and then left it alone for 3 months and re-wrote it in another 6—while on this I worked like a horse from the end of January until nearly the end of August—then the devils own re-writing from Thanksgiving day until the end of January— It seems that much better book—but I'm still so close to it that can't tell if I've made it or only think I've made it— So now we fish and when an installment comes it seems all new and grand—it can't be as good as it seems—and I know the time is coming when it all goes to ashes[9]—that is probably reserved for when it's between covers—but in the meantime there are no worries—finances, nothing can touch me—and my only worry is that I'll die or drown or someone shoot me or some such silly thing before I can write another book. Then, of course, the awakening is when you sit down and are utterly unable to write a story or a line of anything. Started one on the impetus of finishing and after 3 days heard Max would serialize and have been fishing since.

I've bored you enough with this letter. You were fine on the dough of Whitmans.[10] I'm very anxious to know what Kipling said. If you tell me I'd do anything you say. Don't save it till we get a chance to talk. We'll have plenty to talk about.

Yours always,
Ernest Hemingway

Have re-read this and it's a lousy letter full of perpendicular pronouns and conveying nothing of how your instant and splendid support made me feel.

E.H.

LOC, ALS; postmark: KEY WEST / FLA., MAR 5 / 7 AM / 1929

1 In the epilogue of Shakespeare's *As You Like It*, Rosalind muses: "If it be true that good wine needs no bush,' 'tis true that a good play needs no epilogue." After EH told him of his father's suicide and his own new family responsibilities, Wister sent EH a check for $500, which survives with Wister's letter of 25 February 1929 (JFK).

2 Wister had heard a report that EH had offered his own hand "for an expert to throw a knife through" and asked, "Did you?" (27 February 1929, JFK). Baker notes that after EH returned from Italy in 1919, he wrote and told tall tales about his WWI experiences, including a claim that the Italian Arditi troops had schooled him in knife-throwing "and even offered him an Austrian prisoner to practice on" (*Life*, 66).

3 In the same letter, Wister lamented "grievously" that he would not have the chance to talk to EH "as Henry James used to talk to me," saying, "I'm 68 and you're 31, and I'm not an old fogey and you're not a young ass, and so I might say something useful. I'd tell you what Kipling said when I spoke of you to him last November" (JFK). Wister would report in his next letter to EH that Kipling regarded *SAR* as "smut" but liked "The Killers" and told Wister, "If you vouch for him, I'll believe in him" (8 March 1929, JFK).

4 Wister observed that in *SAR*, Bill and Jake could not possibly have gotten off the train at Tours en route to Bayonne. "The Sud Expres doesn't pass Tours ... They got off at St Pierre des Corps," naming the railroad station on the eastern outskirts of Tours (27 February 1929, JFK).

5 Oliver Wendell Holmes, Jr. (1841–1935) served as Associate Justice on the U.S. Supreme Court from 1902 to 1932. In his 27 February letter, Wister had teased EH that, given the chance, he would show EH the "whole of Judge Holmes's letter about The Sun Also Rises."

6 William Rotch Wister (1904–1993) recuperated from the flu during a visit to Jamaica with his father. Charles Kemble Butler Wister (1908–1969), known as Carl, traveled extensively with his father and had met EH and Pauline in Wyoming in 1928. Carl had begun study at Marburg University in Germany.

7 Wister had expressed admiration for Stephen Vincent Benét's *John Brown's Body* (Garden City, N.Y.: Doubleday, Doran, 1928), a book-length epic poem about the American Civil War that was awarded a Pulitzer Prize in 1929 (27 February 1929).

8 EH may refer to Wister's biography *Ulysses S. Grant* (Boston: Small, Maynard, 1900).

9 EH alludes to the burial service from the Anglican Book of Common Prayer: "we commit his body to the ground; earth to earth; ashes to ashes, dust to dust."

10 In his 27 February letter Wister wrote that Walt Whitman's "stuff has the same relation to poetry that dough does to bread."

To Henry and Margaret Strater, [c. 4 March 1929]

Dear Mike and Maggie (or vice versa!)–

It was grand to have you men here and we wish the hell you were still here. You certainly gave us fine presents! Carried away with Champagne!

Youse guys are my idea of how the Very Rich (the ones Scott admires so) should be.[1] Of course by now you spent so much dough here you're probably broke. But Old Hem will look after you.

I got the 300 yds of line Mike and will not use it tho but save it for you to catch Tuna with. Will take good care of the Tackle and send it all in a box. Am using the 300 yds of 15 Denny sent—gee what a swell guy too.[2] I will send the pictures as soon as get them. Hope your eyes cleared up all right.

Since you left have only been in the Gulf once—caught (1) dolphin— Sailfish threw the hook. Will send you the harpoon gun and a world of harpoons. I know its like sending synthetic coals to Newcastle but you might use it.

Waldo arrived very vague and bleary and has gotten vaguer. Had expected so much from the guy and he's an anti climax after youse guys— Broke 16 straight clays yest Charles [Thompson] throwing them way out but it's all right if you dont believe it.

Caught 1 tarpon about 20 lbs—unhooked him and let him go. Charles has an automobile spot light for the little boat and makes [it] fine for the night jumping tarpons.

You guys were certainly fine and Maggie had her nerve to write a thank you letter because I feel youse were the hosts and we the guests.

The fight? at Miami was foul. A careful skilled but gutless Lithuanian vs. an aged acrobat. You would admire Stribling's fighting if it were old Bat. Levinsky or Jack Britton doing it trying to stay the route. We sat among thousands of Georgians and I tried to enliven the evening by yelling "Stribling Stinks. He stinks I tell you!" Anybody who said anything we pushed down. And then you couldnt get a fight. The crowd should have burned up the stands. Even that wouldnt get rid of the stink.[3]

Best love to you both from us, I know I havent thanked you for everything but will write again.

Yrs always

Hem.

Wish the hell we could send Waldo back and get Mike instead. Dos arrives tomorrow.[4] We leave the 23rd I think. Have written for passage.

PUL, ALS

1 In Fitzgerald's story "The Rich Boy" (collected in *All the Sad Young Men* [Scribner's, 1926]), the narrator says, "Let me tell you about the very rich. They are different from you and me." In EH's 1936 story "The Snows of Kilimanjaro," the protagonist mockingly alludes to that statement and counters, "Yes, they have more money."
2 Lansing C. "Denny" Holden, Jr. (1896–1938), Princeton graduate, WWI flying ace, and architect, was a friend of EH and Fitzgerald. Holden and his wife, Edith Harrold Holden (née Gillingham, 1896–1970), visited Key West at the same time as the Straters, and in her letter to EH and Pauline of 25 February [1929], Maggie Strater described the train ride back to New York with the Holdens. Maggie thanked EH and Pauline for "the glorious time" in Key West, saying, "Your hospitality was boundless" (JFK).
3 In the heavyweight elimination fight in Miami on 27 February, Jack Sharkey, of Lithuanian descent, defeated Young Stribling. Stribling, then twenty-five years old, came from a family of vaudeville acrobats and had been fighting professionally since he was sixteen. American light heavyweight boxer Battling Levinsky (né Barney Lebrowitz, 1891–1949). American welterweight boxer Jack Britton (né William J. Breslin, 1885–1962).
4 Dos Passos apparently changed his plans. In an undated letter he would write, "Damn sorry I couldn't get down earlier—but I've been tied up with this damn play." He expected *Airways, Inc.* to fold on Saturday and planned to arrive in Key West "Tuesday or Wednesday" (dated incorrectly as [April 1929], JFK). The play's final performance was held Sunday 17 March; he may have arrived Tuesday, 19 March, or Wednesday, 20 March.

To Mary Pfeiffer, 4 March [1929]

March 4

Dear Mother Pfeiffer—

I've meant to write many times but after the book was done the visitors and one thing and another came. They all come for a week and so have to fish everyminute of the time. Then stay for three weeks—fishing every minute of the time of course. Didn't have a hot meal for six days one stretch—leave befo[r]e breakfast—sandwiches for lunch and supper. But I know Max Perkins serialized my book purely on acct of the tarpon so I suppose it is all a form of literature.

Waldo has arrived seeming very vague and a little blurred. Maybe too many days on the train from Maine—He had the bright idea of buying shells from his local harware store in Bangor and shipping them to me as presents. The express on them from Bangor only being about once and a half as much as you would pay for the shells here. Not to speak of the fact that we have had plenty of shells anyway.

The book—so far and I hope so good—is called A Farewell To Arms—
I've read the book so many times and the title so many that I am not an
authority on either. It starts in the May number of Scribners and runs
through the October number. So far have read proof of the first installment.
It is written in the first person—I wish I could write a novel in the 3rd
person but haven't enough skill to yet. But is not autobiographical.

Your grandson Pat is healthier, browner and more cheerful every day. I
suppose Pauline has written you all the dope. Jinny sounds in wonderful
shape from her letters. I think that maybe having the tonsils out will do an
awful lot for her physically.

We sail the 20th of March or 3rd or 5th of April depending on what
passage we can get.

I wish we were going to see you both before we go—but anyway we'll be
back in two years and Pat should be a fine boy then and able to express
himself. He and Bumby are both too good to be true and I'm glad you go to
the retreat and pray a great deal so that you will have enough credit stored
up so that we may deserve, through you, to have them. I feel about them as
when I'm fishing and have some gigantic and unbelievable fish—knowing
that if anything happens no one will ever believe it—but think of you as a
lying fisherman or only a fond father.

Since this letter was started we have had lunch—and after lunch in the
tropics a head that never works any too good at best ceases to work at all. So
this seems to be the end of the letter[.] You will soon start receiving express
packages of various kinds to store against our return. It looks as though we
were sailing on April 5 on the Hamburg Amerika Line SS. Yorck which may
be German for York. Their only other boat on this run is called Seydlitz
which is undoubtedly German for Seydlitz.

This offers many fine oportunities for joking on the word Seydlitz or
seidlitz all of which I am sure you will be glad I am passing up.[1]

It being after lunch and all maybe you would rather this letter stopped
now and I will write again soon. I'm awfully glad you had such a good trip
and hope everything is going well with you both. My best regards and
greetings from Waldo to Mr/ Pfeiffer. Yours always,

Ernest—

see over

[*On verso:*]

Bumby heard the inauguration on the radio at school and said Papa did you know there's a hoover president of the United States.[2] He said he didn't understand what they said except that they were all getting new offices.

PUL, TLS

1 The *Yorck* and the *Seydlitz*, passenger liners operated by the North German Lloyd (Norddeutscher Lloyd) shipping company, ran a transatlantic route advertised as "The Sunny Route to Europe." The *Yorck* sailed from Havana for France via Spain on 5 April and arrived in Boulogne on 21 April. EH refers to Seidlitz powder, effervescing salts taken as a mild cathartic, named after the Seidlitz Springs in Bohemia.
2 Herbert Hoover (1874–1964) was inaugurated as thirty-first president of the United States on 4 March 1929, the day EH wrote this letter.

To Maxwell Perkins, 4 March [1929]

March 4

Dear Max—

Thanks very much for the two letters enclosing the two checks and royalty report.[1] I wonder if you could send me the amt. of income from Scribners in 1928 so I can make out tax.[2] Don't do this if it's too much bother.

About sailing—have written varoious companies but it looks like the Yorck of Hamburg Amerika Line sailing Havana April 5 for Vigo, Coruna, Gijon and Boulogne—Due Boulogne on April 21. Will know for sure in 3 or 4 days.

I wish as much proof as possible could come down before we go so as to have no delay in getting it back. Also so I'll be well ahead and if there is anything to be discussed there will be time. However we will be in France April 21 and have written the Guaranty Trust Co/ 1, rue des Italiens there to hold all mail for me. So any proof sent there I will look after immediately on getting in and ship directly back to you.

I've caught one small tarpon—slipped him back—20 pounds I guess. Will try to get some good pictures that you can use for publicity. Will shoot this now so you will get it.

yours always,
Ernest Hemingway.

PUL, TLS

1 With his letter of 27 February 1929, Perkins had sent the check for $6,000 that EH had requested (PUL; *TOTTC*, 94), and in his letter of 1 March 1929 he had enclosed a partial royalty report (excluding *SAR*), dated 1 February 1929, and a check for $183.14, the amount of royalties due to EH as shown on the statement (JFK).
2 In his response of 8 March 1929, Perkins would enclose an official 1928 income statement for tax purposes, showing an income of $5,818.35. This included some 1927 payments reported as 1928 income although not a $5000 advance paid in 1928 but technically reportable the following year. The actual amount EH received from Scribner's in 1928 was $8,942.00 (JFK).

To Grace Hall Hemingway, 6 March [1929]

March 6

Dear Mother:-

I was awfully glad to hear you are handling everything so well.

Enclosed is a check for 500\underline{^{00}}$ 400 for the taxes (you pay them please. That's the simplest way) and 100 for this month of March—will send you the other checks as soon as Scribner's check goes through the bank.[1]

Please pardon this note being so brief.

Everyone is well and very happy. We are off for a trip to Marquesas— back Sunday.

Would you ask Leicester to send me the Florida Fishing book I left with him?[2] He was to send it quite awhile ago but know he must have forgotten it.

Best love to all—

Ernie

We leave April 3 or 5th from Havana—

Don't bother to write me a letter thanking for this check— just acknowledge it so I'll know it arrived.

Thank you ever so much for taking so much trouble about Long John—[3] I wish you would keep it for me until I come back—put it in bank vault perhaps— I cant have it in Europe.

UT, ALS

1 This was the first of the monthly checks for $100 that EH would send his mother through March 1930. Using $20,000 from his royalties and $30,000 from Uncle Gus, he would set up a trust fund that provided her with a monthly income of almost $200 and his sister Carol with an annual income of $600, starting in April 1930.
2 Perhaps William H. Gregg and John Gardner's *Where, When, and How to Catch Fish on the East Coast of Florida* (Buffalo and New York: Matthews-Northrup, 1902), which was in EH's personal library (Brasch and Sigman, 170).
3 Grace had asked EH to advise her what she should do with "the old civil war 'Long John'"— his grandfather Anson Hemingway's Civil War pistol, which EH's father had used to kill himself (24 February 1929, JFK). Not having heard back from EH, Grace reported in a letter of 7 March 1929 that she had sent a package by American Railway Express containing the "Old John civil war revolver in holster" as well as "a roll of my two best Desert pictures," cookies for Sunny, a cake for Pauline, salted nuts for EH, and a book for Bumby (JFK).

To Owen Wister, 11 March 1929

March 11, 1929

Dear O. W.——

That Bloody Waldo Frank! Did you ever read what he said about Anderson when Anderson was still a great man to him?[1] Or a book of his called Virgin Spain? There was a book. He has always seemed to me to be a fool but he may be right except this—

Anderson is a man sort of like Old Mother Hubbard in appearance— He wrote some stories that I thought were lovely—all the time he was working as an advertising writer but he wrote simply and to me, anyway, very beautifully—about people and the country and, it's true, best of all about adolescence— He went to New York and a number of Jews—Steiglitz, W. Frank, Paul Rosenfeld got hold of him and turned his head with praise. So that he took all his faults for virtues and all the defects in his writing for characteristics of genius—[2] He was so soft that finally he just flowed all over the place— The convex certainly resembles the concave—but first you must establish that it is the convex and the concave— That is what makes me so impatient with what passes for criticism— They start with something that they never establish to be true and go on with the assumption that it is true and prove everything from that—[3]

I'm no hard boiled or sophisticate (whatever that means) writer—at first I had to write very, almost ridiculously, simple stories to be able to write anything at all. I'd seen I dont know how many hundred baseball games and yet when I wrote about one I did not know what it was in the game that gave me the feeling that I had— I had to find the physical details that produce the aesthetic result (Pardon the terminology) I had to write what I could— always with hundreds I wanted to write and couldnt. I was beginning to get so I could write a little better but always with great defects and awkwardnesses (which already these same jews were praising as "a new style") My life was more or less shot out from under me and I was drinking much too much entirely through my own fault. I was writing better and getting so I could link up sentences occasionally instead of having them all go put put put— Then wrote The Sun Also in 6 weeks— It contains much garbage but no smut[4] and what I hoped to do was contrast the people, most of whom were pretty lousy, with the country which was pretty fine. I tried to give the destruction of character in the woman Brett—that was the main story and I failed to ~~get it across~~ do it.

So I thought the Pamplona part was all right and the rest interesting enough to carry it even though to me it was a failure and I wouldnt have published it except that that was the only way I could get it behind me.

If I'd destroyed it I might later have thought it was better than it was.

Nothing you can say would make me angry— Please always go the limit— It is only amateurs that are angered by criticism— My god all I care about is to do the thing better and I would anytime take 500 insults, 100 untruths to get one true thing. That's why I wish you were criticizing the new book— You show me 5 things wrong with the Sun and I'll show you 50— But this one now I'm blind on—

About Kipling—I suppose no one was ever born with more genius—it is a pleasure even to be damned by him— I have great respect for him as a writer and none for his opinion (abstract opinion of course) You see I have great respect for your opinion because you at (I can't recall the exact advanced age you claim) can write the same story I would write and write it very much better— Kipling could write the same story now and I wouldnt care for it[.] Then too he wouldnt write it— There is no reason why he should continue to write. The early and middle stuff is wonderful enough to stand on— But what happened to him?

I don't know many writers— Ford Madox Ford writes things I cant read and always lies to me— Joyce is a great man and now writes stuff that has to be read out loud by the author to have any point—and how he <u>could</u> write— This letter goes on and on— I'll be damned if I'll write about all the writers— they write enough—

Waldo Frank is a fool— The thing that makes what he writes seem true is the quotation from Taine. I cant claim the 5¢ you offer but it is fine to know I have 50,000¢ (I can't work that out in cents) in your safekeeping. I have word from Max Perkins that he will send you a set of proofs of the book as it appears in the magazine. I must correct the 2nd installment now—[5]

Mrs. Hemingway joins me in all best wishes

Ernest Hemingway.

LOC, ALS; postmark: KEY WEST FLA., MAR 12 / 9 AM

1 In his letter to EH of 8 March 1929, Wister quoted a passage from Waldo Frank's *The Re-discovery of America* (Scribner's, 1929) critical of the work of both Anderson and Hemingway. Years earlier Frank had praised Anderson and predicted his rise to the status of "Genius in America" in an essay titled "Emerging Greatness," which appeared in the first volume of *Seven Arts* (November 1916: 78).

2 American photographer Alfred Stieglitz (1864–1946), Waldo Frank, and American literary critic Paul Rosenfeld had all been early supporters of Anderson's work. In the early 1920s Anderson and Stieglitz mutually admired and praised each other's work, and Frank and Rosenfeld published positive reviews.

3 In *The Re-discovery of America*, Frank wrote: "Thus, the contrast of Anderson with the sophisticate school (in which Ernest Hemingway excels) is but an oscillation of the adolescent mind, from one temper to another. Sentimental tears react into sentimental toughness. Nothing, said Taine, so much resembles convex as concave. Mr. Hemingway has clamped the masque of bravado on the bewildered visage of Anderson's seeker. The world of both is one; the motive of escape beneath their contrasting methods is one, also" (135). After quoting this passage in his letter, Wister wrote, "I'll give you 5 cents if you'll tell me what this means." French critic Hippolyte-Adolphe Taine (1828–1893) espoused a scientific approach to art.

4 Kipling had dismissed *SAR* as "smut" in a November 1928 exchange with Wister.

5 Scribner's sent EH proofs of the second installment of *FTA* on 6 March 1929. Consisting of Chapters 10–16, it would appear in the June 1929 issue of *Scribner's Magazine*.

To Maxwell Perkins, 11 March [1929]

March 11

Dear Max—

Rec'ed the proofs of the 2nd installment when we got home last night from Marquesas.

In galley 2 two omissions have been made—the first of 6 lines in the Mss. The 2nd of 10 lines in the Mss.[1] The 2nd cut has been made so that the resultant dialogue does not make sense—two consecutive sentences are left as dialogue both spoken by the same person. ~~I see no excuse for the cutting when revmoval of one sentence would have handled it.~~

In the first cut the removal of one sentence would have been sufficient.

I thought it was understood that there would be no cutting without consulting me and having my approval.[2] This was cut on the Mss without being set on the proof.

Read it yourself and see what you think.

If any passages are to be eliminated they must be eliminated from the proof so I can see how it looks and clean it up on the proof— I'd rather return the money and call it all off than have arbitrary eliminations made without any mention of the fact they are being made. If that's to be done let some one else sign it—By E.H. and R.B.—[3] Half the writing I do is elimination. If someone else is doing it let them sign it.

[*EH marginal insertion in black ink to the right of the preceding two sentences*: That's just anger!]

<u>Private</u> to you—

I was too damned angry to write Mr. Bridges about it. There was no mention of anything being cut out and the first intimation I get is when the dialogue doesnt make sense on the page. I'll argue any point and if they insist on cutting consent and help the best I can putting the responsibility on the magazine but I'll be damned if it's to be cut in the Mss. without a word to me. It's so awkward to fix—

I suppose I must write Mr. Bridges—that takes 1/2 a day— The chapter (10) was a fine one and it's ruined— I could have fixed the cuts from the galleys so they would make sense—

Ernest Hemingway.

Thanks ever so much for the income tax data—Ive just made it out— We caught 7 tarpon at Marquesas— I got one weighed 96 pounds—

We sail April 5—

Later—[4]

Wrote a calm letter to Mr. Bridges— There was a cut in Galley 10 too that I concede if you think it's necessary—but it doesnt seem so.[5] Would you read the installment and my letter to Mr. Bridges and see if it's all right? You know I'm not just trying to be difficult. Am not sore now— But it was snooty to cut passages on Mss rather than on proof. I think it's fixed up all right.

There's a big norther blowing— Dos Passos read the book and he was very very enthusiastic— He's always been my most bitterly severe critic— Waldo [Peirce] liked it much too— Dos liking it is the best news I've had since you did because he's always been hard as can be and if you, Mike [Strater]— Waldo and Dos all like it that is 4 different views—

I'm not trying to be difficult about the magazine—I want to help however I can—

We got 38 birds I wont mention the name because the season's closed—7 tarpon—a mutton fish—4 kingfish—amberjacks etc.

We sail on the SS. Yorck of North German Lloyd line from Havana April 5—

PUL, ALS

1 Both cuts were to Chapter 10 of the novel, removing Rinaldi's intimation that Frederic and the priest were homosexuals and Rinaldi's comment on the difference between sexual intercourse with a girl and with a woman. Both passages would appear in the book publication of *FTA*.
2 Perkins would respond that the galley revisions were "made for only the one reason of simplifying things and speeding them up," adding, "There is, and was, and never will be, any idea of making any change without your approval" (15 March 1929, PUL; *TOTTC*, 96).
3 R.B., *Scribner's Magazine* editor Robert Bridges.
4 EH wrote the letter up to this point in pencil. After stopping to write the "calm letter" to Bridges dated 11 March 1929 that follows in this volume, he returned to this letter, completing it in black ink and adding marginal notes.
5 This cut was made in the scene between Frederic and Catherine in the hospital in Milan, toward the end of Chapter 14 (Trogdon *Racket*, 72–73, 271). As Reynolds observes, "what may be the shortest seduction scene in literature" was reduced even further by these cuts, "leaving the reader wondering what, if anything, had taken place" (Michael S. Reynolds, *Hemingway's First War: The Making of* A Farewell to Arms [Princeton, New Jersey: Princeton University Press, 1976], 71).

To Robert Bridges, 11 March 1929

March 11, 1929

Dear Mr. Bridges—

We sail on April 5—from Havana for Boulogne via Spanish ports—
Should be in Paris April 22 where my address is care of the Guaranty Trust
Co. of N.Y, 1 rue des Italiens. I hope there will be another installment of
proof before we go and perhaps you will have one in Paris soon after I
arrive. I'll do them the day I receive them.

Am returning the proofs—for June. In galley 2 two omissions had been
made from the Mss. I had not heard of this until (reading) I found that the
Mss. had been cut so that the dialogue in the proof did not make sense. I
have fixed up the two places—eliminating what was desired to be cut but
keeping the sense of the conversation—

In galley 10 I find an omission made which makes the passage
unconvincing to me— I wish you would be perfectly sure that this omission
is necessary— I have worked very hard over that passage and gone over and
over it in order that it might be printed without in any way giving offense
and I hope you will be quite sure that you do not wish to print it as it stands
in the Mss. It is very important that every step in a story be convincing if it is
all to be convincing.

In the future I wish that any cuts of passages could be suggested on the
proof not the Mss. as I might not be where I had a copy of the original
Mss. at hand and I would not like to have to delay the proof until I could
obtain one.

About the introduction at the head of successive chapters—I have never
done this and would probably do it very badly so if you dont mind I would
rather have the magazine do it.[1]

With best wishes.
Yours very truly,
Ernest Hemingway.

UVA, ALS

1 In his letter of 7 March 1929, Bridges told EH it was *Scribner's Magazine*'s practice to provide a brief introduction "at the head of each instalment which leads the new reader, who has missed the earlier instalments, into the story," and offered EH the option of writing his own introductions (PUL).

To Owen Wister, 26 March [1929]

March 26

Dear O.W.

We sail on the Yorck of Nord Deutsche Lloyd from Havana for Boulogne April 5— Then the address in Paris is 6 rue Férou Paris VI— The Guaranty Trust Co. of N.Y. 1, rue des Italiens—forwards all mail— We'll be in Spain from the 1st part of July on—

I asked Max Perkins to send you a set of proofs when they have one— I hope you like it— Herr Bridges does his best to bowdlerize it— So if it makes no sense wait for the book— Then if the book makes no sense do not despair—I'll by then be trying to write one that does— No guarantees—

Have been 8 days on the water in small boat—cruising to Tortugas and around— The house feels like jail and the pen does not feel good in the hand. I'll be looking forward to a letter.

Yrs always,
Ernest Hemingway.

LOC, ALS; postmark: KEY WEST FLA., MAR 26 / 6 PM / 1929

To Archibald MacLeish, 26 [March 1929]

April 26[1]

Dear Archie:—

Papa's too tired to spell correctly.[2] But it was a fine trip (Tortugas)— Yours was a real trip though— It sounded wonderful. We missed not seeing you like hell but understand your not wishing to get shot on acct of not worrying Ada would be plenty of reason alone. I would give my shirt and pants to have made the trip with you— It should be a great poem although count on the boys to say you stole it from Emily Dickinson![3]

My book starts next month in Scribners— Get the 1st because it may be the last number—unless they've bowdlerized <u>after</u> the proofs left here.

We sail on the Yorck of North Gerwan Lloyd line April 5 from Havana for Vigo Coruna Gijon and Boulogne due there April 21— Afterwards at 6 rue Férou—

I wish the hell you were going to be in Paris but Conway will be lovely in the summer— But don't go too long without me seeing you and yr. wife Mrs. MacLeish

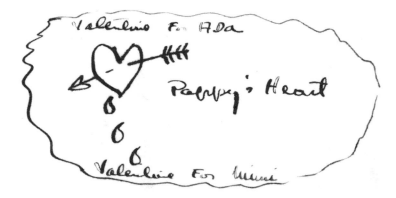

If the serial makes no sense it means they are cutting it so wait for the book— Have been on the water since a week ago yesterday and too pooped —not pooped but fundamentally tired to write a decent letter— Please write

Love to Ada Mimi and Kenny—

Pappy.

LOC, ALS

1 EH mistakenly dated this letter April instead of March, as indicated by internal evidence, including his reference to his pending departure for Europe aboard the *Yorck* on 5 April.

2 EH had written "Aachie" but wrote an "r" over the second "a." After the word "spell" in this sentence, he drew an arrow pointing upward to his correction.

3 In his letter to EH of 11 March 1929, MacLeish described his travels in Mexico. He had taken a mule "over the road between Vera Cruz and Mexico City that Cortes took" because he wanted to write a poem about the Spanish Conquest, and EH had once advised him "never to write about anything I didn't know all about." (MacLeish's epic poem *Conquistador* [1932] would win a Pulitzer Prize in 1933.) He had also planned "to take a

vessel from Vera Cruz to Havana to Key West and drop in on you," MacLeish told EH, but aborted that plan because armed troops had begun seizing the leadership of Mexican states in the course of the country's civil war (JFK). American poet Emily Dickinson (1830–1886) had lived in Amherst, Massachusetts, not far from MacLeish's home outside the nearby town of Conway.

To Maxwell Perkins, [30 March 1929]

Dear Max

Surely you can use Evan Shipman's name— I'm his manager and take responsibility— It will be good for him—[1] He told me you could when I saw him in N.Y— His address is 21 or 23 Beekman Place— It can be verified from phone book— I havent heard from him for several weeks—

This is saturday and we leave Thursday— You were grand to send the Crusades book and the Round Up— All the books you sent go on the boat— I'm saving R. Lardners book for the boat but looked into it and you tell him for me that I know who the best short story writer in America is and that its him.[2] He is certainly a grand American writer— Pauline was knocked over by how very very fine the stories are— Im saving the full enjoyment for the boat

Bumby was overjoyed by the cowboy book—[3]

I'll send the contract before I go—[4] We got 8 tarpon the last two nights at Marquesas— Waldo got one of 107 pounds. Tortugas was such a fine trip[.] I cant tell you anything about it in a letter. Besides there's now a grand rush of proof reading packing and last minute fishing.

Charles said you wrote him the nicest letter he ever got from anyone.

Best from us all—

Ernest Hemingway.

When do I sign the special edition copies?[5] They'd better send me the sheets with the place for signature before they go to bindery. Imagine that would be best. Shipping books back and forth across the Atlantic not money in that— If you want a page of Mss. for reproduction that is O.K.

Bumby reading Carteles saw picture of nude cinema star and said: 'Oh look! a NAKED lady.[6] I must show her to Patrick! Oh Patrick!' and ran off with the magazine. That's masculine and brotherly solidarity.

PUL, ALS

1 In his letter to EH of 25 March 1929, Perkins reported that *Scribner's Magazine* had written to Evan Shipman accepting a poem of his, but had received no response. Perkins wondered if they could print the poem under Shipman's name, recalling having heard something about his publishing only anonymously (PUL). The first work attributed to Shipman in *Scribner's Magazine* would be his poem "Third Heat, 2:12 Trot," published in the February 1931 issue.

2 Perkins may have sent EH a copy of *The Chronicles of the Crusades, Being Contemporary Narratives of the Crusade of Richard Coeur de Lion, by Richard of Devizes and Geoffrey de Vinsauf; and of The Crusade of St. Louis, by Lord John de Joinville* (London: Bohn, 1848). It was among the books in EH's library at his Cuban home, Finca Vigía, where he lived from 1939 to 1960 (Brasch and Sigman, 104). Perkins also sent an advance copy of *Round Up: The Stories of Ring W. Lardner* (New York: Scribner's, 1929).

3 Possibly *Sand* (1929), an illustrated book by Will James (né Joseph-Ernest Nephtali Dufault, 1892–1942), a Canadian writer and illustrator of the American West, or James's *Smoky, the Cowhorse* (1926), winner of the 1927 Newbery Medal, republished in a new edition with color illustrations in 1929. Both books were Scribner's publications.

4 Perkins enclosed the contract for *FTA* in his letter of 14 March 1929 (PUL). EH did not return a signed copy prior to departing for France.

5 Perkins had written to EH about plans for a small limited edition of "say 250 copies, which you should sign. The idea would be that it would have a different type page, be a larger book, have color on the title page, and your signature"—and, with EH's permission, a facsimile of a page from the manuscript (15 March 1929, PUL). Scribner's would actually issue 510 numbered and autographed copies of the so-called Limited Edition of *FTA*.

6 *Carteles*, a weekly magazine published in Cuba from 1919 until 1960, covering Cuban politics, commerce, art, and sports.

To Grace Hall Hemingway, [30 March 1929]

Dear Mother—

Enclosed please find check for 678.$\frac{23}{}$ (578.^{93} for the special assesment taxes and $100 for the month of April.[1] The special assessments were surely tough luck but I am glad to pay them while I can. If you will send me the official location and description of <u>all</u> property—Pauline's uncle has a salesman in that territory who is interested in St. Pete'bg real estate and he will have him look them all up and make a report on them and we may be able to do something about selling.

I am glad to help all I can as long as I have money. I know you will do everything to get things going though because I never know when I may be broke. I can guarantee the 100 a month for this year and next year too (will put it aside now—) but we want to get things going as well as possible. Never worry because I will always fix things up—can always borrow money if I haven't it— So don't ever worry—but go ahead with good confidence and get things going. I am very pleased about the 4 roomers and that you are going to Windermere.[2] Remember you are on your own but have a powerful backer—To whit me.

I will count on Marce and Sterling to do something too. I know Marce is going to have a baby— But we have had one this year too and they are rich and have always been very great friends of the family while I live by my pen and have been more or less of an outcast.[3]

But the main thing is not to worry about money—but to go ahead with courage and confidence. Make Uncle George see you sell the house for a good substantial profit or else he must get the mortgage cancelled. If he has to pay it himself. He did more than any one to kill Dad and he had better do something in reparation. I know his sanctimonious tightness but he is going to do what he ought to do about that house or I will have his hide.[4] I have never written a novel of the H family because I have never wanted to hurt anyones feelings but with the death of the ones I love a period has been put to a great part of it and I may have to undertake it—

This is Saturday[.] We leave next Thursday— Pauline is down with a septic sore throat— Sunny and Pat O.K. but Bumby with a bad throat— Imagine they'll all be O.K. by Thursday Hope so—

Best love to the kids

Yours always

Ernie.

You have been fine about everything. Remember not to worry and not to hold things back from me but dont bother me with general run of stuff— The more I'm let alone and not worried the better I can function— Have paid Sunny's passage etc so imagine she'd have enough for her trip—[5]

PSU, ALS

The conjectured letter date is based on EH's references to his mother's letter dated 24 March 1929 (JFK) and his mention that he was writing on Saturday before leaving Key West for France via Cuba "next Thursday" (4 April). Carlos Baker dates this letter 11 March 1929 (*SL*, 295–96), probably based on postmarks on the copy of the envelope he received from

Madelaine (Sunny) Hemingway, along with a copy of this letter—the originals now in the PSU Special Collections Library. Postmarks on the envelope verso indicate it was sent by registered mail from Key West on 7 March 1929 and received in Oak Park on 11 March 1929. Both the letter and the envelope bear Sunny's notation, "Copied for Baker." However, that envelope most likely belongs with EH's letter of 6 March [1929], now housed at UT.

1 In her letter of 24 March 1929, Grace provided a detailed financial account showing she had paid $409.12 in taxes for the Florida properties but still owed $578.93 in special assessments. Those, she wrote, "came out of the clear sky, when I thought I had everything paid. You see, dear, Dad has been failing for a long time, and last year he just forgot to pay the first instalment on each of these,—consequently they are double this year and a penalty besides" (JFK).
2 In the same letter, Grace wrote that she had taken in four roomers for the spring and that she, Leicester, and Carol would be at Windemere from 9 July to 29 August.
3 Marcelline and her husband, a successful engineer for the Detroit Edison Company, were expecting their second child, James Sanford, who would be born on 29 May 1929.
4 EH blamed his father's brother George Roy Hemingway (1876–1953), a real estate agent in Oak Park, for advising Clarence badly regarding financial investments, including the ill-fated Florida real estate purchases.
5 Sunny would sail with the Hemingways for France, departing from Havana on 5 April.

To Maxwell Perkins, 3 April [1929]

March April 3

Dear Max—

This just a note before we go— Have corrected and am mailing the 4th installment to the magazine— We leave tomorrow morning—in the middle of packing now— We'll try to get Waldo to witness the contract and mail it to you—Pauline got the grippe and is laid up in bed—Sunny worse than useless.[1]

Thanks ever so much for all the grand books— Hope we get off—it seems impossible— I've lost my hat and my coat to blue suit stolen so have nothing to wear— Waldo painted a portrait of me looking like Molly Colum's friend Balzac—wish it was as easy to write like him—not but what he's a hell of a sloppy writer but what an amount of juice![2]

Well as Aiken says Farewell farewell farewell![3]

Ernest

Please dont under any circumstances give Scott [Fitzgerald] our Paris home address— Last time he was in Paris He got us kicked out of one apt.

and in trouble all the time (Insulted the landlord—pee-ed on the front porch—tried to break down the door at 3–4 and 5 a.m. etc.)— Will meet him in public places but have this apt where we're quiet and comfortable and found it with great difficulty and he would get us ousted by only one performance— Bank is only address to give—

I am very fond of Scott but I'll beat him up before I'll let him come and get us ousted from this place—as a matter of fact I'm afraid I'd kill him— It's the best home I've ever had and he would lose it for us without one thought—⁴ It's nothing to do with friendship—that implies obligations on both sides— When I heard he was going to Paris it gave me the horrors.

Sailing SS. Yorck of N German LLoyd via Vigo—Coruña—Gijon for Boulogne—due April <u>21</u>

PUL, ALS

1 EH would write to Perkins from Paris that he did not return the contract because he lacked a witness ([c. 23 April 1929], JFK).
2 Honoré de Balzac (1799–1850), French novelist, author of the multivolume *La Comédie humaine* (1842–1846, 1848, 1855). Molly Colum, pen name of Mary (Gunning Maguire) Colum (1884–1957), Irish American writer and critic who was a frequent contributor to *Scribner's Magazine* and a friend of Perkins. In a letter of 17 September 1928, Perkins had told EH, "Molly Colum says you look like Balzac" (JFK). Her remark might have been prompted by seeing Peirce's portrait of EH with the caption "May 1928 Key West." Here EH refers to Peirce's more recent portrait signed "For Ernest (alias Kid Balzac) Key West— first April /29— WP" (JFK).
3 Conrad Aiken's short story "Farewell! Farewell! Farewell!" appeared in the August 1928 issue of *Scribner's Magazine*.
4 The Hemingways would return to the apartment at 6, rue Férou, in a quiet neighborhood on the Left Bank of Paris, where EH and Pauline had moved during the spring of 1927 after they were married.

VOLUME 3 (1926–1929)
ROSTER OF CORRESPONDENTS

Sherwood Anderson (1876–1941). American fiction writer whose books include *Winesburg, Ohio* (1919), *Many Marriages* (1923), *A Story Teller's Story* (1924), *Dark Laughter* (1925), and *Tar: A Midwest Childhood* (1926). He and EH met in Chicago in 1921, and Anderson provided important letters of introduction when EH followed his advice and moved to Paris that December to pursue writing. Subsequently, EH's opinion of Anderson's work deteriorated, and in 1925 EH wrote a parody of *Dark Laughter* titled *The Torrents of Spring*, which Scribner's published in 1926.

Sylvia Beach (1887–1962). Owner of the Left Bank Paris bookstore Shakespeare and Company at 12, rue de l'Odéon, which also served as a lending library and permanent address for expatriate writers and artists. She published James Joyce's *Ulysses* (1922), and her shop carried the first copies of EH's *Three Stories and Ten Poems* (1923) and *in our time* (1924). EH would later write of her: "No one I ever knew was nicer to me" (*A Moveable Feast*, "Shakespeare and Company").

Glen Walton Blodgett (1882–1956). American autograph collector to whom EH wrote in 1928 after Blodgett solicited a contribution to his collection.

Robert Bridges (1858–1941). An 1879 Princeton University graduate, Bridges wrote literary criticism for *Life* magazine and worked on the staff of the *New York Evening Post* before serving at *Scribner's Magazine* as assistant editor (1887–1914), then as editor in chief (1914–1930).

Louis Bromfield (1896–1956). American novelist who won the 1927 Pulitzer Prize for *Early Autumn* (1926). In 1925 he moved with his family to France, where he had served in the ambulance corps during WWI, and there befriended EH. Later that year, when EH became unhappy with his publisher, Boni & Liveright, Bromfield encouraged him to move to Harcourt, Brace.

Mary Appleton Wood Bromfield (1892–1952). Daughter of Ellen Appleton Smith and prominent New York City attorney Chalmers Wood, Mary married Louis Bromfield in 1921. The couple and their three daughters, Ann Chalmers, Mary Hope, and Ellen Margaret, lived in Europe for thirteen years.

Morley Callaghan (1903–1990). A Toronto native and a 1925 graduate of the University of Toronto, Callaghan was working as a cub reporter at the *Toronto Daily Star* when he met EH in 1923. EH encouraged Callaghan's efforts to write fiction and promoted his work among the Paris literati. Callaghan's first published story appeared in the second number of *This Quarter* (Autumn–Winter 1925–1926) together with EH's "The Undefeated," and he went on to publish *Strange Fugitive* (1928) and *A Native Argosy* (1929). Callaghan would gain fame as the sparring partner who knocked down EH in a 1929 boxing match in Paris refereed by F. Scott Fitzgerald, who forgot to keep time.

Jonathan Cape (1879–1960). British publisher whose firm, founded in 1921, featured the works of many American writers, including Sinclair Lewis, Eugene O'Neill, Sherwood Anderson, Louis Bromfield, Robert Frost, Carl Sandburg, and Edna St. Vincent Millay. Cape's British edition of *In Our Time* (1926) included unauthorized revisions that angered EH. Nevertheless, EH agreed to let him publish British editions of *The Sun Also Rises*, under the title *Fiesta* (1927); *Men Without Women* (1928); and *A Farewell to Arms* (1929).

Eleanor Sawyer Chase (1903–1944). American author of the popular novel *Pennagan Place* (1928). A descendant of a wealthy Wisconsin family and a 1921 University of Wisconsin graduate, she worked for the New York publishing firm J. H. Sears & Company. She associated with members of the Algonquin Round Table, including Robert Benchley and Dorothy Parker. She married noted architect Maurice Fatio in 1929, and the couple lived a fashionable life in Palm Beach, Florida.

Pierre Chautard. Landlord of the cold-water apartment above a sawmill at 113, rue Notre-Dame des Champs in Paris that EH and Hadley kept as their primary residence from February 1924 until their separation in August 1926.

Dorothy Connable (1893–1975). Daughter of Harriet Gridley Connable and Ralph Connable, Sr., and a Red Cross worker in France during WWI. For several months in 1920 EH lived in the Connable home in Toronto as a hired companion to Dorothy's disabled brother Ralph. Dorothy and EH renewed their friendship upon EH's return to Toronto with Hadley in 1923. In 1924 Dorothy moved to New York City, where she began working as a professional photographer in 1926.

John (Jack) Cheney Cowles (1894–1972). A grandson of *Chicago Tribune* co-owner Alfred Cowles, he worked for the newspaper's Paris edition in the early 1920s. He probably met EH through Donald Ogden Stewart (1894–1980), a former Yale classmate of Cowles. During his February 1926 visit to New York City, EH partied with Cowles, who lived in Greenwich Village, and bought liquor from his bootlegger. At that time, EH also wrote a humorous inscription addressed to Cowles in a first edition of *In Our Time* (1925).

Harry Crosby (1898–1929). American writer and expatriate who moved to Paris with his wife, Caresse (née Mary Phelps Jacob, 1892–1970), shortly after they married in 1922. Known for their eccentricities and open marriage, the Crosbys established the Black Sun Press in 1925. Harry Crosby met EH in Gstaad in December 1926 and joined him for the fiesta in Pamplona the following summer. In 1928 Crosby began an affair with Boston socialite Josephine Rotch, who shared his interest in pagan sun rituals and would be found dead of gunshot wounds alongside Crosby in New York City in 1929 in an apparent murder-suicide pact.

Frank Andrew Curtin (1880–1931). A lawyer from Fresno, California, who admired and collected EH's works. In October 1927 EH cooperated with Curtin's request for inscription slips that he wanted to place in EH's books.

Vincent Clement Donovan (1892–1977). A priest at the St. Vincent Ferrer Priory in New York City, Father Donovan wrote to EH in 1927 after learning of EH's conversion to Catholicism. A member of the Dominican Order (O.P., *Ordo Praedicatorum* or Order of Preachers), known for its intellectual tradition and its mission to teach the laity, he delivered popular weekly lectures on liturgical topics at his church and, in 1929, in radio broadcasts.

John Dos Passos (1896–1970). American writer known for his WWI novel *Three Soldiers* (1921) and his innovative fiction, including *Manhattan Transfer* (1925). He served as director of the experimental New Playwrights Theatre until 1929. A political leftist throughout the 1920s, he was a regular contributor to *New Masses* and joined the Sacco-Vanzetti Defense Committee and helped prepare its publication *Facing the Chair* (1927). Dos Passos had met EH in Schio in June 1918, while serving with the American Red Cross Ambulance Service in Italy. Meeting again in 1924 in Paris, the two became close friends, and Dos Passos joined EH in Pamplona for the bullfights in July 1924, in Schruns for skiing in 1926, and in Key

West for fishing in 1928 and 1929. Dos Passos would marry EH's longtime friend, Kate Smith, in 1929.

T. S. (Thomas Stearns) Eliot (1888–1965). Poet, playwright, literary critic, editor, and publisher. His works include the poems "The Love Song of J. Alfred Prufrock" (1915) and *The Waste Land* (1922) as well as literary criticism, such as the essay "Tradition and the Individual Talent" (1920). A St. Louis native and Harvard graduate, Eliot moved to England in 1914 and became a British citizen in 1927. He worked as a clerk for Lloyd's Bank, 1915–1925, while writing poetry and serving as assistant editor at *The Egoist*, 1917–1919. After founding the literary quarterly *Criterion* in 1922, he would serve as its editor until it ceased publication in 1939.

Burton Emmett (1871–1935). Wealthy advertising copywriter and executive in New York City, who served as president of the American Institute of Graphic Arts in the 1920s. He and his wife Mary provided financial support to close friend Sherwood Anderson throughout the 1920s and 1930s. An avid collector of literary manuscripts, Emmett expressed interest as early as 1927 in purchasing the manuscripts of EH's works.

Edith Finch (1900–1978). Educator, publisher, and biographer from New York City. A graduate of Bryn Mawr College (1922) and St. Hilda's College, Oxford (1926), she later returned to Bryn Mawr to teach English literature. In 1926 she co-founded The As Stable Publications, releasing that year a pamphlet series that included Gertrude Stein's "Descriptions of Literature" and EH's "Today is Friday."

F. Scott Fitzgerald (1896–1940). American author who gained immediate success with his novel *This Side of Paradise* (1920) and his stories of the Jazz Age. He met EH in Paris in spring 1925, shortly after the publication of *The Great Gatsby*. An important reader of EH's early manuscripts, Fitzgerald introduced EH's works to his own editor at Scribner's, Maxwell Perkins, and was instrumental in helping EH move from Boni & Liveright to Charles Scribner's Sons in 1926. Soon thereafter, Fitzgerald's career as a novelist stalled. He was paid generously by the *Saturday Evening Post* for his short stories, but he struggled for years to complete his next novel, *Tender Is the Night* (1934).

Zelda Fitzgerald (née Sayre, 1900–1948). American writer, painter, and wife of F. Scott Fitzgerald. Following their marriage in 1920 and the birth of their daughter Frances Scott (Scottie) Fitzgerald in 1921, Zelda pursued a career in ballet. In the winter of 1928–1929 she began writing a series of "girl stories" for

College Humor, partly to pay for her ballet lessons. EH believed that Zelda was harmful to Scott's writing, as he would later recount in *A Moveable Feast* ("Hawks Do Not Share" and "A Matter of Measurements").

Lewis Galantière (1895–1977). Journalist, translator of French literature, and playwright. Born in Chicago to French parents, he worked for the International Chamber of Commerce in Paris from 1920 to 1927, and as "Louis Gay" wrote the column "Reviews and Reflections" for the Paris *Tribune*'s Sunday magazine beginning in 1924. Galantière was among the first of EH's American expatriate friends in Paris, and in 1930 he would write an in-depth, positive review of EH's *A Farewell to Arms* for the *Hound & Horn*.

Isabelle Simmons Godolphin (1901–1964). A next-door neighbor of the Hemingway family, Simmons was a 1920 graduate of Oak Park and River Forest High School and attended the University of Chicago. In 1923 she visited EH and Hadley in Switzerland and Italy. In 1925 she married Francis R. B. "Frisco" Godolphin (1903–1974), a 1924 Princeton graduate who began teaching classics at Princeton in 1927, the same year the couple had the first of their two children, Jeanne and Thomas.

Henry I. Goodman (1893–1991). Romanian-born teacher and translator of Yiddish literature who emigrated to the United States around 1900. For thirty-four years Goodman taught English at Thomas Jefferson High School and at Hunter College in New York City. He included a letter from EH dated 16 January 1928 and EH's short story "The Killers" in his own anthology, *Creating the Short Story* (1929), a collection of advice and writing samples from American writers.

Herbert Sherman Gorman (1893–1954). American writer, critic, and editor for the *New York Times* and the *Herald Tribune*. During the 1920s he contributed book reviews, essays, and poems to various magazines. He also wrote biographies of James Joyce, Henry Wadsworth Longfellow, and Nathaniel Hawthorne, among others. In 1926 Gorman wrote "Hemingway Keeps His Promise," a favorable review of EH's *The Sun Also Rises*, for the *New York World*.

Don Carlos Guffey (1878–1966). Chairman of the Department of Gynecology and Obstetrics at the University of Kansas School of Medicine, Dr. Guffey was chosen by EH and Pauline to deliver their sons Patrick (1928) and Gregory (1931).

John Gunther (1901–1970). Journalist and author from Chicago who published several novels in the 1920s, including *The Red Pavilion* (1926), and who would eventually become known for his memoir *Death Be Not Proud* (1949). From 1927 until 1936 Gunther took assignments in various European capitals while writing for the *Chicago Daily News* in Paris, where he met EH.

Benjamin Tyley Hancock (1848–1933). EH's great-uncle, the brother of EH's maternal grandmother, Caroline Hancock Hall (1843–1895). A traveling sales-man for Miller Hall & Sons (owned by the brother of EH's maternal grandfather), during EH's youth he was the jovial and beloved bachelor uncle who stayed with the Hemingways in Oak Park between business trips, bringing back stories and gifts for the children. In fall 1929 he would settle in Santa Barbara, California.

Harry Hansen (1884–1977). American journalist and critic. After earning a Ph.D. in English from the University of Chicago, he covered WWI and the Paris Peace Conference for the *Chicago Daily News*, then served as its literary editor from 1920 to 1926. His long career as a book reviewer was launched in 1926, when he became "The First Reader" for the *New York World* with a daily review column that was widely syndicated.

Jane Heap (1883–1964). American expatriate artist and writer, co-editor from 1916 to 1923 and sole editor from 1923 to 1929 of the *Little Review*, founded in Chicago in 1914 by Margaret Anderson (1886–1973). The magazine moved in 1917 to New York City, where Heap and Anderson were convicted on obscenity charges in 1921 for the first U.S. publication of portions of James Joyce's *Ulysses*. After relocating to Paris in 1923, the *Little Review* published between 1923 and 1925 some of EH's earliest writing; the magazine ceased publication in 1929. Having met Russian Armenian philosopher George Ivanovich Gurdjieff in 1924, Heap studied at his institute and later led Gurdjieff study groups in Paris and London.

Carol Hemingway (1911–2002). EH's sister and fifth of the six Hemingway children. Though twelve years apart in age, EH and Carol were fond of each other, and EH took over financial responsibility for her in 1928 after their father's death.

Clarence Edmonds Hemingway (1871–1928). EH's father. A native of Oak Park, he attended Oberlin College in Ohio and received his medical degree from Chicago's Rush Medical College in 1896. In addition to practicing medicine, he was an avid hunter and naturalist, and he founded a local chapter of the Agassiz Club for youth in Oak Park. While he and EH seldom saw each other after EH moved to Paris in 1921, Clarence regularly wrote his son loving and supportive letters. By autumn 1928 Clarence had become seriously ill with diabetes and angina pectoris and had grown increasingly concerned about the family's financial situation. Having suffered bouts of severe depression since 1903, he died on 6 December 1928 of a self-inflicted gunshot wound at the age of fifty-seven.

Grace Hall Hemingway (1872–1951). EH's mother. She and Clarence Hemingway met as high school students in Oak Park and married on 1 October 1891. In her youth Grace had aspired to become an opera singer and studied music in New York City from 1895 to 1896. After her marriage and while raising six children, she became a well-known music teacher in Oak Park and later, in the 1920s, an avid painter. A strong-willed woman with progressive views on the role of women in society, Grace lobbied for women's suffrage and was active in civic organizations. Following Clarence's death in 1928, EH assumed financial responsibility for Grace and his two youngest siblings, Carol and Leicester.

Hadley Richardson Hemingway (née Elizabeth Hadley Richardson, 1891–1979). EH's first wife. A native of St. Louis, she attended Mary Institute, a private school for girls, graduating in 1910. She met EH in Chicago in the fall of 1920, and they married in Horton Bay, Michigan, in September 1921 and moved to Paris that December. Their son, John Hadley Nicanor Hemingway (1923–2000), was born in Toronto. After learning that EH and their friend Pauline Pfeiffer were having an affair, Hadley stipulated that she would grant EH a divorce if, after a three-month separation, the two were still in love. EH and Hadley were divorced in 1927. [Hash]

Leicester Hemingway (1915–1982). EH's brother and youngest of the six Hemingway children. From 1921 to 1929 Leicester attended the Oliver Wendell Holmes Elementary School in Oak Park, and he was active in the Boy Scouts of America. As a youth, he was a close companion to his father, and his mother was proud of his violin playing. Growing up to become a journalist and author, he would publish *My Brother, Ernest Hemingway* (1962), a biography of EH. [Les]

Madelaine Hemingway (1904–1995). EH's sister and fourth of the six Hemingway children. In the 1920s she worked as a dental assistant in Oak Park but was eager to see the world. Although her plans to visit EH in Paris in 1927 fell through, she stayed with EH and Pauline in Key West from late 1928 until April 1929, babysitting Patrick and typing the manuscript of *A Farewell to Arms* (1929). She then sailed with the Hemingways to Europe, where she and a friend would tour France, Italy, and Switzerland. [Nunbones, Sunny]

Pauline Pfeiffer Hemingway (1895–1951). EH's second wife, the daughter of Paul and Mary Pfeiffer, a wealthy Roman Catholic family of Piggott, Arkansas. After receiving a degree in journalism from the University of Missouri in 1918, she worked as a writer for *Vanity Fair* and *Vogue* in New York and in Paris. EH and Hadley first met Pauline and her sister, Virginia Pfeiffer (1902–1973), in Paris in 1925. Following his divorce from Hadley, EH married Pauline in Paris on 10 May 1927. The couple had two sons, Patrick (b. 1928) and Gregory (1931–2001).

Barklie McKee Henry (1902–1966). American writer and editor. In 1924 he graduated from Harvard, published his novel *Deceit,* and married Barbara Whitney, daughter of sculptor Gertrude Vanderbilt Whitney and a member of one of America's wealthiest families. In 1925 Henry became an assistant to the editor of the *Boston American* and, in 1926, managing editor for the *Youth's Companion.* He introduced EH's work to Owen Wister in 1926 and the following year served as liaison between the two authors. From 1928 to 1930 he worked in the bond department of the Guaranty Trust Company of New York. [Buz, Buzz]

Josephine Herbst (1892–1969). American journalist and novelist. Her early 1920s writings on Midwestern, proletarian, feminist, and autobiographical topics appeared under the pseudonym Carlotta Greet in the *Smart Set* magazine, owned by H. L. Mencken. In September 1926 she married fellow writer and Midwesterner John Herrmann. In 1928 the couple moved to Erwinna, Pennsylvania, where Herbst wrote her most successful novels, including *Nothing Is Sacred* (1928), for which EH wrote a promotional blurb.

Rafael Hernández Ramírez (1889–1971). Spanish journalist and bullfight critic for the Madrid daily *La Libertad,* he likely met and became friends with EH in 1924. He served as the model for Rafael in Chapter 16 of *The Sun Also Rises* and is mentioned in Chapter 20 of *Death in the Afternoon.*

John Herrmann (1900–1959). American author who wrote about the Midwest. He met EH in 1924 while living in Paris, where he also befriended many writers including Josephine Herbst, whom he married in 1926. After returning to the United States in 1924, Herrmann continued to publish in expatriate avant-garde periodicals, including *transition* and *This Quarter.* His first novel, *What Happens* (1926), published in Paris by Robert McAlmon's Contact Editions, was denied entry into the United States by customs and was officially banned in 1927.

Guy Hickok (1888–1951). Seasoned newspaper reporter and head of the Paris bureau of the *Brooklyn Daily Eagle* starting in 1918. EH met Hickok soon after arriving in Paris in 1921, and the two took a road trip to Italy in March 1927. After EH's return to the United States in spring 1928, Hickok kept him informed about the Paris expatriate scene.

James Joyce (1882–1941). Irish author of *Dubliners* (1914), *A Portrait of the Artist as a Young Man* (1916), and *Ulysses* (1922), which was banned on obscenity charges in both the United States and England after portions were serialized beginning in 1918. Like *Ulysses*, Joyce's volume of poetry, *Pomes Penyeach* (1927), was published in Paris by Sylvia Beach's Shakespeare and Company. His novel-in-progress appeared in magazines for almost two decades before its publication as *Finnegans Wake* in 1939.

James George Leippert (1909–1960). American editor and publisher who as a teenager wrote to EH in 1927 seeking writing advice. Also known as J. Ronald Lane Latimer, he attended Columbia University 1929–1933, edited several literary magazines, and established the Alcestis Press, publishing volumes of modern poetry in the 1930s.

Wyndham Lewis (1882–1957). Canadian-born English writer and painter, best known as a founder of Vorticism and for editing the magazine *Blast: The Review of the Great English Vortex* (1914–1915). He and EH met in 1922 at Ezra Pound's Paris studio. Throughout the 1920s Lewis worked as a painter, edited *The Enemy: A Review of Art and Literature* (1927–1929), and wrote several books, including *Time and Western Man* (1927) and *Paleface: The Philosophy of the Melting Pot* (1929), both of which expressed his strong political views that would become ardently Fascist by the 1930s.

Georgia Lingafelt (1898–1957). American writer, editor, educator, and bookstore owner. After graduating from the University of Chicago, she worked at small magazines in the Chicago area before taking a job teaching journalism and directing publicity for Antioch College. During the late 1920s she worked at Walden Books in Chicago, and from 1933 to 1950 ran her own bookstore, Georgia Lingafelt Books.

Horace Brisbin Liveright (1886–1933). Owner and editor of New York publishing house Boni & Liveright, which published EH's *In Our Time* (1925). With Albert Boni (1892–1981), Liveright founded the firm and its Modern Library series in 1917. In January 1926 Boni & Liveright canceled EH's contract after rejecting *The Torrents of Spring*, which Scribner's then published in May. In spite of Boni & Liveright's success through the 1920s, Liveright's extravagant spending and bad investments left him and the company in serious financial trouble, and he would be forced out of the firm in 1930.

Harold Albert Loeb (1891–1974). American writer, co-founder, and co-editor, with Alfred Kreymborg, of the little magazine *Broom* (1921–1924). Loeb joined EH at the 1925 Fiesta of San Fermín in Pamplona and served as a prototype for Robert Cohn in *The Sun Also Rises*. Boni & Liveright published Loeb's first novel, *Doodab*, in 1925, the same year as EH's *In Our Time*. *Doodab* was not successful, nor were Loeb's second and third novels, *The Professors Like Vodka* (1927) and *Tumbling Mustard* (1929), and he abandoned fiction writing in 1929.

Mildred Longstreth (1900–1968). One of EH's fans in Philadelphia, who had visited Europe with her family in the early 1920s. In 1928 EH wrote to her about his literary depiction of bullfighting.

Archibald MacLeish (1892–1982). Three-time Pulitzer prize-winning American author. A 1915 Yale graduate, WWI military veteran, and 1919 Harvard law school graduate, he left his career as a Boston trial lawyer in 1923 to write poetry in Paris, where he lived with his wife, Ada Taylor Hitchcock, until 1928. EH and the MacLeishes met in Paris in 1924 and became close friends, spending time together on the French Riviera, in Spain, and skiing in Austria and Switzerland. Late in 1928 EH and Pauline visited the MacLeishes at their home in Conway, Massachusetts. MacLeish's many 1920s publications included *Streets in the Moon* (1926) and *The Hamlet of A. MacLeish* (1928).

Robert Menzies McAlmon (1895–1956). American poet, fiction writer, and publisher whose works include *Village: As It Happened Through a Fifteen Year Period* (1924) and *Distinguished Air: Grim Fairy Tales* (1925). In Paris, McAlmon established the Contact Editions press (1922–1929), which published EH's first book, *Three Stories and Ten Poems* (1923), and in 1923 he financed and accompanied EH on his first trip to Spain. Although EH had admired some of McAlmon's writings, including *Village*, by the end of 1925 his feelings had soured. [Mac]

William C. McFarland. University of Michigan student who, as part of his thesis research, wrote to EH in 1927, questioning him about the relationship between the novel and society.

McIntyre. A Pullman porter for the Havana Special train from New York to Key West. On 6 December 1928, after receiving word that his father had died, EH left

Bumby in the porter's care at the North Philadelphia station and rerouted himself on a different train to Oak Park while Bumby continued on to Key West.

Harold Monro (1879–1932). Belgian-born English poet, bookseller, and editor. He edited several magazines, including the *Poetry Review* (1912) and *The Chapbook* (1919–1925), and founded *Poetry and Drama* (1913–1914). He operated the London bookstore and publishing imprint Poetry Bookshop from 1913 to 1922. His poetry collection *The Earth for Sale* was published in 1928.

Gerald Murphy (1888–1964). Wealthy American expatriate and painter, who, with his wife Sara, was at the center of artistic circles in Paris in the 1920s. F. Scott Fitzgerald and John Dos Passos introduced EH to the Murphys in 1925, and in the spring and summer of 1926 the Murphys and Hemingways spent much time together, on the ski slopes of Austria, at the Murphys' Villa America in southern France, and in Spain. After EH and Hadley separated in August 1926, Murphy let EH stay in his Paris studio at 69, rue Froidevaux and surprised EH with $400 in financial support while encouraging him not to return to Hadley. In *A Moveable Feast* EH would characterize the Murphys as "the rich" whose admiration corrupted him ("There Is Never Any End to Paris").

Sara Murphy (née Sara Sherman Wiborg, 1883–1975). Renowned expatriate, along with her husband Gerald. Her father, Frank Bestow Wiborg, became wealthy in the printing ink business and frequently took his family to Europe during Sara's youth. Sara and Gerald met in New York as teenagers and married in 1915; they moved to Europe in early 1921. The couple had three children: Patrick, Baoth, and Honoria.

Paul Daniel Nelson (1895–1979). American-born French artist and architect. After studying literature at Princeton, he fought in France in 1917 with the American Army Air Service. In the 1920s he studied architecture in Paris, where he opened his own firm in 1927. A mutual friend of EH and Pauline, he and EH played tennis together.

George Norton Northrop (1880–1964). American educator and art collector, who was a mutual acquaintance of F. Scott Fitzgerald and EH. After holding faculty positions at the University of Wisconsin and the University of Minnesota, Northrop served as headmaster of the Brearley School in New York 1920–1926, and as head of the Chicago Latin School 1926–1933.

Edward J. O'Brien (1890–1941). Editor of *The Best Short Stories* series of annual anthologies from 1915 to 1940. After meeting EH in Rapallo in 1923 through Ezra Pound, he became an early supporter of EH's work. He dedicated *The Best Short Stories of 1923* to EH, misspelling his name as "Hemenway." Subsequently, O'Brien published "The Undefeated" in the 1926 volume and "The Killers" in the 1927 volume.

Leonore Emily Ovitt (1905–1987). A graduate of Oak Park and River Forest High School, she graduated from the University of Chicago in 1928. Ovitt wrote for the *Oak Parker* from 1923 to 1928, serving as the society editor in 1928. She published a review of EH's work in the newspaper's 29 June 1928 issue.

Waldo Peirce (1884–1970). American painter from Maine. After graduating from Harvard University in 1909, he served as an ambulance driver in WWI. During the 1920s he lived in Paris, where he and EH met in 1927. Sharing with EH a great gusto for life and outdoor adventures, Peirce had a bawdy sense of humor and a habit of illustrating his letters with comic drawings. He memorialized his trip with EH to Pamplona in 1927 with the painting *Bulls at Pamplona*, and he created an illustrated account of his fishing adventures with EH and friends during his visit in Key West in 1928. Scribner's used his 1928 portrait of EH for publicity purposes.

Maxwell Evarts Perkins (1884–1947). Editor at Charles Scribner's Sons from 1914 until his death. One of the most influential literary editors of the twentieth century, he was instrumental in the acquisition and promotion of such authors as F. Scott Fitzgerald, Ring Lardner, Marjorie Kennan Rawlings, Thomas Wolfe, and EH. Perkins's expertise and cordial interaction with EH smoothed the way for the publication of EH's stories in *Scribner's Magazine* and for the publication of *The Torrents of Spring* and *The Sun Also Rises* in 1926; *Men Without Women* in 1927; and *A Farewell to Arms*, serialized in *Scribner's Magazine* and then published in book form in 1929.

Edwin L. Peterson, Jr. (c. 1903–1972). Professor of English at the University of Pittsburgh from 1927 to 1967, and a fan of Hemingway's work, especially *In Our Time* (1925). In a letter of 13 June 1926, he called EH "the only living rival of America's greatest living writer," Sherwood Anderson (JFK).

Gustavus Adolphus Pfeiffer (1872–1953). Paternal uncle of Pauline Pfeiffer. After studying at the Illinois College of Pharmacy, Gus entered the pharmaceutical business that his brother Paul ran in Parkersburg, Iowa. In 1896 Gus married

Louise Foot, and the couple lived with Pauline's family. Their only child died in infancy. Gus doted on his niece throughout her life, and by 1926 Pauline was receiving monthly payments from a large trust fund. After she and EH married in May 1927, Uncle Gus showered the couple with gifts and also provided EH important philosophical and practical advice. EH dedicated *A Farewell to Arms* "To G. A. Pfeiffer."

Mary Pfeiffer (née Mary Alice Downey, 1867–1950). Pauline Pfeiffer's mother. Born into an Irish American family in Parkersburg, Iowa, that valued its Catholic faith and education, Mary was an avid reader. She married Paul Pfeiffer in 1894, and the couple had four children: Pauline Marie, Karl Gustavus, Virginia Ruth, and Paul Max.

Paul Mark Pfeiffer (1868–1944). Pauline Pfeiffer's father. Of German American descent, he was a successful entrepreneur and philanthropist. Paul moved with his wife and first child, Pauline, from Parkersburg, Iowa, to St. Louis in 1901 to join his brothers Gus and Henry in the family pharmaceutical business. Two years after the Pfeiffer Chemical Company was founded in St. Louis, Paul sold his shares and began buying thousands of acres of land near Piggott, Arkansas, where he founded a farmstead-leasing venture and later a cotton processing plant and land company. The family moved to Piggott in 1913.

Josephine Ketcham Piercy (1895–1995). Professor of English at Indiana University, Bloomington, 1926 until her retirement in 1966. She held master's degrees from Indiana University (1919) and Columbia University (1922) and would earn a Ph.D. at Yale in 1937. She and EH corresponded in 1929 regarding his contribution to her book, *Modern Writers at Work* (1930), an anthology of sample works and commentaries by well-known authors including Edith Wharton, Virginia Woolf, Thornton Wilder, and Sherwood Anderson.

Eric Seabrooke Pinker (1891–1973). English literary agent whose father operated the James B. Pinker & Son agency, representing such authors as James Joyce, Wyndham Lewis, H. G. Wells, Ford Madox Ford, Joseph Conrad, and D. H. Lawrence. Upon his father's death in 1922, Pinker became the agency's senior partner.

Ezra Loomis Pound (1885–1972). American poet, author of *The Cantos* (1917–1969), and mentor and advisor to other modernist writers, including T. S. Eliot, H.D. (Hilda Doolittle), Wyndham Lewis, and James Joyce. With a letter of introduction from Sherwood Anderson, EH first met Pound in Paris in 1922.

Pound later became one of EH's earliest and strongest advocates, helping EH develop his writing and negotiate the politics of literary Paris. The letters in this volume trace their changing relationship, with EH advising Pound on literary matters while also ribbing him about his politics. During the 1920s Pound saw the publication of *The Collected Poems of Ezra Pound* (1926), *A Draft of the Cantos 17–27* (1928), and the opera *Le Testament de Villon* (1926). He also won the $2,000 *Dial* prize in 1927 and founded the literary review *The Exile* (1927–1928).

Waverley Lewis Root (1903–1982). American journalist who moved to Paris in 1927 and joined the staff of the Paris *Tribune*, where he wrote news articles, features, literary criticism, and book reviews. In his memoir *The Paris Edition* (1987), Root recalled that whether or not someone knew EH was the "first question asked, inevitably, of anyone who lived in Paris during the 1920s and 1930s."

Marcelline Hemingway Sanford (1898–1963). The eldest of EH's siblings. She and EH graduated together from Oak Park and River Forest High School in 1917, and she married Sterling Skillman Sanford in 1923. The couple lived in Detroit and had three children: Carol Hemingway, James Sterling, and John Edmonds. Marcelline traveled to Spain in the summer of 1928 and visited Hadley and Bumby in Paris. [Ivory, Marce]

Sterling Skillman Sanford (1893–1990). Husband of EH's sister Marcelline. A graduate of the University of Michigan with a degree in mechanical engineering, he was a successful researcher and sales engineer at the Detroit Edison Company from 1920 to 1958. Sterling and Marcelline helped provide financial support for Grace Hemingway after Clarence's death in 1928.

Isidor Schneider (1896–1977). American poet, translator, critic, and editor. Born in Austria-Hungary and educated in New York City, he was a well-known figure on the New York literary scene through the 1940s. During the 1920s he served as publicity director for Boni & Liveright, which published his first novel, *Doctor Transit*, in 1925. That same year, Schneider married Helen Berlin, American writer, editor, and longtime member of the American Communist Party. After EH's break with Boni & Liveright in 1926, Schneider remained on good terms with EH and sent him books. [Issy]

Charles Thomas Scott. Book and autograph collector to whom EH sent autographed photos in response to his request.

Charles Scribner III (1890–1952). American publisher, son of Charles Scribner II (1854–1930). He began working at the family's firm, Charles Scribner's Sons, in 1913. After serving in WWI, he became vice president of the firm in 1926, then president in 1932.

Evan Biddle Shipman (1904–1957). American poet and horse-racing expert whose poetry and journalism appeared in magazines such as *transition*, *Scribner's*, *The Nation*, and *Esquire*. Shipman and EH met in Paris in late 1924 and maintained a lifelong friendship. While in Paris, Shipman lived predominantly on the proceeds from an inheritance, with occasional help from EH. Having dedicated *Men Without Women* to Shipman in 1927, EH would later devote a chapter of his memoirs to him ("Evan Shipman at the Lilas," *A Moveable Feast*).

Luise M. Sillcox (1889–1965). Executive secretary of the Authors' League of America for more than forty years. In January 1929 EH responded to her letter informing him of his election to the League.

Chard Powers Smith (1894–1977). Wealthy American lawyer, author, historian, and expatriate whose marriage was targeted by EH in the story "Mr. and Mrs. Elliott," which appeared in *In Our Time* (1925). Smith published several volumes of poetry in the 1920s, and his work appeared frequently in *Poetry: A Magazine of Verse*, between 1925 and 1933.

William B. Smith, Jr. (1895–1972). EH's friend from summers at Horton Bay, Michigan, and one of his closest companions and confidants, although the two had a falling out between 1921 and 1924. In 1925 Smith visited EH in Paris and joined him for the fiesta at Pamplona, later serving as a partial model for Bill Gorton in *The Sun Also Rises*. While living in Provincetown, Massachusetts, he wrote short stories for sale to magazines, and several appeared in the pulp magazine *Sport Story*. In the spring of 1928 he visited EH and Pauline in Key West. [Bird, Boid]

Russell Spencer. Recipient of a 23 January 1929 letter from EH reporting that Maxwell Perkins would be visiting him in Key West the next week to get the manuscript of a book he had just finished (*A Farewell to Arms*).

John Meloy Stahl (1860–1944). American Midwestern writer who served as president of the Farmers' National Congress and the Drama League of America. As president of the Allied Arts Association, which he founded in Chicago in 1923, he extended an invitation to EH, which EH politely declined in a letter of 26 July 1926, because he was abroad.

Henry Hyacinth Strater (1896–1987). American painter, illustrator, and print-maker who attended Princeton from 1915 to 1917, when he enlisted with the American Red Cross to serve in WWI. Strater and EH met in Paris in 1922 at Ezra Pound's studio, and they soon became friends and boxing partners. A woodcut of Strater's portrait of EH served as the frontispiece of *in our time* (1924). In 1924 the Straters moved to New York City, where Henry kept a studio at 257 W. 57th Street. EH saw Strater on visits to New York in 1926 and 1928; in February 1929 the Straters visited EH and Pauline in Key West. [Mike]

Margaret Strater (née Margaret Yarnall Conner, 1895–1971). Born in Philadelphia, she studied at Vassar College, the Pennsylvania Academy of Fine Arts, and the Art Students League in New York City. She married Henry Strater in June 1920 and moved with him to France, where their first son was born in April 1921. Returning to the United States in 1924, the family lived first in New York City and then moved to Maine. They would have three more children before divorcing in 1942. [Maggie]

Genevieve Taggard (1894–1948). American author and editor whose works include the poetry collections *Words For the Chisel* (1926) and *Traveling Standing Still* (1928). After graduating in 1919 from the University of California at Berkeley, she worked for the avant-garde publisher B. W. Huebsch in New York, and in 1921 she co-founded *Measure: A Magazine of Verse*, for which she served as editor until it ceased publication in 1926. She served as a contributing editor for *New Masses*, as did her husband, Robert Leopold Wolf.

Mildred Stuart Temple (1897–1983). European editorial representative for William Randolph Hearst's International Magazine Company and the Cosmopolitan Book Corporation. She offered EH a contract on behalf of Hearst in 1927, which he declined.

Frances Thorne (1904–1991). Fiancée of EH's friend William D. Horne, Jr., whom she would marry in August 1929. The granddaughter of George R. Thorne, co-founder of Montgomery Ward & Company, Frances was an active member of Chicago society and worked at several Chicago-area bookshops during the 1920s.

Edward William Titus (1870–1952). Polish-born American journalist, editor, and expatriate. His bookstore, At the Sign of the Black Manikin, opened in Paris in 1924. In 1926 he founded the Black Manikin Press, which published the second edition, the so-called authorized edition, of D. H. Lawrence's *Lady Chatterley's Lover* (1929) and the English translation of Alice Prin's racy *Kiki's Memoirs* (1930), for which EH would write the introduction. In 1929 Titus took over as owner and editor of *This Quarter* until it folded in 1932.

Hugh Seymour Walpole (1884–1941; cr. 1937). New Zealand-born English author of some three dozen novels, as well as plays, memoirs, and volumes of short stories. In a 1927 article for *Nation and Athenaeum*, Walpole was complimentary of EH's *In Our Time*, *The Torrents of Spring*, and *The Sun Also Rises*. In "The Best Books of 1929" for the *Saturday Review*, he praised *A Farewell to Arms*. EH mentioned Walpole in his story "The Three-Day Blow" in *In Our Time* (1925).

Ernest Walsh (1895–1926). American poet who with Ethel Moorhead (1869–1955) founded and edited the little magazine *This Quarter*, for which EH served as on-site liaison in Paris for the first number, published in May 1925. Walsh moved around Europe frequently, seeking a healthy climate for his lung condition. In the months before his death, in October 1926, he became romantically involved with American writer Kay Boyle, who gave birth to his daughter in 1927. EH soured on Walsh after he refused to hire EH's friend Bill Smith to work on *This Quarter* in 1925, and his opinion worsened when Walsh's unfavorable review of *The Torrents of Spring* appeared posthumously in *New Masses*. Walsh later would be the subject of EH's cutting sketch "The Man Who Was Marked for Death" in *A Moveable Feast*.

Frederick Charles Wicken (1876–1930). Managing clerk at the British literary agency James B. Pinker & Son in London. In October 1927 EH corresponded with him regarding an offer from the publishing house William Heinemann.

Blanche Colton Williams (1879–1944). American educator and biographer whose books included *Studying the Short Story* (1926). With a Ph.D. from Columbia University (1913), she was a professor of English and department head at Hunter College in New York from 1926 until her retirement in 1939. From 1918 to 1932 she served as chair of the O. Henry Memorial Committee and as editor of the annual volumes of *O. Henry Memorial Award Prize Stories*. In 1927–1928 she corresponded with EH regarding the committee's selection of "The Killers" as winner of the second-place prize.

Mrs. Williams. A fan of EH who wrote to him in 1927, shortly after the publication of *Men Without Women*, to express admiration and to pose a question about the story "Hills Like White Elephants."

Owen Wister (1860–1938). American writer and Harvard graduate who followed the example of his classmate Theodore Roosevelt by going out West, where he discovered the material for his early works, including his celebrated novel *The Virginian* (1902). Barklie McKee Henry sent Wister a copy of EH's *In Our Time* in 1926 and passed along to EH Wister's comments on his work. In 1928 EH visited Wister in Shell, Wyoming, and they began a correspondence.

CALENDAR OF LETTERS

Date of Correspondence	Recipient	Form	Location of Source Text	Previous Publication*
2 January 1926	William B. Smith, Jr.	ALS	Private Collection	unpublished
2 January 1926	Ernest Walsh	ALS	JFK	unpublished
[c. 15 January 1926]	Ernest Walsh	TLS	JFK	*SL*
[mid-January 1926]	Ernest Walsh	ALS	JFK	unpublished
19 January 1926	Harold Monro	ALS	JFK	unpublished
[c. 19 January 1926]	Horace Liveright	ALD	JFK	unpublished
[c. 19 January 1926]	Horace Liveright	TLccFrag	JFK	unpublished
19 January 1926	Horace Liveright	TLS	UDel	*SL*, Trogdon *Reference*
1 February [1926]	Ernest Walsh	ALS	UVA	*SL*
10 February [1926]	Isabelle Simmons Godolphin	ALS	PUL	*SL*
[c. 14 February 1926]	Jack Cowles	Inscription	Biblioctopus	unpublished
[18 February 1926]	William B. Smith, Jr. and Harold Loeb	ALS	Private Collection	unpublished

* Listed are known full-text English-language publications of EH letters, excluding dealer or sale catalog listings and newspaper articles

Date of Correspondence	Recipient	Form	Location of Source Text	Previous Publication*
[25 February 1926]	Isabelle Simmons Godolphin	TLS	PUL	*SL*
5 March 1926	Morley Callaghan	ALS	Private Collection	unpublished
[c. 8 March 1926]	Louis and Mary Bromfield	ALS	Stanford	*SL*
10 March 1926	Maxwell Perkins	TLS	PUL	*SL*
23 March [1926]	Isidor Schneider	TLS with auto-graph postscript	Columbia	unpublished
30 March [1926]	Edwin L. Peterson, Jr.	ALS	Newberry	unpublished
1 April [1926]	Maxwell Perkins	ALS	PUL	*SL*
[c. 4 April 1926]	Herbert Gorman	ALS	UVA	unpublished
7 April 1926	Ernest Walsh	ALS	JFK	unpublished
8 April 1926	Maxwell Perkins	ALS	PUL	unpublished
[c. 10 April 1926]	Maxwell Perkins	ALS	PUL	unpublished
[16] April 1926	F. Scott Fitzgerald	ALS	PUL	Bruccoli *Fitz–Hem, SL*
[17 April 1926]	Ezra Pound	ALS	Yale	unpublished
24 April 1926	Maxwell Perkins	ALS	PUL	*SL, TOTTC*
[c. 2 May 1926]	Ezra Pound	AL/TL with typewritten signature	Yale	unpublished
4 May 1926	Isidor Schneider	ALS	Parke-Bernet catalog	unpublished
4 May [1926]	F. Scott Fitzgerald	ALS	PUL	Bruccoli *Fitz–Hem, SL*

Date of Correspondence	Recipient	Form	Location of Source Text	Previous Publication*
5 May 1926	Maxwell Perkins	ALS	PUL	unpublished
13 May 1926	Robert McAlmon	ALS	Marks	unpublished
[c. 15 May 1926]	F. Scott Fitzgerald	ALS	PUL	Bruccoli *Fitz–Hem*, *SL*
16 May 1926	Lewis Galantière	ALS	Columbia	unpublished
20 May 1926	Maxwell Perkins	TLS	PUL	unpublished
21 May 1926	Sherwood Anderson	TLS	Newberry	*SL*
23 May [1926]	Clarence Hemingway	TLS with autograph postscript	JFK	*SL*
[c. 15 May–27 May 1926]	Rafael Hernández Ramírez	Inscription	Sotheby's catalog	unpublished
5 June 1926	Maxwell Perkins	TLS	PUL	Bruccoli *Sons*, *SL*, *TOTTC* Trogdon *Reference*
[c. 8 June 1926]	Pierre Chautard	ALDS	JFK	unpublished
29 June [1926]	Isidor Schneider	TLS	Columbia	unpublished
1 July 1926	Sherwood Anderson	TLS	Newberry	*SL*
[c. 21 July 1926]	Pierre Chautard	ALD	JFK	unpublished
[c. 24 July 1926]	Pauline Pfeiffer	TN with typewritten signature	JFK	unpublished
24 July 1926	Maxwell Perkins	TLS	PUL	Bruccoli *Sons*, *SL*, *TOTTC*
24 July 1926	Clarence Hemingway	TLS	PSU	unpublished

Date of Correspondence	Recipient	Form	Location of Source Text	Previous Publication*
[24 July 1926]	Henry Strater	TLS	PUL	*SL*
26 July 1926	John M. Stahl	TLS	Knox	unpublished
[7 August 1926]	Ezra Pound	ALS	Yale	unpublished
[7 August 1926]	Genevieve Taggard	ALS	NYPL	unpublished
18 August 1926	Edith Finch	TLS with autograph postscript	Yale	unpublished
21 August 1926	Maxwell Perkins	TLS	PUL	*SL, TOTTC*
[23 August 1926]	Hadley Richardson Hemingway	ALS	JFK	unpublished
26 August [1926]	Maxwell Perkins	TLS	PUL	*SL, TOTTC*
[2 September 1926]	John Gunther	ALS	Alexander Autographs catalog	unpublished
[4 September 1926]	Morley Callaghan	TLS	Private Collection	unpublished
7 September 1926	Maxwell Perkins	TLS	PUL	*SL*
[c. 7 September 1926]	Sherwood Anderson	TLS	Newberry	*SL*
[after 8 September 1926]	F. Scott Fitzgerald	TLS	PUL	Bruccoli *Fitz–Hem, SL*
[c. after 10 September 1926]	Ezra Pound	ALS	Yale	unpublished
[c. 28 September 1926]	Maxwell Perkins	TL	JFK	*TOTTC*
28 September 1926	Maxwell Perkins	TLS	PUL	*SL*
[30 September 1926]	Isidor Schneider	TLS	Columbia	unpublished

Date of Correspondence	Recipient	Form	Location of Source Text	Previous Publication*
30 September 1926	Robert Bridges	TLS	PUL	unpublished
[c. after 16 October 1926]	T. S. Eliot	ALDS	JFK	unpublished
[c. 12–18 October 1926]	Ezra Pound	A Postcard S	Yale	unpublished
22 October 1926	Clarence Hemingway	ALS	JFK	unpublished
25 October 1926	Maxwell Perkins	TLS	PUL	unpublished
[c. 28 October 1926]	Paul Nelson	TLS	JFK	unpublished
[c. 31 October 1926]	Ezra Pound	TLS	Yale	unpublished
[c. 6 November 1926]	Ezra Pound	TL/ALS	Yale	unpublished
12 [November 1926]	Pauline Pfeiffer	TLS	JFK	*SL*
[c. 14 November 1926]	Ezra Pound	TL/ALS	Yale	unpublished
16 November 1926	Maxwell Perkins	TLS	PUL	*SL, TOTTC*
18 November [1926]	Hadley Richardson Hemingway	TLS	JFK	*SL*
[c. late November 1926]	Gerald and Sara Murphy	Inscription with AL and autograph notations	phYale	L. Miller, Trogdon *Reference*
19 November 1926	Maxwell Perkins	TLS	PUL	*SL, TOTTC*
[c. 20 November 1926]	Ezra Pound	TLS	Yale	unpublished
22 November 1926	Maxwell Perkins	TLS	PUL	unpublished
22 November 1926	Maxwell Perkins	ALS	PUL	unpublished
23 November 1926	Maxwell Perkins	TLS	PUL	*SL*

Date of Correspondence	Recipient	Form	Location of Source Text	Previous Publication*
[c. 1 December 1926]	F. Scott Fitzgerald	TLS	PUL	Bruccoli *Fitz–Hem*, *SL*
[1 December 1926]	Clarence and Grace Hall Hemingway	TL/ALS	JFK	*SL*
[c. 2–3 December 1926]	Pauline Pfeiffer	TCD	JFK	unpublished
[2 December 1926]	Pauline Pfeiffer	AL	JFK	unpublished
[3 December 1926]	Pauline Pfeiffer	TL	JFK	*SL*
6 December 1926	Louis and Mary Bromfield	TLS	OSU	unpublished
6 December 1926	Maxwell Perkins	TLS	PUL	*SL*, *TOTTC*
7 December 1926	Maxwell Perkins	TLS	PUL	Bruccoli and Baughman, *SL*, *TOTTC*, Trogdon *Reference*
[10 December 1926]	Pauline Pfeiffer	ACDS	JFK	unpublished
15 December [1926]	Maxwell Perkins	ALS	PUL	unpublished
21 December 1926	Maxwell Perkins	ALS	PUL	*SL*, *TOTTC*
[c. mid-December 1926]	Louis Bromfield	ALS	OSU	unpublished
1 January 1927	Robert Bridges	ALS	PUL	unpublished
[2 January 1927]	Ezra Pound	ALS	Yale	unpublished
[c. 18–20] January [1927]	Isidor Schneider	TLS	Columbia	unpublished
20 January 1927	Maxwell Perkins	TLS	PUL	*SL*
20 January 1927	Maxwell Perkins	Cable	PUL	unpublished

Date of Correspondence	Recipient	Form	Location of Source Text	Previous Publication*
[after 20 January 1927]	Ezra Pound	TL with typewritten signature	Yale	unpublished
1 February [1927]	Director, Spar- und Leihkasse in Thun	TL	JFK	unpublished
[c. 4 February 1927]	*New Yorker*	TCD with typewritten signature	JFK	unpublished
[c. 5 February 1927]	Chard Powers Smith	TLS	JFK	*SL*
5 February [1927]	Clarence and Grace Hall Hemingway	TLS	JFK	*SL*, Trogdon *Reference*
[13 February 1927]	Ezra Pound	TLS	Yale	unpublished
[c. 14 February 1927]	Maxwell Perkins	TLFrag	JFK	unpublished
14 February [1927]	Maxwell Perkins	TLS with autograph postscript	PUL	*SL*
14 February 1927	Isidor Schneider	TLS with autograph postscript	Columbia	unpublished
16 February [1927]	John Dos Passos	TLS with autograph postscript	UVA	unpublished
19 February [1927]	Maxwell Perkins	TLS	PUL	*SL*
5 March [1927]	Isabelle Simmons Godolphin	ALS	PUL	unpublished
[11 March 1927]	Edward J. O'Brien	TLS	UMD	unpublished
[22 March 1927]	Ezra Pound	A Postcard S	Yale	unpublished

Date of Correspondence	Recipient	Form	Location of Source Text	Previous Publication*
[23 March 1927]	Isidor Schneider	T Postcard with typewritten signature	Columbia	unpublished
31 March [1927]	F. Scott Fitzgerald	TLS	PUL	Bruccoli *Fitz–Hem*, *SL*
[c. March 1927]	Edward W. Titus	ALS	IndU	unpublished
[12 April 1927]	Madelaine Hemingway	ALS	PSU	unpublished
14 April 1927	Hugh Walpole	TLS	phNYPL-Berg	unpublished
16 April 1927	Maxwell Perkins	TLS with autograph postscript	PUL	unpublished
18 [April 1927]	Isidor Schneider	ALS	Columbia	unpublished
[c. 25 April 1927]	Maxwell Perkins	TLS	PUL	unpublished
4 May 1927	Maxwell Perkins	TLS	PUL	*SL*
[5 May 1927]	Pierre Chautard	TL	JFK	unpublished
[6 May 1927]	Madelaine Hemingway	ACDS	JFK	unpublished
6 May [1927]	Madelaine Hemingway	ALS	PSU	unpublished
[c. mid- to late May 1927]	Waverley Root	ALS	UMD	unpublished
27 May [1927]	Maxwell Perkins	TLS	PUL	*SL*
[c. 27 May 1927]	Hugh Walpole	TL	JFK	unpublished
7 June 1927	Pierre Chautard	ALS	JFK	unpublished
[after 7 June 1927]	Pierre Chautard	ALD	JFK	unpublished
[c. after 7 June 1927]	Mary Pfeiffer	TLSFrag	PUL	unpublished

Date of Correspondence	Recipient	Form	Location of Source Text	Previous Publication*
10 June [1927]	Maxwell Perkins	TLS	PUL	unpublished
[16 June 1927]	Mildred Temple	TLS	JFK	unpublished
24 June [1927]	Maxwell Perkins	TL/ALS	PUL	*TOTTC*
24 June 1927	Mildred Temple	TLS	PUL	unpublished
27 June 1927	Jonathan Cape	TL	JFK	unpublished
[c. 27 June 1927]	Hugh Walpole	TLS	NYPL-Berg	unpublished
14 July 1927	Barklie McKee Henry	ALS	PUL	unpublished
22 July 1927	Waldo Peirce	ALS	Colby	*SL*
28 July [1927]	William B. Smith, Jr.	TL with type-written signature	PUL	unpublished
[c. 9–13 August 1927]	Barklie McKee Henry	TLS	PUL	*SL*
16 August [1927]	Harry Hansen	ALS	Schulson Autographs catalog	unpublished
17 August [1927]	Maxwell Perkins	TLS	PUL	unpublished
[c. 20 August 1927]	Waldo Peirce	ALS	Colby	unpublished
21 August [1927]	William B. Smith, Jr.	TL with type-written signature	PUL	unpublished
23 August [1927]	Ezra Pound	ALS	Yale	unpublished
29 August [1927]	Archibald MacLeish	TLS	LOC	unpublished
31 August [1927]	Edward J. O'Brien	TLS	UMD	unpublished
31 August [1927]	Maxwell Perkins	TLS	PUL	*SL*

Date of Correspondence	Recipient	Form	Location of Source Text	Previous Publication*
6 September 1927	Maxwell Perkins	Cable	PUL	unpublished
[7 September 1927]	Maxwell Perkins	Cable	PUL	unpublished
7 September 1927	Edward J. O'Brien	TLS	UMD	unpublished
8 September 1927	George Norton Northrop	TLS	James Cummins catalog	unpublished
13 September 1927	Eric Pinker	Cable	NYPL-Berg	unpublished
9–14 September [1927]	Clarence Hemingway	ALS	JFK	*SL*, Trogdon *Reference*
15 September [1927]	Maxwell Perkins	TLS	PUL	*TOTTC*
[c. 15 September 1927]	F. Scott Fitzgerald	TLS	PUL	Bruccoli *Fitz–Hem, SL*
[c. after 20 September 1927]	[Unknown]	ACD	JFK	unpublished
23 September 1927	Eric Pinker	TLS	NYPL-Berg	unpublished
26 September 1927	Eric Pinker	Cable	NYPL-Berg	unpublished
30 September 1927	Charles Scribner's Sons	Cable	PUL	unpublished
1 October 1927	Charles Scribner	TLS	PUL	unpublished
1 October [1927]	Grace Hall Hemingway	TLS with autograph postscript	PSU	unpublished
1 October 1927	Mary Pfeiffer	TLS	PUL	unpublished
3 October 1927	Georgia Lingafelt	TLS	UVA	unpublished
7 October 1927	Frederick Wicken	TLS	NYPL-Berg	unpublished
7 October 1927	Charles Scribner	TLS	PUL	unpublished

Date of Correspondence	Recipient	Form	Location of Source Text	Previous Publication*
8–9 October [1927]	Archibald MacLeish	TLS	LOC	*SL*
10 October 1927	Frederick Wicken	ALS	NYPL-Berg	unpublished
15 October 1927	Burton Emmett	ALS	UNC	unpublished
18 October 1927	Blanche Colton Williams	Letter [transcription]	PUL	unpublished
19 October 1927	Maxwell Perkins	TLS	PUL	unpublished
[c. 19 October 1927]	Ezra Pound	ALFrag	JFK	unpublished
20 October [1927]	Clarence Hemingway	TLS	JFK	unpublished
24 October 1927	Wyndham Lewis	ALS	Cornell	*SL*
[c. 26 October 1927]	Maxwell Perkins	ALS	PUL	*SL*
29 October 1927	Blanche Colton Williams	TCcc	PUL	unpublished
[c. October 1927]	Editor of the *Chicago Tribune* (Paris edition)	TLD	JFK	unpublished
1 November 1927	Frank Curtin	ALS	Meeker	Trogdon *Reference*
1 November [1927]	William B. Smith, Jr.	TL with typewritten signature	PUL	unpublished
[c. 2 November 1927]	F. Scott Fitzgerald	TL	JFK	Bruccoli *Fitz–Hem*, Trogdon *Reference*
[c. 5 November 1927]	Gerald and Sara Murphy	A Postcard S	JFK	unpublished
16 November 1927	Mrs. Williams	ALS	Heritage Auctions catalog	unpublished

Date of Correspondence	Recipient	Form	Location of Source Text	Previous Publication*
[24 November] 1927	Maxwell Perkins	ALS	PUL	unpublished
[17 or 24 November 1927]	Wyndham Lewis	ALS	Cornell	unpublished
November 1927	James George Leippert	ALS	Christie's catalog	unpublished
[c. November 1927]	Grace Hall Hemingway	ALS	PSU	unpublished
[2 December 1927]	Harry Crosby	ALS	SIU	unpublished
5 December [1927]	Isabelle Simmons Godolphin	TLS with autograph postscript	PUL	unpublished
[early December 1927]	Vincent C. Donovan	ALDS	JFK	unpublished
18 and [c. 20] December 1927	F. Scott Fitzgerald	ALS	PUL	Bruccoli *Fitz–Hem*
[c. 25 December 1927]	Clarence and Grace Hall Hemingway	Cable	PSU	unpublished
[c. late December 1927]	William McFarland	TLD	JFK	unpublished
[c. late December 1927]	William McFarland	TL	JFK	unpublished
[late December 1927]	F. Scott Fitzgerald	TL with typewritten signature	PUL	Bruccoli *Fitz–Hem, SL*
[5 January 1928]	Ezra Pound	TL with typewritten signature	Yale	unpublished
[c. 7 January 1928]	Waldo Peirce	TLS	Colby	*SL*
9 January [1928]	Ezra Pound	ALS	Yale	unpublished

Date of Correspondence	Recipient	Form	Location of Source Text	Previous Publication*
15 January [1928]	Maxwell Perkins	ALS	PUL	*SL*
16 January 1928	Henry Goodman	Letter [transcription]	JFK	unpublished
17 January 1928	Mildred Longstreth	ALS	Knox	unpublished
28 January 1928	Glen Walton Blodgett	ALS	HSOPRF	unpublished
30 January 1928	James Joyce	ALS	SUNYB	*SL*
[30 January 1928]	Sylvia Beach	ALS	PUL	unpublished
30 January [1928]	Maxwell Perkins	ALS	PUL	unpublished
[c. 5 February 1928]	Guy Hickok	ALFrag	JFK	unpublished
[c. 10 February 1928]	Madelaine Hemingway	ALS	PSU	unpublished
12 February [1928]	Maxwell Perkins	ALS	PUL	*SL*
[c. 15 February 1928]	Ezra Pound	ALS	JFK	unpublished
[c. 2 March 1928]	Jonathan Cape	TCD with type-written signature	JFK	unpublished
5 March [1928]	Jane Heap	TL with type-written signature	UWMil	Bruccoli and Baughman
11 March [1928]	Editor of the *New York Herald* (Paris edition)	TLD with type-written signature	JFK	unpublished
11 March 1928	Editor of the *New York Herald* (Paris edition)	TLS	JFK	unpublished
16 March 1928	Gustavus Pfeiffer	ALS	JFK	unpublished

Date of Correspondence	Recipient	Form	Location of Source Text	Previous Publication*
16 March 1928	Burton Emmett	TLS	UNC	unpublished
[before 17 March 1928]	Evan Shipman	AL	Channick	unpublished
17 March [1928]	Maxwell Perkins	ALS	PUL	*SL, TOTTC,* Trogdon *Reference*
[c. 28 March 1928]	Pauline Pfeiffer Hemingway	ALS	JFK	*SL*
7 April 1928	Maxwell Perkins	Cable	PUL	unpublished
10 April 1928	Clarence Hemingway	Cable	UT	unpublished
[13 April 1928]	Waldo Peirce	TLS with autograph postscript	Colby	unpublished
21 April 1928	Maxwell Perkins	TL/ALS	PUL	Bruccoli *Sons, SL, TOTTC*
[23 April 1928]	Clarence Hemingway	TLS	JFK	L. Hemingway
[13 May 1928]	Barklie McKee Henry	ALS	PUL	unpublished
13 May [1928]	Henry Strater	ALS	PUL	unpublished
[14 May 1928]	Dorothy Connable	ALS	phPUL	unpublished
31 May [1928]	Maxwell Perkins	ALS	PUL	*SL, TOTTC*
1 June [1928]	Clarence Hemingway	ALS	JFK	unpublished
1 June [1928]	Grace Hall Hemingway	ALS	PSU	unpublished
7 June [1928]	Maxwell Perkins	ALS	PUL	unpublished

Date of Correspondence	Recipient	Form	Location of Source Text	Previous Publication*
[8 June 1928]	Marcelline Hemingway Sanford	ALS	JFK	Sanford
8 June 1928	Marcelline Hemingway Sanford	Cable	JFK	Sanford
12 June 1928	Maxwell Perkins	Cable	PUL	unpublished
17 and [c. 19] June [1928]	Waldo Peirce	TL with type-written signature	Colby	unpublished
[c. after June 1928]	Don Carlos Guffey	Inscription	Christie's catalog	unpublished
[2 and 3 July 1928]	Mary Pfeiffer	TLS	PUL	unpublished
4 July 1928	Clarence and Grace Hall Hemingway	TL with type-written signature	JFK	L. Hemingway
[c. 6 July 1928]	Waldo Peirce	TL with type-written signature	Colby	unpublished
[c. 6 July 1928]	Henry Strater	TL with type-written signature	PUL	unpublished
[c. 6 July 1928]	Evan Shipman	TL	Channick	unpublished
[c. 15 July 1928]	Leonore Ovitt	ACDS	JFK	unpublished
15 July [1928]	Clarence and Grace Hall Hemingway	TL with type-written signature	JFK	L. Hemingway
15 July [1928]	Archibald MacLeish	TLS with autograph postscript	LOC	unpublished

Date of Correspondence	Recipient	Form	Location of Source Text	Previous Publication*
21 July 1928	Benjamin Tyley Hancock	ALS [excerpt]	Sotheby's catalog	unpublished
23 July 1928	Waldo Peirce	ALS	Colby	unpublished
23 July [1928]	Maxwell Perkins	ALS	PUL	*SL*
23 July 1928	Evan Shipman	Cable	Channick	unpublished
[c. 27 July 1928]	Guy Hickok	TLS	phPUL	*SL*
27 July [1928]	Josephine Herbst	ALS	Yale	unpublished
27 July [1928]	Barklie McKee Henry	ALS	JFK	unpublished
9 August [1928]	Waldo Peirce	ALS	Colby	*SL*
[c. 10 August 1928]	Evan Shipman	ALS	Channick	unpublished
[c. 12 August 1928]	Isabelle Simmons Godolphin	ALS	PUL	*SL*
[c. 12 August 1928]	Maxwell Perkins	AL	PUL	unpublished
18 August 1928	Guy Hickok	ALS	Neville	*SL*
25 [August 1928]	Josephine Herbst	Cable	Yale	unpublished
[c. early September 1928]	Waldo Peirce	ALS	Colby	*SL*
[c. early September 1928]	Guy Hickok	ALS	phPUL	Trogdon *Reference*
[c. early September 1928]	Maxwell Perkins	ALS	PUL	*TOTTC*
[c. 7–10 September 1928]	Madelaine Hemingway	ALS	PSU	unpublished
[c. 9–13 September 1928]	Archibald MacLeish	ALS	LOC	unpublished
14 September [1928]	Sylvia Beach	A Postcard S	PUL	unpublished

Date of Correspondence	Recipient	Form	Location of Source Text	Previous Publication*
17 September 1928	Clarence and Grace Hall Hemingway	Cable	PSU	unpublished
23 September [1928]	Henry Strater	TL with type-written signature	PUL	unpublished
[23 September 1928]	Waldo Peirce	TL with type-written signature	Colby	unpublished
24 September [1928]	Sylvia Beach	ALS	PUL	unpublished
26 September [1928]	John Herrmann	ALS	Cohen	unpublished
26 September [1928]	Archibald MacLeish	ALS	LOC	unpublished
27 September [1928]	Guy Hickok	ALS	phPUL	unpublished
27 September [1928]	Owen Wister	ALS	LOC	unpublished
27 September [1928]	Evan Shipman	ALS	Channick	unpublished
[c. 28 September 1928]	F. Scott Fitzgerald	TLS with auto-graph postscript	PUL	Bruccoli *Fitz–Hem*, *SL*
28 September [1928]	Maxwell Perkins	ALS	PUL	*SL*, *TOTTC*
[c. 29 September 1928]	Waldo Peirce	TLS	Colby	unpublished
[c. 1 October 1928]	Waldo Peirce	TLS	PUL	unpublished
1 October [1928]	Madelaine Hemingway	TL with type-written signature	PSU	unpublished
11 October 1928	Maxwell Perkins	TL/ALS	PUL	Bruccoli *Sons*, *SL*, *TOTTC*
12 October 1928	Henry Goodman	ALS	JFK	unpublished

Date of Correspondence	Recipient	Form	Location of Source Text	Previous Publication*
[21 October 1928]	Henry Goodman	TLS [excerpt]	Christie's catalog	unpublished
23 October 1928	Maxwell Perkins	Cable	PUL	unpublished
[31 October 1928]	Waldo Peirce	ALS	Colby	unpublished
13 November [1928]	Madelaine Hemingway	ALS	PSU	unpublished
[18 November 1928]	F. Scott and Zelda Fitzgerald	ALS	PUL	Bruccoli *Fitz–Hem*, *SL*
[c. 3 December 1928]	Archibald MacLeish	ALS	LOC	unpublished
6 December 1928	Maxwell Perkins	Cable	PUL	*TOTTC*
6 December 1928	Maxwell Perkins	Cable	PUL	*TOTTC*
[7 December 1928]	Madelaine Hemingway	ACDS	JFK	unpublished
[c. 7] December 1928	McIntyre (Pullman porter)	ACDS	JFK	unpublished
[7 December 1928]	Pauline Hemingway	ACDS	JFK	unpublished
[c. 8 December 1928]	Eleanor Chase	ACDS	JFK	unpublished
[9 December 1928]	Maxwell Perkins	AL	PUL	*SL*, *TOTTC*
[c. 9 December 1928]	F. Scott Fitzgerald	ALS	PUL	Bruccoli *Fitz–Hem*, *SL*, Trogdon *Reference*
13 December [1928]	Mary Pfeiffer	TLS with autograph postscript	PUL	unpublished

Date of Correspondence	Recipient	Form	Location of Source Text	Previous Publication*
19 December [1928]	Grace Hall, Leicester, and Carol Hemingway	TLS	UT	L. Hemingway
22 December [1928]	Henry Strater	TL with typewritten signature	PUL	unpublished
[c. 23 December 1928]	Archibald MacLeish	ALS	LOC	unpublished
24 December 1928	Grace Hall Hemingway and Family	Cable	UT	unpublished
24 December 1928	Marcelline (Hemingway) and Sterling Sanford	Cable	James Sanford	Sanford
4 January 1929	Mary and Paul Pfeiffer	TL/ALS	PUL	unpublished
4 January 1929	Waldo Peirce	TLS	Colby	unpublished
[4 January 1929]	John Dos Passos	TLS	UVA	unpublished
[4 January 1929]	Henry Strater	TL with typewritten signature	PUL	unpublished
8 January [1929]	Maxwell Perkins	ALS	PUL	*SL*
9 January 1929	Guy Hickok	TLS	phPUL	unpublished
10 January [1929]	Maxwell Perkins	ALS	PUL	*SL*
11 January [1929]	Henry Strater	TLS	PUL	unpublished
[c. 11 January 1929]	Waldo Peirce	ALS	Colby	unpublished
14 January [1929]	Guy Hickok	ALS	phPUL	unpublished
[c. 14 January 1929]	Waldo Peirce	ALS	Colby	unpublished

594

Date of Correspondence	Recipient	Form	Location of Source Text	Previous Publication*
[c. 14 January 1929]	Archibald MacLeish	ALS	LOC	unpublished
[c. 18 January 1929]	Maxwell Perkins	ALS	PUL	*TOTTC*
[c. 18 January 1929]	Waldo Peirce	TLS	Colby	unpublished
[22 January 1929]	Maxwell Perkins	ALS	PUL	*SL*
23 January 1929	Maxwell Perkins	Cable	PUL	unpublished
23 January 1929	Charles Scott	ALS	UVA	unpublished
23 January 1929	Russell Spencer	ALS [excerpt]	Parke-Bernet catalog	unpublished
[23 January 1929]	Henry Strater	ALS	PUL	unpublished
[c. after 23 January 1929]	Josephine Ketcham Piercy	AL	Cohen	unpublished
[c. after 23 January 1929]	Josephine Ketcham Piercy	ALS	IndU	unpublished
27 January 1929	Luise Sillcox	ALS	Private Collection	unpublished
[late January 1929]	Guy Hickok	ACDS	JFK	unpublished
7 February [1929]	Waldo Peirce	TLS	Colby	unpublished
[8] February [1929]	Waldo Peirce	ALS	Colby	unpublished
9 February [1929]	John Dos Passos	ALS	UVA	*SL*
12 February 1929	Frances Thorne	Letter [notes and partial transcription]	PUL	unpublished
12 February [1929]	Sylvia Beach	ALS	PUL	unpublished
14 February 1929	Maxwell Perkins	Cable	PUL	*TOTTC*
16 February [1929]	Maxwell Perkins	ALS	PUL	Bruccoli *Sons*, *TOTTC*

Date of Correspondence	Recipient	Form	Location of Source Text	Previous Publication*
[c. 18 February 1929]	Maxwell Perkins	ALS	PUL	unpublished
[c. 20 February 1929]	Evan Shipman	ALS	Channick	unpublished
20 February 1929	Owen Wister	ALS	LOC	unpublished
[20 February 1929]	Grace Hall Hemingway	ALS	IndU	unpublished
23 February [1929]	Maxwell Perkins	ALS	PUL	*TOTTC*
26 February [1929]	Guy Hickok	ALS	phPUL	unpublished
1 March [1929]	Owen Wister	ALS	LOC	unpublished
[c. 4 March 1929]	Henry and Margaret Strater	ALS	PUL	unpublished
4 March [1929]	Mary Pfeiffer	TLS	PUL	unpublished
4 March [1929]	Maxwell Perkins	TLS	PUL	unpublished
6 March [1929]	Grace Hall Hemingway	ALS	UT	L. Hemingway
11 March 1929	Owen Wister	ALS	LOC	unpublished
11 March [1929]	Maxwell Perkins	ALS	PUL	*TOTTC*
11 March 1929	Robert Bridges	ALS	UVA	unpublished
26 March [1929]	Owen Wister	ALS	LOC	unpublished
26 [March 1929]	Archibald MacLeish	ALS	LOC	unpublished
[30 March 1929]	Maxwell Perkins	ALS	PUL	unpublished
[30 March 1929]	Grace Hall Hemingway	ALS	PSU	*SL*
3 April [1929]	Maxwell Perkins	ALS	PUL	*TOTTC*

INDEX OF RECIPIENTS

In this index of recipients, only the first page of each letter is cited. Letters to more than one person are indexed under each name and marked †.

GENERAL INDEX

References to works by Ernest Hemingway appear under his name. Literary works by others appear alphabetically by the title of the work, as well as under the author's name. Newspapers and magazines are alphabetized by title. Indexed references to baseball players, bicyclists, boxers, bullfighters, and ships are consolidated under those categorical headings. All biblical references are gathered under "Bible." References to localities within a particular city (hotels, restaurants, bars, churches, schools, museums, monuments, and other sites) appear as final subentries under the name of that city. Nicknames are indexed alphabetically with a *See* reference to the person's actual name. Spanish names are alphabetized by the paternal surname, which generally appears next to last in the sequence of a full formal name and is followed by the maternal surname (which is often dropped in common usage). For example, the matador Rafael Gómez Ortega is listed under "bullfighters" as "Gómez Ortega, Rafael."